CHARISMA AND CANON

This volume is dedicated to

Heinrich von Stietencron

Professor of Indology and the Comparative Study of Religions
from 1973 to 1998 at the University of Tuebingen

CHARISMA AND CANON

Essays on the Religious History of the Indian Subcontinent

Edited by

Vasudha Dalmia
Angelika Malinar
Martin Christof

OXFORD
UNIVERSITY PRESS

OXFORD
UNIVERSITY PRESS

YMCA Library Building, Jai Singh Road, New Delhi 110001

Oxford University Press is a department of the University of Oxford.
It furthers the University's objective of excellence in research, scholarship,
and education by publishing worldwide in

Oxford New York

Athens Auckland Bangkok Bogota Buenos Aires Cape Town
Chennai Dar es Salaam Delhi Florence Hong Kong Istanbul Karachi
Kolkata Kuala Lumpur Madrid Melbourne Mexico City Mumbai
Nairobi Paris Sao Paulo Singapore Taipei Tokyo Toronto Warsaw

with associated companies in Berlin Ibadan

Oxford is a registered trade mark of Oxford University Press
in the UK and in certain other countries

Published in India
by Oxford University Press, New Delhi

ISBN 019 565 4536

Typeset in Goudy
by Eleven Arts, Keshav Puram, Delhi 110035
Printed in India by Sai Printo Pack Pvt. Ltd. New Delhi 110020
and published by Manzar Khan, Oxford University Press
YMCA Library Building, Jai Singh Road, New Delhi 110001

Acknowledgements

We are grateful to Nicole Merkel of the University of Tuebingen for the months of patient labour needed to put a large manuscript together. She largely took over the daunting task of eliciting manuscripts from the contributors, of formatting and copy-editing them, as also of co-ordinating the work of the editors themselves, flung far apart by the vicissitudes of fortune. Adrienne Copithorne of the University of California, Berkeley, deserves equally heartfelt thanks for learning with remarkable speed to proofread, copy-edit and correspond with the contributors regarding any number of finer details. Rukun Advani accompanied the process with his usual warm support and suggestions. Grateful thanks to him, as also to the Volkswagen-Stiftung for the generous grant which made possible the symposium that originally brought the contributors together in Blaubeuren, Germany, in May 1997.

Vasudha Dalmia
Angelika Malinar
Martin Christof

Contents

Prophets of the Modern Age

Convergences and Contestations: Contemporary Trends

Introduction

VASUDHA DALMIA, ANGELIKA MALINAR,
MARTIN CHRISTOF

In the nation states of South Asia, perhaps even more intensively than elsewhere in the world, religion continues to play a central role in public life and religious movements of various hues and vintage continue to offer vital sources of personal and collective identity. In fact, the last decades have witnessed the increased significance of religious movements, by no means only fundamentalist, which offer an alternative to current models of identity formation in secular societies by claiming to renew the values of some original religiosity. Recent academic discussions have tended to concern themselves with the contemporary fundamentalist trends which have come to dominate politics, though there have also been readings against the grain, that is, with investigating the plurality of traditions that have existed and proliferated on the subcontinent. However, little attempt has been made to explore how such contradictory trends and pulls have coexisted and interacted with each other. It was not only in order to focus analytically on the nature of these pluralities, but also to explore the homogeneities being forged, that the Institute for Indology and the Comparative Study of Religions at the University of Tuebingen organized a symposium on 'Charisma and Canon: The Formation of Religious Identity in South Asia' in Blaubeuren, Germany, from 17 to 21 May 1997.

Charisma and canon were the two key terms which were to enable this analysis; not so much as absolute concepts defining what constitutes religious traditions and individual and collective religious identities; rather as often present constituents and important points of reference. They were to help by providing new perspectives on the specific potential involved in the legitimization of canonized traditions and of the authority of charismatic religious specialists. The attempt was not so much to set up a typology of various religious traditions; it was rather to explore the relationship between the foundation of a religious community, the formation of canons and the various other devices which made it possible for these traditions to stake their authority. Questions of religious as well as social and political authority, of legitimization, of periodical renewal, of contemporization, but most of all of the connections that the traditions themselves established to each other, could thus be directly addressed.

Indianists and scholars specializing in modern political, sociological and cultural studies were invited to collaborate in an attempt to analyse how modern movements linked themselves anew to those older traditions which they invoked as their own. Though moved by contemporary concerns, our attempt was not just to carry present queries into the past. Rather, the present was to be viewed with past agendas and conflicts in mind. We began with a comparative analysis of medieval religious formations and widened our focus to include the non-Hinduistic religious traditions of the subcontinent when considering colonial and contemporary trends. This volume is a collection of presentations made at the symposium, revised in the light of the discussions that followed and supplemented by a few later submissions.

We still need to gather a vast amount of data before we can begin to compile anything resembling a history of Indian religions. The particular theoretical approach adopted at our symposium, we believe, makes it possible to trace certain lines of development, to set up a first estimate of the kind of fluidities and rigidities—themselves shifting but nevertheless often clearly discernible—which are a part of the religious history of the subcontinent. The essays in this volume offer vivid glimpses of the interdependence and interaction which formed a vital component of various religious traditions, of their particular selection from the same storehouse of key texts, of their overlapping but also sharp demarcations from each other. For us as editors the exercise of gauging and arranging these essays in a meaningful sequence has been somewhat akin to finding and fitting together some of the pieces of a giant jigsaw puzzle spanning several centuries, and regions as far apart as Orissa and Gujarat. We have grouped the essays in clusters suggested not only by chronology but also by phenomenology. In this introduction we shall refrain, as far as possible, from imposing an analytical framework on the arguments offered by the essays. We shall, rather, retrace these arguments and attempt to draw out and establish the links between them, marking both convergences and divergences.

Heinrich von Stietencron, in his keynote essay, presents a broad canvas, historical and conceptual, dealing with charisma and canon as closely interrelated factors in the creation and perpetuation of new religious communities. He traces the historical development of the concept of charisma, seen in the Indian context as the presence of divine energy (*tejas*) in exceptional human beings. Originally a property of kings as long as they were successful, this divine presence came later to be personified as Śrī or Lakṣmī. The concept expanded in the epic and Puranic period to produce the idea of (*aṃśa-*) *avatāra* or *prādurbhāva*, incarnations of the divine, and was, from the Gupta period onwards, also applied to exceptional religious teachers, the *ācārya* or guru, as mediators of grace. From here to the close approximation or virtual fusion of the guru with the deity was a step that could be observed in the later Vaiṣṇava and Śaiva *sampradāyas* or religious communities. Throughout this development it was charisma that provided the authority to introduce changes in religious traditions and set new standards, values and norms of action. It also served to legitimize new sacred scriptures and fresh commentaries on older canonical texts. Seeing himself compelled by the Indian evidence to do so, von Stietencron deliberately expands the notion of charisma as propounded by Max Weber to include the renewal of cults and images in the range of charismatic agendas. The canon, on the other hand, could be conceived, in the Indian context, as comprising textual, ritual and visual/iconographic dimensions. Viewed thus broadly, the canon could become the stabilizing factor that served to consolidate religious group identity in terms of theology, ritual and moral conduct. Although created and preserved in order to defeat the passing of time, the canon, here, as perhaps elsewhere in the world, was eventually overcome by time. Only the fresh influx of charisma was able to legitimize further new interpretations by means of commentary in order to re-adjust the canon to contemporary needs and visions.

As the address by von Stietencron made abundantly clear, religious concepts and practices could not be encompassed by notions of charisma and canon alone.[1] However, both these concepts offered useful analytical points of departure.

Religious Authority in Medieval and Pre-modern India

The first cluster of essays deals with the powerful *sampradāyas* which emerged in the early medieval period. The tensions to be observed here were between the Āgamic and Vedic canonic traditions, between questioning the *varṇāśramadharma* and accepting it in modified form, while negotiating at the same time the relationship between the devotional and the ritual. Whatever the final configuration, as Friedhelm Hardy shows in his essay on Śrīvaiṣṇavism, the religious communities thus constituted considered themselves to be self-contained, irreducible and non-relativizable entities, claiming sole access to divine truth. According to Hardy, charisma as a unique personal quality is problematic in the Indian context since historical information is lacking. He retraces the radical beginnings of the Śrīvaiṣṇavas in the poetry of the Alvars, the primary founder figures, whose doubtlessly charismatic agency in the creation of the *sampradāya* has been lost in the mists of time. Personal charisma with all its unique and idiosyncratic features is transformed in this and other cases into something objective, namely a culturally evolved pattern. It was due to the influence of the charismatic and learned figure of Rāmānuja in the eleventh century that Śrīvaiṣṇavism could impose itself on two *pūjā* traditions—that of the Vaikhānasa and Pāñcarātrins, and acquire control of important Viṣṇu temples. While the external agenda of the *sampradāya* emphasized the vedantic element evolved by Rāmānuja, the internal agenda could be said to recur more often to the Tamil corpus, which, remarkably, also characterizes itself as the fifth 'Veda'. However, though the Tamil songs of the Alvars are constitutive of Śrīvaiṣṇava identity, the conceptual role of the Vedas and their ultimate authority as revelation of the truth remains important. But then again, in the *ācārya paramparās*, the Vedic *ṛṣis* are not mentioned—not even Vyāsa. When invoking the authority of scripture, the most frequent recurrence is to the common pool of canonic texts: the Mahābhārata, Bhagavadgītā, Rāmāyaṇa and the Purāṇas.

Canon-formation in the Indian religious traditions came in most cases to draw upon a storehouse of religious texts. Though, several centuries later, under altered political and social circumstances, this very phenomenon could be seen as forging unity, in the early medieval period and thereafter the individual *sampradāyas* did not view this sharing as creating a larger community. They each brought forth their own specific interpretation of the texts concerned in the massive commentary literature they produced and these interpretations served to divide rather than unite.

The strategies that the 'storehouse' texts themselves employed to represent and legitimize religious authority is examined by Martin Christof in his essay on the *Bhāgavatapurāṇa*, one of the key canonical texts of the great Vaiṣṇava *sampradāyas* through the medieval period. It projects itself, like the Tamil corpus, as the fifth Veda, while identifying Viṣṇu with the non-Vedic deity Kṛṣṇa and simultaneously seeking to transcend Vedic authority. Several pairs of interlocutors, the majority themselves legendary *bhaktas*, enframe the narrative, which links the emotional ecstatic *bhakti* of the Alvars with *Advaita Vedanta*. Dharmaśāstric orthodoxy is not denounced, but it is opened up and the emphases shifted. This allows for a certain latitude in interpretation: either the one or the other philosophical and ideological position can be stressed at the expense of the other, making the text particularly attractive to a variety of groups which, while calling upon its authority, can continue to view themselves as mutually exclusive in their interpretation of it.

There are a variety of early medieval traditions which refer neither to a charismatic founder nor a canonical text as their primary source of authority. As in the following case study, the *ācārya* is the vessel of divine presence during ritual and no specific personal charisma is necessary for his selection and position.[2] This, indeed, is the dominant form in all priestly traditions, as shown by Jörg Gengnagel in his essay on the Sanskrit Śaiva Siddhanta tradition. According to the Śaivāgamas, the canonic texts of Śaiva Siddhanta, written between the ninth and twelfth centuries, the institution of the figure of the *ācārya* provides the main source for establishing the religious identity of the community. The community itself, as presented in the texts of the tradition, is a closed group, a small-scale religious group centred around the *ācārya* and, most likely, his family house. The individual affiliation to the tradition occurs through the initiation performed in a complex ritual by the *ācārya*.

Guru lineages came to form the primary constituents of most late medieval *sampradāyas*. In these later traditions, however, both the charismatic founder as also the canon played a more clearly definable role. The particular vision and (often oral) testimony, as well as the philosophical and theological doctrines and socio-ritual codes that the gurus propagated were frequently supplemented by a selection of texts already in circulation. The one literary genre which contributed enormously to the preservation and recreation of the charisma of the guru was the hagiography, which in turn often achieved canonical status. The influential sacred biography of Śaṅkara is analysed by Angelika Malinar in order to locate the elements which were brought together to vest him with the authority of *jagadguru* or world teacher. The intellectual *vijaya* or conquest of India described in the text, the major parts of which go back to the fourteenth century, served to legitmize and reinforce the universality characteristic of the religious tradition which laid claim to Śaṅkara as its founder.

There were other towering figures in the period who established their own exclusive traditions, rejecting some and accepting other components of the common pool of philosophical-theological tenets and texts, to propagate their own peculiar configurations of belief, ritual and social codes. These new foundings often led to great innovation, a break with parts of orthodoxy, but almost always also recourse to the authority of already established texts, whatever the twist given to their interpretation. Madhvācārya in thirteenth-century Karnataka, a radical in his own time, broke with Śaṅkara's monism on the one hand, while at the same time setting up a canon, exclusive to his own Vaiṣṇava *sampradāya*, which he chose to define as entirely Vedic and orthodox. Thus, even if much was rejected, much continued to be shared. As Robert Zydenbos shows in an analysis of the important fourteenth-century hagiography of Madhva, the charisma of his person, the historical and the hagiographical, was thereby to assume immense importance for later tradition.

What means did these founder figures find to forge their own brand of religious community? The essay by Vasudha Dalmia analyses the workings of Vallabha as *ācārya* and guru in forging one kind of fiercely exclusive Vaiṣṇava community, and as explicated in a seventeenth-century hagiographic text. The radical innovation of his time, which Vallabha shared with founders of other major *sampradāyas* of the period, was the provision, to the initiates, of direct access to the lord by means of the new path of emotional *bhakti*. His own authority derived from his access to, as well as identity with, the Lord. Vallabha polemicized against *māyāvāda*—as he disparagingly termed Śaṅkara's theological edifice—and did away with much of *smārta* or orthodox Vedic ritual. He recognized the *Bhāgavatapurāṇa* as the major canonical text of the community, on which he wrote an equally canonical commentary.

The discussion around the issue of religious authority is expanded by Monika Horstmann to include the role of liturgy and festival in keeping alive both charisma and canon. She places the former within an analytical survey of the great North Indian devotional traditions, *saguṇa* and *nirguṇa*, of the fifteenth to seventeenth centuries, which continue to attract strong affiliation even today.

The nineteenth century was to usher in the new, while continuing to preserve the old. An early-nineteenth-century Vaiṣṇava movement in Gujarat, led by the charismatic Sahajānanda—or Swāmī Nārāyaṇa as he is more popularly known—was to cleanse the movement founded by Vallabha, and with due deliberation initiate the institutionalization of his *sampradāya* during his own lifetime. Peter Schreiner undertakes the exercise of analysing the canonic hagiography written during Sahajānanda's lifetime. But the power of the *sampradāyas* had already begun to be somewhat eroded by the mid-nineteenth century as discussed by Catherine Clémentin-Ojha in her essay on the controversy in the Jaipur royal court between the Vaiṣṇavas and Smārta-Śaivas as to what constituted unimpeachable authority. Backed by the Smārta-Śaiva pandits at the court, the maharaja exerted strong pressure on the Vaiṣṇava *sampradāyas* to conform to *smārta* ritual, whereby the very notion of the *sampradāya* as an autonomous religious institution was put into question, so much so that, in spite of a spirited defence, the Vaiṣṇavas had to retreat, some even to leave Jaipur never to return. Clémentin-Ojha traces some of these pressures back to the influence exercised by the British. With this homogenization in the offing, though as yet only partially realized in Jaipur state, we hover on the brink of the modern age.

Prophets of the Modern Age

In the twentieth century these trends, both to homogenize by knitting together various—what to a later age seemed thinly distinguishable—strands and to define by demarcation not from relatively small *sampradāyas* but from larger groupings, such as the Arya Samaj and Islam for the Sikhs, became more pronounced. Denis Matringe analyses a Panjabi novel of reformist Sikhism which revealed striking analogies with the older hagiographic Janamsākhī literature. He discusses how, in an increasingly modernizing and secularizing world, doctrinal unification, as also clearly defined notions of religious identity, became key issues. These were persuasively presented in the novel by a fictionally recreated modern image of Nānak. Another theme which crystallizes clearly in Matringe's essay is touched upon recurrently by other contributors: apart from the personal charisma radiated by modern religious leaders, the main binding force for the communities thus freshly defined was social reform, as also a much more emphatically defined sense of social service and responsibility.

Revealing also is the contrast between two leaders, Gandhi and Ambedkar—who for all their differences are often clubbed together—when the nature of their charismatic appeal is examined: Gandhi as a secular leader whose very title had religious dimensions, and Ambedkar as a religious leader who remained secular in his appeal. Dieter Conrad traces the usage of the term 'mahātmā' in connection with Gandhi and its various connotations. Most obviously, this was the traditional way of conferring authority upon various holy men. In the late-nineteenth century the term came to signify spiritual authority for a public function. It was also in this period that occult usage was brought into vogue by the theosophists. Finally, there was the more exalted theological-Upanishadic sense of the term, which was also connected explicitly to

Gandhi by Romain Rolland and Ananda Coomaraswamy. Conrad shows how, notwithstanding Gandhi's disclaimers about the applicability of the term to his own person, there persisted an ambivalence in his attitude towards it. If in the late twenties he found it too early for a final submission to the saintly role which he felt went along with it, by the end of his life he seemed to have, at the least, aspired to it.

Ambedkar, on the other hand, as Martin Fuchs points out in his essay, attempted, in his interpretation of Buddhism, to canonize anew a tradition which had been canonized centuries earlier, opening it thereby to the rationalist argumentation of the modern. Fuchs traces links between the socio-ethical dimensions of Ambedkar's depictions of Buddhism and the thinking of John Dewey, whose pupil Ambedkar had been from 1913 to 1916. Ambedkar's Buddhism was based on 'reason' and 'experience', and he felt that it was entirely in accord with modern science. It was not a revelation, it contested divinity; it was much more an inquiry and investigation. Buddhism believed in the regeneration of matter and recognized the principles of social life. Ambedkar was concerned with the establishment of a primarily ethical civil religion. The community that he sought to create was self-organized, non-hierarchical, participatory and non-exclusive. He saw his role in it as an educator-cum-political leader rather than a religious one.

Various forms of social service have been called for by modern-day charismatic leaders. Gandhi's programme of spiritual and social regeneration has been taken up by a Maharashtrian Brahman scholar, Pandurang Vaijnath Athavale, who has reinterpreted upanishadic and vedantic thought to promote devotion towards the communal good. However, he emphasizes that this is a religious rather than social impulse. As Gita Dharampal-Frick illustrates in her essay, Athavale knows how to link up with the socio-cultural equipment of rural India and to organize a number of self-help communities with, and for, the socially marginal.

More urban is the appeal of Sathya Sai Baba. The essay by Smriti Srinivas analyses the new configuration of features which makes for his vast appeal. Apart from his immense personal charisma, part of his appeal surely stems from his efforts to revitalize and reinvigorate a *sanātana dharma* which is based upon and propagates Vedic learning while incorporating the fruits of modern science. He projects himself as an incarnation of Śiva and Śakti, who yet overcomes the old Śaiva-Smārta and Vaiṣṇava divide in that he seeks to absorb Kṛṣṇa and Rāma devotionalism within the symbols and nomenclatures with which he surrounds himself. His millenarian vision offers hope in Kaliyuga. He sees social service as the highest form of devotion. It is offered in the most modern forms by his organization, in pedagogic institutions and highly equipped hospitals—which are also to be seen as an extension of his healing powers.

Both Athavale and Sai Baba represent new forms of affiliation to the older Advaita-Śaiva symbiosis which is, however, diffused by the co-option of Vaiṣṇava deities. Both movements seem to be speeding up, albeit inadvertently, the processes of homogenization of religious discourse and practice which began in the last century. This in turn brings about an erosion of loyalties to older *sampradāyas* and religious communities, thereby smudging the boundaries once held up so stringently by them. Both Athavale and Sathya Sai Baba attract an amorphously defined following, predominantly rural and urban respectively, which does not seek to demarcate and define itself against other sects or religions. According to Dharampal-Frick and Srinivas, both leaders are nonconfrontational in the advocation of their particular brands of faith. They are no supporters of the Hindu right. Their very catholicity, however, could free their followers to sympathize with, if not actually become members of, any political party which seemed to address contemporary issues cogently.

Convergences and Contestations: Contemporary Trends

At the same time, the social transformations and mobilizations make newly vulnerable forms ritually fixed and perpetuated since time immemorial in the largely feudal countryside. Charisma and canon in an oral tradition are constituted by a taut balance of power and functions between patrons, possession priests or media, and professional impersonators of deities. As Heidrun Brueckner shows in her essay on the Tulu-speaking population of coastal South Karnataka, though these ritual and belief systems are resilient and have stood the test of time, their social and cultural context cannot remain impervious to change. A variety of measures have to be resorted to if the delicate balance is to be maintained. The question which crops up inevitably is: how long can this balance be retained?

Twentieth-century efforts to homogenize religious practice and discourse necessarily colour the evolution of Tibetan Buddhism as well. Michael von Brück deals with the Tibetan Tulku tradition and the problem of religious authenticity in considering the history and phenomenology of the present Shugden controversy. Within the framework of the Tibetan history of canonizing spiritual forces and pre-Buddhist cults, his essay looks into tensions within tradition as it is modernized by what he calls the protestant principle that the Dalai Lama seems to apply in condemning Shugden worship.

Similarly exposed to modification are older forms of faith which constituted themselves by exuberant borrowings from neighbouring traditions, whether in conceptual or mythological terms. Explicit Sufi and Yogic crossings, as delineated with admirable lucidity in the joint essay by Gian Guiseppe Fillipi and Thomas Dähnhardt were entirely possible as late as in the mid-nineteenth century. Ramchandra Chaudhary, a bureaucrat in British service, could be initiated both by a Rāmānandī guru and a *pīr* from the Naqsabandīya order, thereby creating his own path to salvation known as the Ānanda mārg. It was feasible for his lineage to have both Hindu and Muslim disciples. In the fifties of the present century, under the tutelage of a more Hindu-minded leader, however, this Yogic-Sufi amalgamation dissolved in favour of the Yogic alone and the Muslim discipleship discontinued its allegiance to the path.

More than ever, it has become then a question of redefining identity in terms of one or the other major religious denominations. How complex it is to retain any fluidity in this respect becomes clear in the essay by Françoise Mallison. The canonical texts of the Ismaili Khojas of India and Pakistan, the Gināns, were composed in the late middle ages. They consisted of verses in indigenous meters and in the indigenous languages of western India, primarily Gujarati and Sindhi, and they borrowed heavily from Hindu mythology and systems of belief. They came to represent the prime markers of the religious identity of the community, serving to distinguish it from the larger Ismaili community, as also from the yet larger Islamic community of the subcontinent and Iran. However, it became important for the Khoja leaders, who came from Iran at the beginning of this century, to legitimize their own claims of leadership in multiple ways. They had to signal both their Islamic affiliation and retain some features which yet served to distinguish the community from the rest. It was the Gināns who became victims of this complex process. The Hindu elements were radically eradicated, and the verses were newly censored, selected and reconstituted. Thus, the canon remained constitutive of community, but had to bow to demands made by the new leadership and the changed political climate.

It is these contrary processes which become most apparent in charting contemporary trends: if there are new fluidities, there are also new rigidities. Both these trends, assimilative as well as resistant, are confirmed once again in the essay by Jamal Malik which analyses the mobilizing potential of what is called the small tradition and the various media for establishing charismatic traditions. As he points out, there is no monolithic Islam.

There are, much more, contradictory opinions, as reflected in competing discourses. Malik scrutinizes the complex intermediary social forces which make for the politicization of Islam and their cultural articulations as exemplified in the writings and work of Abūl A'lā Maudūdī and Abūl Hasan Ali Nadwī. The former Islamicized the political discourse of nationalists, calling for an Islamic state and veering towards pan-Islamicism. The latter, as head of the internationally reputed Nadwat al-'Ulamā, Council of Islamic Scholars, in Lucknow, steers a wary course between allowing for an all-embracing cultural identity which could integrate particular and regional identities, and yet accepting the cultural hegemony of Islam.

The institutionalization of religion on a national scale, in fact, as demonstrated in the essay on the religious leadership of the Vishva Hindu Parishad (VHP) by Christophe Jaffrelot, cannot be a smooth affair. The central organization of Hinduism as sought by the VHP is more effective in terms of popular mobilization than in penetrating older Hindu *sampradāyas* and institutions. It has sought to take over the organization of temples and popular religious festivals, and it has offered a welcome public platform to a sprinkling of modern gurus and sadhus of often diffuse affiliation, who have, however, often exercised their considerable personal charisma to good effect.

Yet, in dealing with the right-wing appropriation of religion, it can only be reductivist to regard the whole as a question of the political instrumentalization of religion. Tanika Sarkar questions the notion of Hindutva as a secular modernist movement. She seeks to locate Sadhvi Rithambhara of the VHP within the larger processes of cultural and institutional transformation within modern Hinduism, and examines why the voice of a female ascetic is necessary to project a form of devotion based on violent aggression. Sadhvi Rithambhara's charismatic personality, transmitted primarily through electronic means, mobilizes people in the nationalist Hindu cause by the emotive use of religious vocabulary. Sacred myths alternate with communalized histories, though interestingly there is no citation from any sacred text nor one complete recall of any mythological event. This is not a doing away of canon, but rather the creation of a new canon, a novel restoration of the spoken word as against the written.

The essays grouped in this cluster demonstrate that the social and political framework of 'religion' has changed in the colonial and post-colonial era, and with that the significance of charisma and canon have also undergone vast changes. Yet the homogenization of religious discourse which all of us speak of and sometimes lament is not a process which can be regarded as an accomplished fact. There are various forms of resistance to the hegemonic claims of a Hinduism which would set out to have a uniform theology, a set pantheon of gods, and, finally, codified rituals and canonic texts. The innovative potential of whole peoples and groups can by no means be regarded as exhausted. We accordingly conclude the volume with an essay by Paula Richman which examines the relationship between canon and the types of innovation that have occurred within the Rāmāyaṇa tradition. She brings three case studies to demonstrate how a peculiar telling of the Rāmāyaṇa consolidates the distinctiveness of a community, to what extent it is seen as authoritative by religious leaders, and to what extent it serves to exclude certain groups from its reading. She discusses a set of women's songs in the Brahmanical milieu of north-eastern Andhra Pradesh which gently shut out the male world of Rāma and Rāvaṇa, as represented in Vālmīki's Rāmāyaṇa, to set up their own everyday world of work and care. The highly abridged and socially subversive telling of the Tulsidas Rāmcaritmānas as venerated by Dalits in Uttar Pradesh simply censors as inauthentic what is regarded as caste-discriminatory. The Dravida Kazhagam tellings in the works of E. V. Ramasami, in which Rāma acts as the villain, once again question the validity of Vālmīki's Rāmāyaṇa.

We are aware that the conclusions which emerge from our investigations and discussions can only be tentative. We hope all the same that they provide new insights into the religious history of the subcontinent, that they hinder reductivist attempts to see developments in some singular direction—however compelling its present dominance—and finally that they open up the field to further investigation.

The symposium from which this volume emerged was organized as a tribute to the work of Heinrich von Stietencron by his colleagues, some of whom had also been his students. This volume is dedicated to him. Professor von Stietencron both consolidated and opened up Indology as a discipline, dexterously intertwining his interest and knowledge of the classical with the modern, both historically and methodologically. His acute awareness of the social and cultural context of texts and events, as also his intimate knowledge of the long religious history of the subcontinent, made the years of his directorship of the Institute of Indology and the Comparative Study of Religions (1973–98) at the University of Tuebingen a period of intense exchange, debate and learning within the institute, as also with scholars in affiliated disciplines in India and Europe. Considering the nature of his involvement, it seemed only natural, then, that we did not exclude him from this tribute, as is usually the case with such festivities, but placed him at the centre of it, as the source of continuing inspiration and interaction. A select bibliography of his works to date is appended to this volume.

Notes

1. Von Stietencron discusses these two concepts in detail. The reader is referred to his essay for bibliographical references.
2. The notion of charisma in a *mat*, or faith, considered to be divine revelation, would relate most prominently to Max Weber's notion of the charisma of office.

Charisma and Canon: The Dynamics of Legitimization and Innovation in Indian Religions

HEINRICH VON STIETENCRON

The juxtaposition of charisma[1] and canon[2] invites a number of questions. Why choose these two phenomena as anchor-points or cornerstones in a discourse that is meant to throw light on the dynamics of religious movements in India's past and present? How precisely do these phenomena relate to each other? At one level they seem to be opposites, representing the dynamic and the static operating in religious communities. At another level they appear to be interdependent. But do they really interact? And if so, in what manner and for what purpose?

These queries may appear to be abstract and academic, but they are relevant. Put in simple everyday language, they address the question: What keeps religions alive? It is this question that underlies my essay.

In the context of religion, a canon is the result of a deliberate attempt to collect, arrange and preserve the original message of a religious community, and to protect it against all corruption. It transforms haphazard individual recollection into authoritative tradition or sacred scripture. As such, it itself becomes endowed with an aura of sacredness[3] which derives both from the original seers, *ṛṣis*, prophets or teachers who formulated the message, and from the eternal truth which is thought to be encapsulated in the text of canonical scripture. Such a canon is one of the strongest possible forms of defining and securing a specific religious identity. In its contrast with the doctrines of other creeds, the canon is a continuous source of self-awareness and self-definition. It provides meaning and direction to the community as a whole and to each individual member by representing both the ultimate truth and the means of attaining it.

In a world subject to perpetual change, the formation of a canon is a device to arrest time, or rather to pick out and separate from the change-inducing flow of time a selected set of elements that are considered essential and eternally valid: values, guidelines, exemplary representations of true religion and wholesome conduct that together provide lasting orientation to the community.

Ideally a canon, once fixed, is permanent. Nothing is to be added, nothing to be taken away. The canon is a perfect body that defeats time. Entrusted to the collective memory of specialists (or later to writing and re-writing, or to print), it seems to be the one human possession that approaches the ideal of permanence.[4]

Charisma, on the other hand, is a power operating in time. It is not the rule, but the exception: a spark of divine presence flashing into ordinary life and legitimizing leadership and change. It is divine agency operating through man, a power temporarily conferred on him which creates extraordinary authority: a gift or fruit of the Holy Spirit or other divinities, it is clearly of superhuman origin and superhuman effect. Such charismatic authority stands at the origin of a new doctrine or a new religion. It takes precedence over the canon by bringing into convincing shape those innovative ideas, concepts, models of behaviour and approaches to the divine that create a new religious movement. It is to the credit of charisma if such elements of religious content can be successfully propagated against the natural resistance of established religion—and there is no period other than mythic time in which a new religious movement was not confronted with one or several pre-existing religions. Charisma, i.e. personal charisma, pushes a new configuration of religious ideas into public acceptance and gains for them a following that may be able to survive the founder.[5] This innovative impulse is often also revolutionary in nature, in as much as it rejects essential parts of earlier established traditions or questions and changes earlier law.

Thus, while canon stands for permanence, charisma stands for innovation. This leads us directly into the dialectics of timelessness *versus* time-governed life, of transcendence *versus* worldly existence, of permanence *versus* change. They are opposing yet interacting principles that are constitutive for all religions and, indeed, for all human effort at creating and implementing order in a cosmos that is materially and biologically constituted and, therefore, equally liable to chaotic growth and decay.[6]

The canon, while attempting to preserve the essential, also fixes it in a particular historical expression: in the language of a certain region and time; in stories, examples, arguments and prescriptions that relate to that particular social and cultural context in which the charismatic founder of the movement or the redactors of the canon lived. The result is a snapshot that preserves for collective memory one moment out of many in cultural evolution.

Such unavoidable historicity is the one major defect in every canon. Several generations later, spoken language may have changed so much that people have difficulty understanding the original message. Social and economic structures may have undergone drastic transformations, different paradigms of thought may have redirected human intellectual attention to entirely different topics. Even if the language problem were solved, people might not later be able to derive from canonic texts meanings relevant for their problems, their times. In other words the very object of the canon—to fix a timeless truth or guideline—also inevitably leads to a continually growing gap between the canon and its addressees, to people living in time and changing with time.

As can be seen, this is a dilemma that all religions have to face, whether their sacred tradition is remembered or written down—most notably the so-called 'high' religions that refer to a transcendent reality and claim universal truth.

It is here that charisma comes in again. The original message must be translated, transformed and made meaningful for a changed society and altered circumstances. The commentary now becomes an exegetic tool of prime importance, so much so that it too requires charismatic legitimization. Often it becomes canonic scripture in its own right, as evident in India, for instance, in the various Vedānta traditions.[7]

We thus have an interdependence between charisma and canon; they not only alternate, but also form a chain of religious legitimization. Experienced charisma legitimizes innovation and the establishment of new law—and here I use the word 'law' in its most general sense of wholesome guideline for individual, social or religious conduct (all included in the Indian term *dharma*). Aleida and Jan Assmann have described how canonizing that law is a process of selection and emphasis, including the necessity of censoring and rejecting disturbing elements, of adjusting or reshaping others, and of attempting some sort of systematic organization.[8] Drawn from the memory of elders who were themselves witness to the life, words and deeds of a charismatic leader, this canon draws its legitimacy partly from actual experience or memory of charisma, and partly from the collective consent of learned religious leaders of the community.[9] The law, thus established and canonized, becomes subject to transmission and interpretation for many generations, until a point comes when the gap between the original message and the social and spiritual needs of a changed society becomes too wide. At such a point new charisma is required for the renewal of meaning and authority. Should it fail to appear, the movement is bound to lose some of its importance.

This brief analysis shows that the repeated presence of charisma is of vital importance for religious movements. From charisma religions derive their primary legitimacy. And whatever secondary legitimacy may vest in institutions, offices or sacred texts and rituals, it inevitably requires, from time to time, an actualization by means of a renewed influx of charisma.

The relation between charisma and canon has, therefore, a vertical and a horizontal dimension. The first has to do with the structure of the *sacred* as against the *systematic* and with the former's legitimizing impact; the second has to do with historical processes in which the sacred must be actualized and adapted in order to be understood and exert influence. This directs attention to social constellations in which religions arise and establish themselves, i.e. in a given social setting, or in which they fight for survival under conditions of social, economic, political or ideological change. Both cases provoke questions (and suggest answers) as to the necessary conditions for a religious movement to come into being, to gain recognition, to adapt to changing contexts, and to preserve all the same an identity over time.

The Indian Context

The next few steps of my argument, while leaving the general frame and turning to Hindu India, will focus on charisma in its revitalizing aspect. How do Hindu religions provide their devotees with sufficiently frequent charismatic experiences to keep both their emotional engagement and their intellectual interest in religion alive? It will be clear by now that both charisma and canon serve the same end, namely the defeat of *kāla*, time, and its degenerating effect. In India, the general frame of reference is not an evolution that tends to produce ever-more complex and more capable organisms, but the opposite vision of a pure and perfect creation which, under the influence of time, exhausts itself in gradual deterioration at all levels of physical and spiritual existence. After several cycles of rejuvenation and decay, it will be finally consumed in a cleansing cosmic cataclysm from which—after an interval—it will reappear in its pristine purity. Gods, kings, and saints all serve the same purpose—to counteract the agents of time and decay. They may not be successful in the end, but they can stop the process for the time being, and here charisma plays a decisive role.

This overall picture gets complicated by the fact that a considerable number of different religious communities co-exist—and have co-existed all along. They competed for patronage and political influence, stimulating each other in terms of ritual and literary presentation, as well as challenging each other as to the logic and validity of theological or systematic argument. There was never, in any of these religions, a set of religious institutions powerful enough to impose doctrinal uniformity and ban sectarian deviations. Nor did the cyclical concept of time—present since the early Upanishadic period—favour an emphasis on the uniqueness of any manifestation of divine agency in historical time. Moments of the special influx of divine grace or divine law in human history comparable to those experienced by Abraham, Moses, the apostles of Christ, or Muhammad are recorded in India, too; but in cyclical time they appear only as recurrent sparks of light in an endless sequence of time cycles. And while an incarnate Messiah or Son of God can be claimed to mark an absolute turning point for humanity in linear time, this is not thinkable in the cycle of *yugas* and *manvantaras*. Incarnations occur again and again when there is a need for order to be restored.[10] And each of the Indian religions can present their own *avatāras* or *aṃśāvatāras* of the divine, whether Śaivas, Vaiṣṇavas, Śāktas, Bauddhas, Vedāntins or followers of *nirguṇa sampradāya* sants.

The very plurality of religious thought requires mechanisms to establish eternal truth and assert the legitimacy of its exegesis. One of these is the *guruparamparā*, the line of authorized transmission from fully trained teacher to tested student both of sacred scripture and its interpretation. It is in the latter that innovation is required from time to time and does, indeed, occur. Yet in order to make it acceptable, in order to convince a following of the eternal truth of a new idea or form of conduct proffered in the garb of commentary on the original canon, fresh charisma is needed. But what, exactly, does 'charisma' mean in the Indian context? Is there complete agreement with the conclusions of Max Weber and others[11] whose results were based on the Greek Bible, on epics and sagas from various religious traditions, and on the ethnographic literature about shamans, yogis, miracle workers and medicine men around the world?

In the Indian literary tradition, the notion of charisma is first and primarily linked to the king. It is a kind of radiating power and unfailing fortune that distinguishes its bearer from other persons or entities. It can be directly experienced in the encounter with a charismatic person. Both in ancient Iranian and Indian tradition, charisma was conceived of as a kind of subtle, luminous substance that could be conferred on a deserving person by a God or by ritual action. This concept goes back to the second millennium BC, when the Indian and Iranian Aryans had not yet separated.

The ancient Persians called this substance *xˇarənah*,[12] (the corresponding Sanskrit word is *svarṇa* or *suvarṇa*, with *śrī* or *tejas* as alternative designations), and it described the faculty to know and achieve what others were unable to know and do, as well as that golden radiance which can be perceived in a victor or in a powerful, successful king. Already in Vedic times the election of a leader included contests of various kinds in order to test skill, wisdom and luck in chariot races (skill), poetry contests (divine inspiration), and the throwing of dice (luck). The God Indra himself was thought to guide the horses, the words, and the dice of the winner. Charisma was thus God-given. It was a more-than-ordinary performance and luck which characterized the charismatic leader and thus directly corresponded to the gifts of grace, the *charisma* of the Greek,[13] which was a reference to the miraculous powers of outstanding persons. Later Indian mythology also sees royal charisma as a property of the divine, particularly of Viṣṇu. Its manifestation in the human realm signals divine presence. In kings it is a spark of the success-promoting nature of the Goddess Śrī or Lakṣmī, the consort of Viṣṇu. The king himself, equated with Viṣṇu on account of his task to protect and uphold the world order, is conceived of as the husband of Lakṣmī, whose place was at the bosom of the king. As long as this divine power was present, a king would not meet with defeat, nature would provide ample crops and every sort of benefit, and there would be prosperity and justice in the king's realm.

But charisma (or Śrī) was not a property of the king nor a result of inborn character. It was conceived of as an independent agent, related to *dhārmic* kingship rather than to the king as a person. It could leave him abruptly if he failed to protect the *dharma* or misused his power for selfish ends. It could simply run away and thereby bring disaster to the country.

There is an Iranian myth, where this royal fortune (*xˇarənah*) disappears after the misconduct of Yima, first man and first king, and hides in a pond. As a consequence, moral order is corrupted, the powers of darkness gain the upper hand, and the king is slain by the usurper Azhi Dahāka, a tyrant serpent king who assumes power and takes all the riches for himself. At this stage a young hero named Thrita Āthwya or Thraetaona (the Farīdūn of later texts), born in the royal line, finds the hidden royal fortune in the pond. He conquers the snake, is elected king, and restores order and prosperity to the country.[14] This myth belongs to a period when kingship is already considered a divine institution but not yet hereditary. All its elements can be found in the Indian mythic tradition as well, although in different contexts. An important part can be recognized in the well-known Vedic narrative of the slaying of the serpent Vṛtra in a version where the hero and slayer of the demon is Trita Āptya, a double or precursor of Indra.[15] Charisma, according to the Iranian version of this myth, descends from the throne of Ahura Mazdāh and then moves from one righteous ruler to the next. It is something conferred on a person when merited and withdrawn from him when merit fails. Both in India and Iran it can arise spontaneously, can be given by the celestials, and conferred by ritual consecration. Its nature is fire (*tejas*): it radiates and illuminates the entourage of its possessor; it also consumes his foes and dispels the forces of darkness.

The presence of divine agency—an agency substantially different from that of ordinary humans[16]—is thus a characteristic of charisma, of royal glory, of unusual success and power. This power often, but not necessarily, requires ritual confirmation, as can be seen in the ceremony of royal consecration (*rājasūya*). We shall see that this is not only the case with the king, but with other charismatic agents as well. The problem is that charismatic kingship is difficult to regulate and control. This is much easier in institutionalized hereditary kingship, where stability and continuity are provided for by princely education, regular succession, and a group of experienced ministers responsible for the administrative processes of government. In contrast, the inherent revolutionary power of a charismatic leader tends to overthrow the dynastic line rather than continue it. In ancient Indian law-books, therefore, a deliberate attempt is made to institutionalize royal charisma by locating it in kingship as such. In the Manusmṛti the king is represented as an embodiment of the eight guardian deities of the world[17] and his task mirrors theirs: to protect the established order of the world. The more famous and slightly later version of a similar idea of divine incarnation is the concept of *prādurbhāva* or *avatāra*, according to which the God Viṣṇu himself 'becomes manifest' or 'descends' and incorporates himself, or part of himself, on earth. The Bhagavadgītā (4.6-7) declares that Kṛṣṇa appears in every age, whenever there is a need to destroy the wicked and uphold *dharma*. It is the presence of divine agency in human form that is common to these concepts.

Such presence of the divine in a human body, when institutionalized in kingship, is an invaluable source for the legitimizing of charisma and it was, indeed, one of the major preconditions for the development of strong and organized kingdoms in ancient India. To some extent the monastic orders of the Buddhists and Jains succeeded in developing organizational structures that were also able to channel charismatic leadership in high offices, such as that of the head of the *vinaya*. But late Vedic polytheism and the various new religions centred on a single supreme divinity that arose and propagated their *dharma* in the centuries from *ca.* 300 BC to AD 400 did not evolve corresponding institutions. A similar technique of domesticating charisma could, therefore, not be applied for achieving the rejuvenation of a stagnant or disinterested religious community. The danger, and indeed the dominant historical fact, was rather that charisma inaugurated fresh and compelling authority outside the existing community, thereby weakening instead of strengthening it.[18]

Of course, Brahmin priests knew the potential inherent in the concept of institutionalized charisma. Since Vedic times, *ṛṣis* had been considered recipients of divine inspiration, and during the heyday of Vedic ritual the priesthood as such was sanctified by mediations between ordinary mortals and Vedic Gods: so much so that Weber considered the Brahmin caste as a prime example of institutionalized charisma. But those golden times for Brahmanism had passed. Ideas and social conditions had begun to change drastically in northern India around the middle of the first millennium BC, when common borders with the powerful Achaemenid empire in the West had led to a fresh influx of Near Eastern culture, trade and organization. There was rising discontent, in a growing urban society, with antiquated patterns of Vedic ritual that had been inherited from a cattle-breeding and semi-nomadic way of life, and with the Brahmin claim to monopoly on religious knowledge and practice. This expressed itself vigorously via the rise of a number of intellectual reform movements led by charismatic non-Brahmin teachers in the lower Ganges valley. Such movements, particularly those of the Buddhists, Jains and materialists whose new lines of thought proved to be of great attraction, diverted patronage and political influence from the fifth century onwards from the Brahmin community. The fourth or early third century saw the rise of new religious movements that adopted image worship in temples from the non-twice-born population; these also tended to supplant Vedic ritual among the twice-born.[19] It should be remembered in this context that the poetic and ritual tradition of Vedic religion had distinguished itself sharply and proudly from popular religion. But with a growing participation of Śūdras in the rural and urban economy as well as in politics, these divisions could no more be strictly maintained. And as if these internal factors contributing to a gradual erosion of priestly dominance were not enough, there were soon to follow repeatedly successful inroads of foreign *mleccha* invaders into northern India which unsettled traditional structures of power and patronage.

This decline of the Brahmins was not uniform, nor did it affect all regions in similar measure. There were, for example, Brahmin revivals under Kāṇva and Śatavāhana rule. But in northern India an unfavourable situation began—at the latest with the reign of the Nandas in the fourth century BC—and lasted, with intervals, for roughly 600 years, until the later part of Kuṣāṇa rule. These were the centuries of self-assertion by the Kṣatriyas. In the Upanishads, in Buddhism and in Jainism, they all claimed higher knowledge on ritual than Brahmin experts. And when the foreign invaders came to rule north-western India, they too were not dependent on Brahmin services but felt free to adopt or reject them according to their pleasure. The notion of divine kingship, with its long tradition in Egypt and western Asia, had informed developments in ancient Iran, in the Hellenistic world, in Central Asia, and in the Maurya empire as well as its successor states all the way down to the Kuṣāṇa empire.

Over these centuries Brahmins did not participate in the benefits of the institutionalization of the charisma of office in the same way that Kṣatriyas did. On the contrary, they were further threatened with marginalization when the *bhakti* concept of a personal relation between devotee and God gained momentum and reduced once again the need for a mediating priest. The repeated verbal claim that the Brahmins were 'living Gods on earth' reflected social reality no more. Their strictly 'religious' qualifications, such as knowledge of the Vedas and ritual skills, were less in demand in this period. It was rather their literacy and their learning in law, politics, administration and the traditional sciences that secured them an influential position and made them indispensable to every ruler. Dominance in religious affairs was regained only when they condescended to earn their living with temple worship,[20] when they started appropriating the leadership of popular religious movements—such as the cults of Kṛṣṇa, Nārāyaṇa, Rudra/Śiva, Sūrya, Skanda/Kumāra/Mahāsena and others—and when they gave a theological form to the growing monotheistic religions. It was at this stage that a new priesthood in a changed society could again claim to be entitled to the charisma of office. Now it only needed a theologically justified transfer of this concept from Kṣatriya to Brahmin, from king to priest. Kṛṣṇa himself is still mainly a king. It is the myth of Paraśurāma (cf. Gail 1977), who is primarily *ṛṣi* but also warrior, that marks the transition.

The new concept arose in the Gupta period. It linked divine presence, and therefore also divine grace, with outstanding religious leaders. The first historical evidence is the (posthumous) identification of Lakulīśa, the famous Śaiva teacher of the second century, with Śiva himself.[21] This seems to have happened in the fourth century and it was a turning point: it ended the long and painful decline of Brahmin priestly power in India. The priestly class now regained much of its former influence. Among Vaiṣṇavas it extended the *avatāra* concept beyond the Kṣatriyas Rāma, Balarāma and Kṛṣṇa to include also Brahmins like Paraśurāma, Kapila and Dattātreya. It appropriated *purāṇic* literature and added the *māhātmya* and *tīrthayātrā* sections, as well as long expositions on ritual, theology, Sāṃkhya and Yoga. The gradually evolving Smārta religion, consisting of a combination of monistic philosophy with the *pañcāyatana* worship of a set of five major deities, offered new possibilities for the king to honour and control the more important Gods of his kingdom with the help of priests. From the sixth century onwards, an increasing number of Brahmins[22] began to associate with, and domesticate, the *bhakti* movement. Also, from the sixth or early-seventh century, the concept of *jīvanmukti* gained wide recognition, with the result that the old words guru and *ācārya*, traditionally signifying teachers, acquired an additional shade of meaning in which was implied closeness to a divine state. From the *Viṣṇudharmottarapurāṇa* we may deduct that by the middle of the seventh century priests had regained their position as mediators between man and God. And from the eighth or ninth century this mediatorship took a modified, ritually controlled and highly effective form. The new role gave the guru an important place in a line of transmission of grace that linked the highest God with the *bhakta* or *dāsa*, the devoted but imperfect and unworthy slave.

It is not yet clear where the concept took initial shape, whether in a Vaiṣṇava (i.e. Sāttvata or Pāñcarātra) or a Śaiva context. The point is that *dīkṣā* or initiation as a symbolic act confirming access to, and acceptance in, a religious group, now became a condition for the attainment of divine grace. The *dīkṣāguru* was, as it were, the arm of God—to hand out grace or withhold it. In this way, Brahmin ritual-control over communication with the divine that, with the decline of *śrauta* sacrifice had been reduced to the mere performance of *saṃskāra* rituals, was finally re-established.

In Śaivism the concept of *śaktipāta*, the descent of the Lord's cleansing energy which destroys the primordial *mala* or dirt attached to the soul and thus prepares the individual devotee for participation in God's grace, made the guru the last and most immediately important member in a chain of spiritual intermediaries. *Īśvara*, the Lord Himself, remains aloof from defiling contact with the material world. In later Vaiṣṇavism it is the *ācārya* who performs a similar service of initiation, though it is not the destruction of *mala* but the entrance into the community of saints which is decisive. In both cases, the charisma clearly rests in the guru or *ācārya* who assumes the role of representative or mouthpiece of God. And in both traditions, God and guru in their relation to the devotee tend to become exchangeable and almost identical.[23]

Evidence of this tendency is not restricted to the literary tradition of hagiography in both Śaiva and Vaiṣṇava traditions. Archaeological evidence shows that already in the seventh century, and possibly earlier, Pāśupata teachers were thought to become identical with Śiva in the moment of death, and temples were erected with the *liṅga* installed bearing their name.

With the full development of this new type of adult initiation[24] we have reached a point where the exceptional religious specialist, the guru or *ācārya*, is *ex officio*, i.e. through appointment to succession in a line of spiritual transmission or *guruparamparā*, endowed with charisma. He is the mediator of grace and so close to God—and at the same time so much easier to approach—that in the eyes of the devotees he can become almost a substitute for God himself. It is he who is the immediate source of divine blessings.

It is obvious that our observations, derived from South Asian sources of the Smṛti literature onwards, correspond exactly to what Weber has called the routinization of charisma.[25] If the original charisma is not linked to an office but to a person, it is unstable by its very nature of being a divine gift depending on purpose and merit. But the community attracted and formed by it requires stability in order to continue to exist, it requires the continuation of charismatic authority. This is where the transformation from personal to institutional charisma takes place. Whether succession to charisma is inherited[26] or occurs through appointment or ritual initiation,[27] or is again divinely revealed through visions and signs,[28] it always implies the appropriation of special powers inherent in the office or necessary for the office through ritual transmission of charismatic authority, i.e. through initiation, coronation, or investiture. This was already true for the two major early institutions in human society: kingship and priesthood. The example of righteous kingship quoted above shows that charisma could be seen as conferred on a person through ritual action or be gained by individual righteousness, but was itself of a non-personal divine nature, and linked to the ideal of a divine institution such as kingship. This would apply similarly for later priestly offices like that of the Pope or the *jagadguru* or *dīkṣāguru*. Of course, charisma can also be invested in a radiant individual person without office, making that person eligible for office.

Our analysis up to this point has shown that although charisma is always experienced in the office-holder, the king, priest, prophet, healer or magician, its foundation is often not in the person but in the social function he represents. We shall now go a step further and see that charisma, though still defined as divine agency in an inner-worldly context of gross material bodies, can also be experienced in things—things, that is, that have something divine about them.

When the tenth guru of the Sikh community, Guru Govind Singh, closed the line of spiritual succession and stated that henceforth the sacred scripture was to be taken as the only guru, he not only prevented future rivalries for the office, he also invested the book itself with the status of ultimate spiritual guide and source of grace. Henceforth the guru became the *Guru Granth Sāhib*, a guru in non-human form that was yet able to speak the Truth: a canon was declared guru and became the charismatic centre of the Sikh community, located in the Golden Temple at Amritsar.

The history of religion provides many examples of divine agency experienced as residing in things and acting through things: these are not persons but objects endowed with 'gifts of grace', with the power of working miracles and enchanting devotees, like the famous shroud of Turin, or a splinter from the cross on which Christ died. Still more remotely linked to the charismatic person, and yet powerful, are mere symbols of divine presence, such as the footprints of Buddha or Viṣṇu. Evidence shows that an exclusive link between charisma and a human personality is not universal. Rather, it is the presence of some superhuman agency that is perceived as charisma in persons and elsewhere. This is the case in kingship and even more so in the *avatāra* (who need not take human form),[29] and in the guru. Is it also true for another important embodiment of the divine, for the ritually consecrated image of God?

I am conscious of the fact that in making this step from the charismatic person to the charismatic object or symbol, I am extending the concept of charisma into a domain that Weber did not envisage. I am equally conscious of the common belief on the part of the devotee that the image of God is, indeed, God Himself—a belief that is beautifully expressed in much South Indian devotional poetry. Nevertheless there are compelling reasons for the historian of religion to also see the parallels that exist between the charismatic processes discussed so far, and those that manifest themselves in image worship. The identification of image and deity arises out of the emotional urge of one's *bhakti* to visualize and actually *see* the Lord, prostrate before Him and serve Him. Yet this attitude is accompanied by the knowledge that God is in the image only when ritually invoked or visualized in it, and that He could, in principle, be invoked or visualized everywhere since He is omnipresent. His nearest presence is, in fact, in the devotee's own heart. The image is important because it constitutes a focus of identification that allows for a personal relation not only for one individual but for many, that creates community, that asks for duties to be fulfilled, that allots tasks and rewards. It is, in this respect, comparable to the charismatic person and to the guru. And if the guru, like the image, is also seen as a visible manifestation of the Lord Himself, this only enhances the comparability between the charismatic experience of divine presence in front of an image of God and that experienced in front of a guru.

We will, therefore, extend our investigation to include the charisma of divine images and the canons of their visual representation and ritual consecration. And anticipating the objection that this amounts to a virtual equation of charisma with God or divinity itself, I would protest that this is not my intention. As in all the other cases discussed so far, we have to do here with divine agency operating through a material body that is only temporarily—mostly through ritual transfer—inhabited by it. Here, in precise analogy to the allegorical equation of the king's body with the heavenly guardians of the quarters, the presence of divine agency is established through ritual consecration. And again, as in the other cases, this body is *purposefully* endowed with divine agency, in this case to hand out grace and to produce in the mind of the devotee a blissful or transforming and motivating charismatic experience. There is, therefore, sufficient reason to look at the image of God as another source of charismatic experience and to investigate whether the pattern of charismatic renewal encountered earlier applies to the image of God as well.

There are basically two variants of the *mūrti* or image of God: the image in the household shrine and that in the temple. In both, there is the presence of God in ritual performance. But they serve different purposes and cater to different needs.

While worship of the household deity is intensely centred on individual devotion and service, the temple deity is instrumental in creating a community and a public religious sphere. In the privacy of the house it is primarily *premabhakti* or *vātsalya-bhakti*, where the God is to be cared for with emotions derived from, and increased beyond, those emotions that are commonly experienced in receiving a welcome guest, in caring for a child, in pining for a beloved, or in devotedly serving a beloved husband. In the temple it is primarily *dāsya* and *prapatti*, the complete submission of the servant to his master, or of the unworthy and helpless soul to the source of grace. Here the God is a king and treated as a king. He gives both blessing and protection to his people, secures prosperity for subjects, and unites them in their concentration on the master so as to form a community of devotees, the *sajjana* or good people, those who share the same beliefs, the same rules of conduct, and the same grace. With others than these, a devotee needs to avoid contact for fear of being defiled.

The differences between home and temple are slight, but significant: decorating the image of the deity in the home emphasizes the beauty of the beloved, decorating it in the temple emphasizes His or Her majesty. Here the visual transmission of divine charisma is important. That is why the eyes of the deity are accentuated: *darśana*, eye-contact between the Lord and his devotee, is of prime importance even in the darkness of the *garbhagṛha* and across the space reserved for the priesthood—and often also across crowds of other devotees. Here, the presence of God manifests itself in a flash of vision. It touches the innermost being of some devotees and inspires them to produce the most fervent songs of praise; it also induces those less sensitive to go there again and again, hoping for the same miracle to happen to them. The miracle is indeed, necessary for the continuing attraction of the cult. Where it does not happen because charismatic experiences tend to be rare within an established tradition, it must be re-enacted, called back to memory, artificially renewed. The hagiography, its recitation or, more important, its re-enactment in procession—such as the yearly *yātrā* of saints to Pandharpur in Maharashtra[30]—is one of the means to charismatic renewal. Another possibility, rarely made use of on account of high costs though highly effective, is the renewal of God's image. In this latter case, the canon is that of the art of the craftsmen (*śilpaśāstra*) and that of ritual procedure:[31] an established norm for the symbolic representation of God in visual form with all His attributes and the accompanying *mantras*, *yantras*, rites and paraphernalia. The charisma is that of a person-to-be-born, still encapsulated in the process of a miraculous transformation. The whole process involves a vision of divine command, omens that direct a search for the divinely inhabited person-to-be,[32] his self-revelation and taking shape, and, finally, his awakening to life and showering grace on his devotees.

If the image is life-size and made of stone, as is the case in most temples, the costs of renewal are so high and the time required is so long that this option is usually not resorted to except in case of serious damage to the old image. If, on the other hand, the image is made of wood or clay, its periodic renewal is easier and affordable and can lead to another culmination in the ritual life of a cult. As an outstanding instance I would cite Lord Jagannātha, one of the most compelling manifestations of God in a Vaiṣṇava, more specifically Kṛṣṇaite, context. And since this is an extention of the Weberian concept of charisma, it is useful to add a case study to substantiate my point.

Navakalevara, the New Body of Lord Jagannātha

The images of the Jagannātha triad in Puri are renewed from time to time. This happens whenever an intercalary *āṣāḍha* month has to be inserted in order to re-adjust the solar and lunar calendar, an event which occurs at irregular intervals of between eight to nineteen years. At that time the Gods receive a new body: in Sanskrit *navakalevara*, the most important ritual in Puri.[33] Its last occurrence was in 1996.

When compared to the age of the temple,[34] this ritual is not very old. Its first recorded occurrence was in 1587.[35] Nineteen years earlier, in 1568, the army of the Afghan Sultan Sulaiman Karrāṇi of Bengal had conquered Orissa, killed its ruler and destroyed its main symbol of power—Lord Puruṣottama-Jagannātha of Puri, in whose name the kings of both the Eastern Gaṅga and the Sūrya dynasties had been ruling as human representatives of the God.[36]

There are several accounts of what happened. The Muslim general (called Kalāpāhāḍ, the 'Black Rock' in Orissan tradition) seized the images, mounted them on elephants and carried them in triumph to the seashore,[37] or to the bank of a river (the Ganges[38] or the Mahānadī[39]) where they were solemnly burnt in public.[40] The 'Lord of the World' suffered total destruction.

However, in the Orissa chronicles the episode does not end here. A Vaiṣṇava named Biśara Mahānti had gone to see the destruction of the Gods. Later he returned to the spot, searched for a piece that had not been entirely consumed by the flames, hid it away in his *mṛdaṅga* drum, and took it secretly to the fortress Kujanga.[41] This is the *brahma-padārtha* or Brahma element, a fraction of divine substance, which was rescued at the time. Nineteen years later, Rāmacandra I, founder of the Bhoi dynasty, had established and fortified a new principality in Khurda and ordered new images of the Jagannātha triad to be made. According to the Mādalā Pāñjī, the *brahma-padārtha* was brought from Kujanga and inserted into a cavity of the new statue of Jagannātha. The Cakaḍā Pothi claims that it was Lord Jagannātha Himself who told the king in a dream about His presence in Kujanga and ordered the king to have new images made.[42] Symbolically, the essence of the old body of God was transferred to his new form. Evidently, it was the emphatic claim of preserving continuity even in a case of apparent total discontinuity and change that prompted this ingenious device.

King Rāmacandra I of Khurda installed the new images of Jagannātha, Balabhadra and Subhadrā at first in his own temple in Khurda. Two years later they were transferred to Puri. But there the Gods were by no means safe during the reigns of Ramacandra I and his son Puruṣottama. The Muslims made repeated efforts to purloin the images again, but meanwhile the priests in Puri had learnt their lesson and were more vigilant. They managed to carry the images away in time, brought them in a boat across Cilkā Lake, and kept them in hiding in Gañjām district. Several times they carried them back to the temple and as many times they had to flee again and hide their Gods in the jungle, where the statues suffered rain and gradual decay.[43] The weakness and vulnerability of the Puri temple is evident, but instead of total defeat there is now a story of priestly heroism, of success in fooling even as powerful an enemy as the Muslim governors of Cuttack.

Rāmacandra I was a charismatic leader and political genius. He did not belong to the royal family and yet succeeded in gaining the vacant throne of Orissa. In the face of the ruling Afghans, he dared to set up new images of the Jagannātha triad in his small principality of Khurda. This extraordinary event gave him an advantage over other more legitimate but less active claimants to the throne. The priests of Puri and the people of Orissa applauded him. It also justified his claim to be chosen by the Lord Himself as *rāuta*, as son and rightful deputy of Jagannātha. He later moved both the images and his court to Puri and settled Brahmins from elsewhere in five new *śāsana* villages near Puri in order to obtain an independent basis of support. In Rāmacandra I we encounter a charismatic person setting in motion a highly charismatic event.

For the population and pilgrims the renewal of the cult in Puri—a real resurrection after total annihilation—proved a tremendous success, so much so that the priests understood the message: it is renewal that radiates charisma and stimulates religious fervour. The Lord himself, they claimed, had shown he wanted to give up his old body and get a new one from time to time; he even used Muslims to get that message across. And they did what any authority with any sensitivity to charisma would have done: they institutionalised the event.

The *navakalevara* ritual has been periodically repeated ever since. It is construed in such a way that evidence of God's presence in the new body is established beyond all reasonable doubt. The preparations begin six months ahead of time. After careful ritual purification, a party comprising both tribal and Brahmin priests is sent out to find the *dāru*, the wood required for the new bodies of the Gods. Lord Jagannātha himself or the Goddess Maṅgalā show the direction in a dream. They must find a *nīm* tree big enough to provide the wood for all three large statues and the Sudarśana pole that represents the discus of Jagannātha, or several trees. But not any big *nīm* tree will do. The Lords manifest the future body they want to animate by unmistakable signs. The tree to be chosen must bear, clearly visible, the natural signs of the disc and the conch, symbols of Viṣṇu.

The search can last several months. When a corresponding tree is finally found, a *vanayāga* takes place, a sacrifice meant to pacify the forest and all animals and spirits that have used the tree as shelter. They are requested to leave and the tree itself is requested to consent to reveal the new body of the lords. Only after a successful sacrifice which signals acceptance by the tree is it felled, its branches buried, and the usable logs taken back to Puri. It takes the entire month of *āṣāḍha* to shape and paint the new images, a procedure which largely follows and re-actualizes the traditional canon of the craftsmen and ritual specialists but can, if necessary, introduce innovations. A case in point is the change from the threefold *mūrti* of Jagannātha, Saṃkarṣaṇa and Subhadrā attested to in the earlier texts to a fourfold *mūrti* which contains Sudarśana (as symbol of both the *cakra* and Narasiṃha) in addition and is attested only in later texts.[44] Such innovation can happen only at the time of the renewal of the statues, and it affirms and strongly legitimizes modified theological concepts, introduces significant changes in ritual procedure, and adds new forms to the traditions of the craftsmen.

The process of creating the new images of the Jagannātha triad follows in principle the example set in the late-sixteenth century, but takes later changes and additions into account. The *brahma-padārtha* of the old statue is taken out by a tribal priest who is blindfolded and has his hands wrapped so that he can neither see nor feel what he is taking out. That unseen and unfelt substance is carefully inserted into the new body of the Lord, filling with it a cavity that has been prepared for the purpose, and is then closed and sealed. No one is to witness this moment of mysterious transfer of divine substance that guarantees the continuity of the divine essence in the new image. When covered with various layers of cloth, resins and colours, its outer appearance will, of course, be almost identical with the previous one.

Here we have a ritual enactment of innovation and continuity that closely parallels the results of our analysis of the relation between charisma and canon. Even the presence of God in an image, a prime source of charismatic experience, can be enhanced and actualized by occasional renewal.

The extension of our investigation into charisma and canon to include 'charismatic events' such as the renewal of an image (and canons other than holy scripture such as canons of visual art and ritual) has not changed the pattern arrived at earlier. In all cases, charisma was instrumental in creating, keeping alive, changing, and rejuvenating a canonical tradition. While the context shifted, the relation between charisma and canon remained similar. The new image corresponds to a new charismatic leader who is able to instil fresh life into an old cult and canonic ritual tradition, as well as new or enhanced commitment in the community of believers.[45]

Weber, when enumerating pure types of legitimate authority, characterized these as 'resting on devotion to the specific and exceptional sanctity, heroism or exemplary character of an individual person, and of the normative patterns or order revealed by him' (1964: 328). His emphasis, in this context, was on the personal relationship of devotion and the recognition of superiority that results from the *experience* of charisma by those who encounter a charismatic leader.[46] One could go further and ask whether charisma is something a person *possesses* or something another person *perceives*. A charismatic person whom nobody recognizes as such would go unnoticed and have no impact. Charisma, therefore, reveals itself always in interaction. Nevertheless, our sources confirm that charisma is first and foremost believed to be an uncommon quality that someone (or something) *possesses*. This is shown not only by the biblical conception of *charismata* mentioned earlier, but also by reports about miracles of the Buddha, or by the phenomena of possession, shamanism, magic and communication with ancestral spirits known from so-called 'primitive' religions around the world. Weber himself understands charisma as something that is possessed, and he also acknowledges several forms of 'routinized' charisma as distinguished from 'pure' charisma. It is in the logic of things that the former is more common than the latter and that it is only 'pure' charisma that develops revolutionary power and causes radical change. Both forms of charisma have to do with the creation and reinterpretation of a canon. They differ not only in degree of intensity but also in their direction of commitment: pure charisma overthrows existing norms or institutions and creates new ones. Institutionalized charisma adapts existing norms and institutions to changing times and thereby keeps them alive.

To summarize, a religious community comes into being through the agency of one or more charismatic leaders.[47] With the formation of a canon it provides itself with a doctrine and religious practice based on initial charisma and meant to be timelessly valid. This also constitutes an unassailable referent for collective group identity, which is most important for the survival of a religion. But as time goes on, doctrine and practice have to be updated because a stagnant religion is likely to die. The task is to legitimize change and preserve identity in change. This is possible through an actualization of the initial canon that may affect theology and social value system, ritual practice, visual representation of the divinity, or rules of conduct for devotees. For all cases of important change as well as for arousing new enthusiasm in the community, fresh legitimizing charisma is required. More often than not, it is institutionalized charisma (which may well be enhanced by the personal charisma of the office-bearer) that is at work in constructive change. For the community it is charismatic experience that rejuvenates aging religion and facilitates change. It is the experience of an uncommon presence of divine agency in exceptional humans, in sacred scripture or holy objects, in the faith-inspiring image of God and, of course, in all kinds of extraordinary events and miracles. The more often this happens, the safer is the religion from obsolescence.

The most common form to achieve the task of rejuvenation is ritual renovation and reconfirmation as practised, for instance, in the yearly festival calendar. It is also, and very prominently so, achieved by a charismatic guru and by the act of succession from one guru to the next. Here we have a moment of crisis and rebirth with a tremendous cathartic potential, if the succession proves a success. In the case of the image of God, this too can be a source of charismatic experience. A renewal is not normally necessary but if it happens this constitutes another occasion for change and another climax in the ritual revitalization of a cult.

Notes

1. Derived from the Greek *charis*, meaning grace, favour; the *charismata* (pl. of *charisma*) mentioned in the Greek Bible were 'gifts of grace' or special powers attributed to the agency of the Holy Spirit but operating in exceptional human beings. They included the gift of healing, prophecy, exorcism of evil spirits, working miracles, unusual knowledge, wisdom, faith or love, as well as *glossolalia* (speaking in tongues, ecstatic incoherent utterances as sign of possession by the Holy Spirit); the ability to interpret these utterances and unusual oratorical capacities in general (see, e.g., Paul in I. Cor. 12.1-14.40; Acts 2:1-12). These examples were derived from the life of Christ and his immediate disciples and were later expanded to include unbending heroism, fearless testimony in martyrdom, visions, and communication with superhuman beings. For important works on charisma prior to Max Weber, see Sohm (1892–1923) and Holl (1898). Other cultures have basically similar notions, with additional emphasis on the special powers of the hero, the shaman, the yogi or the magician, etc. These are extensively listed in Parrinder (1987: 218-22).

   Max Weber, the most important modern theoretician on charisma, whose wide erudition included much that was known in his time about different cultures and civilizations, defined it as 'a certain quality of individual personality by virtue of which he is set apart from ordinary men and treated as endowed with supernatural, superhuman, or at least specifically exceptional powers or qualities.' (Weber 1964: 358).

2. The Greek term *kanōn* is a loan word derived from Semitic languages, signifying originally a reed, used as a straight measuring rod or standard of length. In its application in Greek, the term acquired the two basic meanings of 'norm', 'formal basis for distinguishing truth from falsehood,' and 'complete enumeration', 'scientific list'. In early Christianity it was used for the binding norms of true Christian faith (the Latin counterpart being *regula*) and for authorized collections of sayings, decisions, or laws.
3. Holy scripture, conceived of as a collection of God's own words, enshrines in its letters an element of divinity that can, in ritual performance, induce charismatic experience in a perceptive audience. Instances of this kind are the unveiling and unrolling of the *Torah*, and the unwrapping of the *Qur'ān* or the *Guru Granth Sāhib*.
4. Although voiced by seers, prophets, poets or gurus, the sacred scripture is generally not considered a human creation, but something given, revealed, received in inspiration, or mysteriously found inscribed on clay tablets or stone blocks.
5. Weber (1964: 324-8 and 363ff.) distinguished charismatic authority from the authority of both tradition and law. According to him, it is the transformation into general routine that marks the transition from charismatic authority to 'tradition' or 'law'.
6. This view of bio-physical processes of nature seems to retain its validity in spite of the discovery of recurrent patterns in chaos theory: even chaos that overwhelms existing structures may have its own basic order.
7. This is, for example, the case with Śaṅkara, Rāmānuja and Madhva, whose commentaries were all based on the same set of basic texts but established different systems of philosophy.
8. Cf. Assmann and Assmann (1987: 19–23).
9. The formation of canonical scripture is fairly well documented in the Jewish, Christian and Islamic traditions, in Buddhism, Jainism and the Indian Vedānta schools. The typology derivable from these as well as from the Roman canonization of law renders the myth of Vedavyāsa's one-man-achievement of collecting and arranging all the Vedic hymns rather unlikely. Its approximate date might also require reconsideration on the basis of archaeological evidence regarding patterns of settlement and social organization in early North India.
10. For a famous passage to this effect refer to *Bhagavadgītā* 4.7-8.
11. Weber (1964: 328) quotes Sohm (1892–1923) and Holl (1898). See note 1.
12. Pronounced *hvarenah*; related to Persian *farnah*: glory.
13. See note 1.

14. Yašt 19, 21–38; the entire Yašt, named Zamyād Yašt, praises the kingly (and priestly) glory (Kavaém xˇarənah). See Kanga 1962, part II, pp. 654–82 for the text in *nagar* characters and Darmesteter 1883, reprint 1965, pp. 286–309 for a translation. The legend is elaborated in Firdausi's *Shah-nāma*. For the parallel myths of Iranian Yima-asaeta, son of Vivahant (the Djamshad of later texts) and the Indian Yama, son of Vivasvant, see Christensen (1917–34).
15. Only a few indications of the myth of Indra's slaying the serpent Vṛtra borrowing from traditions about Trita Āptya are preserved in the *Ṛgveda*: such as RV 1.187.1 or 8.7.24 and passages where Indra gets the *soma* from Trita or is supported in battle by Trita. But Trita is also an earlier hero in two other myths ordinarily associated with Indra, namely the freeing of cows (the vala myth in RV 1.52.5) and the killing of Triśiras/Viśvarūpa (RV 10.8.8). The quoted Iranian tradition has further partial Indian parallels in the myth of Yama and in the legend of the wicked king, Vena, and his successor Pṛthu.
16. This agency was believed to emanate from divine *substance*, so that the charismatic person was seen as possessing an extra element in addition to his human nature.
17. Manu V, 96–7; VII, 3–7. For the consequences of this concept see Stietencron (1998, especially 497ff.). See also Ghoshal (1966: 29f., 163f.).
18. Similar processes were precisely the reason for the early Christian church to try to contain and eventually ban anarchic charismatic activities such as *glossolalia* (spontaneous, not always coherent inspirational speech), prophecy, miracles and new revelations in the Christian community. The effort to create an authoritative canon to counteract unwanted additional revelations began with the so-called Didachē containing the teachings of the twelve apostles (early second century) and ended in 367, when Bishop Athanasius of Alexandria established a final selection of 'canonical' revelation considered binding for the Christian faith.
19. Information on these developments in North and North-west India is as yet restricted to a limited number of coins and random hints in the *sūtra* literature. It appears that the rise of these cults—mainly clan deities of successful warrior clans like the Yaudheyas, Vṛṣṇis and others—has to be seen in the context of major military operations of the Nandas and the Mauryas that required recruitment and the social integration of mercenary troops and their gods or clan heroes. See Stietencron (1977a); Härtel (1987) and Jaiswal (1967).
20. Stietencron (1977a, *passim*). The fact that some of the new temple cults developed monotheistic theologies (Viṣṇu, Śiva, Sūrya) may be seen in the context of links with the Hellenistic Seleucid empire since the early Mauryan period and the influence of Zoroastrianism from Eastern Iran.
21. The Mathurā pillar inscription of Candragupta II, regnal year 5, Gupta year 61, i.e. AD 380 mentions a Śaiva guru who was tenth in succession from Kuśika, one of the four main disciples of Lakulīśa (Bhandarkar 1931–2; Sircar

1993: 277–9). This gives us a basis for an approximate date of Lakulīśa. His identification with Śiva is accomplished at the time of the inscription, but probably not much earlier.

22. If some passages in the *Bhagavadgītā* suggest a Brahmin participation in its formulation, this would imply a priestly involvement in early *bhakta* thought. But orthodox Brahmin opposition remained strong due to considerable low-caste participation in the *bhakti* movement.
23. In the case of the Sikhs, the tenth guru, Govind Singh, closed the line of succession by transferring guruship on the sacred scripture, the *Guru Granth Sāhib*. Henceforth it was the book that carried the charisma of the guru.
24. *Dīkṣā* was already a Vedic rite of purification and initiation which was a prerequisite for the *yajamāna* or patron of all major rituals. Its effect was supposed to last only as long as the period of ritual engagement, usually a clearly defined and limited number of days, in some *sattra* sacrifices longer. In the case of royal consecration, the period of initiation into office would last as long as the reign. In the early medieval concept of *dīkṣā* there are two forms: (*a*) initiation of the novice into the religious community by the *ācārya* or *dīkṣāguru*; and (*b*) the transfer of divine power to a religious specialist who thereby becomes an *ācārya* or *dīkṣāguru* himself. For these two there is no time limit, since the first is meant to last for the whole life (unless invalidated by another *dīkṣā*) and the second is expected to yield liberation while still living (*jīvanmukti*), either with the initiation or during his lifetime or at the moment of death at the very latest.
25. On various forms of the routinization of charisma, see Weber (1964: 363–73). He distinguishes six different types: (*a*) traditionalization, i.e. search for a person who displays certain pre-established distinguishing characteristics; (*b*) revelation through oracles, lots, divine judgments etc.; (*c*) designation of a successor by the charismatic leader himself; (*d*) designation of a successor by an elite of qualified followers, prominent example: the Pope; (*e*) heredity (here, a stabilization occurs only where the law of primogeniture is observed, otherwise, fights for succession are not uncommon); (*f*) transmission by ritual.
26. Often in the case of *Pīrs*, but also in several *saguṇa* and *nirguṇa sampradāyas* from the sixteenth century onwards. Weber includes in this category the Indian caste system which he considers the classical case of hereditary charisma. 'All occupational qualifications, and in particular all the qualifications for positions of authority and power, have there come to be regarded as strictly bound to the inheritance of charisma' (Weber 1964: 372).
27. Dominant in traditions demanding abstention from sexual contact with women as a condition for priestly office; also prominent in traditions characterized either by a strong guru-*śiṣya* relationship or by the development of central institutions and functionaries.
28. A prominent example is the search for, and selection of, the Dalai Lama and other prominent Tulku leaders of Tibetan Lamaism. (See Brück 2000; Weber 1964: 364).
29. See the *avatāras* in animal or half-animal shape. Even the *mūrti* or

consecrated stone image can be considered an *avatāra*, both by Śaivas and by Vaiṣṇavas.

30. Sontheimer (1989). Compare the mystery plays of the birth and passion of Christ or the grief for Hussein on the tenth day of muharram.
31. Codified in the *kriyā* sections of the *Āgamas* and in the *pūjāpaddhatis* and other manuals for the officiating priest.
32. Before creating an image of a deity, the stone to be used is carefully selected. Both the type of stone and its quality are relevant. The latter is tested by the sound it produces when knocked against. For the selection of the wood for a wooden image, see below.
33. For a detailed description of the ritual see Tripathi 1978 (according to textual prescription) and Hardenberg 1998 (according to actual practice).
34. The temple was consecrated in 1197 after almost seventy years of building activity. For a discussion of the date see Stietencron (1977b).
35. According to Kulke (1979:122–3) this event has to be dated two years later. S. N. Rajguru (1996: 63) believes the first renewal to have taken place in 1308.
36. This policy of projecting the king as representative of God was introduced in Orissa by the Eastern Gaṅga king, Anaṅgabhīma III (ruled 1211–38), in the year 1216. In his Kanchipuram inscription no. 1 he declared himself to be the son and representative of Puruṣottama, Rudra and Durgā, the three major deities of Orissa. From 1230/1 on he dropped Rudra and Durgā and reigned on behalf of Puruṣottama alone. With only a few exceptions, this remained a royal policy for most of his successors up to the present.
37. Abū'l Fazl Allāmī (1948–9: 140).
38. Mahānti (ed.)[1940] 1969: 61. The Mādalā Pāñjī calls this period *arājaka*, without king, Lord Jagannātha being the missing king. See Kulke (1979:126).
39. Pattanaik (ed.) 1959: 5-6.
40. These accounts emphasize the religious zeal of the conqueror who is not content with destroying the images on the spot: what he wants is publicity for everyone to witness the superiority of Allah the Almighty, who easily reduces to ashes even the highest god of the infidels.
41. Mahānti (ed.) [1940] 1969: 61–2; Pattanaik (ed.) 1959: 5–6.
42. Mahānti (ed.) [1940] 1969: 61, Pattanaik (ed.) 1959: 6
43. Mahānti (ed.) [1940] 1969: 62ff.
44. See Stietencron (1980).
45. Since it is a periodic and ritualized process, it is 'routinized' or institutionalized charisma that is displayed here.
46. Weber (1964: 359): 'It is recognition on the part of those subject to authority which is decisive for the validity of charisma. This is freely given and guaranteed by what is held to be a 'sign' or proof, originally always a miracle ... But where charisma is genuine, it is not this which is the basis of the claim to legitimacy. This basis lies rather in the conception that it is the *duty* of those who have been called to a charismatic mission to recognize its quality and to act accordingly. Psychologically this "recognition" is

a matter of complete personal devotion to the possessor of the quality, arising out of enthusiasm, or of despair and hope.'

47. Most charismatic movements do not survive their founders for long. It is only when the charismatic leader does find able successors who keep the community together, and who systematize the scattered utterances of the founder, that the new movement is able to survive.

References

Abū'l Fazl Allāmī.1948–9. *Āīn-I-Akbarī*, vol. II, trans. into English by H. S. Jarrett, 2nd corrected ed. by Jadunath Sarkar. Calcutta: Royal Asiatic Society of Bengal.

Assmann, Aleida, and Jan Assmann.1987. Kanon und Zensur. In *Kanon und Zensur. Beiträge zur Archäologie der literarischen Kommunikation II*, ed. by Aleida Assmann and Jan Assmann, 7–27. München: Wilhelm Fink Verlag.

Bhandarkar, D. R. 1931–2. Mathura Pillar Inscription of Chandragupta II: G. E. 61. *Epigraphia Indica* 21: 1–9.

Brück, Michael von. 2000. Canonicity and Divine Interference. The Tulkus and the Shugden-Controversy. In the present volume pp. 328–349.

Christensen, Arthur. 1917–34. *Les types du premier homme et premier roi dans l'histoire légendaire des Iraniens*. Vols I and II, Stockholm: Norstedt, and Leiden: Brill.

Darmesteter, James. 1883. *The Zend Avesta*, Part II, (Sacred Books of the East, Vol. 23). Oxford. Oxford University Press; reprint Delhi: Motilal Banarsidass, 1965.

Gail, Adalbert. 1977. *Paraśurāma, Brahmane und Krieger: Untersuchungen über Ursprung und Entwicklung eines Avatāra Viṣṇus und Bhakta Śivas in der indischen Literatur*. Wiesbaden: Harrassowitz.

Ghoshal, U. N. 1966. *A History of Indian Political Ideas. The Ancient Period and the Transition to the Middle Ages*. London: Oxford University Press.

Hardenberg, Roland.1998. *Die Wiedergeburt der Götter. Ritual und Gesellschaft in Orissa*. Hamburg: Verlag Dr Korvac.

Härtel, Herbert. 1987. Archaeological Evidence on Early Vāsudeva Worship. In *Orientalia: Iosephi Tucci memoriae dicata*, ed. by G. Gnoli. Vol. 2, 573–87. Roma: Istituto Italiano per il Medio ed Estremo Oriente.

Holl, Karl. 1898. *Enthusiasmus und Bussgewalt beim griechischen Mönchtum. Eine Studie zu Symeon dem neuen Theologen*. Leipzig: Hinrich.

Jaiswal, Suvira. 1967. *The Origin and Development of Vaiṣṇavism (Vaiṣṇavism from 200 BC to AD 500)*. Delhi: Munshiram Manoharlal.

Kanga, M.F. 1962. *Avesta: The Sacred Scripture of the Porsees, Part II: Khordesh Avesta and Yasts*, ed. by F.M. Kanga and N.S. Sontakke. Poona: Vaidika Samçodhana Mandala.

Kulke, Hermann. 1979. *Jagannātha-Kult und Gajapati-Königtum. Ein Beitrag zur Geschichte religiöser Legitimation hinduistischer Herrscher* (Schriftenreihe des Südasien-Instituts der Universität Heidelberg 23). Wiesbaden: Franz Steiner.

Mahānti, Ārtta Ballabha (ed.). [1940] 1969. *Mādaḷā Pāñjī*. Cuttack: Prācī Samiti, reprint Bhubaneswar: Utkal University, 1969.

Parrinder, Geoffrey. 1987. Charisma. In *The Encyclopedia of Religion*, ed. by Mircea Eliade. Vol. 3.: 218–22. New York: Macmillan.

Pattanaik, Sudhākara (ed.). 1959. *Cakaḍā Pothi o Cakaḍā Basāṇa bā Cayini Cakaḍā*. Cuttack: Sudhakara Pattanaik.

Rajguru, S.N. 1996. 'The Starting of Navakalevara: A Glimpse'. In *Navakalevara of Lord Jagannath*, ed. Surat Chandra Mahapatra, 60–6, Puri: Sri Jagannath Research Centre.

Sircar, Dinesh Chandra. 1993. *Select Inscriptions Bearing on Indian History and Civilization*. Vol. 1, reprint Delhi: V. K. Publishing House.

Sohm, Rudolf. 1892–1923. *Kirchenrecht. Systematisches Handbuch der deutschen Rechtswissenschaft*. 2 vols. München.

Sontheimer, G.-D. 1989. *Pastoral Deities in Western India*, trans. by A. Feldhaus. New York: Oxford University Press.

Stietencron, Heinrich von. 1977a. Orthodox Attitudes Towards Temple Service and Image Worship in Ancient India. *Central Asiatic Journal* 21.2: 126–37.

———. 1977b. The Date of the Jagannāth Temple: Literary Sources Reconsidered. In *Sidelights on the History and Culture of Orissa*, ed. by Manmath Nath Das, 516–32. Cuttack: Vidyapuri.

———. 1980. Die Stellvertreterrolle des Narasiṃha im Kult des Jagannātha. In *Studien zur Indologie und Iranistik* 5/6: Festschrift Paul Thieme zur Vollendung des 75. Lebensjahres dargebracht von Schülern und Freunden, ed. G. Buddruss and A. Wezler, 245–78. Reinbek: Dr Inge Wezler.

———. 1998. The Non-Existence of Impurity and the Legitimation of Kings. In *Lex et Litterae. Studies in Honour of Professor Oscar Botto*, ed. by Siegfried Lienhard, 489-508. Torino: Edizioni dell'Orso.

Tripathi, Gaya Charan. 1978. Navakalevara, The Unique Ceremony of the 'Birth' and the 'Death' of the 'Lord of the World'. In *The Cult of Jagannāth and the Regional Tradition of Orissa*, ed. by A. Eschmann *et al.*, 223–64. New Delhi: Manohar.

Weber, Max. 1964. *The Theory of Social and Economic Organization* [Wirtschaft und Gesellschaft, Teil I], trans. by A. M. Henderson and Talcott Parsons, ed. by Talcott Parsons. New York: Free Press.

Religious Authority in Medieval and Pre-modern India

The Formation of Śrīvaiṣṇavism

FRIEDHELM HARDY

The conceptual framework suggested by the terms 'charisma' and 'canon' implies the existence of a community which is not only socially distinct and demarcated, but which also explicitly defines its self-identity. Such a group, then, is a primary object of study for the historian of religion. A further task for such a historian is to investigate whether, in terms of its self-definition, this group closes itself off against all other groups to be found in a shared culture, by making claims to the absolute truth or whether it opens itself to a wider arena by acknowledging that absolute truth is shared with other groups. Only in the latter case can the use of an umbrella-term for all communities that express a common identity be legitimate. In any case, it is possible to assess each individual case *empirically*, by analysing documented beliefs.

In India, there has been a tendency to either subsume a vast variety of religious practice and beliefs under some high-order umbrella ('Hinduism'), or express a kind of epistemological agnosticism ('each religion can only grasp limited aspects of the truth'). In the latter case, the metaphor of blind men touching different parts of an elephant's anatomy has been frequently invoked. One might speculate on the reasons for this tendency and think, for example, of the stunning complexity of religion in India; of the claim by one group (e.g. the Advaita-Vedānta) to represent a meta-system in which all others find their fulfilment; of the participation by many different groups in one religious event; of the fashionable idea of 'interconnectedness'; or of tendencies to create a modern, unified 'Hinduism' for political reasons. But none of this removes the need for straightforward empirical work within which 'truth' as such cannot figure; attempts at relativizing the beliefs of a particular community must be avoided at all costs.

The present essay will focus on one religious tradition of South India, the Śrīvaiṣṇavas, and explore the themes of charisma and canon in their history. When turning to their religious identity it will become apparent that—and here I am anticipating the results of the investigation—according to Śrīvaiṣṇava belief, they constitute a self-contained, irreducible and non-relativizeable entity.

Charisma

A central element in the self-definition of a religious movement is the specific construction of its past history. Such constructions usually point towards some unique access to revelation or the 'truth'. Rāmānuja (traditionally 1017–1137), the famous author of the *Śrībhāṣya*, must without doubt be regarded as the central figure in the evolution of Śrīvaiṣṇavism, both as a comprehensive theological edifice that fused the devotionalism of *bhakti* with the philosophy and meditation of the Vedānta, and as a cohesive religious movement associated with the Viṣṇu temples of South India as well as a corpus of scriptures in Tamil. The majority of scholars have tended to select from this complex whole a single feature—by more or less exclusively locating Rāmānuja within the tradition of the Vedānta and its various interpretations of Bādarāyaṇa's *Brahmasūtras*. In this context, little more than an incidental glance is cast upon Yāmunācārya (traditionally 916–1038) as the sole predecessor of Rāmānuja. But religion in India is more than its philosophy, a point made abundantly clear in the Śrīvaiṣṇava construction of its spiritual past.

Great historical events sometimes have very innocuous or accidental catalysts. The fusion of Tamil and Sanskrit religious material was such an event, but within the Śrīvaiṣṇava tradition itself this is presented with the utmost simplicity. The setting is a village called Kāṭṭumaṉṉanārūr in Tamil (Vīranārāyaṇapuram in Sanskrit texts), about sixteen miles south-east of Chidambaram, with its temple dedicated to Viṣṇu, called (Kāṭṭu-) Maṉṉaṉār (Skt.: Rājagopāla). It is the late ninth, or early-tenth century, and the brahmin temple priests Īśvaramuni and his son Nāthamuni[1] have settled here after a lengthy and doubtless prestigious pilgrimage to North India, and after staying in the village of Govardhana on the banks of the Yamunā. Nāthamuni is renowned both for the depth of his yogic trances and his skill in singing.

One day some Śrivaiṣṇavas from Tirunakari arrived and visited Maṉṉaṉār to pay their respect to Him. By reciting the Tamil song that begins with 'O you nectar that never satiates one ...' they cultivated the enjoyment of His physical qualities. When Nāthamuni witnessed this, he became fascinated by it and thought: 'To cultivate the enjoyment of His physical qualities by means of this Tamil song is so much sweeter than experiencing Kṛṣṇa by means of *yoga*.' He prostrated himself before them, and he received from them that song ... Then he asked them: 'Please give me all the thousand stanzas, for Caṭakōpaṉ of Kurukūr speaks of "this song of ten stanzas among the thousand ..."' But they replied: 'Although Tirunakari is our home-town ... we learnt the song in Tirukkuṭantai. More we do not know.'[2]

A single religious song in Tamil, accidentally brought to his attention by some pilgrims, opens up an entire new religious universe for the *yogī* Nāthamuni, and he is eager to explore it further. The final stanza of the song has given him all the clues he needs (the name of an author, his home-town, and the size of his work) and he sets out to recover the whole composition. Kurukūr (Skt.: Kurukā) or Tirunakari is the modern Alvartirunagari in Tirunelvely District of southern Tamil Nadu, and this is where he goes.[3] When he arrives there, initially his mission seems to have failed, because in Kurukūr too nobody knows any further songs.[4] But there is a Viṣṇu temple with a separate shrine for Caṭakōpaṉ (Skt.: Śaṭhakopa) and his disciple Madhurakavi—who were born about four thousand years earlier, towards the beginning of *kali-yuga*. Appropriately, a late version asks: 'How could there exist a teacher–pupil relationship between Śaṭhāri and Nāthamuni?'[5]

Now it happens that there is a Vaiṣṇava called Parāṅkuśadāsa, who has learnt another Tamil poem, the *kaṇṇi nuṇ ciṟu ttāmpu*, composed by Madhurakavi in honour of his guru Śaṭhakopa. Nāthamuni learns it, becomes absorbed in his powerful yoga, and recites it 12,000 times in front of the temple statue of Caṭakōpaṉ. The texts state very elaborately that this makes Nāthamuni a 'disciple', by the definitions of the *śāstras*, worthy of the compassion of his chosen guru, Caṭakōpaṉ. Thus the latter grants Nāthamuni a divine eye,[6] and manifests himself before him to teach him the primordial truth of Viṣṇu religion, including, naturally, his entire Tamil poetry—the Tiruvāymoḻi, from which the pilgrims' song on Kuṭantai was taken, and three other Tamil works.[7] Nāthamuni returns home to institute a tradition of singing the scriptures that have been revealed to him, called the 'Tamil Veda',[8] in a 'religious style' (*deva-gāna*, as opposed to 'secular style', *martya-gāna*).[9] But Nāthamuni is not merely the founder of a new musical tradition. The Tamil Veda revealed to him has to be interpreted, and serves as the interpretative tool, in the context of reflections on the primordial truth. Thus the great *yogī*, musician and *bhakta* (by virtue of his *Kṛṣṇa-guṇānubhava* approach to religion) gathers disciples, among whom Puṇḍarīkākṣa (Tamil: Uyyakkoṇṭār) is the most important. He in turn entrusts[10] his foremost disciple Rāmamiśra (Tamil: Maṇakkāl Nampi) with the task of looking after the spiritual education of Nāthamuni's grandson Yāmunācārya. This he does, and the latter, at least indirectly—through a number of his own disciples—provides religious education to Rāmānuja.[11]

Now, what precisely are we dealing with? From the account given so far it is clear that Nāthamuni received one large collection of religious songs, the *Tiruvāymoli* (Skt.: *Sahasragīti*), and three shorter works, all by Caṭakōpaṉ, and this is at least the core of the 'Tamil Veda'. But our texts are careful to add an 'etc.' when listing the content of what Nāthamuni was taught in Kurukūr. The reason for this is clear: in the Śrīvaiṣṇava tradition, Nāthamuni is credited with the compilation of a larger corpus of Tamil scriptures, 23 in all, which add up to a perfect 4000 stanzas. This is the *Nāl āyira tivya pirapantam*, 'the Holy Scripture of 4000', or in short, the *Prabandham*. Twelve of the works contained in the *Prabandham* carry the names of their authors (similar to the northern *bhaṇitā*), and this allows us to identify seven different poets, including one woman. Thus it is only tradition that furnishes us with the names of five further (male) poets and their authorship of the remaining eleven works in the *Prabandham*. These twelve poets are known as the Āḻvār (kaḷ) or, in Sanskrit, *(divya)sūris*. All versions of the Śrivaiṣṇava *guruparamparā* begin with accounts of their lives. They are regarded as the human 'founders' of the tradition. Nammāḻvār (viz. Caṭakōpaṉ, Śaṭhakopa) in particular provides the medium through which Viṣṇu's eternal truth is channelled. The figure of Viṣvaksena, Viṣṇu's heavenly general (who can be regarded as a Vaiṣṇava parallel to Gaṇapati and who is basically of Pāñcarātra origin) is presented as the direct teacher of Nammāḻvār. In short, the line of transmission runs as follows: Viṣṇu, (Lakṣmī), Viṣvaksena, Nammāḻvār, (Madhurakavi), Nāthamuni, Yāmuna, Rāmānuja, and the later Ācāryas. What is particularly striking here is the fact that all the Vedic *ṛṣis* are ignored, and even Vyāsa is not mentioned!

Let us note in passing that there is one important constraint on this hagiography: it wants to say something about the authors of a particular set of religious poems which play an important role in the transmission of the primordial truth, the Veda, and its correct interpretation; they are not presented as 'ideal *bhaktas*'. Thereby it differs significantly from otherwise comparable Śaiva material where only some of the 63 traditional Śaiva saints (Nāyaṉār) are poets included in the Śaiva Tamil canon (the *Tirumuṟai*), and not all poets are included in the list of the 63 Nāyaṉār.

It would obviously be of central interest in an essay dealing with charisma to look at these Āḻvārs (and Nāthamuni) in greater detail. Unfortunately, this is impossible. The reason is simple: while we do have their poetry, there is absolutely no independent biographical information. What they tell us about themselves in the concluding stanzas to their songs allows us to say that two were brahmin temple priests, that the one woman among them was possibly the daughter of one of them, that a further two were chieftains of some kind, and that one (Nammāḻvār) was the son of an agricultural landlord. Madhurakavi mentions no more than his name, and for the five remaining Āḻvārs we have no reference at all within the *Prabandham*. Moreover, we have no information as to their personalities or role in society, the social position of their poetry, any possible link or contact between them, and nothing about their precise dates. To speak of the sixth to the early tenth century as the period of the Āḻvārs is no more than tentative.[12] No work by Nāthamuni himself has come down to us, and his life-story is not independently documented.

This does not now imply that Śrīvaiṣṇavism has little to say about its primary founder-figures. Quite the contrary! Very elaborate life-stories are told in a variety of works. As mentioned above, the official *guruparamparās* in Tamil (and their Sanskrit derivations) always begin with accounts of their lives. Various similar works in Sanskrit (including a *mahākāvya*) add further detail, and in some cases we have the *sthalapurāṇa* associated with an Āḻvār's birthplace which may well provide us with a rather different life-story. All this is basically hagiographical in character; that in itself can provide much entertaining and interesting material for a separate essay.[13] But hagiography is probably not the appropriate term because in Śrīvaiṣṇava perception Āḻvārs are only partially seen as ideal exemplars of *bhaktas* or saints. All the stories are set within a special 'hermeneutical frame' which continues for the various teachers in the *paramparā* after the Āḻvārs. According to Śrīvaiṣṇava theology, Viṣṇu is not just an absolute, 'passive' truth or transcendental reality, *brahman*; he is very active in the world, pursuing the salvation of mankind. The primordial truth, to be revealed and transmitted, is the means for this salvation, but his own actions are the driving force underlying the process of salvation. This means that the written versions of the *guruparamparā* introduce the hagiography of the Āḻvārs with an account, set in Vaikuṇṭha, of Viṣṇu's dissatisfaction with the success rate of the classical *avatāras*, and his decision to initiate a much more effective stratagem. An apparently very old verse (probably pre-Rāmānuja) says:

[Thus] were the liberated souls commanded by the ocean of mercy, Madhu's Enemy [= Viṣṇu], and once again these beings in heaven descended into *saṃsāra*, to be born on earth in the many temple towns, such as Śrīraṅgam; for the words of a teacher must not be disobeyed.[14]

What this means is that Viṣṇu has decided to incarnate himself in the many temples as their *arcās*, temple statues, and that many of the eternally liberated beings (*nitya-sūris*), such as his 'general' Viṣvaksena, his 'weapons' Sudarśana, Pañcajanya, Kaumodakī, Nandaka, and also Bhūmi, will be born on earth to sing his praise in a language comprehensible to all (which is Tamil!) and promulgate the saving truth. These incarnated heavenly beings are the Āḻvārs and the subsequent Ācāryas. Each Āḻvār is therefore the embodiment of a being who has never been in *saṃsāra* and now is also free from the influence of karma. His or her life on earth is purely due to an order by Viṣṇu and is meant to be part of a grand and more effective new stratagem of salvation. It should be clear how different this makes the Āḻvārs from 'saints' or 'ideal *bhaktas*'. As earthly embodiments of a heavenly discus, sword, conch, club, etc., and as poets who express an eternal, saving truth, their lives are bound to be different from those of ordinary mortals who live by the rules of karma and dharma. Incidentally, Nammāḻvār in this construction is the embodiment of Viṣvaksena, and Rāmānuja that of Ananta.

The poetry of the Āḻvārs has shaped Śrīvaiṣṇavism in many other ways. Aiyangar Tamil is pervaded by expressions and words that derive from the *Prabandham*; a special tradition of professional reciters, the Araiyar, who also employ a simple form of *abhinaya*, which can be found in various temples. But above all else, it is the production of commentaries on the *Prabandham* that must be mentioned. Supposedly at the direct suggestion of Rāmānuja, these commentaries began to be written initially on Nammāḻvār's *Tiruvāymoḻi* and eventually on all the poems. The bulk of all this material is probably twice the size of the *Mahābhārata*.

Before leaving the Āḻvārs, a few additional comments on one of them, viz. Tirumaḻicai-Āḻvār,[15] might be appropriate. His real name is not known to us since the two poems in the *Prabandham* ascribed to him by tradition are not 'signed'. His Sanskrit name is Bhaktisāra, while in Tamil he is simply referred to by the name of the town near which he is said to have been born: Tirumaḻicai (Skt.: Mahīsāra, in the vicinity of Ceṉṉai or Madras). In a sense he is the most interesting and colourful of all the Āḻvārs. Legends tell us that he was the son of the sage Bhṛgu and an *apsara*, that he was brought up by low-caste wood-cutters, and that he acquired the magic sciences (*siddhis*). He defeated the *siddha* Koṅkaṇa and Śiva himself in battles of sorcery (in which magic pills are flung about, etc.), and humiliated brahmins who reviled him for his low-caste origin. Seated in a cave outside Kāñcīpuram, he emitted a bright light which the three, so-called 'early', Āḻvārs saw and followed to its source, then to become his disciples. (Somehow the biblical story of the three magi appears to have entered the realm of Tamil hagiography!) But most important is the fact that the accounts of his life are unanimous in mentioning that he studied all the religious systems, decided that the Viṣṇu religion was the only true one, and constructed its *matam*, its doctrinal system.[16] He is the *only* Āḻvār about whom this is said; even Nammāḻvār is not credited with the creation of a theological edifice derived from the study of other belief systems.

Thus one might venture the theory that an earlier stratum of Tamil Vaiṣṇavism, which referred to Bhaktisāra for its doctrinal foundations, was superseded and more or less forgotten due to the central role attributed at a later stage to Nammāḻvār. It has even been suggested (rather fancifully, in my opinion) that Tirumaḻica-Āḻvār was the Dramiḍācārya quoted in commentaries on the *Brahmasūtras*.[17] He is also said to have been originally the *siddha* called Śivavākiyar (prior to his conversion to Vaiṣṇavism); indeed there is a slight overlap between some of his stanzas and those attributed to Śivāvakiyar.[18] (Koṅkaṇa's poetry too is included in Tamil collections of *siddha* poetry.) We may never find the answers to all these interesting and puzzling hints and questions. The few traces that hagiography has preserved of this Āḻvār's life certainly would suggest that we are dealing with a highly unusual and individual 'charismatic' figure. The marginal role he plays in the *guruparamparās*, in spite of having established the Vaiṣṇava *matam*, might suggest that he was just too outrageous for later taste. Incidentally, something similar happened to the type of devotion the Āḻvārs actually express in their poetry. Whatever prominence may be given to the Tamil Veda as a source of theological authority, in the post-Rāmānuja period only some traces of the highly emotional, erotic and ecstatic *bhakti* of most of the Āḻvārs have been retained.

Canon

Let me turn now to the scriptural heritage of the Śrīvaiṣṇavas in general. Obviously, the ultimate 'authority' of the Vedas as revelation of the truth is accepted by Śrīvaiṣṇavism, just as it is taken for granted that as a good brahmin one ought to know Vedic material by heart. Moreover, Rāmānuja's writings within the Vedānta tradition are among his central contributions to the movement. Certainly later teachers continued this enterprise by writing commentaries and sub-commentaries on the *Śrībhāṣya*. Since the days of Yāmunācārya, the *Bhagavadgītā* has been a scripture that enjoyed intense study by many teachers (including, obviously, Rāmānuja himself). But, again from the time of Yāmuna onwards, scriptural authority encompassed a wider range, by including what in certain quarters were regarded as non-Vedic scriptures, the Saṃhitās of the Pāñcarātra tradition. From the days of the Āḻvārs, the movement has been very closely connected with South Indian Viṣṇu temples. Soon after them, most likely before Rāmānuja, an exegesis of the *Prabandham* was carried out that yielded a list of 108 temples referred to by the Āḻvārs. Now within these most prestigious—and in many other—Viṣṇu temples, a variety of professional *pūjā* traditions were found. Without going into details, which in any event are still rather obscure, we can say that, due to the influence of Rāmānuja, Śrīvaiṣṇavism could superimpose itself on two *pūjā* traditions—that of the Vaikhānasas and Pāñcarātrins (failing to take control over temples looked after by Nambudiris, Dīkṣitars, Gurukal and later Mādhvas). Yāmuna produced a justification for regarding the Pāñcarātra scriptures as authoritative,[19] and Rāmānuja maintained this in his turn. In his commentary on Brahmasūtra II, 2, 40–3, he states, for instance:

> The wise Lord Hari ... extracted the essential meaning of all the Vedānta-texts and condensed it in easy form.[20]
>
> The Lord ... called Highest Brahman ... with a view to enable his devotees to grasp the true meaning of the Vedas, himself composed the Pāñcarātra-Śāstra.[21]

Thus theoretically Śrīvaiṣṇavism is in possession of a further vast corpus of Sanskrit scriptures. But the fact that Rāmānuja himself only quotes from three Saṃhitās and includes altogether no more than five quotations[22] from them indicates the position of the Pāñcarātra within Śrīvaiṣṇavism. No commentaries on any of the Saṃhitās were ever written, as far as I know. Pāñcarātra influence on Śrīvaiṣṇavism was much more indirect and selective, and it involved individual features (such as the veneration of Viṣvaksena, Sudarśana and Garuḍa, the theory of the *vyūhas* and the concept of the *arcāvatāra*, Viṣṇu's incarnation in the statues of the temples, apart from a stereotypical set of quotes on the nature of *prapatti*). Moreover, we are not really dealing here with a fixed corpus, but a continuing literary development. For instance, from the thirteenth century on, a new work, the Lakṣmī-Tantra, begins to attract the attention of various Śrīvaiṣṇava theologians.

Finally, we can return briefly to the Tamil Veda. It is presented very much in the way that Rāmānuja interprets the Pāñcarātra scriptures. But instead of merely saying that this is an 'easy' summary of the Vedas, his emphasis is on the fact that all can understand it, since it is in the vernacular; moreover, it allowed Rāmānuja to solve the puzzles and problems that arose in his study of the *Brahmasūtras*.

What has been building up over the centuries of the Śrīvaiṣṇava movement is a massive collection of scriptures, all of which, in one way or another, are regarded as authoritative, or, if you like, as 'canonical'. But such a list does not by itself offer much of an insight into the precise use that was made of this vast heritage for theological and practical purposes. Moreover, it obscures historical trends and shifts in emphasis. To produce a more detailed picture of how Śrīvaiṣṇavism has drawn on its scriptural heritage would involve a major study, which I have not undertaken. Instead I would like simply to offer one illustration. Veṅkaṭanātha (better known by his title of Vedāntadeśika) wrote a large treatise in Tamil and Maṇipravāḷa, the *Rahasyatrayasāram*, in which we find, very roughly speaking, 1500 quotations or '*pramāṇams*', 'authoritative quotations from scripture'. Here is an approximate list of percentages.

Tiruvāymoḻi:	10%	
other Āḻvārs:	10%	Āḻvārs total: 20%
Bhagavadgītā:	7%	
rest of *Mahābhārata:*	12%	total MBh: 19%
Rāmāyaṇa:	8%	
previous Ācāryas:	14%	
Viṣṇu-purāṇa:	6%	
other (11) Purāṇas:	7%	total Purs: 13%
(10) *smṛtis:*	7%	
(13) *Saṃhitās:*	5%	
Brahmasūtras:	2%	
Lakṣmītantra:	2%	

only 6 quotations from Rāmānuja's *Śrībhāṣya*, but 30 from *Gadyatraya*

I wonder whether I am alone in thinking that such a list is rather unexpected, in view of the catalogue of sacred scriptures mentioned previously and of the general perception of Śrīvaiṣṇavism. But I think the picture presented here is not unrepresentative of post-Rāmānuja Śrīvaiṣṇavism and it is possible to get a glimpse of the underlying rationale. The thinkers after Rāmānuja (and probably also his contemporaries) set themselves, on the whole, a rather different task from that accomplished in the *Śrībhāṣya*. This task could be described as the endeavour to present a logically coherent exposition of Śrīvaiṣṇava beliefs and practices as they appear from *inside* the tradition, and not as structured according to an *outside* agenda (the *Brahmasūtras* with their alien conceptual structure). The internal agenda builds on schemata such as that of the *tattva-traya* (matter, souls, God) and the *artha-pañcaka* (God, the soul, the means towards, and the nature of, salvation, and *karma* as its obstacle), but above all on the *rahasya-traya*, often incorporating the former. Here now an agenda is provided that on the surface looks most puzzling or incongruous and entirely different from that of the Vedānta.

What are these three *rahasyams*, 'secrets'? They are a set of three minute scriptural passages that are regarded not just as the summary of the whole Veda but also as containing the entire theology of Śrīvaiṣṇavism in a nutshell—a new miniature (or minimalist) canon. The first *rahasyam* is the mantra '*Oṃ namo Nārāyaṇāya*', the second is called *Dvayam* and consists of the two (thus '*dvaya*') sentences: *Śrīman-Nārāyaṇa-caraṇau śaraṇaṃ prapadye* | *Śrīmate Nārāyaṇāya namaḥ*. (I take my refuge at the feet of Nārāyaṇa [who is joined with Lakṣmī]. Honour be to Nārāyaṇa [who is joined with Lakṣmī].' The third is verse 18.66 of the *Gītā: sarva-dharmān parityajya mām ekaṃ śaraṇaṃ vraja* | *ahaṃ tvā sarva-pāpebhyo mokṣayiṣyāmi. mā śucaḥ* || 'Having abandoned all religious exercises, come to me as your sole refuge. I shall free you from all evil *karma*. Do not grieve!'

This is not the occasion for details of the interpretation of these three fundamental scriptural authorities. Let it suffice to illustrate, very briefly, with an example. The syllable *oṃ* is analysed as consisting of *a*, *u*, and *m*. *A* signifies Viṣṇu, according to Sanskrit dictionaries. Also still recorded in the dictionaries is *u* as meaning 'exclusively'. More inventive is the interpretation of *m* as 'soul'. But *m* figures as the twenty-fifth consonant in the Sanskrit alphabet, and the twenty-fifth category of the Sāṃkhya is, as it happens, *puruṣa*. When *a* is treated as implying a dative case, the following meaningful sentence emerges: 'the soul exists exclusively for the benefit of Viṣṇu'.

It is clear now how the whole of Śrīvaiṣṇava ontology (the *tattva-traya*, the nature of Viṣṇu, of the soul and of matter) can be accommodated here. Moreover, soteriology is implied: the human being finds salvation by acknowledging his fundamental ontological dependence on Viṣṇu. This act of acknowledgement implies an act of submission, of seeking refuge, referred to in the two *śaraṇas* and in *prapadye*. *Prapatti* becomes the central concept denoting the religious act that can achieve liberation from *saṃsāra*. In discussions of this, the vast scriptural heritage of Śrīvaiṣṇavism finds a new focal point.

We witness in the literature an almost obsessive preoccupation with the three *rahasyams*. I said earlier that a massive literature of commentaries was produced on the poems of the Āḻvārs. Not only do these commentaries seek to interpret the originals in the light of Rāmānuja's thought, they appear even more interested in demonstrating how the Tamil verses implicate and explicate the *rahasyams*. Moreover, we have an equally massive literature dealing directly with the *rahasyams* and using their traditional structure to present theological discussion. Looking at all this activity, one is tempted to see Rāmānuja's Vedānta as an almost incidental achievement: the outside world demanded something like it, it was delivered; after that, one could turn to the central religious concerns of Śrīvaiṣṇava thought.

That such a view is not totally frivolous can be illustrated from another work by the Vedāntadeśika, his Maṇipravāḷa treatise *Paramatabhaṅgam*.[23] This is a neatly laid-out account of sixteen different *matams*, religious systems, with a carefully worked out hierarchy. The first *matam* (that of the Lokāyatas) is the furthest removed from the truth, the sixteenth and last is the only one that fully contains the truth. What is interesting to the present discussion is the fact that no Vedānta appears here. Śaṅkara and his followers (in position 6, between the Vaibhāṣika Buddhists and the Jainas), Bhāskara (in position 8, between the Jainas and the grammarians), etc. are treated separately, and the author's own tradition, the Bhagavacchāstra or Pāñcarātra, culminates the whole edifice. 'Vedānta' does not appear as anything that could provide a common framework for Śaṅkara, Bhāskara and Rāmānuja, and at least here, it is not even mentioned in the Vedāntadeśika's self-definition.

Religious Identity

Thus, as far as the religious identity of Śrīvaiṣṇavism is concerned, it is clear that we are not dealing here with a ('sectarian') variant of the Vedānta, but with a unique and independent *matam*. Let us explore the question of religious identity further by looking at the relationship of the Śrīvaiṣṇavas with society at large. As background to this exploration it seems appropriate to draw attention to the fact that, for most of the period under discussion, South Indian society can be described as basically functioning between two poles: a small minority of 'twice-born', almost exclusively represented by brahmins, and a large indigenous majority (naturally subdivided into various, partly hierarchically ordered groups) which the *varṇa* system would classify as *śūdra* and *pañcama*, 'untouchables'. Inscriptions, by referring to an organization called the *cāturvarṇyam*, imply some kind of functional interaction between the brahmin minority and the Tamil majority. In that context, the 'discovery' of a *śūdra's* Tamil Veda by a South Indian brahmin looks somewhat less striking.[24] Nevertheless, it is a bit surprising to find that the brahmin Āḻvārs are responsible for the most 'popular', almost 'folksy', poems, and that the most learned and sophisticated works in the *Prabandham* are the creation of Āḻvārs either directly identifiable as *śūdras* (this includes Nammāḻvār), or labelled as such by later hagiography. Not only that: one Āḻvār is identified as untouchable, and yet his poem, the first three stanzas of which begin with *a*, *u* and *m* respectively, is highly praised as a condensed Veda by even the more Sanskritic teachers.[25] Rāmānuja is said to have proclaimed to the general public the mantra '*Oṃ namo Nārāyaṇāya*', which he had received from his teacher in Tirukkōṭṭiyūr as a great secret.[26] Moreover, after his break with his Vedānta teacher Yādavaprakāśa, Rāmānuja is said to have served in the Varadarāja temple under the *śūdra* Tirukkacci Nampi (Skt. Kāñcī-pūrṇa).[27] All this seems to suggest that Śrīvaiṣṇavism presented itself as a religious programme that could be universally adopted. Certainly, today its followers are not only Aiyangar brahmins but also members of social groups such as the Piḷḷai, Mutaliyar, and, further down the hierarchical scale, Vēḷāḷar, Kaḷḷar, and Iṭaiyar.

Returning once again to Rāmānuja's *Śrībhāṣya*, it will come as a real surprise to find his comments on who is permitted access to salvation. A longish section discussing Brahmasūtra I, 3.32–9 makes it perfectly clear that a *śūdra* is 'not qualified for knowledge of Brahman'—let us not forget that *brahman* is Viṣṇu and that 'The prohibition of learning [the Vedas] thus implies the prohibition of understanding and whatever depends on it.'[28] It is the Advaitin that Rāmānuja accuses of permitting, by the logic of his philosophy, that a *śūdra* can gain an understanding of this ultimate nature and knowledge of *brahman*. Rāmānuja appears to reject this idea totally.

Somehow Śrīvaiṣṇavism managed to extricate itself from such an uncompromising position. By interpreting the poetry of the Āḻvārs as a summary in the vernacular of and commentary on the Vedas, it became possible, also theoretically, to give *śūdras* access to divine knowledge. But more happened: we noticed previously that the saving religious act became defined as *prapatti*. While in Rāmānuja it is *bhakti-yoga*, which includes meditation that allows a person to achieve liberation, among the later authors this *bhakti-yoga* is either contrasted as an extremely difficult method—of which only the privileged few are capable—with the 'easy' means of *prapatti*; or it is rejected outright as a sign of human arrogance *vis-à-vis* the availability of divine grace. By virtue of being human, everyone has access to *prapatti*. This now has the potential of being turned into a most radical and revolutionary social programme. Indeed the outlines of such a programme were produced, in the thirteenth century, in a Tamil work, the *Ācāryahṛdayam*, by Aḻakiya Maṇavāḷa Perumāḷ Nāyaṉār.[29] Here the religion of *prapatti* presents itself as a total replacement of the Vedic tradition. Of course such an extreme position found few followers, at least in practice.

Whatever views Śrīvaiṣṇavism may have concerning social structure and adherence to the Vedas and a Vedic lifestyle, and however strongly these issues were debated, the movement is at the same time busy defining its external expression. Many works were written, popular ones in Tamil and learned ones in Sanskrit, that enjoined typically Śrīvaiṣṇava features. Rules for daily rituals (the *tinacari* in Tamil, *nityam* or *āhnika* in Skt.) are laid down; these include the prescription that every morning Viṣṇu's twelve *nāmams* have to be painted on the body—a public statement of religious identity. The details of the *ūrdhvapuṇḍram*, the three vertical lines of the *nāmam*, are reflected upon. In a special sacrament, a male follower is branded on his body with the symbols of Viṣṇu, his discus and conch.[30] Going to Viṣṇu temples, or better still living near one, is advocated, and entrance into Śiva temples (not to mention worshipping there) prohibited (not to speak of worshipping him).[31] Indeed, even a simple entry into shrines containing Viṣṇu shrines is prohibited if the *pūjārīs* there are Śaivite. Children were taught a special form of Śrīvaiṣṇava Tamil, with words, phrases, idioms, etc. peculiar to the community and different from other varieties of brahmin Tamil.[32] With these and many other devices the Śrīvaiṣṇava community defines itself internally and marks itself off from the rest of society.

So far I have ignored one important event in the formation of Śrīvaiṣṇavism, namely the major schism due to which the movement broke up into two separate branches. Here again we could look at the role of a charismatic figure, in many ways comparable to Rāmānuja, and that is the figure of Maṇavāḷa mā muṉi (fifteenth century). Unfortunately, the issues underlying the schism are far too complex for me to explore within this essay. At various points I have alluded to possible tensions within this enormously complex religious heritage. Thus, we had a combination of Sanskrit and Tamil scriptures and culture; the shift from *bhakti* to *prapatti*; the degree of social openness; the relevance of all the rites established in the Smṛtis; and so on. Together with economic factors, such as control over temple revenues, and social ones, such as the organization of a network of *maṭhas* and loyalty of gurus associated with them, over a number of centuries these tensions and diverse viewpoints split the community into two (unequal) parts. These came eventually to be known as the Teṉkalai and the Vaṭakalai. As I said, there is no easy way of describing the issues underlying the split or defining the terms themselves, just as the historical developments leading up to the modern, very rigid divide, are still rather obscure. In conclusion, I would like to ignore the schism and concentrate on the single movement prior to its break-up.

In terms of the methodological remarks made at the beginning of this paper, Śrīvaiṣṇavism clearly defines itself as a 'closed' community since it consciously rejects any possible higher system of which it could be part. Note in particular that the ontological category of 'Īśvara' (God) is represented exclusively by Viṣṇu. But what do we call it? Well, personally I am happy to call it a religion, using the word in the straightforward sense of everyday speech. Of course, one then has to say that there are many such religions in India, comparable entities that share certain common characteristics and structures and draw on a similar range of religious source material. I am thinking here of examples such as the Mādhvas, Vallabhites, Caitanyites, Smārtas, etc. But it is essential to keep in mind that only an outsider to these would construct, on the basis of this common ground, a metasystem. Such a metasystem does not possess any credibility in the insider's mind; to an insider his religion seems exclusive and irreducible, just as it would seem to a Jew, a Christian or a Muslim that their religions are distinct, notwithstanding certain common features shared by Judaism, Christianity and Islam.[33]

Moreover, I am aware that my label 'religion' is simplistic and requires refinement. In fact, I regard this as one of the major tasks of Indology when dealing with the religious history of India: namely, to interact with the social sciences and develop a differentiated and more sophisticated system of social organization and religious identities. Thus, how do we describe individually the Teṉkalai and Vaṭakalai that together make up the 'religion' Śrīvaiṣṇavism? What title should we give to the Varkari 'movement' in Maharashtra or the 'cult' of Yellamma? On the other hand, I am not suggesting that everything gathered together under the title of 'Hinduism' allows for the type of particularist description which I have applied selectively here.

But, finally it seems appropriate to draw one major distinction, and that is between 'philosophy' (in a technical sense) and the concrete religious realities of India. The historian of Indian religion cannot simply use frameworks that the historian of Indian philosophy finds useful or appropriate. Rāmānuja's *Śrībhāṣya* is quite legitimately placed within the framework of a *philosophical* discussion alongside other interpretations of the *Vedānta-sūtras*. But I would compare this to the study of the discourse shared between Averroes, Avicenna, Maimonides, Abelard, and Aquinas in medieval Europe. To trace the nature of a *religion* is a rather different task.

Some Concluding Remarks

My earlier observations have highlighted certain problematic features in the application of the conceptual triangle of charisma—canon—religious identity to Indian material. To analyse charisma as a special and unique personal quality is only possible on the basis of detailed information about that individual. We have to know his or her biography, manner of attracting people, communication skills, etc., quite apart from what precisely the charismatic individual actually said or taught. Such information has simply not been retained in traditional India. Instead, we witness the almost instantaneous transformation of personal charisma, with all its unique and idiosyncratic features, into something 'objective', i.e. a culturally evolved pattern. We are offered a more or less stereotypical picture which allows us to do little more than study the character and types of such patterns. What is handed down is already a perception, and not the more immediate details, of a charismatic life, and later generations develop merely the former, not the latter. No doubt the history of Śrīvaiṣṇavism has been activated by charismatic individuals—the Āḻvārs, Rāmānuja,[34] Veṅkaṭanātha, Maṇavāḷa mā muṉi, etc.—but they are more or less lost to us as historical individuals.[35]

The institutionalization of charisma, the construction of a scriptural canon and the evolution of a religious identity have revealed themselves as complex processes. In one sense it could be claimed that the Tamil songs of the Āḻvārs constitute a Śrīvaiṣṇava religious identity. Yet the conceptual role of the Vedas remains important; this can be seen not just in the conceptualization of a 'Tamil Veda', but also in the practical, philosophical engagement with the Vedānta. This itself became conceptualized in the idea of the 'ubhaya-Vedānta', the twofold Vedānta. In addition, Pāñcarātra (and far less conspicuously, Vaikhānasa) scriptures appear in an authoritative role. De facto *smṛti*, above all the *Rāmāyaṇa* and the *Mahābhārata*, has influenced Śrīvaiṣṇava thought considerably.

But a mere list of such canonical traditions is not sufficient. We have seen that it is possible to distinguish different focal points, depending on an external or an internal agenda. The Vedānta is resorted to in the case of the former, the Tamil Veda of the latter. Finally, we have noticed a shift in time—the almost exclusive preöccupation with the *rahasya-trayam*, not just as a highly condensed form of canon, but also as the structuring mechanism of theological exploration. The role of charismatic individuals in all these trends and shifts and choices is only very indirectly discernible. But what emerges with all clarity is a unique, well-defined religious community which derives its identity from its belief in possessing the ultimate truth. Due to this self-understanding, no further relativization is possible. To impose this from the outside ('but they are part of Hinduism') would mean to apply a philosophical monism to religious history in the form of a social monism, namely the construction of a single 'Hinduism'. Only the mystic may be permitted to abstract some 'underlying essence' from the data provided by religious history, but not the religious historian.

Notes

1. Kulacēkaraṉ suggests, somewhat surprisingly, very precise dates (pp. 232–7) for Nāthamuni and events during his life-time: 913–78 for his life, 940 for his visit to northern India, 945 for his visit to Kurukūr, 958 for the beginning of the tradition of reciting the *Tiruvāymoḻi* in Śrīraṅgam, 960 for the birth of Nāthamuni's son Īśvaramuni, and 970 for a second pilgrimage to North India (1996: 232–7).
2. *Appōtu cila Tiru Nakari Śrīvaiṣṇavarkaḷ eḻunt' aruḷi Maṉṉaṉārai sēvittu 'Ārāv amutē' eṉkiṟa tiruvāymoḻiyai anusantittu kkuṇānupavam paṇṇa, atai kkaṇṭu Nātamunikaḷum 'yōkattālē Kaṇṇaṉai anupavikkum atai kkāṭṭilum ittiruvāymoḻiyālē kuṇānupavam paṇṇukiṟa itu iṉiyat' āy iruntatu' eṉṟu makiḻnt' aruḷi, avarkaḷai taṇṭaṉ samarppittu anta ttiruvāymoḻiyai krahittu … itu āyiram pāṭṭ' uṭaiyat' āy itu pattu ppāṭṭ' āy … Kurukūr Caṭakōpaṉ aruḷi cceytat' ākaiyālē ivv āyirattaiyum prasātikka vēṇum eṉṟu avarkaḷai kēṭka, avarkaḷum 'eṅkaḷukkut tTiru Nakari janma-pūmiy ākilum … Tiru kKuṭantaiy ēṟa vantu … ippattu ppāṭṭukkaḷaiyum apyasittōm, maṟṟat' aṟiyōm' eṉṉa* (3000) *Kuruparamparāprapāvam*, p. 50). Atypically, this Vaṭakalai account is more detailed than the parallel in (6000) *Kuruparamparāprapāvam*, p. 101. The song in question is Tiruvāymoḻi V, 8. Of particular interest is the conscious contrast between yoga and a different type of religious practice, called *guṇānubhava* here. *Divyasūricarita*, ch. XVI has a mere four lines (vv. 13f), and *Prapannāmṛta* (107, 1–17) follows the 6000.
3. Some accounts complicate matters. Since the song is dedicated to Viṣṇu in Kuṭantai, namely modern Kumbhakonam, they add that he first went there, but was once again directed (by Viṣṇu himself, or the temple priests) to Kurukūr.
4. A very late version tries to explain the loss of the whole work by telling a rather strange story. Caṭakōpaṉ's Tamil poetry was so efficient that everyone

who studied it died and achieved *mokṣa* instantly. People who worried about the future of mankind threw the work into the Tāmraparṇī river so that nobody is accidentally 'killed' by it. But after a year the song dedicated to Viṣṇu in Kumbhakonam is found floating on the water of the river and is rescued (*Prapannāmṛta* 107, 23–37).

5. *Prapannāmṛta* 106, 5. Different versions provide slightly different dates but it hardly matters whether it is three or four thousand years that intervene between Nāthamuni and the next link in the *guruparamparā*, Caṭakōpaṉ.
6. The parallel of *Bhagavadgītā* XI, 8 is explicitly stated in *Prapannāmṛta* and the 6000.
7. As to the precise content of that teaching, the different accounts differ considerably, and all the details cannot be explored here. They all seem to agree, at least by implication, that the teaching included the whole of the Tamil *Prabandham*.
8. On the Tamil Veda and its *śūdra* author Nammāḻvār (Caṭakōpaṉ is most commonly known as Nammāḻvār, but also by the Sanskritised version of his name, i.e. Śaṭhakopa, Śaṭhāri, Śaṭhārati) see Hardy (1979).
9. I leave out of the present discussion the accounts of how he demonstrated to the Cōḻa king the superiority of the first over the second. Issues that certainly in the cultural history of India were important are alluded to in such a fragmentary and non-technical manner that their proper evaluation is very difficult. It is clear that today, even what could be called the 'classical' Śrīvaiṣṇava style of reciting the *Prabandham* (and given the nature of musical history in India, I dare not speculate how closely this would correspond to the musical style taught by Nāthamuni) is near extinction, only four temples still preserving the *Araiyar* tradition. Those interested in this topic may profitably consult the writings and audio cassettes of Srirāma Bhārati, a modern *rasika* in search of recovering a (nearly) lost ancient heritage.
10. This is only mentioned explicitly in *Divyasūricarita* XVI, 42f. See Garuḍavāhana-paṇḍita (1978).
11. There are many ways of commenting on the mathematics of the *guruparamparā*. The Occidental concept of 'hagiography' often seems to imply a totally free play of the imagination, but what impresses me most in the case of the Śrīvaiṣṇava versions is the apparent *rationale* of the seemingly irrational construction. Lives of 120 years' duration, teacher–pupil relationships spanning three or four thousand years, etc. become only possible when a fundamental faithfulness is maintained with certain *historical* facts. These hagiographies do not deceive us concerning the *facts* that Rāmānuja was never directly taught by Yāmuna, that the intellectual relationship between Yāmuna and Nāthamuni is a distant one, and that Nāthamuni's contact with the Tamil Viṣṇu *bhakti* tradition is very indirect indeed. What is done here is to establish an inner continuity *inspite of* the chronological problems. That such problems are acknowledged, and not simply wiped away by means of a truly fabricated and merely seemingly logical account, is the impressive feature I am commenting on.

12. For further information on the Āḻvārs and their poetry see Hardy (1983: 239–480).
13. I have written on the hagiography of three Āḻvārs in three articles: Hardy (1979, 1991 and 1992). On Tirumaḻicai see below.
14. *Divyasūricarita* I, 93: *nirdiṣṭā Madhu-ripuṇā dayakareṇa Śrīraṅgādiṣu bahu-dhāmasu kṣamāyām | muktās te punar api sūrayo Ho'vatīrṇāḥ saṃsāre na guru-vaco hi laghunīyam ||*
The verse is also quoted in the (3000) Vaṭakaḷai *Kuruparamparāprapāvam* (p. 6, variant *śubha-guṇa* for *punar api*), ascribed to Vankipuratt' Ācci, and identified as a quote in the *Divyasūricarita* by Garuḍavāhana-paṇḍita. Since the 3000 (p. 47) mentions this Vankipuratt' Ācci as Nāthamuni's father-in-law, this conception of a second, grandiose series of *avatāras* would seem to go back to the very beginnings of the Śrivaiṣṇava tradition.
15. The following comments derive from a study of this Āḻvār which I am preparing.
16. The *Periyatirumuṭiyaṭaivu* states succinctly: *para-mata-nirasaṉa-pūrvakam āka sva-mata-sthāpaṉam paṇṇinār*, 'first he demolished the other religious systems, and then he established his own doctrinal system'. See Kantāṭai Nayan (1968: 5).
17. By Kuppuswami Sastri (1981: 17–22).
18. See for instance *Prapannāmṛtam*, 79, 30–5 in Anantācārya (1966) for the identification, and Subramania Iyer (1969: 34–146) for a closer comparison of the poetry. *Siddha* poetry in Tamil can be found in collections such as the *Cittar periy ñāṉakkōvai*, edited by Ramanātaṉ (1959). On the Tamil *siddhas* generally see Zvelebil, with some examples of Civavākkiyar's poetry in translation (1973: 84f).
19. See van Buitenen (1966: 26–32).
20. Rāmānuja in Thibaut's translation (1971: 527).
21. Ibid., pp. 527f; 529.
22. *Pauṣkara-*, *Sātvata-* and *Parama-saṃhitā*. Ibid., pp. 525–7.
23. This is a substantial work, one of the longest of his *Rahasyams*. It includes a set of fifty-four stanzas in Tamil which, in a most interesting and ingenious manner, summarize the elaborate argumentation. A commentary on these stanzas can be found in Śrīrāmatēcikācārya ([1941] 1958: 142–206); the following comments are primarily derived from there.
24. See Hardy (1979) on the role of *śūdras* and the *cāturvarṇyam*.
25. This Āḻvār is TirupPāṇ, on whom see Hardy (1991).
26. See for instance (6000) Piṉp' Aḻakiya Perumāḷ Jīyar (1968: 174–7).
27. See ibid. (1968: 135–47).
28. Rāmānuja in Thibaut's translation (1971: 343).
29. Some aspects of the work have been discussed in Hardy (1995).
30. Restricting ourselves to the literary output of Veṅkaṭanātha (Vedāntadeśika), the following works may be listed. The *Ṣrīvaiṣṇavatiṉacari*, *Paṉṉirunāmam*, and *Āhāraniyaman* are short Tamil poems, included in the *Śrī-Tēcikappirpantam (Deśikaprabandham)*, which deal with daily rituals, the twelve *nāmams*,

and restrictions on food. The *Saccaritarakṣa* is a learned treatise in Sanskrit, dealing with the *lāñchanas* and *ūrdhvapuṇḍram*. Matters concerning the *nityam* are discussed in Veṅkaṭanātha (1969: 329), where we hear *devatāntarasyānārādhyatvam*, 'deities other [than] Viṣṇu must not be worshipped'.

31. See for example Vedāntadeśika's *Rahasyatrayasāram*, ch. 15 (*Uttarakṛtyādhikāram*, 'The chapter on what one must do after *prapatti*').
32. See e.g. *Śrīvaiṣṇavasatācārasaṅkraham*, published as recently as 1968, for vocabulary, sample conversations and correct letter formats (52–64).
33. Similar suggestions, namely that instead of 'Hinduism' we should deploy the idea of a variety of 'religions' in India, have been made by Stietencron (1986, 1988 and 1995). I fail to understand how B.M. Sullivan, author of a *Historical Dictionary of Hinduism* (1997), who explicitly quotes Stietencron (1995), can then conclude that '[f]or the purpose of this volume, it will not be necessary to settle the question whether Hinduism is one religion with a number of sectarian groups, or several religions ...' (1) Surely the definition of any term in a dictionary will fundamentally depend on whether or not a global 'Hinduism' can legitimately provide the semantic framework.
34. In his case, the 'perception' of his charismatic role can be found not only in hagiographic and legendary writings, but also in poetic symbolism. I have in preparation a study of about a dozen poems on Rāmānuja, the overall impression of which is one of 'military symbols': the mighty warrior who fights battles with representatives of other belief systems. A few samples are given in F. Hardy, *The Religious Culture of India*. Cambridge, 1994: 118f; 563, n. 29.
35. This is not to say that we cannot distinguish a scale of degrees to which stereotypical hagiography might incorporate biographical and historical data. In the case of Parakāla, for instance, tradition has accumulated so many divergent features that the resulting picture is far larger than (any realistically possible single) life; it has ended up by being more or less a pastiche of many divergent cultural patterns. See Hardy (1992: 105–14). At the opposite end of the scale one might want to place for instance Mhaiṃbhaṭ's account of the life of the thirteenth-century Maharashtrian saint Cakradhara. See S.G. Tulpule, *An Old Marathi Reader*. Pune, 1960: 112f. But even here a closer look at the material will reveal how hazardous it would be to treat this as critically biographical.

References

Anantācārya. 1966. *Prapannāmṛtam*, ed. Ramanārāyaṇācārya. In Devanāgarī characters. 2 vols. Vol. 2: Hindi translation. Vārāṇasī.

Anon. [1966] 1968. *Śrīvaiṣṇava satācāra saṅkraham*. Ceṉṉai: Ti Liṭṭil Pḷavar Kampeṉi.

Buitenen, J.A.B. van. [1966] 1968. On the archaism of the Bhāgavata Purāṇa. In *Krishna: Myths, Rites, and Attitudes*, ed. M. Singer, 23–40. Chicago: The University of Chicago Press.

Civavākkiyar. 1959. Pāṭal. In *Cittar periya ñāṉakkovai*. See Rāmanātaṉ 1959: 135–90.

Garuḍavāhana-paṇḍita. 1978. *Divyasūricaritam*, ed. T.A. Sampatkumārācarya with Hindī translation by Mādhavācārya. In Devanāgarī characters. Bombay: Ananthacarya Research Institute.

Hardy, Friedhelm. 1979. The Tamil-Veda of a Śūdra Saint: the Śrīvaiṣṇava interpretation of Nammāḻvār. In *Contributions to South Asian Studies*, ed. Gopal Krishna, 29–87. Vol. 1. Delhi: Oxford University Press.

———. 1983. *Viraha-bhakti: The Early History of Kṛṣṇa Devotion in South India*. Delhi: Oxford University Press.

———. 1991. TirupPāṇ-Āḻvār: the Untouchable Who Rode Piggy-back on the Brahmin. In *Devotion Divine: Bhakti Traditions from the Regions of India. Studies in Honour of Charlotte Vaudeville*, ed. D.L. Eck and F. Mallison, 129–54. Groningen: Egbert Forsten.

———. 1992. The Śrīvaiṣṇava Hagiography of Parakāla. In *The Indian Narrative: Perspectives and Patterns*, ed. C. Shackle and R. Snell, 81–116. Wiesbaden: Harrassowitz.

———. 1995. A Radical Reassessment of the Vedic Heritage: The *Ācāryahṛdayam* and its Wider Implications. In *Representing Hinduism: The Construction of Religious Traditions and National Identity*, ed. V. Dalmia and H. von Stietencron, 35–50. Delhi: Sage Publications.

Kantāṭai Nāyaṉ, K. 1968. *Periyatirumuṭiyaṭaivu*, ed. S. Kiruṣṇasvāmi Ayyaṅkār. (Śrīsūktimālā; 23). Tirucci.

Kulacēkaraṉ, Cu. 1996. *Nāta vaiṇavam*. Ceṉṉai.

Koṅkaṇa-nāyaṉār. 1959. Vālaikkummi. In *Cittar periya ñāṉakkōvai*. See Rāmanātaṉ 1959: 243–55.

Kuppuswami Sastri. 1981. Bodhayana and Dramidacarya [:] Two old Vedantins presupposed by Ramanuja. In *Kuppuswami Sastri Birth Centenary Commemoration Volume*, ed. S.S. Janaki, 14–22. Madras: Kuppuswami Sastri Research Institute.

Piṉp' Aḻakiya Perumāḷ Jīyar. 1968. *Āṟ'āyira ppaṭi (=6000) Kuru-paramparā-prapāvam*, ed. S. Kiruṣṇasvāmi Ayyaṅkar. (Śrīsūktimālā 23). Tirucci.

Rāmanātaṉ, A. (ed.). 1959. *Cittar periya ñāṉakkōvai*. Ceṉṉai.

Rāmānuja. 1971. *The Vedānta-sūtras with the commentary by Rāmānuja*, trans. G. Thibaut (Sacred Books of the East 48). Reprint. Delhi.

Śrīrāmatēcikācāryar, V.N. [1941] 1958. *Śrī-Tēcika-ppirapantam-urai*. 206–44. Tañjāvūr.

Stietencron, Heinrich von. 1986. Hinduismus. *Theologische Realenzyklopädie*. Vol. 15, Lieferung 3/4: 346–55.

———. 1988. Voraussetzungen westlicher Hinduismusforschung und ihre Folgen. In ... *Aus der anmuthigen Gelehrsamkeit: Tübinger Studien zum 18. Jahrhundert*, ed. Eberhard Müller, 123–53. Tübingen: Attempto.

———. 1995. Religious Configurations in Pre-Muslim India and the Modern Concept of Hinduism. In *Representing Hinduism: The Construction of Religious*

Traditions and National Identity, ed. V. Dalmia and H. von Stietencron, 51–81. Delhi: Sage Publications.

Subramania Iyer., A.V. 1969. *The Poetry and the Philosophy of the Tamil Siddhas*. Chidambaram.

The Third Brahmatantrasvatantra-svāmi. 1968. *Guruparamparāprapāvam* (in 3000 paṭis), ed. K. Śrīnivāsācāriyar. Ceṉṉai.

Veṅkaṭanātha (Vedāntadeśika). 1920. *Rahasyatrayasāram*, ed. with Maṇipravāḷa commentary by Narasimmācārya-svāmī. Tamil in Grantha characters. Ceṉṉai.

———. 1969. *Pāñcarātra-rakṣā*. In *Rakṣā-granthāḥ*, ed. with commentary by U. Vīrarāghavācāryar, 279–519. Madras: Ubhaya-Vedānta-Granthamālā.

———. 1969. Saccaritra-rakṣā. In *Rakṣā-granthāḥ*, ed. with commentary by U. Vīrarāghavācāryar, 123–62. Sanskrit in Devanāgarī characters. Madras: Ubhaya-Vedānta-Granthamālā.

———. 1972. *Paramatapaṅkam*. In Tamil and Devanāgarī characters. Śrītēcik-atarcanasapai, Poṉṉayintai.

Zvelebil, K.V. 1973. *The Poets of the Power*. London: Rider & Co.

The Legitimation of Textual Authority in the *Bhāgavatapurāṇa*

MARTIN CHRISTOF

Introduction

The *Bhāgavatapurāṇa (BhāgP)*, for the Vaiṣṇavas the most popular of all Purāṇas, probably belongs to South India and is datable to the ninth–tenth century. It could be designated as a consciously engendered canonical text, composed in order to be recognized as *the* holy book of Bhāgavatism. Following Hardy (1983: 484), one could describe it as a translation of the emotional Kṛṣṇa *bhakti* of the Āḻvārs into a Purāṇa claiming to be *the* Veda for *kaliyuga*. It was built on a blueprint of the Kṛṣṇa story received from the North—represented inter alia by the *Viṣṇupurāṇa* and the *Harivaṃśa*. While it was commented on by authors belonging to different schools of thought, Vallabha introduced it as a canonical text into the group of authoritative scriptures formerly consisting of the *Upaniṣads*, the *Bhagavadgītā* and the *Brahmasūtras*. He conferred upon it the status of the final decisive text in relation to uncertainties raised in the other *prasthānas*, i.e. authoritative sources (Glasenapp 1933–4: 277f. and Sheridan 1986: 123). It was accepted as canonical or authoritative in the Vaiṣṇava schools of Madhva and Caitanya as well. Its lasting influence is reflected in the number of translations and adaptations that were made of it—in part or as a whole—in the vernaculars.

Since textual authority is a prerequisite of canonicity, it is worth analysing what it is that imbues a text with authority.

In most religions there are religious texts which are not necessarily sacred.[1] The sacredness of a text is discernible in its careful preservation; in the care over its transmission; the dignity of its contents; the way it is recited or used in ritual or healing; and very often by the fact that it is written down in the first place. Communities that preserve such textual traditions set themselves apart from their social context in terms of organization, self-image and religious way of life. The text comes to embody some kind of normative value for the community (cf. Colpe 1987). There remains, however, a difference between sacred texts and canonical texts. Though sacred texts show a tendency to normativity and provide a direction, they are open to additions and interpretations. A canon, however, is the institutionalization of permanence, and is believed to be based on an ahistorical connection with primeval times. None of these great traditions and canons are 'self-stabilizing'; institutions in each community are engaged in creating a sense of permanence. First, there is the institution of censorship. Once the canon has been defined via the selection of a certain part of a broad sacred tradition and the rejection of other parts, censorship keeps the other—the apocrypha and the marginalized—from encroaching on the canon. It also tries to make the canon immune against change. Techniques for the preservation of the expressive aspects of a text which aim at fixing a text word by word and letter by letter, and even fixing the intonation, are employed by those responsible for conserving the text. By this means, the expressive dimension of the text is made taboo.

An obvious example from the Indian tradition is the Veda, where the fixed expressive dimension of the holy scripture has become 'a temple made of speech'. But, fixing the letter might easily lead, as time goes by, to growing obscurity in relation to the meaning of the text. Therefore, in order to create a successful canon, conservation of meaning needs to compensate for semantic losses on account of conserving the letter. It is this combination of texts being made taboo, allied with the conservation of meaning, which defines a canon.

Most traditional cultures have specialists whose task it is to interpret the canon and relate it to the changing world. In the Indian tradition, the prototype of these specialists is the brahmin. A central method of fulfilling his function is the writing of a commentary. The canonic commentary must relate the text to the world, mediate between the closure of a canon and the openness of reality—which it claims to interpret comprehensively. To put it differently, the canon is the result of an often arbitrary limitation whereas the commentary represents an effort to overcome this limitation by ingenuity on the part of an exegete, whose task it is to extend the domain of the closed canon over everything that is known or exists (cf. J.Z. Smith 1982: 48f). The commentary, in turn, serves as the legitimising basis for innovation. Thus, the conservation of meaning—if it does not end in dogmatism—may lead to new interpretations and new meanings.

A further characteristic of the canon is its absolute claim to salvation, which is paired to an often small group for which this claim holds good. This leads to a further distinction: between the 'canon from above' and the 'canon from below' as the two poles of a continuum in which we find different forms of canons and differing relations with censorship. The 'canon from above' is a power-related canon aiming at unification and standardization. It seems to be related to high cultures and trans-regional types of rule; it is based on a homogeneous upper class. The 'canon from below' is based on a special source of meaning, charisma, a truth which is not bound to an institution but to a person or situation. It involves a charismatic leader and his followers, who are bound by a personal and emotional relationship. Charisma is the most absolute and yet most transient form of power, and it is fundamentally uncanonical. Yet charisma may develop into a canon when the charismatic message is conserved. However, when the message is subjected to inscription and institutionalization, the canon is changed considerably.

Keeping the above definitions and notions in mind, I will try to locate the status of the *BhāgP* within a broad range of sacred/canonic 'texts', using a typology of the Word in India as proposed by Coburn (1984: 452–4) while discussing the term 'scripture' in relation to Hinduism. The typology is designed to indicate the varied ways in which Hindus have related to a range of 'holy verbal events'. Given the scope of the term Hindu, we could deduce that Coburn is not presenting a typology of canonic 'texts' or verbal events, but rather a typology of sacred 'texts'. The canonicity of the examples he offers for his different types depends on the existence of a specific religious community which relates to the exemplary 'texts' analysed. He begins with the cautioning note that in India 'scripture' is not necessarily written. There is verbal material in a highly 'crystallized' form, i.e. quite specific, bounded, and even written, but other manifestations of it are dynamic and open-ended rather than bounded and reified. Another feature of scripture in India is the primacy of the experiential factor: a holy verbal event is first and foremost an oral or aural experience, the holiness of holy words not being a function of their intelligibility. On the contrary, sanctity often appears to be inversely related to comprehensibility: 'Hindus have affirmed that the holiness of the Word is intrinsic, and that one participates in it, not by understanding, but by hearing and reciting it' (447). He further describes the central dynamic of the Hindu treatment of the Word:

That dynamic revolves around the tension between (1) the desire to preserve and recite, and not necessarily to understand, a verbally fixed (usually oral) text, and (2) the desire to understand, both for oneself and for others, religious ideas that are presented in verbal form" (449).

Allowing for a continuity between the literal preservation and the dynamic re-creation of the Word as well as for overlap between the types, he begins his typology with (1) the Word being frozen, captured verbatim, having thus a mantric quality, being eternal, intrinsically powerful and supremely authoritative. It is recited verbatim, but more often than not it is not intelligible to the majority—a point in case being the Veda, especially the *Ṛgveda*. Then, there are (2) certain stories, such as the Kṛṣṇa myth, which are regarded as routes to salvation, and/or normative. Being told again and again, the prime concern is now their intelligibility, which might make translations or transcreations necessary. Further, there are (3) commentaries, making some embodiments of the Word intelligible for present times—making sacred texts accessible and meaningful. Next, there are (4) the imitations which some texts have generated as a further type of the Word, as for example the many Gītās claiming to be similar or superior to the *Bhagavadgītā (BhG)*. Finally, there are (5) those embodiments of the Word which have lived on via accretions, as did the Purāṇas.

In a second typology, Coburn juxtaposes scripture (basically the first type of the Word as mentioned above) with story, covering the other four types. He holds that the first type, being treated as eternal and immutable, comes closest to 'scripture' as a generic phenomenon since it is compact, bounded, and therefore capable of being canonized. Other instances of the Word, when treated as dynamic, spawn all manner of elaboration. It seems to me, however, that a text in its historical development might partake of the features of more than one 'verbal event' as enumerated by Coburn, especially if the point of view of a specific segment rather then the totality of 'Hindus' is taken into account. Further, it should be mentioned that in another place within the same work (1984: 450) Coburn holds that 'canonized' in the Hindu case means 'worthy of being recited verbatim'. We would argue, on the other hand with Assmann and Assmann (1987: *passim*) that both the literal preservation and the dynamic re-creation of sacred texts are characteristics of the canon.

In what follows it will become obvious that the *BhāgP* transcends the boundaries of Coburn's typologies—at least of the second typology, which unduly emphasizes conservation of the letter and the static quality of the canon, as against the conservation of meaning and dynamic aspects of the canon.

Textual Authority and the Veda

What techniques are employed in the *BhāgP* to establish its authority?

There is, first of all, a recurrence of the Veda, within it, this being a privileged means of establishing textual authority in the Indian tradition. This is a feature common to other Purāṇas[2] as well. The *paurāṇikas* claimed that the Purāṇas as a genre are a necessary complement of the Veda, the teachings of which they reinforce and amplify. This process makes them accessible to those who were either intellectually incapable of understanding the Veda or socially excluded from Vedic recitation. This function is described by the tradition as *upabṛṃhaṇa*, confirming elaboration. Thus, the *paurāṇikas* did not negate the canonicity of the Veda, but they stretched the limits of that canon by introducing new concepts. In other words, the Purāṇas claim to be canonic commentaries which are able to relate the text commented upon, namely the Veda, to the world.

In the *BhāgP* this use of the Veda does not stop with the attempt to attain status as a commentary; there is an additional emphasis. The author claims that the *BhāgP* is itself equivalent to the Veda, if not the essence of the Veda (cf. 1,1.3f, which states that the Bhāgavata is the fruit of the wish-yielding tree of Veda, dropped on earth from the mouth of Śuka). It is described as the fifth Veda (1,4.20) or the Veda of *kaliyuga*, and therefore the Veda appropriate for the present age. That these claims were subsequently accepted by some of the Vaiṣṇava schools is evident from the title 'Viṣṇuveda' conferred upon it. F.M. Smith[3] maintains that in North India people today refer to the *BhāgP* when they speak of the Veda. This is telling evidence of how deeply the intimate relation between the Purāṇa and the old canonical tradition is entrenched in the minds of devotees.

The *BhāgP* does then claim a special relation to the Veda. How can this claim be substantiated? At the linguistic level, as Buitenen (1966) points out, the author(s) responsible for the final version of the *BhāgP* wanted the book to sound archaic. The Purāṇa not only seeks to be orthodox in the Vedic tradition, it tries to sound like the Veda. This may have been a reaction to pressures exerted by orthodox South Indian brahmins, an attempt of the authors of the *BhāgP* to prove the orthodoxy of their teachings. Thus, while its use of Vedic Sanskrit is unique, its Vedicism, according to Hardy, 'is part of an overall Southern Vaiṣṇava preoccupation. It shows that a whole culture is struggling to preserve its identity by relating itself to the most powerful symbol with which the North has been challenging it'. (1983: 489–90) The *BhāgP* takes both the Veda and Vedic ritual and reshapes them to meet its own ideological and ritual needs, thus sustaining its claim of being legitimate in the orthodox tradition (cf. F.M. Smith 1993). Moreover, the authors of the *BhāgP* claim that the Veda itself was created by Viṣṇu and identify Nārāyaṇa, the *puruṣottama* or highest being, with the Vedic *puruṣa*, the primeval man. Further, they establish the identity of Viṣṇu and Kṛṣṇa, the latter probably being a non-Vedic deity. They argue thus for the teachings of Kṛṣṇa being the Veda, and for the Purāṇa being the infallible vehicle of those teachings. As consciously engendered canon, the Purāṇa appropriated the territory held by the Veda, and, as a dynamic re-creation of it, it takes pieces of Vedic imagery and lore and presents them in a new setting. It thereby recontextualizes them and produces a new, contemporary image and meaning.

Textual Authority and Purāṇic *Paramparā*

The Purāṇas themselves provide a *paramparā* of textual transmission from the divine author to the final text. There are three levels in this transmission: that of the deity, that of the *munis* and *ṛṣis*, and that of the redactor who finally communicates the text to his pupils. There are 38 such lists of transmission given at various places in different Mahāpurāṇas.[4] Their purpose is to substantiate the claim to divine origin, to establish the character of revelation, and to provide a seamless line of transmission that guarantees the authority of the teaching. These several levels of narration are also significant for the concept of originality and authorship as perceived in the Purāṇic genre, which opts not for individual creativity in the sense of originality, but for a fresh retelling of a received or revealed tradition.

For the *BhāgP*, the *paramparā* begins with Viṣṇu-Nārāyaṇa, who, at the beginning of creation, revealed the matchless lamp of wisdom to Brahmā (first level), who taught it to Nārada, who again taught it to Vedavyāsa (second level), who taught it to his son, the sage Śuka, who again taught it to King Parīkṣit (third level) (*BhāgP* 12,13.19–21).

If, however, one follows the narrative of the *BhāgP* from its beginning, one first encounters an anonymous author who sets the frame for the Purāṇic recitation. It begins in a conventional setting—the Naimiṣa forest, where Śaunaka and the other *ṛṣis* are about to engage in a *sattra*, lasting for a thousand years. When Sūta Ugraśravas arrives, he is asked by the *ṛṣis* about the deeds of Bhagavān. The Sūta proceeds to recite the *BhāgP*, which had been composed by Vyāsa, who taught it to his son Śuka, who recited it to Parīkṣit during his fast unto death, at which occasion Sūta also happened to be present to hear it. In what follows,

Sūta tells how Vyāsa came to compose the *BhāgP* —I will return to this shortly. From 1,7.12 onwards, Sūta narrates what happened at the time of the *Mahābhārata* battle, as well as the story leading up to the birth of Parīkṣit and his life up to the point when the king enters his fast unto death and meets Śuka. From 2,1 onwards, the text consists of the recitation of Śuka to Parīkṣit, ending in 12,6, when Parīkṣit attains *mokṣa*, and Śaunaka and the Sūta take over again as interlocutors. In the main body of the text recited by Śuka, there are embedded narratives in which other interlocutors come to the fore, as for example Uddhava and Vidura (3,1–3,4), Vidura and Maitreya (3,5–4,31) or Nārada and Yudhiṣṭhira (7,1–7,11). They are conceived of as so many pairs of guru, teacher, and *śiṣya*, student.

We will return to these pairs of teachers and students and to the message they propagate or listen to in due course. For now, let us concentrate on the level of interlocution or *paramparā* connected with Vyāsa. There is nothing extraordinary about Vyāsa being credited with the composition of the *BhāgP*. What is unique is the explanation of how Vyāsa came to compose it.

BhāgP 1,4 describes how Vyāsa first divided the original single Veda into four, to enable mortals thus to retain it in parts, and then composed the *Mahābhārata (MBh)* for the sake of those who were not allowed to listen to the Veda. Afterwards he still felt uneasy at heart and despondent, 'sorrowing with the feeling that something was wanting in him' (1,4.32ab). *BhāgP* 1,5 has Nārada arrive and explain to Vyāsa what is lacking in the Vedic and epic literature Vyāsa has so far arranged and composed. He says that though Vyāsa has produced the most wonderful *MBh* which fully deals with all the objects of human pursuit, as dharma, etc., and has realized the eternal brahman, delineating spiritual knowledge for the welfare of living beings, he has failed to sing adequately the stainless glory of the Lord:

> I consider that wisdom to be deficient, which does not tend to please the Lord. (8) O chief of sages, you have not so fully described the glory of Bhagavān Vāsudeva as you have dealt with the objects of human pursuit such as dharma etc. (9) Speech, which though full of figurative expressions, never utters the world-sanctifying praises of Śrī Hari, is considered to be the delight of voluptuous men, who wallow in the pleasures of sense like crows that feed upon the dirty leavings of food. Like swans, having their abode in the Mānasarovar lake, devotees who ever abide in His heart never take delight in such speech. (10) On the other hand, that composition which, though faulty in diction, consists of verses each of which contains the names of the immortal Lord, bearing the impress of his glory, wipes out the sins of the people; it is such composition that

> pious men love to hear, sing and repeat to an audience (11). That wisdom too which is free from blemish and is a direct means to the attainment of liberation does not adorn one's soul so much if it is devoid of devotion to Lord Achyuta ... (12) ... Therefore, with a concentrated mind now recall the exploits of Śrī Hari, who wields unthinkable power, with a view to the liberation of the entire humanity. (13cd) The man who desires to talk of anything else than the Lord's exploits falls into the trap of the manifold names and forms, evolved by such desire and sees diversity everywhere. Like a boat beaten by a blast, his unsteady mind finds no rest anywhere. (14)[5]

The important thing, according to Nārada, is that Bhagavān is the reality at the base of the entire universe. This knowledge, if it finds expression in devotion to Him, is the only means leading to salvation. Therefore Vyāsa, himself a ray of the supreme spirit, should describe the exploits of Bhagavān in their full glory. He should highlight the fact that Bhagavān is to be perceived in everything and is the foundation of everything—a teaching that, according to Nārada, was lacking in the *MBh*.

An interesting evaluation of the *BhāgP* is given in the text itself. As answer to their question as to whom dharma has gone for refuge, now that its defender, Kṛṣṇa, is no longer on earth (1,1.23), Sūta tells Śaunaka and the other *ṛṣis* that the replacement for Kṛṣṇa in *kaliyuga* is 'this Purāṇa called Bhāgavata which is equal in exellency to the spiritual essence of the Vedas' (*idam bhāgavatam nāma purāṇam brahma-sammitam*, 1,3.40). Further, 'Kṛṣṇa having returned to his own abode, together with *dharma*, knowledge and the rest, this sun in *purāṇa* form has now arisen for the benefit of those who have lost their sight in the *kaliyuga*' (1,3.43b-44a) (cf. Matchett 1993: 97).[6]

Thus, the *BhāgP*, via the identification of Vyāsa as its author, refers back to his previous work, the Veda and the epic. It links up with their prestige as canonical or authoritative texts. At the same time, it highlights the fact that it is superior, being the culmination of the creative process of Vyāsa, the one scripture for *kaliyuga*—when Bhagavān himself is absent—which teaches us about his ultimate immanence.

The Message of the *Bhāgavatapurāṇa* and Textual Authority

If *bhakti* [7] is the central concern of the text, it should be added that it is emotional *bhakti*, as archetypically represented by the *gopīs*' or milkmaids' relation to Kṛṣṇa, that is highlighted in the *BhāgP*. Intellectual *bhakti*, which Hacker (1959: 92ff) claimed for the Viṣṇupurāṇa, one of the sources of the Kṛṣṇa story then being reworked by the Āḻvārs, also finds a place in the *BhāgP*, pointing to its *advaita* heritage. Emotional *bhakti* is focused on Kṛṣṇa, the supreme Lord, and even *mokṣa* tends to be seen in terms of *parabhakti*, the highest devotion. *Bhakti* is the way for spiritual fulfilment and it is the goal: *bhakti* leads to *mokṣa*, which, again, is *parabhakti*, the final *satsaṅga*, which means being united with other *bhaktas* in ultimate devotion to Kṛṣṇa (cf. Anand 1996: 201–18). Yet, even in the teachings that the authors of the *BhāgP* put in the mouth of Kṛṣṇa in *BhāgP* 11,7-29, *bhakti* is often described as a means for reaching liberation in terms of self-realization or knowledge of one's being identical with brahman, as against some eternal relationship with a personal god. In 11,11, Kṛṣṇa recommends listening to and singing stories of Him, and associating with good people. The ideal *bhakta* worships His images, serves fellow devotees, sings and listens to stories of Kṛṣṇa, meditates upon Him, serves Him, takes part in His festivals, pilgrimage, etc., and all this without interest in reward (11,11.34–41). In 11,12, *satsaṅga* and devotion are highlighted by Kṛṣṇa as the most effective ways to union with him. Correct *bhakti* behaviour is important, more so than notions of the *varṇāśramadharma* which are nevertheless still preserved in the *BhāgP*. The life and teachings of people who narrate or teach the *BhāgP* bear witness to this. They tend to belong to circles of ideal *bhaktas*, *mahābhāgavatas*, i.e. great devotees of Bhagavān Kṛṣṇa, or *bhakti* teachers.

Turning to the interlocutors of the *BhāgP* in terms of their mythological background and their qualifications as teachers of *bhakti*—the ultimate teacher being Kṛṣṇa himself—it is worth taking a closer look at Śuka and Parīkṣit. Here, we touch again upon the issue of the *BhāgP* referring back to the *MBh*.[8]

Whereas Vyāsa is, in the *BhāgP* as well as in the *MBh*, present in the framing story and in the main narrative, and is introduced as the composer of the *BhāgP*, the main interlocutors, namely Śuka and Parīkṣit, belong to the generation of sons and grandsons. Thus the narrative situation of the *BhāgP* is placed in the aftermath of the *MBh*—its place being at the fast unto death by Parīkṣit who had been cursed by a brahmin boy to die of snake-bite. This situation consciously echoes the one in which the *MBh* professes to be told, namely the snake sacrifice of Janamejaya, with which he wishes to avenge the death of his father Parīkṣit.

What is it in the characters of Śuka and Parīkṣit that qualifies them as the main dialogue partners of the *BhāgP*? What is it that makes Parīkṣit worthy as a *bhakta* to ask the right questions about Bhagavān? In what way is Śuka, the son of Vyāsa, the composer of the *BhāgP*, more suited to answer Parīkṣit's questions than his father? Parīkṣit has special devotion to Kṛṣṇa because he had *darśana* or vision of him while still in the womb.

When attacked by Aśvatthāman with the *brahmāstra*, in an attempt to kill the last of the Pāṇḍava heirs, he was saved and revived by Kṛṣṇa. After that *darśana* he spent the rest of his life looking for Kṛṣṇa, in the end inviting Śuka to expound on Bhagavān. Having listened to the teachings of Śuka, Parīkṣit finds Bhagavān again, and without further delay attains final release.

Śuka, in his turn, is introduced as the silent sage and son of Vyāsa, who went forth to become ascetic though he had not received his initiatory thread (1,2.2). He is the guru of sages who, out of his compassion, narrates the secret Purāṇa (1,2.3). Further, he is described as having renounced all passion. Again, it is declared that he was without ties, a *yogi* even in the womb—compare Parīkṣit who has his first *darśana* in the womb. Losing all self-interest, he was devoted to Kṛṣṇa, and practised disinterested devotion, *ahaitukī bhakti* (1,7.10). He was fascinated by the virtues of Kṛṣṇa, which induced him to learn the *BhāgP* from his father. This absolute detachment and renunciation finally qualify him to recite the Bhāgavata, setting him off against his more worldly father, who longed for sons and did eventually father them, being actively involved in the action of the *MBh*. His greater spirituality, his having attained *mokṣa* and dissolving his body to merge with all the elements, make Śuka fit to recite the *BhāgP* with its additional subtlety and spirituality. Since it is superior to the *MBh* in terms of its potential for providing Salvation, it requires a reciter superior to Vyāsa in detachment and renunciation.[9]

Another of the dialogue partners of the *BhāgP*, Uddhava, the Yādava, friend and minister of Kṛṣṇa, is similar to Parīkṣit. He too expresses the greatness of his devotion by the enthusiasm with which he receives instruction. Maitreya resembles Śuka in that he spends his time in telling the stories of Bhagavān to those who need to hear them.

Nārada, in his turn, enters the Purāṇa at many places in the role of teacher and adviser—note his instructions to Vyāsa, Dhruva, Priyavrata, etc.—and narrates almost all of *BhāgP* 7 relating the story of Prahlāda, his narration to Yudhiṣṭhira being 'cited' by Śuka to Parīkṣit.

Prahlāda, again, is one of the *mahābhāgavatas*, and not mainly an interlocutor of the Purāṇa, but all the more important as a demon—devoid of demonic qualities—who is a teacher of *bhakti* and a model devotee. Amongst the different modes of emotion which can turn one's mind to Vāsudeva, there is, according to the teaching of Nārada to Yudhiṣṭhira (*BhāgP* 7,1), hostility (*dveṣa*), characterizing the *asuras*, as for example Śiśupāla, who have their minds fixed on Kṛṣṇa as their enemy. Yet, though Prahlāda is an *asura*, it is *bhakti* in the narrower sense of *ahaitukī bhakti* which draws him to the Lord. He shows love to Lord Vāsudeva from the beginning of his life, imitating the childhood play of Kṛṣṇa and showing, out of his deep devotion, outwardly incoherent behaviour, such as shouting and singing aloud, sitting silent or weeping, etc.

Another significant characteristic of most of the *mahābhāgavatas* is their missionary zeal, the desire to share their beliefs and feelings with others, to spread the *bhakti* ideal, to communicate their experience to others. This highlights again the fact that telling and listening to the stories of the Lord is a major feature of the life of Kṛṣṇa's *mahābhāgavatas* (cf. Matchett 1993: 103).

Nārada, Prahlāda and Śuka belong to those *mahābhāgavatas* who, in the course of the narration of the *BhāgP*, act as teachers of *bhakti* in a more definite sense. Here, in their exhortations, we find not only emotional *bhakti*, but also 'intellectual' *bhakti*—paired, as it is for example in most of the teachings of Nārada, with *advaita* doctrines and *dharmaśāstra* material. Śuka, when measured by his more personal advice to Parīkṣit as against his 'teaching' consisting of most of the *BhāgP*, also seems to favour advaitic ideas. Prahlāda, in his teachings to his fellow demon youngsters, praises a path which combines *jñāna*, *yoga* and *bhakti*, devotion to Govinda Kṛṣṇa being, however, the highest goal for all beings in the world.

Thus, we have seen how the interlocutors of the *BhāgP* are themselves teachers of the central message of the text, namely *bhakti* in its emotional and intellectual variant as sanctioned by Kṛṣṇa himself, the addressee of the devotion. At the same time, they are embodiments of the very ideals they teach. There is then a strong internal consistency concerning the message of the text and its 'messengers'.

Textual Authority and Canonicity

Coming back to the typologies of the Word in India as cited earlier, it has become obvious that the *BhāgP* is not confinable either to the status of 'scripture' or 'story'; rather, in the course of history, it combined features of more than one of Coburn's types.

The *BhāgP* started out as the prototype of a normative story and route to salvation, the foremost concern being its intelligibility, even if it contains passages in archaic Sanskrit. The author(s) of the *BhāgP* obtain sanction for their text and its message by reconnecting with the Veda in terms of the *paramparā* claimed for the text. It is held to be the culmination of the creative process of Vyāsa, the one who arranged the Veda and author of the *MBh*. In addition, Kṛṣṇa is shown to be identical with the Vedic *puruṣa* via the chain of identities with Viṣṇu and *puruṣottama*. Kṛṣṇa's teaching is thus shown to be as old as the Veda, even the true essence of the Veda.

But, while accepting the Veda as a point of reference for its own authority, the authors try to establish the *BhāgP* as a text which is ultimately more authoritative than the Veda itself. It not only claims to be a canonic commentary on the Veda in the sense of *upabṛṃhaṇa* or confirming elaboration (making it accessible and meaningful in *kaliyuga*), but also claims to be the Veda, the authoritative scripture, for the new times. Textual authority is to an important degree due to the quality of the text as a route to salvation, as well as to the text's ability to define the position of man and his duties in relation to the cosmic whole, the key to these questions given in the *BhāgP* being *bhakti*.

The *BhāgP* as authoritative text with its message of *bhakti* paired with *advaita* awaited a community which would adopt it. Neither Rāmānuja nor Nimbārka refer to the *BhāgP*. The adoption took place in the Vaiṣṇava *sampradāyas* of Madhva, Caitanya, and last but not least Vallabha, whose doctrine has been characterized as 'a systematization of the Bhāgavatapurāṇa in the light of certain epistemological views and sectarian ideas' (Glasenapp 1933–4: 319).

As one of the canonical texts of the aforementioned *sampradāyas*, the *BhāgP* gave rise to its own library of commentaries being commented upon and interpreted according to a variety of doctrines of the Vedāntic tradition from *dvaita* via *śuddhādvaita* to *acintyabhedābheda*, the doctrine of the 'ineffable duality in non-duality'.[10]

Due to its importance as a theological text and the stabilizing effect of its commentaries, the *BhāgP* reached a stage where it was no longer changed, as the other Purāṇas were. This is attested to by the manuscript tradition, which is rather uniform and devoid of significant textual variations.

Further indication of the *BhāgP*'s canonical status, showing features of Coburn's category of 'scripture', is to be found in the *Bhāgavatamāhātmyas* (*BhāgMā*). One of these, claiming to be part of the *Padmapurāṇa*, has been conveniently put before the text of the *BhāgP* in the Gītā Press edition. Here, in *BhāgMā* 1.20, it is said that the *ṛṣi* came to regard the *Bhāgavata* as an embodiment of the Lord in *kaliyuga*, capable of conferring the reward of speedy access to Vaikuṇṭha by merely being read or heard. Especially salving is the reading of the *BhāgP* in a week's time,[11] this imbues *bhakti*, *jñāna*, and *vairāgya*, asceticism personified, with new vigour (*BhāgMā* 3 passim). Further, the exposition of the *BhāgP* in its true spirit leads to the attainment of equality with Kṛṣṇa for both the expounder and the listener (*BhāgMā* 3.74). And, naturally, the *BhāgP* is the only text leading to salvation—due to the charismatic presence of Kṛṣṇa in it.[12] Thus, at this late stage of development, the *BhāgP* attains the mantric efficacy of a stable text. When recited verbatim and with proper devotion, it leads to salvation.

The lasting influence of the *BhāgP* is attested to by the amount of Sanskrit literature refering back to it for inspiration. Apart from commentaries and poetic reworkings, etc. to be found in the classical language, there exist innumerable translations, transcreations and poetic treatments in all the vernaculars of India (cf. Prasad 1984: 259–97). Those texts amount to a body of popular commentary, making the story-turned-scripture accessible to later centuries and to people who cannot understand the archaic Sanskrit of the text. This is also visible in the practice, often encountered in contemporary India, of reciting the *BhāgP* interspersed with oral commentary in the vernacular.

In conclusion, the *BhāgP* in its development is proof of the dynamics of the canonicity of texts in the Indian tradition over the last 3000 years—the dynamics that revolve around the tension between a literal preservation of sacred or canonical texts and their dynamic re-creation.

Notes

1. For what follows, cf. Assmann and Assmann (1987).
2. For a discussion of the dynamic canon of the Purāṇas as evident from the Purāṇic texts themselves, see Bonazzoli (1979). It has to be kept in mind that the canonicity of the Purāṇas is probably more of the kind characteristic of a literary canon: such a canon acknowledges a series of—be it religious—works which belong to a certain genre of literature as rightly claiming a place within this genre. The genre as a whole claims a certain authority whose canonicity—in the sense of normative texts for a certain community—is however difficult to prove.
3. (1993: 125 n12), quoting an observation by Philip Lutgendorf.
4. For the following, cf. Bonazzoli (1980).
5. The translation follows that of Goswami, i.e. *BhāgP* ([1971] 1982,1: 18), with minor modifications.
6. For a lucid exposition of the role of absence or separation, *viraha*, in the narrative structure and for the interpretation of the *BhāgP*, as well as some perceptive comments on the framing of the narrative, see Huberman (1994). He holds the *BhāgP* to be a narrative as response to *viraha*, which the *bhakta* is bound to suffer in *kaliyuga*, when Kṛṣṇa is no longer visible on earth; *harikathā* being the antidote to separation.
7. For the concept of *bhakti* in the *BhāgP*, cf. Gail (1969).
8. Cf. Brown (1996), Doniger (1993) and Huberman (1994).
9. Cf. Doniger (1993), referring to the story of Śuka as told in the *MBh* and

in the *Devībhāgavatapurāṇa* (*DBhāgP*) to elucidate Śuka's role in the *BhāgP*. Compare the discussion of Śuka in the *MBh*, *BhāgP* and *DBhāgP* in relation to different modes of perfected living as given in Brown (1996).

10. For a concise discussion of those interpretations of the *BhāgP*, cf. Sheridan (1986: 118–35).
11. This practice is also mentioned in a passage from the Pratisargaparvan of the *Bhaviṣyapurāṇa* (*BhvP* 3/3,28.7-19), where a list of eighteen Purāṇas is given. They are qualified according to the gods to whom they are dedicated, and it is stated that the *bhāgavataśāstra*, i.e. the *BhāgP*, is the first and foremost of these eighteen.
12. Brown (1986: 82) highlights the fact that in the *BhāgMā* of *Padmapurāṇa*, the *BhāgP* is treated as a manifestation of god's grace and love for his devotees, infused with his real presence, so that the *BhāgP* in this view qualifies as a *mūrti* or form of Bhagavān.

References

Anand, Subhash. 1996. *The Way of Love: The Bhāgavata Doctrine of Bhakti*. New Delhi: Munshiram Manoharlal.

Assmann, Aleida and Jan Assmann. 1987. Kanon und Zensur. In *Kanon und Zensur. Beiträge zur Archäologie der literarischen Kommunikation II*, ed. Aleida Assmann and Jan Assmann, 7-27. München: Wilhelm Fink Verlag.

Bhāgavatapurāṇa. [1971] 1982. *Śrīmad Bhāgavata Mahāpurāṇa (with Sanskrit text and English translation)*. Rendered into English by C. L. Goswami. 2 Pts. Gorakhpur: Gita Press.

Bhaviṣyapurāṇa. 1959. *Bhaviṣya Mahāpurāṇa*. Ed. Kṣemarāja Śrīkṛṣṇadāsa. 3rd ed. Bambaī: Śrīveṅkateśvara Presa.

Bonazzoli, Giorgio. 1979. The Dynamic Canon of the Purāṇa-s. *Purāṇa* 21.2: 116–66.

———. 1980. Purāṇic Paramparā. *Purāṇa* 22.1: 33-60.

Brown, C. Mackenzie. 1986. Purāṇa as Scripture: From Sound to Image of the Holy Word in the Hindu Tradition. *History of Religion* 26.1: 68–86.

———. 1996. Modes of Perfected Living in the Mahābhārata and the Purāṇas: The Different Faces of Śuka the Renouncer. In *Living liberation in Hindu thought*, ed. Andrew O. Fort and Patricia Y. Mumme, 157–83. Albany: State University of New York Press.

Buitenen, J. A. B. van. 1966. On the Archaism of the Bhāgavata Purāṇa. In *Krishna: myths, rites, attitudes*, ed. Milton Singer, 23–40. Chicago and London: University of Chicago Press.

Coburn, Thomas B. 1984. 'Scripture' in India: Towards a Typology of the Word in Hindu Life. *Journal of the American Academy of Religion* 52.3: 435–59.

Colpe, Carsten. 1987. Sakralisierung von Texten und Filiationen von Kanons. In *Kanon und Zensur. Beiträge zur Archäologie der literarischen Kommunikation II*, ed. Aleida Assmann and Jan Assmann, 80–92. München: Wilhelm Fink Verlag.

Doniger, Wendy. 1993. Echoes of the Mahābhārata: Why is a Parrot the Narrator of the Bhāgavata Purāṇa and the Devībhāgavatapurāṇa? In *Purāṇa perennis. Reciprocity and Transformation in Hindu and Jaina Texts*, ed. Wendy Doniger, 31–57. Albany: State University of New York Press.

Gail, Adalbert. 1969. *Bhakti im Bhāgavatapurāṇa. Religionsgeschichtliche Studie zur Idee der Gottesliebe in Kult und Mystik des Viṣṇuismus*. Wiesbaden: Harrassowitz. (Münchner Indologische Studien 6).

Glasenapp, Helmuth von. 1933–4. Die Lehre Vallabhacāryas. *Zeitschrift für Indologie und Iranistik* 9: 268–330.

Hacker, Paul. 1959. *Prahlāda: Werden und Wandlungen einer Idealgestalt*. Mainz: Akademie der Wissenschaften und der Literatur.

Hardy, Friedhelm. 1983. *Viraha-bhakti: The Early History of Kṛṣṇa Devotion in South India*. Delhi: Oxford University Press.

Huberman, Eric. 1994. The Semiotics of Separation: Narratives of Absence in the Bhāgavata Purāṇa. *Journal of Vaiṣṇava Studies* 2.3: 87–112.

Matchett, Freda. 1993. The Pervasiveness of *Bhakti* in the Bhāgavata Purāṇa. In *Love Divine: Studies in Bhakti and Devotional Mysticism*, ed. Karel Werner, 95–115. Richmond: Curzon.

Prasad, Sheo Shanker. 1984. *The Bhāgavata Purāṇa: A Literary Study*. Delhi: Capital.

Sheridan, Daniel P. 1986. *The Advaitic Theism of the Bhāgavata Purāṇa*. Delhi: Motilal Banarsidass.

Smith, Frederick M. 1993. Purāṇaveda. In *Authority, Anxiety and Canon: Essays in Vedic Interpretation*, ed. Laurie L. Patton, 97–138. Albany: State University of New York Press.

Smith, Jonathan Z. 1982. Sacred Persistence: Toward a Redescription of Canon. In *Imagining Religion: From Babylon to Jamestown*, 36–52. Chicago and London: University of Chicago Press.

The Śaiva Siddhānta Ācārya as Mediator of Religious Identity[1]

JÖRG GENGNAGEL

This article deals with a specific exegetical tradition within the Sanskrit Śaiva Siddhānta and explores how religious identity is created by focusing on the role of the Śaiva Ācārya. First I will show that the ritual specialists of the religious community and bearers of this tradition, the Ācāryas, present themselves as a closed group dealing with a specific set of texts. Second, I will deal with the various categories of initiated Śaiva Siddhāntins who constitute the religious community, and with the position of the Ācārya amongst them. An analysis of the Ācārya's function as the mediator of religious identity will follow. The Ācārya places the school's own canon of revealed literature within the larger framework of sacred Śaiva scriptures in general and at the same time transmits a specific textual tradition to his successor and his pupils. Finally, in exploring the issue of charisma I shall try to show that the Ācārya's position is created by his being a vessel of divine presence during ritual; no specific personal charisma is necessary for his selection or position as Ācārya.

The school of Śaiva Siddhānta is to be placed within the larger framework of Tantric Śaivism. Theology and ritual are defined basically by two factors: individual affiliation to the tradition through the initiation (*dīkṣā*), performed in a complex ritual procedure by the Ācārya, and the acceptance of a corpus of authoritative literature, the canon of 28 Tantras[2] and a large number of subsidiary Tantras. Both groups of texts are believed to be directly or indirectly revealed by Śiva. The Sanskrit Śaiva Siddhānta school of Śaivism to which I am referring has to be distinguished from the later Tamil Śaiva Siddhānta, a South Indian tradition with Tamil and Sanskrit scriptures developing out of the Śaiva Siddhānta school prominent in Kashmir but not exclusively confined to this region. The Sanskrit Śaiva Siddhānta tradition is characterized by a dualistic theology separating Śiva as efficient cause (*nimittakāraṇa*) from the material cause (*upādānakāraṇa*) of the universe and insisting that even the liberated soul does not achieve identity with Śiva.[3] The Siddhānta does maintain the dharmaśāstric rules of purity in its ritual practice and represents therefore an orthodox strand within Tantric Śaivism. The liturgical tradition is based on the worship of Sadāśiva. In this context it should be noted that the vedic initiation rituals (*saṃskāra*) are not neglected; rather a higher and more powerful level of Śaiva initiations is added to it.[4]

The Lineage of Ācāryas

The lineage of Śaiva Ācāryas is linked to a period of Śaiva exegetical literary traditions which bases itself on a huge corpus of Śaiva revelatory literature, formed roughly between the sixth and tenth centuries. During and after this period we find both a process of canonization of this revelatory literature and the emergence of various exegetical traditions. The first preserved non-scriptural texts of the Śaiva Siddhānta were composed in the eighth or ninth century by the Śaiva Ācārya Sadyojyotis. The literature of the school had reached a highly systematized terminology and theology at the time of Aghoraśivācārya in the twelfth century. One must add that the process of canonization obviously included the redaction as well as the composition of new Tantras, sometimes under the name of older works.[5]

Looking at the Sanskrit literature of dualistic Śaivism we find an exegetical tradition consisting of texts written by Śaiva Ācāryas that bases itself on the canon of Tantras mentioned above. At least three types of texts constitute the non-scriptural literature of the Siddhānta: commentaries and subcommentaries on the revealed literature, independent treatises, and ritual handbooks (*paddhati*) based on ritual sections (*kriyāpāda*) of the Tantras. These texts are closely interrelated by sharing a limited repertoire of quotations from Tantric literature. Independent treatises of this textual tradition as well as commentaries by earlier authors are frequently cited and commented upon by succeeding Ācāryas.

The most prominent figure and point of reference for the successive Śaiva Ācāryas is certainly Ācārya Sadyojyotis. We find Sadyojyotis already quoted by the Kashmiri idealist Somānanda (around AD 900) and later by Abhinavagupta.[6] He composed independent treatises as well as commentaries on Tantras.[7] Though the position of Sadyojyotis is very important, one has to bear in mind that he is not considered the founder of the tradition. He himself refers to his predecessors, but the works of these authors are unknown to us. A lineage of Śaiva teachers with their names ending in 'Kaṇṭha' shows a strong dependence on the work of Sadyojyotis, but we do not have precise information about a familial or teacher–pupil relation between the Kaṇṭha lineage and Sadyojyotis. The situation is different with the Kaṇṭhas: they do show close family relations and share a documented teaching tradition. The first Kaṇṭha known to us is a Rāmakaṇṭha, of whom we only know that he had Śrīkaṇṭha—author of the *Ratnatrayaparīkṣā*—and Vidyākaṇṭha as his pupils. This second pupil, Vidyākaṇṭha, is the father of Nārāyaṇakaṇṭha, author of an important tenth-century commentary on the *Mṛgendra*. The son of this Nārāyaṇakaṇṭha is the very influential author Rāmakaṇṭha II (end of the tenth century), who composed several important and sophisticated commentaries on Tantras and on the works of Sadyojyotis. Aghoraśiva (twelfth century) stands last in this line, again like Sadyojyotis without familial or direct teacher–pupil affiliation, but drawing heavily on the texts of the authors mentioned above. He also composed the well-known ritual manual *Kriyākramadyotikā* which is still in use in the Tamil-speaking areas of South India.[8]

In summing up we can say that, in the given succession of Ācāryas, we do find close family ties, an interrelated corpus of exegetical literature, as well as a relatively homogeneous repertoire of authoritative texts quoted and commented upon. If we now try to get more information about the early historical, social and geographical background of this tradition, we have to admit that the available data are scarce.[9] I shall try to deduce information about the internal structure of the school by considering the normative statements contained in the textual tradition. As textual sources for this study I focus on the sections on ritual and conduct of the *Mṛgendra* (composed roughly before the tenth century) and the ritual manual *Somaśambhupaddhati* or *Karmakāṇḍakramāvalī* (eleventh century). Both these āgamic sections on ritual and conduct and the ritual manuals of the Śaiva Siddhānta school allow a closer look at the role of the Ācārya as mediator of religious identity. This will also help us to shed some light on the structure of the given Ācārya lineage and the transmission of textual traditions.

Ācārya, Sādhaka, Putraka and Samayin

The role of the Śaiva Ācārya in the Sanskrit Śaiva Siddhānta tradition has to be defined within a framework of a complex system of hierarchically arranged levels of initiations (*dīkṣā*) and ordinations (*abhiṣeka*). Analysing the different categories of initiated Śaivas (*dīkṣita*) will allow us to get a clearer view of the specific position of the Ācārya within this tradition.

There are four basic categories of initiates: On a first level of introductory initiation the novice receives his new *dīkṣā*-name and is thus admitted into the Śaiva Siddhānta community represented by the initiating Ācārya. During this ritual, the Ācārya enumerates certain rules of conduct (*samayācāra*). Besides the rules to never censure Śiva, his teachings, and the initiated Śaivas, the Ācārya declares that the adept is obliged to perform regular worship to Śiva, to fire, and to his guru from now until the end of his life. The ritual ends with the handing over of the marks of observance (*vratāṅga*).[10] Those considered incapable of following the given rules—the handicapped, the old and sick as well as children and women—receive an initiation that does not depend on the observation of all of the duties (*nirbījadīkṣā*).[11] They receive an initiation in relation to their individual capacities and are thus not excluded from liberation.[12]

After this first level of initiation called 'initiation into the state of a follower of the rules' (*samayadīkṣā*), the initiate is called 'Samayin'.[13] The Samayin is entitled to receive a liberating initiation (*nirvāṇadīkṣā*), but only after a thorough examination by his Ācārya. Thereby the initiated is liberated from his basic fetter 'impurity' (*mala*) through the action of Śiva, who is thought to be present in the body of the Ācārya in charge of the ritual. This basic fetter is seen as a substance that functions as a beginningless cover of the soul and obstructs its capacity to know and to act (*jñāna* and *kriyā*). Śiva alone has the capacity to remove this cover of the soul during the process of liberating initiation. He thus bestows his liberating grace on this soul. Having received this *nirvāṇadīkṣā*, the *dīkṣita* is called Putraka,[14] 'son [of Śiva]', and as a liberated soul (*muktātman*) he will reach a state almost equal to that of Śiva after his death.

Only a Putraka initiated in this way can be selected by an Ācārya as his successor and will be ordained as an Ācārya through the performance of a consecration ritual (*ācāryābhiṣeka*). It should be added that the consecration of the Ācārya entitles him to perform all three types of ritual acts classified as daily and regular (*nitya*), occasional (*naimittika*) and for specific wishes (*kāmya*). As the thus initiated and consecrated Ācārya is qualified to perform rituals for himself as well as for others, his initiation—and the initiation of the Sādhaka—is called 'initiation which bestows authority' (*sādhikāradīkṣā*). On the other hand, the initiation of the Samayin and Putraka is called 'without authority' (*niradhikāra*). These two are only entitled to perform the obligatory ritual (*nityapūjā*) on their own; for other types of ritual they need the assistance of an officiant.[15]

In addition to the categories of Samayin, Putraka and Ācārya we find a fourth level of initiation leading to the position of a Sādhaka, which is difficult to place within the tradition. The Samayin who wants to receive further initiations has the choice between two options. If he is primarily interested in liberation after death, if he is a *mumukṣu*, he will receive the liberating initiation (*nirvāṇadīkṣā*) and can eventually become an Ācārya. But if his main interest is in gaining certain faculties and powers during his lifetime, if he is a *bubhukṣu*, he will receive a special type of liberating initiation called *sādhakadīkṣā*, and will be consecrated as Sādhaka through a *sādhakābhiṣeka*. He will try to gain the desired faculties in a suitable, secluded place (*kṣetra*) by seeking power and control over his specific Mantra (*sādhyamantra*) and the deity that it designates. Dealing with this status of the Sādhaka, one has to keep in mind that the Śaiva Siddhānta perceives itself as the highest and purest tradition within Tantric Śaivism, and is critical of the nondualist, esoteric traditions:

> The religious practice of the Siddhānta was dualistic (*dvaitācāraḥ*) in the sense that it accepted the orthodox (Vedic) distinctions between the pure and the impure and remained strictly within the boundaries of the former. The Trika, by contrast, advocated the practice of nonduality (*advaitācāraḥ*), in as much as its rituals involved contact with impure persons and/or substances. (Sanderson 1995: 17)

The Śaiva Siddhānta's relation to Tantric heteropraxy can be outlined as follows:

> Whatever connections that Tantric system may have had with the heterodox culture of the cremation-grounds, they had no doubt been long concealed and forgotten beneath a systematic epistemology, ontology and injunctive orientation which aligned it, inspite of its theism, with the orthodox world-view of the Mīmāṃsakas. (Sanderson 1985: 203)

It is the figure of the power-seeking Sādhaka which obviously presents a link between these elements of the heterodox practice of the cremation-grounds to the orthodox, exoteric orientation of Śaiva Siddhānta.[16] These heterodox elements are almost exclusively limited to the Sādhaka. This observation is confirmed by the position of the Sādhaka in the later Tamil Śaiva Siddhānta. There we find a complete negation of the heterodox elements, with the consequence that the figure of the Sādhaka is reduced to an almost irrelevant category.[17]

The Role of the Ācārya within the Tradition

In what type of religious community did the adepts of the early Śaiva Siddhānta live? The picture varies according to the texts one refers to. We find a group of texts that deals only with private worship (*ātmārthapūjā*), no specific public temple worship (*parārthapūjā*) being described or listed under the Ācārya's duties.[18] Following these texts the instruction of pupils takes place at the house of the guru (*dhāman*, *gurugṛha*). The Samayin and Putraka live there after they have finished their general studies of basic śāstric literature.[19] From one of the injunctions—that after sexual intercourse the Ācārya must bathe before teaching his students—we can conclude that he was not necessarily celibate.[20] It seems quite likely that he was a married householder (*gṛhastha*). We do have indications that the Ācārya could be both, a *brahmacārin* or a *gṛhastha*, but in the textual traditions which give both options only the *gṛhastha* is entitled to confer consecration upon both the Ācārya and the Sādhaka, and therefore his status is to be judged as higher.[21] One should add that, in the texts which exclusively describe private worship, the Ācārya consecrates his immediate successor just before he retires.[22] All these facts point to a small-scale religious community centred around the Ācārya and most likely his family's house.[23]

The position and role of the Ācārya differs in a set of texts dealing mainly with public temple worship.[24] His function there is not only confined to his immediate pupils but extends to the sphere of public places of worship. Brunner describes the relation between the officiants of public worship and the Ācārya of the small community as follows: 'the ritual preparation and theoretical qualifications of the officiating priests of a temple have been largely borrowed from the texts which know the *ācārya* solely as a spiritual and religious master. Assuredly there was a time when the priest of a temple was not obliged to receive the same *abhiṣeka* as the one given to the guru of a *maṭha*, and still less the *nirvāṇa-dīkṣā* which necessarily precedes it ... (1990: 17).' The structure of temple ritual with its need for specialized officiating priests obviously had its impact on the mode of consecrating Ācāryas. Whereas in the small-scale religious community the Ācārya was the sole person[25] to teach and perform rituals, in the context of public worship the authorization to perform these rituals had to be shared by more than one member of the community: 'However, they [the texts dealing with *parārthapūjā* – J.G.] generally avoid the phrase which reveals the fact that each *ācārya* anoints only one disciple, his successor: this rule would not suit the necessities of temple life (1990: 16).' When we look at the issue of *varṇa* we find no specific rules in Somaśambhu's manual. But Sadyojyotis makes it clear in his *Mokṣakārikā*, that all four *varṇas* are entitled to receive initiation, though the rank of an Ācārya is only open to a Brahman. This is also confirmed by his commentator Rāmakaṇṭha.[26] Another tradition puts it a little differently: there the three lower *varṇas* are not excluded from becoming Ācāryas but their authority is restricted to their own and lower *varṇas*.[27] In texts which deal with temple ritual, the officiating priest has to be not only a Brahman but also an Ādiśaiva or Śivabrāhmaṇa, a descendant of the sages that are believed to be initiated directly by Śiva.[28] One might add that a conversion to the religious community of the Śaiva Siddhānta is possible and described as a specific ritual act called *liṅgoddhāra* ('removal of the sect-marks'), but the convert will never attain the right to be ordained as an Ācārya or Sādhaka.[29]

The mutual and historical relations between the Ācārya's position in a limited community of followers and the Śaiva temple priest and his public function are complex and chronological speculations should be made with the greatest care,[30] though it seems reasonable to suggest that the texts dealing exclusively with personal worship reflect an earlier stage within the Śaiva Siddhānta tradition.[31] In order to further characterize the Ācārya's function in the self-definition and self-representation of his tradition I will focus on the texts which describe private worship.

The Handing Over of Religious Tradition

The Ācārya wishing to retire selects one suitable pupil who has already received the *nirvāṇadīkṣā* and transfers his own authority to him by consecrating the new Ācārya. These following basic duties are handed over: the new Ācārya is obliged to confer the different types of initiation on his pupils after carefully examining the state of his pupils' souls. He must protect his own religious tradition and lineage of teachers (*gurusantati*) by studying the teachings of Śiva (*śivajñāna*) and handing it over to his pupils.[32] The *Mṛgendra* adds that the consecration of idols (*pratiṣṭhā*) is another duty of the Ācārya.[33] In order to prevent the Ācarya from neglecting his duties, his personal religious activities should be restricted. The *Somaśambhupaddhati* says: 'He should daily recite a little, practise some fire oblation and meditate a little. This is the constant Mantra of the guru.'[34] This description of the Ācārya's duties points to the two-fold character of his role in handing over the religious tradition. He has received the right and the duty to initiate new members into his religious community and has to secure the continuity of the school by selecting a suitable successor before his retirement. Added to this is the duty to study the revealed Śaiva literature and teach it to his pupils. In order to learn more about textual transmission within the tradition, one must look at descriptions of the ritual transfer of authority. The handing over of the school's specific texts can only take place after the Ācārya has ordained his successor. This ritual process is accompanied by the handing-over of two sorts of items: on the one hand, the typical royal insignia of an Ācārya and, on the other, the sacrificial utensils: 'The guru transfers the authority (*adhikāra*) to his pupil [by handing over the insignia] turban, crown, parasol, sandals, chowrie, elephant, horse, palanquin etc. and [the sacrificial utensils] scissors, drawing-string (*karaṇī*), pot, rosaries, darbha-grass, the small and large wooden laddle, the book etc.'[35] This transfer of 'the Book' (*pustakam*) as one of the sacrificial utensils indicates that the Ācārya is transmitting a specific textual tradition, and the accompanying ritual authorization, which was handed over to him by his predecessor.[36] The new Ācārya is not only admitted to a specific lineage of Ācāryas but also gains the right to teach and interpret a specific text or set of texts, forming a part of the larger corpus of Śaiva Siddhānta literature. The Ācārya and his lineage then apparently represent a specific ritual tradition within the Śaiva Siddhānta.

In the *Mṛgendra* the manner in which a newly ordained Ācārya begins teaching is described as follows: the instruction has to take place at a suitable place, and it has to be made sure that no uninitiated persons (*paśu*) are able to listen to the teachings of the Ācārya. After the worship of Śiva, Gaṇeśa and the teacher of the Ācārya, the carefully protected book (*pustakam*) will be opened and the Ācārya will ask one of his pupils to start reading.[37] Then he begins commenting upon the text (*vyākhyāna*) by pointing to the structure of the textual tradition in which the book is to be placed and which the Ācārya himself represents. The Śaiva Siddhānta canon of twenty-eight Tantras is enumerated and connected with a larger five-fold framework of revealed Śaiva scriptures. These five 'streams' (*srotas*) of literature originated out of the five faces of Sadāśiva, in a hierarchical order. The canon of Śaiva Siddhānta Tantras arises out of the upper face of Īśāna: these twenty-eight Tantras are said to be directly revealed by Śiva to ten Śivas and eighteen Rudras, both created by him. The other scriptures are said to emanate from the other four faces of Sadāśiva.[38] Clearly, the Ācārya locates his own tradition by hierarchically structuring the canonical Śaiva Tantric literature, then identifying a specific canon of the Śaiva Siddhānta, and finally by relating the book lying in front of him to this canonical tradition.

The Ācārya is thus the head of a small religious community which is part of the school of Śaiva Siddhānta in general and defined by a specific lineage of Ācāryas as well as a specific textual tradition. The Samayins and Putrakas that the Ācārya teaches are either initiated by himself or by his predecessor. In this position the Ācārya plays a central role in the continuity but also change of the school's theological and religious teachings. I would like to give one example of how the reinterpretation of tradition can be performed by the Ācārya without openly contradicting the textual tradition. In verse 25 of the *Tattvaprakāśa* Bhoja defines the highest of the 36 *tattvas*, the *śivatattva*, as having knowledge and action as its very nature (*jñāna kriyā svabhāvam*).[39] Since in Śaiva Siddhānta knowledge and action (*jñāna* and *kriyā*) are attributes of pure consciousness (*cit*), it is obvious that Bhoja identifies the *śivatattva* with the highest entity, i.e. Śiva. Aghoraśiva, in commenting upon this passage in his *Tattvaprakāśavṛtti*, faces the problem that the *śivatattva*, as the first *tattva* of the succeeding 35 *tattvas*, can never said to be Śiva. For Aghoraśiva all *tattvas* are unconscious (*acit*) entities. Śiva and his Śakti transcend the sphere of *tattvas* (*tattvātīta*).[40] Aghoraśiva solves the problem by not openly contradicting Bhoja. Instead he reinterprets the passage, arguing in the end that Bhoja wants to state that the *śivatattva* is *not* of the nature of knowledge and action. This purpose is achieved by a common exegetical method. Aghoraśiva plays with the ambiguity inherent in the combination of vowels in compounds. Without changing the text he simply postulates an *alpha privativum*, reading *jñāna-kriyā-asvabhāva* instead of *jñāna-kriyā-svabhāva*, thus understanding the compound in the sense that 'knowledge and action is *not* the very nature' of the *śivatattva*. At that point, the interpretation fits perfectly well into Aghoraśiva's understanding of the *tattva* structure, but no longer into that of Bhoja.[41]

This example might suffice to show that the reinterpretation of textual statements is not openly admitted. One reason for this has to be seen as an attempt to fight against competing exegetical traditions. Aghoraśiva explicitly states that his exegetical effort in the *Tattvaprakāśavṛtti* is caused by 'others who have—overpowered by non-dualist ideas and without knowledge of the Siddhānta—interpreted [the text] differently.'[42] Rāmakaṇṭha mentions in his introduction to the *Mataṅgapārameśvaravṛtti* the various interpretations influenced by the vedic tradition, by the non-dualistic Kula, and by the school of Nyāya as reasons for writing his own commentary.[43] By interpreting the given texts along the lines of dualistic Siddhānta, the text's canonical status within the school is defended. This is obvious for the Tantra *Mataṅgapārameśvara*, but given the influential position of the *Tattvaprakāśa* one must say that the text did gain a quasi canonical status within the school because of the commentary of Aghoraśiva.[44] This attempt to unify the Siddhānta's textual tradition obviously does not allow the admission of divergent options within one's own school.

The Ācārya as Śiva and Śiva as the Ācārya

For the Samayins, Sādhakas and Putrakas mentioned above, the Ācārya is a godlike figure, equivalent to Śiva. The Ācārya possesses—like every *nirvāṇadīkṣita*—the six divine qualities (*divyaguṇa*), i.e. omniscience (*sarvajñatva*), contentment (*paritṛpti*), eternal insight (*anādibodha*), independence (*svātantrya*), and everpresent as well as unlimited power (*alupta-* and *anantaśakti*).[45] During the ritual of initiation the Ācārya becomes a vessel for Śiva's presence (*sādhikaraṇadīkṣā*). He reaches a state in which he is Śiva and acts as Śiva. The Ācārya mentally envisages this state during the *samayadīkṣā*: 'I am connected with the qualities omniscience etc., I am standing above all paths (*adhvan*), a part of me is the place of the union [between the soul and Śiva], I preside over the great sacrifice, I am Śiva!'[46] Certainly, much value is given to respectful behaviour towards the Ācārya; it is also stressed that he should behave according to his status.[47] The *Mṛgendra*, for example, refers to a situation in which a Samayin or Putraka has come to know something new (*kiṃcid apūrvakam*)[48] and wishes to convey this to his Ācārya. In this context it is important that the communication between the teacher and his pupil is formalized so that the difference in status between the two is not neglected. This is avoided through two prerequisites. Firstly, the pupil must gain the permission of the Ācārya to convey the information. Secondly, it can only be handed over in a ritualized context—the Ācārya must be seated on his special seat or throne (*pīṭha*) when he receives the new information through his pupil. If the Ācārya is travelling and meets another Ācārya who wishes to impart new information to him, then a teacher–pupil constellation should be avoided. The Ācārya whom the travelling Ācārya meets on the road should not be sitting on his special seat when he is communicating the news. This means that the Ācārya who has left his home should not get into a position where he could be perceived as the pupil of another Ācārya, since this would be difficult to reconcile with his status and his omniscience, etc.[49]

Conclusion

The Śaiva Siddhānta Ācārya is the most important mediator of religious identity, embodying in person a lineage of Siddhānta Ācāryas and their specific ritual and theological tradition. The Ācārya's body is the vessel for Śiva's liberating grace and his ritual authorization is necessary for the admission of new pupils as well as for the selection of the succeeding Ācārya. The necessary qualifications for a Siddhānta Ācārya seem to confirm the general characteristics of an esteemed teacher and officiant of a religious community. The domain of heterodox and exceptional behaviour is mainly restricted to the figure of the Tantric Sādhaka. This might reflect the Siddhānta's self-perception as an orthodox community within the Śaiva traditions. The Ācārya's position is central in bestowing initiation and consecration to his pupils and in handing over and interpreting the textual tradition that he represents. By becoming an initiated member (*dīkṣita*) of this religious group the new pupil gets linked to the lineage of Ācāryas that his own Ācārya represents. He is a member of a small-scale religious community headed by an Ācārya who is part of a specific local lineage. The Ācārya has to place the textual tradition that he transmits within the larger framework of the canonical literature of Tantric Śaivism and to identify its place within the Śaiva Siddhānta's own canon. By enumerating the school's canon and commenting upon the revealed texts along the lines of the school's dualistic theology, the Ācārya takes active part in the process of canonization. The attempt to formalize his role in the passing on of a specific canonized Śaiva tradition might be interpreted as an effort to protect his own school against exegetical efforts of rival religious traditions.

Notes

1. I would like to thank Srilata Raman, Reutlingen, who went through an earlier version of this paper and helped me to polish the English, my colleagues and friends Dominic Goodall, Oxford, and Jürgen Hanneder, Munich, for stimulating discussions and helpful comments, and finally the editors, especially Angelika Malinar, for careful reading and suggestions.
2. I am using the term Tantra for the revealed Śaiva literature in general, since the distinction between South Indian 'Āgamas' and North Indian 'Tantras', found in secondary literature and modern editions, is not confirmed by the texts (Gengnagel 1996: 2, n3 and Goodall 1998: xxxvii-xxxix).
3. The liberated souls (*muktātman*) gain equality (*samatā, tulyatā*) with Śiva but they do not lose their individual identity. These souls are the many '*śivas*' in contrast to the one and eternally liberated Śiva. For this basic distinction see *Tattvaprakāśa* 6 and the discussion in Aghoraśiva's *Vṛtti*.
4. See Sanderson (1990, 1995) for more details. For a study of basic doctrinal aspects of dualistic Śaiva Siddhānta see Gengnagel (1996).
5. Compare Goodall: 'Of the twenty-eight tantras that are listed as scriptures of the Śaiva Siddhānta very few are demonstrably early works. Most are

South Indian redactions or entirely fresh compositions (...).' (1998: xxxix).

6. See *Śivadṛṣṭi* 3.13cd–14 and *Tantrāloka* 9.262cd. In both passages the given name is 'Kheṭapāla' which is the worldly name of Sadyojyotis. See Jayaratha's commentary on the passage in Tantrāloka.
7. The *Nareśvaraparīkṣā*, *Tattvasaṅgraha*, and *Tattvatrayanirṇaya* belong to the first category the *Svāyaṃbhuvasūtrasaṅgrahaṭīkā* to the last. Goodall (1998: xx–xxi) has shown that Sadyojyotis' *Bhogakārikā*, *Mokṣakārikā*, *Paramokṣanirāsakārikā* as well as the lost *Mantravārttika* are most likely partial commentaries on the *Rauravatantra*.
8. See Surdam in his introduction to the translation of the *dīkṣāvidhi*-section of the *Kriyākramadyotikā*: 'the rituals performed in Śiva temples in the area of Tamil Nadu north of Tanjore are governed by the *paddhati* of Aghoraśivācārya; from Tanjore south, by that of Īśānaśiva.' (1984: xiv). One might add that Carl Gustav Diehl's often quoted study *Instrument and Purpose* bases its study of Śaiva rituals on editions of Aghoraśiva's handbook. In an extensive footnote Goodall has now shown that the edition of Aghoraśiva's *Mahotsavavidhi* section from the *Kriyākramadyotikā*

   > actually contains much else that is manifestly not by the hand of Aghoraśiva and nothing that can be proved to be his. (...) Various (...) texts belonging to the category of *parārthapūjā* have been published as parts of Aghoraśiva's *Kriyākramadyotikā*. Not all are quite as muddled as the *Mahotsavavidhi*, but all are suspect. (1998: xiii, n24)

9. A lot of research on the history of Śaivism remains to be done and it is beyond the scope of this article to present and discuss the available data. See Davis (1991: 3–21) for a general introduction.
10. See *Somaśambhupaddhati* 3 *viśeṣadīkṣā* 25 for the *vratāṅgas*.
11. See Sanderson (1995: 26) who adds the categories of kings (*bhūbhṛt*) and renouncers (*saṃnyāsin*) to this list. The term *nirbījadīkṣā* is applied because the initiation for those who are not capable to follow the rules does not lead to daily ritual duties, it is without effect (*nirbīja*) in that respect.
12. See *Somaśambhupaddhati* 3 *viśeṣadīkṣāvidhiḥ* 22–24, *Mṛgendra kriyāpāda* 8.170cd–174ab and Surdam's translation of *Kriyākramadyotikā* (1984: 108–109). Compare also the parallels in *Svacchandatantra* 5.43cd–52ab and 4.87–88ab.
13. For the twofold subdivision of the *samayadīkṣā* in *sāmānyasamayadīkṣā* with the name-giving ceremony and *viśeṣasamayadīkṣā* or *saṃskāradīkṣā* with the handing over of the rules and the *vratāṅgas* see *Somaśambhupaddhati* 3: 142–144, n45 and 47.
14. It is a matter of dispute on what level the status 'Putraka' occurs. Either after the second form of *samayadīkṣā* for the *viśeṣadīkṣita* or *saṃskāradīkṣita* (see previous note) or after the liberating initiation for the *nirvāṇadīkṣita*. Brunner discusses this question at length (*Somaśambhupaddhati* 3: 416–24, n457), holding that only the *nirvāṇadīkṣita* should be seen as a Putraka. This is also clearly shown by the table given in Brunner 1975: 415. In contrast Davis states—

If *samayadīkṣā* is predominantly a rite of entry, *viśeṣadīkṣā* (...) is in essence a rite of rebirth. The initiating guru ritually removes the initiate's soul from his body, (...) and (...) subjects it to a series of life-cycle rites (*saṃskāras*) replicating birth. When the soul is then returned to the novice's body, he has been reborn as a 'son of Śiva' (*putraka*) (1991: 91).

15. For this distinction see *Somaśambhupaddhati* 3 *samayadīkṣāvidhiḥ* 10–11.
16. Sanderson (1985: 215, n119) points to chapter 9 of *Mataṅgapārameśvara, caryāpāda* (1982: 407–13). Here a *rudravrata* of the Sādhaka, including practice on cremation-grounds (*śmaśāna*), is described. Bhatt (1982: 408, n1) gives a parallel passage in the *caryāpāda* of the Kiraṇa (20.8–10). See also text and translation of this passage (20.8–15) in Brunner (1975: 433, n72).
17. For a closer consideration of the role of the Sādhaka see Brunner (1975).
18. The *Mṛgendra* and *Mataṅgapārameśvara* as well as the handbook *Somaśambhupaddhati* belong to this category, most probably also Aghoraśiva's *Kriyākramadyotikā*. Brunner adds *Sārdhatriśatikālottara* and *Svacchanda* to this list (1990: 5 and 21, n2).
19. See *Mṛgendra caryāpāda* 1.67. Provided the Ācārya gives his permission, the Putraka is not obliged to live in the house of his guru (1.73ab).
20. See *Mṛgendra caryāpāda* 1.30.
21. See *Somaśambhupaddhati* 3.17, n17.
22. This is clearly indicated in *Mṛgendra kriyāpāda* 8.208:

    brūyāt: samarpito yo 'yam adhikāro mayādhunā | sa kartavyas tvayā tāvad yāvat saṃkrāmito 'nyataḥ. [The Ācārya] says: You should hold the office that I have just handed over until you will transfer it to somebody else.

23. To my knowledge, we do not have clear epigraphical indications of a connection between Sadyojyotis and especially the Kaṇṭha-lineage on the one hand, and some of the documented monastic traditions on the other. Śaiva Siddhānta scriptures are mentioned by the Pallava king Narasimhavarman II in inscriptions around AD 700 (Davis 1991: 12); monastic traditions seem to exist at the same time (168, n24).
24. Brunner (1990: 21, n2) enumerates *Ajita, Kāmika, Kāraṇa, Kiraṇa, Raurava* and *Suprabheda.*
25. One has, however, to keep in mind that the Sādhaka, like the Ācārya, receives an initiation with authority (*sādhikāra*) to perform rituals for others. To what extent the Sādhaka participates in the ritual acts and teachings of the Ācārya needs further investigation.
26. See *Mokṣakārikā* 99, Rāmakaṇṭha's Vṛtti (*Aṣṭaprakaraṇa* 1988: 265) and the parallel passage in Rāmakaṇṭha's commentary on *Mataṅgapārameśvara kriyāpāda* 5.93.
27. See for example *Kiraṇa āśramācāryavidhi* 4–5 as explained and quoted in Brunner (1964: 461–2; 472, n34).
28. Brunner states that 'this rule cannot be very old, for there are several Āgamas and *paddhatis* which ignore this concept ....' (1990: 12). See also the study on social categories among the Śaiva Siddhāntins in Brunner (1964).

29. *Mṛgendra caryāpāda* 1.27–8. See also the description of *liṅgoddhāra* in *Somaśambhupaddhati* 3, *vratoddhāra* 6cd–17.
30. See Brunner (1990: 17) where she states that Śaiva Siddhānta temple cult is not necessarily a later development and describes the mutual influence between elements of temple worship and private cult (1990: 12–14).
31. For a more detailed discussion see Brunner (1990).
32. See *Mṛgendra caryāpāda* 1.23–6, 29 and *Somaśambhupaddhati* 3 *ācāryābhiṣeka* 25.
33. *Mṛgendra kriyāpāda* 8.216c.
34. '*svalpam ahni japaṃ kuryāt svalpam agnau ca homayet | svalpaṃ vai dhyānam ātiṣṭhet. mantra eṣa sadā guroḥ.*' *Somaśambhupaddhati* 3 *ācāryābhiṣeka* 26cd–27ab. See the parallel passage in *Mṛgendra kriyāpāda* 8.217.
35. *Somaśambhupaddhati* 3 *ācāryābhiṣeka* 17–18: *uṣṇīṣaṃ makuṭam chatraṃ pādukācāmarāṇi ca | gajāśvaśibikādīni kartarīṃ karaṇīṃ ghaṭīm | akṣamālāṃś ca darbhāṃś ca sruksruvau pustakādi ca | adhikāraṃ gurus tasmai śiṣyāya vinivedayet.* Compare also *Mṛgendra kriyāpāda* 8.205–8 and *Svacchanda* 4.470–1c.
36. Brunner discusses the usage of *pustakam* in *Mṛgendra* and states that this term could refer to a collection of texts but more likely hints at the specific Āgama or Tantra of the Ācārya's lineage (1985: 263). See also the reference to *pustakam* in *Svacchanda* 4.471b (1985: 263).
37. See *Mṛgendra caryāpāda* 1.31–3.
38. Aghora (South: Bhairava/Asitāṅga), Vāmadeva (North: Vāma/Saṃmoha), Tatpuruṣa (East: Garuḍa/Trotala) and Sadyojāta (West: Bhūta/Caṇḍāsidhāra), compare *Mṛgendra caryāpāda* 1.35–6ab.
39. See *Tattvaprakāśa* 25 (*Aṣṭaprakaraṇam* 1988: 46).
40. This is already stated in the first introductory verse to Aghora's *Tattvaprakāśavṛtti* (*Tattvaprakāśa* 1988: 6). The relevant systematic framework is discussed in Gengnagel (1996: 43–9).
41. Linked with this problem is the interpretation of *Tattvaprakāśa* 32 where Bhoja neglects the existence of a succession (*krama*) among the first five *tattvas* and Aghoraśiva states the opposite, suggesting that the verse should be regarded as an interpolation.
42. See *Tattvaprakāśavṛtti*, opening verse 2 (1988: 6): *advaitavāsanāviṣṭaiḥ siddhāntajñānavarjitaiḥ | vyākhyāto 'trānyathā 'nyair yat sa tato 'smākam udyamaḥ.*
43. *Mataṅgapārameśvaravṛtti vidyāpāda*, opening verse 4 (1977: 1–2), see also text and translation in Goodall (1998: xxxi, n71).
44. The *Tattvaprakāśavṛtti* has, for example, strongly influenced chapter 7 on *śaivadarśana* in the *Sarvadarśanasaṅgraha*. See Gengnagel (1996: 32–5).
45. See *Somaśambhupaddhati* 3 *nirvāṇadīkṣā* (399)
46. *Somaśambhupaddhati* 3 *samayadīkṣā* 95cd–96c: *sarvajñatvādiyukto 'haṃ, samastādhvopari sthitaḥ | mamāṃśo yojanāsthānam, adhiṣṭhātā mahādhvare | śivo 'ham!* The meditation 'I am Śiva' should not be taken as an indicator for a non-dualistic doctrine. The involved souls become similar to Śiva but never

identical. The ritual process clearly shows that souls never lose their individual identity.

47. See for example *Mṛgendra caryāpāda* 1.63–5.
48. See *caryāpāda* 1.61–2, it is not clear if this refers to worldly or doctrinal information.
49. See *Mṛgendra caryāpāda* 1.61–2.

References

Primary Sources

Aṣṭaprakaraṇam. Tattvaprakāśa-tattvasaṃgraha-tattvatrayanirṇaya-ratnatraya-bhogakārikā-nādakārikā-mokṣakārikā-paramokṣanirāsakārikākhya-siddhāntaśaivīyāṣṭagranthānāṃ saṭīkānāṃ samāhāraḥ. Ed. Vrajavallabha Dvivedī. Vārāṇasī: Sampurnananda Sanskrit University, 1988 (Yogatantra-Granthamālā 12).

Īśānaśivagurudevapaddhati of Īśānaśivagurudeva. Ed. T. Gaṇapati Sāstri. 4 vols. Reprint. Delhi: Bharatiya Vidya Prakashan, 1988 (First published: Trivandrum 1920–1922, 1925).

Karmakanda-Kramavali by Sri Somashambhu (Outlines briefly the procedure of Shaivaistic Sandhya, Diksha, & other ritual). Ed. Pandit Jagaddhar Zadoo. Srinagar: 1947 (The Kashmir Series of Text & Studies 73).

Mataṅgapārameśvarāgama (Vidyāpāda) avec le Commentaire de Bhaṭṭa Rāmakaṇṭha. Ed. N. R. Bhatt. Pondichéry: Institut Français d'Indologie, 1977 (Publications de l'Institut Français d'Indologie 56).

Mataṅgapārameśvarāgama (Kriyāpāda, Yogapāda et Caryāpāda) avec le Commentaire de Bhaṭṭa Rāmakaṇṭha. Ed. N. R. Bhatt. Pondichéry: Institut Français d'Indologie, 1982. (Publications de l'Institut Français d'Indologie 65).

Mṛgendrāgama. (Kriyāpāda et Caryāpāda) avec le Commentaire de Bhaṭṭa-Nārāyaṇakaṇṭha. Ed. N. R. Bhatt. Pondichéry: Institut Français d'Indologie, 1962 (Publications de l'Institut Français d'Indologie 23).

Mokṣakārikā. Sadyojyotiḥśivācāryapraṇītā. Bhaṭṭarāmakaṇṭhakṛtavyākhyāsahitā. In *Aṣṭaprakaraṇam*, 245–78.

Śaivāgamaparibhāṣāmañjarī de Vedajñāna. Le Florilège de la doctrine śivaïte. Ed. Bruno Dagens. Pondichéry: Institut Français d'Indologie, 1979 (Publications de l'Institut Français d'Indologie 60).

Śivadṛṣṭi of Srisomānanda with the Vṛtti by Utpaladeva. Ed. Madhusudan Kaul Shāstri. Srinagar: 1934 (Kashmir Series of Texts & Studies 64).

Somaśambhupaddhati. Vol. 1: Le rituel quotidien dans la tradition śivaïte de l'Inde du Sud selon Somaśambhu. Vol. 2: Rituels occasionnels I: Pavitrārohaṇa, Damanapūjā et Prāyaścitta. Vol. 3: Rituels occasionnels II: dīkṣā, abhiṣeka, vratoddhāra, antyeṣṭi, śrāddha. Ed. Hélène Brunner-Lachaux. Pondichéry: Institut Français d'Indologie, 1963, 1968, 1977 (Publications de l'Institut Français d'Indologie 25. 1.3).

Svacchandatantram with Commentary 'Udyota' by Kṣemarājācārya. Ed. Vraj Vallabh Dwivedi. 2 vols. Delhi: Parimal Publications, 1985.

Tantrāloka of Abhinavagupta with the Commentary of Jayaratha. Ed. R. C. Dwivedi and Navajivan Rastogi. 8 vols. Delhi: Motilal Banarsidass, 1987.

Tattvaprakāśaḥ. Śrīkumārakṛtayā tātparyadīpikayā Śrīmadaghoraśivācārya-praṇītayā vṛttyā ca sahitaḥ. In *Aṣṭaprakaraṇam*, 1–114.

Secondary Sources

Brunner, Hélène. 1964. Les catégories sociales védiques dans le Śivaisme du Sud. *Journal Asiatique* 252: 451–72.

———. 1975. Le Sādhaka, personnage oublié du Śivaisme du Sud. *Journal Asiatique* 263: 411–43.

———. 1985. *Mṛgendrāgama. Section des Rites et Section du Comportement. Avec la Vṛtti de Bhaṭṭanārāyaṇakaṇṭha*. Traduction, Introduction et Notes par Hélène Brunner-Lachaux. Pondichéry: Institut Français d'Indologie.

———. 1988. L'ācārya śivaite: du guru au gurukkal. *Bulletin d'Études Indiennes* 6: 145–76.

———. 1990. Ātmārthapūjā versus Parārthapūjā in the Śaiva tradition. In *The Sanskrit Tradition and Tantrism*, ed. Teun Goudriaan, 4–23 (Panels of the VIIth World Sanskrit Conference). Leiden: Brill.

Davis, Richard H. 1991. *Ritual in an Oscillating Universe: Worshiping Śiva in Medieval India*. Princeton: Princeton University Press.

Diehl, Carl Gustav. 1956. *Instrument and Purpose. Studies on Rites and Rituals in South India*. Lund: CWK Gleerup.

Gengnagel, Jörg. 1996. *Māyā, Puruṣa und Śiva: Die dualistische Tradition des Śivaismus nach Aghoraśivācāryas Tattvaprakāśavṛtti*. Wiesbaden: Harrassowitz.

Goodall, Dominic. 1998. *Bhaṭṭa Rāmakaṇṭha's Commentary on the Kiraṇatantra*. Vol. 1: Chapters 1-6. Critical edition and annotated translation. Pondicherry: Institute Français de Pondicherry (Publications du Départment d'Indologie 86).

Sanderson, Alexis. 1985. Purity and Power Among the Brahmins of Kashmir. In *The Category of the Person. Anthropology, Philosophy, History*, ed. M. Carrithers *et al.*, 190–216. Cambridge: Cambridge University Press.

———. 1990. Śaivism and the Tantric Traditions. In *The World's Religions: The Religions of Asia*, ed. F. Hardy, 128–72. London: Routledge.

———. 1995. Meaning in Tantric Ritual. In *Essais sur le Rituels III: Colloque du Centenaire de la Section des Sciences religieuses de l'École Pratique des Hautes Études*, ed. A.-M. Blondeau and K. Schipper, 15–95. Louvain-Paris: Peeters.

Surdam, Wayne Edward. 1984. South Indian Śaiva Rites of Initiation: The Dīkṣāvidhi of Aghoraśivācārya's Kriyākramadyotikā. Ph.D. dissertation, University of California, Berkeley.

Śaṅkara as *Jagadguru* According to *Śaṅkara-Digvijaya*

ANGELIKA MALINAR

The philosopher Śaṅkara is claimed as the founder of the monastic institutions (*maṭha*) of the Daśanāmi orders and of the Advaita *sampradāya*. This position is elaborated and continously re-created in numerous hagiographies, in which Śaṅkara is depicted as a *saṃnyāsin* who sets off on a journey through India in order to propagate his philosophical insights in public debates, and thus to bring 'heretic' teachers into his fold. The claim of the *mahants* of the monasteries, and thus the leaders of the Advaita *sampradāya*, to represent an all-India authority is retrospectively projected on the personality of Śaṅkarācārya and summed up by ascribing to him the title 'teacher of the world' (*jagadguru*). This canonization of Śaṅkara's status as a *jagadguru* allows for claims of royal patronage as well as for sustaining the leader-position of succeeding *jagadgurus*, who are also called Śaṅkarācārya. This reflects the assertion of the *sampradāya*'s continuity through an uninterrupted tradition of teachers, starting with the 'first Śaṅkara' (*Ādi-Śaṅkara*), as well as the self-perception of the office-holders as representatives of Śaṅkara. The hagiographical accounts—the so-called *vijayas* (lit.: conquests)—contributed, through their reconfirmation of this special position, to the preservation of this claim to overarching authority over the centuries until today.[1] Seen from the angle of what Max Weber called the 'institutionalization of charisma',[2] the codification of the life-history of a charismatic founder-figure can be valued as a factor in this process. On the other hand, it is stressed by Keyes (1982: 8) that charisma is always enacted or manifested in regard to models that, in a given culture, have already been recognized as sacred signs (this also holds true for what Weber calls 'original charisma'). This is confirmed by the very existence of 'sacred biographies', in which charisma 'is adjudged with reference to the authority of existing cultural understandings of the sacred'. Such adjudgements will also be considered in the following analysis of some of the 'biographical images'[3] provided by *Śaṅkara-Digvijaya* (ŚDV). However, it will be shown that those (traditional) elements, which are taken as signs of charisma, are blended in a specific way in order to preserve Śaṅkara's individuality and thus to create more than a replica of traditional icons. In addition to this, the fact that 'sacred biographies' of the founder of a religious community have been fabricated in different periods seems to be closely connected with the necessity of holding one's ground as a religious institution in a competitive environment. This can also be noted in the ŚDV, and that on two levels—the narrative set-up itself, and in the historical circumstances indicated by the text. It will be considered how a referential framework is established which allows Śaṅkara to be re-created as a founder-figure.

Before dealing with the devices employed in ŚDV for making Śaṅkara the founder of a religious community I shall briefly introduce the text: amongst the numerous[4] but only partially available *vijaya*-texts which describe Śaṅkara's 'conquest of the regions', the 'Śaṅkara-Digvijaya' (ŚDV) ascribed to Mādhavācārya or Vidyāraṇyamuni is transmitted as one of the most popular.[5] The exact date of the text and its authorship are matters of some controversy.[6] Traditionally, the authorship is ascribed to Vidyāraṇya, who was the successor of Bhāratī Tīrtha as the twelfth *mahant* of the Śaṅkara *maṭha* in Śṛṅgeri between 1380 and 1386. The text is a compilation from several other *vijaya* texts and was perhaps written in the early seventeenth or eighteenth century.[7] The major part of the text seems, however, to be identical with texts from the fifteenth and sixteenth century, texts which in their turn were probably based on traditions from the thirteenth century onwards.[8]

Apart from these textual historical considerations, it is not without significance that the text is presented as a work by Mādhava/Vidyāraṇya. Thereby the text is connected with a time when the Śṛṅgeri *maṭha* played a crucial role in the process of setting up the Vijayanagara empire in the middle of the fourteenth century. As documented in several land-grants, the *maṭha* was entitled to claim taxes from the villages attached to it.[9] Moreover, it does not seem to be pure coincidence that the production of *vijaya* texts went hand in hand with claiming royal patronage, and later also with defending the grants. In fact, several features of the ŚDV, especially the connection of certain localities with specific Śaiva-cults, point to the historical context of the Vijayanagara empire. In addition to this external function, the continuous text-production might also have had the internal function of re-creating the position of the original founder, the Ādi-

Śaṅkara, as an intellectual world-conqueror with royal support who nevertheless kept to his ascetic lifestyle. Thus he could continue to serve as a model for the community to emulate in times when the *maṭha* had become a firm institution. As such, it had to compete with other recipients of royal patronage and to defend its claim for an all-India authority, when its influence was by and large confined to the South. The re-compilation of available *vijaya* texts resulted, in the case of the ŚDV, in a most influential hagiography. Its composition (if the proposed date, seventeenth to early eighteenth century, is accepted) corresponds with the re-establishment of the Śṛṅgeri *maṭha* after several raids, which followed upon the downfall of the Vijayanagara empire. This included new assignments of land grants and villages for taxation as well as the clearance of all debts by Somaśekhara Nāyaka II (1714–38).[10]

It has also to be taken into account that in the hagiographies the hierarchy between the different *maṭhas* was negotiated. This holds especially true for the tensions between the *maṭhas* of Śṛṅgeri and Kāñcī. The latter was viewed by the Daśanāmi-Saṃnyāsins as an additional fifth *pīṭha* without legitimation. It nevertheless tried to claim authority by asserting (for example in the Śaṅkarajaya of Anantānandagiri; see Antarkar 1960a) that Śaṅkara attained '*siddhi*', i.e. gave up his body, in Kāñcī and not in the Himālaya as maintained in the ŚDV. There was even the rumour that the Śṛṅgeri *maṭha* produced the ŚDV as evidence for their right to perform a ritual for the goddess Akhilāṇḍeśvarī in a law-suit against the claims of the Kāñcī *maṭha*.[11]

Thus, the comprehensive presentation of Śaṅkara as *jagadguru* can also be seen as a reaction to the situation that, although the *jagadgurus* were still vested with a universalist claim, they in fact ended up as heads of one of many *sampradāyas*, their influence depending on larger political considerations. In the *vijaya* texts the overarching claim is maintained by ascribing to Śaṅkara the royal function of conquering the quarters. His religious mission was thus vested with a political dimension, which a king or any other political leader could not neglect if he aspired to all-India rule, or at least for hegemony in a specific region.[12] However, this royal function has to be ascribed to Śaṅkara in a way that would not make his asceticism dubious or corrupt his moral demands. In the text this is achieved by depicting Śaṅkara as the embodiment (*avatāra*) of Śiva, while distributing the martial tasks of an *avatāra* amongst his four disciples.

The text is divided into 16 *sargas* or books composed in different metres. It is presented as a *carita*, an account of a life-history, and is thus aligned with a well-known literary genre. Moreover, the author presents himself as the 'New Kālīdāsa' (*navakālīdāsa*; 1.9), who, after having earlier in his career praised rather unwillingly the vanity of kings, now wants to use his skill to bring 'the wondrous and cooling nectar of Śaṅkara's life-story'—which is in fact the story of a conquest and thus close to royal panegyrics—to a larger audience. The narrative follows the chronology of important events in Śaṅkara's life, sometimes highlighting their miraculous[13] aspect: e.g. his becoming a *saṃnyāsin*, the instruction by his teacher Govindapāda, his stay in Kāśī and at the Bādarī-āśrama to write his commentaries, his debate with Maṇḍanamiśra and Sarasvatī, his final conquering of the 'seat of omniscients'—the Śāradā *pīṭha* in Kashmir with a subsequent establishment of a Śāradā-temple in Śṛṅgeri. In the account of his mission, descriptions of his emotional relationship with his mother, his gurus and his own disciples are inserted.

Turning now to the ŚDV, I shall raise the following questions: what are the characteristics which, according to the text, allow for ascribing the exceptional status of a *jagadguru* to Śaṅkara? How is the institutionalization of the Advaita *sampradāya* legitimized in the text? With regard to the first question I will argue that the exceptional is not seen in Śaṅkara's opposition to the traditional, i.e. Vedic authority, but in his very reclaiming of that authority through a recombination of already accepted values.[14] His position as leader is explained and manufactured by connecting his status with traditional—especially epic and purāṇic—discourses on saints and saviours. In addition to this, a 'triple identity' is ascribed to the *jagadguru* as he is made to represent the following three value-structures, which otherwise might represent different ways of life: (1) He is vested with the martial, royal task of the 'conqueror of the regions' for the sake of Vedic tradition, i.e. the prescriptions of *varṇāśramadharma*, as the 'king of teachers' (*gururāja*, 4.101; *deśikendra*, 6.1; *deśikasārvabhauma* 12.8; etc.); (2) he is made to advocate theism (i.e. *saguṇa brahman*);[15] (3) he is made the representative of the highest knowledge of salvation, the 'king of ascetics' (*yatīndra*, 1.44, 8.60; *bhikṣurāja*, 8.48 etc.). The position of the *jagadguru* is created in the text by presenting all these three value-structures as harmoniously blended in the persona of Śaṅkarācārya. The three elements correspond to what in the text is called the 'three parts' of Vedic tradition (*karma-*, *upāsana-*, and *jnāna-kāṇḍa*). Thus, Śaṅkara is Vedic tradition incarnate. Another important aspect implied in this is the blending of Vaiṣṇava and Śaiva elements in Śaṅkara. The text also reconfirms the legitimacy of the procedures of succession prevalent in the *sampradāya* by placing Śaṅkara in the line of teachers through encounters with his predecessors. Correspondingly, the tradition is projected into the future by Śaṅkara's selection of successors. Thus, the text does not allow for an application of the categories of charisma and institution, or charisma and canon, in an antagonistic manner. In the following, I shall deal with this 'triple identity' by pointing to two referential frameworks which are decisive for the creation of Śaṅkara's status as a *jagadguru* in the narrative: his being an *avatāra* of Śiva, and his successful victory over different opponents.

Śaṅkara as *Avatāra*

In the ŚDV, the *avatāra* doctrine is used as the 'classical' or stereotypical way of dealing with the temporality of what is interpreted as transtemporal; it serves also as an explanation for the historicity of truth-claims and for the propagation of 'new' truths which at the same time are seen as eternal and omnipresent. The ascription of an *avatāra* status to historical figures is a practice that can be traced within many sacred biographies. It has the function of providing an interpretive pattern for the appearance of exceptional teachers, founder-figures, and religious leaders. It is seen as a necessary but also as a recurring event, designed not only for one saviour to come, as for example in messianic soteriologies, but for several saviours or restorers of some original teaching. Crisis, disorder and decadence as rationalized in the *kaliyuga* axiom[16] provide the constant background against which time and again these various *avatāras* have to appear. Śaṅkara's unique philosophical and ethical ideals, his appearance as restorer of Vedic tradition and as the founder of monastic institutions, can thus be interpreted as a divine institution—as it is actually done in the ŚDV. Nevertheless, the description of Śaṅkara's enactment of the typical task takes account of the special features of his personality and also of some of his Advaita-Vedāntic teachings.

In fact, the whole of ŚDV is embedded in the overarching referential framework of Śaṅkara as an embodiment (*avatāra*) of Śiva, the all-knowing Yogin, the destroyer of desire (the god Kāma). This framework is established through a description of the pre-history of Śaṅkara's birth in the heavenly regions, a pre-history familiar from Purāṇa-literature: The gods complain to Śiva about the consequences of Viṣṇu's incarnation as the Buddha. The prescriptions of the Vedic tradition are no longer followed and heretics of different affiliations have become dominant,[17] not only Buddhists but also different schools of Śaivas and Vaiṣṇavas who follow their own canonical texts (*āgama*) and practices (like the head-offering of the worshippers of Bhairava). The gods ask Śiva to restore the 'path of the *śruti*' (*vartma śrautram*). Śiva promises that he will rescue the Vedic tradition in its three parts (*kāṇḍatrayātmaka*; 1.48; i.e. *varṇāśramadharma* (*karmakāṇḍa*); *upāsana-yoga*; and *jñāna* as the highest; 1.49-52). The connection with Śiva is again established in the account of Śaṅkara's birth. When numerous ritual activities do not help them obtain a son, Śaṅkara's parents resort to *Sadāśiva-upāsanā* (2.49-50). Śiva grants them a son, but they have to choose between a 'normal' child or an exceptionally wise one who, however, will die early. The father opts for the latter, i.e. for obtaining a *mahātmā* (2.54). In the account of the pregnancy and Śaṅkara's early childhood, time and again the 'avatāric' nature of the events is hinted at.[18]

However, it is also pointed out that Śaṅkara's task of 'conquest' and re-establishment of the true meaning of Vedic tradition is actually a task traditionally associated with Viṣṇu. As Viṣṇu does not seem to interfere in the catastrophic consequences of his incarnation as the Buddha (1.30) and since, as mentioned above, the Vaiṣṇavas have started to follow the canon of the *āgamas* instead of the *jñānamārga* taught in the *śruti*-texts (1.35), Śaṅkara has become the true 'highest abode of Viṣṇu' (*viṣṇuparamaṃ padam*; 5.111), surpassing even Viṣṇu's ten incarnations (ibid.). His speech is sweeter and more salutary than that of Ādiśeṣa (1.5). Thus, together with his four disciples, he has become the true four-armed Hari of the Kaliyuga (1.42).[19] However, Śaṅkara is never directly involved in the violence which goes along with the *avatāra* function. This task is ascribed to his disciples, first and foremost to Padmapāda, who even acts as Narasiṃha incarnate.[20] Śaṅkara himself defeats his opponents only through his superior knowledge, which is the *jagadguru*'s weapon (6.79-80; 9.28). This taking-over of mythologems and symbols associated with Viṣṇu is an aspect of Śaṅkara's identity as the *avatāra* of Śiva, which provides a theological legitimation for the universalist claim of his teaching and his status. This special elaboration of Śaṅkara's *avatāra* status is one element constituting what I previously called his triple identity as *jagadguru*.[21] The interest of Paramaśiva in uplifting the world through knowledge of the self as embodied in Śaṅkara prevails through the distribution of different aspects of the *avatāra* function, traditionally allotted to Viṣṇu, between Śaṅkara and his disciples. Thereby the opposition between the duties of the ascetic, whose renunciation of worldly activities indicates his 'self-knowledge', and the sometimes violent task of restoring Vedic 'world-order', is dissolved through the distribution of functions between Śaṅkara and his disciples.

Conquest of the Regions (*Dig-vijaya*)

As he appears as a form of a god, an *avatāra* depends on a corresponding theological and, most important, an iconographic elaboration. If the god takes a 'human form' (*mānuṣī tanu*), as is the case of Śaṅkara, this is indicated by a specific, i.e. selective, combination of characteristics common to exceptional or 'super-human' (*atimānuṣa*; cf. 5.10: *atimartya*) figures. Thus, though he is neither the first nor the last *avatāra*, through his blending of Śaiva and Vaiṣṇava elements in his *avatāra* identity Śaṅkara can be distinguished from other *avatāras*. He can also be identified by the modified duty ascribed to him as an *avatāra*. The 'ordinary' task of an *avatāra*, according to the purāṇic interpretation, consists in the restoration of order. It is usually fulfilled by killing singular demons who gained absolute, i.e. despotic, power over the 'triple world'. In contrast, Śaṅkara's task involves an intellectual 'conquest' of the different regions of India, each dominated by different rulers with various religious affiliations. The *dig-vijaya* is an enterprise traditionally ascribed to a king. In fact, Śaṅkara is projected as having performed what had once been part of the Vedic ritual of the consecration of the king, the *digvyāsthāpanam*, the 'mounting of the quarters of space', which precedes the actual consecration (*abhiṣeka*) (Heesterman 1957: 103–5). As shown by Buitenen (1988: 311–12), this part of the ceremony has been dramatized and elaborated in the account of the *dig-vijaya* of the Pāṇḍavas in the Sabhāparvan of the Mahābhārata. In the ŚDV the theme of the recovery of the predominance of the 'Vedic lifestyle' is connected with the ritual dimension of establishing legitimate rule. However, as Śaṅkara first and foremost represents the ascetic tradition, he has to renounce violent actions and the normal military equipment. His weapon is his knowledge and his *śrī*, i.e. the female power granting the prosperity of the king, is the *advaita* doctrine (*advaitaśrī*; 4.78).[22] As will be shown, the more violent aspects of the conquest are accorded to his disciples, or to kings who fight for Śaṅkara's cause.

In Śaṅkara's case the part of the 'demons' is distributed, roughly speaking, among three groups: firstly, there are those opponents who could be potential allies if they were made to give up their wrong interpretations of *śruti*-texts, stopped in their denial of the *īśvara-tattva* (the principle of a highest God), and made to accept the Advaitic interpretation of the 'knowledge of the self' (*ātmajñāna*). As they already deal either with the Vedic tradition or with ascetic values, they are promising objects of attempts at conversion. Secondly, there are those who directly oppose the *vedamārga*, e.g. the Buddhists and the Jainas, as well as those who neglect it, e.g. the Vaiṣṇava and Śaiva *sampradāyas* which follow their *āgamas* rather than the *śruti*. These groups are only incidentally presented as having been converted; rather they meet destruction.[23] Then there is a third group, only mentioned but not included in the conquest: the *abhinava-yavana*, the new foreigners (presumably the Muslims), who destroy temples and practice cow-slaughter. The text asks: 'How can salvation be obtained by *bhaktas*, if these people have pervaded the whole country?' (9.32),[24] and offers the following general answer: 'When, however, those, who have the speaker of truth [i.e. Śaṅkara, AM] as their king, who have shunned the defilements of *kaliyuga*, who ardently follow the principle of Viṣṇu, expand from all sides by being active in each and every region, why should I then worry because of this [presence of foreigners]?'[25] The reference to the adherence to *viṣṇu-tattva* again indicates that the *jagadguru* and his followers have taken over the task of preservation from Viṣṇu and his *avatāras*. At the same time, the conquest of the first two groups is in this passage presented as a precondition for the defeat of the foreigners.

Conversion of Maṇḍanamiśra and the Slaying of a Kāpālika

The text depicts in great detail Śaṅkara's encounters with the first two groups, the wrong interpreters of Vedic tradition and the adherents of other *sampradāyas*, especially Śaiva ascetics. In the following, one example from each group will be given.

First there is the conversion of Maṇḍanamiśra, a proud and apparently choleric brahmin scholar. Maṇḍana's lack of self-control and his subsequent violent behaviour are presented as the dark side of the brahmanical status. Maṇḍana denies the existence of an *īśvara* and advocates *karman*, i.e. ritual activity, as the only way to salvation (*mokṣa*). Śaṅkara sets out to defeat Maṇḍana after his dispute with Vyāsa, who precedes him in the *guruparamparā* as one of his teachers. Vyāsa grants Śaṅkara a *darśana* and prolongs his limited lifetime, so that he will be able to defeat those still undefeated. After a meeting with the Mīmāṃsā scholar Kumārilabhaṭṭa (7.61-111), who has to undergo penance for his denial of God and for his inability to defeat the Buddhists, Śaṅkara reaches Maṇḍana's home in Mahiṣmatī, where he lives with his wife Ubhayabhāratī. Previously it had been related that Maṇḍana is an incarnation of Brahmā (1.56), while his wife Ubhayabhāratī is the incarnation of Sarasvatī (3.9). Śaṅkara enters their home through his yogic 'power' (*yogaśaktyā*; 8.11) at a moment when Maṇḍana is worshipping Vyāsa and Jaimini. Maṇḍana becomes almost mad with anger when he sees Śaṅkara standing next to his gurus and can only be stopped by Vyāsa. Nevertheless, the opponents agree to enter into a regular debate, a *vivāda*, and both promise to adopt the other's lifestyle in case of defeat. Maṇḍana's wife, Ubhayabhāratī, is made the judge. For several days they engage in a dispute, which is, as pointed out in the text, full of dignity and erudition. The account of the dispute includes an exposition of the principal teachings of both sides and presents as the core of the conflict a disagreement with regard to the interpretation of the Upaniṣads. Śaṅkara wins with the argument that the authority of Vedānta is established by a teaching which can only be known through the testimony of these texts, because all other means of knowledge would fail. Whereas difference can be seen, heard and inferred everywhere, non-difference is that knowledge which is revealed only in the Upaniṣads. This knowledge has for the first time been truly understood and communicated by Śaṅkara.

After this final blow against Maṇḍana, his wife Ubhayabhāratī immediately leaves the *sabhā*, eager to cook the *bhikṣā*-meal of the *saṃnyāsin*, this time not only for Śaṅkara but also for her husband. Maṇḍana accepts becoming a *saṃnyāsin* and, in consequence, Śaṅkara's disciple under the new name 'Sureśvara'. Śaṅkara then proceeds to defeat Ubhayabhāratī as she in fact represents the position Śaṅkara is about to achieve. She is the *sarvajñatāpadam*, the abode of omniscience. After winning the debate with Ubhayabhāratī, Śaṅkara promises to establish the worship of the goddess in Śṛṅgeri, and thus in Southern India (10.70–2). Śaṅkara actually does this after having conquered the Śāradā-*pīṭha* in Kashmir and giving the (not further specified) teachers already resident in Śṛṅgeri instructions on the Advaita-doctrine (12.68–9).[26] I will come back to this aspect of the conquest, the re-connection of the North with the South, in the next paragraph. But first, this 'winning-over', this conversion of an opponent, shall be contrasted with the depiction of Śaṅkara's encounter with a Kāpālika ascetic.

On his route through South India Śaṅkara defeats the Pāśupatas, Vīra-Śaivas and Vaiṣṇavas. Next he reaches the well-known Śaiva centre (*kṣetra*) Śrīśailam in order to worship Śiva in the form of Mallikārjuna (10.106).[27] One day a Kāpālika ascetic approaches Śaṅkara. After displaying his knowledge of Śaṅkara's teachings on the illusionary existence of the body, the Kāpālika asks Śaṅkara to let him have his head. The Kāpālika explains his wish by referring to Kāpāli-Śiva's promise that only when he offers his oblations in the skull of a king or an omniscient person will he reap the fruits of his ascetic practices. Śaṅkara, in conformity with his teachings, answers: 'With pleasure I give you my head!' (11.25). He only asks the Kāpālika to behead him in a hidden place (in order to prevent his disciples from interfering), and during his *samādhi*. When the Kāpālika finally stands behind Śaṅkara to chop off the head, Padmapāda, the most yogic of Śaṅkara's disciples, has a vision of the scene and immediately appears on the spot in the form of Narasiṃha. He seizes the Kāpālika and tears his belly apart, just as, the text states, Narasiṃha did with Hiraṇyakaśipu to save Prahlāda. Then follows an explanation of Padmapāda's ability to become Narasiṃha and a hymnic praise of

Narasiṃha-Padmapāda by Śaṅkara. Padmapāda here, as also in another incident, becomes the most violent and one of the most worshipped[28] *avatāras* of Viṣṇu. As such he has a duty to rescue Śiva in the form of Śaṅkara from the violent practices of certain Śaiva ascetics. It is made clear that Śaṅkara would never actively engage in violent action as this would mean betraying his doctrine and vow as a *saṃnyāsin*. His disciples, however, have the duty to act as *avatāra*, and punish a demon-like Kāpālika or other such for their selfish exploitation of Śaṅkara's Advaitic indifference in personal matters.

In contrasting these two episodes, a marked difference with regard to the results can be observed: while encounters with self-forgetful and god-denying teachers of the *pravṛttimārga* like Kumārila Bhaṭṭa or Maṇḍanamiśra, or with teachers like Bhāskara, end up with submission or conversion, the encounters with the Pāśupatas, Kāpālikas and finally with Abhinavagupta—who is depicted as indulging in black magic—lead to their destruction (16.1–32).[29] Śaṅkara, face to face with competing *ācāryas*, is first and foremost the scholar and *bhāṣyakāra*, and 'knower of the self' (*ātmajñānin*). Confronted with wild ascetics he is presented as a yogi who, instead of using his yogic powers, sticks to his principles and willingly renounces his body to the dignity of *samādhi*. It is left to his disciples to save the beloved guru from deliberate death before his mission is fulfilled and a succession properly arranged. The encounters in the 'battle of arguments' (*vivādakalaha*) with Vedic or ascetic scholars combine two aspects of Śaṅkara's 'triple identity': although he is as an ascetic no longer involved in social transactions, he advocates conformity to Vedic rules and prescriptions in daily life. This is aptly symbolized in the statement that Śaṅkara with his ascetic's staff (*daṇḍa*) leads the 'old cow of Vedic tradition' back on the right path (5.88). The stories of victory over Śaiva ascetics illustrate the already mentioned integration of aspects of the *avatāras* of Viṣṇu in the depiction of Śaṅkara as Śiva's incarnation. In these, his disciples play a decisive role, they are indeed passionately attached to the 'principle of Viṣṇu' in saving their guru. The full acceptance of this theistic, i.e. *saguṇa*, dimension for the fulfilment of his mission is the third element which constitutes Śaṅkara's identity as a *jagadguru* in the ŚDV.[30]

Inclusion of South India: Śaṅkara and the Śāradā-pīṭha

The conversion of misguided opponents is in the text presented as a precondition for the most important achievement and in fact the culmination of Śaṅkara's victory-tour over India. He conquers the 'seat of omniscients', the *pīṭha* of the goddess Śāradā-Sarasvatī in Kashmir. Thus, the *ācārya* gets hold of the most prestigious institution, which permits the title *jagadguru* to be ascribed to him. What is exceptional in Śaṅkara's accession to the *pīṭha* is the connection between, if not reunification of, North and South India.[31] The account starts with a depiction of Śaṅkara who, one morning on the banks of the Gaṅgā, overhears the following 'popular rumour' (*lokavārtā*; 16.54):

> Here on this earth, Jambūdvīpa is especially praised; there [in Jambūdvīpa] the region of Bhārata has the highest esteem; in Bhārata again the region called Kaśmīr is praised as the best. There rules Śāradā, the empress of learned speech. There is the abode of the Goddess, the 'seat of omniscients' equipped with four gates belonging to the temple. Only omniscient and good men are allowed to ascend to this place; no other people. When they are opening the respective gate, these omniscient people go to the Eastern gate, when they are from the East, to the Western gate, when they are from the West, and to the Northern gate, when they are from the North. Those from the South did not [yet] open the closed Southern gate. (16.55–7)[32]

While listening to this talk, Śaṅkara realizes that in the core of his heart he is a South Indian. Therefore, he decides to go to Kashmir immediately in order to contradict the opinion that in South India one does not find 'omniscient' scholars. After passing all examinations by scholars gathering around the threshold of the *pīṭha*, Śaṅkara is the first to enter the temple of Śāradā through the Southern gate. The opening of this gate makes not only the *dig-vijaya* complete, it also includes the South of India in the overarching authority of the *pīṭha*. But also, conversely, the authority of the *pīṭha* is only complete with the Southern door opened, with Śaṅkara's southern-bound omniscience included.

I will finally and briefly turn to the process of the institutionalization as depicted in the text through *sampradāya-paripālana*, i.e. through the protection and preservation of the traditional line of teachers. This is presented as one of the duties of the *jagadguru*.

Protecting the Line of Transmission

Although Śaṅkara is described as an *avatāra* of Śiva, the text explains that Śaṅkara's existence in a human body subjects him to traditional rules and regulations. Moreover, only by obeying these can he serve as the measure and ideal (*pramāṇa*) for his mostly human followers. The author of the text, therefore, relates in detail Śaṅkara's behaviour as a disciple and how he places himself in the succession of teachers who represent the pre-history of the *sampradāya* that Śaṅkara is said to have established. Correspondingly, the relationship between Śaṅkara and his four disciples is the subject of several episodes. In one of these it is related that after his decision to become a *saṃnyāsin*—a decision much resisted by his mother—Śaṅkara approaches Govinda Bhagavatpāda, who lives in a cave near the Narmadā river. After receiving Śaṅkara's homage to him as the guru, Govinda Bhagavatpāda asks Śaṅkara to introduce himself. Śaṅkara replies with the following formula which, according to the ŚDV, comprises the knowledge taught in the Advaita-darśana: 'Who as the only one is the highest, that Śiva am I'. (*yaḥ kevalo 'sti paramaḥ sa śivo 'ham asmi*; 5.99). After reconfirming the truth of this assertion by the insight gained through *samādhi*, Govindapāda stretches his feet out of the cave. Śaṅkara immediately worships the feet and thereby becomes the pupil (*śiṣya*) of Govindapāda. The text explains that although for Śaṅkara there is nothing left to learn, this behaviour is motivated by Śaṅkara's understanding of the necessity of protecting and preserving the *sampradāya* (5.102: *sampradāyaparipālanabuddhyā*). Correspondingly, he is instructed by Govindapāda in the interpretation of the Brahmasūtras, which are declared as belonging to the *sampradāya*. In this context the tradition of teachers (*guruparamparā*) of the *sampradāya* is completely listed: it began with Vyāsa, was handed to his son Śuka, then to Gauḍapāda and Govindapāda, and now to Śaṅkara (5.105).

Not satisfied with establishing this direct succession, Śaṅkara, after having received his instruction from Govindapāda, is granted the *darśana* of the first teacher Vyāsa. This, however, only after he has been exposed to a 'battle of words' for several days (7.1–9). When Śaṅkara realizes that he is disputing with Vyāsa, he asks the author of the *sūtra* text to correct his commentary. As Vyāsa finds no mistakes in the text, the final sanction for the commentary to become the canonical text for the *sampradāya* has been given (7.40–50). This realignment of Śaṅkara's authority is again illustrated in a conversation between Śaṅkara and his teacher's teacher Gauḍapāda just before his conquest of the Śāradā *pīṭha*. Moreover, Gauḍapāda is presented as directly accepting Śaṅkara's interpretation of his *Māṇḍūkyakārikās*. This tradition of reconfirming new commentaries on what is to become the canonical literature of the *sampradāya* by one's teacher, ideally by the *jagadguru* himself, is also continued with Śaṅkara's disciples. This implies the canonization of those texts, which are to be accepted as authoritative. Knowing both the strength and weakness of his disciples, Śaṅkara asks only Sureśvara and Padmapāda to comment upon his commentary. Śaṅkara is shown as agreeing fully with Sureśvara-Maṇḍanamiśra's tract *Naiṣkārmyasiddhi* and with his sub-commentaries (*vārttikas*) on some of his Upaniṣad-commentaries. Padmapāda's sub-commentary on the Brahmasūtrabhāṣya is even memorized by Śaṅkara after Padmapāda has lost the power of his mind (as a result of having been poisoned by his relatives). As has already been demonstrated, the intellectual guidance provided by the guru is balanced by the physical care and protection the disciples offer Śaṅkara in their affection for him (*gurubhakti*). Śaṅkara is also depicted as settling quarrells between his four disciples by alloting them different tasks. This is the subject of chapter 13 of the ŚDV, in which is discussed Sureśvara's wish to write a commentary on the Brahmasūtrabhāṣya. The other disciples express their distrust of Sureśvara, because he is only a convert and therefore might distort the true teaching. Śaṅkara requests Sureśvara to refrain from his project and to write instead an independent treatise in order to prevent further rivalries. The task of writing a commentary is accorded to Padmapāda, who is Śaṅkara's first disciple (6.1–5, 65–71) and whose intense devotion is seen by the other disciples as making him predestined for the scholarly task. His sub-commentary on Śaṅkara's Brahmsūtrabhāṣya, however, is ill-fated. It is destroyed by his relatives and only partially restored (14.75–170). Thus, placing oneself in a line of predecessors and duly arranging the succession by balancing the competitive claims of the disciples are depicted as belonging to the duties of the *jagadguru*. At the same time they are decisive factors in the legitimation of his status.

Final Remarks

Being an incarnation of all-knowing Śiva, fulfilling the royal duties ascribed to Viṣṇu, revealing the true importance of the Veda and restoring the validity of the *varṇāśramadharma*, personifying the power and truth of ascetic values and accepting the necessity of theism—these are the elements that are joined together in the ŚDV in order to establish Śaṅkara's status as a *jagadguru*. In his persona three different structures of value, normally ascribed to different sections of society and lifestyles, are united. This blending of those structures of value is in the ŚDV presented as the basis for the successful conquest of the regions. On a geographical level this achievement is symbolized in his opening, allegedly for the first time, the Southern gate of the Śāradā-*pīṭha* as the culmination of his all-India intellectual conquest. Through this inclusion of South India the claim of the *pīṭha* to represent omniscience is completely realized. To win an institution and even to become identical with it is not seen as a 'fate' of normalization of an exceptional founder-figure—as is suggested in Weber's model. Rather, this achievement is seen as an essential task of an exceptional founder-figure which proves and explains his outstanding position. Thus, it is only through institutionalization and an uninterrupted succession of *jagadgurus* that the special claim of Ādi-Śaṅkara can be re-enacted and preserved. The ŚDV shows that this position is rooted exactly in those activities that accompany the conquest of the regions. Finally, the claim for an overarching authority is represented through the four—or with the inclusion of Kāñcī five—*maṭhas* located at the periphery, in the four cardinal directions of India. These encompass all the other centres, if those would only accept subordination to the authority of the Vedānta *pīṭhas*, with their claims to truth interpreted according to the Advaita-Vedānta hierarchy of knowledge. With regard to this, the Advaita *sampradāya* seems to share the paradoxical qualities implied in the institutionalization of exceptional claims to truth: the doctrine of 'non-difference' is presented as the teaching which distinguishes the *jagadguru* from all the other teachers, and permits the demand for its acceptance from those who insist on difference.

Notes

1. Cf. Lütt (1978) and Cenkner (1983: 109–34). For the involvement of different Śaṅkarācāryas in the activities of the Vishva Hindu Parishad see Jaffrelot (1993: 355–8).
2. The different forms of 'institutionalization of charisma' (e.g. rules for succession, festivals, hagiographies) are for Weber attempts to cope with the 'fate of normalization' ('Veralltäglichung') of the charismatic experience (1964: 179–88, 832–73). For a discussion of Weber's propositions see Seyfarth (1979) and Schluchter (1988). On the paradoxical structures implied in the 'normalization' of the exceptional compare O'Dea (1960). In the context of the discussions on 'genuine'- versus 'pseudo'-charisma, hagiographies might be viewed as an instance of 'manufactured charisma.' Cf. Bensman, and Givant (1986); Bell (1986) and Glassman (1986). Potter (1982: 121) is rather critical of this kind of 'remake' of the 'historical' Śaṅkara in the hagiographies and states: 'The philosopher acquires charisma by virtue of adulation based on a completely erroneous assessment of his philosophy.'
3. This term has been used by Reynolds and Capps (1976: 4) with regard to 'mythical ideals' created in sacred biographies, which generally take precedence over the historical facts. While using 'sacred biography' I do not imply to follow the distinction between 'sacred biography' and 'hagiography', which Reynolds and Capps propose in the same article: firstly, because it is not based on a study of narrative devices, but solely on a hierarchy of central characters (i.e. 'founders' in sacred biographies and 'lesser figures' in hagiographies). Secondly, it is exceeded in view of Keyes' 1982 analysis of the interplay between charisma and sacred biography.

4. Antarkar (1960: 113, n1) gives a list of ten Sanskrit hagiographies.
5. Antarkar (1972: 1) comments: 'religious preachers like the kirtankaras rely on this work only for his life-history.' Compare also Sawai (1992), who uses the text for his analysis of the faith of the lay community of the Śṛṅgeri *maṭha*.
6. Antarkar (1972: 1) stresses that the title of the text found in the work itself is '*Saṅkṣepa Śaṅkara Jaya*' with Mādhavācārya as author. However, it became popular as 'Śaṅkara-Digvijaya', and the authorship was ascribed to Vidyāraṇyamuni. On the association with the foundation of Vijayanagara compare Kulke (1985: 124ff).
7. Antarkar traces the quotations from other *vijaya* texts in the ŚDV (1972: 3ff, 22).
8. Ungemach (1992: 7–8) points to the polemic depiction of Śaṅkara in *Maṇimañjarī*, a hagiographical biography of Madhva by Nārāyaṇapaṇḍita (early fourteenth century). Some episodes of Śaṅkara's life correspond to those to be found in the *vijaya* texts. He comments: 'Diese Episoden aus Śaṅkaras Leben müssen zur Zeit, als die M.M. [Maṇimañjarī AM] abgefaßt wurde, bereits bekannt gewesen sein, denn [...] es ist unwahrscheinlich, daß die Verfasser der Śaṅkara-Legenden sich von den Schmähschriften ihrer Gegner über Śaṅkara inspirieren ließen.' (8).
9. Cf. Kulke (1985), Shastry (1982: 17–26) and Verghese (1995: 8, 111–20).
10. The Nāyakas of Keḷadi, who did rise to power under the Vijayanagara rulers, established an independent kingdom and ruled in west Karnāṭaka. Cf. Shastry (1982: 26–34).
11. Cf. Antarkar (1972: 3–5), see also Sawai (1992: 28, n45) and Cenkner (1984: 114ff.).
12. This is corroborated by the continuation of the *vijaya* practice by succeeding *jagadgurus*, who re-enact the example set by the Ādi-Śaṅkara. For recent dates see Cenkner (1984: 131ff.).
13. Although Śaṅkara's ability to perform miracles is only rarely demonstrated, it is nevertheless an indispensable aspect of his presence. As examples may serve: (1) the episode in which he induces the Pūrṇa river to come closer to the house of his family by a hymnic praise (5.5–9); (2) when he rescues villagers from the floods of the Narmadā by *mantra*-recitation. For the difference between the miracles performed by Śaṅkara according to his status as a *bhakta*, *saṃnyāsin*, and yogin see Sawai (1992: 91–9). For the use of 'black magic' in the story of the defeat of Abhinavagupta in ŚDV in comparison with Nārāyaṇācāryas's Maṇimañjari see Granoff (1985: 464f.).
14. This is to be stressed in contrast to Weber's characterisation of the charismatic leader as a revolutionary, who advocates heterodox doctrines.
15. On the 'historical' Śaṅkara's attitudes toward theism cf. Hacker (1965).
16. Cf. Stietencron (1986).
17. It is pointed out that people now follow Buddhism, hate those who practice *varṇāśramadharma* (*varṇāśramasamācārān dviṣanti*; 1.32), and neglect their ritual duties (*sandhyādīni karmāṇi*; 1.33).

18. Thus, the peacefulness of animals and the harmony of nature on the eve of his birth are contrasted with the fear of Śaṅkara's potential opponents; the astrological constellation is auspicious, the gods pour flowers from heaven (2.57–93). The baby illuminates his cradle in the night by his own lustre (*tejas*; 2.81–3). For parallels with purāṇic accounts of Kṛṣṇa's childhood see Lorenzen (1976: 94; 9ff). These elements however can already be traced in the accounts of the birth of the Buddha (cf. Buddhacaritam 1.1–30). In ŚDV 3.80–83 Śaṅkara's childhood is explicitly compared with Kṛṣṇa's infancy.
19. The whole passage 1.39–45 is a variation on Bhagavadgītā (BhG) 4.6–8, in which Kṛṣṇa declares the purpose of his 'divine birth'. The four-armed Hari is referred to in BhG 11.46. The ŚDV at this point does not explicitly refer to the purāṇic tradition of Śiva's 28 incarnations (e.g. Vāyupurāṇa I,23; Kūrmapurāṇa 1,51.10). In the account in Liṅgapurāṇa 1,24.141 Śiva is accompanied by four disciples, i.e. his ascetic sons, who practise Yoga. In one of his incarnations he appears as Lakulīśa, the founder of the Pāśupata-school (Liṅgapurāṇa 1,24.130; also Vāyupurāna I,23, 208–10). In the ŚDV (6.25–40) Śiva challenges Śaṅkara in the disguise of a Caṇḍāla accompanied by four dogs (i.e. the four Vedas). A connection of Śaṅkara's *avatāra* status with the four *yugas* and a succession of teachers is established in one passage (9.22): According to the 'Purāṇa belonging to Śiva' the knowledge (*jñāna*) was in *kṛtayuga* spread by Kapila (*sattvamuni*), in *tretāyuga* by Datta(ātreya), in *dvāparayuga* by Vyāsa and in *kaliyuga* by Śaṅkara.
20. A similar 'division of labour' can be observed with regard to the Jaina classification of Baladevas and Vāsudevas, who rule jointly the earth during those intervals, when a *cakravartin* is absent: 'the intention of the ācāryas seems to be to depict the one (Baladeva) as leading the life of an ideal Jaina layman, ... and to portray the other (Vāsudeva) as the hero's companion, who is capable of carrying out terrible destruction.' (Jaini 1993: 211).
21. Therefore I cannot subscribe to Lorenzen's view, that the ŚDV primarily contrasts Śaivism and Vaiṣṇavism by comparing the biography of Kṛṣṇa with that of Śaṅkara. According to him, the text therewith depicts the 'basic tension in the Indian world view between the desire for and fear of human freedom and individuality, between the ascetic who is an individual-outside-the-world and the insubstantial man-in-the-world of caste society' (Lorenzen 1976: 104).
22. See also 4.80 praising Advaita as the path of salvation free from 'thorns' (*advaite parimuktakaṇṭakapathe*).
23. Compare the refutation of the *īśvara* doctrine of the Pāśupatas. It is not explicitly stated that they were converted, rather their 'pride' (*abhimāna*) has been shattered (6.72–8). In one passage it is stated that some of the defeated theists give up their creed, while others decide to take revenge (10.115–16): 'The Pāśupatas, Vaiṣṇavas, Vīraśaivas and Maheśvaras were in fact defeated by Sureśvara and the other [pupils]. Some of them gave up their creed completely and became pupils of that one [Śaṅkara] as their

envy and the defilements of their mind had vanished. Others however, became obsessed with wrath, they, being full of thoughts for revenge, spent their time thinking about [means to bring about] his [Śaṅkara's] death.'

([...] *pāśupatavaiṣṇavavīraśaivamāheśvarāś ca vijitā hi sureśvarādyaiḥ* // 10.115/ *kecid visṛjya matam ātmyam amuṣya śiṣyabhāvaṃ gatā vigatamatsaramānadoṣā* / *anye tu manyuvaśam etya jaghanyacittā ninyuḥ kṣaṇaṃ nidhanam asya nirīkṣamāṇāḥ* // 10.116/).

24. *vyāptā sarveyam urvī kva jagati bhajatāṃ kaiva muktiprasaktiḥ* /9.32/
25. *yad vā sadvādirājā vijitakalimalā viṣṇutattvānuraktā* / *ujjṛmbhante samantād diśi diśi kṛtinaḥ kiṃ tayā cintayā me* //9.32/
26. On the importance of the Śāradā temple as a place of pilgrimage for the lay community, compare Sawai (1992: 71–82). The establishment of a larger Śāradā temple in Śṛṅgeri is associated with Vidyāraṇya's pontificate (Sawai 1992: 32).
27. The temple in Śrīśailam enshrining the Mallikārjuna *liṅga*, one of the twelve especially important *jyotir liṅgas*, was one of the greatest within the Vijayanagara empire (Verghese 1995: 26–7). Śrīśailam was also one of the centres of the Bhairava cult of the Kālāmukhas. The ŚDV identifies them with the Kāpālikas.
28. On the importance of the cult of Narasiṃha for the non-Śaiva cults in the Vijayanagara empire which was later (sixteenth century) overshadowed by the cult of Viṭṭhala and Veṅkateśvara, see Verghese (1995: 34-41).
29. Especially devastating for a large group of Kāpālikas led by Krachaka is their encounter with Śaṅkara, who is supported by the army of King Sudhanvā (15.11–28). Śiva himself kills Krachaka when he is asked to take revenge for the many Kāpālikas who have been killed.
30. Another incident, which corroborates this analysis, is his immediate acceptance of his mother's final wish to be initiated to a *saguṇa-deva* as she in her hour of death cannot find comfort with a reality (*tattva*) she cannot grasp (14.36).
31. There are other instances, in which this dimension of Śaṅkara's mission is indicated, as for example the establishment of the Śāradā temple in Śṛṅgeri. Significant in this respect is also the account of the marriage between Maṇḍanamiśra (Brahmā incarnate) and Ubhayabhāratī (Sarasvatī-Śāradā incarnate): Maṇḍana's family lives in the North, in Kashmir, while Sarasvatī lives in the South. That this might arouse problems is indicated in a brief conversation between Sarasvatī's parents about the marriage proposal (3.26ff). It is pointed out, that the bridegroom comes from the North, where habits and customs are different. Finally, the marriage is arranged, and Sarasvatī leaves for Kashmir. Thus this North-South marriage is acknowledged and 'divorced' at the same time, when Śaṅkara installs her in the Śāradā temple in Śṛṅgeri.
32. *jambūdvīpaṃ śasyate 'syāṃ pṛthivyāṃ tatrāpy etan maṇḍalaṃ bhāratākhyam* / *kāśmīrākhyaṃ maṇḍalaṃ tatra śastaṃ yatrāste 'sau śāradā vāgadhīśā* //16.55/

dvārair yuktaṃ māṇḍapais tac caturbhir devyā gehaṃ yatra sarvajñapīṭham /
yatrārohe sarvavitsajjanānāṃ nānye sarve yat praveṣṭum kṣamante //16.56/
prācyāḥ prācyāḥ paścimāḥ paścimāyāṃ ye codīcyās tām udīcīṃ prapannāḥ /
sarvajñās taddvāram udghāṭayanto dākṣā naddhaṃ no tad udghāṭayanti //16.57/

References

Antarkar, W. R. 1960. *Bṛhat-Śaṅkara-Vijaya* of Citsukhācārya and Prācīna-Śaṅkara-Vijaya of Ānandagiri as Ānanda-Jñāna. *Journal of the University of Bombay* 29, n.s. 35: 113–21.

———. 1960a. *Śaṅkara-Vijaya* of Anantānandagiri. *Journal of the University of Bombay* 29, n.s. 35: 73–80.

———. 1972. *Saṅkṣepa Śaṅkara Jaya* of Mādhavācārya or Śaṅkara Digvijaya of Śrī Vidyāraṇyamuni. *Journal of the University of Bombay* 41, n.s. 77: 1–23.

Bell, Richard S. 1986. Charisma and Illegitimate Authority. In *Charisma, History and Social Structure*, ed. by Ronald M. Glassman and William H. Swatos, 57–70. New York: Greenwood.

Bensman, J. and M. Givant. 1986. Charisma and Modernity: The Use and Abuse of a Concept. In *Charisma, History, and Social Structure*, ed. by Ronald M. Glassman and William H. Swatos, 27–56. New York: Greenwood.

Buitenen, J. A. B. van. 1988. On the structure of the *Sabhāparvan* of the *Mahābhārata*. In *Studies in Indian Literature and Philosophy. Collected papers by J. A. B. van Buitenen*, ed. Ludo Rocher, 305–22. New Delhi: American Institute of Indian Studies.

Cenkner, W. 1983. *A Tradition of Teachers: Śaṅkara and the Jagadguru Today.* Delhi: Motilal Banarsidass.

Gebhardt, W. 1993. Charisma und Ordnung. Formen des institutionalisierten Charisma—Überlegungen im Anschluß and Max Weber. In *Charisma. Theorie—Religion—Politik*, ed. Winfried Gebhardt, Arnold Zingerle and Michael N. Ebertz, 47–68. Berlin, New York: de Gruyter.

Glassman, Ronald M. 1986. Manufactured Charisma and Legitimacy. In *Charisma, History, and Social Structure*, ed. by Ronald M. Glassman and William H. Swatos, 115–28. New York: Greenwood.

Granoff, Phyllis. 1985. Scholars and Wonder-workers: Some Remarks on the Role of the Supernatural in Philosophical Contests in Vedānta Hagiographies. *Journal of the American Oriental Society* 105.3: 459–68.

Hacker, P. 1965. Relations of Early Advaitins to Vaiṣṇavism. *Wiener Zeitschrift für die Kunde Südasiens* 9: 147–54.

Heesterman, J. C. 1957. *The Ancient Indian Royal Consecration. The* Rājasūya *Described according to the Yajus Texts and Annotated.* Gravenhagen: Mouton.

Jaini, Padmanabh S. 1993. Jaina Purāṇas: A Purāṇic Counter-tradition. In *Purāṇa Perennis, Reciprocity and Transformation in Hindu and Jaina Texts*, ed. Wendy Doniger, 207–49. Albany: State University of New York Press.

Jaffrelot, C. 1993. *The Hindu Nationalist Movement and Indian Politics, 1925 to the*

1990s. Strategies of Identity-building, Implantation and Mobilisation (with Special Reference to Central India). London: Hurst.

Keyes, Charles F. 1982. Introduction: Charisma: From Social Life to Sacred Biography. In *Charisma and Sacred Biography*, ed. Michael A. Williams,1–22. Missoula, Mont.: American Academy of Religion.

Kulke, H. 1985. Mahārajas, Mahants and Historians. Reflections on the Historiography of Early Vijayanagara and Sringeri. In *Vijayanagara—City and Empire. New Currents of Research*, ed. by A. L. Dallapiccola, 120–43. vol. 1. Wiesbaden: Steiner.

Kūrmapurāṇa 1972. *The Kūrma Purāṇa (with English translation)*, ed. Ananda Swarup Gupta. Varanasi: All-India Kashi Raj Trust.

Liṅgapurāṇa 1885. *Lingapurana by Maharshivedavyasa*, ed. Jibananda Vidyasagara. Calcutta: New Valmiki Press.

Lorenzen, David N. 1976. The Life of Śaṅkarācārya. In *The Biographical Process. Studies in the History and Psychology of Religion*, ed. F. E. Reynolds and D. Capps, 87–107. The Hague, Paris: Mouton.

Lütt, J. 1978. The Śaṅkarācārya of Puri. In *The Cult of Jagannath and the Regional Tradition of Orissa*, ed. by Anncharlott Eschmann *et al.*, 411–19. Delhi: Manohar.

O'Dea, T. F. 1964. Die fünf Dilemmas der Institutionalisierung der Religion. In *Religionssoziologie*, ed. Friedrich Fürstenberg, 207–13. Neuwied: Luchterhand.

Potter, Karl H. 1982. Śaṃkarācārya: The Myth and the Man. In *Charisma and Sacred Biography*, ed. Michael A. Williams, 111–25. Missoula, Mont.: American Academy of Religion.

Reynolds, F. E.; Capps, Donald 1976. Introduction. In *The Biographical Process. Studies in the History and Psychology of Religion*, ed. F. E. Reynolds and D. Capps, 1–33. The Hague, Paris: Mouton.

Śaṅkaradigvijaya. 1891. *Śrīvidyāraṇyaviracitaḥ śrīmacchaṃkaradigvijayaḥ, advaitarājyalakṣmītīkāntargataviśeṣavibhāgaṭippaṇībhis tathā dhanapatisūrikṛtaḍiṇimākhyaṭīkayā ca sametaḥ, etat pustakam ānandāśramasthapaṇḍitaiḥ saṃśodhitam tac ca mahādeva cimaṇāji āpṭe*. Poona: Ānandāśrama.

Sawai, Y. 1992. *The Faith of Ascetics and Lay Smārtas. A Study of the Śaṅkaran Tradition in Śṛṅgeri*. Vienna: Sammlung de Nobili.

Schluchter, W. 1988. Umbildung des Charismas. Überlegungen zur Herrschaftssoziologie. In *Religion und Lebensführung. Studien zu Max Webers Religions- und Herrschaftssoziologie*, ed. by W. Schluchter, vol. 2: 535–54. Frankfurt: Suhrkamp.

Seyfarth, C. 1979. Alltag und Charisma bei Max Weber. Eine Studie zur Grundlegung der 'verstehenden' Soziologie. In *Alfred Schütz und die Idee des Alltags in den Sozialwissenschaften*, ed. Walter M. Sprondel and Richard Grathoff, 155–77. Stuttgart: Enke.

Shastry, A. K. 1982. *A History of Śriṅgeri*. Dharwad: Karnatak University.

Stietencron, H. v. 1986. Kalkulierter Religionsverfall: Das Kaliyuga in Indien. In *Der Untergang von Religionen*, ed. H. Zinser, 135–50. Berlin: Dietrich Reimer.

Ungemach, A. 1992. *Śaṃkara-Mandara-Saurabh, Eine Legende über das Leben des Philosophen Śaṃkara. Text, Übersetzung, Einleitung.* Stuttgart: Steiner.

Vāyupurāṇa 1880, 1888. *The Vāyu Purāṇa: A System of Hindu Mythology and Tradition*, ed. Rājendralāla Mitra; Vol. One, 1880; Vol. Two, 1888. Calcutta: Kalika Press (Bibliotheca Indica).

Verghese, A. 1995. *Religious Traditions at Vijayanagara as Revealed Through its Monuments.* New Delhi: Manohar.

Weber, M. 1964. *Wirtschaft und Gesellschaft. Grundriss der verstehenden Soziologie*, ed. Johannes Winckelmann. 2 Vols. Köln: Kiepenheuer & Witsch.

Madhva and the Reform of Vaiṣṇavism in Karnataka

ROBERT J. ZYDENBOS

In south-western India the word 'Vaiṣṇavism' practically always refers to the school of religious thought introduced by Madhvācārya (1238–1317).[1] In Karnataka this school today is one of the most prominent and socially active forms of Hinduism, and it has held a place of intellectual and cultural importance ever since its beginnings. Madhva described his religious and philosophical thought as *tattvavāda* or 'realism', in contradistinction to the *māyāvāda* or 'illusionism' of the Advaita school of Vedānta which prevailed in south-western Karnataka in his time. More popularly, Madhva's theology is known as Dvaita-Vedānta, a term which Madhva himself did not use but which obviously expresses the opposition of this school to the monism implied in the name 'Advaita'. Today, the followers of Madhva customarily refer to themselves as 'Mādhvas'. Apart from the Tamil-speaking Śrīvaiṣṇava brahmins, who are concentrated in south-eastern Karnataka, all the other brahmins of Karnataka are either Smārta or Mādhva, and we may assume that in several districts the majority of the brahmins are Mādhvas.

Not much is known about the presence of Vaiṣṇavism in Karnataka before Madhva's time. There was no outspokenly Vaiṣṇava literature predating Madhva in Kannada or any other language spoken in what was a predominantly Jaina and Śaiva land. A little about Madhva's religious background can be reconstructed from what we read in the *Madhvavijaya*, the main hagiographical document and the main source of information about events in the life of Madhva. Madhva was from a Smārta family which apparently had Vaiṣṇava leanings, as the names of his relatives suggest, and the Bhāgavatapurāṇa was evidently considered an important religious text: it is mentioned a few times in the *Madhvavijaya*, and there

Madhva is said to have understood the text at a very early age. It has been suggested that Madhva's background was that of the *Bhāgavata-sampradāya*, a syncretistic current of apparently Śaiva origin which later largely merged with Śrīvaiṣṇavism and Mādhva Vaiṣṇavism.[2]

Madhva probably knew about Rāmānuja, who had lived two centuries earlier, and there are some obvious similarities between the two thinkers: they rejected Advaitin *māyāvāda*, they recognized the Pāñcarātra *āgamas* as scripture, *bhakti* plays an important part in their theology, and they unambiguously declared Viṣṇu the supreme being. Perhaps these very similarities explain why Madhva did not undertake any polemics against the school of Rāmānuja:[3] his priorities lay elsewhere. But Rāmānuja's Vedānta was *viśiṣṭādvaita*, a 'qualified' monism, and Madhva rejected monism altogether: his system stresses the *pañcabheda* or fivefold absolute difference between god and souls, one soul and another, god and matter, soul and matter, and matter and matter.

śrīmadmadhvamate hariḥ paratarah satyaṃ jagat tattvato
bhedo jīvagaṇā harer anucarā nīcoccabhāvagatāḥ |
muktir naijasukhānubhūtir amalā bhaktiś ca tatsādhanaṃ
hy akṣāditritayaṃ pramāṇam akhilāmnāyaikavedyo hariḥ | |

— this is the traditional and oft-quoted verse[4] that lists some of the most prominent characteristics of Madhva's system of thought. The world is real, the souls are the servants of the supreme lord Hari, *bhakti* is the means to liberation, and Hari is the only subject of all scripture. To propagate such ideas it was inevitable that Madhva should break with the orthodoxy into which he was born, just as the Śaiva brahmin Basava did several decades earlier when he organized the Vīraśaiva community in northern Karnataka. But there were two important differences between Basava and Madhva: first, Basava totally rejected the traditional *varṇa* system, whereas Madhva did not; secondly, Basava was not alone but gave form to a socio-religious reform which was already being carried out by a considerable number of like-minded people, whereas Madhva was the originator of a reform and at first had to struggle single-handedly. For the later development of the tradition this meant that the person Madhva, both the historical and the hagiographical, assumed immense importance.

Madhva's hagiography tells us that he was born into the Smārta brahminical theological establishment of his time. In this part of India, all the Smārtas are at least nominally Advaitins, and as Renou (1983: 92–3) has mentioned, their ritualism and religiosity are quite eclectic, while they are often misleadingly portrayed as 'orthodox' in modern literature. Śaṅkara's theory of the absolute as *nirguṇa brahman*, along with his disapproval of the theology of the *āgamas*, probably obstructed the development of a theory of temple ritual, and lent no support to the development of a theology of devotion to any particular god. As a result, Smārta devotionalism remained rather inchoate and eclectic, with a large number of divinities being possible objects of devotion without the theology of any of those divinities being particularly elaborated and developed. In practice, there was (and still is) a semblance of a Śaiva orientation, and Śaṅkara is depicted in popular iconography with the horizontal Śaiva lines of ash on his forehead, although he did not show any penchant towards Śaivism in his authentic writings.

Madhva's philosophical writings show us a radical break with a number of traditional Advaitin tenets, as a result of a fundamentally different understanding of the ontological status of the world and of life in the world. He refused to dismiss the phenomenal world as a mere illusion and asserted its absolute reality in all its diversity. Similarly, for him the absolute being was not *nirguṇa* (which would lead to the philosophical problem of the origin of phenomena which do have characteristics) but, on the contrary, it possessed all possible characteristics to a perfect degree. This irreducibility of empirical reality furthermore led to the assertion of the irreducibility of the soul's individuality: just as each soul leads an individual life in this world, the souls remain separate individuals in the state of final liberation instead of losing their individuality and merging in the *nirguṇa brahman*. What is also evident from Madhva's writings is that he was an immensely well-read person. He employs the whole of his Vedic learning to demonstrate that his doctrine should be considered a reflection of the correct understanding of the Vedic heritage. Thus we see Madhva claiming his doctrine to be Vedic, while on several cardinal issues it was diametrically opposed to the conventional brahminical teachings and practices of his time.

In defence of his position, Madhva followed two lines of argumentation. The first and most formidable was purely rational: a critique of Advaitin epistemology and ontology in which Madhva and his followers made a highly able use of logic. But this was insufficient against the Advaitin doctrine of *māyā*, because logic is based on experience of the phenomenal world, which, according to Advaita, is illusory. The Advaitins claimed that a higher type of knowledge, transcending *māyā*, is found in Vedic revelation, and that the so-called *mahāvākyas* of the Upaniṣads faithfully summarized the whole of Upaniṣadic thought. There is of course a good deal of wishful thinking involved here, since the Upaniṣads do not show a uniformity of thought. Therefore, secondly, Madhva set out to demonstrate that the Advaitin exegesis of scripture is faulty, mainly because the

Advaitins interpreted scriptural passages out of context. Madhva was quick to point out that besides the *abhedaśrutis*, such as *sarvaṃ khalv idaṃ brahma*, there are also *bhedaśrutis*, passages which are hard to explain in a monistic manner. In a great exegetic effort, Madhva and his followers argued that the Vedic truths are Vaiṣṇava truths: the entire Vedic literature points to Viṣṇu as the supreme lord, and acceptance of this tenet implied, for them, that one must accept the theology of Madhva.

On the other hand, Madhva broadened the criterion of what constituted valid scripture to include texts which supported his own views, and this brings us to the question of what is authoritative Vedic literature. Madhva states this explicitly in one of his main works, the *Viṣṇutattvanirṇaya*, where he quotes a verse from the *Brahmāṇḍapurāṇa*:

Ṛgādyā Bhāratam caiva Pañcarātram athākhilam | Mūlarāmāyaṇaṃ caiva Purāṇaṃ caitadātmakam || ye cānuyāyinas tv eṣāṃ sarve te ca sadāgamāḥ |

The four Vedasamhitās, the Mahābhārata, the entire Pañcarātra, the original Rāmāyaṇa, the Purāṇas which are in agreement with these, and all those writings which follow these aforementioned ones are valid scripture.

This is an open-ended definition which allows for the inclusion of many more unnamed writings, provided that these are 'in agreement'. From Jayatīrtha's commentary on this passage we can see what Mādhvas soon considered to be the real criterion: *tatra kās tā Nārāyaṇasya sadāgamaika-vedyatvaṃ pratipādayantyaḥ saduktaya ity ata āha.* Valid scripture is what teaches solely about Nārāyaṇa. (This was taken rather liberally. According to Jayatīrtha, in this same fragment, this criterion also meant that, for example, the Manusmṛti was to be included.) Obviously there was the danger of a circular argument here, but a solution to this was found already by Madhva himself. He had been initiated as a renunciant under the name Pūrṇaprajña and later, when he became an *ācārya*, was renamed Ānandatīrtha, and still later he gave himself the name 'Madhva' and declared that his coming had been foretold in the Ṛgveda. He was an incarnation of Vāyu: the third, after Hanumat and Bhīma. His followers believed him, and this obviously lent much more weight to his views about Vedic religion.

Madhva was very explicit about being an *avatāra*. At the end of the *Viṣṇutattvanirṇaya* he says:

yasya trīny uditāni vedavacane rūpāṇi divyāny alaṃ baṭ taddarśatam eva nihitaṃ devasya bhargo mahat | Vāyo Rāmavaconayaṃ prathamakaṃ pṛkso dvitīyaṃ vapur Madhvo yat tu tṛtīyam etad amunā granthaḥ kṛtaḥ Keśave ||

The greatly splendorous god Vāyu had three divine forms which are mentioned in the Veda: the first was the form that conveyed the words of Rāma (as a message to Sītā, or in the form of the Rāmāyaṇa to students, according to the sub-commentary by Rāghavendrayati), the second form destroyed the army of the Kauravas, and the third form is Madhva,[5] by whom this work was written about Keśava.

This verse echoes parts of the *Baḷitthā-sūkta* (Ṛgveda 1:141), which is quoted in Madhva's *Mahābhāratatātparyanirṇaya* (2:154–8) in a fragment which is presumed to explain the greatness of Vāyu. Numerous portions of the Vedas are obscure; already in ancient times there were great differences of opinion among scholars about how those portions of this holy text are at all to be understood,[6] and the Madhva interpretation of this *sūkta* is an example of how in the course of time creativity has done remarkable things with the eternal Veda. The idea that the Veda would already refer to characters from the Rāmāyaṇa and Mahābhārata demands very much from a historically conscious reader, and the exegesis that supports this idea barely convinces as an example of the common practice of juggling with single syllables that supposedly form abbreviations: for instance, Rāghavendra, and later Śrīnivāsatīrtha, explain the word *pṛkṣa* in this *sūkta* as an abbreviation of *pṛtanākṣayakaram* or 'destroying an army *(pṛtanā)*'. They ask us to assume that the army referred to is that of the Kauravas. If one believes, as many orthodox Hindu scholars do, that all scripture has been given to us by Vedavyāsa, then questions of chronology cease to exist and anything can refer to anything else, provided that there is some theological cogency. In any case, the notion that Madhva was an *avatāra* took root quickly and was elaborated in the *Madhvavijaya*.[7]

The *Madhva-* or *Sumadhvavijaya* of Nārāyaṇapaṇḍitācārya is the hagiographic document which established itself as the main source of information about the life of Madhva and of the miraculous events in it. The author may have lived *ca.* 1295–1370. This *mahākāvya* of 1008 verses in 16 cantos has been published several times and has been translated more than once into Kannada. As I have already dealt in detail with the *Madhvavijaya* elsewhere,[8] I will give here only a few illustrations of how Madhva has been described in this text.

In the first chapter of this text, it is mentioned that Madhva is an *avatāra* of Vāyu. After earlier incarnations as Hanumat and Bhīma, Vāyu returns on earth at Viṣṇu's request to fight the demon Maṇimat, whom Bhīma killed in a previous age and now is reborn as Śaṅkara, who has set out to pervert the minds of people with his crypto-Buddhist teachings. Vāyu descends to earth near Rūpyapīṭha (Udupi), expels the soul that was inhabiting the body of a yet unborn child, and is thus born in a pious brahminical family where he is named Vāsudeva. He grows up a healthy and strong child, and already at a young age he displays feats of remarkable intellect, courage and physical strength. He becomes an embarrassingly good student who understands the purport of ancient texts better than his father and teachers do.

Vāsudeva desires to become a renunciant because he knows that he will earn the respect of people by thus showing his detachment from worldly things. One day, God tells the learned ascetic Acyutaprajña[9] in Udupi that he will know the Lord through a splendid disciple, who is yet to come. Vāsudeva becomes Acyutaprajña's pupil, and after a while God takes possession of a person who tells Acyutaprajña that Vāsudeva is that promised pupil. When Acyutaprajña teaches his pupils the *Iṣṭasiddhi* of Vimuktātman, Vāsudeva explains how the very first verse of this Advaitin work contains thirty-two errors. He also explains the fifth chapter of the Bhāgavatapurāṇa, which he already knew in previous births. Acyutaprajña anoints him as his successor, giving him the name 'Pūrṇaprajña'; later, when he becomes *ācārya*, he receives the name 'Ānandatīrtha'; still later, he gives himself the name 'Madhva'. Many scholars come to test his learning but Madhva defeats them all in debates; some opponents actually surreptitiously flee at night to escape the impending humiliation. A leader of the *māyāvādins* (Advaitins) is defeated by Madhva in a debate. Meanwhile Madhva's books are stolen by other *māyāvādins*, who hope to thus weaken this formidable adversary; but the local king sees to it that the books are returned. On another occasion he declares that the *Viṣṇusahasranāma* has 100 meanings; other brahmins challenge him to demonstrate this, and he challenges them to repeat the meanings which he tells them; he begins with the name '*viśva*', and the brahmins quickly admit defeat.

He goes on a pilgrimage to Badari and from there proceeds to Uttarabadari (northern Badari), where he meets Vedavyāsa, who embraces him and gives him the true knowledge of the *itihāsas*, *purāṇas*, *sūtras* and *Pañcarātra.* He also sees the Lord Nārāyaṇa himself, who requests him to write a *bhāṣya* on the Brahmasūtra. Madhva then writes that *bhāṣya*, which refutes many other corrupt commentaries and itself is irrefutable. He then returns to Udupi, converts his own teacher to his views, and the custom of wearing *mudrā*[10] is instituted.

Several episodes of the *Madhvavijaya* illustrate Madhva's physical prowess. When, one day, Acyutaprajña and Madhva receive their *bhikṣā* (offerings of food), Acyutaprajña is astonished that Madhva eats 200 bananas; Madhva simply explains that the divine force in his belly is the same that consumes the world at the time of *pralaya*. Later, in Goa, he eats 4000 bananas and drinks 30 pitchers of milk. On the coast, the heavy image of Lord Kṛṣṇa, which was worshipped by Rukmiṇī and the *gopikās* and cannot be carried by 30 people, is recovered from a ship, carried by Madhva to Udupi, and installed there in the Kṛṣṇamaṭha. Madhva demonstrates his strength by defeating his disciples in wrestling matches, taking on fifteen of them at a time. But on another occasion he climbs on the back of a small boy and has the boy carry him around a temple. His mystical knowledge of the workings of the world is such that he makes blossoms and fruit appear on a tree by means of his knowledge of music. He demonstrates the effectiveness of the Vedas by having some grains sprout, blossom and bear seed by means of a Vedic *sūkta*. On one occasion he satisfies a group of people with a quantity of food that otherwise would have been sufficient for only a quarter of their number. When, one night, his students have no light to study by, he helps them by producing light from the tip of the nail of his big toe. Various gods and saintly personalities appear in the course of the narrative, praising Madhva and exhorting his students to follow his teachings.

It is necessary to distinguish between, on the one hand, what have probably been Madhva's own intentions and, on the other, what his later followers have made of the new tradition. Madhva himself was a revolutionary character who rebelled against the brahminical orthodoxy into which he was born. His oeuvre and the theology expressed in it are a spectacular intellectual feat and display an independent mind. He is the only of the three major Vedāntācāryas who wrote a commentary on the Ṛgveda, that most holy of orthodox Hindu texts; he is also the only of three who wrote a commentary on the Bhāgavatapurāṇa. He wrote four different commentaries on the Brahmasūtras and two on the Bhagavadgītā, which reveal to us an astute mind with an eye for textual criticism.[11] As we have seen earlier, he accepted 'the entire Pañcarātra' as valid scripture, and his interest in the āgamic tradition is seen in the many quotations from Pañcarātra texts in his commentaries as well as in his *Tantrasārasaṅgraha*, a manual in which he explains how, in his view, the *āgamas* are to be read, and in which he provides details concerning temple construction, the installation of images in temples, the use of mantras and ritual worship; here too he broke with the Śaṅkarite Advaitin tradition. In scriptural matters he was not a diehard conservative, but neither was he willing to neglect the traditional canonical heritage, in which he saw relevance and to which he obviously felt personally attracted. Some of the peculiarities of Madhva's Sanskrit have been traced to his fondness for pre-Pāṇinian usage, which critics in rival schools of

Vedānta found eccentric and which they turned into a target for ridicule.

Madhva's writings give us reason to believe that his views of society were in opposition to the orthodoxy in which he was brought up. He was so staunchly Vaiṣṇava that he wrote a notorious verse in his *Kṛṣṇāmṛtamahārṇava*, saying that when a person's forehead is devoid of the *ūrdhvapuṇḍra*, the vertical Vaiṣṇava sign, it looks like a cremation ground, and if one is so unfortunate as to see that, one should look at the sun to purify one's sight.[12] Here we should recall that in Karnataka the Smārta practice was, and still is, to apply the three horizontal Śaiva lines; the Mādhvas themselves apply their own distinctive single vertical black line or *nāma* on the forehead, to which is often added at the lower end, near the eyebrows, a round dot of *akṣata*, a dark red or blackish substance. Further distinctive outer signs of the Mādhvas are the necklace of *tulasī* beads and the two kinds of *mudrā* or 'seals': marks of the conch and the discus in a very thin paste of *gopicandana* (a fine variety of clay, brought from holy localities) which are applied on the cheekbones with metal stamps, and the *taptamudrā* or similar signs which are branded on the arms.[13]

Madhva also seems to have wanted a redefinition of the concept of *varṇa* in the final chapter of his second commentary on the Bhagavadgītā, the *Bhagavadgītātātparyanirṇaya*, where Kṛṣṇa explains what the four *varṇas* are. Śaṅkara took the word *svabhāvaja*, 'natural, inborn,' in verses like

śamo damas tapaḥ śaucaṃ kṣāntir ārjavam eva ca | jñānaṃ vijñānam āstikyaṃ viprakarma svabhāvajam | | (18:42)

Peacefulness, restraint, austerity, purity, forbearance, uprightness, knowledge, wisdom and piety are the inborn duties of a brahmin.

to refer to the nature of one's caste (*brahmakarma brāhmaṇajāteh karma svabhāvajam*, 'brahmakarma is the natural duty of [those of] brahmin birth'). But the text of the Bhagavadgītā does not mention 'birth' (jāti), and so Madhva felt justified in interpreting *svabhāvajam* as 'originating from one's own individual nature'. The qualities which are listed in these verses as *varṇa* qualities are, in Madhva's view, not collective but individual qualities. Quoting an unnamed source, Madhva adds:

adhikāś ced guṇāḥ śūdre brāhmaṇādiḥ sa ucyate | brāhmaṇo 'pi alpaguṇakaḥ śūdra eveti kīrtitaḥ | naro 'pi yo devaguṇo devo jñeyo nṛtāṃ gataḥ | |

If these qualities are found to a greater extent in a śūdra, he is called a brahmin etc., and a brahmin in whom these qualities are deficient is known to be a śūdra.

Also a man who possesses the qualities of a god is to be known as a god who has assumed manhood.

He furthermore discusses how, although an individual's proclivities are of one kind, and in agreement with one *varṇa* he may take up activities which are characteristic of another *varṇa*; and although people have their inborn proclivities *(naisargikā bhāvāḥ)*, a proclivity that is not inborn (*anisarga)* should also be encouraged if it is a pure and beneficial one; in other words, Madhva was clearly not a conservative in matters of traditionally prescribed *varṇa* behaviour.

The Mādhvas broke away from the brahminical mainstream, but they maintained that not they, but the Smārtas, were deviants. Vaiṣṇava literature was quoted in support of this view, just as typically Vaiṣṇava texts like the Bhagavadgītā eminently suited Madhva's realistic theistic system of thought. The situation was conducive to such a reform. Jainism, the old aristocratic religion of the Kannada land, was very strong in Madhva's home region. (Madhva was born in a village only a few kilometres from the capital of a missionarily inclined Jaina king.) It has been noted by other scholars that two of the main Mādhva temples in the middle of Udupi (dedicated to Ananteśvara and Candreśvara) were originally Jaina temples.[14] A century earlier, the socially revolutionary Vīraśaiva movement had begun in northern Karnataka. Both Jainism and Vīraśaivism are basically egalitarian religious systems which give no position of any particular importance to the brahmin *varṇa* in society.

The Jaina influence is clear from certain doctrinal features in Madhva's writings. Part of Madhva's epistemology (his views about internal perception, *manas* and *mānasapratyakṣa*), his theory of inherent tendencies of the soul, the possibility of *pramā* (correct knowledge) being a *pramāṇa* (means of knowledge), his twofold categorization of the *pramāṇas*, and his doctrine of *saviśeṣābheda* are all departures from earlier Vedānta but were current in Jaina thought already, centuries before Madhva.[15] Madhva did not borrow random notions from Jainism but a coherent system of concepts that supported the development of a school of philosophical realism.

Madhva also composed devotional verses in Sanskrit, such as his *Dvādaśastotras* and *Narasiṃhanakhastuti*, and the Mādhvas see this as the beginning of a development that led to the institution of the *haridāsas*, the composers of devotional Vaiṣṇava hymns in Kannada, which were meant for the common people. The Kannada Haridāsas obviously were largely inspired by the earlier Āḻvārs in Tamil as well as by the Vīraśaiva Vacanakāras, but in any case it is true that the Kannada Haridāsas explicitly owe allegiance to the school of Madhva, and several hymns by Purandaradāsa and Kanakadāsa—the foremost Haridāsas of the sixteenth century, the golden age of Haridāsa literature—openly praise 'Madhvamuni' as a saviour who has brought the light of true devotion into the world. Mādhva authors of the period were divided into two categories: the *dāsakūṭa*, who wrote hymns in Kannada and who could be from any caste, and the *vyāsakūṭa*, who wrote learned treatises in Sanskrit and were brahmins. Occasionally, a person could belong to both these *kūṭas*, e.g. Vādirāja, who was a highly gifted author in both Sanskrit and Kannada, and who also composed a work in Tulu 'for the benefit of outcastes', as his hagiographer says.[16] Although the Mādhva leadership gave some recognition to the lower castes (as well as to women) and to their creative contributions, the traditional *cāturvarṇya*—which according to the Bhagavadgītā had been instituted by God himself—remained, and thus from a social point of view Mādhva Vaiṣṇavism seems to have occupied, at least for some time, a half-way position between earlier Smārta Hinduism on the one hand and Jainism and Vīraśaivism on the other.

It is not generally known outside the Mādhva community that this community is not a monolithic whole. In the fourth volume of his *History of Indian Philosophy*, S. N. Dasgupta mentions the Mādhva *guruparamparā*, quoting R. G. Bhandarkar.[17] Bhandarkar gave this list on the basis of lists which he found in *maṭhas* in Pune and Belgaum; but what he did not realize was that there is not just one Mādhva *guruparamparā*, and that the list he was given was that of the Uttarādimaṭha, the largest single *maṭha*, to which most of the Mādhvas in Maharashtra and in eastern and northern Karnataka adhere. Actually several spiritual lineages go back directly to Madhva, e.g. those of the eight *maṭhas* of Udupi.

There are three quite distinct social subdivisions among the Mādhvas, which we may call sub-castes. One immediately obvious distinction is that of the mother-tongues of the members of those subdivisions, namely Tulu, Kannada and Konkani. A Marathi-speaking group has merged with the Kannada-speaking group. Each of these three groups is organized in a system of adherence to *maṭhas*. The dozen Taulava or Tulu-speaking *maṭhas* are all named after the town where they were founded (e.g. Palimāru, Puttige, Subrahmanya, Pejāvara). The Deśastha or Kannada-Marathi Mādhvas have a few *maṭhas*, of which the Uttarādimaṭha is the largest; the origin of this name is unclear.[18] The Uttarādimaṭha claims that it is the original *maṭha* of Madhva and his teacher (although both of them were Taulavas from the west coast), that it was founded by the Lord Viṣṇu himself, and that over 80 per cent of all Mādhvas are its followers (Rao 1984: 27–8). Also the Konkani-speaking Mādhvas or Gauḍa Sārasvata Brahmins (who are colloquially referred to as 'GSBs', and who according to legend have migrated from Bengal), have two *maṭhas*. The three subdivisions have different customs and mores; for instance, the Taulavas generally do not allow the GSBs to have meals together with them on auspicious occasions, because the GSBs also eat fish. For this reason some Taulava Mādhvas do not consider the GSBs true brahmins. As commonly happens in such situations, the GSBs have their own reasoning for considering themselves 'superior'. While the GSBs tend to be a religiously self-contained community, the Taulavas and Deśasthas are more sought after for priestly services by other communities. There are numerous other cultural differences between these three subdivisions.

All Mādhvas respect a common corpus of canonical texts and commentaries written on those texts, as well as a considerable quantity of later literature, largely devotional, in Kannada and Sanskrit, which is imbued with a Mādhva world view. But there are different attitudes with regard to how this literary heritage is to be integrated within the whole of the doctrine that governs the lives of the believers. Among the Deśasthas, we see a tendency towards a more strictly literal and legalistic interpretation of the entire textual corpus, whereas among the Taulavas, the later commentaries are no doubt of great importance but are considered theological and philosophical documents which are open to theological discussion. They are not considered quasi-legal documents of absolute binding validity. An incident in the late 1960s illustrates this difference in attitudes. There exist two recensions of the writings of Madhva: one is popularly known as the *pracalitapāṭha* or 'current reading', which was used by Jayatīrtha, the most popular commentator of Madhva's writings; the other is known as the *mūlapāṭha* or 'original reading', which has been preserved in the oldest existing manuscript of Madhva's works, written by Hṛṣikeśatīrtha, one of Madhva's direct disciples. When Hṛṣikeśa's manuscript was edited and published, there was unrest among Mādhva scholars: not only were there differences in the text of the known writings of Madhva, but the manuscript also contained two smaller writings of Madhva which were previously unknown. Rather than rejoice in the discovery of these two new texts, traditionalists objected that these texts could not be real because Jayatīrtha had not commented on them. (Ironically, Jayatīrtha mentions that he was aware of the existence of the *mūlapāṭha*, and that he used a different recension.) Philologically, it seems that the *mūlapāṭha* gives more coherent and therefore truer readings than the *pracalitapāṭha*. Typically, the opposition to the *mūlapāṭha* was stronger among the Deśasthas than among the Taulavas, because Jayatīrtha is a link in the Deśastha *guruparamparā* and still later sub-commentaries are largely based on Jayatīrtha's commentaries. The *mūlapāṭha* versus *pracalitapāṭha* issue has never been decisively resolved.

and till today there are authors who refuse to acknowledge that Madhva has left forty works.

Other cultural differences include different views about the place of the Mādhvas in society. There is an ongoing debate about the definition of a 'Mādhva': can only brahmins be considered Mādhvas, or does anyone who believes in the tenets of Madhva's religion qualify to be called a Mādhva, irrespective of his standing in *varṇa* and *jāti* hierarchies? Here the Deśasthas apparently tend more towards an exclusively brahminical use of the term 'Mādhva' than the Taulavas do, though there is no absolute, clear-cut division on this matter. In any case it is clear that the Deśasthas are far more rigid in maintaining norms of orthodox behaviour both within their community (e.g. demanding an austere lifestyle from widows, involving the shaving of their heads, etc.) as well as in their relationships with persons outside the community (i.e. maintaining the traditional rules of ritual purity in contacts with others). Thus we have the odd phenomenon that the sixteenth-century Kanakadāsa, who extolled Madhva in his writings and declared that Madhva's teachings are the way to salvation, is respected by many Mādhva brahmins who, however, will not consider him a 'Mādhva' because he is not a brahmin. On the other hand, Kanakadāsa has been commemorated with an architectural peculiarity—a 'chink'—in the holiest of Mādhva temples, the Kṛṣṇamaṭha at Udupi.[19]

The differences between Taulavas and Deśasthas are illustrated by another incident which took place in Bangalore several years ago. The head of Pejāvara Maṭha in Udupi, the learned Śrī Viśveśatīrtha, during one of his visits to Bangalore, not only visited a Harijana colony but actually entered the dwellings of some Harijanas, and this led to an outcry in the Mādhva community of Bangalore. The incident became the subject of a short study by a European sociologist of religion, whose findings were later published in the form of an article (van der Burg 1991: 205–36). One crucial matter which the sociologist overlooked was that behind this commotion lay the fact that Viśveśatīrtha is a Taulava, and that the local Deśasthas of Bangalore took up this issue as proof that they were socially more exclusive and therefore 'purer' and 'better' Mādhvas than the Taulavas. The sociologist obviously was unaware of this point because the Mādhvas preserve their solidarity as a group *vis-à-vis* outsiders, and hence the questionnaire which he drew up contained no questions about the matter of subdivisional differences.

It would be very wrong, however, to conclude from this incident that Śrī Viśveśatīrtha is a progressive religious leader. He strives to overcome Mādhva factionalism, and in practice this means that he is the most conservative of the eight *maṭhādhipatis* of Udupi. At least one of his writings shows a tendency towards xenophobia,[20] and he is a publicly active supporter of the 'Sangh Parivar'.[21] Whereas he is interested in uniting the Mādhvas and also Hindudom as a whole, his militant hatred of Islam is well known. For instance, he was arrested at Ayodhya before the demolition of the Babri Masjid, and he was also present when the mosque was demolished. He also formally initiated the right-wing political activist Umā Bhāratī as a Hindu renunciant.[22] Viśveśatīrtha's militancy and his open association with the Sangh Parivar appear not to have tarnished his image in the Mādhva community as a whole, although the famous writer U. R. Anantha Murthy, who for some time was his follower, openly broke with him, saying that he was unfit to be a *dharmaguru*.

To sum up, the following conclusions about the Mādhva tradition seem reasonable. Madhva drew an appreciable deal of material from Jaina philosophy, which was the leading school of realistic philosophy in his time and region, to build up his own realistic Vedānta, and it seems that he believed that this philosophical realism was needed to justify *bhakti*, which occupies a place of cardinal importance in his theology. Not only had he new ideas about what had to be considered valid scripture, he also declared that the Rāmāyaṇa of Vālmīki was not the original text. He quoted from texts which he considered authoritative but which apparently nobody else had ever seen, and this led to the accusation that he fabricated his own authoritative texts to fit his own needs.[23] Some of his ideas meant a profound break with the orthodox mainstream of his time, and he dismissed the worries of the doubtful by stating that his words could be taken as authoritative because he was an incarnation of Vāyu. He was a highly creative thinker who tried to encompass in one theological framework a huge canonical heritage, starting with the Ṛgveda and ending with texts which were recent in his time, and he invited his readers to read and rethink the whole corpus along with him. He wished to liberalize society through a new application of the concept of *varṇa*.

Ironically, Madhva's claim to being an *avatāra* seems to have frustrated part of his purpose. After his apotheosis came the apotheoses of others less creative who did not share his innovative tendencies. Rather than inspiring their followers to active thinking, the statements of these latter *devāṃśabhūtas* acquired a near-absolute authority. With this there developed a scholasticism which is almost Semitic in character, with earlier authors in the tradition, particularly Jayatīrtha (who later was thought of as an incarnation of Indra),[24] assuming positions similarly unquestionable to that of Biblical prophets. The Mādhva way of life is grounded in this devotion to the gurus of the tradition, which is one of the mainstays of a distinct

Mādhva identity. Outwardly, the Mādhvas give great importance to orthodox forms of social behaviour, and this puritanism, together with the heavy scholasticism of their polemics against rival schools of thought, suggests that the Mādhvas are perhaps, collectively, historically aware of their specialness in Hinduism and concerned about proving their credentials as orthodox Vaidikas.

Relatively few modern studies of the tradition have been undertaken, and relatively little is known about it outside the community that sets it forth. This is in spite of the role of some of its members in the development of later Hinduism (since, I take it, they have not participated as a block) and its prominence in south-western India. But the faith of the Mādhvas is strong, and recent events in Karnataka suggest that they are likely to assert their presence even more strongly.

Notes

1. Other dates are also found in secondary literature, but those given above seem firmly established on the basis of literary and epigraphical evidence. Cf. Bannanje Govindacharya (1984: 38–40) and Siauve (1968: 4–5).
2. Siauve (1968: 11, n. 4) quotes C. M. Padmanabha Char's *The Life and Teachings of Sri Madhvacharya* (Coimbatore, 1909), who also mentions that nowadays the *Bhāgavata-sampradāya* has become so similar to the Mādhvas that the two groups intermarry.
3. 'Madhva himself says litle or nothing which may be interpreted as a direct attack upon his predecessor Rāmānuja', writes Dasgupta (1975: 94–5). Later, as the schools of both Rāmānuja and Madhva were further elaborated, polemical exchanges did take place.
4. This verse has been ascribed to Vyāsatīrtha, but its authorship has not been established yet.
5. *ānandarūpasya Hareḥ pratipādakaśāstranirmātṛ*, says Rāghavendra. In another sub-commentary, Śrīnivāsatīrtha tries to derive an etymology from this phrase for the name 'Madhva'.
6. See for instance Macdonell (1990: 49–50).
7. Cf. the first chapter, and also explicitly in later verses, e.g. 2:26: *Vāyur ayam āvirabhūt pṛthivyām*.
8. Zydenbos (1994).
9. In my article (Zydenbos 1994) I gave the name of Madhva's teacher as 'Acyutaprekṣa', as most authors do, following *Madhvavijaya* 4:6. But Bannanje Govindacharya (1984: 41–2) has argued quite convincingly on the basis of Nārāyaṇapaṇḍitācārya's own commentary and other documents that 'Acyutaprajña' was the teacher's true name.
10. See below.
11. See e.g. Zydenbos (1997a: 55–63) on how Madhva's interpretation of

vyaktopāsana and *avyaktopāsana* differs from the common one of the followers of Śaṅkara.

12. *ūrdhvapuṇḍravihīnasya smaśānasadṛśaṃ mukham / avalokya mukhaṃ teṣām ādityam avalokayet // Kṛṣṇāmṛtamahārṇava* vs. 217.
13. In my earlier article (Zydenbos 1994: 173, n. 11) the descriptions of the two types of *mudrā* have erroneously been mixed together.
14. Siauve (1968: 8, n. 4) and Rāmacandrarāv (1968: 44).
15. I have dealt with this matter in detail in my article 'On the Jaina Background of Dvaitavedānta'. See Zydenbos (1991).
16. At present I am about to complete an English translation of this hagiographical text, the *Śrīmadvādirājaguruvaracaritāmṛta* of Rāmacandra. The hagiography of Vādirāja has been discussed in detail in my forthcoming article 'Vādirāja (1480–1600), saint de la tradition mādhva du Karnataka'. See Zydenbos (1997b).
17. Dasgupta (1975, 4: 56). An alternative list is also mentioned, drawn up by one Baladeva, which appears to show the link which the Gauḍīya Vaiṣṇavas make with Madhva; the same list, with only minor differences in two of the names, is part of the longer list of names given as the *guruparamparā* in the publications of the International Society for Krishna Consciousness (ISKCON).
18. C. R. Rao's short book *Srimat Uttaradi Mutt* (1984) is an illustration of how the rivalries between Mādhva *maṭhas* and between Mādhva social divisions are argued out in quite bizarre and hateful ways.
19. Quite unconventionally, the image of Kṛṣṇa in the Kṛṣṇamaṭha faces west, and the traditional explanation for this is as follows: Kanakadāsa, of ritually low birth, was not allowed to enter the temple and see the image which Madhva had installed there. He then sang hymns to the god while standing outside the temple, and the image of the god responded by turning around in the direction where Kanakadāsa was standing and breaching the temple wall, so that Kanakadāsa could see the image from outside the building. A chink in the wall, directly opposite the image of Kṛṣṇa and known as the 'Kanakana kiṇḍi' or 'chink of Kanaka', is still there and is prominently marked for visitors.
20. In a small collection of essays on the Mahābhārata he mentions that at Kurukṣetra Jarāsandha, 'overpowered by Kṛṣṇa, requested the king of Gāndhāra (present Afghanistan) to assist him with soldiers for his selfish benefit; thus the great sinner Jarāsandha did not desist from casting aside patriotism and accepting the help of foreigners to plunder his fatherland' (1984: 49–50). He also urges officials 'to prevent citizens from betraying their country with the help of foreigners' (23).
21. The collective name for various related right-wing Hindu organizations, such as the RSS, Vishwa Hindu Parishad, Bharatiya Janata Party, the student organization ABVP, etc.
22. *Hinduism Today* magazine, front page, September 1993. This was brought to my attention by Ms. K. Komenda of Santa Barbara.

23. Recently a new, full-length study on this contentious matter has appeared by Mesquita (1997).
24. '... an avatar of Indra with Aavesha of Sesha and blessed by goddess Durga (Sri Mahalakshmi)' (Rao 1984: 38–9).

References

Bannanje Govindacharya. 1984. *Madhvacharya*. Udupi: Sri Pejawar Mutt.

Dasgupta, S. N. 1975. *History of Indian Philosophy*. Vol. 4. Reprint. New Delhi: Motilal Banarsidass.

Macdonell, Arthur A. 1990. *A History of Sanskrit Literature*. Reprint. New Delhi: Motilal Banarsidass.

Mesquita, Roque. 1997. *Madhva und seine unbekannten literarischen Quellen: Einige Beobachtungen*. Wien: Gerold.

Rāmacandrarāv, S. K. 1968. *Pūrṇaprajña-praśasti*. Mysore: Geetha Book House.

Rao, C. R. 1984. *Srimat Uttaradi Mutt*. Bangalore: The Author.

Renou, Louis. 1983. *L, 'hindouisme*. Paris: Presses Universitaires de France.

Siauve, S. 1968. *La doctrine de Madhva*. Pondichéry: Institut Français d'Indologie.

Śrī Viśveśatīrtha. 1984. *Mahābhāratada Beḷaku*. Bangalore: Akhila Bhārata Mādhva Mahāmaṇḍala.

van der Burg, C. J. G. 1991. A Traditional Élite in a Transitional Society: Bangalore Brahmins and the Dilemma of Social Interaction. In *Gender, Caste and Power in South Asia: Social Status and Mobility in a Transitional Society*, ed. J. P. Neelsen, 205–36. New Delhi: Manohar.

Zydenbos, Robert J. 1991. On the Jaina Background of Dvaitavedānta. *Journal of Indian Philosophy* 19: 249–71.

———. 1994. Some Examples from Mādhva Hagiography. In *According to Tradition: Hagiographical Writing in India*, ed. W. M. Callewaert and R. Snell, 169–89. Wiesbaden: Harrassowitz.

———. 1997a. Is Kṛṣṇa Seen Or Not? Madhvācārya on *Bhagavadgītā* 12:1. *Journal of Vaiṣṇava Studies* 5.3: 55–63.

———. 1997b. Vādirāja (1480–1600), saint de la tradition mādhva du Karnataka. In *Constructions hagiographiques dans le monde indien. Entre mythe et histoire*, ed. Françoise Mallison. Paris: École des Hautes Études.

Forging Community: The Guru in a Seventeenth-century Vaiṣṇava Hagiography

VASUDHA DALMIA

Modern Hinduism is based to a large extent on great monotheistic devotional movements. Many of these, emerging from the South, swept through and occupied North India from the fifteenth century onwards. Transformations in these great movements which set in during the eighteenth century with colonialism, and the subsequent reconfigurations, within them, have never really been subjected to close scrutiny. Nor has there been a systematic study of the theological and sociological relationship of the devotional communities to each other and to the brahmanical orthodoxy of the day.

The movements themselves fall into two somewhat heterogeneous clusters. The first cluster consists of those communities of believers that practised *nirguṇa* or aniconic devotion, the second comprises communities which believed in *saguṇa* or iconic worship. There were antagonisms within these clusters as well as between them. What were the bonds which forged the respective devotional communities, what made for the similarities, and what distinguished them from each other? What, if any, were the features shared by the two clusters? *Saguṇa* and *nirguṇa* are valid theological classifications, but should they also be extended to the social dimension?

Scholars today often suggest that belief in a personal god, in reincarnation, and in *varṇāśramadharma*[1] are to be regarded as some of the main features of the vastly influential *saguṇa bhakti* or iconic devotional traditions. With the exception of the belief in *varṇāśramadharma*, as I hope to show below, it would be possible to accept these features as characteristic of the *saguṇa* traditions. However, the question is whether these features alone justify the contemporary view, which is to see these movements as brahmanical, catering only to the élites, and ultimately fathering what is today known as 'Hindutva'.[2]

An approach which confounds 'Hindutva' with the loose coalition which is modern Hinduism can, I would suggest, at best be described as reductivist. A perspective so coloured by contemporary prejudices can only serve to distort rather than clear the view. In fact, much spadework remains to be done before we can even begin to formulate satisfactory questions, leave alone answers, regarding religious constellations in post-medieval India and their relationship to Hindu formations today. How elitist were these *saguṇa bhakti* formations and in what relationship did they stand to the orthodoxy of the day? The information we have at this stage is tentative; it has to be drawn from texts which speak, in however convention-ridden a manner, about actual people and the social groups initiating and participating in the fledgling movements. In reviewing the representation of community formation in a central text from the Vallabha *sampradāya*—one of the Vaiṣṇava *saguṇa bhakti* traditions which emerged at the end of the fifteenth century—what I shall be putting forward, then, are explorations rather than final results. My focus will be on the guru as the charismatic figure in the process of winning over disciples and welding them into fellowship.

The four great Vaiṣṇava communities, or *catuḥsampradāya* as they were collectively known, existed in some kind of a loose coalition from the seventeenth century onwards.[3] The life-spans of the founders of two of the most prominent movements, Caitanya (1476–1533) and Vallabha (1478–1530) were almost coterminous. The remarkable coincidence of the rise and spread of their *sampradāyas*, as also their relationship to each other, await detailed study.[4] The founders' decisive role in the actual formation of community has also tended to be overlooked by scholars. This is because more attention has been devoted to the *nirguṇa* or aniconic devotional traditions—which were more obviously centred around the figure of the guru.[5] It is certainly true that in the *saguṇa bhakti* traditions there were a number of other authoritative instances which bound the devotional community and embedded it in a tradition which claimed immemorial existence. Apart from the central image or icon of the deity worshipped, there were the older scriptures—the *Bhāgavatapurāṇa* for the Krishnaite and the *Rāmāyaṇa* for the Ramaite traditions—which could be viewed as fountainheads of the newly forming canons. Yet, though linking up with the older canonic texts, the founders of the new *sampradāyas* were opening up radically new paths which were also to find expression in popular literary genres. Two other categories of religious literature proliferated under the patronage of the *sampradāya*, that of the *pada* or verse composed for singing; and the hagiography, termed *vārtā* by the Vallabhites.[6] Both addressed a completely different audience than did the Sanskrit works. This audience was often a non-literate one, and the transmission of these literatures required congregational activity, since they were primarily oral in character. The *vārtā* literature is particularly valuable for the investigation in this essay. It contains a mass of information about the social and political formations of the day, but most of all it offers insights into the nature of the popular appeal of the founding figures and the ideologies they embodied.

The first two preceptors of the *sampradāya*, Vallabha as a migrant from the South and his son Viṭṭhala (1515–85), had written learned treatises in Sanskrit, the pan-Indian mode of communication. From the third generation onwards, Brajbhāṣā, which was understood and spoken by a majority of the following, took over as the literary and liturgical language. The *padas*, devotional verse, of poets who later came to be known collectively as the *aṣṭachāp*, eight seals, vividly expressed an emotional relationship to the lord. This relationship was newly vested with a literary-religious aesthetics of its own. These *padas* became part of the official canon, endowing both the language and the *sampradāya* with new prestige. The earliest extended narrative prose in Brajbhāṣā, relating the lives of devotees, was also a major literary contribution. This popular narrative genre, *bāt* or *vārtā*—loosely translatable as tale—which was taken over and transformed for this purpose, had originally consisted of incidents strung together, chiefly with the aim of sustaining suspense as to the outcome of the story. These were now endowed with a new didactic goal. Tales which related the lives of devotees who had the fortune to be initiated by the first two preceptors were collected, and then ordered and enriched with a commentary in the century and a half following Vallabha.[7]

The *Puṣṭimārg*, or 'way of fulfilment', as the *sampradāya* came to be known, boasts of two major hagiographic compilations. The first relates *prasaṅgas* or episodes in the lives of 84 followers of Ācāryajī, or preceptor (as Vallabha was called in the narrative). The second is a collection of the lives of the 252, i.e. three times 84, followers of his son Viṭṭhala. In this essay I concentrate upon the first collection, the *Caurāsī vaiṣṇavan kī vārtā*, or tales of the 84 Vaiṣṇavas, of which a good edition based on the manuscripts of 1695 and 1721 is fortunately available.[8] The lives of the *bhaktas* as related in these compendia came to form an explicit part of the official canon. They were *daivī jīvas*, godly beings, whose specific destiny it was to serve according to the will of the lord and the guru. Their peculiar form of bondage to this will, and to each other, served to distinguish them from all the other communities surrounding them.

Hagiography as Canon

According to the tradition current in the *sampradāya* and recorded in the second compilation, the *vārtās* came into being as part of the pious ritual of telling and hearing of the lives of the men and women who had first formed the core of the community. Ācāryajī himself had been known to indulge in this virtuous pastime, but it became the particular addiction of Gokulnāthjī (1557–1640) who, in the third generation, came luckily to possess a version written by an ardent devotee. This written version was reduplicated and added to, till his nephew and pupil Harirāyjī (1590–1721!), in the fourth generation, placed the episodes within the framework of a *Bhāv prakāś* or commentary. This commentary related details of the previous lives of the devotees, thus motivating the course of events related in the main *vārtā*.[9] It added incidents from the lives of those connected with them, and interpreted the whole in the light of theological developments in the late seventeenth century.[10]

In his commentary Harirāyjī drew an explicit axiom—he called it *siddhānta*—from each life, and it was with this that he rounded up each *vārtā*. It was the *siddhānta* that endowed the compendium with lasting value and raised it to canonical status, for it was here that the teachings of Ācāryajī, his charisma and authority, were explicitly articulated in the life of the devotee. This is how the compendium introduces itself in the *Bhāv prakāś* of Harirāyjī: as *bhagavadvārtā*, or godly discourse, in stature and splendour higher than the *Bhāgavatapurāṇa* itself, or Ācāryajī 's commentary thereof, the *Subodhinī*. It called forth ecstatic listening:

> So one day while discoursing on the eighty-four Vaiṣṇavas, Śrī Gokulnāth was so immersed in *rasa*, pleasure, that he heeded not to [the daily ritual of] the telling of the *kathā*, the tales of the *Subodhinī* and midnight approached. Then one Vaiṣṇava asked Śrī Gokulnāth, Maharājādhirāj, when will you relate the tales today ? Midnight is past. Then with his illustrious mouth Śrī Gokulnāth said, you must take all fruits [of the *kathā*] to be in the discourse on the Vaiṣṇavas. There is no other *padārtha*, principle, besides the Vaiṣṇavas. This is the path of *puṣṭi*, fulfilment, which gains fruition through the Vaiṣṇavas. Ācāryajī himself used to say, Damlā [the name of his first disciple], this path has been manifested for you. Hence the discourse on the Vaiṣṇavas is to be understood as supreme. The eighty-four Vaiṣṇavas are to be considered foremost in the *nirguṇa* or qualityless aspect of Ācāryajī. (2)[11]

Thus the central importance of the tale of the devotees, for whom the path was created and who, by moving on it, kept it intact. However, the listeners and readers of the compendium were ever reminded that the life of the devotee, as centrally constituent of the canon, was not related in and for itself but selected and steered by the guru. It was the charisma he radiated which formed the central focus of the compendium.

Since the individual *vārtās* can stem from different stages in the evolution of the community, they are not always theologically consistent or homogenous in style and perspective. Inevitably, there are certain contradictions and tensions, as also an occasional need to interpret and temper the original radical message. Vallabha's teachings are sometimes overlaid with the workings of the much more sensuous Gosāīṁjī, as Viṭṭhala was called, who was said to incorporate *parakīyā bhāva*— the extramarital erotic relationship to the lord as beloved and as one path of access to the lord. Later redactions also tended to place Gosāīṁjī at par with his father, or even at times to supersede him. Right at the beginning of the compendium, for instance, the first disciple, Dāmodardās Harsānī, is made to recognize the primacy of Gosāīṁjī after Vallabha. However, obviously in some faithfulness to the historic situation, Dāmodardās cannot be kept from chiding the new incumbent for, upon occasion, simply whiling away time in laughter. It is, as he points out, a serious and painful task that Gosāīṁjī has taken upon himself; it demands study, self-control and concentration.

Ācāryajī as Mediator of Direct Access to the Lord and as Identical with the Lord

The main *vārtā* text begins by proclaiming that the way of *bhakti* was created for Damlā or Dāmodardās Harsānī. However, it is at pains to emphasize the prime role of the guru as mediator. Before initiating Damlā, Ācāryajī is to be seen steeped in anxiety:

> There this anxiety grew in Ācāryajī. Why? Ṭhākurjī, the lord, has ordered that *jīvas*, human souls, be bound to him (*brahmasambandha*), but as Ācāryajī reflected, if human souls are full of *doṣa*, impurities, and Srīpuruṣottama is the treasure of good qualities, how can this binding take place. As this anxiety grew, he became exceedingly restless.
>
> At this moment, and at once Ṭhākurjī manifested himself and asked Ācāryajī, why are you so restless and anxious? Then Ācāryajī himself said, you know the *svarūpa*, self-form or image, of human souls, it is full of impurities. So how can this binding with you take place? Then Ṭhākurjī said, if you impart the name to human souls then all their impurities will be checked, therefore accept them as your own [the term used is *aṅgīkār kar*]. (4)

It thus becomes clear that only when Ācāryajī mediates and hands over a devotee to Ṭhākurjī, does he become the eternal concern of the lord.

It is Ācāryajī who decides what form of initiation is best suited to a particular devotee, and what kind of *sevā* or service to the lord he is best capable of fulfilling thereafter.

Initiation consisted of (1) *ṇam nivedan* or *nām sunāna*, that is, communicating the name of the lord to the devotee; (2) *brahma-sambandha*, imparting the *mantra*; and, finally (3) *lāljī padhrānā*, presenting a *svarūpa* or self-image of the lord. Not all three were followed with each devotee, and the kind of initiation determined the kind of *sevā* to be undertaken by the devotee.

The *sevā* at home, as described in the *vārtā*, was a private, even secret, ritual, intensely intimate and tender. No priestly mediation was necessary. *Karmakāṇḍa*, and brahmans who specialized in it—as the tales are at pains to emphasize—were absolute anathema to Ācāryajī. The *sevā* could even be idiosyncratic, provided it was performed with intense devotion. Once a *sevak* had proved his or her mettle, then it was in this private sphere that Ṭhākurjī himself began to hold communion with the devotee and communicate his wishes. *Sānubhāvatā janānā*, or causing experience of the lord, is the term that the *vārtā* uses for this communion. This intimate experience of the lord was the prime fruit of the path. However, even here Ācāryajī remained mediatory, he was present even in his absence. If a devotee disregarded some intimate need of Ṭhākurjī, he complained immediately to Ācāryajī or Gosāīṁjī, who then reprimanded and corrected him.[12] This form of domestic devotion, this intense immediacy of experience—at once intimate and transcendent, unmediated by brahmanical ritual, not requiring years of withdrawal, asceticism and self discipline—seems commonplace to us today. It needs to be stressed that it was obviously the radical innovation of its time.

The stories relate what befell devotees from the time that they had been initiated and received instructions on *sevā* till they attained the state of grace. The devotees were by no means perfect models of virtue. If there were some amongst them who followed a relatively straight path, there were those who faltered, fell, and who had to be picked up. It was left to Ācāryajī to intervene and correct them. Often, their failings were then highlighted, for these served to substantiate a *siddhānta* more effectively than virtues.

Ācāryajī's following was numerous and heterogeneous in its composition. His followers came from all walks of life and from a variety of castes—mostly lower to middling.[13] In principle, the path was open to all. However, *jāti* rules were observed in qualified form: in fact information on the *jāti* of the follower was scrupulously documented in the *vārtās*. But even those regarded as entirely inauspicious and marginal could be integrated into the community by Ācāryajī's mediation and gain a privileged place within it. When initiating a follower from one of the lower castes, Ācāryajī would ask the question: how will you carry out the *sevā* ritual in your environment? The devotee-to-be is inevitably reassuring that he will distance himself from non-Vaiṣṇavas, as also from other varieties of Vaiṣṇavas.

Initiation into the *sampradāya*, with its scrupulous attention to details of personal purity and morality, then, clearly signified upward mobility for the clean *śūdra* castes. The founder of a new *sampradāya* had to have something new to offer, and this ensured a radical flexibility, at least in the early stages of community formation. Ācāryajī was certainly aware of Shastric norms. But it was against these that he explicitly set up new norms which, he claimed, were based on practice, and which he knew to be radical in their departure from the old. What was regarded as orthodoxy or custom, *ved aur lok*, was invoked negatively time and again.

The devotee could share his or her life in *sevā*, which formed the kernel of human existence, only with those who were similarly disposed. If family members dissented or even went so far as to oppose the initiation, and the new way of life which followed upon it, some kind of separation was called for, often within the house. This sometimes meant that the devotee would have to separate his or her kitchen from that of the rest of the family, if the family could not be persuaded to follow the same path, or if Ācāryajī declared that they were not *daivī jīvas*. Ācāryajī did not tolerate even the barest suggestion of asceticism, and clearly this has to be understood as part of his determined opposition to the practice of certain *nirguṇa sampradāyas*. The family setting was important for the community. However, the family in its turn had to be amenable to integration within the greater social unit which was the community.

The figure of Vallabha in the *vārtās* comes across, then, not so much as the learned Paṇḍit and theologian as much as the popular, charismatic teacher to be observed in his manifold dealings with his disciples.[14] Ācāryajī often accosts them on the many journeys that he makes. At the beginning of the compendium we are told that he thrice made the *pṛthvī parikrama*, circumambulation of the world. Considering the arduousness of the routes that led to the great pilgrim centres, we find Ācāryajī setting out on these long journeys, surprisingly often, either to Dvārikā, Purī or, in one instance, to the South. As other sources specify, in all Ācāryajī spent nineteen years, from the founding of the *sampradāya* in 1493 to 1512, roaming over the subcontinent.

The *vārtās* remain somewhat ambiguous as to the nature of Ācāryajī's connection with Jagannāthdhām and Dvārikā. He is often to be found in one of these centres, attracting new followers and, surely in some measure, deriving his authority from the charisma radiating from the deities there. In some of the tales the devotees are made to realize that he is not only mediator to the lord but in fact identical with him. Thus the *vārtā* of Gopāldās Baṁsvāṛe, Khatrī, relates how Gopāldās wins over two influential devotees by revealing to them that Ācāryajī is in fact Raṇchoṛjī himself: '*Aṛel meṁ Śrīraṇchoṛjī pragaṭ bhaye haiṁ. So sab soṁ bolat batrāt haiṁ.*' (168) Śrīraṇchoṛjī has manifested himself in Aṛel and he talks and holds converse with all. And indeed Ācāryajī obliges these devotees by appearing as Raṇchoṛjī, divining and resolving all their secret doubts. In other episodes, which take place either in Dvārikā or on the way to it, Raṇchoṛjī is demoted to the status of a slightly subsidiary manifestation. The case of the lord in Purī is similar. In the *vārtā* of the two brothers Jagannāth Jośī and Narhari Jośī, sent by their mother to Aṛel to become disciples of Ācāryajī's, we hear that he himself has, in fact, left for Puruṣottampurī to obtain *darśan* of Śrī Jagannāthjī. For fear of their mother the brothers follow Ācārayajī to Purī. When they find him, he asks in all innocence—have you already been to the temple? The brothers obligingly run there, to find Ācāryajī standing next to the deity. Has he taken another route to the temple and overtaken them, they wonder. They run back to him, to find him seated as they had left him. The two brothers pray to him: '*ham ajñānī haiṁ, jo sandeh kiyo, āpu sākṣāt puruṣottam ho*' (188), we are ignorant to have harboured doubt. You yourself are Puruṣottam. The guru is represented as omnipresent and closely associated, if not identical, with the great Vaiṣṇava deities: he is capable of divining thoughts, forecasting events and performing any number of miracles almost casually. And this happens early in the tradition, since this information is offered by the *vārtā* text, not the *Bhāv prakāś*.

But it is not Ācāryajī's ability to perform miracles which is highlighted in the *vārtās*; nor that of his followers, who seem to imbibe, as casually, the same capacity from him. Ācāryajī's power is not to be confused with mere *siddhis* or magic of lower varieties. The *vārtās* take pain to establish his distance from this kind of wonder-working and the devotees are, in fact, positively discouraged from interfering in the way of the world by performing any sort of miracle. For one thing, miracles disturb the normal run of things because they put more emphasis on worldly gains; for another, they mean that either Ṭhākurjī or Ācāryajī or even both exert themselves on the devotee's behalf.[15] Therefore, restraint is to be exercised.

Ācāryajī's primary task in the *vārtās* is to attract and hold followers. He comes across as wise, tolerant, compassionate, full of *vātsalya*, himself a living representation and model for the central form of relating to the child Kṛṣṇa. He comes to stand for compassion with the downtrodden, for people in the extremes of sorrow; but most of all for people looking for the truth. To these he opens the way for authentic religious experience.

He is to be seen at dawn, bathing on the banks of a holy river, or in the evening, discoursing. It is here that he encounters souls in distress, crouching in various postures of despair. Often it is his voice, expounding on tales from the *Bhāgavatapurāṇa*, which attracts their attention and they come to him for succour. He does not seek out the affluent and the powerful, though they are welcome too. The *vārtās*, it can hardly be emphasized enough, revolve around the lives of the marginalized and the oppressed, offering them the possibility of entering into their own intense, at times highly whimsical, relationship with the lord. *Sevā*, it is true, had its own ritual, but even here, the code laid down by Ācāryajī himself could be transcended, if it was dictated by *prīti*, love of the lord. The present scholarly view—which ascribes élite following and brahmanical manipulation to all *saguṇa sampradāyas*—obviously falls victim to the stereotypes it creates.

It is from the humblest people that this community of the elect is chosen. Often they are nameless, for, as the *Bhāv prakāś* tells us, the devotees were often people with rustic names which the teachers did not see fit to hold fast for posterity: 'Now here and there Gokulnāthjī has not preserved the names. For the parents kept the names, some were called Phakīrā, others Ghasīṭā. Of such Vaiṣṇavas Śrīgokulnāthjī does not say the name. Therefore the names of sundry Vaiṣṇavas have not been disclosed.' (252) These are common, everyday people who rise to special status by the grace of Ācāryajī and Ṭhākurjī. It is to these everyday lives that I now turn, in order to review how the compendium represents the constitution of the first community as bound together by the working of the guru.[16]

Laying Down the Path and Demarcating It

The *vārtās* show Ācāryajī at his most skilful, blending visionary power and compassion with a stern demarcation of his community from bordering or encroaching belief systems. Ācāryajī sees the many Bairāgīs and Jogīs, whose specific provenance is often left unspecified, as so many charlatans who haunt the very places he himself frequents—river banks and pilgrimage sites. He spares no effort to dislocate their authority and, where possible, demolish it. This is a feature common to all gurus of the period, irrespective of *nirguṇa* or *saguṇa* calling. No authority outside their own is allowed to hold its ground, not even in matters as trivial as those which call for the help of a soothsayer.[17]

The authority generated by places of pilgrimage, by ritual, asceticism, even traditional Sanskritic learning,[18] is displaced, if not entirely denied. But the *vārtās* leave us in no doubt that Ācāryajī considers the paths promising *mukti*, redemption, fitting only for those who choose to be satisfied with lower states of being. If *mukti* has any standing at all, it is made quite clear that it is a decidedly inferior state than that of *bhakti*. In fact the principle of *māyā*, which sees the world as illusory, is vigorously disputed. It stands in direct opposition to *puṣṭi*, which comes about in this world and within family and community. *Māyāvād*, as Śaṅkara's theological edifice is disparagingly called, is a blind alley for those who have once begun to tread the path of *bhakti* and *vairāgya*. The kind of detachment which shrugs off responsibility towards others and makes for arrogance can be no other than the way of the erring. Thus it is that *māyāvād* and the cluster of concepts surrounding it, including *vairāgya*, detachment and the asceticism which it calls for, and *maryādāmārg*, which is associated with *smārta* ritual and the brahmans specializing in it, are seen as being in stark opposition to *bhakti*.[19]

In order to understand the nature of these polemics—i.e. the authorities Ācāryajī seeks to dispel in order to establish his own—it is imperative that we recognize the nature of the relationship of this *sampradāya* to what it views as orthodoxy. The other imperative is to identify clearly the terms of reference within which Ācāryajī and his followers operate: *daivī jīv*, *sevā*, *mahāprasād*, *sānubhāvatā janānā*, *bhagvadvārtā*. Though they exist within banal, everyday reality, this reality is now shot through with the new ecstasy of being in communion with the lord. This makes for the special tone of the text. While the everyday speech in which the tales are related grant it a quality of easy accessibility, the intense emotion and spiritual power radiated by Ācāryajī raises these episodes to the level of the extraordinary and even the lyrical.The tales need to be told and heard in their entirety if we are to appreciate the nature of the world they delineate.

The following *vārtās* offer vivid sketches of lives, lost and erring, which regain their footing by the grace of Ācāryajī. In the first of these we have the tale of an adolescent in crisis.

The story, as related in the *Bhāv prakāś*, is that of Rāmdās Sāṁcorā of Rājnagar or Ahmedabad. From early youth he showed signs of *vairāgya*, disinclination for pleasures of the world. When he was nine years old his parents married him to an eight-year-old girl. But he was attached to no one, conversed with no one. His parents had him taught much but he learnt nothing. One day, he was sitting on the banks of a tank in Rājnagar. A *teli* or oil-presser came by with his oxcarts to give his oxen water. One of the animals drank the water and fell down dead. The oil-presser began to cry. The ten-year-old said, why don't you take hold of him and raise him? The oil-presser said, how will it rise now, it has no life. Then, just like the young Siddhārtha, the little boy asked, does everyone die, just like him? The oil-presser said, this is how it comes about, it is only a question of a day here or there. Hearing this, Rāmdās ran from that place. In a few days he reached Dvārikā and took *darśan* of Raṇchoṛjī. Here, Ācāryajī was to be found, relating tales from the *Subodhinī*. And it came to Rāmdās's mind that he wanted to stay with Ācāryajī for a while and listen to the *kathā*. He thought it would be to his good if he could serve him. And so it came about that he became his follower.

It is here that the *vārtā* makes itself felt in. Ācāryajī initiated him and gave him a *svarūpa*. But it was Ācāryajī's way, once *bhakti* had gained firm root in the disciple, to send him back home, even if it wrenched him to do so. Rāmdās had a wife, herself a creature of god, *daivī jīv*, who pined at home for him; and he had parents. For the deliverance of their souls, it was necessary that Rāmdās go back.

Rāmdās does go back, his parents are dead, his wife is at her parents' place. She joins him but Rāmdās does not accept her and, in two or three days, he sets forth alone on a journey to Dvārikā. She follows him, eats his left-overs, but he throws stones at her. And then Raṇchoṛjī begins to speak to him: why did you marry her? You are a follower of Ācāryajī, so accept her. He makes the first overtures, and upon reaching Dvārikā she receives her first initiation. Ācāryajī comes by and seals the bond. It is not seemly, Rāmdās thinks, to wander through the world with her. We should stay at one place and sing of the lord. And so it comes about.

The commentary which frames the actual tale serves to make the hearer realize that *vairāgya* was a trait that Rāmdās had been literally born with. But this did not equip him with the means to resolve the dilemmas of existence. He had merely to witness one incident of life's impermanence to lose all sense of direction. He could, of course, have become a Bairāgī or a Jogī. Instead, he was so fortunate as to win Ācāryajī's favour and be early awarded a *svarūpa*. But Ācāryajī did not allow him to stay away from his own social world and sent him back to take up his rightful position within it. However, left to his own devices, Rāmdās once again set off for Dvārikā. His leanings seemed incorrigibly non-familial. But Ācāryajī remained ever vigilant. He caused Raṇchoṛjī to follow him and made him realize that devotion to Ṭhākurjī took place *within* the world, and with his wife at his side. Both had a duty towards the other Vaiṣṇavas, *saguṇa* or not. Interestingly enough, at no stage in this tale, is there any mention of a temple or any obligation to serve the lord in Dvārikā. The emphasis is upon service to the *svarūpa* granted him, and to the community.

Thus also the story, as related by the *Bhāv Prakāś*, of two Khatrī brothers: Ānanddās and Viśvambhardās from Prayāg also tended to *vairāgya* from early youth. They refused to marry, ran away from their home to Citrakūṭ, and had to be brought back by a remorseful father. Once, they were sitting on the banks of the Yamunā, mourning the eternal passages of birth and rebirth and seeing themselves condemned to being born ever again without ever having recognized the lord. And so overwrought were they with the sorrow of it that they beat their heads and cried out until they lost all consciousness. They lay there the night, upon the sand. It was then that Ṭhākurjī approached Ācāryajī and said: two boys lie up on the sand on the other bank of the Yamunā. They are in great agony over me. Present yourself to them and accept (*aṅgīkār*) them into the fold. And so they were initiated—but they were sent back home: 'And mother and father were both filled with great happiness. The sons were at home; if they had not been found, then what would have happened?' (249)

As the *vārtā* tells us, the brothers spent the rest of their lives in *bhagvadvārtā*, stretching the story-telling hours so long that one would drop off to sleep while the other talked on. Then, in order to bring the story to fruition, Ṭhākurjī himself—who had begun early to let them experience his self (*sānubhāvatā janānā*)—would step in to punctuate the story with his listener's 'yes' (*hūṁkārī bharnā*) to prevent the flow being inauspiciously interrupted: 'And so from childhood onwards, the two brothers knew not the ways of *lok*, custom, and of *ved*, ritual, and the agony and sorrow of *saṃsāra* could not prevail.' (249) Ṭhākurjī needs the services of Ācāryajī in order to save the two brothers from their own detachment and award them access to his *sevā*, though once again this is to take place within the world and within the framework of family life. Vallabha's opposition to ascetic orders and the itenerant life was decisive and firm.

Since *sevā* itself was a domestic rite, the *svarūpa* became a privileged member of the family, to be fed, clothed, laid to rest with more care, love and respect than anyone else. For the marginalized and the isolated, *sevā* became a means of integration into the community.[20] Ācāryajī even goes so far as to tolerate the relationship of a devotee to a prostitute, commending this for raising the spiritual status both of the devotee and the fallen woman. As the *vārtā* relates the tale: Once, when Śrīācāryajī arrived in

Kaṛā, Vaiṣṇavas said to him: *Mahārāj*, Mādhodās has kept a prostitute. Then Ācāryajī asked, well Mādhodās, have you kept a prostitute? Mādhodās said, my mind is intensely attached to her. This is why I have kept her. In this manner, Ācāryajī put the question to him thrice. And all three times Mādhodās said to him, *mahārāj*, my mind is intensely attached to her. This is why I have kept her. Then Ācāryajī maintained a long silence. Upon this the Vaiṣṇavas said to Ācāryajī: *Mahāprabhu, mahārāj*, your honour has been preserved until now. He will only be rid of her once you have spoken to him. Have you said nothing to him? Ācāryajī resolved their doubts by saying: Do not be anxious. His mind is intensely attached to her, so how long will it take for Ṭhākurjī to turn it? And Ghadādardās has given his blessing to him, so that his devotion to Hari will be firm, such is Mādhodās. Then all the Vaiṣṇavas were satisfied and they were silent a long while. After this Mādhodās's mind turned, and so he put the prostitute far from him. He adopted the way and dignity of the Vaiṣṇavas and he became a good Vaiṣṇava. (92)

The *vārtā* offers the bare skeleton of this story; but the *Bhāv prakāś* goes on to provide much vivid detail as well as moral and social comment. Further, it carries the tale into Gosāīṁjī's time and spins the tale of the prostitute into an almost autonomous narrative. The words *veśyā dūrī kīnī* are interpreted to mean that the prostitute, *veśyā*, was told that she was a *sakhī*, friend, companion to Gosāīṁjī. Thus, she is said to have waited for him for all of fifteen years, existing only on dry bread. When he arrived, she asked to be accepted into the fold. Gosāīṁjī's reaction was curt: we do not make *veśyās* into our *sevaks*, devotees. Thereupon she took to a hunger strike. On the ninth day of his visit, as he was making preparations to depart, the *veśyā* came into his presence, supported on the arms of two people. She said, *mahārāj*, today is the ninth day. Without food and water, my *prāṇ*, life's breath, will leave if you do not accept me. Gosāīṁjī knew then that she had been purified and he carried out the ceremonies of initiation. Not only this, he gave her a small *svarūpa*, Lāljī, for worship and care. The Vaiṣṇavas admonished him: teach her the way of *sevā*. Thus performing *sevā*, it came about that her menstruation set in. Then the Vaiṣṇavas forbade her to touch water etc. for four days. But her love was so immense that she could not bear to forego *sevā*, and she simply carried it out. The other Vaiṣṇavas ceased all communication with her. After some days Gosāīṁjī arrived once again in Kaṛā, and the Vaiṣṇavas complained to him. When questioned by him the *veśyā's* reply was direct and straightforward: *mahārāj*, I have had as many worldly masters as the hairs on my body. It was because of you that they could be discarded. Now, through your grace, I have acquired an unworldly master. How can I live without him for four whole days? ... I'll do as you say. Gosāīṁjī saw that Ṭhākurjī was pleased with her, so he said: Continue doing as you have until now. And thus resolving her doubts he sent her home: hurry, Ṭhākurjī will be waiting for you. He told the other Vaiṣṇavas that she was to be allowed to do as she did. She must not be admonished. But her case was a special one and he expressly charged the other Vaiṣṇavas to desist from following her ways. (93)

Another story, of an old woman, poor and inauspicious in her widowhood, whom Ācāryajī endows with the most privileged form of *sevā*, presents him at his most compassionate and nurturing.

The *Bhāv prakāś* introduces this tale of a nameless Brāhmaṇī from Aṛel who was married at nine years of age to a sickly man. When she was forty-five years old her husband took ill and died. (It is hinted that she had a difficult life, tending a sickly husband who left her no progeny.) This Brāhmaṇī had never experienced worldly happiness and comfort at home. When she was left alone, her thoughts turned to the service of the lord, and, living as she did at home, she thought she would become a follower of Ācāryajī. Saying, I have spent all my life in the service of my worldly master, now he is dead, I seek refuge with you, she began to cry. Ācāryajī had compassion for her. He not only imparted the name to her, but on the next day gave her a *svarūpa* that had been given to him by a brahman from the South who had departed to Kāśī to take *saṃnyāsa*. Being awarded a *svarūpa* was a great privilege, and it was jealously watched by the other Vaiṣṇavas. Not only did the Brāhmaṇī at once enter into the very heart of *sevā*, Ṭhākurjī began to favour her almost at once with *sānubhāvatā*, that is, she began to hold the most intimate communion with him. This Brāhmaṇī was most guileless and simple in her ways and had no wealth or goods. She would place an earthen vessel before the lord; her abode was narrow and tiny, the same room housing at once the kitchen, the temple and the material for Ṭhākurjī's *sevā*. She understood little of *ācāra*, proper ritual conduct, and her eyesight was poor. But she would serve with great love and it was this which kept Ṭhākurjī happy. She made do with those of her husband's former clients that were sent her. The Vaiṣṇavas began to mutter amongst themselves. Why has Ācāryajī favoured her with *bhagvadsevā*? If he had bestowed this upon us, we would have performed the appropriate service. One day, the Vaiṣṇavas could hold themselves back no longer; they went to Ācāryajī and lodged a complaint. Ācāryajī said, it is not ritual conduct, sacrificial act or wealth which makes me happy, it is *prīti*, love of Ṭhākurjī, that I need, and it is of this quality that the Brāhmaṇī has plenty. Therefore Ṭhākurjī acquiesces to whatever the Brāhmaṇī manages to do. Then the

Vaiṣṇavas fell silent. After having performed his evening prayer to Yamunā, Ācāryajī betook himself in the direction of the Brāhmaṇī's house. The Vaiṣṇavas said, *mahārāj*, you can give her your *darśan* and see for yourself what kind of *sevā* she performs. She was busy preparing the evening meal and took no heed of Ācāryajī's coming. The Brāhmaṇī was dim of vision and so she could not see much. She would make a *roṭī*, daub it with *ghī*, Ṭhākurjī would pick it up and partake of it. She would fumble for the *roṭī* and not find it. Then she would say, either the cats or the mice have taken it. She would bang the floor and make another *roṭī*. Then Ācāryajī told her, Ṭhākurjī has partaken of it, not cats and mice. It is your great good fortune. The Brāhmaṇī said, it is because of you that Ṭhākurjī has partaken of it. But Ācāryajī said, whatever you do will agree with Ṭhākurjī and please him. And afterwards he told the Vaiṣṇavas, it is affection that Ṭhākurjī hungers for and he is pleased with the Brāhmaṇī (150–1).

The nameless Brāhmaṇī, apparently without being aware of her immensely privileged status, exists on terms of easy familiarity with the lord, watched over and protected by Ācāryajī. Her poverty is no barrier to the lord granting her *sānubhāvatā*, nor is her widowed state. *Smārta* ritual or *maryādāmārg* would have denied her, as also the prostitute, participation in auspicious ritual, but the path of *bhakti* opens up the possibility of new ritual relationships which create their own laws. Remarkably, while both women refer to the devotion they gave their worldly masters or lords, the *veśyā* speaks unashamedly of them in the plural. It is from the shortcomings experienced in these relationships that the women, in fact, draw their right to serve Ṭhākurjī and shower him with the whimsy and ecstasy of their devotion. However, their inclusion in the community and their erratic behaviour are not accepted without protest. Not only do the other Vaiṣṇavas watch jealously over the privileges granted these poor, polluted women, they are quick to point out transgressions. In both cases, however, the gurus concerned make special concessions for the women's extraordinary devotion; and in the widow's case we see Ṭhākurjī himself validating her behaviour. Clearly, Ṭhākurjī and Ācāryajī prescribe no absolutely binding path for devotion to the lord.

Thus it is that people entangled in some form of woe or despair, adolescents in crisis, those looking for answers in life, widows, prostitutes, and *śūdras*, all find refuge at the feet of Ācāryajī.

However, lest the Vaiṣṇava community seem to exist in idyllic and splendid isolation, we need to take note of the stern bounds with which Ācāryajī cordons it off. The greatest emphasis is laid on keeping a clear distance from those who in fact seem the nearest. Thus, the lines demarcating Puṣṭimārg and other Vaiṣṇava traditions, *maryādāmārgī* Vaiṣṇavas as they are called in the *vārtās*, are the most resolutely drawn. The sacred texts can be shared, but there are differences in interpretation and there is always the issue of ritual authority. Ācāryajī can endow this on brahman or non-brahman alike, depending on ability and talent. Here *jāti* hierarchies cease to function

In the tale of Mukunddās Sahaniyā, Kāyasth of Malwa country, these issues are dealt with in some detail. The *Bhāv prakāś* introduces the two brothers, Dinkardās and Mukunddās, who stayed with Ācāryajī and learnt the ways of the *mārg*. But they did not receive a *svarūpa*, only a letter of *brahmasambandha* which they were to serve. Their women were not *daivī*, therefore there was to be no commensality with them. Mukunddās had received *caraṇamṛta* from Ācāryajī, therefore he knew all the *śāstras*, *vedas* and *purāṇas* by heart. The *vārtā* comes in here with the information that Mukunddās composed beautiful verses, including a *Mukundsāgar*. This was a compilation of *padas* which contained and explicated the twelfth *skandha* of the *Bhāgavatapurāṇa*. The brahmans and pandits of Ujjain would come to him and say, come, we shall narrate the *Bhāgavatapurāṇa* to you.[21] But Mukunddās always said that he would listen to them only when he had the leisure. And so, many days passed. Once, they caught him playing the game of *caupaṛ*. And they said, you have leisure to play *caupaṛ*, but not to listen to the Bhāgavata. But as they were not *mārgīya* brahmans, he could not hear the *kathā* from them (129). The *Bhāv prakāś* enters at this stage into a long exposition of why this is so: The fruit to be gained from *maryādāmārg* is *mukti*, redemption, whereas in Puṣṭimārg, it is *ekāṅgī puṣṭibhakti*, which could only be gained by seeking refuge with Ācāryajī, so that all kinds of *ānanda*, joy, connected with Ācāryajī entered the heart. It could only take firm root in the heart if godly discourse could be heard from the mouths of the Vaiṣṇavas of the Vallabhakula. If one listened with love to another, then it was to be regarded as *anyāśraya*, seeking refuge of another. '*tātem̐ anyamārgīya som̐ na bhagavaddharam kī bāt pūchanī na apnī kahnī*.' (130) Therefore one was neither to ask of matters connected with *Bhagavaddharma* from those following another path, nor speak of one's own.

The *vārtā* takes up the tale here. There was an eclipse of the sun and Mukunddās was standing in the river invoking the lord, when the Pandit from Ujjain chanced upon him again. And this time he did not let go till Mukunddās relented and held discourse. He embarked upon an exegesis of a *śloka* from the *Bhāgavatapurāṇa*. Day became night and day again. The people of the village came to bathe in the river. Will you now be done with the meaning of this *śloka*? And Mukunddās said, it shall take a full six months. Then that Pandit was quite exhausted. He said, the lord has endowed you with this ability. What can a *jīva* know of it? And he acknowledged defeat. If at times he came again to put a question to him, Mukunddās found so many faults with the question that the Pandit gave up coming. (131)

Mukunddās obviously disobeys the injunctions of Ācāryajī when he holds forth on the Bhāgavata to one of alien belief. It is not quite clear whether he is at all interested in mediating his knowledge and insight of the text to the Pandit, or whether he wishes merely to take care of the Pandit's pretensions once and for all. The Pandit does allow himself to be convinced of his prowess and it is this which is portrayed as exemplary, as also his firm refusal to enter into the world of their discourse. The *Bhāv prakāś* warns clearly: 'There is no impurity greater than *anyāśraya*, seeking refuge of another. Just as a woman's entire *dharma* leaves her if she abandons her own husband to seek another, similarly a Vaiṣṇava's *dharma* is destroyed if he indulges in taking refuge of another. This is the *siddhānta* illustrated by the *vārtā*.' (34–5) The tale is important also for an illustration of the fact that even a text as sacred as the *Bhāgavatapurāṇa* cannot be considered sacred in and of itself. Taken by itself it generates no knowledge, radiates no authority. It needs training and authorization by Ācāryajī, and later by those of his *kula*, for the exponent to gain the insight to interpret it for himself and to others. And as we have seen, this authority is not restricted to brahmans. It can be granted to a Kāyasth who happens to be a gifted poet. He can then be further gifted by Ācāryajī so that he comes to possess the linguistic skills and vast reading needed to interpret an intricate poetic text in a manner which might put learned brahmans to shame.

Demarcating the path was obviously a tricky task in a period where so many similar, if not overlapping, belief systems competed for the allegiance of presumably the same classes of people. The *vārtās*, which so precisely delineated the authority of Ācāryajī in all its ramifications and illustrated his teachings as operative in the tiny details of daily life, were themselves early raised to canonic status, not to be imparted to the unworthy even within the community.

The immense power generated by the *vārtās* is illustrated in the story of Puruṣottam Jośī, Sāṁcora brahman from Gujarat, who visited Kṛṣṇa Bhaṭṭ in Ujjain, the son of Padmārāval. Puruṣottam Jośī would indulge in relating *Bhagavadvārtā*, tales of the godly, secretly at night to his wife, for he thought that Kṛṣṇa Bhaṭṭ was not yet worthy of it. Four days passed and Kṛṣṇa Bhaṭṭ knew that they discoursed thus. When they were about to depart and Puruṣottam Jośī already sat astride his horse, Kṛṣṇa Bhaṭṭ held his horse from the one side and himself launched forth in *Bhagavadvārtā*. He did this in such a way that Puruṣottam Jośī lost all consciousness of being and was so engrossed in *rasa* that he made to alight from the horse. But he continued on his journey and Kṛṣṇa Bhaṭṭ accompanied him to Gokul and they discoursed thus all the way. He lost all sense of time and did not know when they had accomplished the first stage of their journey. When he realized this, Puruṣottam Jośī pulled himself together, but *bhagvadvartā kā āveś utaryo nahīṁ*, the ecstasy of *Bhagavadvārtā* would not wear off (180). And so he also began to talk to Kṛṣṇa Bhaṭṭ, and night and day they indulged in this pastime, and so they reached Gokul where Gosāīṁjī (for it is already a later period and we do not hear Ācāryajī's voice in this tale) put Puruṣottam Jośī's mind at rest regarding the worthiness of Kṛṣṇa Bhaṭṭ.

Thus it is that while tales of community-formation shape the *vārtās*, the compendium in its turn acquires the function of further forming and perpetuating the community. This makes for the canonic status of the *vārtās*, raising them to a level above that of the *Bhāgavatapurāṇa* and even the *Subodhinī*, Ācāryajī's own commentary on the *purāṇa*. The *Bhāgavatapurāṇa* remains central, but it is superseded, at least in their own representation, by the *vārtas*, which had clearly originated as oral texts composed in everyday speech.

The main if not the sole authoritative instance in the tales is the charismatic person of Ācāryajī. His authority and his sometimes idiosyncratic choices supersede the power of the deities in the well-known Vaiṣṇava temples and of the well-known Vaiṣṇava scriptures. It is he who selects his chief disciples, recognizing and consolidating their godly destiny, it is he who then also proceeds to form and shape the community of the elect, validating one mode of worship over another, correcting and guiding. His own special brand of *bhakti*, the ecstatic recognition of the lord, the communion with him, and the lifestyles associated with this form of devotion, all remain centrally connected to his person.

Conclusion

Doubtlessly, the *vārtās*, in that they set up models, idealize. Yet we must take note of what it is that they idealize. It is the poor and the lowly who are accorded such importance in the tales they tell. And the guru of this *saguṇa sampradāya* comes across primarily not only as an *ācārya* but as a popular teacher, mingling with the common folk. He has knowledge of Sanskrit texts, of the classical schools of philosophy, of the *dharmaśāstras*, and of *smārta* ritual. But he does not derive his authority from any of these venerable instances. In fact he uses his knowledge of these to show up the hollowness of the traditions that they enshrine and to distance himself from these. His authority, which derives much more from his own peculiar experience of and communion with the lord, overrides that of pilgrimage centres and temple images—as we saw in the tales of the Khatrī brothers who rushed to Purī and Rāmdas Saṁcorā who hovered near Dwārikā. As *ācārya* and guru he confidently overrules *varṇa* hierarchies. He allows Mukunddās Sahaniyā, a Kāyasth, to offer an exegesis of the *Bhāgavatapurāṇa* so powerful that it shames a brahman into silence. He communicates with those whom he finds most in need of his message, regardless of their *varṇa* allegiance. He comes to their rescue in crises familiar to most healers, as with the Khatrī brothers, and holds public discourse in terms which reach the unlettered and the simple, as well as the learned and the reclusive. He explicitly questions and defies *ved aur lok*, the norms laid down by the *dharmaśāstras* and by custom. In fact, he rejects brahmanic ritual, coining his own simple form of worship. He allows the marginalized and the despised, such as the poor brahman widow and the prostitute, to practice this form of worship and allows for the most idiosyncratic modifications of even the simple ritual he prescribes if they are performed with love. In fact, it is the reciprocal and easy familiarity of the women with the lord that, according to him, puts them above the rest of the community. And he proceeds to protect these women in all the deviations they unwittingly practice, from the wrath of the righteous in the community.

We need then to question the stereotypes set up both by later *sampradāya* tradition and taken over by contemporary scholarship, which would set forth the rather simplistic and partisan view of *saguṇa* and *nirguṇa* traditions as polar opposites, both theologically and socially. If there is one clear difference from the *nirguṇa*, it lies in the stress laid by Vallabha and his successors on family and communitarian formations and the need to practice, as far as possible, the new forms of worship within these. Apart from this, Vallabha and the *saguṇa* traditions of the day are as keen as *nirguṇa* to set themselves off from *smārta* ritual. They award as much importance to the figure of the *ācārya*, and offer as direct and unmediated access to the lord. Many of the features they stress present little difference from those preached by the great *nirguṇa* gurus. In fact, the analysis of both clusters of tradition calls for a finer differentiation and possibly much more sociological data before we as scholars are able, in our turn, to overcome and transcend sectarian prejudices. In short, we need to assess both the similarities and differences more carefully. At the least, it seems risky to conflate movements—laying such great stress on their particularity—with the many others, within and without the *saguṇa* and *nirguṇa* clusters, though today they seem similarly configured.

Many questions remain to be asked, then, before we can satisfactorily locate these movements in their respective socio-religious and political constellations through the five centuries of their existence. Minute attention to the aesthetic details of *sevā*, as also the hereditary authority invested in members of his family, the misuse of power which reached the zenith of notoriety in the Maharaja Libel Case of 1862, have done much to shape the nineteenth-century image of the *sampradāya*. But these developments need in their turn to be regarded historically so that we do not lose sight of their beginnings. The later opulence of Vallabha's *sampradāya* has effectively blocked access to its initially radical message, as also its relative social flexibility. When did Vallabha's *sampradāya* become more exclusive and opulent? In what ways did it relate to others in the *catuḥsampradāya*? Was this only a strategic alliance, which agreed to take no cognizance of difference at one level while at others observing the strictest segregation? What of the many Vaiṣṇavas who belonged to the drifting mass of people that visited temples and holy sites of particular *sampradāyas* but as easily drifted to others? There are obviously no simple equations.

The end of the eighteenth century and the beginning of the nineteenth saw the construction of the neo-traditional framework with a renewed importance of *dharmaśāstras* and *varṇāśramadharma*, within which the colonial regime chose to operate. The nationalist endeavours were to create their own balances and imbalances. There were certain pan-Indian alignments, sanskritizing moves. But this did not necessarily only lead to the formation and domination of élite groups, which in any case were constituted differently over the centuries.

Modern Hinduism, which operates both with monotheistic and vedantic monistic claims, has seen fit to melt entirely the differences between the *nirguṇa* and *saguṇa sampradāya* clusters, and of these again to the *smārta* orthodoxy of their day. The balance it seems to have achieved is fraught with tensions of a kind which still needs to be adequately assessed. But the way even thus far has been stony, and there have obviously been many intermediary stages. The original egalitarianism, which, as I hope to have shown, once made for the great popularity and success of Vallabha's *sampradāya*, could at later stages look for other channels to realize itself. There could be other schisms and alliances. If the Vaiṣṇava *sampradāyas* by and large once offered means to middling and lower-middle *jātis* to rise in status, then it is entirely possible that these very *jātis*, in a changed political constellation, might seek the support of the still lower to come into power.[22]

How is socio-religious power to be shared with others, with the post independence state, if we in fact choose to look at it in these terms alone? Even the absolute authority of the guru, though it might seem to point the way to state authoritarianism and right-wing Hinduism, could as well stand in the way of it.[23] Thus, though it may be possible to trace certain tendencies in present-day Hinduism back into the Vedic period, can present political developments be similarly projected into beginnings? Can Hindutva be read backwards?

Notes

1. Thus for instance Lorenzen in the introduction ('The Historical Vicissitudes of the Bhakti Religion') to his edited volume on the *bhakti* religions of north India: 'The second pillar of saguṇī ethics is, of course, the doctrine of varṇāśramadharma (the law of social classes and stages of life). According to this doctrine, one obtains a better rebirth precisely by following the rules of conduct appropriate to the varṇa (roughly 'class') and *jāti* (caste) in which one was born. The rules of behaviour for *varṇas* are set out in elaborate detail in the legal texts of Hindu tradition: the dharmasūtras, dharmaśāstras and legal digests.' (1995: 16) The Vaiṣṇavas, as I hope to show in the course of this essay, in fact developed their own ritual and social codes in express opposition to the *dharmaśāstra*.
2. To quote Lorenzen once again: 'Kings are more often portrayed as the allies of *saguṇī* saints, while their opponents may either be fellow Brahmin philosophers (with whom they have mostly polite intellectual debates) or low 'heretics' who are generally dispatched by force (either by the saint's magical power or by the physical power of his royal ally) ... Is it too far fetched to see these alliances as early precursors of the curiously similar political alliances of present-day India between the social base of the Congress and Janata Dal Parties (richer peasants, Untouchables, poor labourers, and Muslims), on the one side, and the social base of the Bharatiya Janata Party (merchants and traders, lesser peasants, and many white-collar professionals), on the other?' (1995: 189) Have the same groups retained elite positions across the centuries? In which category would we, by this definition, include the Sikhs, surely a *nirguṇa* formation?
3. Burghart's pioneering essay (1978) on the meeting of the four *sampradāyas* in Galta which brought about the coalition still remains the only sustained treatment of the theme.
4. As Satish Chandra has pointed out, '[w]e have yet to asses the social and economic background and the historical significance of this second phase of the bhakti movement as it was, or popular (saguna) bhakti as distinguished from the earlier movement which has been called popular monotheism. Was the "success" of saguna bhakti in large parts due to its being more traditional,

and hence arousing less hostility from the orthodox Brahmans? Was its appeal specifically more rural, as compared to the earlier movement which drew support from city based artisans and traders?' (1996: 130). Satish Chandra then does go on to postulate that 'the triumph of saguna bhakti over the more radical school of popular monotheism in the Gangetic valley may, to some extent, be considered as the triumph of the conservatism of the countryside over the latent radicalism of the towns.' (131) As my investigation to date shows, it is not really possible to stipulate any kind of rural–urban divide. The followers of the *sampradāya* in fact come much more from lower to middling castes and from small town and city rather than village, though later the *sampradāya* does seem to profit from Rajput patronage. There is, then, even in this second *saguṇa* phase of the *bhakti* movement, a decided radicalism which has been largely overshadowed by later developments.

5. Here there seems to have been some inadvertent glorification of the *nirguṇa* tradition (in such accounts necessarily viewed as homogeneous), which is celebrated somewhat uncritically as radical and resistant from often rather hazy beginnings in time through the Mughal period (Akbar's role remains fuzzy in such narratives) into the present. See Gold (1987: 210, 211).
6. For a comprehensive account of the hagiographic literature of the period see Dube (1968).
7. The central motifs in the individual tales, as Lorenzen has shown (1995: 181–211), often repeat themselves in the hagiographies of the various *sampradāyas*, crossing, as I have found, the boundaries of *nirguṇa* and *saguṇa*. However, since the frame of reference does not stay the same, it is entirely legitimate to treat each episode, even if it has already occurred in another compendium, as unique in its own context.
8. The citations in this essay are from this text as edited by Dvārikādās Pārikh (1971).
9. The commentary began always by providing information about the devotees' favoured initial position in Kṛṣṇa's heaven, from which they fell temporarily only to be gathered up and taken into the fold again by the deity, after their lives on earth were spent. As Caroline Bynum in her study of women's religiosity in the Christian middle ages has noted: 'Indeed, medieval hagiographers pointed out repeatedly that saints are not even primarily "models" for ordinary mortals; the saints are far too dangerous for that. Like Christ himself, they could not and should not be imitated in their full extravagance and power. Rather (so their admirers say), they should be loved, venerated, and meditated upon as moments in which the other that is God breaks through into the mundane worlds, saturating it with meaning.' (1987: 7)
10. The *vārtās* are available in three kinds of compilations: the first seem to be random collections of tales, without any discernible organizational pattern; the second, possibly later, compilations, have been arranged in the sequence of 84 and 252 lives as we know them today, and the third go further still and

arrange the tales within a commentarial frame. For details, see Ṭaṇḍan (1960: 44ff.).

11. All translations are by the author. The *saguṇa* aspect was ordered and subsumed under Gosāīṁjī.
12. When Ṭhākurjī was served a *khīr* dish too carelessly prepared and it scalded his mouth, he complained at once to Ācāryajī (p. 173).
13. Thus the Bhāṭiyā and Lohāṇa in Gujarat, who Cohen describes as 'at best former Rajpūts on the fringe of Hindu society' (1984: 69) and the Kaṇbīs , 'an old, well entrenched, landed Śudra caste of agriculturists' (70) who effected upward mobility through entering the Vallabhite Vaiṣṇava community. Pinch in his study of the Rāmānandīs (one of the four Vaiṣṇava *sampradāyas*) has similarly noted that the early nineteenth-century ethnographic accounts of religious denominations in Eastern U. P. by Francis Buchanan show clearly the upward social mobility brought about by acceptance into the Vaiṣṇava fold. Firstly, 'Buchanan's remarks on religious practice in the Gangetic core, together with comments by other observers through the nineteenth century, indicate that Vaishnava gurus (and Ramanandis in particular) pursued a far more aggressive program of social and religious reform in comparison with their Dasnami and Nanakpanthi counterparts. Consequently, Vaishnava bairagis were drawn from the entire varna spectrum and included not only brahmans but many shudras.' (1996: 38) Secondly, these bairagis encouraged their lay followers to adhere to a rigid moral code and a strict regimen. 'Describing Vaishnavas as "everywhere the most strict," Buchanan noted that "some few of them here [Bihar and Patna] will neither pray nor even show common civility to any god but those of his own sect." The emphasis on a pure life applied as well to daily diet: "All the Hindus, brahmans or sudra, of the sect of Vishnu, are remarkably strict in eating, reject altogether rice cleaned by boiling, all parched grains, and animal food." By contrast, Buchanan observed that "all the Sudras, except those of the sect of Vishnu, drink avowedly."' (38–9)
14. Vallabha was a scholar and a learned exegete of traditional texts. In this sense, he was more 'ācārya' then 'guru'. The two terms have been used interchangeably in the Sanskrit tradition, almost as synonyms, but there is a connotational difference which has continued to be operative as well. As Minoru Hara has shown, the *ācārya* is a specialist of particular fields of knowledge, which he mediates to his pupil over a period of time. Built into the relationship is respect and distance, though intellectual difference of opinion is, in principle, possible. In later classical tradition, guru also came to be used for teacher, though the term continued to mean respected elders as well. The guru-disciple bond was more emotional than intellectual and called for absolute obedience by the disciple. Hara's distinctions seem then to be turned upside down in our case. Though Vallabha's designation is *ācārya*, in fact, in the hagiographical compendia at least, he functions more as a 'guru'. He has himself a highly emotional relationship to the lord as well as to his disciples and he mediates between the two in an entirely

intimate, albeit authoritarian, manner. In this respect, Vallabha as *saguṇa guru* seems very close indeed to the *gurus* of the *nirguṇa sampradāyas*.

15. See for instance the tales of Padmanābhdās (40) and Tripurdās (151). Both devotees are made to realize that giving in to the temptation to perform miracles has meant that Ṭhākurjī had to labour on their behalf.
16. I have chosen to focus on the lives of humble devotees rather than the eight famous poets of the *sampradāya*, known as the *aṣṭachāp*, or eight seals, whose *vārtās* have been translated and analysed by Richard Barz (1976, 1992, 1994). The eight poets have been pressed into service as a special group within the two compendia. For the possible appropriation of Sūrdās, the most well known of the eight, by the Vallabhite community, see Hawley (1983).
17. This is a typical feature of all such accounts, as Simon Digby has remarked in connection with the Sikh hagiographical literature of the period, which could be characterized as firmly *nirguṇa* in provenance: 'Those who write about the harmony of syncretistic movements in medieval India should perhaps reflect that the number of anecdotes in medieval hagiography depicting the universal kindness and benevolence of religious leaders is small compared to the quantity of those depicting their formidable powers, their triumphs over their rivals and the awful consequences of their wrath.' (1970: 306) The tale of Dāmodardās Sambhalvāre, Khatrī of Kannauj, one of Ācāryajī's most devoted followers, illustrates well how Ācāryajī disposes of the authority of others in matters connected with his followers: Many a time when Ācāryajī would alight upon his house, Dāmodardās would serve him by pressing his feet. Once he was asked to wish for something he had always wanted, but he said he had no wishes. Thereupon Ācāryajī bade him ask his wife. She said all she wanted was a son. Ācāryajī assured her that this wish would be fulfilled. Ācāryajī left for Jatīpura. She was soon with child. But this is when she committed a fatal mistake. Along with the wives of other *smārtas*, she ran to a soothsayer (Ḍakotiā) to ask about the sex of the child and was told it would be a boy. After some time, when Ācāryajī came to Kannauj, and Dāmodardās made to touch his feet, Ācāryajī said, don't touch me. '*tokoṁ anyāśraya bhayau hai*', you have sought refuge with another (33). Dāmodardās pleaded innocence; whereupon he was told to ask his wife, who duly enlightened him. Then Ācāryajī pronounced his awful curse: a son would be born to them, but he would become a mleccha. So strong was the wife's wish to remain within the fold that she in fact asked her mother to take away the son the moment he was born. And so he was raised at his grandmother's home. When Dāmodardās died of old age, the wife put all his goods in a boat and sent it to Ācāryajī in Aṛel, so that the son, who had indeed become a *turak*, a Muslim, could not possess it. She would depend forthwith on the succour of the other Vaiṣṇavas. In short, seeking advice from an authority other than Ācāryajī brought destitution and loneliness upon a woman who had once set her heart on becoming a mother.
18. There is the tale of the boy Būlā Miśra from Lahore, who was so dim-witted that no amount of teaching could drill knowledge into him. In despair he

attempted suicide by drowning in the river Gaṅgā, at a remote site a little outside Kāśī. But Sarasvatī refused to become incriminated in this enterprise and came to his rescue, granting him boundless knowledge of the *śāstras*. He became a pandit of stature, but, even with Sarasvatī to back him, he could not defeat Ācāryajī. It was only when he sought refuge with him that he became a true pandit (264–5). But he was not allowed to partake of the fruit of this pleasure and take up residence in Kāśī as an *ācārya* of note. He was sent back home, like all devotees before to him, to waiting parents, to take up family life again. So much for the worth of Sanskritic learning.

19. See Glasenapp (1934) and Barz ([1976] 1992) for the delineation of Vallabha's theological edifice.
20. See Dalmia (forthcoming) for a discussion of the special place awarded to women in the devotional community.
21. This was obviously an attempt by *smārta* Vaiṣṇavas to either dismantle and reduce his claims to being a talented poet and exegete, or subsume him within their own context.
22. As Pinch points out in connection with the social aspirations of the Rāmānandis in the earlier part of this century, upward mobility emanating from claims to be both Vaiṣṇava and *kṣatriya* could mean 'two socio-religiously related but distinct cultural processes; for radical Ramanandis, Vaishnavism entailed a philosophical stance against all forms of elitism, social or religious; for Yadavs, Kurmis, Kushvahas and many other "reformed ksatriyas", Vaishnavism provided the discursive and historical frame for a new, elite status that drew on a hierarchical world. In this sense, though the ideological poles of this study stand in rigid opposition, both represented reasonable and compelling options for the millions of ordinary people long stigmatized by the term shudra.' (1996: 140)
23. As Christophe Jaffrelot's essay in this volume amply illustrates.

References

Barz, Richard. [1976] 1992. *The Bhakti Sect of Vallabhācārya*. Delhi: Munshiram Manoharlal.

———. 1992. Kṛṣṇādās Adhikārī: An Irascible Devotee's Approach to the Divine. In *Bhakti Studies*, ed. G. M. Bailey and I. Kesarcodi-Watson, 236–50. Delhi: Sterling Publishers.

———. 1994. The Caurāsī Vaiṣṇavan kī Vārtā. In *According to Tradition. Hagiographical Writing in India*, ed. Winand Callewaert and Rupert Snell, 43–64. Wiesbaden: Harrassowitz.

Burghart, Richard. 1978. The Founding of the Rāmānandī Sect. *Ethnohistory* 25: 122–39.

Bynum, Caroline Walker. 1987. *Holy Feast and Holy Fast: The Religious Significance of Food to Medieval Women*. Berkeley & Los Angeles: University of California Press.

Callewaert, Winand & Rupert Snell (eds.). 1994. *According to Tradition. Hagiographical Writing in India.* Wiesbaden: Harrassowitz.

Cohen, Richard J. 1984. Sectarian Vaishnavism: The Vallabha Sampradāya. In *Identity and Division in Cults and Sects in South Asia*, ed. Peter Gaeffke and David A. Utz. Proceedings of South Asia Seminar, 1980–1, 69–72. Philadelphia: Department of South Asia Regional Studies, University of Pennsylvania.

Dalmia, Vasudha. Forthcoming. Women, Duty and Sanctified Space in a Vaiṣṇava Hagiography of the Seventeenth Century. In *Constructions Hagiographiques dans le Monde Indien: Entre Mythe et Histoire*, ed. Françoise Mallison. Paris.

Dūbe, Lāltā Prasād. 1968. *Hindī bhakta-vārtā sāhitya*. Dehradun: Sāhitya Sadan.

Digby, Simon. 1970. Review of *Guru Nanak and the Sikh Religion* by W.H. McLeod. *The Indian Economic and Social History Review* 7.2: 301–13.

Glasenapp, Helmuth von. 1934. Die Lehre Vallabhacaryas. *Zeitschrift für Indologie und Iranistik* 9.3: 268–330.

Gold, Daniel. 1987. *The Lord as Guru. Hindi Sants in the Northern Indian Tradition.* New York, Oxford: Oxford University Press.

Hara, Minoru. Hindu Concepts of Teacher: Sanskrit Guru and Ācārya. In *Sanskrit and Indian Studies in Honour of Daniel H. H. Ingalls*, ed. M. Nagatomi, B. K. Matilal, J. M. Masson and E. C. Dimock, Jr., 93–118. Dordrecht: D. Reidel.

Hawley, John Stratton. 1983. The Sectarian Logic of the Sūr Dās kī Vārtā. In *Bhakti in Current Research, 1979–1982*, ed. by Monika Thiel-Horstmann, 157–69. Berlin: Dietrich Reimer.

Lorenzen, David (ed.). 1995. *Bhakti Religion in North India: Community Identity and Political Action*. Albany: State University of New York Press.

Mulji, Karsandas. 1865. *History of the Sect of the Maharajas, Or Vallabhacharyas in Western India.* London: Trübner & Co.

Pārīkh, Dvārikādās (ed.) 1971. *Caurāsī vaiṣṇavan kī vārtā (tīn janma kī līlā bhāvanā vālī)*. Mathura: Śrī Bajraṅg Pustakālay.

Pinch, William R. 1996. *Peasants and Monks in British India.* Berkeley and Los Angeles: University of California Press.

Satish Chandra. 1996. Historical Background to the Rise of the Bhakti Movement. In *Historiography, Religion and State in Medieval India*, 110–31. Delhi: Har-Anand Publications.

Ṭaṇḍan, Hariharnāth. 1960. *Vārtā sāhitya. Ek bṛhat adhyayan.* Aligarh: Bhārat Prakāśan Mandir.

Institutionalization of Charisma: The Case of Sahajānanda

PETER SCHREINER

The Swaminarayan Movement[1] began as a Hindu reform movement in the nineteenth century in Gujarat. It is today influential mostly in Gujarat and in countries with a sizeable Gujarati section of the population, formerly in Africa, now mainly in Great Britain, and to a lesser extent in the USA. The movement is no longer a homogeneous organization but has developed its own 'sects' and 'reform movements'.[2]

It is not to be qualified unambiguously as 'neo-hindu', since there is no evidence for a reinterpretation of traditional concepts in the light of modern, Western influences. It is a movement with strong regional roots (Gujarat) and an impetus towards universality[3] in which the founder figure, Swami Sahajānanda (1781–1830), is a focal point for the identity of the movement.

If one accepts charisma as a code for conceptualizing a person's influence on his or her followers who develop (possibly at a later stage, i.e. after the founder's death) the religious identity of what outsiders call a 'sect', then the fact that the Swaminarayan Movement has turned out to be a successful religious movement within the fold of modern Hinduism would allow us to postulate that its founder, Swami Sahajānanda, called Swaminarayan (*svāmīnārāyaṇa*) by his followers,[4] did indeed have personal charisma.

Sahajānanda was born in a Brahmin subcaste in the village Capaiyā near Ayodhyā in Uttar Pradesh and was named Ghanaśyāma. His education included the study of the fundamental texts of the Rāmānuja tradition and the *Bhāgavatapurāṇa*.[5]

At the age of eleven years, after his parents' death, he left home and wandered through India in search of a teacher who could let him 'see Kṛṣṇa'. He successfully learned yoga. During this period of his life he is called Nīlakaṇṭha; this Śaivite name underscores a certain discrepancy between the supposedly Vaiṣṇava and *bhakti* background of the family and the young ascetic's personal search through asceticism and yoga. Possibly, the Vaiṣṇava background belongs to the later creations of legendary traditions about Swaminarayan, though what is told about the biography of his parents seems to confirm their Vaiṣṇava attitude: it is their teacher, Swami Rāmānanda, who makes their son his successor. After seven years of wandering, Nīlakaṇṭha joins a group of Vaiṣṇava *saṃnyāsins* whom he meets at Lojpur in Gujarat and who follow a movement called Uddhava-sampradāya, led by Swami Rāmānanda. Nīlakaṇṭha is initiated and renamed Swami Sahajānanda. At the tender age of twenty-one, he is made Rāmānanda's successor as leader of the movement. In this function he moves through Gujarat, actively opposing all forms of ritual and religion which involve animal sacrifice or alcohol and engages in reforming society according to the ideals of caste and strict morals. With these aims he preaches and performs elaborate rituals and celebrations of festivals.

When seen against the background of this record of successful public activities and of the resulting religious group identity, is it plausible to consider 'charisma' as the decisive factor for this success and as foundation of this religious identity? To examine the charisma of a historical personality is thus inseparable from reflection about the source(s) which documents and institutionalizes it. For the purpose of this paper, the singular is appropriate since only a single source will be examined, the *Satsaṅgijīvanam* (SSJ; [Śatānandamuni] 1987 V.S. = AD 1930).

The *Satsaṅgijīvanam*

The SSJ is one of the oldest and most authentic sources on the life and person of Swami Sahajānanda; it is a lengthy Sanskrit work (16.536 verses)[6] by Swami Śatānanda, a close devotee of Sahajānanda from 1814 onwards.[7] It was written during the lifetime of Sahajānanda and supposedly approved by the latter. The colophons to each chapter contain the characterization of the work as *nārāyaṇacaritra* and *dharmaśāstra*.[8]

The SSJ is divided into five parts (*prakaraṇa*). The first part (60 chapters) tells about a pilgrimage of the author, Śatānanda, to Badarīkā, where his wish to 'sing Nārāyaṇa's glory' is granted. He is directed to Gujarat, where the Lord is living in human form (ch. 1–3). Upon his encounter with Sahajānanda, Śatānanda is granted omniscience about the past, present and future—which serves to explain how the SSJ can in consequence narrate about the (mythological) pre-history to Nārāyaṇa's appearance as Sahajānanda (ch. 4–10). Part I continues with the life-story of Sahajānanda's parents (ch. 11–21), including an excursus about the life of Swami Rāmānanda, (ch. 13–16), his birth (ch. 22) and boyhood, education, initiation, departure into homelessness (after the parents' death) (ch. 23–42), wanderings including defeating various proud or otherwise misguided teachers (ch. 43–9), and his encounter with the monks following Swami Rāmānanda (ch. 50–4); he is initiated by Rāmānanda and is appointed as his successor to lead the monks (ch. 55–60).

Part II (52 chapters) narrates the establishment of Sahajānanda's authority by defeating opponents and by transposing people into a state of yogic absorption or trance (*samādhi*) (ch. 5). He is committed to establishing a religion of non-violence in opposing the blood-sacrifices current among the ruling Śāktas (e.g. ch. 19 and ch. 45–6) and by celebrating festivals and preaching the true dharma.

Part III (64 chapters) is situated mainly in Durgapura (modern Gaḍhaḍā) and describes in detail how the food festival (*annakūṭa*, ch. 4–22) and the Prabodhinī festival (ch. 23–45) are celebrated there, and the Swing festival (ch. 46-64) in Vṛttālaya (modern Vaḍatāla).

Part IV (73 chapters) begins with regulations about the recitation of Purāṇas, about celebrating the Janmāṣṭamī festival, about vows, etc. taught during visits to different towns; it contains an account of the foundation of temples and discussions of the rank of Sahajānanda as *avatāra*, the appointment of Ācāryas (cf. below, section 5), the writing of the Śikṣāpatrī (ch. 44, cf. below, section 3), regulations concerning initiation (ch. 46–53) and about the annual cycle of festivals; it ends with teachings about 'knowledge' (cosmology, Sāṃkhya).

Part V (70 chapters) is almost exclusively devoted to teaching dharma (ch. 1–48) and contains teachings on the duties of castes and stages of life (*varṇāśramadharma*) and expiation (*prāyaścitta*); it recounts the installation of temples (5,49; 5,55) and teaches specifically about the dharma of life-long celibates (5,50–4) and about yoga (ch. 56–65); it narrates Sahajānanda's death (ch. 68) and the writing of the SSJ (ch. 66).[9]

It would be false to consider the SSJ as a primarily historical document; on the other hand, there can be little doubt that the author had a sense of historical reality. Many events are dated precisely, and occasional lists of names (of persons present) give the impression of calling upon eye-witnesses. In any case, there seems to be no source which allows closer access to the historical reality of Sahajānanda's personality. As already indicated, the SSJ institutionalizes Sahajānanda's personal charisma by documenting instances of its display. This is done by a combination of several elements which allow for Sahajānanda's depiction as the charismatic founder of the movement, e.g. by an idealized presentation of his spiritual power, by defining a specific textual tradition, through the foundation of temples and the establishment of ritualized access to the guru, and by providing for the continuation of charisma through hereditary succession.

'Spiritualization'—Personal Encounters with Sahajānanda

The achievement of spiritual power and its display in personal encounters with adepts or adversaries is in the text presented as the foundation-stone of Sahajānanda's power. Amongst the many instances, I shall first single out the encounter of Sahajānanda with the disciples of Swami Rāmānanda (SSJ 1,50–4). Sahajānanda reaches Lojapura on the sixth day of bright Śrāvaṇa V.S. 1856 (AD 1799) after seven years and one month of asceticism practised while wandering through India (SSJ 1,50.32–4). The image which is drawn of the young ascetic and his behaviour must be considered stereotyped and idealized; its elements, however, may be considered as the constituents of his charisma:

— Missionary zeal (he spreads 'the true dharma')
— Personal authority (he defeats heretic teachers)
— Integrity of character and behaviour (patience, desirelessness, fearlessness, lack of pride)
— Spiritual power (he conveys liberation to those who desire it and attracts other ascetics while the proud flee him)
— Appeal to scriptural authority by display of learnedness (he defends doctrines which are in accordance with true authoritative scriptures, i.e. *sacchāstra*)
— Asceticism (consisting in lack of protection through dress or housing, restricted food, detachment from sensual objects and in particular women)
— Yoga (practice of breath-control and yogic postures)
— Ritually expressed devotion to Kṛṣṇa (expressed through regular daily worship and observance of festivals). (SSJ 1,50.15–30)

Sahajānanda agrees to pay a visit to Muktānanda, the leader of the group of monks who are impressed by Sahajānanda's asceticism and consider him a liberated being. The relationship to the group is established by a theological discussion: Sahajānanda asks about the soul (*jīva*), God (*īśvara*), illusion (*māyā*,) and the absolute (*brahman*). Muktānanda answers to his satisfaction. The theological agreement between the monks and the newly-arrived ascetic is confirmed by Sahajānanda introducing himself as one who meditates on Kṛṣṇa (1,52.3–7). When he is told about Rāmānanda he recognizes in him his parents' guru and wants to meet him. While waiting for the teacher's arrival he shares the daily routines with the monks without abandoning his dharma, his asceticism, his yogic exercises; the influence which he thereby exercises over the monks is expressed by their identifying him with Kṛṣṇa, with Rāmānanda, etc. (SSJ 1,52.33–7).

Nīlakaṇṭha becomes impatient and Muktānanda writes a letter to Rāmānanda informing him about the newly-arrived guest, which repeats and confirms (1,53.17–38) the above-mentioned elements (asceticism, Yoga, wordly detachment, scholarly expertise, spiritual influence).

The passage which contains the written message is in Sanskrit of a highly literary style (in Indravajrā metre); we cannot assume that it has preserved the wording or even the language (which may have been Gujarati) of the original letter, yet the historical fact of such a letter need not be doubted; and the content does at least reflect memories of how the young Sahajānanda was seen by Rāmānanda's disciples. These memories are strikingly in accordance with what Sahajānanda says about himself in a letter written by him where he introduces himself to Rāmānanda: the contents include asceticism with the goal of seeing Kṛṣṇa; emaciation; mastery of yoga; opposition to all who oppose Kṛṣṇa; detachment in relation to women, fame, luxury, food (1,54.4 and 36).

The two letters document the agreement of self-image (on the part of Sahajānanda) and interpretation (how Rāmānanda's disciples see him). Personality, behaviour, spiritual qualification and scholarship combine to create a model (1,50.29, where it is explicitly stated that the monks consider Sahajānanda their model) in which conventional expectations and individual peculiarities enhance each other. Even if Sahajānanda's letter to Rāmānanda is a literary fiction, it tells us that he gave his fellow monks the impression of consciously and intentionally fulfilling expectations created by the model. His charisma appears as theologically and spiritually justified, but it appears also as something accepted and employed by Sahajānanda.

The second instance of the working of Sahajānanda's charisma (SSJ 2,5) is situated towards the beginning of his activities as a wandering teacher and religious leader. Sahajānanda's yogic powers apparently included the capacity to transport others in a state of visionary trance (in the text called *samādhi*); the object of the vision is generally that of the 'chosen deity' (*iṣṭadevatā*); the trance is described as a condition of total absorption in which the bodily functions practically come to a standstill. In the case of the Jain merchants (narrated in SSJ 2,5.1–9), the families of those in trance become worried that their relatives may have died, since the condition lasts nine hours. Sahajānanda recalls them to their waking state; and they come back with detailed recollections of what they have seen as well as with a sense of indifference towards the body.

The chapter continues by mentioning the types and classes of people who make up Sahajānanda's followers and visitors:

> There were in this city other people belonging to the three [upper] castes [*traivarṇika*], followers of the sects of Śrī Vallabha, followers of Nimbārka, Madhva, adherents of Śrīmad Rāmānuja and of Rāmānanda, some adherents of Śaṅkarācārya; devotees of the Sun [*saura*], the Goddess [*śākta*], Gaṇeśa [*gāṇapatya*], Śiva [*śaiva*]; and [further] Śūdras, women, renouncers, celibates [*varṇin*] and 'those without attachment' [*vītarāgin*, which the commentary explains as 'those called in vernacular 'Berāgī'] and others without appellation, who came there by the thousands. (2,5.10–12)

Seeing Sahajānanda's deed (of having bestowed the Jains with a visionary trance) they beg to be granted a vision of their favourite deities. The text includes two verses reporting Sahajānanda's thoughts. He reflects that if through his yogic power he grants them a vision of their favourite deities, they will afterwards consider *him* God (*tarhi māṃ vidyur īśvaram*), they will abandon their fake dharma (*dharmābhāsāṃś ca hitvā*), and they will practice devotion to him (SSJ 2,5.15–16).

By merely looking at him they are transported into *samādhi*; their breath stops and they see their favourite deities: Śrī Kṛṣṇa as playful child for the followers of Vallabha, Lakṣmī Nārāyaṇa for the followers of Rāmānuja, Rāma and Sītā for the followers of Rāmānanda, the light of *brahman* (*brahmajyotiḥ*) for the followers of Śaṅkara, Śiva (*śaṅkara*) with Umā for Śaivites, a golden man in the orbit of the sun (*hiraṇmayaṃ puruṣaṃ sūryamaṇḍale*) for adherents of Sūrya, Gaṇeśa for devotees of *mahāgaṇapati*, 'their own goddess' (*nijāṃ devīm*) for devotees of Śakti (*śaktibhakta*). Having been brought back to the waking state they all recognize Nīlakaṇṭha as 'assuming all forms' (*sarvarūpadhara*) and as Nārāyaṇa, the highest Lord, himself. Even Muslims approach him and ask to be shown their prophets (plural!, *paigambarān*) (SSJ 2,5.33–8).[10] All of the visualizations mentioned identify religions or religious groups (Jainas, Muslims, adherents of specific personalities like Śaṅkara or Rāmānuja, devotees of specific deities like Kṛṣṇa, Rāma, Gaṇeśa, etc.),[11] and all of them fall under the verdict quoted concerning 'fake dharma' (SSJ 2,5.15–16). They are identified by their founder or by their (iconographically identifiable) concept of god. It is tempting to transfer these criteria to Swaminarayan's own followers, and to their sense of identity as defined with reference to the concept of god and/or to the personality of the founder.

In the event cited, personal encounter leads to a spiritual experience which changes the ideas which those who have this experience had about that person; various aspects of divinity are projected upon the person.[12] The power to grant such visions is interpreted as receiving his grace. I propose to label this aspect of Sahajānanda's use of his charisma 'spiritualization'. It presupposes the spiritual dimension in Sahajānanda's personality; it designates the employment of this dimension in transpersonal transactions. The effect on those graced with such experience must be termed a conversion, since it involves a change of personal adherence from one 'founder figure' to another; since adherents of different deities have this experience, Sahajānanda is identified with the visualized forms of different deities. The 'religion' (dharma) thus established is primarily one of worldly behaviour: no drink, no meat, no adultery, no theft, no violence, no mixing of castes (SSJ 2,5.41). There is no reason to doubt that Sahajānanda did have these yogic powers; the text also leaves no doubt that he used them deliberately for the purpose of his missionary activity and to strengthen social and religious reform.

Charisma appears in the above instances as a matter of a personal spiritual experience which is subjected to intentional guidance and, if directed at adversaries, may result in their conversion. There are other aspects of Sahajānanda's actions and instructions concerning the effect and institutionalization of charisma in different realms: the experience of a divine leader is 'textualized' by the creation of a canon (of traditional texts on the one hand, of new texts on the other), it is 'ritualized' by the construction of temples in which the founder's image is venerated along with other aspects of Viṣṇu-Nārāyaṇa, and it is 'legalized' by establishing the principle of hereditary succession for the Ācāryas.

'Textualization'—The Formation of a Canon

It may be an exaggeration to call the Swaminarayan Movement a 'religion of the book', but it is certainly a movement in which texts contribute essentially to the definition of identity. Texts are mentioned in a number of contexts: they form part of the (religious) education of Sahajānanda, Rāmānanda (Sahajānanda's teacher), Śatānanda (the author of the SSJ); the regular listening to or recitation of these texts is part of public festivals as well as of private spirituality (e.g. in preparing for one's death);

authoritative texts (*śāstra*) are constantly referred to in order to enhance the authority of the teachings of dharma, behaviour, ritual, etc.; and to know these authoritative texts is a standard qualification of religious functionaries (reciters, priests, Brahmins in general).

In the SSJ, the text most frequently mentioned by name is the *Bhāgavatapurāṇa* (BhP).[13] This text is also included in the list of eight texts which are explicitly listed and recommended for study: *Vedas*, *Brahmasūtras*, *Bhāgavatapurāṇa*, *Viṣṇusahasranāma*, *Bhagavadgītā*, *Viduranīti*, *Vāsudevamāhātmya* of the *Skandapurāṇa*, *Yājñavalkyasmṛti* with the commentary *Mitākṣarā* (SSJ 4,44.93–102). These texts are thus defined as constituting a canon of authoritative texts from tradition.[14]

The definition of the canon of eight authoritative texts[15] is itself part of a text, the SSJ, the writing of which is attributed to Sahajānanda himself. The tradition of texts constitutive of the identity of a religious group is thus continued;[16] to the traditional canon is added another canon of new texts which owe their origin to the founder of that movement. Two of these canonical texts are in Sanskrit.

The so-called Śikṣāpatrī (contained in SSJ 4,44) is a brief summary of rules and regulations on religious practice; it calls itself 'the essence of all authoritative texts' (4,44.203); the connection with the 'traditional' canon is established by referring the reader to those texts for further details.[17] On the other hand, the new text is made 'canonical' when the followers of Sahajānanda are told that it should be read daily and that those who do not practice its instructions are to be considered expelled from the group of followers (4,44.205–10).

The other text which is endowed with comparable importance within the Swaminarayan Movement is the SSJ itself. The high estimation which the text claims for the followers of Sahajānanda is summarized (SSJ 1,1.17–22) by characterizing the SSJ as the essence of all Vedas, as propounding 'the dharma directed towards one single goal', i.e. an exclusive, absolute doctrine and code of conduct (*aikāntikadharma*) as cause of liberation from the bonds of existence, as describing the life of Sahajānanda, and as source of merit only for the good. Thus, the text is invested not only with the greatest authority, it is also made into a means of salvation which distinguishes the followers of Sahajānanda from everybody else and is accessible only to them.

The story framing the dialogue during which the text is repeated to a king from Gujarat in Jagannāthapurī adds another detail concerning the religious significance of the SSJ: the king asks Suvrata, the reciter, how he can see the Lord (i.e. Sahajānanda) directly (1,2.48). Since it is not possible to meet him in person (as Suvrata did), the narrated encounter substitutes for the personal encounter. This is an episode which puts into practice what Sahajānanda promised to Śatānanda when granting him, as a boon, that he should write a book about him (SSJ 5,68.28–31); Śatānanda will be a great support for his followers after his disappearance.

As if to test Śatānanda's literary qualification,[18] he is given the task 'to first compose the *Śikṣāpatrī*, which was written by me, promptly, in *anuṣṭubh* verses and thereby make it a great book' (5,68.32). This may mean that the *Śikṣāpatrī* was originally written either in (Sanskrit) prose or even in the vernacular; it clearly states that the text of the *Śikṣāpatrī* contained as chapter 4,44 in the SSJ was formulated not by Sahajānanda but by Śatānanda. Śatānanda thus is the author of the two works which constitute the original canon of (Sanskrit) texts of the Swaminarayan Movement. Both texts are authorized by the founder, the *Śikṣāpatrī* by the claim to authorship, the SSJ by explicit approval (cf. 5,68.16–18). Each section of the SSJ is read in the presence of Sahajānanda who is satisfied.[19] They incorporate and to a certain degree replace Sahajānanda's words, teachings, and personality. This textualization is rooted in Sahajānanda's arrangements for the time after his death and can thus be considered a deliberate attempt to replace personal encounter and guarantee the continued functioning of what was charisma during his lifetime. In continuation of a textual tradition, in which texts are appealed to as authoritative, new texts are created to institutionalize the founder's sayings and personality. The use of these texts seems to be the same as that of the traditional texts, particularly as sources for personal edification and public recitation.

Both texts of the 'new canon' are presented as the continuation of a scriptural tradition which serves to define group identity (*saṃpradāya*). The doctrinal content of these texts provides a point of reference for the theoretical teachings as well as for the regulations of behaviour and ritual in the group. Another aspect of how a traditional text, specifically the *Bhāgavatapurāṇa*, serves as point of reference (and thus another aspect of the textualization of Sahajānanda's person and charisma) are those instances in the life of Sahajānanda for which an episode of the *Bhāgavatapurāṇa* or general acquaintance with that text is mentioned as the motive.

Thus, the decision to appoint Ācāryas as hereditary successors (cf. below) is motivated by Sahajānanda's desire to lead a life like Jaḍa-Bharata.

> Presently, due to listening again and again to the fifth skandha (of the *Bhāgavatapurāṇa*), I am eager to remain distant from worldly activity, like the stupid Bharata. I have renounced the duty of active involvement; reading and listening to the tenth skandha (of the *Bhāgavatapurāṇa*) daily, I shall practice devotion to Kṛṣṇa and nothing else. (4,44.14–15)

The same story is mentioned in the episode of Sahajānanda's departure into homelessness (1,42). It is told that he wanders for a month towards the Himālaya, welcoming whatever hardship he has to bear. 'By listening etc. to the story of Bharata, Hari had obtained an attitude of detachment; he was very eager to practice asceticism in the hermitage of Pulaha' (1,42.56). It is the hermitage of Pulaha to which Bharata retires according to *Bhāgavatapurāṇa* 5,7.8. In a brief 'autobiography' (2,37.18–36) Sahajānanda mentions that the *Bhāgavatapurāṇa* had made him want to see Kṛṣṇa; thus he left home and wandered, visiting places of pilgrimage.

SSJ 2,22–3 tells us about a local king who anticipates that Kṛṣṇa's incarnation is to be expected after having recited the *Bhāgavatapurāṇa* and having reflected about it. His meeting with Sahajānanda verifies this anticipation and serves at the same time to give scriptural authorization to the recognition of Sahajānanda as an *avatāra*.

Another example (and more examples could probably be found in the SSJ) of this interpretation of Sahajānanda's personality and behaviour in the light of 'canonical' texts occurs in Muktānanda's letter to Rāmānanda (cf. above, section 2). The strict fasting habits of the young ascetics are interpreted as an example of what is said about liberated beings living on the White Continent (*śvetadvīpa*) without food. The commentary attributes this to 'the Purāṇas etc.' (*iti purāṇādau śrūyate*).[20]

'Ritualization'—The Foundation of Temples

The SSJ leaves no doubt that Sahajānanda is considered as the embodiment of Śrī Kṛṣṇa, the highest God, in his aspect as Nara-Nārāyaṇa. Yet, the boy Ghanaśyāma, later wandering ascetic Nīlakaṇṭha, then monastic leader Sahajānanda, is described as someone on an earnest spiritual search, ready to change affiliations and masters and eager to learn in theory and practice. He may have reminded his parents of Kṛṣṇa, he may have been considered by his fellow ascetics as a model of divine devotion, he may have been identified by those who came under the influence of his yogic powers with the form of the divine which they saw in their vision; however, the SSJ does not completely conceal the fact that Sahajānanda did not consider himself divine from the very beginning of his public career.[21]

The SSJ presents Sahajānanda's decision to construct temples in which his image (identified with various forms of Kṛṣṇa-Viṣṇu) is installed as one aspect of the secret resolve by which he prepares for the time after his death. The brief chapter SSJ 4,24 is something like an inner monologue (*acintayat sa manasā*) attributed to Sahajānanda. He reflects that the purpose of his descent (*avatāra*) has been fulfilled; after his disappearance, however, his followers will be without support. He wishes to support them in three ways: (1) by the construction of temples, (2) by the appointment of a leader and religious teacher from his family, (3) by the composition of a book by Śatānanda (i.e. the SSJ).

In terms of literary criticism one needs to ask how Śatānanda could have known about Sahajānanda's secret thoughts (*gūḍha-saṃkalpa*, as the colophon calls it). The endowment with omniscience granted by Sahajānanda serves as a kind of 'fictional' authorization; it is also not impossible that Sahajānanda did communicate his decisions and plans to somebody as close to the inner group of monks as Śatānanda. The literary device of a 'secret resolve' would then betray the author's desire to let Sahajānanda appear as the true master of all events; everything happens according to his wish.

This literary and/or theological intention anticipates the next chapter when the people of Ahmedabad (*Śrīnagara*) approach Sahajānanda with the wish to construct a temple. Without the preceding chapter one would have to read this as a further incident of a deification by the people accepted by Sahajānanda; in its context the event appears as divinely motivated. One can sense the same distance between historical event and theological justification when, after the completion of the construction and just before the installation of the images in the temple, Sahajānanda confirms that the construction of the temple happened in accordance with Nārāyaṇa's will (4,25.60–1); he could have said 'my will'.

This distance has disappeared in the speech by which the installation ceremonies conclude:

O people, listen everybody to my words because I speak for your benefit. Our favourite deity is Śrī Kṛṣṇa, the highest Puruṣa. He, who stays within a circle of brilliance in Goloka, appears on earth for the good of all beings. When Dharmadeva and Mūrti meditated on him with utmost firm devotion, he became manifest from their body, comprising two forms [*dvirūpa*], accepting the lifestyle of a celibate. Then, satisfying them by a boon for the good of human beings, he—under the name Nara-Nārāyaṇa—went to the forest Badarī. He resides there practising asceticism for the sake of the enjoyment and liberation of those human beings who have taken refuge in the land of actions, Bhārata. But when requested by Brahmā and others for the sake of removing the burden of the earth, Śrī Kṛṣṇa gracefully became manifest in the clan of the Yādavas. Nara was born under the name Arjuna in the Kuru clan as friend of Hari; combined with this Arjuna, he (Hari) is remembered as Nara-Nārāyaṇa. This same Nara-Nārāyaṇa has been installed here by me; there is no doubt that the good of human beings will come about through devotion to him. (SSJ 4,25.82–9)

Without clear distinction of levels of reality or time-scale, a number of aspects of divinity are amalgamated: the one highest deity (Śrī Kṛṣṇa), his double aspect as Nara and Nārāyaṇa who are identified with two personages from the Mahābhārata (Kṛṣṇa and Arjuna) and with the god in the double aspect of ascetic and deity of a place of pilgrimage in India; the purposes of any divine manifestation or embodiment (removal of the burden of earth, increase of devotion to Śrī Kṛṣṇa, fulfilment of human desires and achievement of liberation) is transferred also to the mission of Sahajānanda as son of Dharmadeva and Mūrti. Thus, the image of Nara-Nārāyaṇa in the temple of Ahmedabad is or becomes the image of Sahajānanda.[22] By visiting the temple daily and via *darśana* of its idol, people will obtain 'enjoyments and liberation' (4,25.90–2). As if to demonstrate the effectiveness of his commitment to his followers, the chapter ends by describing how Sahajānanda satisfies the people (and Brahmins in particular!) by donations and by feeding them a sumptuous meal.

In the context of a deliberate institutionalization of charisma the foundation of temples can be seen as the ritualization of a previously personal relationship: Sahajānanda spent the second half of his life presenting himself to his followers and devotees as a recipient of honours, gifts, worship, and as the distributor of instructions, donations and grace. By replacing personal contact with the ritual of temple service he remains in conformity with a model which is traditional and accepted.

'Legalization'—Hereditary Succession

The same may be the case for the regulation of succession by inheritance within the family which Sahajānanda instituted (according to 4,24.12): 'For the sake of the thriving of the way of devotion, initiation by means of the sacred formula is required; therefore I should establish the office of sacred teacher among the pure descendants of Dharma.' Such a regulation had been established by Vallabhācārya for the so-called *Puṣṭimārga*; acquaintance with this movement and a considerable closeness in matters of religious practice and liturgy is evident in the SSJ.[23]

The chapter which relates the appointment of Ācāryas (4,40) does not give any reasons why *two* successors are appointed. One can only speculate that it was the family as a whole that should guarantee the succession and that the regulation of succession was not the result of any personal preference for an individual or a favour. Since Sahajānanda had two married brothers, there had to be two successors; the territory, the rights of property and income were consequently divided by two. One may also speculate that Sahajānanda was aware of the fact that a restriction to a single lineage involved considerable risks in cases of childlessness. Such considerations are at least suggested by the fact that the adoption of a son (who would be the hereditary successor) from within the family is explicitly permitted; Sahajānanda's elder brother had three sons, his younger brother five. Still, it deserves mention that the right of the first born is abolished (4,40.50: *na jyeṣṭha-niyamaḥ atra*).

In the light of the insistence on Brahmin privileges attributed to Sahajānanda throughout the SSJ and of the great importance given to caste divisions (there are, e.g. special regulations for the initiation of Śūdras) it seems that Sahajānanda interpreted his personal charisma in the sense of an *adhikāra*, a right and privilege, which was due to his person no less than to his family and which was due to his family not least of all *because* it produced a personality like him.[24]

Conclusion

The SSJ presents Sahajānanda as a personality who undoubtedly did have charisma, but who utilized that charisma consciously to serve his missionary intentions (reform of dharma, abolition of social and religious abuses). He seems to have had a realistic estimate of the role of personal influence ('charisma') on the sense of identity of his followers; and he planned for the time when (after his death) this identity would have to continue and thrive without this factor. The different elements in the institutionalization of his charisma have been labelled 'spiritualization', 'textualization', 'ritualization' and 'legalization'. To the extent to which Sahajānanda may be assumed to have chosen these elements deliberately, one might even call them strategies. Śatānanda in the SSJ may have wanted to present all the events in Sahajānanda's life, including his appearance on earth, as effect of (his) divine will; therefore the presentation of these 'strategic' decisions must be interpreted also as literary device and not only as historical information. Nevertheless, the SSJ allows the conclusion that the canonization of Sahajānanda's charisma is not something effected by his followers. That is, it is not or not primarily a historical process falling into the realm of Sahajānanda's *Wirkungsgeschichte*; rather it is something which he himself consciously wanted, programmed and directed during his lifetime.

Notes

1. Thus the anglicized transliteration, used also in the literature produced by the Movement itself, which I adopt in this paper. 'Movement' translates

what from the insider's point of view is called *saṃpradāya*, while the (Western, Christian) outsider's perspective is accentuated where the Movement is called 'sect'.

2. For background information about the history of the movement and its teachings see Williams (1984). The Swaminarayan Movement has not received as much attention in academic research as other movements which originated at about the same period, e.g. the Brahmo Samāj, the Ramakrishna Mission, Sri Aurobindo's movements etc. It is beyond the scope of this paper to attempt any comparison, but the evidence provided by the Swaminarayan Movement and its scriptures invites such comparison, especially within the framework of a typology of Hindu religious movements.
3. See Williams (1984: 201–4).
4. The name of Swami Sahajānanda changed several times during his life: born as Ghanaśyāma and called Hari, he became Nīlakaṇṭha as wandering ascetic; Swami Rāmānanda renamed him Sahajānanda upon his initiation; by his followers (including Śatānanda in the *Satsaṅgijīvanam*) he is called Svāminārāyaṇa Muni. In this paper I use Sahajānanda uniformly.
5. The *Bhāgavatapurāṇa* is not among the texts quoted by Rāmānuja.
6. I gratefully wish to acknowledge the support for research on this text granted by the Swiss National Funds by financing a project (1992–4) at the Abteilung für Indologie, University of Zürich. The complete text was transliterated in machine-readable form, meticulously carried out by Dr Jaydev Jani. Further, an English summary of contents of the whole text has been prepared by Dr Jani and myself. Dr Jani's contribution to this research is indeed everywhere evident in this paper.
7. Cf. SSJ 2,48.37.
8. Each colophon further identifies the part (*prakaraṇa*), sometimes the subsection (e.g. 'in the context of teaching *dharma*'), and then gives the number of the chapter and indicates the subject-matter.
9. 5,69 gives the regulations for celebrating Harijayantī; 5,70 contains a summary outline of the SSJ.
10. Another episode of induced yogic trance is narrated in SSJ 2,44. There the absorption experienced by uneducated people is tested by learned Brahmins; they fail to wake these people up (even by inflicting pain upon them). The Brahmins have to acknowledge that what the people report as the content of their vision corresponds to descriptions found in the holy scriptures. Thus, in this episode the spiritual experience is verified by reference to the scriptures—an instance of 'textualization' (cf. below, section 3).
11. Cf. above for the translated passage 2,5.10–12, where these 'religions' figure as groups or classes of people.
12. For Muslims the change of mind or loyalty is restricted to the wordly sphere in that they submit to his instructions (*tad-ājñayām avartata*).
13. Schreiner (1999).
14. Cf. also 2,2.32–33; 2,37.104–11. The mention of texts or the use of texts in

the SSJ leads one to suspect that the Vedas do not play an important role in the religious practice of the movement. On the other hand, there are lists of texts recited on certain occasions which differ from this canon. In 4,9 the recitation of these texts is narrated as a public event; the Vedas are represented by the *Sāmaveda*; the *Brahmasūtras* are missing.

15. The same canon is mentioned in the context of appointing Ācāryas (cf. below, section 5); the Ācāryas are instructed to behave according to these 8 texts: *yuvābhyāṃ manmatān granthān aṣṭāv āśritya nityadā* | *vṛtyaṃ śiṣyā vartanīyāḥ saṃpradāyānusārataḥ* | | (4,40.46).
16. In Sahajānanda's disputes with representatives of Śāktism the fact that these persons read the wrong texts (e.g. *Kaulāgama*) is often mentioned; to give up wrong beliefs entails a change of authoritative scriptures; cf. for instance SSJ 2,45.37–50 where a Śākta is told to give up his authoritative scriptures (the *Kaulāgama*).
17. *iti saṃkṣepato dharmāḥ sarveṣāṃ likhitāmayā* | *sāṃpradāyikagranthebhyo jñeya eṣāṃ tu vistaraḥ* | | (4,44.203).
18. Or perhaps in order to establish a kind of shared authorship between Sahajānanda and Śatānanda for both of the texts of the new canon?
19. After Sahajānanda's death a group of monks collected and redacted the sermons given by Sahajānanda in Gujarati; this collection, the *Vacanāmṛta*, is certainly of equal importance in the religious life of the movement.
20. The reference is probably to the Nārāyaṇīya (*Mahābhārata* 12,322.9).
21. It would require a separate article to trace the change in the use of proper names employed by the author in referring to Sahajānanda's behaviour in public, which developed from ascetic refusal to acceptance of pompous honours and divine worship.
22. Cf. 1,3.16 where Nara-Nārayaṇa speaks to Śatānanda, who is visiting Badarī on a pilgrimage, and tells him that he has presently been born on earth; the same simultaneity of atemporal and historical divine presence is expressed and, as far as Śatānanda is concerned, experienced here.
23. Cf. for example 2,37.51–5.
24. Cf. 4,44.12, where Sahajānanda uses the word *adhikāra* when describing how the function as popular teacher had been transferred to him by Rāmānanda: *yo 'yam janagurutve 'trādhikāro vartate mama* | *nyasto 'sti sa balād eva śrīsvāmicaraṇair mayi*.

References

[Śatānandamuni]. 1987 V.S. [A. D. 1930]. *Satsaṃgijīvanam: śrīśatānandamunivi-racitam: śrīśukānandamuni-viracitayā hetu-saṃjñayā ṭīkayā, sa. dha. dhu. ācār-ya-śrī-vihārilāla-mahārāja-viracitayā bhāvaprabodhinyākhyayā vyākhyayā ca sametam*. Mumbayyām: Sārikākhyamudraṇālaye.

Schreiner, Peter. 1999. The Bhāgavatapurāṇa as Model for the Satsaṅgijīvanam.

In *Composing a Tradition: Concepts, Techniques and Relationships. Proceedings of the First Dubrovnik International Conference on the Sanskrit Epics and Purāṇas*, ed. Mary Brockington and Peter Schreiner. 257–78. Zagreb: Croatian Academy of Science and Arts.

Williams, Raymond Brady. 1984. *A New Face of Hinduism: The Swaminarayan Religion*. Cambridge: Cambridge University Press.

Charisma, Transfer of Charisma and Canon in North Indian Bhakti

MONIKA HORSTMANN

Introduction

This essay is concerned with the fate of charisma in *bhakti* groups which owe their existence to a charismatic leader. Its first section addresses the way in which succession is regulated in these groups. Succession is the key event by which the continuity of a group is secured, and this requires that a group, in order to legitimize itself, have recourse to its own charismatic beginnings. It is thus a locus of the transition of charisma, both in the sense of a move on the time-axis (from the first generation to subsequent ones) and in the sense of a transformation in quality and consolidation of structure. In Weber's study of charisma (1985) succession occupied a prominent position. According to him, the preservation of the prime charisma, which, as he contended, was poorly structured and operated in a spontaneous assembly of the charismatic leader's followers, was perpetuated in the structured institution. Most prominent and most essential for the survival of the group is the institution of succession. Thus the transition from charisma to institution equals the transformation of the unstructured into the structured. Wolfgang Schluchter (1991: 238–43) highlighted two aspects of Weber's concept, namely (1) charisma vested in the person of a succeeding office-holder, and (2) charisma vested in the office itself and not in the office-holder. This two-fold distinction may be used to review the modes of succession to be found in the groups which I have chosen as examples.

The second section deals with the various ways in which *bhakti* groups rescue their prime charisma. Generally, this happens by providing a structured frame within which institutions or events are allowed and encouraged to operate in ways which invoke the affective immediacy of the communities' prime.

In the third and final section I refer to the relationship between charisma and canon. I will review the concept of charisma as being transformed and, as it were, superseded by the structure of the canon with its fixed texts, dogmas and regulations enjoined on the community.

Three *bhakti* groups will serve as examples, namely, the sects[1] of Caitanya (in its North Indian, Braj form), of Vallabha, and of Dādū.[2]

Charisma and Office

The Dādūpanth (DP), the sect of Dādū, provides an example of a sect in which personal charisma came to be institutionalized. Therefore, it belongs to the model of charisma vested in the person of the individual gurus, in the nomenclature of the sect, the *svāmī*, abbot (*mahant*)-in-chief, and the *mahants* or abbots subordinate to him. This concept springs from the monastic key-concept of the sect according to which the Supreme is found within. He who has realized the Supreme most perfectly is the guru. The Supreme is called the 'real guru' (*satguru*) who resides within, while the human *satguru* is the corporeal Supreme.[3]

The succession which relies on personal charisma is a frail construction, for an office-holder may fail. This has led to developments, in the DP as well as in other sects, which passed through an initial stage of about two generations after the generation of the founder during which it was still assumed or hoped that the successor to the office might bear the founder's charisma. Succession would take place within the founder's family or by different processes of selection. However, at a stage increasingly remote from the prime charisma, a crisis seems to have been almost inevitable. This is especially evident in groups with a heterogeneous clientele. Moreover, in the DP there existed a potentially fissiparous factor. The charisma became vested in spirited individuals within the sect who could justly claim to participate in the prime charisma embodied by guru Dādū. These in turn made disciples of their own, so that the community soon became fragmented. This process was spurred by inherited and often differing religious traditions and life-styles which influenced the sect's clientele. Over the generations the sect split up into innumerable branches, which blurred and also weakened the relation between the centre and its branches. Moreover, some new lineages attracted a lay clientele which was at times able to provide these lineages with considerable prestige, support and hence independence. All this made the office of abbot-in-chief vulnerable. Consequently, before long the DP was threatened by dissolution. The crisis that befell it and ultimately led to a regulated, predictable procedure of succession, according to which the new abbot would be designated by his predecessor-guru, was resolved in a telling fashion. In 1693, a faction within the DP which was opposed to descendants of Dādū and their relatives—who had not been able to hold the sect together—opted for Jaitrām as abbot-in-chief. Jaitrām reorganized the sect and after him succession was always bestowed by timely designation of the future office-holder. Hagiography has it that the oracle, Dādū's heavenly voice itself, had pointed to him as his successor (Kanīrām 1986: 15). All this goes to say that Jaitrām had been found to be graced with Dādū's charisma. The case exemplifies how the claim to personal charisma is normally sought to be underpinned by a supportive strategy, in this case succession regulated by designation.[4]

In both the Caitanya and Vallabha sects succession runs in the male line, i.e. from the office-holder to his son or adopted son. Thus, they follow the model of charisma principally vested in the office with a strong, stabilizing admixture of what Weber called *Gentilcharisma*. Smooth succession is safeguarded by the timely designation of a successor. The legitimization of succession is not or at least not entirely vested in the founders of the sect, although these are conjured up in many ways in the life of the community, e.g. hagiography, theological works authored by Vallabha. The succession is rather linked with the icons (the *vigrahas* or *svarūps*) of Kṛṣṇa. The authority of the office, as has always been emphasized, rested on these right from the beginning, especially as the authority over certain icons was and has remained disputed among the various sects and among lineages of the same sect.[5] The office itself participates in and partakes of the divine presence enshrined in the icons. The office-holder is the caretaker of the deity's mundane interests and its juridical representative, his *adhikārī*.

The early generations of communities paid much attention to the firm foundation of the principles underpinning their legitimacy. In the case of the Caitanyas this created no major problem (endless problems, however, cropped up later as lineages fought over the authority over icons and their worldly gains). Caitanya himself appointed the Six Gosvāmīs to carry on his religion, although this must by no means be taken at face value, for the legitimacy of the link between Caitanya and his disciples was emphasized to great and constitutionally lasting effect by Caitanya's early hagiographer Kṛṣṇadās Kavirāj (Entwistle 1987: 149). The various lineages springing from the Six Gosvāmīs and other Caitanyites developed according to much the same pattern: the devotee serving a divine image, which he handed down to his successor along with the wealth vested in the deity and, usually, his personal property.

It would be incorrect to assume that the office-holder's authority is conceived of as solely derivative, merely as that of a caretaker. It is also supported by the authority rooted in the concept of the guru, which is antecedent to all individual sects discussed here. The concept of the guru was essential in settling the question why, if *bhakti* was the free flow of God's grace, the office should exist. As would be expected, the answer did not openly address a vital problem that also lingered within the debate. The problem was how the economic continuity of a community, which relied on income provided by the state, devotees and its own economic transactions could be secured. It ran as follows—the guru surpassed God himself, because he was the mediator of grace. The Caitanyites, for example, formulated this with clarity in words such as those of Gopālabhaṭṭa's 'Praise of the guru's greatness' (*Gurumāhātmya*) (HBV, chapter 4, stanzas 346–66), which consists almost entirely of citations from earlier scriptural authorities. The debate as it was conducted in the sect of Vallabha is reflected in its hagiography, the *vārtās*. An excellent example of this would be the *Dāmodardās Harsānī ki vārtā*, the first hagiographical text of the CVV. Hagiographies such as this one put emphasis on *gurubhāva*, the affection for the guru without which *puṣṭi*, grace, cannot be attained. The question, 'What is greater, the gift [of grace; MH] or the giver?' is answered in favour of the giver, namely, the guru (HBV 1986: 8ff.). From this there ensues a mutual enhancement of the rank of the icon and the office-holder, and, of course, of their mutual dependence.

While the various modes of institutionalized charisma, as it prevails in succession, are regulated and, accordingly, are somewhat closed structures, there are many more ways in which the prime charisma can be guarded, rescued and become revitalized. The affective, personal relationship, through which prime charisma was mainly transported, is put afresh into effect by these means, albeit within a structured frame (cf. Gebhardt 1993).

One of the means would be the affective relationship to one's personal guru. In a much more structured way, the affective relationship between the lay community and a monk or an abbot is strengthened by the institution of the *caumāsā*, as it is observed in the DP. During that period of the rainy season a monk observes *stabilitas loci*. He may be or, for religious leaders, will almost certainly be invited by a family and thus a local community to spend his *caumāsā* with them. The religious activities and the personal communication taking place during that period greatly strengthen the affective relationship between the laity and their guru. Other ways to intensify an affective relationship consist of festivals and religious feasts in which the entire community or subgroups interact and co-operate, often over a period of several days. This certainly does not take place within a rank-free context, but in a non-routine context determined by the requirements of religious service, *sevā*. The most striking example of the enormous affective release and the locus of realization of the divine presence are, I feel, the meticulously structured 'divine feasts' organized by the Vaiṣṇavas, in a most sophisticated and certainly most complicated way in the sect of Vallabha. Here I am thinking especially of the Annakūṭa festival, in which the intrusion of many folk elements into the normally observed rites cause a 'dislocation', in the course of which inversive symbols and behaviours intrude in the ritual and widen its interpretive horizon (Toomey 1994: 106–16).

The structural limitations governing life-styles are not necessarily barriers to the flow of charisma. This is also evident in the social role of renunciation in *bhakti*. In principle, in *bhakti* renunciation is not a means to an end, namely, release (*mokṣa*), but the result of being irresistibly attracted to the object of one's *bhakti* and thus being pulled away from the world. This principle is found to be modified in many respects, because other ideals and ideas about renunciation mix with it. However, a *bhakti* monk or nun is the exemplar of *bhakti*, having matured under the spell of the Supreme as it was transported by the charisma of the guru. The monk or nun serves as an example of how the spirit of *bhakti*, if taken to its radical end, works on the devotee. The life of these exemplars of *bhakti* and their interaction with the world is regulated, but within these structures they represent the effect of unconditional grace. This is not dissimilar to what Tambiah (1987: 126) said of Buddhist forest monks: 'Rather than creating doctrine, they bring doctrine to life, especially for the lay communities. They are capable of circulating their grace and radiating their charisma as quintessential achievers of the highest values of faith.'

Charisma and Canon

In this last section of my paper I will dwell on the relationship between charisma and canon. Do we encounter a duality of the poorly structured *versus* structure in this relationship, of the spontaneous, original *versus* the constituted, consolidated continuity? If we take canon to comprise the body of scriptures, dogmas, visible and actional symbols authored or adopted by a given group, this duality cannot be readily established, for, in principle, this canon may work both ways—it may stifle, but it may also preserve and enhance the charismatic flow. If we think mainly of tacitly or openly apologetic texts and *mores* we may find it easier to highlight such a duality.

In light of the well-known history of Christian monastic orders, it is a little surprising that a duality of this kind should enjoy popularity. Saints Benedict, Francis of Assisi and Ignatius of Loyola, for example, all created their specific rules of discipline and spiritual exercises during their lifetime. The bodies of prescriptions both preserved charisma in a structured way and served as models to enact it. A similar situation existed in the *bhakti* tradition. Leaving aside the scholastic exercises which are likely to obliterate the vestiges of a charismatic spirit, one must avoid thinking of the canon in terms of an element of somehow subordinate or frozen charismatic potential. The history of the groups, which we know relatively well, rather suggests structures both being inherited by and evolving anew in the first generation of a group, notwithstanding the fact that structures have been questioned as long as groups have been able to rescue vestiges of the charismatic spirit as they saw it governing their life. The *bhakti* movements, which eventually consolidated as sects, had charismatic founders, but had these founders denounced, abandoned, let alone discarded, the canon in which they had grown up?

For both the Caitanya and the Vallabha sects this has to be denied. Their founders were saturated with a theological tradition which was prerequisite to their own doctrines, which modified the tradition. Tradition conditioned what they were to preach and how they were to act. Apart from an extraordinary, individual disposition which we must account for, the rapture into which Caitanya is reported to have fallen in front of Kṛṣṇa, or when visualizing him, is informed by and derives its meaning from the theological concept of the '*bhakti* of disinterested love', *premabhakti*, which had been canonized in scripture long before Caitanya.[6] Also, physical symbols of mystic rapture were preconditioned and to this day have been handed down by subsequent generations as models, to the extent that charismatic affect or mere affectation follows a relatively well-defined pattern.[7] The canon, first created by Caitanya's disciples and overshadowing Caitanya himself, sets meticulous rules both of a theological and a ritual kind and, although it serves the end of legitimizing the status of religious officials (Weber 1985: 297), it is also a locus of charisma made reliably tangible. It sets the rules of how to serve the divine image, it reinterprets the religious *mores* in aesthetic terms and thus provides for the theatrical enactment of *bhakti*.

In other words, the canon delineates and sets models for how affective relationships are to be acted out. It provides the pattern for the 'imitation of Kṛṣṇa'.

In the case of Vallabha, the formation of the canon was begun by himself and further developed by his disciples. As the *ācārya,* he spoke with canonical authority. The Vallabhite canon is the vehicle of the charismatic in giving enduring models for helping to perpetuate *bhāva*, the emotion that transports the devotee from the mundane to the eternal level and that unites the devotees, and has therefore an essential social impact.

In both the Caitanya and Vallabha sects the elaborate daily ritual and special festivals represent a canonized way of making accessible the spirit of the beginnings of their respective movements. Through these rituals the devotee conceives of himself as sharing in divine grace. He complies with canonical rules but is, at the same time, liberated to expand his experience in a broad and individual scope. I will illustrate what I have in mind by a recent incident. It concerns the Caitanya sect and shows how canonically sanctioned operations may well set in motion a charismatic flow, particularly if additional circumstances add to them, and how this can be channelled back into the routine management of a religious group. The incident took place in 1992 and was recorded on videotape. Also in 1994, when I watched it first, it served as a powerful medium of religious edification. I will now quote from a text which, since that incident, happened to be circulated as a kind of follow-up *māhātmya* of the Bhramarghāṭ, a sacred place in Vrindaban.

[In the fall of 1992,] Jayasiṃha Gherā [the house of Jaisiṅgh II. at Vrindaban and now the central building of the Sri Caitanya Prema Sansthana] was the site of an *aṣṭayāma līlā* ... The script was prepared from a traditional text, the rich costumes and sets were made with careful attention to each detail, the troupe of boys and men who are sponsored by the ashram rehearsed under Maharaj ji's [Puruṣottama Gosvāmījī, the leading priest of the Rādhāramaṇa temple lineage, which is traced back to Gopālabhaṭṭa Gosvāmī] close supervision.

But before the lila [*sic!*] could begin, it was necessary to invoke the eternal performers, to bring space and the time to life ... [The text goes on recording the brahmins performing].

After they all had spoken, Maharaj ji asked one of his devotees, a gifted dancer, to speak. Just as she finished, a large black insect, about three inches long, flew into the tent in front of her. The visitor danced on the ground and flew up to dance in the air, alighting two or three more times—long enough to be captured on video. After less than a minute it flew off again. ... Maharaj ji spoke, saying that the divine spirit can take any form, and for those who could see with devotion and love, it was Kṛṣṇa's presence that had become visible. He declared that a beautiful bower should be created to commemorate this manifestation … [The *bhramara* appeared again on three more days. On the third and the penultimate day it installed itself in the central eight-petalled lotus made on the spot in the newly erected bower where it had first appeared].

A sacred space is a place where two worlds intersect. At Jayasimha Ghera [*sic!*] the spirals of time measured in Kṛṣṇa's boyhood, Śrī Caitanya's ecstatic discoveries, Jayasiṃha's building—came together under Maharaj ji's direction with the time measured in hours and minutes—the daily activities of the deity, the regular recitation of sacred text, and the offerings of music and song that defined and filled the space. … In the moment, what had been and what eternally is came together to create a new beginning… (Anonymous n.d.: 2–4).

The effect of the insect's appearance was clearly interpreted as the charismatic infusion of Kṛṣṇa's renewed presence in Braj. As late as January 1994 the incident was much talked of and memory of it often refreshed by presentations of the video recording. This event would have been pointless except that it was rooted in the canon of sacred literature, such as the *Bhāgavata Purāṇa* and numerous treatments of the incident in Kṛṣṇa poetry. As the writer put it, the incident was seen as an intersection of canonically enjoined ritual activities and a manifestation of the divine. By 1994 conjurations of the event had become quasi-routinized, with many side-effects relating to the growing religious popularity of the Bhramarghāṭ—which further underpinned the significant role of the lineage of Gosvāmīs who manage the place.

In the case of the Dādūpanthīs, too, we can be sure that the way in which the community lived and enacted their faith was informed by tradition: communal singing with a sort of skeleton ritual beginning with the invocation of Gaṇeśa, and concluding with *āratī*, festivals and feasting. The canon of scripture grew effortlessly, starting in the first generation of the sect subsequent to the founder, then already comprising the founder's own words as well as those of at least one of his disciples. This was Sundardās the younger (1596–1689), who was to become the author of the bulk of Dādūpanthī liturgy and theological treatises. A similar pattern may have evolved in the Sikh community. Thus the growth of patterns which became canonized does not establish a case for the juxtaposition of the category of charisma, as anti-structure against that of structure.

In a final example, which is again taken from the DP, I will dwell more specifically on the relevance of the fixed ritual prescriptions, namely the liturgy on the revitalization of charisma. As for the example presently quoted, I take it both as the product of the founder's charismatic impact on the author of it as much as the product of the theological reasoning and eventual distilling in quasi-orthodox terms that was important for the first generation of the DP's followers. Dādū's message had centred on interior religion and the monistic fusion of the soul and the Supreme. It was a message taken to have been authenticated by personal experience. In the very first generation of Dādū's disciples there started the process of making Dādū himself the pivot of the message. This shift put great emphasis on Dādū's identity with the Supreme. He himself became the Compassionate [Redeemer] which was expressed by the epithet '[Dādū] Dayāl' and the mantra and greeting formula *dādūrām satyarām*, 'Dādū is Rām, Rām is the Truth'. This then also meant that his disciples had lived in the presence of the Supreme and that, accordingly, their own religious quest had borne fruit. The most perfect result of this process is represented by the litanies written by Sundardās, Dādū's direct disciple. These texts are now part of the DP's liturgy. The majority of them are written in musical *stuti* metres, allowing for powerful, rhythmic communal recital. The liturgy of the DP does not distinguish between the daily and the occasional liturgy. Hence, everyone knows the liturgy by heart: it is part of routine religious life. However, that which is routine can be raised to the level of the extraordinary on special occasions. It is a very different matter to chant the *āratī* prayer quickly between the delivery of other chores or to celebrate it on the day when the descent of the Supreme Being, Dādū himself, is commemorated, or on a hilly desert graveyard where the bodies of Dādūpanthīs, who are believed to have conquered death, are exposed to the forces of nature. To reach this place you have to travel through several miles of hilly desert area, and this is what pilgrims do once a year—a pilgrimage infamous for the accidents that often occur when vehicles traverse sand dunes. One section of the liturgy is called 'The Octave of the Gift of Fearlessness'. It is concerned with the gift of eternal life in union with the Supreme and is chanted at dawn after the *jāgaraṇ* which follows the ascent to the hill sanctuary. I am quoting this text which captures faithfully the foregoing experience of both pilgrimages—this particular one and the lifelong pilgrimage:

(1) O Divine Master, I am ignorant, subject to passions,
Have mercy upon me, give me the gift of Fearlessness!

(2) It was only good fortune that I attained your feet,
Beholding you I will live. Give me …

(3) O Lord, I am helpless, clasp my hand,
Why do you not take mercy on me? Give me …

(4) Tell the unhappy, distressed creatures the words of the Supreme
So that their hearts be steeped in love. Give me ...

(5) I have seen ascetics and noticed observances of every kind,
But my mind will find rest only with you. Give me ...

(6) I have travelled region after region, [I became a monk and] shaved my head,
But this did not comfort me. Give me ...

(7) My life is all exhausted, sorrow presses heavily on me,
My body is wasting away, in vain. Give me ...

(8) Let wisdom be my joy
So that I may drink eternally the Nectar. Give me ...

(Sundardās 1993: 261)

I argue that a routinized canon can be revitalized and come to breathe the presence of the charismatic redeemer. In the case mentioned last, the author of an important part of the canon itself has provided for this. By a carefully devised shift of emphasis, the makers of the liturgy (as well as of theological treatises) made Dādū and the Supreme merge. Thus, to invoke Dādū is not only to conjure up but also to make available to the devotee the lived reality of the Supreme. Doing so on the extraordinary occasion of pilgrimage, when its physical and mental effects are felt strongly to be in consonance with the liturgical texts, can infuse fresh spirit into a liturgy rehearsed most of the time in unspectacular ways.

Canonically enjoined practices like the ones mentioned above provide for the transfer of charisma through ritualized techniques (Tambiah 1987: 123), and thus allow it to flow back into and add renewed meaning to the everyday practice of religion.

Abbreviations

CVV. *See* Harirāy 2027 V.S.
HBV. *See* Gopālabhaṭṭa 1986.

Notes

1. I am using the admittedly unsatisfying and possibly misleading term 'sect' for the Indian terms *sampradāya*, 'line of tradition' and *panth*, 'path'.
2. The *floruit* of the founders of these groups were the fifteenth and sixteenth centuries, respectively (Caitanya 1486–1533; Vallabha 1476–1530; Dādū 1544/45–1604).

3. In a related sect, the Nānakpanth (Sikhs), this ideal is most clearly expressed by the fact that all author-gurus, who contributed to the *Ādigranth*, the Sikh scripture, bear the name of Nānak, all of them are vessels of the divine presence that resides within Nānak himself.
4. To mention an opposite example, in the initial phase of the Nānakpanth (gurus 2–4) the successor guru was selected according to his personal ability which made the line of succession rather fluid and, within limits, unpredictable. However, from the fourth generation succession took place within the male line of the Soḍhī family. Thus personal charisma became effectively stabilized and the material resources going along with the office were handed down in a calculable way.
5. Recall, for example, the disagreement of the Caitanyites and Vallabhites on the issue of authority over the image of Śrīnāthjī (Entwistle 1987: 153) or the inner-sectarian Caitanyite conflicts so vividly reflected by the documents calendared by Habib (1996).
6. The most important early ritual text of the Caitanyites, HBV (before 1541, according to De 1961: 139), does not even care to mention Kṛṣṇa by his name but sparsely, and most of the time speaks of Viṣṇu. This is quite in accordance with the indebtedness of HBV to the larger Vaiṣṇava tradition, mainly the Pāñcarātra (Filliozat in Joshi 1959: 6–7).
7. Cf. the images of Caitanya and Nityānanda depicted as being carried away by the rapture of *bhakti* and *kīrtana* (Entwistle 1987: 436, Ill. 6a). Their gestures and mimics serve as models for devotees. For a published photograph of this see the front cover of *The India Magazine* 7 (1987).

References

Anonymous. [c. 1993]. *Jayasiṃha Gherā*. [typescript]

De, Sushil Kumar. 1961. *Early History of the Vaisnava Faith and Movement in Bengal*. Calcutta: Firma K.L.M.

Entwistle, Alan W. 1987. *Braj: Centre of Krishna Pilgrimage*. Groningen: Forsten.

Gebhardt, Winfried. 1993. Charisma und Ordnung. Formen des institutionalisierten Charisma: Überlegungen im Anschluß an Max Weber. In *Charisma: Theologie, Religion und Politik*, ed. W. Gebhardt, A. Zingerle, and M. N. Eberts. Berlin: de Gruyter.

Gopālabhaṭṭa Gosvāmī. 1986. *Haribhaktivilāsa*, ed. with Sanātana Gosvāmī's Digdarśinī commentary by Haridās Śāstrī. 3 vols. Vṛndāvana: Śrīgadādhara-gauraharipresa.

Habib, Irfan. 1996. A Documentary History of the Gosā'ins (Gosvāmīs) of the Caitanya Sect at Vṛndāvana. In *Govindadeva: A Dialogue in Stone*, ed. Margaret H. Case, photographs by Robin Beeche, 133–59. New Delhi: Indira Gandhi National Centre for the Arts.

Harirāy. 2027 V.S. [1969]. *Caurāsī Vaiṣṇavan kī Vārtā*, ed. Dvārkādās Parīkh. Mathura: Śrī Bajraṃg Pustakālay.

Joshi, Rasik Vihari. 1959. *Le rituel de la dévotion kṛṣṇaite*. Pondichéry: Institut Français d'Indologie.
Kanīrām. 1986. *Śrī Jayanta-prakāśa*. Bhivani: Śrīcandra Goyal.
Schluchter, Wolfgang. 1991. *Religion und Lebensführung: Studien zu Max Webers Religions- und Herrschaftssoziologie*. Vol. 2. Frankfurt a.M.: Suhrkamp.
Sundardās. 1993 V.S. [1935]. *Sundar-granthāvalī*, ed. Purohit Harinārāyaṇ Śarmā. Kalakattā: Rājasthāna Risarca Sosāiṭī.
Tambiah, Stanley J. 1987. The Buddhist Arahant: Classical Paradigm and Modern Thai Manifestations. In *Saints and Virtues*, ed. John Stratton Hawley, 111–26. Berkeley: University of California Press.
Toomey, Paul M. 1994. *Food from the Mouth of Krishna: Feasts and Festivities in a North Indian Pilgrimage Centre*. Delhi: Hindustan.
Weber, Max. 1985. *Wirtschaft und Gesellschaft: Grundriß der verstehenden Soziologie*. 5th rev. ed. Johannes Winckelmann. Tübingen: Mohr.

A Mid-nineteenth-century Controversy over Religious Authority

CATHERINE CLÉMENTIN-OJHA

In the mid-nineteenth century the Brahmo Samāj (under the leadership of Debendranath Tagore) officially rejected the doctrine of the infallibility of the *Veda*. It maintained that other means of knowing the ultimate truth were applicable—such as 'nature' and 'intuition' (Rambachan 1994: 22–3). However, not all reformists of the period denied the notions of scriptural and Vedic authority. Dayānand Sarasvatī did not. Yet it would be misleading to picture him as the 'solitary champion of Vedic authority and infallibility' (Rambachan 1994: 38–9). For in this respect Dayānand shared the basic presuppositions then accepted in north-west India by classical scholars (*paṇḍita*), that is by those Brahmins who had received a training in Sanskrit grammar, *dharmaśāstra*, logic and other *darśanas*, who lived inside traditional society and did not question its founding principles. In fact, Dayānand's intellectual formation had been similar to theirs. Until his visit to Calcutta in December 1872, he had preached and debated in Sanskrit alone (Jones 1989: 34). However, even before the foundation of the Ārya Samāj (1875), Dayānand no longer believed in hierarchy and separation in social and religious life (*adhikāra-bheda*) and for this reason he was rejected by the traditional Hindu milieu, whereas the Brahmin protagonists of Jaipur, to whom we shall turn in a moment, belonged to that milieu without any restriction.

In the mid-nineteenth century, then, the problem of the 'limit of scriptures' (Rambachan 1994) did not bother the intellectual and religious élites of north-west India—they were trained in the old ways—as much as it did the Brahmos. Rather, they accepted the notion of *śabda-pramāṇa*. That is, they recognized the final validity of the *Veda*, the *śabda* par excellence, or, in other words, they considered the scriptures to constitute absolutely reliable means of knowledge (*pramāṇa*) of the ultimate reality. But despite this general agreement, the question of the validity of scriptures was not outside the sphere of dispute, for they differed amongst themselves as to the *nature of the relation* between the *Veda* and other sources of authority, textual or non-textual.

The validity of scriptures other than the *Veda* has been a central problem in the development of Indian classical thought. As Wilhelm Halbfass puts it: 'The extent to which other traditions and branches of knowledge possess an authoritative status of their own alongside or independently of the Veda or the degree to which their authority is merely secondary, derivative, and dependent upon the Veda has remained the subject of controversy'. (1988: 359) The histories of Indian philosophy testify that the established *darśanas* have treated the issue in a variety of ways and that there is no agreement among them about the 'orthodox' position in this matter. Rather, as if to underline the fact that orthodoxy is not a static position, each school has maintained the correctness of its own interpretation and the heterodoxy of its adversaries. That such debates continued in the second half of the nineteenth century is exemplified by the religious crisis that engulfed Jaipur in 1864, when Brahmin advisors of the Mahārāja accused the Vaiṣṇavas of the *Catuḥ sampradāya* of being heretics (*pāṣaṇḍa*). The controversy that ensued forms the background of the case study presented here. It also serves to remind the historian of modern Hinduism not to overlook the tensions that manifested themselves among traditional élites while they were busy counter-attacking the newer trends of the reformists.

The Problem and Its Setting

Following Śaṅkara and his school, and their advaitic interpretation of the *vedānta*, the religious advisors of the Mahārāja of Jaipur took the *śruti* to be the source of all knowledge. And they recognized the validity of the *smṛti* only insofar as it accorded with the texts of the Vedic revelation. On their side, the Vaiṣṇavas of the *Catuḥ sampradāya*—the four established schools of theistic interpretation of the *vedānta*—accepted the *śruti* and the *smṛti* as equally authoritative.[1] They also held that the Vaiṣṇava scriptures, being revealed by God (Viṣṇu), presented a self-valid and self-existent knowledge, just as the *Veda* did. Their position was therefore quite different from the Śaṅkarian non-theistic school for whom *śruti* alone, being *apauruṣeya*, authorless and eternal, was characterized by an intrinsic validity (*svataḥ prāmāṇya*) whereas *smṛti*, being memorized tradition, had no independent validity apart from the *śruti* (*parataḥ prāmāṇya*). But the four schools of Vaiṣṇavas also differed among themselves regarding the canonicity of texts. Some, like the disciples of Rāmānuja and Nimbārka (thirteenth century), ascribed to the *Veda*, the *smṛti* (the *Rāmāyaṇa*, the *Mahābhārata*, the *Bhagavad-gītā*), and the *Pāñcarātra* the status of authoritative scriptures.[2] Others, like the Vallabhīs and the Mādhva-Gauḍīya-Vaiṣṇavas, regarded as canonical another set of texts: the *Veda*, the *Bhagavad-gītā*, the *Brahma-sūtra* and the *Bhāgavata-purāṇa*. For the Vallabhīs, the *Bhāgavata-purāṇa*'s authority was not only on par with the *Veda*'s, it was to be treated as the final source of authority.[3] Such a position was of course unacceptable to the Mahārāja's religious advisors. They did not recognize the Rāmānujīs' and the Nimbārkīs' scriptures either, for unlike them they did not consider the *Pāñcarātra* as a canonical text. Since the Vaiṣṇava sects did not have their foundation or root (*mūla*) exclusively in the *Veda*, they considered their faith to be based on *nirmūlatva*, or rootlessness. Here I shall concentrate on the arguments that they exchanged with the Nimbārkīs and Vallabhīs.

The definition of scripture was not the sole bone of contention between the debaters of Jaipur. For the Nimbārkīs and the Vallabhīs held that their traditions rested not only upon scriptures but also upon an uninterrupted transmission (*sampradāya*) of knowledge. Their sectarian lineages constituted, in their eyes, valid sources of religious authority. Again, there were some differences among them regarding the right to transmit the tradition. The Nimbārkīs left it to Brahmins (ascetics or lay people) who had been duly initiated into sectarian preceptorhood, whereas among the Vallabhīs only those who had been born into Vallabha's family (although Brahmins also) were qualified transmitters. But for both sects the eligibility of its different lineages rested on the charismatic power which they had all received from the founder himself through a succession of gurus. It all boiled down to the eligibility of the first guru. As we shall see, their claim was contested by the religious advisors of the Mahārāja, who questioned this very religious authority of their founders.

The controversy between the traditional Brahmins of Jaipur was brought about by the change of religious allegiance by Mahārāja Rām Singh II (r. 1851–80). Since the early eighteenth century, the Kachvāhā dynasty to which he belonged had generously patronized and endowed the temples and religious houses of the Nimbārkīs, Vallabhīs and other Vaiṣṇavas, so that by the mid-nineteenth century their sects were well settled in the kingdom. Political patronage had also bestowed status upon them. The Kachvāhā dynasty had further placed itself under the protection of two powerful Vaiṣṇava deities, Sītārāmajī and Govindadevajī, whose guardians were respectively the Galta branch of Rāmānandīs and the Gauḍīya-Vaiṣṇavas. But in 1862 Rām Singh II installed a Śiva temple inside his palace, thus making it publicly known that he considered Śiva his personal deity. At that time the Mahārāja, who was thirty years old, had been on the throne of Jaipur for twelve years. He had established his reputation as an able administrator on whom the British, who had signed a treaty of protection with Jaipur in 1818, could rely. In fact, Rām Singh's education had been supervised by British political agents from his childhood, following the sudden death of his father Jai Singh III in 1835, and he had remained their close ally ever since. The young Mahārāja had amply demonstrated his loyalty to the British during the Mutiny of 1857. In the following years he earned further favour by introducing several measures to rationalize and centralize the state administration, for such homogenizing efforts were complementary to theirs and in keeping with the tendencies of the imperial Raj (Stern 1988). It is my contention that the religious options he adopted from 1863 onwards were very much in the same line (Clémentin-Ojha, forthcoming).

Like his predecessors, Rām Singh II had been raised as a Vaiṣṇava. He had even received two Vaiṣṇava initiations (*dīkṣā*) during his childhood, a rather unusual occurrence since one cannot normally belong to two sects simultaneously. First, he had been initiated into the Kankroli branch of the Vallabha *sampradāya* (June 1844) and then, some months later, into the Galta branch of the Rāmānandīs (February 1845). He had also been duly invested with the sacred thread in January 1845.[4] The very fact that his *upanayana* had been performed *after* his first Vaiṣṇava *dīkṣā*, and not before any other initiation—as would have been required by the Brahmanic code of religious law (*dharmaśāstra*)—also bears witness to the Vaiṣṇava orientation of the milieu in which Rām Singh had been brought up.

Rām Singh's conversion to Śiva worship was the first sign of the religious controversy that culminated in 1865. This controversy is known locally as the *tilaka-vivāda*, or the quarrel about religious marks (*tilaka*). Those whom it brought into conflict displayed different symbolic signs on their bodies: the Vaiṣṇavas bore two or three *vertical* lines (*ūrdhvapuṇḍra*), their contenders three *horizontal* lines (*tripuṇḍra*). Among the latter, one found a handful of religious figures, priests and learned pandits who had acquired an important position at the palace since the beginning of the 1860s. From 1863 they acted as the royal religious advisers in a more or less direct connection with a state Dharma-sabhā which the Mahārāja had organized that year. One of their demands was that the Vaiṣṇavas renounce their own religious marks and adopt the *tripuṇḍra*.

It seems appropriate to qualify the overall leaning of the Jaipur Dharma-sabhā as Smārta-śaiva, even if this expression is not to be found in the records. The Dharma-sabhā members themselves refered to their system as that propounding the 'true *dharma*' (*sad-dharma*, *satya-dharma*). But the Dharma-sabhā of Jaipur was Smārta-śaiva. In the realm of regulation of social behaviour it strictly abided by the rules of the *dharmaśāstra*, ritually it promoted the cult of the [image of the] Five deities (*pāñcāyatanā-pūjā*) with Śiva in the middle, and philosophically it followed the *advaita* or non-theistic interpretation of the *vedānta* of the Śaṅkara school. The religious policy of the state Dharma-sabhā entailed imposing these three sets of principles on the superior castes of the society, primarily on the Brahmins. The *tilaka-vivāda* was born from the Vaiṣṇavas' refusal to comply with this programme which threatened the very ritual and theological foundation of their sectarian formations. For, according to their theology, Viṣṇu, being the supreme deity, could never be worshipped on par with other gods. It was through him and through him alone that one could get salvation even if other gods' favours could be asked for. But the Vaiṣṇavas of Jaipur had to submit to the Dharma-sabhā for the simple reason that its Smārta-śaiva homogenizing tendencies coincided with the centralizing concerns of the Mahārāja which, in the context of the Raj, could not be postponed. The political motivations of the *tilaka-vivāda* are well underlined by records which show that the palace exerted economic and social pressures on the Vaiṣṇavas to make them renounce their sectarian practices and adopt the Smārta-śaiva system, or the true dharma (*satya-dharma*). Exactions from and persecutions of Vaiṣṇavas, notably of their Brahmin members whose social conduct did not strictly conform to the *smṛti* norms, reached such a point of tension that, in July 1865, the Vallabhī custodians of the Fifth and Seventh Houses fled with hundreds of their servants to the adjacent kingdom of Bikaner, abandoning their belongings in Jaipur. At the beginning of 1867 the properties of the Nimbārkīs were seized by the state and handed over to new protegés of the Mahārāja. Their superior, Śrī jī Mahārāj, who had taken refuge in his monastery of Salemabad (in the nearby kingdom of Kishangarh) in mid-1864, never returned to the Kachvāhā kingdom.

A Defence of the Vallabhīs

I first select for discussion a letter the Vallabhīs wrote to the Dharma-sabhā some time in the middle of the year 1865, a few weeks before their departure from Jaipur. At that time the controversy of Jaipur had been going on for about three years. To follow the letter's content it is sufficient to know that the discussions had been framed within a sixty-four point questionnaire. This series of questions had been prepared by the state Dharma-sabhā in order to examine the Vaiṣṇava sects and come to a final judgment regarding the dharma (*dharma-nirṇaya*). In their letter, the Vallabhīs outline the main arguments of their defense.[5]

Hail to Śrī Gokulendu (*Śrī Gokulendur jayatī*)
Answer to the Sabhā [assembled to take] a decision regarding the *dharma* (*dharma-nirṇaya-sabhā*)

Homage to Śrī Kṛṣṇa (*Śrī Kṛṣṇāya namaḥ*)

As you all know, there has been a decision (*nirṇaya*) [concerning] *dharma*. This is the reply to that.

[1] There are two kinds (*prakāra*) of *dharma: varṇāśrama* and *upāsanā dharma*, among which the *varṇāśrama dharma* has been determined (*nirṇaya*) by Manu and others. There one should not expect (*apekṣā*) differences in the determination (*nirṇayāntara*). And there are also different kinds of *upāsanā dharma*. In the *Mahīmna* they are: 'the Pāśupati doctrine and Vaiṣṇava [doctrine]. Persons follow different paths—straight or crooked—due to the difference in temperaments' and also according to the *Bhāgavata-purāṇa*: 'the *yoga* of devotion, o beautiful lady, is as manifold as the paths' and other such statements have also determined (*nirṇaya*) the [different kinds of *upāsanā*].[6] We do not aspire (*ākāṃkṣā*) to a modern (*adhunika*) *nirṇaya*.

[2] You have written that on our side it has been three years that you have not received any answer but, in fact (*yathārtha*), we have already given a condensed (*saṃkṣepa*) answer. Anyway what is asked again, one says also again.

[3] And you have written that this *sabhā* had made great efforts to investigate (*heran*) the handed down tradition (*sampradāya*). We answer that *sampradāyas* have been going on all the time (*sanātana*). The *śruti* etc. prove it, thus in the *śruti*: 'Those who know *brahman* say that the great divine sages (*ṛṣi*) started the transmission (*sampradāya*) of the revered knowledge of *brahman*.'[7]

[4] And you have written that eminent pandits (*paṇḍita mahānubhāva*) in Kashi etc. have taken their decision (*niścaya*), but we have not known anything [about it]. The very best (*āche āche*) eminent pandits of Calcutta, Nadiya etc. have [also] pronounced their judgement (*nirṇaya*). Their particulars (*taphsīl*) [are] like this: from Kashi, besides Kākārāmajī, [there was] Rādhāmohana Bhaṭṭācārya, Bhāū Śāstrī, the treasurer (*dānādyakṣa*) of the Peswa, Sakhārāma Bhaṭṭa [and] Gaṅgādhara,[8] etc.; besides the Maharashtrians, [there were] the Bengalis such as Bastīrāma etc.; from the Government [Sanskrit] College (*sarkārī pāṭaśālā*) of Calcutta, [there were] Jayanārāyaṇa Tarkapañcānana and Mahes Bhavasaṅkara [sic] etc.; and from Nadiya, Brajavidyāratna, Rāmanātha Tarkasiddhānta, Harimohana Cuḍāmaṇi, etc. [All] have [written] in a letter of approval (*saṃmata patra*) that they agreed (*saṃmati*) that the *sampradāya* of Śrī Vallabhajī was agreeing with (*saṃmata*) the *vedasāstra*. This is a well known fact. [If you have] any doubt then send for them and ascertain from them.

[5] And you have written that there was no doubt regarding the decision (*nirṇaya*) which had been pronounced [by the Dharma-sabhā]. To this we answer that all determine (*nirṇaya*) their own (*apne apne*) *dharma*. And you should have shown us the conclusion (*siddhānta*) you had reached along with your regulation (*vyavasthā*). What have you decided (*nirṇaya*)?

[6] And you have written that the usage (*riti*) of the *dharmaśāstra* has been fixed (*cuknā*) and all must accept (*grahaṇa*) it. To this we reply that the usage of the *dharmaśāstra* [concerns] the *varṇāśramadharma*. Concerning the Śaiva and Vaiṣṇava (*śaiva-vaiṣṇava upari*), all accept the *dharma* whose law (*vidhāna*) is written in the *Mayūkhanirṇayasindhu*, the *Dharmasindhu*, the *Ācārārka*, the *Jayasiṃhakalpadruma* in accordance with (*anusāra*) their authority (*adhikāra*).

[7] And you have written that whosoever keeps aways from this usage (*rīti*) must be considered as outside the dharma. To this we reply that one who does not follow his dharma is outside that dharma. As it is said [in the Bhagavad-gītā, III. 35]: 'Better is one's dharma, though defective, than the dharma of another well performed. Death in one's dharma is better, the dharma of another is fraught with fear,'[9] and other sentences (*vākya*) state it too: it is not proper (*ucita*) to give up (*tyāga*) one's dharma (*apnā dharma*).

[8] And you have written that one has to abide by the judgement (*nirṇaya*) of *dharma* that has been passed. To this we answer that just as the followers of the *sampradāya* of Śaṅkara, Nīlakaṇṭha etc. have a special (*viśeṣa*) faith (*śraddhā*) in their *sampradāya*, in the same way we have always (*sarvadā*) faith in our *sampradāya*.

[9] And the great late (*vaikuṇṭha-vāsī*) Mahārāja Savai Jai Singh had an *aśvamedha* and several other sacrifices performed. He had the [*Jayasiṃha*] *Kalpadruma* treatise composed in which is the pure knowledge (*vidyā*). He established (*sthāpana*) different schools (*aneka bheda*) and there were several uprisings (*upadravana*) and revolts (*viplava*), but then he protected the *dharma* properly (*yathāvat*) in different ways. And he has established (*sthāpana*) the Vaiṣṇava *sampradāyas* in this city knowing that they agreed with the *śruti*, *smṛti* and *purāṇa*. Until today this is well known.

The relevant statements made in this letter are the following.

Point 1 showed that the Vallabhīs distinguished between two kinds of dharma, the *varṇāśrama*-dharma (i.e. the dharma of social classes and stages of life) and the *upāsanā*-dharma (i.e. the dharma of adoration). Each dharma was governed by a specific set of regulations, each established on equally specific authoritative texts. But whereas socio-religious behaviour pertaining to one's birth and age was determined by a single source of scriptural authority recognized by all (the *dharmaśāstra*), salvation oriented observances (*upāsanā-dharma*) obeyed a plurality of textual sources that fell into two categories: Vaiṣṇava and Śaiva.

Point 3 stated two things about the handed-down traditions or *sampradāyas*: they come from times immemorial (*sanātana*), and they originated from *ṛṣis*, or authoritative sources par excellence.

Point 4 contested the condemnation by the Dharma-sabhā and therefore challenged its proclaimed absolute control in matters of dharma. It did so by referring to the support which the sect of Vallabha had received from some Brahmin authorities recognized within the traditional milieu. It is worth noting that this support was sought from Eastern high centres of classical learning (Banaras, Calcutta, Nadiya), not from anywhere closer to Jaipur. The probable reason is that the West was still associated with the famous Bombay Libel Case of 1862 which had proved so disastrous for the reputation of the Vallabhīs.

Point 5 claimed equal competence with the Dharma-sabhā in the matter of dharma.

Point 6, like point 1, distinguished between two kinds of dharma and again opposed two sets of scriptural authority. But whereas earlier the opposition was between the *dharmaśāstra* on one side and the *Mahīmna* and the *Bhāgavata-purāṇa* on the other, this time it was between the *dharmaśāstra* and four corpora of Śaiva and Vaiṣṇava rules (*vidhāna*). These are the *Mayūkhanirṇayasindhu*, the *Dharmasindhu*, the *Ācārārka* and the *Jayasiṃhakalpadruma*. The *Jayasiṃhakalpadruma*, a compendium on dharma drawing from the *dharmaśāstra* literature as well as from puranic traditions, displays a Vaiṣṇava orientation. If one is to judge the contents of the three other texts by the orientation of its content, and the context of the letter allows it, they too must have sectarian leanings.[10]

Point 7 displayed once more the Vallabhīs' ambiguous use of the word 'dharma' and that by '*svadharma*' they refered to '*Vaiṣṇava-dharma*.' Note that this usage was traditional within the sect (Barz 1976: 214).

Point 8 reiterated point 5 with the argument of faith (*śraddhā*): our faith in our *sampradāya* is worth your faith in yours, just as our competence in dharmic matters is worth yours.

Finally, point 9 appealed to the ultimate legitimator of the Vaiṣṇavas of Jaipur, Jai Singh II (1699–1743), the founder of Jaipur and the most famous ancestor of Rām Singh II, at whose request the *Jayasiṃhakalpadruma*, mentioned in point 6 as a scriptural authority, had been composed.

These statements make it clear that the Vallabhīs did not consider themselves outside Brahmanic society. They recognized the bindings of the *dharmaśāstra* usage in respect of caste, etc. But in two other respects they stressed their right to abide by other scriptural authorities. Thus they declared that they followed the *Bhāgavata-purāṇa* in the realm of *upāsanā* or devotional practices, and some other texts in a second realm defined as *Vaiṣṇava-dharma*. But they did not specify how these two sets of regulations related to the *dharmaśāstra* and what the course to be followed was in case they did not tally, etc. Their emphasis lay elsewhere, namely on the fact that they belonged to a religious tradition different from that of the members of the Dharma-sabhā, different and autonomous. They firmly asserted their right to be different. Their main line of argumentation was that there was not one single uninterrupted tradition, one single set of rules, one single version of the socio-religious norm (dharma), but several. Each category was defined in reference to certain key practices and also in contrast to what it was not. The Vallabhīs' line of defence was therefore to plead for religious diversity. They argued that every religious tradition was legitimate insofar as it was established on the *pramāṇa* of relevant scriptural sources (Śaiva or Vaiṣṇava), and had been handed down (*sampradāya*) since time immemorial (*sanātana*) through lineages made eligible by the prestige of their founders. As a consequence, they denied the Dharma-sabhā any claim to superiority, any right to award or withhold a certificate of legitimacy. In other words, the religious advisors of the Mahārāja did not represent orthodoxy in their eyes, but some other religious traditions existing side by side with their own, such as those formed by the *sampradāyas* of Śaṅkara or Nīlakaṇṭha.

The Nimbārkīs Refuted

I now turn to the document which is a refutation of the Nimbārkīs by the Dharma-sabhā of Jaipur. Let us examine in particular some of the Dharma-sabhā's reactions to the Nimbārkīs' conception of *sampradāya*:[11]

About your *sampradāya*, the question was what is the meaning of the word '*sampradāya*'.

You have answered that the meaning of the word '*sampradāya*' indicated the conduct (*śīla*) followed in a continuous manner (*uttarottara*) transmitted by an eternal tradition (*anādi paraṃparayā*) and expressed by the words 'practices of the good' (*sad-ācāra*), 'proper teaching' (*sad-upadeśa*) etc.

It is not so. Your *sampradāya*, having been started by an *ācārya* called Nimbārka who lived one thousand years ago, cannot be found earlier, or since it cannot be said to have been started before the birth of your *ācārya*, it is impossible to hold its 'beginninglessness' (*anāditva*). As for the meaning of the words 'practices of the good' and 'proper teaching' it is that of *sampradāya* whose sole meaning is the manifold (*vikalpita*) conduct (*vyavahāra*) established by the *śāstra*. The name of your *sampradāya* procuring [the meaning] of the word *sampradāya* such a state of things (*tathātvam*) is not possible.[12] (...) Then [referring to the question] of how long [your *sampradāya*] has existed: [we object that] if it has existed since a long time [as you say] how do you prove (*pramāṇa*) its features (*vilakṣaṇa*) since it is not seen in Manu and other treatises?[13]

The Dharma-sabhā invalidated the Nimbārkīs' reply with two related arguments. First, the Nimbārka *sampradāya* had a human origin, therefore it was not eternal, literally 'without beginning'. By contrast, as we have seen earlier, the Smārta-śaivas held that their tradition was '*anādi*' since it has its roots in the *Veda* which is itself eternal. The second argument was that it is *śāstra* which gives authority (*pramāṇa*) to a *sampradāya*. By '*śāstra*' the Dharma-sabhā had in mind the *dharmaśāstra*, and particularly the *Manu-smṛti* (with the commentary by Kullūka) and the *Yājñavalkya-smṛti* (with *Mitākṣarā*) which, for all practical purposes, were its references during the deliberations. The fact that the Nimbārka *sampradāya* was not found in *śāstras* such as Manu etc. was further proof that it was not ancient. Being neither eternal nor ancient, the Nimbārka *sampradāya* was bereft of sanction.

In its next argument, which I sum up here, the Dharma-sabhā refuted the assertion that Nimbārka was an *āpta*, a trustworthy person or 'a person who, being in possession of true knowledge, is qualified to transmit it to others' (Chemparathy 1987: 40). To do so it first ridiculed the claim that the name Nimbārka was found in Hemādri (thirteenth century) etc. saying that the word '*nimbārka*' [sun of the margosa tree] did not refer to Nimbārka-the-*ācārya* at all but to the sun. Next, the Dharma-sabhā refuted the comparison between Nimbārka and Vyāsa by stressing that they were incomparable since Vyāsa had lived long before Nimbārka. The whole claim of the Nimbārkīs, it concluded, amounted to making a new (*ādhunika*) and artificial (*kṛtrima*) river flow and calling it a *tīrtha* (*Nimbārkamatakhaṇḍana*, p. 5).

In the Dharma-sabhā's refutation of the Nimbārkīs' legitimacy one finds two ideas, both connected with the notion of antiquity. First, there is the idea that the past was more perfect than the present. In this conception, which is central to Indian classical thought, the present as Halbfass has written 'lags behind the past' (1988: 364; Deshpande 1979: 10–11; Pollock 1985: 512). Therefore those who had lived earlier were more qualified than those who had followed them, or, a Vyāsa was more able than a Nimbārka. Second, there is the conception that antiquity and therefore quality could be ascertained through certain categories of authorized textual sources, such as the *dharmaśāstra*. This in turn implied the primordiality of scriptures or, as Sheldon Pollock has argued, the anteriority of śāstric norms in general to any human activity (1985: 512). Having originated in the most remote past, *śāstras* sanctioned whomsoever they happened to have mentioned and invalidated all others. What was not in the *śāstras* was by definition posterior and represented an innovation. And as Manu had said, all innovations were suspect for what is *more modern* (*arvāk-*

kālika-tā) is worthless (*niṣphala*) (*Manusmṛti* XII, 95–6). In this scheme, error and novelty were one and the same thing.

Conclusion

The tendency to attribute greater abilities to works of the remote past was common to many thinkers of the period of the *tilaka-vivāda*. One can recognize this archaist turn in Dayānand Sarasvatī's model of knowledge. Dayānand treated the *mantra-saṃhitā* sections of the Vedic corpus as independent means of knowledge (*svataḥ pramāṇa*). He also recognized the remaining texts (*brāhmaṇas*, *āraṇyakas* and *upaniṣads*) as *ārṣa*, or authoritative, insofar as they were dependent (*parataḥ pramāṇa*) on the *ṛṣis* who had revealed them (Llewellyn 1993: 93), thereby reduplicating somewhat the relative degree of validity attributed by the Smārta-śaivas to the *śruti* and *smṛti*. As for such Vaiṣṇava texts as the *Bhāgavata-purāṇa*, all posterior to the *ārṣa* revelation, Dayānand considered them totally devoid of authority (Llewellyn 1993: 161). That is to say that in his quest for the most authoritative source of the Hindu tradition Dayānand went to the earliest layers of the Vedic texts (the *saṃhitā*) and relegated the sections of the *Veda* composed later to a lower level of authority. Implicit in his selection was a vision of the relation between the present and the past which had been and remained central for the traditional milieu, one in which 'the present can be restored only when [the] original past has been recovered' (Van Buitenen 1966: 36–7; Pollock 1985: 515). But, at the same time, Dayānand's notion that the *mantra-saṃhitās* had an intrinsic superiority to the rest of the Vedic texts was an original idea, for the traditional milieu regarded the *whole śruti* as equally valid and ancient. It is likely that Dayānand had been influenced, even if indirectly, by the findings of the Orientalists' historical-critical method which had established the relative antiquity of each section of the Veda. Thus, his was a new notion of the past superimposed over the past notion of the past.

The findings of the Orientalists also supported some of the criticisms that were directed against the Vallabhīs during the Bombay Libel Case (1862). A perusal of the newspaper article which originated the Libel Case shows that its writer (the editor Karsandas Mulji) commended the 'original ancient religion' and condemned the 'modern sects.' His four main points were:

(1) the Vallabha *sampradāya* belongs to the Kali yuga and is therefore false;[14]
(2) at the beginning there was one single original religion, therefore the different sects born in the Kali yuga represent so many heresies;

(3) this has been established by the *Veda*, the *purāṇa*, etc.;
(4) the [Vallabhī] Maharaj's behaviour with the wives and daughters of devotees is outrageous (*History of the Sect of Maharajas or Vallabhacharyas, in Western India*: 172–4). During his examination at the time of the trial, Karsandas Mulji kept opposing the 'old' or 'ancient religion' to the 'sect of Vallabha' and he declared that none of the other sects represented 'the ancient Hindu religion'. It was the 'learned Brahmins' who taught 'the doctrines of the ancient religion', not the Vallabhī Maharaj. He also declared that he did not 'believe in the modern stories in books which [were] written after the Vedas,' adding, rather inconsistently, 'which I have not read' (Appendix 12–22).

In this criticism, emanating from the English-speaking and English-educated élite, one sees that the condemnation of 'modernity' was closely interrelated with the condemnation of diversity. 'Religion' was viewed as being opposed to 'sect' on two levels: recent/modern and united/divided. The same kind of judgment was implicit in Dayānand's programme to replace all practices he considered erroneous by the Ārya dharma, that is by a tradition that was both unique and most ancient. For, from a single source of scriptural authority (i.e. the *Vedas*) there could only flow *one* homogeneous religious current. Dayānand claimed to represent that single religious tradition. In fact, and as a consequence of his ideas, he never attempted to start a new *sampradāya*, for it would have meant vesting authority in yet another religious group, or empowering yet another division.

There were of course several important differences between the religious advisors of the Mahārāja of Jaipur and reformists like Dayānand and Karsandas Mulji, as well as between the reformists themselves. For instance, Dayānand would not have agreed with a Karsandas Mulji who put the *purāṇas* on par with the *Vedas* and thought that traditionally trained Brahmins were the true exponents of the ancient religion. But Dayānand's opposition to members of the Dharma-sabhā of Jaipur on one side,[15] and to rival reformists on the other, did not preclude his adopting some strong anti-Vaiṣṇava feelings very similar to those that both groups entertained. One of the reasons why these different personalities opposed the Vaiṣṇavas at that time was that they maintained the superiority of textual authority over any other source of authority, as well as the superiority of ancient times over modern. All extolled antiquity, and unity over diversity and newness. All perceived religious diversity as a late development. The Vaiṣṇava sects, who relied on a different corpus of scriptures that were relatively recent, were seen as threats to these principles.

The Vaiṣṇava records examined earlier highlight the fact that at the time of the *tilaka-vivāda* the Vallabhīs and the Nimbārkīs' position was rather complex. On the one hand, both sects claimed that their *sampradāyas* were beyond the pale of ordinary diachronic time. They were *sanātana* or had existed since time immemorial. Their validity was guaranteed by scriptures a well as by the fact that, as the result of an unbroken transmission, their original and divine source was made ever available to the present. It did not age. The Vaiṣṇavas did not attempt to establish their legitimacy on new grounds. Rather, they shared their opponents' contempt for 'modern' sources of validity. Yet, on the other hand, the Nimbārkīs and the Vallabhīs looked at their movement from a chronological and, therefore, dynamic perspective. Their supreme authority being incarnated in a person (Vallabha or Nimbārka) possessing a biography, they referred over and over again to the story of their origin. Thus they pointed to a time when they had not been in existence. Their acute knowledge of the genealogical succession of their teachers (which they committed to heart), of their hagiographies, of the celebrations of their birthdays, all bore witness to their awareness of the historicity of their movement. From their point of view, therefore, paradoxically, their *sampradāya* could be both ahistorical and historical.

Giving authority to one's teachings by referring them to a transmission of knowledge was quite normative among the Smārtas too. Many examples could be given to illustrate that it was commonly held among them that, although ultimate truth cannot have a human origin and can only be known through scriptures or authoritative texts, a degree of human agency is required for their correct interpretation. Had not Śaṅkara's relationship to Gauḍapāda's teaching (Dasgupta [1922] 1969: 423) served this purpose? So the construction of his legitimacy as a teacher had required both conformity to valid scriptures as well as his belonging to an eligible tradition of interpreters. It should be observed here that neither Nimbārka's nor Vallabha's legitimacy had been established according to this pattern. Thus it is striking that, in contrast with the other great Vaiṣṇava teacher Rāmānuja, Nimbārka and Vallabha did not refer to any guru in their philosophical and theological works.[16] Within their own tradition, they have not been associated with any human teacher; they have been considered as *avatāra*. Their disciples regarded their teachings as directly derived from the revealed words of God, which amounted to claiming they were the divine source itself. However, it was by an explicit reference to a handed-down tradition that the Nimbārkīs and the Vallabhīs, in Jaipur and elsewhere, defined their own social and religious identity and secured the authority of their sect. In that respect, these Vaiṣṇavas obeyed the model of legitimization followed by Śaṅkara himself. A model in which ahistorical sources of religious authority display a certain in-built historicity.

So it is not the case that the Smārta-śaivas had altogether rejected 'historical precedent (...) as sources of religious truth' (Lorenzen 1995: 181). Their difference with the Vaiṣṇavas lay elsewhere. Whereas Śaṅkara's religious authority derived only in part from knowledge acquired from a competent historical person, Nimbārka's or Vallabha's was grounded on charisma, or on a personal direct experience of the divine. Therefore their role in the formation of the religious identity of their followers was of an altogether different nature. And it was precisely its cruciality and centrality to the Vaiṣṇavas' religious and social life that was unacceptable to the Dharma-sabhā. To start with, its members contested the eligibility of their founders on the ground that they had lived in recent times. Besides, the near absolute authority which the Vaiṣṇavas attributed to their god-like teachers, and beyond them to the sectarian institution itself, particularly in matters of conduct, introduced a plurality of socio-religious norms not conductive to social unity. At that time the Dharma-sabhā was bent upon doing away with all sectarian divisions in order to homogenize the religious practices of the kingdom of Jaipur. The Smārta-śaiva tradition provided the overarching principles of the rules of *varṇāśramadharma* and of *pāñcāyatanā-pūjā*. The Vaiṣṇavas were asked to accommodate their socio-religious practices within this frame. Rām Singh II and his Dharma-sabhā insisted that all of them adopt the religious mark (*tilaka*) of the *tripuṇḍra* as a symbol of their submission. This religious policy was attuned to the political agenda of the ruler of centralizing the state around his own authority and of monopolizing the social control of the subjects of his kingdom (particularly the Brahmins). Far from adhering to this unique system, the Vaiṣṇavas of Jaipur argued in favour of religious 'plurality'. And rather than giving in to the pressures of their royal patron, the Nimbārkīs and the Vallabhīs placed themselves under the protection of neighbouring Mahārājas and abandoned the kingdom of Jaipur.

But in the following years the Vaiṣṇavas of north India would learn their lesson from the Bombay Libel Case (1862) and the Jaipur *tilaka-vivāda* (1863–72). Like their reformist and traditional opponents, they too would begin to lament over their sectarian divisions. The need to rise above religious differentiation had finally caught up with them as well. It led them to view their sectarian formations as parts of broader and more homogeneous social and religious units. One of the earliest attempts came from Bharatendu Hariścandra (1850–85), the intellectual descendant of a Vallabhī merchant family of Banaras who, in 1873, founded the Tadīya Samāj in order to propagate social and theological solidarity amongst the Vaiṣṇava sects. In this quest Hariścandra defended the '*veda purāṇa vihita ārya dharma*', or the religious tradition common to all those who considered the *purāṇas* as authoritative as the *Veda*. Centred on the immemorial practice of image-worship (*mūrti-pūjā*), but devoid of any precise theological and ritual references, this frame was wide and hazy enough to accommodate all the Vaiṣṇava sects (Dalmia 1998: 77).

Later, in the fast transforming social and political context of the late nineteenth and early twentieth century, this new self-perception of the Vaiṣṇavas was one of the factors which helped to bridge the great divide that had existed between them and the Smārta-śaiva. A movement set in that led to the consolidation of *sanātana-dharma*, and, in the process, the debates about the relative validity or canonicity of the *śruti*, *smṛti* and Vaiṣṇava scriptures ceased to appear essential.

Notes

1. At that time, the representatives of the *Catuḥ sampradāya* in Jaipur were: the Rāmānandīs (who were considered, and considered themselves, as belonging to the Śrī-sampradāya of Rāmānuja), the Nimbārkīs (of the Sanaka *sampradāya* of Nimbārka), the Mādhva-Gauḍīya (i.e. the Caitanya section of the Brahma *sampradāya* of Madhva) and the Vallabhīs (or the *Puṣṭīmārga* which had grafted itself on the old [and by then defunct] Viṣṇusvāmi *sampradāya*). Among them, it was Rāmānuja (eleventh century) who had first accorded the same status to the *śruti* and *smṛti*. He had based his interpretation on the *mīmāṃsā* principle of *aikārthya* (the *artha*, or meaning, of all scriptures is fundamentally the same). Van Buitenen (1968: 30–2).
2. In his commentary on *Brahma-sūtra* II,2,43, Rāmānuja held that the Pāñcarātra had been composed by Vāsudeva himself and was therefore as fully authoritative as the Veda (Thibaut [1904] 1966: 529–30). Nimbārka made the same point (*Brahma-sūtra* I,1,3). See also Bose (1943: 27–9).
3. Vallabha himself had written that if doubts still arose after one had consulted successively the Veda, the *Bhagavad-gītā* and the *Brahma-sūtra*, one had to abide by the teachings of the *Bhāgavata-purāṇa* (Dasgupta [1949] 1966: 346; Barz 1976: 56). In Vallabha's view therefore, the *Bhāgavata-purāṇa* helped to ascertain the meaning of the Veda.
4. The Vallabha *sampradāya* comprises seven 'Houses' since the time of Vallabha's grandsons, the Kankroli branch belonging to its Third House. The House of Kankroli had established a religious relationship with the Kachvāhā since the time of Madho Singh I. The Rāmānandīs of Galta were the custodians of the famous monastery situated on the hill of Galta (near Jaipur) which had been founded by Krishnadas Payohari in the sixteenth century, the guru of Prithvi Singh of Amber. See Clémentin-Ojha (forthcoming).

5. This letter is part of the rare *contemporary* evidence of the Vallabhīs of the Fifth and Seventh Houses who were involved in the *tilaka-vivāda* discussions. At the time they wrote it, they had received the sixty-four point questionnaire but they had not yet published their answers. By the time they did, in 1867, they had already fled Jaipur and taken refuge in Bikaner. Since the Vallabhīs left Jaipur in July 1865, they must have sent their letter sometime between March and July 1865. A copy of the letter is kept in the private archives of the seat of Galta (Rāmānandī *sampradāya*), Jaipur.
6. The *Mahīmna*, for *Śiva-mahimnaḥ stotra* or *Mahimnaḥ stava*, is a famous hymn to the greatness of Śiva. See Farquhar ([1920] 1967: 383). The Sanskrit original in the letter is the following: *Paśupati-mataṃ vaiṣṇavam iti rucīnāṃ vaicitryād ṛju-kuṭila-nānā-pantha-juṣāṃ bhāgavate 'pi bhakti-yogo bahuvidho mārgair bhāmini bhāvyate*. It is difficult to make sense of this sentence for it assembles two incomplete quotes from two texts, the *Śiva-mahimnaḥ stotra* and the *Bhāgavata-purāṇa*. I am extremely grateful to Gerdi Gerschheimer for having helped me out of this conundrum as well as for locating the relevant original passages. The first half of the quoted sentence comes from the *Śiva-mahimnaḥ stotra* (stanza 7): *trayī sāṃkyaṃ yogaḥ paśupati-mataṃ vaiṣṇavam iti prabhinne prasthāne paramidamadaḥ pathyamiti ca/ rucīnāṃ vaicitryād ṛju-kuṭila-nānā-pantha-juṣāṃ nṛṇāmeko gamyastvamasi payasāmarṇava iva//*: 'There are different paths as enjoined by the three [Veda], Sāṃkhya, Yoga, Pāśupati doctrine and Vaiṣṇava [doctrine]. Persons following different paths—straight or crooked—according as they consider that this path is best or that one is proper due to the difference in temperaments, reach Thee alone just as rivers enter the ocean.' The second part of the quoted sentence comes from the *Bhāgavata-purāṇa* (III,29,7): *Śrībhagavānuvāca // bhakti-yogo bahuvidho mārgair bhāmini bhāvyate // svabhāva-guṇa-mārgeṇa puṃsāṃ bhāvo vibhidyate //*: Bhagavān said: 'the yoga of devotion, o beautiful lady, is as manyfolded as the paths [taken by men] to practice it; and men's temperaments are as varied as inherent dispositions with their diverse qualities.'
7. *Namasparamarṣibhyo namobrahmavidyāsampradāyakartṛbhyo brahmavādino vadanti*.
8. I have not been able to identify these personalities. The person called Kākārāma is different from Kākārāma Śāstrī since the latter died in 1860 (Upadhyaya 1994: 182).
9. *Śreyān svadharmo viguṇaḥ paradharmāt svanuṣṭhitāt // svadharme nidhanaṃ śreyaḥ paradharmo bhayāvahaḥ*.
10. None of these texts is mentioned by Farquhar ([1920] 1967).
11. They are exposed in the *Nimbārkamatakhaṇḍana*, (the refutation of the doctrine of Nimbārka) a manuscript kept in the archives of Maharaja Sawai Man Singh II Museum, City Palace, Jaipur (Bahura 1976: manuscript 623).
12. *atha bhavat-sampradāyas tatra sampradāya-śabdasya ko 'rtha iti praśnas // tatra anādi paraṃparayā pravartamāna uttarottarānuvartamānaśīlāḥ sadācāra-sadupadeśādi padair abhidhīyamānaḥ sampradāya-padasyārtha ity uttaram uktaṃ // tan na samīcīnaṃ // bhavat-sampradāyasya bhavad-ācārya-pravartitatvena*

tasya ca nimbārkābhidhasya varṣa-sahasrātpūrvam anulabdhatvena tat-pūrva-tat-pravartita-sampradāyasya tv arthād anupalabdhyā bhavad-ācārya-janmārabhyai vopalabhyamānatvena ca anāditvāsaṃbhavāt // kiṃ ca sadācāra-sadupadeśādi-padair abhidīyamāno yo 'rthas tad arthakatvaṃ śāstrīya-vikalpitārtha-vyavasthāpaka-vyavahāramātrārthaka-sampradāya-śabdasya bhavatu // nāma-bhavat-sampradāya-ghaṭaka-sampradāya-śabdasya tu na tathātvaṃ sambhavati (*Nimbārkamatakhaṇḍana*, p. 1).

13. *atha kiyatkālāt pravṛttaḥ tatra bahokālāt pravṛttaścenmanvādigrantheṣvadṛṣṭatvāt tad-vilakṣaṇatvāc ca kathaṃ pramāṇam iti* (*Nimbārkamatakhaṇḍana*, p.4 b).
14. This kind of statement was yet another evidence that mental attitudes belonging to the traditional milieu were still to be found among those who advised radical reforms for it did not reflect the understanding of history taught in the Anglicized colleges where Karsandas Mulji and others of his time had been educated. Rather, it reflected the traditional historical vision for which the characteristics of a given period determined the nature of the events. According to this view, in the Kaliyuga everything was bound to be corrupt since it was the Kaliyuga.
15. This opposition was to manifest itself during the *tilaka-vivāda* itself, for Dayānand was present at Jaipur at that time (between October 1865 and March 1866 and again in October 1866). As he has recorded in an autobiographical speech delivered ten years later in Poona, Dayānand first sided with the Dharma-sabhā against the Vaiṣṇavas but later he incurred the displeasure of the Mahārāja and of his religious advisors when they realized he did not share all their ideas. On his side, Dayānand who had hoped to enrol Rām Singh II in his campaign against all unauthoritative (*anarṣa*) literature, was frustrated by the Jaipur episode (*Pūnā pravacana*).
16. Rāmānuja acknowledged his debts to Yamunācārya: in his commentary of the Bhagavad-gītā, he not only dedicated his work to him, but he also quoted his words frequently. Van Buitenen (1968: 9–12).

References

Arya, K. S. and Sastri, P. D. 1987. *Swami Dayananda Saraswati. A Study of his Life and Work*. Delhi: Manohar.

Bahura, G. N. 1976. *Literary Heritage of the Rulers of Amber and Jaipur*. Jaipur: Maharaja Sawai Man Singh II Museum.

Barz, R. 1976. *The Bhakti Sect of Vallabhācārya*. Faridabad: Thomson Press.

Bose, R. 1943. *Vedānta-pārija-saurabha of Nimbārka and Vedānta-kaustubha of Śrīnivāsa:* (Commentaries on the Brahma-sūtra). Translated and annoted by Roma Bose. Calcutta: Royal Asiatic Society of Bengal.

Chemparathy, G. 1987. Nature and Role of Apta in the Nyaya-Vaisesika Thought. In *Kusumāñjali. New Interpretation of Indian Art and Culture. Sh. C. Sivaramamurti Commemoration Volume*, ed. M. S. Nagaraja Rao, 39–47. Vol. 1. Delhi: Agam Kala Prakashan.

Clémentin-Ojha, C. [forthcoming]. *Discussions religieuses au palais. Les vishnouïtes et le pouvoir royal à Jaipur (1863–1867)*.
Dalmia, V. 1998. The Modernity of Tradition: Hariścandra of Banaras and the Defence of Hindū Dharma. In *Vivekananda and the Modernisation of Hinduism*, ed. W. Radice. Delhi: Oxford University Press.
Dasgupta, S. 1969. *A History of Indian Philosophy*. Vol. 1 ([1922] 1969), Vol. 4 ([1949] 1966). Cambridge: Cambridge University Press.
De, S. K. 1986. *Early History of the Vaiṣṇava Faith and Movement in Bengal. From Sanskrit and Bengali Sources*. Calcutta: Firma KLM.
Deshpande, M. 1979. History, Change and Permanence: A Classical Indian Perspective. In *Contributions to South Asian Studies* 1, ed. G. Krishna, 1–28. Delhi: Oxford University Press.
Elkman, S. 1986. *Tattvasandarbha. A Study on the Philosophical and Sectarian Development of the Gauḍīya Vaiṣṇava Movement*. Delhi: Motilal Banarsidass.
Farquhar, J. N. [1920] 1967. *An Outline of the Religious Literature of India*. Reprint. Delhi: Motilal Barnarsidass.
Gonda, J. 1965. *Change and Continuity in Indian Religion*. London: Mouton & Co.
Halbfass, W. 1988. *India and Europe. An Essay in Understanding*. Albany: State University of New York Press.
History of the Sect of Maharajas or Vallabhacharyas, in Western India. London: Trübner & Co, 1865.
Hara, M. 1980. Hindu Concepts of Teacher, Sanskrit Guru and Ācārya. In *Sanskrit and Indian Studies. Essays in Honour of Daniel H. H. Ingalls*, ed. M. Nagatomi, B. K. Matilal, J. M. Mason, E. C. Dimock, 93–118. Dordrecht: D. Reidel Publishing Company.
Jones, K. W. 1989. *Arya Dharm. Hindu Consciousness in 19th-Century Punjab*. Delhi: Manohar.
Llewellyn, J. E. 1993. *The Arya Samaj as a Fundamentalist Movement. A Study in Comparative Fundamentalism*. Delhi: Manohar.
Lorenzen, D. N. 1995. The Lives of Nirguṇī Saints. In *Bhakti Religion in North India. Community Identity and Political Action*, ed. D. N. Lorenzen, 181–211. Albany: State University of New York Press.
Pollock, S. 1985. The Theory of Practice and the Practice of Theory in Indian Intellectual History. *Journal of the American Oriental Society* 105.3: 499–519.
———. 1989a. The Idea of Śāstra in Traditional India. In *Shastric Traditions in Indian Arts*, ed. A. Libera Dallapiccola, 17-36. Vol. 1. Stuttgart: Steiner.
———. 1989b. Playing by the Rules: Śāstra and Sanskrit Literature. In *Shastric Traditions in Indian Arts*, ed. A. Libera Dallapiccola, 301–12. Vol. 1. Stuttgart: Steiner.
Pūnā pravacana (Upadeśa-mañjarī), Svāmī Dayānanda Sarasvatī ke pandrah vyākhyān. Ajmer: Vaidik Pustakalay, 1985.
Rambachan, A. 1994. *The Limits of Scripture. Vivekananda's Reinterpretation of the Vedas*. Honolulu: University of Hawaii Press.
Renou, L. 1956. *Histoire de la langue sanskrite*. Lyon: Paris, IAC.

———. 1960. *Le destin du Veda dans l'Inde*. Paris: Editions E. de Boccard.

Rosu, A. 1978. *Les conceptions psychologiques dans les textes médicaux indiens*. Paris: Collège de France (Institut de civilisation indienne).

Stern, R. W. 1988. *The Cat and the Lion. Jaipur State in the British Raj*. Leiden: E. J. Brill.

Thibaut, G. [1904] 1966. *The Vedānta-sūtras with the Commentary by Rāmānuja.* Transl. G. Thibaut. Delhi: Motilal Banarsidass.

Upadhyaya, B. 1994. *Kāśī kī pāṇḍitya paramparā* (A Comprehensive Historical Account of the Sanskrit Pandits of Varanasi with their Biography and Works, Literary Attainments and Reminiscences, 1200–1980). Varanasi: Vishvavidyala Prakashan.

Van Buitenen, J. A. B. 1966. On the Archaism of the *Bhāgavata purāṇa*. In *Krishna: Myths, Rites and Attitudes*, ed. M. Singer, 23–40. Honolulu: The University of Hawaii Press.

———. 1968. *Rāmānuja on the Bhagavadgītā: A Condensed Rendering of his Gītābhāṣya with Copious Notes and an Introduction*. Delhi: Motilal Banarsidass.

Prophets of the Modern Age

The Re-enactment of Gurū Nānak's Charisma in an Early-twentieth-century Panjabi Narrative

DENIS MATRINGE

'Later Kālū heard that Nānak had built a village and settled down. Taking all the members of his family, Kālū went there. They were all very happy. Work, donations and devotion were going on. The Bābā's seat was set under a pipal. A long time passed. A large community gathered.'[1]

This is how one of the traditional eighteenth-century hagiographies of Nānak (1469–1539), the *Janam-sākhīs*, refers to the foundation by the first Sikh Gurū of the small town of Kartārpur ('the city of the Creator'). It lay on the right bank of the river Ravi, in a place now located in Pakistani Panjab. According to these sources, Nānak settled here after twenty years of travel through the Eastern world, and here he taught and preached among the first and ideal community of his disciples, instituting practices which are still part of the Sikh canon. These practices include rising early, bathing, and reciting his long poem the *Japu-jī* (*Ādi Granth* 1962–4: 1–8), working all day, assembling in the evening to listen to his sermons, and singing two of his other compositions, *Sodara* (*Ādi Granth* 1962–4: 8–10) and *Āratī* (*Ādi Granth* 1962–4: 13), before retiring to rest.

This image of the first Sikh community living happily in Kartārpur around Gurū Nānak had a strong and lasting impact on the religious consciousness of Sikhs.[2] It is thus no surprise that it came to be used in various ways by reformers of the Siṅgh Sabhā in the late-nineteenth and early-twentieth century, at a time of intense religious controversies in Panjab.[3] The proclaimed aim of the Siṅgh Sabhā was to restore Sikhism to its pristine purity, to get rid of later Hindu accretions, to attempt doctrinal unification with a sustained effort to produce a clear Sikh identity. The main means to which the Siṅgh Sabhā resorted were education, social reform and literature. Taking full advantage of the development of the printing press, numerous books, booklets and tracts were published, mostly in the fields of history, scriptural commentary and apologetics.

One of the most prolific and talented writers of the Siṅgh Sabhā milieu was Bhāī Vīr Siṅgh (1872–1957). He produced scholarly editions of Sikh classics and a commentary on the *Ādi Granth*, wrote biographies of Gurū Nānak (1469–1539) and Gurū Gobind (1666–1708, Gurū: 1675), plays, pamphlets, articles, historical novels, lyrical poems, as well as a long spiritual epic entitled *Rāṇā Sūrat Siṅgh*, and a reformist narrative which is the subject of the present article.[4]

The full title of the work is *Subhāg jī dā sudhār hatthī Bābā Naudh Siṅgh* (lit. 'the reform of Subhāg by the hands of Bābā Naudh Siṅgh'); but according to common practice in Panjabi literary circles, we shall refer to it as *Bābā Naudh Siṅgh*. This work, first printed in 1921, is in fact a compilation of episodes published from 1907 onwards in the *Khālsā Samācār* ('Khalsa News'), a weekly started by Bhāī Vīr Siṅgh in 1899 for spreading 'education' as well as 'national and religious advancement' among the Sikh community (Singh 1972: 38–41). It is a massive volume of 304 densely written pages. Since its publication, it has had impressive success—the 1979 reprint was the twenty-first, with a run of 2100 copies. This is impressive, even if *Bābā Naudh Siṅgh*, like *Rāṇā Sūrat Siṅgh*, is often purchased more for the bookshelf than to be read.

The nucleus of the story is the fate of an inconsolable young Hindu widow who, after having been deceived by various religious charlatans, is converted to Sikhism by a charismatic exemplary man, Bābā Naudh Siṅgh, the leader of an ideal village strongly reminiscent of Kartārpur in the *Janam-sākhīs*. Important also are the successful encounters of the Bābā with representatives of Ārya Samājī and Brahmo Samājī Hinduism,[5] Islam, Christianity and western rationalism, all of whom come to the village.

This story, despite obvious differences, has some important characteristics in common with *Rāṇā Sūrat Siṅgh*. In both cases the heroine is a widow who, after many travails, finds beatitude in practising the true religion. Both texts have the same macro-structure: a predominantly narrative first part, and a long and heavy appendix of 'neo-Sikh' preaching.[6] But a major difference lies in the fact that whereas there is no charismatic figure in *Rāṇā Sūrat Siṅgh* apart from the deceased husband, *Bābā Naudh Siṅgh's* central character shows a highly charismatic spiritual and group leader. Since this character disappears completely in the second part of the narrative, we shall concentrate on the first part. Examining first the surface content of the narrative, we shall study the relation between charisma and identity. We shall then see how the figure of Nānak in the *Janam-sākhīs* was used as a model for Bābā Naudh Siṅgh's charisma. Lastly, we shall concentrate on the internal structure of the book and analyse the instrumentalization of charisma in this 'exemplary narrative'.

Charisma and Reformist Identity: The Surface Content of the Narrative

Surface Content

The first part of the narrative consists of twenty-two chapters (I. 1–22: 1–159) divided into three main sections. In the first of them, Jamnā, once widowed, is cheated by selfish religious impostors before finally settling in Bābā Naudh Siṅgh's house after having met a Sikh hermit who renames her Subhāg (I. 1–8: 1–24). The second section is devoted to encounters between Bābā Naudh Siṅgh and various characters: an Ārya Samājī (I. 9: 24–28), a Muslim 'elder' (*buzurg*)[7] and a local Christian pastor (*pādrī*) (I. 11: 35–45). The last and by far longest section of the first part revolves around the stay in the village, after a severe car accident, of a Panjabi barrister and his wife. After various events and long discussions, both are finally converted from western atheistic rationalism to the simple Sikh faith of the villagers (I. 12–22: 45–159).

The main narrative continues in the first three sections of *Bābā Naudh Siṅgh*'s second part. Initially, Subhāg figures in the forefront. Very much like Rāj Kaur in *Rāṇā Sūrat Siṅgh*, she is seized by the memory of her deceased husband and sinks into despair, from which she is brought back to serenity and faith by the preaching of the Bābā.[8] Afterwards, Subhāg disappears from the stage, while a traveller comes to the village. He presents himself as a 'school master' and a 'philanthropist' who has come to the village to distribute free 'homeopathic' medicines (II. 3: 169). His humanist, scientist and rationalist discourse indicates that he is most likely a Brahmo Samājī. In conversation with the Bābā, he begins to admire him. He awakens in him a keen interest in Sikhism.[9] Finally, the Bābā offers him a book, the contents of which occupy the last 109 pages of *Bābā Naudh Siṅgh* (II: 195–304). The book deals with a saintly man, Sāīdās, who was closely related to and a devotee of the sixth Gurū of the Sikhs, Hargobind (1595–1644, Gurū: 1606).[10] Through this literary device of a story within the story, Bhāī Vīr Siṅgh, relating at length the events in the life of the Gurū, of his family and of his disciples, shows how, in his own imaginary reconstruction, Sikhism was taught in words and in action by Gurū Hargobind, who first institutionalized the militarization of the Sikh *panth*. He also describes how true religion was lived by a faithful believer and his wife, Rāmo, thus establishing a striking parallel between these seventeenth-century characters on the one hand, and Bābā Naudh Siṅgh and his wife on the other.

This sketchy outline will make clear that the true subject of the book is the Bābā's charisma, and we shall now turn our attention towards the various ways in which Bābā Naudh Siṅgh enacts this gift of divine origin. We shall see how he successfully counters ill-inspired preachers, how he changes the heart of misled individuals and how he motivates a village to follow the values of the true religion.

Defeating the Preachers

Though it was initially published in episodes and despite long digressions and a heavy appendix, *Bābā Naudh Siṅgh* is built up in such a way that the Bābā's charisma is clearly thrown into relief. In the first part of the book, for instance, the two first groups of chapters are arranged in a kind of mirror structure, contrasting strongly the deeds of negatively characterized religious persons in the absence of the Bābā, and then in his presence.

Before her meeting with Bābā Naudh Siṅgh, Jamnā is cruelly deceived by a Hindu miracle-maker who, pretending to offer a vision of her husband, deprives her of her belongings and tries to push her to her death.[11] She is then betrayed by a Christian preacher who converts her to Christianity under the name of Miss Ḍumelī (Dumaily) and in whose establishment she receives marriage proposals 'from some very dark-skinned sweepers and leather workers who had converted [to Christianity].' (I. 4: 6–8). Escaping to Lahore, she falls pray to a *maulvī* who makes her a Muslim under the name of Gulām Fātmā and then tries to marry her.[12]

In the second group of chapters, when religious characters appear again, Jamnā has been rescued by the Sikh hermit, who calls her Subhāg, and adopted by Bābā Naudh Siṅgh.[13] This time, the Ārya Samājī, the Muslim *buzurg* and the Christian *pādrī* try either to convert the villagers or to sow communal disharmony. The Bābā convinces the first two that true religion cannot accommodate hatred. The Ārya Samājī finally converts to Sikhism and is granted permission to settle in the village. Saif Dīn, the *buzurg* who tried to convince the Muslims to stay away from the Sikhs, is converted by the Bābā to the religion of love.[14] He too asks to stay in the village and place himself under the spiritual guidance of Bābā Naudh Siṅgh. As for the Christian *pādrī*, who had falsely accused a Muslim of assaulting his wife, he is made to realize the wrong he has committed through the Bābā's intervention. But when the bishop wants to prosecute him, the Bābā asks for and obtains his pardon. Thus, in strong contrast with the first group of chapters, where religious imposters remained villains, the Bābā's charisma converts to true religion three potential imposters by addressing them from within their own religion in a manner quite similar to Gurū Nānak's approach (Matringe 1991: 50–1).

Changing the Hearts

While in all these chapters the Bābā's charisma is exerted in the context of religious controversies, in a whole section of the book it is directed at changing in depth the heart, the worldview and the ethics of two individuals. This part of *Bābā Naudh Siṅgh* mostly consists of conversations between the Bābā, Subhāg and a pious Sikh Doctor on one side, and the westernized alcoholic Hindu barrister Mādho Dās and his wife on the other. The latter are staying with the Bābā after a car accident in which a child from the village died and they were themselves seriously injured. The barrister, during his long stay in England, has become an atheist and is convinced that 'self interest is the true principle' (p. 70). But gradually the charismatic Bābā, through preaching the basic tenets of Sikhism and through the recitation of passages from the *Ādi Granth*, cultivates a change of heart, in the barrister and his wife until they become true Sikhs, believing in the virtue of unselfishness and love, convinced of the prime importance of the inner life and ready to adopt the simple Sikh way of existence. The barrister also renounces drink, and his wife and he finally experience an ecstatic vision while listening to a last sermon of Bābā Naudh Siṅgh (I. 22: 156–9).

More than once, the barrister expresses his astonishment at the Bābā's knowledge, wisdom and persuasiveness.[15] When he asks Bābā Naudh Siṅgh how he attained this clear consciousness, the Bābā answers that he was taught by a person whom he calls a 'master' (*ustād*) and a 'great man' (*mahā purakh*) (I. 22: 153). There is thus the indication of a tradition, which continues through Subhāg. She has followed the teaching of Bābā Naudh Siṅgh with great fervour and inherited his charisma. We see her using it when she helps the doctor's wife to overcome her suffering and distress after the death of her brother—himself a doctor and devout Sikh—in the First World War (I. 19: 99–129). At this point, Bhāī Vīr Siṅgh resorts to a literary device which he appreciates: a story within a story. In his narrative he causes Subhāg to read out to the doctor's wife an enlightening Sikh story in newspaper episodes. This story, entitled *Satt aukhīā rātā* ('Seven Awful Nights'), tells how the mother of Gurū Gobind Siṅgh's wife is successively grieved at the death of her husband and then of her daughter, at the destruction of Anandpur and the massacre of heroic Sikh fighters, at the killing of the two elder sons of the Gurū, of his two younger sons, and finally of the Gurū himself.[16] Each time, and more and more, religious meditation and, above all, taking part in religious congregations (*satsaṅgat*) and in the collective singing of hymns (*kīrtan*) help her to overcome her pain and finally to enter a state of blessedness (I. 19: 101–28). Through this reading and her inspired comments, Subhāg succeeds in enlightening the heart of the doctor's wife, who thanks her, embraces her, and tells her: 'I was dead and you have restored me' (128).

Managing the Village

The Bābā's charisma does not apply only to religious matters, but also to social and material problems concerning the life of the village. At the social level, the Baba's main concern is communal harmony, which he has made the fundamental law of the place. As the group leader, Bābā Naudh Siṅgh has also taken particular measures to favour both good relations and healthy life: for instance, corruption is fought with determination[17] and nobody drinks alcohol in the village (I. 20: 132).

Healthy life, hygiene and purity of food are indeed the Bābā's constant preoccupations, as is evident from his conversations with the barrister after the latter has recovered and can walk around the village (I. 20 & 21: 129–51). Bābā Naudh Siṅgh contrasts the simplicity and salubriousness of village life to the pollution and unhygienic conditions which prevail in cities. He criticizes corrupt practices such as food adulteration and Western habits such as 'tea addiction' (*cāh dī bīmārī*)—introduced in the villages by retired army men (I. 21: 149)—and drinking soda water. Concerning the latter, the Bābā tells the barrister how, once, his wife and he were so thirsty while travelling by train that they thought of drinking soda water. But they forgot about this when they saw, to their utter disgust, that the soda vendor had dirty clothes and unclean hands and was serving water from the same glass to the 'Sāhib-jī' and to 'Lālājī', to the 'Bābū' and to the sick (I. 20: 135). According to the Bābā, because Panjabis have gone astray from healthy food habits based on wheat and milk products, they have become weaker: 'Like this, "I look quite strong", he says, "but I am shorter than my father"'. (I. 20: 140). Consequently, the Bābā is regularly nostalgic about the good old days. He proposes solutions which all point towards a life more simple and more sincerely religious:

> The divine Gurū Nānak, when he preached the true religion, taught the people these principles:

Do your work,
Share the fruit of it and
Meditate upon the Name.[18]

Bābā Naudh Siṅgh himself does nothing else. He works hard, helps people in all sorts of ways, regularly meditates, and repeats '*vāhigurū*' (lit. 'Praise to the Guru')—the popular name by which the Sikhs refer to God.[19] Besides this personal and inner practice of religion, he strongly reminds one of Gurū Nānak as portrayed in the *Janam-sākhīs*: he engages in religious controversies and emerges victorious, he preaches, and he uses his charisma to make Sikhs adhere to the canon of their religion. Thereby he offers his co-religionists a renewed and 'purified' identity.

Re-enacting Charisma: Bābā Naudh Siṅgh and the *Janam-sākhīs*

Similarities between the Bābā and the Gurū are echoed in the resemblance between the village imagined by Bhāī Vīr Siṅgh and the Kartārpur of the *Janam-sākhīs*. There are, in fact, some striking parallels between *Bābā Naudh Siṅgh* and the *Janam-sākhīs* in terms of purpose and function, of structure, and of relations to history.

Purpose and Function[20]

Like the hagiographical narratives of the *sufi* and *bhakti* traditions, the purpose of the *Janam-sākhīs* is to engage readers and listeners with the way to salvation. In the context of the late-nineteenth and early-twentieth century Sikh revival, *Bābā Naudh Siṅgh* has the same purpose. We find in it some of the key features of the way to salvation proposed in the *Janam-sākhīs*. For instance, in the discourse of the Bābā and of his 'disciples'—his wife, the doctor and Subhāg—there is a strong emphasis on such basic tenets of Sikhism as hearkening to the divine word, meditating upon the Divine Name, participating in the congregation of the faithful (*satsaṅgat*), and collectively singing God's praises (*kīrtan*). *Satsaṅgat* and *kīrtan* are accepted as normative by the narrators of the *Janam-sākhīs*, one of their purposes being precisely to encourage their practice (McLeod 1980: 241). In *Bābā Naudh Siṅgh*, *satsaṅgat* and *kīrtan* are present at three levels:[21] the main character and his close relations engage regularly in these salutary activities;[22] as does Gurū Gobind's mother-in-law, as referred to in the work 'Seven Awful Nights';[23] lastly, the narrator himself recites the *gurbāṇī* by quoting it in the epigraph of many chapters of the book.[24]

Two other *Janam-sākhī* features relating to salvation are also very important in *Bābā Naudh Siṅgh*: teaching others—in which Bābā Naudh Siṅgh is so often engaged; and *darśan*—in the sense of a salutary 'vision' of the Gurū (McLeod 1980: 241). *Darśan*, in the book, is of three kinds. At the most obvious level, mere sight of the Bābā has a powerful effect. Such is the case, for instance, when Bābā Naudh Siṅgh joins the Muslims of the village around the *buzurg* Saif Dīn, who is advocating communal division. When they see the Bābā full of love and radiance the people say: 'The Bābā has come! The Bābā has come!' Their faces light up and the Bābā is invited to sit among them. The predicator is shattered and immediately changes his topic (I. 10: 29). There is also a more mysterious type of *darśan* when the young and beautiful hermit, who seems to have overcome joy and pain, rescues Jamnā from drowning in the Ravi, teaches her to keep hope in humanity and reject selfishness and doubt, offers her a book of prayers, and changes her name to Subhāg. The young widow, listening to him, experiences sweet and peaceful ecstasy. When she comes back to her senses he has disappeared, replaced by an old lady who takes her to Bābā Naudh Siṅgh's house (I. 7: 11–20). Lastly, the book *Bābā Naudh Siṅgh* itself, by staging such a character as the Bābā, offers its readers a *darśan* of that eminent man, whose example and teaching they are implicitly invited to follow.

With this latter aspect, we come close to the purpose of the narrators of the *Janam-sākhīs*: setting forth a soteriological interpretation of the life of Gurū Nānak and constructing a myth around his person (McLeod 1980: 243). Bhāī Vīr Siṅgh's narrative is entirely directed towards an identical interpretation of the Bābā's life. The character can be read as an attempt at creating a new myth for a new age: the myth of a charismatic leader, faithful and perceptive enough to derive from Sikhism, in its supposedly pristine purity, answers to all the questions and problems of contemporary life, and able to set forth a model of dedicated social work, of deep religiosity, and of an exemplary re-enactment of the old Sikh ethics (working, sharing, meditating on the Name).

If we now think in terms of function, we see such texts as *Bābā Naudh Siṅgh* acting among the Sikh reading élite as a strong cohesive factor, just as the *Janam-sākhīs* did in their own time, when they provided the Sikhs, through the myth of the community's first teacher, with 'a single focus for a common loyalty.' (McLeod 1980: 245) In the context of the Siṅgh Sabhā renewal movement, *Bābā Naudh Siṅgh* and *Rāṇā Sūrat Siṅgh* were some of the few widely circulated works which, in comparison with such negative pamphlets as the famous *Ham hindū nahī* ('We are not Hindus') by Kāhn Siṅgh Nābhā,[25] efficiently succeeded in proposing a model for a new positive Sikh identity (Matringe 1996b: 60).

Structure

Serving the same sort of purpose and playing an analogous role in their respective time, *Bābā Naudh Siṅgh* and the *Janam-sākhīs* also share some common structural characteristics. Let us first consider the global architecture of both these works. At first glance, the *Janam-sākhīs* give the impression of a profoundly diverse tradition. A closer scrutiny reveals that, to a very large extent, the *Bālā Janam-sākhī*, the *Purātan Janam-sākhī*, the *Ādi Sākhī*, the '*Mihrbān*' *Janam-sākhīs*, the *Gyān ratnāvalī* and the 'Mahimā *Prakāś*' *Janam-sākhīs* are based on the same stock of episodes and traditions, themselves derived from various sources and presented in diverse forms—mostly anecdotes and discourses.[26] In terms of their composition, the *Janam-sākhī* tradition is basically a particular way of assembling episodes or groups of episodes. In every case, the structure is very loose. We spring from one episode to the next without transition, or with such formulae as: '*Sākhī sampūran hoī. Sākhī hor calī*', which may be translated as: 'A story is finished. Here is another story.'

Published over several months in a magazine, *Bābā Naudh Siṅgh* displays the same two distinctive characteristics. First, as we have seen, the narrative consists of a succession of loosely linked episodes and groups of episodes. Second, in congruence with such a structure, we do not find in *Bābā Naudh Siṅgh* a continuous narration supporting a tightly knitted plot but, as in the *Janam-sākhīs*, an almost bare succession of anecdotes and discourses.

If we now zoom in on the internal fabric of the smaller narrative units, we discover new structural analogies between *Bābā Naudh Siṅgh* and the *Janam-sākhīs* concerning both the most typical situation met with in a particular episode, and the contextualization of the *gurbāṇī*.

In a standard *Janam-sākhī* episode, Gurū Nānak arrives somewhere, has an encounter with followers of another faith and, through his discourses and poetry, convinces them of the superiority of the Sikh way to salvation and of the necessity of propagating it. We have seen that this sequence of encountering, preaching and converting or convincing is met with again and again in *Bābā Naudh Siṅgh*. Similarly, the Bābā's perfection and charisma play, in the twentieth-century narrative, the same structural role as the miracles through which conversions are operated in the *Janam-sākhīs*. However, there is a difference. In the *Janam-sākhī*, Gurū Nānak travels because he has to propagate what had become, at the time of these hagiographies, a new religion, whereas in Bhāī Vīr Siṅgh's narrative people come to the Bābā's village. The result is a sharp contrast between a young and conquering religion and an island of ideal life—personal, social and religious—successfully resisting aggression, and enemies turning into allies thanks to the charisma of its leader. It is difficult not to relate this difference to the fact that, while Siṅgh Sabhā intellectuals thought the favourable treatment which the Sikhs were enjoying in *Pax britannica* before the First World War offered suitable conditions for their attempt at purifying and reviving their religion, they were also conscious of the considerable threat arising from fast advancing Western modernity.

Besides the analogies of composition and the internal structure of episodes, *Bābā Naudh Siṅgh* re-creates, if we get into further detail, another distinctive characteristic of the *Janam-sākhīs*. A recurrent pattern of the latter consists in inventing a narrative context for a hymn of Nānak and sometimes, anachronistically, for a poem of one of his successors. Let us take an example common to all the *Janam-sākhī* traditions—the meeting with Kaliyug.[27] After having subdued female magicians and their queen Nūrśāh who ruled over the land of Kāvarū, Gurū Nānak and his faithful bard Mardānā are resting in a wilderness. At God's command, amidst natural phenomena that terrify Mardānā, Kaliyug appears in the form of a giant demon. But coming closer to the Gurū, he is finally reduced to the size of a man. Respectfully greeting Gurū Nānak, he tells him:

Take something from me (...).
— What do you have, asked then Gurū Bābā.
— I have got everything, replied Kaliyug. If you say so, I shall erect a palace made of pearls and studded with rubies (...).
Then the Gurū sang an hymn in the *rāg Srī*:
'If a palace was raised made of pearls and studded with jewels,
Deliciously anointed with musk, saffron, aloes and sandal,
May it not be that seeing it I should become oblivious and that Your Name should not come to my mind!
Without God, let my soul burn and be consumed.
Asking my Gurū, I saw that there was no other abode for me [but He].'[28]

Hearing this, Kaliyug makes increasing offers of gifts, even his entire kingdom, but each time Gurū Nānak refuses. Kaliyug finally asks him what he wants, and Nānak answers that he only asks the safety of his Sikhs; in reward of this the demon will attain salvation. Kaliyug complies with Nānak's wish and falls at his feet.

We see the same pattern at work in *Bābā Naudh Siṅgh*, precisely with the invention of another context for the same hymn of Gurū Nānak. The episode has been previously referred to—of the Muslim who is arrested, having been falsely accused by a *pādrī* of having assaulted his wife. The Bābā goes to the bishop (*angrez pādrī sāhab*, the only British character in the narrative!) to ask his intervention. The bishop agrees and, after writing a letter to the police officer, takes the Bābā to his drawing room.

Entering there, the Bābā forgot his tiredness. The room was cool, the walls painted in fresh tin-blue, there were beautiful statues, astonishing curtains at the doors, European chairs, Persian carpets on the floor: it was an image of paradise. One could not but think that it was like a paradise on earth. How many virtuous deeds could have brought all this to that man? But the next moment, the Bābā had changed his mind and he began an inner recitation:

'If a palace were raised made of pearls and studded with jewels...' (I. 11: 40–1)

Thanks to the bishop's intervention, Rājhā the Muslim is released. Finally, the bishop comes to the village and the pastor's lie is discovered. But the Bābā successfully insists that he should be pardoned. Thus, a typically modern context has been imagined for quoting the same hymn as in the Kaliyug episode of the *Janam-sākhī*. But while the hymn had an instant effect on his interlocutor when sung by the Guru-poet, when remembered by a twentieth-century Sikh at a time of confusion it helps him remain faithful to the canon of his religion.

Comparing an episode from *Bābā Naudh Siṅgh* with a traditional *sākhī* allows us to point to yet another purpose of Bhāī Vīr Siṅgh's narrative. The *Janam-sākhīs*, by using hagiography in order to invent contexts for Gurū Nānak's compositions, aimed at concretely explaining their meaning. Creating new contexts for the hymns of the *Ādi Granth* and deploying spokesmen engaged in social and religious reform (such as the Bābā), serves the purpose of showing, at the same time, their present relevance and eternal value.

Canon, Charisma and History

This raises the wider question of the respective historical situation of the *Janam-sākhīs* and of *Bābā Naudh Siṅgh*. The *Janam-sākhīs* flourished between the late-sixteenth and the late-eighteenth century, when changes linked to the spread of Sikhism altered its initial form of a rather unorganized mystical fraternity. Both the necessity of a stronger temporal management and the absorption within the *panth* of more and more people of various social origins led to the need for cohesive factors, and of these, as we have seen, the *Janam-sākhīs* were one.

But in the new historical circumstances the prominence attributed to Gurū Nānak's myth gradually gave ground to the other charismatic pole of Sikhism—the militant image of Gurū Gobind. In the turmoil of the conquest of Panjab by the Sikhs, when the need was felt for a more specific religious code of conduct, two new branches of Sikh religious literature developed at the expense of the *Janam-sākhīs*' popularity: the *Rahit-nāmas* ('Code textbooks') which codify new norms of behaviour and the *Gur-bilās* ('Guru's pleasure') which sing of the great martial deeds of Gurū Hargobind and Gurū Gobind.[29] Both manifest a drastic shift towards the dominance of Gurū Gobind's mythology.

In a way, the history of the Sikh *panth* can be seen as an oscillation between these two charismatic poles. After the fall of the Sikh kingdom of Panjab, in the context of the *Pax britannica* and the Christian presence—when such missionary works as the *Bāibal dīā kahāṇīā* projected a strong and appealing image of Jesus (Matringe 1985: 428)— the need was felt in Sikh intellectual circles to re-enact Gurū Nānak's charisma. This became one of the aims of the Siṅgh Sabhā and *Bābā Naudh Siṅgh* was the greatest achievement to that end: this despite what might be considered its shortcomings when viewed from a too narrowly literary viewpoint. As for Gurū Gobind's image, it remained in the background and was linked to the reconstruction of Sikh history by the Siṅgh Sabhāites, as well as to their attempt at codifying Sikh identity anew.[30] Similarly, in *Bābā Naudh Siṅgh* itself, Gurū Gobind is sometimes referred to, but either from a distance, as in the story of the 'Seven Awful Nights', or in passing. When, for instance, while remembering with regret the good old days he refers in an already quoted statement to Nānak's teaching of the Sikh ethics,[31] the Bābā adds that Gurū Gobind instituted the Khālsā 'so that one could pay attention on the one hand to God's creation, and on the other hand to righteous action.'[32]

Bābā Naudh Siṅgh as an Exemplary Narrative

Replacing *Bābā Naudh Siṅgh* thus in the ideological context in which it was written allows a better understanding of its semantic and structural proximity to the *Janam-sākhīs* and of the historical meaning of its re-enactment of Gurū Nānak's charisma. But we are still left with the task of exploring the relationship between the purpose of the book and its literary form.

It has hopefully become evident that *Bābā Naudh Siṅgh* is not a 'realistic novel' in the sense of being inherited from the nineteenth century. It is not based on an aesthetics of plausibility and representation, and it does not narrate the fate of characters given as real and moving in a world which corresponds, at least nominally, to that of the reader's daily experience.[33] So loose is its structure, so stereotyped its characters and so tiny its plot that the book cannot be characterized as 'a novel with a message'. It does not combine captivating story and demonstration, skilful narrration and doctrine, nor uses fiction to impose a particular truth and a specific way of life.[34]

In fact, with *Bābā Naudh Siṅgh* we are structurally and functionally much closer to such 'exemplary narratives' as the *Janam-sākhīs* or the '*exempla*' of medieval Europe, both of which used existing stories only for the sake of their interpretation.[35] Thus, in several episodes of *Bābā Naudh Siṅgh*, a story is told, it is interpreted, and then follows, explicitly or implicitly, an injunction. To these narrative, interpretive and pragmatic levels correspond appropriate discursive forms: narrative for the fable (ex.: the Ārya Samājī insults the Sikh Gurūs, thus hurting the feelings of the people and failing to convince them), interpretive when a commentary draws out the meaning (the Ārya Samājī failed because hatred underlay his preaching) and pragmatic when a rule of action is derived from the interpretation (in substance: 'preach a religion of love and enact it, first of all, through your own behaviour'). Sometimes, the interpretation and the injunction may be missing, as in Chapter three (when Jamnā follows the miracle maker), or in Chapter Five (when she is forcibly converted to Islam and about to be married to the *maulvī*). But the story is so 'exemplary' that it conveys the interpretation and the injunction by itself.

Once Jamnā has become Subhāg and lives in the village, most of the injunctions are uttered by the Bābā and derive their efficiency from his charisma: 'keep the village clean', 'do not be individualistic', 'work, share and meditate on the Name', 'participate in *satsaṅgat*', etc. But behind the dialogue between the main character and his interlocutors, there is another—that between the narrator and the audience which, as in any exemplary narrative, is supposed to be well acquainted with the doctrine preached to them through the narrative. Thus, staging the Bābā, the narrator manifests his utopian project of changing the reader's heart and his actions. Writing an exemplary narrative about a charismatic character, he exerts his own charisma, using as tools his doctrinal mastership, his literary skill and his prodigious linguistic craftsmanship. The latter aspect deserves thorough study. Suffice it to say that *Bābā Naudh Siṅgh* is the first modern prose narrative of such scope and size written in Panjabi. In his narrative, Bhāī Vīr Siṅgh created a literary idiom—based on the *mājhī* ('central') dialect of the Lahore-Amritsar area—which is close to the spoken language,[36] with Perso-Arabic loanwords. It possesses a remarkable syntactic flexibility and is rich in the numerous semantic nuances required by the wide range of its themes, historical and contemporary, social and psychological, secular and religious. This language was to become, thanks to the pioneering efforts of Bhāī

Vīr Siṅgh and his emulators, what is called contemporary standard Panjabi.[37]

Through the type of relation established with his reader, Bhāī Vīr Siṅgh was following the example of the *Janam-sākhī* narrators, producing with *Bābā Naudh Siṅgh* the last Panjabi masterpiece of the tradition of religious didactic anecdotes, which has enjoyed lasting fortune in India. But in the context of the colonial presence, of acrimonious religious controversies and of the increasing impact of European literature on the cultural expectations of the Panjabi reading élite, he also radically transformed this traditional genre. He invented a new literary language and introduced contemporary situations and a modern hero endowed with the charismatic qualities of Gurū Nānak. But he used them to confront—albeit in a utopian way—the great social and religious problems of his time. Just like *Rāṇā Sūrat Siṅgh* in the field of poetry, *Bābā Naudh Siṅgh* is a unique phenomenon in the history of Panjabi literature, an isolated classic, both post-traditional and pre-modern.

Notes

1. *Janam-sākhī Śrī Gurū Nānak Dev Jī* (India Office Library manuscript Panj. B 40), 76(o), p. 74. This translation is mine, but the whole of this particular *Janam-sākhī* has been translated into English by W. H. McLeod (see Bibliography, under 'Sources', B–40 *Janam-sākhī*). On the *Janam-sākhīs* in general, see McLeod (1980).
2. See Matringe (1991).
3. Having dealt elsewhere with the new conditions of literary production in early-twentieth century Panjab, I shall not develop them here (Matringe 1985: 425–34; 1996a: 35–8; 1996b: 41–3). The most illuminating study of the Siṅgh Sabhā movement is Oberoi (1994). For a quicker presentation, see McLeod (1989b: 62–81). For a general survey of religious polemics in Panjab in the late-nineteenth and early-twentieth century, see Jones (1989: 85–121).
4. On Bhāī Vīr Siṅgh, see, for instance, Singh (1972). For a study of *Rāṇā Sūrat Siṅgh*, see Matringe (1996b).
5. On the Ārya Samāj in the Panjab, see Jones (1976). On the Brahmo Samāj, see Kopf (1979).
6. 'Neo-Sikhism' was one of the terms used by British officials to describe the Sikh reformist movement which they regarded with suspicion. See Matringe (1996a: 58; fn 66).
7. (I. 10: 28–35). *Buzurg* is traditionally used by Muslims to refer to a holy man.
8. (II. 1-2: 160–9). Rāj Kaur experiences the same type of salvation by joining a congregation (*satsaṅgat*) led by a saintly spiritual guide (*gurmukh*).

9. (II. 3-4: 169–95). On the Brahmo Samāj and more particularly on the Brahmo Samāj in the Panjab, see Kopf (1979: 320–1; 331).
10. On Sāīdās, see Nābhā ([1930] 1981: 175). On Gurū Hargobind, see Grewal (1990: 64–7).
11. (I. 2–4: 2–6). The narrator then reveals that the miracle-maker was in fact a *ṭhagg* from Central India (*madh-hindustān*), descending from Sajjaṇ, a *ṭhagg* rescued from a life of sin by Gurū Nānak (pp. 5–6). This is an allusion to a *Janam-sākhī* episode, entitled 'Sajjaṇ ṭhagg' in the *Purātan janam-sākhī* (no 13: 51–3) which Bhāī Vīr Siṅgh knew quite well, since he edited that text in 1926. On the *Purātan janam-sākhī*, see McLeod (1980: 22-30). A certain Šaix Sajjaṇ has built a temple and a mosque next to his house, theoretically for the convenience of both Hindu and Muslim travellers, but in fact in order to attract them and then throw them into a well. When Nānak and his bard Mardānā come to his house, he invites them to rest. But before doing so, Nānak sings a hymn which changes the heart of Sajjaṇ and makes him implore the Gurū's forgiveness, which is granted to him on the condition that he return the goods (*basatu*) which he had stolen. Kāhn Siṅgh Nābhā states, without refering to a source, that Sajjaṇ was from the region of Multan (Nābhā [1930] 1981: 145).
12. (I. 5: 8–9). Gulām Fātmā stands for the Perso-Arabic Gulām-i Fāṭima ('slave of Fāṭima', the daughter of Muḥammad and wife of 'Ali).
13. Subhāg means the fortunate one, literally 'one who got a good share'.
14. Saif Dīn stands for Perso-Arabic Saif-i Dīn, 'Sword of the Religion'.
15. See for instance I. 22: 152—'In which college did you study? I remain astonished at what you say.'
16. For a balanced approach to Gurū Gobind's career, see Grewal (1990: 73–81).
17. Chapter I. 17: 89–95 tells how, thanks to the intervention of the Bābā and the doctor, a family of Muslim cultivators gets back irrigation water which it had been deprived of after greedy neighbours bribed the irrigation officers.
18. '*Kirat karnī, vaṇḍ chakṇā te nām japṇā*.' The formula appears several times in the discourses of Bābā Naudh Siṅgh. The oft-quoted passage of the *Ādi Granth* to which it refers is a *salok* of Gurū Nānak inserted in a hymn in Rāg Sāraṅg by Gurū Rām Dās (1534–81; Gurū: 1574). It says: 'The one who eats from what he earned working hard and who shares some of it, o Nānak, that one knows the way.' (*Ādi Granth* 1962–4, 9: 86). This *salok* is used by Bhāī Vīr Siṅgh as an epigraph for the eighth chapter of *Bābā Naudh Siṅgh*, where Subhāg, having been adopted by Bābā Naudh Siṅgh and his wife, discovers happiness in hard work and meditation on the Name ([1921] 1979: 20–24). This meditation on the Name is the fundamental discipline of the Sikh religion. See for instance McLeod (1976: 214–19).
19. The expression is already found in the *Ādi Granth*, but only in the panegyrics written by bards in praise of the first five Gurūs. See, for instance, *Savaīe Mahale Cauthe ke 4, Jholanā* 1.6: 1402. It is common in the *Janam-sākhīs* where it is used for meditation upon the Name, as it is still today.

20. Concerning the *Janam-sākhīs*, this distinction is sensibly made and soundly argued in McLeod (1980: 137–47) who, contrasting 'function' (role actually played) to 'purpose' (conscious intention of an author), refers to Merton (1957).
21. On the same type of emphasis on these practices in *Rāṇā Sūrat Siṅgh*, see Matringe (1996b).
22. There is thus a striking scene in I. 20 when, while the barrister and his wife are conversing, the Bābā arrives reciting the *Sukhmanī* ('Pearl of peace', *Ādi Granth*, 1962–4: 262–96), a masterpiece written by Gurū Arjan (1563–1606; Gurū: 1581, compiler of the *Ādi Granth*). The barrister and his wife invite the Bābā to sit with them. He finishes his recitation and then says the ritual prayer of the Sikhs (*ardās*): the *Sukhmanī* brings peace to the hearts of the barrister and his wife, while the prayer moves them to tears (132).
23. See above.
24. *Gurbāṇī* literally means 'the speech of the Gurūs' and refers *stricto sensu* to the compositions of the Sikh Gurūs. However, the term is commonly used to refer to any composition found in the *Ādi Granth*.
25. Nābhā (1899). For a study of the role of that text, see Jones (1973).
26. The synopsis presented in McLeod (1976: 73–6) gives a good idea of the relation between the various *Janam-sākhī* traditions.
27. In the *Janam-sākhī*, Kaliyug is an incarnation of the complete degeneration characterizing the last era of a cosmic cycle. More concretely, it was considered an evil person living in Jagannāth-Purī, who was finally converted by Gurū Nānak. See Nābhā ([1930] 1981: 310).
    Once again, we shall follow the *Purātan Janam-sākhī* edited by Bhāī Vīr Siṅgh. The Kaliyug episode is narrated in *sākhī* 24: 79–82.
28. *Rāgu sirīrāgu Mahalā pahilā 1 Gharu 1*, *Ādi Granth* (1962–4: 14).
29. On this evolution see McLeod (1989a: 98–101) and (1989b: 23–61).
30. See McLeod (1984: 11–13) and (1989b: 62–81).
31. I. 20: 139. See above note 18.
32. Ibid. In *Rāṇā Sūrat Siṅgh* too, the militant aspect of Sikhism is hardly mentioned, and always in connection with the past. See Matringe (1996b: 62).
33. For theoritical reflections on the 'realistic novel', see for instance *Poétique* 16 (1973), *Communications* 11 (1968), Barthes (1970a), and also Auerbach (1969), Decottignies (1979) and Mitterrand (1980).
34. On the novel with a message see Rubin-Suleiman (1983).
35. For a concise historical survey of the medieval '*exemplum*' see Mosher (1911). For a detailed study of the genre see Welter (1927); for modern approaches see Barthes (1970b), Zumthor (1972) and, on a related subject, the thought provoking Chabrol and Marin (1974).
36. As for the *Janam-sākhī* narrators, they had adopted a popular literary idiom based on Khaṛī Bolī, with a noticeable Panjabi element. Khaṛī Bolī had for long been current in Panjab and was closer to Panjabi than the Brajbhāṣā used in such works as the *Dasam Granth*, the second sacred book of the Sikhs, reputedly compiled by Gurū Gobind. See McGregor (1984: 140–1; 213) and McLeod (1989a: 89-92).

37. For an introduction to the question of the beginnings of contemporary standard Panjabi, see Shackle (1988).

References

Primary Material

Ādi Granth (Srī Gurū Granth Sāhib Darpan). 1962–4. Gen. ed. Sāhib Siṅgh. 10 vols. Jalandhar: Rāj Publications.

B-40 Janam-Sākhī. 1980. An English translation with an introduction and annotation by W. H. McLeod. Amritsar: Guru Nanak Dev University.

Bhāī Vīr Siṅgh. [1905] 1980. *Rāṇā Sūrat Siṅgh*. Amritsar: Khālsā Samācār.

———. [1921] 1979. *Subhāg jī dā sudhār hatthī Bābā Naudh Siṅgh*. Amritsar: Khālsā Samācār.

Janam-sākhī Srī Gurū Nānak Dev Jī. 1974. Ed. Piār Siṅgh. Amritsar: Gurū Nānak University. (India Office Library manuscript Panj. B 40)

Nābhā, Kāhn Siṅgh. 1899. *Ham hindū nahī*. Amritsar: Khalsa Press.

Purātan Janam-sākhī. [1926] 1982. Ed. Bhāī Vīr Siṅgh. Amritsar: Khālsā Samācār.

Criticism

Auerbach, Erich. 1969. *La Représentation de la réalité dans la littérature occidentale*. Paris: Gallimard.

Barthes, Roland. 1970a. *S/Z*. Paris: Seuil.

———. 1970b. L'Ancienne rhétorique. *Communications* 16: 172–229.

Chabrol, Claude and Louis Marin. 1974. *Le Récit évangélique*. Paris: Aubier-Montaigne, Éditions du Cerf and Delachaux-Niestlé.

Communications 11 (1968). Special issue: Le Vraisemblable.

Decottignies, Jean. 1979. *L'Écriture de la fiction. Situation idéologique du roman*. Paris: Presses Universitaires de France.

Grewal, J. S. 1990. *The Sikhs of the Punjab*. Cambridge: Cambridge University Press.

Jones, Kenneth W. 1973. Ham hindu nahin. Arya-Sikh Relations, 1877–1905. *Journal of Asian Studies* 32.3: 457–75.

———. 1976. *Arya Dharm. Hindu Consciousness in 19th Century Punjab*. Berkeley: University of California Press.

———. 1989. *Socio-religious Reform Movements in British India*. Cambridge: Cambridge University Press.

Kopf, David. 1979. *Brahmo Samaj and the Shaping of the Modern Indian Mind*. Princeton: Princeton University Press.

Matringe, Denis. 1985. L'Apparition de la nouvelle et du roman en panjabi (1930–1947). *Journal Asiatique* 273.3-4: 425–54.

———. 1991. Images de la première communauté Sikhe. In *Littératures médiévales de l'Inde du Nord*, ed. by FranŚoise Mallison, 39–54. Paris: École Française d'Extrême-Orient.

———. 1996a. Punjabi Lyricism and Sikh Reformism: Bhāī Vīr Siṅgh's Poetry

in the 1920s. In *Punjabi Identity: Continuity and Change*, ed. Gurharpal Singh and Ian Talbot, 35–59. New Delhi: Manohar.
———. 1996b. Histoire du Sikhisme et littérature panjabie: *Rāṇā Sūrat Siṅgh* de Bhāī Vīr Siṅgh. *Revue de l'Histoire des Religions* 213.1: 39–74.
McGregor, Ronald Stuart. 1984. *Hindi Literature from its Beginnings to the Nineteenth Century*. vol. VIII. Fasc. 6 of A *History of Indian Literature*, ed. Jan Gonda. Wiesbaden: Otto Harrassowitz.
McLeod, W. H. 1976. *Gurū Nānak and the Sikh Religion*. 2nd ed. Delhi: Oxford University Press.
———. 1980. *Early Sikh Tradition. A Study of the Janam-sākhīs*. Oxford: Clarendon Press.
———. 1984. *Textual Sources for the Study of Sikhism*. Manchester: Manchester University Press.
———. 1989a. *The Sikhs. History, Religion and Society*. New York: Columbia University Press.
———. 1989b. *Who is a Sikh?* Oxford: Clarendon Press.
Merton, Robert K. 1957. Manifest and Latent Functions. In *Social Theory and Social Structure*, ed. Robert K. Merton, 19–84. Glencoe: The Free Press.
Mitterrand, Henri. 1980. *Le Discours du roman*. Paris: Presses Universitaires de France.
Mosher, J. A. 1911. *The Exemplum in the Early Religious and Didactic Literature of England*. New York: Columbia University Press.
Nābhā, Kāhn Siṅgh. [1930] 1981. *Mahān Koś*. Patiala: Bhāṣā Vibhāg, Pañjāb.
Oberoi, Harjot. 1994. *The Construction of Religious Boundaries*. Delhi: Oxford University Press.
Poétique 16 (1973). Special issue: Le Discours réaliste.
Rubin-Suleiman, Susan. 1983. *Le Roman à thèse ou l'autorité fictive*. Paris: Presses Universitaires de France, coll. 'Écriture'.
Shackle, Christopher. 1988. Some Observations on the Evolution of Modern Standard Punjabi. In *Sikh History and Religion in the Twentieth Century*, ed. Joseph T. O'Connell *et al*. Toronto: University of Toronto, Centre for South Asian Studies.
Singh, Harbans. 1972. *Bhāī Vīr Siṅgh. Makers of Indian Literature*. New Delhi: Sahitya Akademi.
Welter, J.-Th. 1927. *L'Exemplum dans la littérature religieuse et didactique du Moyen Âge*. Paris: E.-H. Guitard.
Zumthor, Paul. 1972. *Essai de poétique médiévale*. Paris: Seuil.

Gandhi as Mahatma: Political Semantics in an Age of Cultural Ambiguity

DIETER CONRAD

The reverential designation of Gandhi as *Mahatma Gandhi* has become a natural compound, a formula used virtually as his proper name. It seems artificial now to refer to Gandhi as 'Mr Gandhi', or to use his initials, 'M. K. Gandhi'. The honorific has melted into the proper name, but also *vice versa;* the historical event which was Gandhi's personality and life seems to have appropriated the title *Mahatma.* If we speak of *Mahatma* without further specification, it goes without saying that we are referring to Mahatma Gandhi. Books on Gandhi are published under the title *Mahatma*, as notably the 8-volume biography by G. D. Tendulkar (Tendulkar 1960), but also a book of which the title might have suggested itself for this essay: *The Making of the Mahatma*—a study on Gandhi's early years by Chandran D. S. Devanesan (1969). Recently, a film by Shyam Benegal dealing with Gandhi's South African years has used that title.[1]

It is better, however, not to be tempted by these titles because what is treated there is not the issue which interests me—the semantic potential of a name or designation. What did *Mahatma* mean, how did the title come to be fixed on Gandhi, and what became both of Gandhi and the title in the process? All this is taken for granted in Devanesan's book. What that work deals with is the formation of Gandhi's personality, presupposing the existence of his 'mahatmaship'. To quote from a review: 'The process that makes a man is indeed difficult to analyse and that of a *mahatma* much more so.' (Chavda 1972–3: 70). Perhaps it is even more difficult to analyse what is meant by such a statement. Devanesan's study concludes with the following sentence: 'It was South Africa that made the Mahatma' (Devanesan 1969: xi)—a formulation misleading in a specific sense. Whatever might be said about the formation of Gandhi's personality, the title *Mahatma* was conferred on him not until after his return to India, and only in India was his charismatic appeal expressed by that designation. Its significance appears in the context of a peculiar colonial cultural situation where influences from various Indian traditions and Western perceptions mingled in an unclear manner to create a halo with politico-religious potential.

Should we really bother so much about the title? In the Indian subcontinent there is a widespread custom of using traditional titles such as Pundit, Shastri, Acharya, Svami or, on the Muslim side, Maulana, Moulvi, Sheikh, Pir, etc. More characteristically, personal honorifics are coined and used, such as *Lokamanya* for B. G. Tilak, *Deshbandhu* for C. R. Das, *Bangabandhu* for Sheikh Mujibur Rahman, *Netaji* for S. C. Bose, *Qaid-i-Azam* for M. A. Jinnah, *Qaid-i-Millat* for Liaqat Ali Khan, etc. If such is the custom, and its practice and extension so familiar in the South Asian milieu, why wonder about *Mahatma*?

Few indeed have wondered. It is amazing how the use of the honorific has become a matter of course in East and West. Only once in the historical literature have I come across an author betraying sensitivity towards the phenomenon and this, characteristically, in a book not on Gandhi but as a passing reference in a book on Bal Gangadhar Tilak (Cashman 1975: 2 ff.). Introducing his subject, the author writes that after the 'myth of the *Lokamanya*' (*lit.* 'the one revered by the people') one of the most powerful political myths in India was the myth of the *Mahatma*. He mentions earlier attempts with the *Mahatma* concept: during the Ganpati-festivals, when Tilak in popular parlance was sometimes identified with Maharashtrian saints as '*Mahatma* Bhagwan Tilak'.[2] But in its true form the *Mahatma* myth 'was established to describe the career of India's foremost leader, Mohandas Karamchand Gandhi. The Mahatma-concept underlined Gandhi's efforts to combine religion and politics, non-violence, spiritual end, asceticism.' And later: 'As a shrewd politician Gandhi recognized the potential of the myth and succeeded in capturing it. But it was not Gandhi who created the myth; it was the myth, and the circumstances that produced it, which established Gandhi as the Mahatma, the chief symbol of the nationalist movement.' (Cashman 1975: 220).

Whether the 'shrewd politician' Gandhi 'capturing the myth of Mahatma' is an adequate description that answers the motivational complexities of the process is open to discussion. In any case—writing primarily on Tilak—Cashman does not explain himself more specifically. Nor is a closer analysis of his concept of 'myth' called for in our context.

But there is no doubt that, in a general sense, the use of the epithet *Mahatma* has helped create a kind of mythical halo around Gandhi, particularly in the West where the term is scarcely understood. An example is the UNESCO Symposium on Human Rights assembling contributions by various thinkers and savants in the context of the UN Universal Declaration of Human Rights 1948 and including a letter on the subject by Gandhi. In the appendix, which provides particulars on contributors such as Aldous Huxley, Harold Laski, Salvador de Madariaga, Kurt Riezler *et al.*, each with full name, professional position and some publications, Gandhi is listed not with such mundane information but simply as 'Mahatma Gandhi. The Father of Modern India.' (UNESCO 1949: 282).

The mythical aura is not exclusive to Western orientalism. The monumental biography by Tendulkar, published by the Director, Publications Division, Government of India, has already been mentioned. The title is not, as one might expect 'Life of Mahatma Gandhi' but 'Mahatma. Life of Mohandas Karamchand Gandhi'. This is followed, on the title page, by four lines of verse which I put here in full:

He is the One Luminous, Creator of All, Mahatma
Always in the hearts of the people enshrined,
Revealed through Love, Intuition, and Thought,
Whoever knows Him, Immortal becomes.

No quotation or explanation is given. As we shall see, this is a verse from the *Svetasvatara Upanishad.*[3] Its position and literal understanding here, where the reader must take it to be a direct reference to the historical person of Gandhi, seems strange to a Western mind attuned towards a certain prejudice against the deification of mortals. But ironically it is a Western mind—Romain Rolland in his book on Gandhi—that reverentially reports this stanza from the *Svetasvatara Upanishad* being recited as salutation to 'the Apostle' by Tagore on his visit to Gandhi's ashram in December 1922 (Rolland 1924: introductory page, unnumbered).[4]

On the reverse there is another passage attributed to Rabindranath Tagore:

He stopped at the threshold of the huts of the thousands of dispossessed, dressed like one of their own. He spoke to them in their own language. Here was living truth at last, and not only quotations from books. For this reason the Mahatma, the name given to him by the people of India, is his real name. Who else has felt like him that all Indians are his own flesh and blood? When love came to the door of India that door was opened wide. At Gandhi's call India blossomed forth to new greatness, just as once before, in earlier times, when the Buddha proclaimed the truth of fellow-feeling and compassion among all living creatures.

This, upon closer inspection, again turns out to be a paraphrase of a section in Romain Rolland's *Mahatma Gandhi* (1924: 84–5), which in turn paraphrases a passage in Tagore's article of 1921 'The Call of Truth' (Chander 1945: 48–9). The comparison with Buddha is much more subtle there, though unmistakable. Another variation is significant: the key sentence by Tagore reads: 'So the name of Mahatma, which was given to him, is his true name.' With Rolland, and Tendulkar, this is rendered: 'Mahatma, the name given by the people of India to Gandhi, is his real name.'

We may note, in passing, the emphasis on 'true' and 'real'. For Tagore, the name was simply 'given' to Gandhi—this perhaps reflects a tradition and conviction that it was Tagore himself, rather than 'the people of India', who bestowed the title on Gandhi. But, as we shall see, there are other aspirants. The question is: who were the Indian people giving that name, or was it 'captured' by the 'shrewd politician Gandhi'—and what was its political significance?

That there was in fact some political significance involved, and that the matter cannot be relegated to some more or less familiar and likeable Indian habit, can be seen from certain voices of dissent—Indians who did not want to use the title *Mahatma*. A first harmless case is Jawaharlal Nehru. In his autobiography he mentions an incident from the year 1923–4. Nehru had been made secretary of the All-India National Congress by its president, Mohammad Ali. He reports how he tried to introduce a policy of referring to all Congress members only by their name, leaving off the abundant and useless prefixes, suffixes, honorifics and the like. He was stopped by Congress President Mohammad Ali who sent 'a frantic telegram' directing him 'as President' to revert to the old practice and, in particular, always to address Gandhiji as *Mahatma* (Nehru 1962: 117).

Why should this Muslim politician and leading Khilafatist be bothered by the use of a Hindu epithet such as *Mahatma*? For Nehru, this was mainly a question of taste and convenience. But there were others who definitely objected to the title. M. A. Jinnah, for instance, in his later years[5] studiously avoided it, speaking of Gandhi as 'Mr Gandhi' in a pointed manner. It is hardly accidental, either, that B. R. Ambedkar wrote a pamphlet in 1943 under the title '*Mr* Gandhi and the Emancipation of Untouchables' while shortly thereafter dedicating a book to the nineteenth-century Maharashtrian reformer '*Mahatma* Jotiba Fule' (Ambedkar 1946, emph. add).[6]

II

The ordinary dictionary meaning of *mahatma* is usually rendered as *maha atma* (Skt. *atman*)—a great soul, 'an honorific given to men of outstanding character and spiritual qualities'.[7] The designation seems traditionally to have been in use in an unspecific sense of 'holy man', 'saint' or *sannyasi*, particularly in west and north-west India. A few stray examples may be given. For its traditional use, reference may be made to the *lilacaritra* of the bhakti saint Cakradhar who lived in the kingdom of Devagiri in the thirteenth century. (Sontheimer 1982: 329 ff.) *Mahatma* is here used to denote an ascetic. Cakradhar, on being questioned by people on whether he is a Gosavi, replies 'I am a Bikhsu Mahatma.' (Sontheimer 1982 : 356, see also 338). From the nineteenth century there is the tentative conferment of the title on Tilak (as mentioned). Jyotiba Phule, according to his biographer D. J. Keer, was ceremoniously proclaimed *Mahatma* at a public function in Bombay in 1888 (Keer 1964: 235 f.). But it seems that, in informal usage, various personages of differing degrees of sanctity were popularly called *mahatma*. In his autobiography Swami Shraddhanand (formerly known as Mahatma Munshi Ram) mentions a *Mahatma Shankar of Puri* living near Jullunder who impressed him favourably in contrast with certain other dubious *sannyasins* in the vicinity (Swami Shraddhanand 1961: 83). The Rowlatt Committee, tracing suspect influences on the early career of Vinayak Damodar Savarkar, lists his affiliation, in Nasik 1905, to a certain *Mahatma Sri Agamya Guru Paramhansa* who preached fearlessness against government and founded a political society (Sedition Committee 1918: 4). In the Khilafat Conference in Delhi 1920, one *Mahatma Anand Prasad* is mentioned as representing 'the Hindus of Bareilly' (Government of Maharashtra 1965: 240, 242). In such instances we may discern a certain tendency towards political use of the religious honorific.

There was a well-known and frequent but mostly unexplained use of the *Mahatma* title in the history of the Arya Samaj in Punjab. With the split into two factions over the issue of English or Sanskrit education in 1891, the party that was expelled from the Dayananda Anglo-Vedic College Lahore came to be known as 'Mahatma Party'. It subsequently founded the Gurukul in Hardwar.The split has to do with a general divergence of religious outlook centring on various issues like meat-eating, the importance of religious propaganda (*prachar*), Sanskrit *vs.* English education, the education of girls, etc. In this dispute the religiously committed anti-college group 'became variously called the "Mahatma Party", the "Gurukul Party" or simply "the radicals"' (Jordens 1981: 31), in contradistinction to the 'cultured party' favouring English education and remaining in control of the Anglo-Vedic College in Lahore. Munshi Ram, who insists that the educational difference rather than the question of meat-eating was the crucial issue, gives the following description: 'Those who held the view that English and science were the most important, declared that the rest of us were religious fanatics and debarred us from the management of the College.' (Lajpat Rai 1915: 196 f.). From the ironic description as 'religious fanatic' it might be inferred that the label 'Mahatma Party' was also given half jokingly or ironically (see also Lele 1946: 9). This is confirmed by Lala Lajpat Rai who, in his autobiography, explains the label 'Mahatma Party' as a mockery of the group's constant appeal to religious principles.[8]

Yet, besides this polemical use, the title *Mahatma* was applied to leading figures of the Arya Samaj in a reverential, un-ironic sense. In such manner it had been conferred on Munshi Ram after his return from a successful fund-raising tour undertaken through Punjab, U.P. and Hyderabad in order to procure means for the foundation of the Gurukul, in 1900: 'On his return a triumphal procession was taken out in Lahore, and this astounding achievement of single-minded dedication earned him the title of Mahatma.' (Jordens 1981: 58). Munshi Ram was definitely called Mahatma in a reverential sense, quite independently from his role as leader of the 'Mahatma Party'. Again, it is noteworthy that *Mahatma* came to be used and claimed also for the other, the 'cultured' faction: the head of the Dayananda Anglo-Vedic College in Lahore, Lala Hansraj, was called Mahatma Hansraj (Sri Ram Sharma 1965). Munshi Ram himself, it seems, referred to him under that honorific title at the time of the factional dispute leading to the split in 1891. In his *Autobiography*, when dealing with the dispute, he calls him a 'Chief and Mahatma', but goes on to discuss the question whether this was compatible with meat-eating. 'I sang and revered Mahatmajis, but their love for flesh [*sic*] had lessened my respect towards the Lahore Arya Samaj leaders' (Swami Shraddhanand 1961: 107).[9]

While these varied applications generally point to a rather informal and easy use of the title, a new element appears with ceremonious conferment upon a particular date and at a public gathering—something like a public appointment. In this respect the conferment on Munshi Ram was reminiscent—by its emphasis on social service and by public reception and public acclaim—of an earlier ceremony described by Keer in his biography of Jyotiba Phule (Keer 1964). According to Keer, Phule was formally proclaimed Mahatma on 11 May 1888 at a gathering of his followers at the old custom house (Mandvi), Bombay. This was done, as Keer puts it, in recognition of his unflagging work for the uplift of the downtrodden, and for his matchless life full of service, struggle and sacrifice for the glory of God. Keer goes on to state: 'Jotirao was *now* a Mahatma. A *real Mahatma*. A high-souled personage .... The title was conferred upon him by the common people. Such examples are rare. Jotirao was the first great man in modern India to receive this highest of titles at the hands of the lower classes. A Mahatma is a patriot of humanity and such was the Mahatma in Jotirao Phooley.' (Keer 1964: 236, emph. add.). In the case of Munshi Ram, we saw that he was taken out in procession after his return to Lahore in 1900 and publicly acclaimed *Mahatma*. We read: 'Mahatma—the title affectionately bestowed on him by the Aryan public of the Punjab' (Jambunathan 1961: 141). If we compare Romain Rolland's and Tagore's preconisation of Mahatma Gandhi, certain similarities and a pattern begin to appear. In distinction to the older and more informal use, the title now is to be conferred by somebody, preferably 'the people' or 'the public' (or by whoever may act on their behalf) and it conveys spiritual authority *for a public function*.

With Munshi Ram we are close to Gandhi. Gandhi became acquainted with Munshi Ram through C. F. Andrews and, in a letter written from South Africa, addressed him as Mahatma.[10] Later, on his return to India, Gandhi visited the *gurukul* in April 1915.[11] On the occasion of this visit Munshi Ram claims to have 'dubbed' him Mahatma, or significantly, 'the great Mahatma' (Shraddhanand 1946: 40, 49). Gandhi does not appear to have accepted this at the time. In a later comment, remembering the incident at the inauguration of the Banaras Hindu University in 1916, he explains:

> I had not then been made a 'Mahatma', and if anyone called me by that name I knew I must have been mistaken for Mahatma Munshiramji, as the late Swami Shraddhanandji was then called. *For, there cannot be a number of Mahatmas*, and I knew even when I was in South Africa that Munshiramji's great work had entitled him to that name.[12] (*emph. add.*).

A strange comment. First of all we note the modern emphasis on social or public work as a credential for mahatmaship—something one would not normally associate with the traditional role of a *sadhu* or *sannyasi*. But secondly and more significantly: why could there not be more than one mahatma? As we have seen, there was a traditional and rather loose way of conferring the title to various 'holy men', and within the Punjab Arya Samaj in particular quite 'a number of mahatmas' happily coexisted. It had never been suggested that there could only be one. Gandhi himself had tried to confer the honorific on Rajchandra (*CW* 13, 144 from *Bombay Chronicle* 23. 11. 1915) and repeatedly on G. K. Gokhale.[13] Some change seems to have taken place by the turn of the century. On 13 April 1917 Munshi Ram became a *sannyasi*, adopting the name of Swami Shraddhanand; at the same time he resigned from the governorship of the *gurukul* and formally renounced mahatmaship.[14] In a sense the post of the one pre-eminent Mahatma— if there could only be one—had become free from then on.

III

In order to understand the idea that 'there cannot be a number of mahatmas' we have to take note of a second, or perhaps the primary meaning of 'Mahatma', which is eminently in the singular. Apart from the colloquial use of the term to designate a 'holy man', an ascetic or *sannyasi*, 'mahatma' occurs, in the classical scriptures and particularly in the Upanishadic speculation, as a name of the divinity. *Mahānātman*: the great Self, the 'large atman' is the creator manifesting himself and embodying himself in creation ...'itself resulting from and, in effect, identical with the creator's self-recognition' (van Buitenen 1964: 109). This meaning is explained by Ananda Coomaraswamy in a congratulatory volume for 'Mahatma Gandhi' edited by Radhakrishnan in 1939. Coomaraswamy's article on 'Mahatma' opens with the sentence: 'The term "Mahatma" has been much abused but has precise and intelligible meanings and a long history.' (Coomaraswamy 1939: 63). He goes on to identify the term 'Mahatma' as the name of God, 'the Spiritual-Essence of all that is (RV, I, 115, 1). The Great Self is the only Witness, Agent and Knower, at the same time immanent and transcendent. To have found Him is to have abandoned all the peripheries of our existence and returned to its centre of being.' (ibid.: 66). *Mahān ātman* is the unity of the cosmic and the transcendental individual self. In this sense it is used in the verses from *Svetasvatara Upanishad* quoted above; in Max Müller's translation: 'That God, the Maker of all things, the great Self, always dwelling in the heart of man, is perceived by the heart, the soul, the man; they who know it, become immortal.'

A derivative sense is indicated here: one who realizes this absolute identity of self becomes immortal, partaking in the transcendental unity and, in that sense, *mahatma* himself. 'To call a man Mahatma then is to say that he has been liberated in this life (*jivan mukta* ...) or in some life.' (Coomaraswamy 1939: 66). In this sense the *Bhagavadgita* uses the word in 8,15: 'Having come to Me, these great souls (mahatmas) never return to birth, the place of sorrow, impermanent, for they have reached the highest perfection.'[15] The relationship of the two meanings is, however, not entirely clear.[16] The double meaning still recurs in modern standard

Hindi dictionaries. *Mahatma* is rendered as 'I a pure soul, a personality with high ideals, a sadhu, sannyasi, a great ascetic; II *Paramatma*—the highest God.'

IV

Obviously the second meaning has a theological potential of a quite different order. It is unlikely that the word was used with this connotation by Arya Samajists—who adhere to a doctrine of metaphysical dualism. But it is to be expected that the ancient speculative sense, with its strong currents of neo-Vedantism, would influence perceptions in Bengal. We saw from this tradition that Tagore personally conferred the title upon Gandhi. Often, it is confidently asserted that this happened on the occasion of Gandhi's first visit to Santiniketan in February 1915 (Hay 1970: 282; Sengupta 1948: 23), but upon closer examination the evidence seems to evaporate.[17] Tagore's first letter to Gandhi, written in late 1914 and welcoming Gandhi's 'Phoenix boys' in Shantiniketan, adresses him as 'Dear Mr. Gandhi'. On Gandhi's own visit to Shantiniketan on 17 February 1915 Tagore had absented himself and gone to Calcutta. From Calcutta, however, on 18 February he wrote a letter to C. F. Andrews who was to receive Gandhi in Bolpur, using the epithet for the first time, though in a rather conventional or casual way: 'I hope that Mahatma and Mrs. Gandhi have arrived in Bolpur ...' (Tendulkar 1960, I:160). It appears, then, that Tagore did use the honorific at the time, though he did not publicly commit himself and did not, in the way it is alleged, pointedly confer it on Gandhi.

A different though slightly vague story is provided by Fischer (1954: 50): 'In India, Gandhi's spiritual qualities were quickly perceived. After his return in January, 1915, audiences at meetings shouted 'Mahatmaji' 'Mahatmaji'...and *some time later* the title of Mahatma was conferred on him by Rabindranath Tagore ...'Great Soul in *peasant's* garb', the poet *wrote*, and the crown sat forever on the Politician-saint's head.'

In a later version (Fischer 1955: 159) it reads: 'It was Tagore, *apparently*, who conferred on Gandhi the title of Mahatma; "the Great Soul in *beggar's* garb", Tagore *said*.' (emphasis added throughout) Obviously the two versions differ so as to create doubts as to time and authenticity. When or where Tagore wrote or said this, I have not been able to trace. I would submit that at least the expression 'beggar's garb' indicates a later phase, after Gandhi had turned to wearing a simple loincloth (on 22 September 1921; Gandhi *CW* 21: 180).

Tagore did commit himself to the honorific at a later juncture, in a famous letter he wrote on 12 April 1919, during the days of the Rowlatt

Satyagraha. The date is significant. The letter was written in reply to a direct request by Gandhi (Gandhi 5. 4. 1919, *CW* 15, 179 f.) and conveyed Tagore's public blessings to Gandhi's satyagraha campaign. The letter was published by Gandhi—it was destined for publication.[18] It addresses Gandhi as 'Dear Mahatmaji.' And it goes on, after warning against the irrationality of all 'power', to preconize Gandhi as a 'great leader of men' who appeared in the hour of crisis to proclaim his faith in the Indian ideal. 'You have said, as Lord Buddha has done in his time and for all time to come: "Conquer anger by the power of non-anger and evil by the power of good".' This leads up to a solemn invocation: 'And you have come to your motherland in the time of her need to remind her of her mission, to lead her in the true path of conquest...' etc. (Chander 1945:10 ff.). The analogy with the appearance of the Buddha is again taken up and expanded in Tagore's later article 'The Call of Truth' (1921; Chander 1945: 39 ff.), of which Romain Rolland's paraphrase has already been cited. The analogy is of crucial significance. It links Tagore's use of the Mahatma title to the philosophy of another great Bengali: the *avatara* doctrine of Vivekananda.

In a lecture on 'Krishna', given in California on 1 April 1890, Vivekananda quotes *Bhagavadgita* 4,7:

> Whenever virtue subsides and irreligion prevails, I come down. Again and again I come (i.e. Lord Krishna re-incarnating himself). Therefore, whenever thou seest a *great soul* struggling to uplift mankind, know that I am come and worship ... A Hindu devotee would say: It is God himself who became Christ and Krishna and Buddha and all these. A Hindu philosopher would say: These are the *great souls*; they are already free. ... Glory unto the great souls whose lives we have been studying. They are the living gods of the world. (Vivekananda 1955–9, 1: 437 ff. emph. add.)

'Christ and Krishna and Buddha and all these': here we have the series to which Gandhi will later be added. Tagore's letter by using the term 'great soul', reforms a public canonization. We are now in a position to appreciate the report of Tagore's visit to Gandhi's Sabarmati Ashram in 1922 (?)[19] as given by Andrews and adopted by Rolland. On that visit Tagore is said to have recited verses from the *Svetasvatara Upanishad*, referring to 'the apostle', as Rolland puts it. At a later stage there is a report of Tagore's speech on his visit to Gandhi in Poona the day after Gandhi ended his historic Poona fast. On this occasion Tagore expressed himself in a most solemn and explicit manner:

> We know, that, in the Upanishads, the God who ever dwells in the hearts of all men, has been mentioned as the Mahatma. The epithet is rightly given to the

man of God, whom we are honouring today, for his dwelling is not within a narrow enclosure of individual consciousness. His dwelling is in the heart of the untold multitude who are born and who are yet to come, and this greatness of his soul, which has power to comprehend other souls, has made possible what never has happened in our history ...

In such speeches and eulogies Tagore clearly adopts the full speculative meaning of the term and, in this emphatic sense, bestows the title on Gandhi. In this light we have to read Rolland's full title (1924): 'Mahatma Gandhi. The Man Who Became One With Universal Being'. This is quite different from the occasional shouts of 'Mahatmaji' in popular gatherings, as often reported. Such diffuse popular acclaim seems to have sprung up—whether spontaneously or engineered from interested quarters it is difficult to tell—from an early date after Gandhi's arrival in India. In his initial years of political activity it seems to have grown and mixed with all sorts of superstitious expectations in the popular mind (Tendulkar 1960: 258; Amin 1984). Such scenes often annoyed Gandhi. But it is also clear that he sensed the change brought about by Tagore's ambitious conferment of the honorific. Remembering his Indian agitation tour for the abolition of indentured labour in 1917, Gandhi writes in his autobiography (5, 11): 'Fortunately I had not then received the stamp of Mahatmaship, though the shout of that name was quite common where people knew me.' The *stamp of Mahatmaship* was precisely Tagore's exalted understanding of that title, conveyed by his conferment and persistent application of it to Gandhi. In this understanding 'mahatma' was not just one popular designation of a 'holy man' but conveyed a speculative and soteriological claim epitomizing Gandhi's uniquely Indian blend of political and spiritual charisma.

Coomaraswamy, in his 'historical explanation' of the word 'mahatma', feels compelled to add a note of caution. While by common consent this name has been given to Gandhi, perhaps in the general sense of 'Saint', and while in some of its connotations the term may justly be applied to him, he expressly disclaims any intention to discuss the applicability of the term 'in its full meaning' to any individual: 'for that must ever remain a secret between himself and God.' (Coomaraswamy 1939: 67). This is in a congratulatory volume dedicated to 'Mahatma Gandhi': as explicit as one might wish. It is equally clear that Tagore's thinking had been moving in this very direction—of fusing the colloquial with the full theological sense of the term. This line of thought, in fact, antedates the appearance of Gandhi as a national figure. In 1908, in *Purva o Pascim*, he had applied the epithet to Vivekananda: 'The Mahatma who died in Bengal some time back was Vivekananda who could strike a balanced position, with Orient on his right and Occident on his left.'[20] This shows the influence of Vivekananda's teaching on Tagore's speculation. It is not far-fetched to assume that Vivekananda's use of the translation 'Great Soul' may have helped blur the distinction between the two meanings of 'mahatma'. We are dealing with a cultural situation and an age where Hindu tradition is significantly influenced by English translation.

V

But there is more than a question of translation. We may note in the first instance that Vivekananda also occasionally uses the Indian term 'mahatma'. But when he does, we can sense a polemical overtone. A typical statement would be: 'Him I call Mahatman (great soul) whose heart bleeds for the poor, otherwise he is a Duratman (wicked soul)' (Vivekananda 1955–9, 5: 58, letter to Alasinga, Chicago 1894). Apparently there is a certain tension and an urge to contrast a true mahatma with a fake one, a caricature. This leads us to consider a further source and another influence which comes into play and which only fully explains what happened in 1919. In 1896 the well-known Oxford Indologist, Friedrich Max Müller published, in the magazine *The Nineteenth Century*, an article entitled 'A Real Mahatman' (Müller 1896: 306 ff.) This article chiefly centres on Ramakrishna, whom Müller had come to know from publications by Vivekananda and via correspondence with Indian friends. The gist of the argument is that the recently discussed term *mahatma* is a common Sanskrit word and means nothing except, literally, a great-souled, high-minded, noble person; that it is used as a complimentary term and applied as an equivalent to refer to a *sadhu* or *sannyasi*; and that there are still serious and honest saints of that description in India—apart from a number of impostors and hypocrites. One of the truly saintly figures was Ramakrishna, who 'seems to have been, not only a high-souled man, a real *Mahatman*, but a man of original thought.' (Müller 1896: 309). He goes on to analyse Ramakrishna's teaching against the background of Indian theological tradition, notes an interesting blend of European thought in his utterances, and finally adds a selection of translated sayings or 'Precepts of Ramakrishna Paramahansa'. The Upanishadic term and theology of *mahatma* are not mentioned at all in this context.

We are left with the question provoked by the pronounced title 'A Real Mahatman': if this is a 'real' mahatma, are there false mahatmas, and who are they? No further indication is given in the article, except for a phrase in a Postscript providing further detail of the Mahatma's life; Müller's correspondent Protap Chunder Mozoomdar is quoted as saying that Ramakrishna emphatically disclaimed the knowledge of secrets and mysteries. Müller adds a comment: 'This shows that he never was an occultist or esoteric Mahatman' (317). In a later book (Müller 1952: 83) he inserts a chapter inscribed 'The Mahatmans'. He mentions the intention of his earlier article to protest against wild and overcharged accounts of saints and sages living in India and to dispel claims by Western visitors to have discovered with these Indian mahatmans knowledge of ancient or even primeval wisdom and superhuman powers: 'I wished to show at the same time that behind such strange names as Indian Theosophy, and Esoteric Buddhism and all the rest, there was something real, something worth knowing ...'. There is no direct reference to H. P. Blavatsky, but it is clear from the context, and must have been obvious to contemporaries, that he is referring to the Theosophical Society founded in 1875 by Blavatsky and Colonel H. Olcott in New York.

The Theosophical Society had originally been a spiritualist venture of Western (American) vintage. But in December 1878 Blavatsky and Olcott travelled to India and in Bombay, in January 1879, declared themselves Buddhists. At the same time they expounded a new theory, or rather the myth—it is still not clear on what inspiration—according to which there is a 'white brotherhood', an occult hierarchy of 'adepts' called 'Mahatmas' or 'Masters', great souls who have passed the stage of transmigration and attained salvation, residing somewhere in Tibet and steering, through supernatural power and their influence on chosen human individuals, the historical progress or salvation of mankind. Blavatsky claimed to have migrated to Tibet after 1848 and to have sat 'at the feet of the Masters, or Mahatmas' who directed her to found the Theosophical Society (Taylor 1992: 229; see generally Farquhar 1915: 227 ff.). Later she pretended to have received written messages from the mahatmas, notably her special mentors, Mahatmas Moriya and Koot Hoomi. With these revelations she was able to attract curiosity and attention among intellectuals in India. It appears that A. O. Hume, later founder of the Indian National Congress, felt himself to be under 'mahatmaic' influence (Martin 1969: 62 ff.; McLane 1977: 45). Olcott was convinced that the Masters had chosen him for the task of directing the Theosophical Society under Blavatsky's guidance. After Blavatsky's death, in a letter to Max Müller dated 25 April 1893, he sought the latter's support and further enlightenment on his 'esoteric Buddhism'. He was, however, rebuked by Müller, who replied that there was nothing esoteric in Buddhism and who earnestly warned him against Blavatsky's influence (Taylor 1992: 231 ff.; Chaudhury 1974: 328; Müller's letter to Olcott dated 10 June 1893). This correspondence throws some light on the background of Max Müller's article in *The Nineteenth Century*. At the time of the correspondence, however, the Mahatma myth had already been exploded, or so it seemed. During a temporary absence of Blavatsky and Olcott from the Theosophical Society's headquarters at Adyar, Madras, it had been discovered that the 'Mahatma letters' and messages allegedly received by Blavatsky in a miraculous way had in fact been manipulated by trickery: through the device of a double-panelled cupboard in Blavatsky's private room. This discovery had created a sensation and must have been the talk in intellectual circles in London. '"Theosophistry" was a splendid public joke. Mahatmas turned up everywhere.' *The Westminster Gazette* published a series under the title (in allusion to the title of Blavatsky's book 'Isis Unveiled', 1877): 'Isis Very Much Unveiled: The Truth About the Great Mahatma Hoax' (Taylor 1992: 274).

Strangely enough, the Mahatma myth survived the scandal. This was largely due to the intervention of Mrs Annie Besant, who was 'converted' to theosophy in 1888 by reading Blavatsky's new book 'The Secret Doctrine'. Her spectacular mutation from being a close collaborator of Charles Bradlaugh to a theosophist and close confidente of Blavatsky again created a stir in intellectual London circles, notably in the Fabian society. In 1888 the Esoteric School of Theosophy was inaugurated by Blavatsky and Olcott; after Blavatsky's death in 1891 it was led by Besant and Leadbeater. Besant from the beginning came out in defence of the Mahatma theory, which she declared to be a crucial element of theosophy: 'If there are no Masters, the Theosophical Society is an absurdity' (Besant 1890: 10). In later lectures and publications she expanded the doctrine, clarifying that Masters and Mahatmas are synonymous terms (Besant 1907). This is important since, in later years, as a consequence of the ascendancy of Gandhi's mahatmaship, theosophical authors have tended to employ only the term 'Masters'. 'Great is this ideal of the Mahatma—despite the idle laughter that has been used—for the name is merely the Sanskrit for Great Spirit. ... For who is the Mahatma? He is the man who has become perfect, he is the man who has reached union with the Divine.' (1895, in Besant 1973: 17f.). The companionship of such superhuman beings who have reached what Hindus and Buddhists call liberation form the Inner Government of the World: 'These, behind all that we call "powers" in this world, are the superhuman Powers ... they are the true Rulers and the true Teachers; they are the real Powers that guide our world in evolution.' (Besant 1921: 20)

Annie Besant went to India in 1893 and became the leading figure in the Indian Theosophical Society. In 1907, when Olcott died, she was made President of the Society. Her investiture took the form of an apparition of 'the Masters' at Olcott's deathbed, instructing him to nominate her to succeed him (Taylor 1992: 285). This enthronement through an astral epiphany may not have been to the liking of all members of the Society, but it proved effective. From then on she led the Theosophical Society and imbued it with her very personal stamp of spiritual and political activity. In later years she became more and more a political figure in the context of the Indian national movement, and the Mahatma doctrine always remained in the background. She claimed to have received directives by a member of the Hierarchy, the Rishi Agastya, to work for Indian self-government. This corresponded to a great master plan of the Hierarchy to keep India within the British Empire in the interest—identified rather naively—of the evolution of Humanity. (Besant 1921: 19 f. and 102; 1922: 47; H. N. Datta, 1938: 139; Taylor 1992: 294). The metaphysical motive behind imperial loyalty may to some extent explain the acrimony of her later polemics against Gandhi's national campaigns. It remains to be said that belief in guidance from an occult brotherhood stayed with Besant throughout her life, though in course of time she may have become more cautious in referring to it within political context. Still, in 1930, she sent a public message to her followers in the *New India* of 24 April 1930 (Besant 1942: 90): 'The Masters note each worker for the Motherland and send their blessings to all who render Her faithful service'. The belief even survived her in the Theosophical Society (Arundale 1941: 17ff).[21] It still appears in an *Oxford Companion to English Literature* in the following definition (Harvey 1953: 486): '*Mahatma*, Sanscrit *mahatman*, meaning "great-souled"; in esoteric Buddhism, one of a class of persons with preternatural powers imagined to exist in India and Tibet. The word is also used by Theosophists.' The most scurrilous survival of the Mahatma myth is perhaps to be found in the circle surrounding the late Russian painter, living in India, N. K. Roerich, who is portrayed as the direct messenger of the Mahatma Maitreya Morya known from Blavatsky's days (Augustat 1993: 43ff) as 'the Mahatma of today's Russia'. (*Statesman Weekly* 11 Jan. 1997)

From the early years of Besant's Indian career we have critical comments on theosophy by Vivekananda. In an interview with *The Westminster Gazette* on 23 October 1895 he pointedly declares: 'I teach no authority proceeding from hidden beings speaking through visible agents.' (Vivekananda 1955–9, 5: 187). Interviewed by the *Madras Times* in 1897 he finds complimentary words for Mrs Besant but criticizes the Mahatma doctrine (Vivekananda 1955–9, 5: 224). Among the papers found after his death is a sharply critical manuscript 'Stray Remarks on Theosophy' presumably dating from 1900 (Vivekananda 1955–9, 4: 317 ff.) Here he ridicules 'this Indian grafting of American Spiritualism—with only a few Sanskrit words taking the place of spiritualistic jargon—Mahatma missiles taking the place of ghostly raps and taps, and Mahatmic inspiration that of obsession by ghosts.' He notes that 'modern theosophy is Mrs. Besant. Blavatskism and Olcottism seem to have taken a back seat. Mrs. Besant means well at least—and nobody can deny her perseverance and zeal.'

The latter remark has a prophetic ring. Besant's energy and perseverance made her a very influential figure in Indian politics, culminating in her presidentship of the Indian National Congress in 1917 and the agitational politics of her Home Rule League (Owen 1968:159 ff; Kumar 1981). In her public activities there was no overt assertion of 'mahatmaic' inspiration. But she did annoy Indian politicians with her claims. Thus Gandhi, who in his earlier years had been an admirer of Mrs Besant, in a letter to Pranjivan Mehta of 8 May 1911 (CW 11, 64 ff.) speaks of the 'occult humbug' associated with theosophy and criticizes Besant for her desire to pass off as 'the Master'. From Tilak's later years we have a more outspoken, even angry letter which, in view of later developments, is of some significance:

> Though I admire her eloquence, learning, and unfailing energy for work, I cannot bear for a moment the supremacy which she claims for her opinions in matters political under the guise that she is inspired by the Great Souls and that such orders from them as she professes to receive must be unquestionably obeyed. Autocracy may be, and sometimes is, tolerated in theological and Theosophical Society matters, but in democratic politics we must go by the decisions of the majority ... Congress recognizes no Mahatma to rule over it except the Mahatma of majority. (quoted from Taylor 1992: 315)[22]

It is amazing to see how, shortly after this vehement protestation, indeed even before Tilak's death, Gandhi was proclaimed as 'the Mahatma' and soon came to be recognized as the charismatic leader and, for all practical purposes, the ruler of Congress. The decisive turn of events occurred in early 1919 in connection with the launching of Gandhi's first national campaign, the so-called Rowlatt Satyagraha. In this context Gandhi seems to have abandoned his former reluctance against the occasional use of the epithet and seems to have sanctioned the use of 'Mahatma' in documents published under his control,[23] e.g. a printed version of his hartal declaration of 24 March 1919 under the title '*Mahatma Gandhi ka moqqadas hukam*' or 'Mahatma Gandhi's Holy Order' (V. N. Datta, 1975: VI, 429) or in leaflets issued by the Satyagraha Sabha, e.g. 12 April 1919 entitled 'Mahatma Gandhi's Warning to Satyagrahis and Sympathizers' (ibid. 433, cf. Satyagraha Leaflet No. 5, 17–4–1919 CW

15, 236f.; No. 10, 30–40–1919, CW 15, 260). In this time also, as we noted, Tagore publicly conferred the title Mahatma on Gandhi and, as it were, canonized him in the full sense of the term. From then onwards the designation became all but official. In 1920, Motilal Nehru in his Congress Presidential Address addressed him as 'Mahatmaji' (Erikson 1970: 392).

If we ask ourselves why the occasional and sporadic use of the honorific was regularized and adopted as a matter of policy in early 1919, one possible reason comes to mind. In 1919 Gandhi had not yet 'conquered' the Indian National Congress. He was trying to establish his influence through various other organizations. In Bombay the most important group to work with was Annie Besant's Home Rule League, inaugurated in 1916. The Bombay branch of the Home Rule League was largely dominated by Theosophists; in fact Besant systematically used her influence with Theosophists to employ them as lieutenants and agents in the build-up of the new organization (Owen 1968: 172ff.). In the opening session in Bombay, 68 among 70 members were Theosophists, mainly young Gujaratis like the Dwarkadas brothers (Masselos 1971:153ff.; Munshi 1967: 6). Some outsiders 'who owed no personal allegiance to Mrs. Besant' decided to bring in Gandhi as President of the All-India Home Rule League (Munshi 1967: 13). Gandhi soon thereafter changed the designation of the Home Rule League into 'Swarajiya Sabha' and also changed its declared aims so as to make it an instrument in his Satyagraha campaign. This change contrived with some procedural impropriety prompted M. A. Jinnah to leave the Home Rule League under protest.

It is well known that Annie Besant did not take kindly to the use of her Home Rule League organization as an instrument of Gandhi's satyagraha and to what she considered the desertion of her Bombay Home Rule Leaguers, prominently Kanji and Jamnadas Dwarkadas. In May 1919 she resigned as President of the Home Rule League—being 'forced out' as she complained (Taylor 1992: 315ff.; for Gandhi's 'capture of the Home Rule League' see also Brown 1972: 169). She founded her own National Home Rule League and henceforth became a vocal critic of Gandhi's 'dictatorial' methods and 'anarchical' aims. In the end she largely lost her influential position in Indian national politics (Roy Chaudhury 1972: 20).

In the struggle for control over the Home Rule League and for the allegiance of the Theosophist members in the League, one significant element in our context may now be noted. As we know, Besant in her direction of the Theosophical Society relied on her claimed mandate from 'the Masters' or Mahatmas and demanded obedience on account of the transcendental authority speaking through her. In wresting control of the Home Rule League from her, it may have been an obvious advantage to field a counter-mahatma, as it were, to contest the allegiance of Besant's Theosophical followers to the occult mahatmas. Gandhi could appear as a 'real mahatma', an Indian authentic and living saint as against the spurious claims of the astral entities enunciating their will through the medium of Mrs Besant, an Irishwoman. The growing popular acclaim of Gandhi as mahatma at this juncture may have come handy. Naturally, these things were not brusquely and crudely spelt out, just as Tilak, as we have seen, voiced his antipathy against the mahatma claims only in a private letter. We cannot know, therefore, what Gandhi's role was in this manipulation, whether he simply acquiesced in the political use of the term, or whether he took a more active part himself. But it is noteworthy that in April 1919 he was, all of a sudden, clothed with the full paraphernalia of the Vedantic mahatma myth through Tagore's public message.

There are certain incidents which point to the fact that a contest had been transferred to the 'metaphysical' plane. One is the affair of Dr Sir Subramaniam Iyer, a very respected retired judge of the Madras High Court, Honorary President of the All-India Home Rule League and Theosophist of long standing.[24] Gandhi had offered him the vice-presidentship of the Satyagraha Sabha. Iyer had declined on the plea that to accept the offer would mean for him breaking a long friendship with Mrs Besant and the relation as co-worker with her in work she had been doing for the country, by arraying himself against her in what she viewed as a party proceeding (23 March 1919, SN 6465). Gandhi replied in a polite, cautious letter (23 March 1919, *CW* 15, 147) but subsequently received a letter from Mrs Besant in which she explained Iyer's position in a different and outspoken manner (10 May 1919, SN 6605 A). The central issue was Iyer's original signing of the Satyagraha Pledge, including a civil pledge to break such laws as a Committee under Gandhi's direction might specify. Besant's letter states, on behalf of Dr Subramaniam Iyer:

> He has had through myself for more than 25 years, and before that through H. P. Blavatsky, a close relationship with a great Indian Rishi, whom he has faithfully served. Overpersuaded, he took your pledge, thinking it did not affect his spiritual relations. He learns that, unintentionally, he has done a thing disapproved by his Master ... He asks me to say that his older pledges prevent his resumption of your vow.

Gandhi reacts in letters to Subramaniam Iyer directly as well as to Mrs Besant. (*CW* 15, 300 and 309).[25] He insists that one cannot 'possibly deviate from the true path even at the dictation of a great *rishi*' and in the letter to Mrs. Besant, more aggressively, that: 'I would certainly advise everyone to break all the pledges he might have taken if they are contrary to Truth. You deprive a fellow-being of his or her human dignity when you interpose between him and his conscience, an outsider, no matter how high-placed in spirituality he may appear to be.' In his final reply Iyer maintains that: 'I cannot avoid the conclusion that, so far as this (i.e. the lawbreaking) part of the pledge is concerned not to withdraw from it would conflict with a previous pledge of mine taken long ago as a member of a school to which I still belong and of which I have no intention of ceasing to be a member' (19 June 1919, SN 6484 a).

This correspondence would show that there was indeed a struggle going on with claims from a 'supra-mundane' plane, even if Iyer, in contrast to Besant, expresses himself in a most guarded manner. The correspondence does not directly show the role of Gandhi's Mahatma title, except for a studious avoidance of that title by both correspondents. Later, during the non-co-operation campaign, Besant polemically attacked Gandhi and the excesses of the 'Gandhi Raj': 'Mob support is obtained ... by giving to Mr. Gandhi high religious names, such as Mahatma and Avatara, assigning to him supernatural powers and the like' (Besant 1922: 97ff.).

There is a later incident further illustrating the tension: in a gathering at the Excelsior Theatre in Bombay on 31 August 1924, Jamnadas Dwarakadas, speaking to the audience in the presence of Gandhi, had been interrupted by shouts from the crowd demanding that he address Gandhi as 'Mahatma Gandhi'—which he steadfastly refused (31 August 1924, *CW* 25, 69). Dwarakadas was a Theosophist and leading member of the Home Rule League; he had been one of the first Home Rulers to sign Gandhi's satyagraha pledge in 1919, but had subsequently been forced out of the Satyagraha Sabha by Gandhi, who told him that as a satyagrahi he could not continue to be a member of the National Home Rule League of Besant (Gopalaswami 1969: 89). Here we are faced with the same conflict of compatibility, from the other side, as in Subramaniam Iyer's case. The incident in the Excelsior Theatre, however, prompted an energetic intervention from Gandhi which for its significance may be quoted here (*CW* 25, 56ff): 'Much dirty work has been done in the shadow of 'Mahatma'. The word 'Mahatma' stinks in my nostrils; and, in addition to that, when somebody insists that every one must call me a 'Mahatma' I get nausea, I do not wish to live ... In the Ashram where I live, every child, brother and sister has orders not to use the word 'Mahatma'. None should refer to me as 'Mahatma' even in writing. I should be referred to as Gandhi or Gandhiji.'

He goes on, with an intrinsic though not apparent connection of thought, to give a report of his visit to the 'scholarly Mrs Besant' with whom he had talked like a son with his mother. Why was he referring to 'much dirty work ... done in the shadow of 'Mahatma', and what was in his mind? In any case, in 1924 the struggle of 1919 was a thing of the past; Gandhi had moved to a leading position in the Congress, he could well afford to pay his 'filial' respects to Mrs Besant, and he could weigh the implications of the Mahatma title in a detached manner. In many utterances from that time he repudiates the honour thrust on him with that title, and he often disclaims role expectations associated therewith in the public mind. In the introduction to his autobiography he attributes the conferment on him to his political, as distinguished from his spiritual, experiments. 'For me, they have not much value; and the title of "Mahatma" that they have won for me has, therefore, even less.' This assessment reflects the modern tradition of relating the title to outstanding public service, as we saw it in the cases of Mahatma Phule and Mahatma Munshi Ram. As such it already represents a certain distance from the exaggerated projections coming from Bengal and its Vedantic speculation. But even beyond such sober reduction there is a growing unease, almost revulsion, at the title and the aspirations associated with it. 'I am Tired of Mahatma' (*Young India* 12 June 1924, *CW* 24, 232) or, in his dispute with the Communist Saklatwala: 'I shall gladly subscribe to a bill to make it criminal for anybody to call me Mahatma and to touch my feet. Where I can impose the law myself, i.e. at the Ashram, the practice is criminal' (*Young India* 17 March 1927 'No and Yes', *CW* 33, 167), or: 'the epithet 'Mahatma' has always galled me and it almost sounds to me like a term of abuse' (*CW* 40, 212). Such statements abound, and there is no doubt that in personal communication he preferred less extravagant forms of address, such as 'Bapu' or 'Gandhiji'. There is also no reason to doubt the sincerity of the frequent disclaimers. But having said this, we must also note that a certain ambivalence remained. Some of his statements betray an inclination to measure himself against the normative implications of the title, and to repudiate it for the time being, as a gesture of modesty. This attitude appears early, e.g. in a public meeting at Nadiad during the Kheda campaign, where the British Commissioner Pratt had introduced Gandhi as Mahatma and as a very holy man, unfortunately ignorant of politics. Gandhi's reply is: Mr. Pratt has described me as a sannyasi [note his avoidance of the term Mahatma]. He was both right and wrong. I do not claim to be a sannyasi. I am as liable to err as you; the difference is, that I desire to be a sannyasi and constantly strive to be one.' (12 April 1918, *CW* 14, 549). To a newspaper correspondent putting the favourite question, whether he was a politician or a saint, his reply is: 'To clothe me with sainthood is *too early even if it is possible*. I myself do not feel saint in any shape or form. But I do feel that I am a votary of Truth ...' (*Young India* 20 Jan. 1927, *CW* 32, 587, emph. add.). In this vein further: 'It is my knowledge of my limitations and my nothingness which has so far saved me from the oppressiveness of the "mahatmaship"' (*Young India* 1 November 1928, *CW* 37, 409).

We can see a growing recognition of the dimensions of the title and critical self-evaluation in relation to its implications. This is the process—well-known and documented as a historical fact—of Gandhi's gradual absorption of the title so as to become one with it. It explains how, towards the end of his life, he could be found advising Tendulkar on his monumental biography, which was to appear under a title (Mahatma) that had originally been galling to Gandhi. In an impressive way he finally submitted to the role projected for him and transformed it in a singular manner.

From his last days we have a moving document in a diary entry by his niece Manubehn Gandhi (Gandhi, Manubehn 1962: 297–8). After the first attempt on his life Gandhi is reported to have said: 'If I were to die of disease or even a pimple, you must shout to the world from housetops that I was a false mahatma ... people might well swear at you for my sake; yet, if I died of illness, you should declare me a false or hypocritical mahatma. And if an explosion took place, as it did last week, or somebody shot at me and I received his bullet on my bare chest, without a sigh and with Rama's name on my lips, only then you should say that I was a true mahatma. This will benefit the Indian people.'

I cite this text with some hesitation. It is difficult to verify, and it has the sound of an *ex post* construction. It is impossible to judge whether these truly were Gandhi's words. We do have, from the last months of his life, a number of utterances expressing a premonition of his impending death. There is in fact a closely similar statement from September 1947 transmitted, however, again solely and at a later date, by Manubehn Gandhi.[26] Be that as it may, what interests us in any case is the specific atmosphere surrounding him—of which this text, authentic or not, is indicative. It is still the problem of the 'real Mahatma'. What has happened since Max Müller wrote his article is a realization of the Mahatma myth in the life of one extraordinary individual, and the extinction of its many dubious and superstitious ingredients through his performance. It is unlikely that in the foreseeable future anyone else will dare aspire to mahatmaship after the event that was Gandhi. And this, we may say in conclusion, will benefit the Indian people.

Notes

1. Shyam Benegal, 'The Making of the Mahatma', first released in Johannesburg in April 1996, cf. *Hindu Weekly* 25. 5. 1996, p. 6.
2. Ibid. p. 3, citing Keer (1964: 372–83).
3. *Svetasvatara Upanishad* 4,17. The translation seems to be taken from Catherine D. Groth's translation in Rolland (1924). Other translations give a quite different impression, e.g. Max Müller (1884):

   That God, the Maker of all things, the great Self,
   always dwelling in the hearts of man,
   is perceived by the heart, the soul, the man;
   they who know it, become immortal.

   In the German translation by Deussen (1921:303):
   Ja, dieser Gott, allschaffend, hohen Sinnes
   Ist stets zu finden in der Geschöpfe Herzen;
   Nur wer an Herz und Sinn und Geist bereitet,—
   Unsterblich werden, die ihn also kennen.

4. Rolland probably got this information from C. F. Andrews who, with comments, assisted him in composing his essay (Rolland 1969: 192 ff., letters to Luc Durtain 1. 6. 1923 and A. J. Taupin 7. 6. 1923; ibid. 427, Rolland's *Journal*). Concerning 'apostle' we learn that Andrews wholeheartedly approved of Rolland comparing Gandhi with St Paul (*Journal*, ibid. 428), but himself compared him with Christ (Andrews' Letter to Rolland 2. 3. 1924, ibid. 433). The date given by Rolland, however, is definitely wrong: in December 1922 Gandhi was already detained in Yeravda prison and could not be visited in his Ashram.
5. Earlier, during the Amritsar Congress of 1918, Jinnah appears to have referred to 'Mahatma Gandhi' while supporting a resolution moved by him (Jayakar 1958: 310).
6. The dedication runs: 'Inscribed to the Memory of Mahatma Jotiba Fule [*sic*] (1827–1890) the Greatest Shudra of Modern India who made the lower classes of Hindus conscious of their slavery to the higher classes and who preached the gospel that for India social democracy was more vital than independence from foreign rule.'
7. This is, for example, the explanation given in Walker (1968: 438), s.v. *hierophant*, but similarly in many standard Hindi dictionaries; cf. for Sanskrit Monier-Williams 1899: 796 s.v. *mahatman*: high-souled, high-minded, noble, having a great or noble nature.
8. *Lajpat Rai-Ji Ki Atmakatha*. Lahaur n. d. (between 1910 and 1920) p. 112. I owe this reference to Harald Fischer-Tiné.
9. For the probable date of this controversy, cf. ibid. 103: 'Pandit Gurudutt, the late Lala Sain Dass and Mahatma Hansraj ... arrived at 12 on the 25th December 1888.'

10. Gandhi to Munshi Ram 27. 3. 1914, *CW* 12: 400: 'I hope therefore that you will pardon me for addressing you by the title which both Mr. Andrews and I have used in discussing you and your work.'
11. Entry in Gandhi's diary (*CW* 13, 156 ff.), on 6 April 1915: 'Gurukul. Meeting with Mahatmaji'.
12. Speech on the Silver Jubilee Convocation of Benares Hindu University, 21 Jan. 1942 (*CW* 75, 240).
13. Article in the Gujarati paper *Bhagini Samaj Patrika*, 4. 2. 1916 (*CW* 13, 202); Speech after Gokhale's death, 12. 11. 1917 (*CW* 14, 83); *Preface* to a Gujarati edition of Gokhale's speeches (*CW* 14, 198 ff.): 'the late mahatma Gokhale'.
14. This renunciation in itself is significant because, as we shall see, *mahatma* had often been taken as just one more name for a *sannyasi* (cf. Müller 1896: 306).
15. Translation from Radhakrishnan (1963: 232). Cf. *BhG*. 9,13.
16. Prof. Hermann Berger, with whom I discussed this, suggested that *mahatma* may really be a homonym for two separate words: (I) someone who *has* a great soul, (II) the one who *is* the Great Soul.
17. Both sources cited by Hay, (1970), namely Andrews (1931: 23 f.), and Chaturvedi/Sykes (1950: 90–3) do not give that information.
18. In his letter of 5 April 1919 Gandhi had explicitly asked Tagore for a 'message for publication'.
19. Concerning this date cf. n. 4 *supra*.
20. I owe this reference, as well as the translation from the original Bengali, to Dr Alokeranjan Dasgupta.
21. In this curious book Arundale reports appearances of Besant after her death on 20 Sept. 1933 in which the world government through the Masters figures large. 'The Society needs a thorough overhauling if it is to be once more the instrument the Masters need.' (p. 11ff.). The providential link between India and the British Empire is again emphasized, and leads to the conclusion that the President of the Theosophical Society 'for various occult and karmic reasons' must be an Englishman (p. 23). We are not surprised to learn that G. S. Arundale is recommended for the position.
22. Anne Taylor unfortunately neither cites the recipient of the letter nor the date. She gives as her source Adyar Archives, Indian National Congress Papers, 585. I cannot at the moment trace the date, but from the context would assume that it belongs to the period following Besant's release from detention, when there was growing criticism of her dictatorial methods of leadership.
23. Already in 1918 Gandhi's nephew Mathurdas Trikumji had prepared a selection from Gandhi's writings translated into Gujarati, published under the title: '*Mahatma Gandhini vicharrishti*' in January 1919. Gandhi had been advising him on this edition (cf. letters 14 Jan. 1918, 21 Jan. 1918, 25 Jan. 1918, *CW* 14, 148, 163 and 174). The title is not mentioned or discussed in this correspondence.
24. The exchange is documented, though in an all too fragmentary selection

in *CW* 15, 146 and 300 f. the *CW* give only Gandhi's letters to Annie Besant and Subramania Iyer, without the two important letters from Iyer to Gandhi, and Mrs Besant's letter to Gandhi. The reader therefore is not in a position to fully understand the controversy. Iyer's and Besant's letters are cited here from the original manuscripts, available in the Gandhi Memorial Library at Sabarmati Ashram, Ahmedabad, Sabarmati Nidhi (Symbol SN + serial number).

25. The dates of the letters given in *CW* are problematic. In two cases—Gandhi's letter to Iyer of 23 March 1919 and his letter to Besant of 10 May 1919—they are identical with the dates of the letters addressed to Gandhi from Mylapore or from a moving train respectively. This coincidence would imply a miraculous speed of the mails not to speak of the time required for writing a reply.
26. This is from an account of a discussion with J. B. Kripalani, on 9 September 1947 (CW 89, 235). Gandhi's words as reported are: 'I am not being arrogant when I say that I know the art of dying but I have the courage to say it. But God alone knows if I will run away when I am being shot at or attacked with knives or will get angry with the attacker. If this happens then also there is no harm because the people will come to know that the man they looked upon as a Mahatma was not a true Mahatma. I too shall come to know where I stand. It is possible that I may still utter 'Rama Rama' when I am shot or attacked. Let the outcome be either, ultimately it will be for the good.' (From Gandhi, Manubehn 1964, originally in Gujarati).

References

Ambedkar, B. R. 1943. Mr. *Gandhi and the Emancipation of the Untouchables*. Bombay: Thacker Press.

———. 1946. *Who Were the Shudras?* Bombay: Thacker Press.

Amin, Shahid. 1984. Gandhi as Mahatma. In Ranajit Guha (ed.), *Subaltern Studies* III: 1–61.

Andrews, C. F. 1931. The Poet. In *The Golden Book of Tagore*, ed. R. A. Chatterjee, 23–6. Calcutta: Modern Review Office.

Arundale, G. S. 1941. *Conversations with Dr. Besant Sept. 20–Oct. 1st, 1933*. Adyar: Theosophical Publishing House.

Augustat, W. 1993. *Das Geheimnis des Nicholas Roerich. Agni Yoga und die geheimen Lehrer*. Muenchen: Heyne Verlag.

Besant, A. 1890. *The Theosophical Society and Helena Petrowna Blavatsky*. London Theosophical Publishing Society.

———. 1907. *H. P. Blavatsky and the Masters of Wisdom*. London: Theosophical Publishing Society.

———. 1921. *Britain's Place in the Great Plan*. London: Theosophical Publishing House.

———. 1922. *The Future of Indian Politics* containing *inter alia* 'The Great Plan',

1920 on the providential connection between England and India]. Adyar, Madras: Theosophical Publishing House.

———. 1942. *Builders of New India*. Adyar, Madras: Theosophical Publishing House.

———. [1912] 1973. *The Masters* [containing a lecture 'The Masters as Facts and Ideals', London 1895]. 4. repr., Adyar, Madras: Theosophical Publishing House.

Brown, Judith M. 1972. *Gandhi's Rise to Power: Indian Politics 1915–22. Cambridge*. Cambridge Univ. Press (South Asian Studies Series no. 11).

Cashman, R. 1975. *The Myth of the Lokamanya. Tilak and Mass Politics in Maharashtra*. Berkeley: University of California Press.

Chander, J. P. 1945. *Tagore and Gandhi Argue*. Lahore: Indian Printing Works.

Chaturvedi, B. and M. Sykes, 1950. *Charles Freer Andrews. A Narrative*. New York: Harper and Bros.

Chaudhuri, N. 1974. *Scholar Extraordinary. The Life of Professor the Rt. Hon. Friedrich Max Müller*, P. C. New Delhi: Oxford University Press.

Chavda, V. K. 1972–3. Review of Devanesan (1969). In *Quarterly Review of Historical Studies (Calcutta)* 12: 70-71.

Coomaraswamy, A. 1939. Mahatma. In *Mahatma Gandhi. Essays and Reflections on his Life and Work*, ed. S. Radhakrishnan, 63ff. London: George Allen & Unwin.

Datta, H. N. 1938. *Theosophical Gleanings*. Adyar, Madras: Theosophical Publishing House.

Datta, V. N. 1975. *New Light on the Punjab Disturbances in 1919*. Vol. VI and VII of Disorders Inquiry Committee. Simla: Institute of Advanced Study.

Deussen, P. 1905. *Sechzig Upanishad's des Veda*. 3. Aufl. Leipzig: Brockhaus.

Devanesan, C. D. S. 1969. *The Making of the Mahatma*. Madras: Orient Longmans.

Erikson, E. H. 1970. *Gandhi's Truth*. London: Faber & Faber.

Farquhar, J. N. 1915. *Modern Religious Movements in India*. New York: MacMillan, repr. Delhi, 1967.

Fischer, L. 1954. *Gandhi. His Life and Message for the World*. New York: New American Library.

———. 1955. *The Life of Mahatma Gandhi*. Part I. Bombay: Bharatiya Vidya Bhavan.

Gandhi, Manubehn 1962. *Last Glimpses of Bapu*. Delhi: Siva Lal Agarwala.

———. 1964. *Dilhiman Gandhiji*. Ahmedabad: Navajivan Publishing House. (Gujarati).

Gandhi, M. K. 1958 ff. *The Collected Works of Mahatma Gandhi* (cit. *CW*, volume and page). New Delhi: Publications Division, Government of India.

Gopalaswami, K. 1969. *Gandhi and Bombay*. Bombay: Gandhi Smarak Nidhi/ Bombay: Bharatiya Vidya Bhawan.

Government of Maharashtra. 1965. *Source Material for a History of the Freedom Movement in India (Collected from Bombay Government Records) Vol. III Mahatma Gandhi*. Compiled by B. N. Pathak. Bombay.

Harvey, P. 1953. *The Oxford Companion to English Literature*. Oxford: Clarendon Press, 3rd ed.

Hay, S. 1970. *Asian Ideas of East and West. Tagore and His Critics in Japan, China, and India*. Cambridge, Mass: Harvard University Press. (East Asia Series 40).
Jambunathan, M. R. 1961. Editor's epilogue. In Shraddhanand 1961.
Jayakar, M. R. 1958. *The Story of my Life*. Vol. I. Bombay: Asia Publishing House.
Jordens, J. T. F. 1981. *Swami Shraddhananda*. Delhi: Oxford University Press.
Keer, D. J. 1964. *Mahatma Jotirao Phooley. Father of Our Social Revolution*. Bombay: Popular Prakashan.
Kumar, R. 1981. *Annie Besant's Rise to Power in Indian Politics 1914–1917*. Delhi: Concept.
Lajpat Rai. 1915. *The Arya Samaj. An Account of its Origine, Doctrines, and Activities, with a Biographical Sketch of its Founder*. London: Longmans & Green.
Lele, P. R. 1946. Introduction to: Swami Shraddhanand, *Inside Congress*. Bombay.
Martin, Briton. 1969. *New India: British Official Policy and the Emergence of the Indian National Congress*. Berkeley: University of California Press.
Masselos, J. 1971. Some Aspects of Bombay City Politics in 1919. In *Essays on Gandhian Politics: The Rowlatt Satyagraha of 1919*, ed. R. Kumar, 145–88. Oxford: Clarendon Press.
McLane, J. R. 1977. *Indian Nationalism and the Early Congress*. Princeton: Princeton University Press.
Monier-Williams, Monier 1899. *A Sanskrit-English Dictionary*. Oxford: Clarendon Press.
Müller, F. Max 1884. *The Upanishads*. In *Sacred Books of the East*, Vol. 15. Oxford: Clarendon Press.
———. 1896. A Real Mahatman. *The Nineteenth Century* 40: 306.
———. 1952. *Rammohan to Ramakrishna*. Calcutta: Susil Gupta [abridged from Müller, *Ramakrishna: His Life and Sayings* (1898) and My *Indian Friends* (1899)].
Munshi, K. M. 1967. *Pilgrimage to Freedom*. Bombay: Bharatiya Vidya Bhavan.
Nehru, J. 1962. *An Autobiography; With Musings on Recent Events in India*. repr. 1942, Indian ed. Bombay: Allied Publishers.
Owen, H. F. 1968. Toward Nationwide Agitation & Organisation: The Home Rule Leagues, 1915-1918. In *Soundings in Modern South Asian History*, ed. D. A. Low. 159ff. London: Weidenfeld & Nicolson.
Radhakrishnan, S. 1963. *The Bhagavadgita. With an Introductory Essay, Sanskrit Text, English Translation and Notes*. 6th impression. London: George Allen & Unwin.
Rolland, R. 1924. *Mahatma Gandhi*. Translation from the French by Catherine D. Groth, London 1924, repr. by Publications Division, Government of India, 1968.
———. 1969. *Cahiers Romain Rolland 19: Gandhi et Romain Rolland*. Paris: A. Michel.
Roy Chaudhury, P. C. 1972. *Gandhi and His Contemporaries*. Jullundur: Sterling Publications.
Sengupta, S. C. 1948. *The Great Sentinel. A Study of Rabindranath Tagore*. Calcutta: A. Mukherjee.

Sharma, Sri Ram. 1965. *Mahatma Hansraj. Maker of the Modern Punjab*. 2. ed. Jullundur: Institute of Public Administration.
Sontheimer, G.D. 1982. God, Dharma and Society in the Yadava Kingdom of Devagiri According to the Lilacaritra of Cakradhar. In *Indology and Law. Studies in Honour of Professor J. Duncan M. Derrett*, ed. G.D. Sontheimer and P. K. Aithal, 329ff. Wiesbaden: F. Steiner Verlag.
Sedition Committee. 1918. *Report*. Calcutta: Bengal Secretariat Press.
Shraddhanand, Swami. 1946. *Inside Congress*. Bombay: Dhawale.
———. 1961. *Autobiography*. English ed. M. R. Jambunathan. Bombay: Phoenix Publishing.
Tagore, Rabindranath. 1921. The Call of Truth (*Modern Law Review* 1921). In: Chander 1945: 39 ff.
Taylor, A. 1992. *Annie Besant. A Biography*. Oxford, N. York: Oxford University Press.
Tendulkar, G. D. 1960. *Mahatma. Life of Mohandas Karamchand Gandhi*. New (revised) edition in 8 vols. Delhi: Publications Division.
UNESCO. 1949. *Human Rights. Comments and Interpretations. A Symposium*. Edited UNESCO with an introduction by Jacques Maritain. New York.
Van Buitenen, J. A. B. 1964. The Large Atman. *History of Religions* 4: 103–114.
Vivekananda. 1955–9. The Complete Works of Swami Vivekananda. Mayavati Memorial Edition. 8 vols. 3rd-10th ed. Calcutta: Advaita Ashrama.
Walker, Benjamin. 1968. *Hindu World: An Encyclopaedic Survey of Hinduism*. 2 vols. London. George Allen & Unwin.

A Religion for Civil Society? Ambedkar's Buddhism, the Dalit Issue and the Imagination of Emergent Possibilities

MARTIN FUCHS

> *... the reality of ideal ends as ideals is vouched for by their undeniable power in action. An ideal is not an illusion because imagination is the organ through which it is apprehended. For all possibilities reach us through the imagination. In a definite sense the only meaning that can be assigned the term 'imagination' is that things unrealized in fact come home to us and have power to stir us.*
>
> *The aims and ideals that move us are generated by the imagination. But they are not made out of imaginary stuff. They are made out of the hard stuff of the world of physical and social experience. ... The new vision does not arise out of nothing, but emerges through seeing, in terms of possibilities, that is, of imagination, old things in new relations serving a new end which the new end aids in creating.*
>
> (John Dewey [1934] 1962: 43, 49; emphasis added)

Introductory Remarks

After a long delay, and still only sporadically, Bhimrao Ambedkar's thinking is beginning to receive the attention it deserves in the general intellectual and academic discourse.[1] This delay has to do, above all, with the oppositional stand which he took—and into which he was pressed—against Gandhi and the Gandhian concept of national reconstruction. But in addition to this, his 'conversion', as it was seen, to Buddhism at the end of his life did not meet with understanding everywhere. From within a rationalist or 'secularist' framework a return to religion by a secular political leader, and above all a reinvention of a religion no longer alive in the society in question, is not easily intelligible. Often it is understood as an opportunistic and strategic move, attending to the traditionalistic or irrational needs of one's mass following. Of course, convinced Hindus take the decision as a vote of non-confidence in their own religion, which it certainly also was. Only in recent years have efforts been made to understand what religion, and the choice of a new one, could have meant for the rationalist intellectual that Ambedkar was, as well as for the political and apparently materialist movement he represented.[2]

For those who undertook it, the 'conversion' had a direct practical significance. However, it had also broader social, political and cultural significance, for it was at the same time an appeal for the reconstruction of society. In the context of this volume the existential significance, its social, socio-psychological or emotional, and even the cognitive meaning of the turn to Buddhism for converted Dalits, and for the cause of 'Ex-Untouchables' in general, is not at issue.[3] More relevant here is its importance as interpretive intervention. In addressing this issue I hope to uncover some of the hermeneutical implications of this event which have been largely disregarded by those authors who see Dalit movements only as straightforward struggles for status, power, resources and social advancement.

What I would like to emphasize in particular is Ambedkar's effort to shift the co-ordinates of public discourse and the modalities of social interaction in India. This touches upon the quest for alternative options of modernity. There are certain links between the socio-ethical dimensions of Ambedkar's depiction of Buddhism and the thinking of John Dewey. According to Ambedkar himself, Dewey impressed and influenced him strongly while he was a student at Columbia University in New York in 1913-16.[4] Something of the interaction or affinity between the two is reflected in Ambedkar's approach to Buddhism. Ambedkar, like Dewey, pursued the idea of what has been termed by some a *religion civile*, a new religious, or rather ethical, concept for modern civil society. But both thinkers differed in their conclusions in respect of the way they related to the tradition of religion.

Ambedkar has not expounded in any detail upon his intellectual encounter with Dewey's thought and there seems to be as yet no research on this issue. In regard to the topic considered here this has perhaps to do with the fact that Dewey's book on religion (*A Common Faith* [1934] 1962) was to appear eighteen years after Ambedkar had studied under him.[5]

Elementary Religion: Buddhism and Society

Bhimrao Ramji (Dr Babasaheb) Ambedkar lived from 1891 to 1956. Just two months before his death he underwent public initiation into

Buddhism in a self-invented *dīkṣā* ceremony together with a large number of followers, most of them from his own *jāti* of Mahars. It is said that along with him around half a million people converted on that day and on the day following. Back in 1935, Ambedkar had publicly declared that he would 'not die a Hindu'. In his last years, in fact up to the night he died, he had been working on a text that he considered should assume the role of a Buddhist bible: *The Buddha and His Dhamma* (Ambedkar [1950] 1970: 14f). Published a year after his death, the book still shows parts which have not been worked out thoroughly and are not as trenchant as others. There are also a few uneliminated repetitions. He sets out to deliberately rewrite parts of what is treated as the Buddhist canonical tradition in order to give to Buddha's teachings a distinct interpretation. He obviously has a very mixed readership in mind: Dalits, people who have been already practising Buddhism, followers of other religions—and ultimately society at large (cf. Ambedkar [1950] 1970). As with every systematic exposition—and especially one which tries to present in broad outline fundamental teachings on the human condition while at the same time inevitably addressing specific socio-historical conditions—one can discern certain tensions within his basic assumptions.

Ambedkar addresses his contemporaries, people of the modern world. But what does he aim at? Is he attempting a contingent, contextual reading or the reconstruction of an eternal yet forgotten truth? A modern message in an ancient garb—or rather an ancient message for modern men and women? 'If the *new* world ... must have a religion—and the *new* world needs religion far more than the old world did—then it can only be the religion of the Buddha.' (Ambedkar [1950] 1970: 13; emphasis Ambedkar's)[6] From the 1930s onwards, Ambedkar had been engaged in evaluating different non-Hindu religions with regard to their suitability as means of offering an escape from the stranglehold of the caste system. Ambedkar did not mean to project a religion for the Untouchables or Dalits, i.e. for *one* community only. One cannot even depict Ambedkar's presentation of Buddhism as that of a religion of resentment, in the sense of Nietzsche's idea, which is supposed to serve the feelings of impotence and revenge of the underprivileged against the powerful. On the contrary, Ambedkar was looking for a broadly humanist and social religion, which he found best realized in Buddhism.[7]

While putting forth his conception of Buddhism Ambedkar was very conscious of what he was setting out to do. He pursued what one might term a counter-modern modernist project. Like a modern student of society and religion—which he had been *de facto* since he went to the United States and England for his studies—he thought of religion in the plural, representing competing interpretations of the world. From such a perspective, the respective universalist claims of the different religions appeared as contingent, particularist truths, relative to the concepts of divinity on which they were based ([1950] 1970: 3f; [1957] 1974: 226, 229, 231). Ambedkar used the yardstick of modern science, and its universalist claim to reason, and subjected the different world religions to a 'test', as he phrased it ([1950] 1970: 13f). He did this not in order to disown religion, but rather to find out and reclaim ancient moral insights—which had proved their trans-historical validity—and return them to his contemporaries. This mode of dealing with religion, this way of installing a 'new' religion, takes for granted that religion has been differentiated from other social domains, and developed into a sphere that follows its own inner logic.[8] Only then does it become at all possible to think of making a religious choice in the abstract manner Ambedkar did. He saw Hinduism, against which he fought, as keeping religion directly implicated in the institution of society. The turn to Buddhism thus signified the 'liberation' of religion from the social entanglement and social strain, making religion free to address itself to society, to give (individual) guidance and (collective) orientation. Only in this way would a religion—in principle—be able to bridge the gap between divergent experiences and opposite outlooks, between those marginalized and excluded and those who wield the logic of exclusion. Unlike many new religious leaders, Ambedkar is not arrogating any particular religious qualities—or 'charisma'—to himself, he only wants to revive a forgotten truth, and the charisma of the Buddha.

To understand the relation between religion and society in Ambedkar's thought, I will sketch some basic propositions of his conception of Buddhism and indicate some of the liberties he took in his interpretation of older Buddhist canons.

Basic Propositions

It is not so much an authoritative set of convictions and soteriological practices that Ambedkar tries to fix; rather, he wants to induce a certain humanistic attitude. Ambedkar's interpretation of Buddhism rests on: (a) the contention that Buddhism is based on 'reason' (or rationalism) and 'experience' and that it is 'in accord with science', (b) its contestation of divinity, and (c) the claim that it recognizes the fundamental principles of social life.

'Buddha's religion is not a revelation', Ambedkar states ([1957] 1974: 153). Buddhism, he emphasizes, denies the reality of God, understood as creator or as absolute, ultimate entity (in the mode of *brahma*). Ambedkar is certain that Buddha did not claim a divine or supernatural status or supernatural powers for himself, nor did he claim divine status or 'infallibility' for his word. Buddha, in this understanding, was no prophet (see [1950] 1970: 3f, 12; 1974: 63, 68, 151, 153, 156–7).

Buddhism, on the contrary, is 'discovery', is the 'result of *inquiry and investigation* into the conditions of human life on earth' ([1957] 1974: 153; emphasis mine). '[The Buddha] was nothing if not rational, if not logical' ([1957] 1974: 255). Consistent with this rationalist attitude, Buddha is presented as having declared his message open. It can be 'questioned' or 'tested' and his followers are 'free to modify or even to abandon any of his teachings if it was found that at a given time and in given circumstances they did not apply' ([1957] 1974: 157, 1970: 4).[9]

For Ambedkar Buddha was a *mārgadātā*—he showed the way—he was not a *mokṣadātā*, i.e. he did not *give* salvation ([1950] 1970: 4; [1957] 1974: 153, 156). The concept of *bodhisattva*, as far as I can make out, makes a single appearance only in Ambedkar's book on Buddhism and remains rather unconnected to the rest of the text.[10] The concept of *bodhisattva* does not match well with those parts of Ambedkar's argument in which he expresses strong scepticism toward the theory of rebirth, or (personal) identity beyond death. The Buddha, says Ambedkar, 'believed in the regeneration of matter' ('energy is never lost'), but rejected the existence of a soul and thus denied the idea of the rebirth of the soul. He is, of course, opposed to the theory of karmic retribution *beyond* actual life. It would have taken all 'responsibility for the condition of the poor and the lowly' from society or the state ([1957] 1974, book IV, part II: 235–48).

Buddhism helps to realize fundamental values. A religion which abides by a moral standard, Ambedkar declares, must 'recognise the fundamental tenets of liberty, equality and fraternity' ([1950] 1970: 13). Ambedkar does not mean that Buddha expressed these principles in such modern language—Ambedkar to some extent respects the difference between religion and society and between historical epochs—but he thinks that Buddha fostered thinking along these lines. Buddha was the 'earliest and staunchest upholder of equality' ([1957] 1974: 216). He laid the ideal of a 'brotherhood of men' before the social actors, the 'men-in-the-world' ([1957] 1974: 234). Buddhism demanded compassion for every human being, not differentiated according to status or gender. The practice of the 'Noble Eightfold Path'—*Ashtanga Marga* or Path of Righteousness—together with the 'Path of Purity' and the 'Path of Virtue'[11] 'remove(s) all injustice and inhumanity' ([1957] 1974: 89; also 83–8). Ambedkar argues against an interpretation of Buddhism as a 'gospel of pessimism' and gives a distinct interpretation to the 'Four Aryan (noble) Truths' and to the striving for *nirvāṇa* or *nibbāna*.[12] Suffering is not so much contingent on men's clinging to this world, but, more prosaically, it means living 'in sorrow, in misery and poverty' ([1957] 1974: 83). Suffering, the way Ambedkar conceives it, is primarily being inflicted by man upon man, through pursuit of gain, lastly by 'class struggle' ([1957] 1974: 168f, 424).[13] The recognition of the existence of suffering is counterbalanced by an '*equal stress* on the removal of suffering' ([1957] 1974: 90; emphasis mine). *Nibbāna* does not so much mean loosening the relationship with the material world, instead Ambedkar declares: 'It was vain to attempt to escape from the world. ... What is necessary is to change the world and to make it better.' ([1957] 1974: 78). Again and again Ambedkar contrasts the Buddhist tenets with Hinduism which for him advocates the principle(s) of inequality, dependency and divisiveness.[14] Ambedkar is also very outspoken in his rejection of the assumption that religion should, or Buddhism would, 'sanctify or ennoble poverty'. Rather the other way round, 'riches are welcome', but must be subject to *vinaya*: acquired lawfully, without craving, and be used to give to others ([1950] 1970: 13; [1957] 1974: 168, 332, 423, 424).

A Religion of Laymen

Ambedkar himself had put the main emphasis on the *message* of the old-new religion. He paid no attention to contemplation (Zelliot 1992: 194) and he was only little concerned with building it up institutionally, or rather he seemed hesitant to give it a fixed institutional structure and create a distinct body of spiritual and ritual specialists who might attempt to distance themselves from the laity and form a separate body. Ambedkar hinted at his disappointment with the performance of the historical *sangha*, as it was to be observed in the neighbouring countries of India ([1950] 1970: 16f; [1957] 1974: xlii; comp. Zelliot 1992: 243f). Although Neo-Buddhist supporters sometimes, and more or less metaphorically, employ the title 'human saviour' for him, it becomes apparent again that Ambedkar understood himself not as a religious leader in the common sense of the term but that he rather saw himself as an educator-*cum*-political leader. The *dīkṣā*, the initiation ceremony he had conducted for himself and others and for which he conceived the procedure as well as the vow to be spoken,[15] was an initiation into the Buddhist *dhamma* and not, as elsewhere in Buddhism, into the *sangha* (Zelliot 1992: 244; cf. Ambedkar [1957] 1974: 328).

The only step Ambedkar himself took to give to Buddhism an institutional base was the founding of the *Buddhist Society of India* in

1955 with its head-office in Bombay. This maintains only loose ties with its local branches and gives little by way of directions (Zelliot 1992: 228f). Of course Ambedkar, already very ill on the day of his *dīkṣā* (14. Oct. 1956), had no time to pursue organizational work, but I think it fits very well with his conception of religion and its social significance not to have an élite body of spiritual *virtuosi*. In any case he also lacked the decisive prerequisites for creating a *sangha*. Within his larger *jāti*, the Mahars, renunciation or celibate scholarship and piety had no tradition (Zelliot 1992: 246). And then there was the lack of resources. Buddhist missionary activities would have had to be financed from other sources. He himself had hoped that Buddhists from other Asian countries would step in ([1950] 1970: 17).

Although over the years a number of *bhikkhus* have been visiting the new Buddhists, especially in Maharashtra—*bhikkhus* who hail from various backgrounds and countries (Thai, English, Tibetan *and* Mahar)—the life of the Neo-Buddhist communities for long has basically been a local affair, run by local leaders. Local residents, men as well as women, may conduct (daily, mostly weekly) *vandanās* (paying of deference) at the local *vihāra*, hold speeches on Buddhism or give some training to children, conduct festivals and processions[16] or collective singing, collect money, plan and build new *vihāras* (Zelliot 1992: 226f, 229, 244f). The concept of *vihāra* is now being used for meeting places(*-cum-*shrines) and not any more, or at least not primarily, for a residence of Buddhist monks. Many of the *bhikkhus* who first attended to the new Buddhist communities did not manage or attempt to learn any of the languages spoken in the regions, and thus had been in any case restricted in their interactions with them.

While very exceptional for a new, or reinstated, religious movement, the significance of the lay factor and the decentralized structure of this new Indian Buddhism makes it appear very modern: a self-organized, non-hierarchical, participatory and non-exclusive community. On the other hand, as Eleanor Zelliot suggests, there may be very traditional roots, or at least a traditional model, for this kind of organization without a clear leadership pattern: the *bhakti* movement, still vital in Maharashtra. We only need to think of the *vārkarīs*, who also seem to have flourished on dispersed leadership, a shared tradition and group singing.[17] However, the Buddhists do not have a geographical ceremonial centre, as the *vārkarīs* have Pandharpur, as point of pilgrimage. 'Neo'-Buddhists have only Ambedkar as their focal point (Zelliot 1992: 244f).

But there are signs of stronger 'professionalization' and 'spiritualization' in recent times. The Trailokya Bauddha Mahasangha Sahayaka Gana

(TBMSG), founded in 1979, is acting as institutional disseminator of Buddhist knowledge. It has introduced the practice of meditation among 'Neo'-Buddhists, but it also does educational work and runs health centres and other welfare projects. Originally founded by British Buddhists, with a parent or parallel body, the '(Friends of the) Western Buddhist Order' in Great Britain, it represents a combination of *sangha* and developmental NGO (non-governmental organization). The number of ordinated and affiliated members from within the group of Mahars seems to be slowly increasing. The intention of the TBM is not to be a monastic order in the traditional sense (e.g. no obligation for celibacy). In consonance with Ambedkar the TBM(SG) wants to avoid a sharp distinction and division between lay members and *bhikkhus*. Forming an institutionally distinct body it does not cover the whole expanse of 'Neo'-Buddhist communities in Maharashtra, even less so other places in India. Thus, different models of Buddhist practice coexist in Maharashtra today.[18]

A Religion for Society

Buddhism, in the eyes of Ambedkar, carried a strong social message ([1957] 1974: 159). Ambedkar took to Buddhism to give a new foundation to society. The central term around which all revolves is *dhamma*. This is not the place to discuss the whole spectrum of connotations this term has received in Ambedkar's writings, and even more so in the Buddhist literature in general. What I am concerned with is the special role that *dhamma* is given in Ambedkar's attempt to (re-)construct the Buddhist canon. It is his endeavour to translate the individual's search for salvation from suffering into a social, or even sociological demand, so that it can form a guideline for society. On the one hand Ambedkar does take account of the concern to strive for purity of body, speech and mind, to control the passions and reach perfection and to strive for *nibbāna* ([1957] 1974: 160ff et passim).[19] On the other hand he makes this orientation a very this-worldly one. He rejects the idea of a soul and with this the idea of salvation after death: *nibbāna* in the Buddhist way of Ambedkar means 'happiness of the sentient being in *Samsara* while he is alive' ([1957] 1974: 164).[20] Buddha's 'main concern', Ambedkar states, 'was to give salvation to man in his life on earth and not to promise it to him in heaven after he is dead' ([1950] 1970: 14). While *dhamma* does refer to the control of the individual over him- or herself, Ambedkar is very firm in his resolution that '*dhamma* is social'. 'It is fundamentally and essentially so', he adds ([1957] 1974: 226). Because suffering, the way Ambedkar conceives it, is primarily inflicted upon man by man, *dhamma* is needed to recognize it and 'to remove this suffering from the world'

([1957] 1974: 83). 'Dhamma is righteousness, which means right relations between man and man in all spheres of life .... one man if he is alone does not need Dhamma .... But when there are two men living in relation to each other they must find a place for Dhamma whether they like it or not. ... In other words, Society cannot do without Dhamma.' ([1957] 1974: 226) One may take this as a point of departure in the struggle for liberty ([1957] 1974: 227).

This is a strong claim with regard to the social message of Buddhism, but it is even more so in a theoretical sense. When there is no *dhamma*, no Buddhism, then there is no society, no society at least that allows (fraternal) coexistence. Ambedkar introduces a remarkable perspectival shift into the interpretation of Buddhism. A religion which originates in a critique and questioning of the prevalent attitude in social life, calling upon men to renounce and transcend the world while formulating principles of ethical conduct for those who remain 'in the world', is here being converted into a *prerequisite* essential to secure *the working* of society.[21] *Dhamma* at one and the same time is seen as a moral code—for both the individual's conduct of life and social interaction—*and* as a constitutional necessity for society. 'Morality in Dhamma arises from the direct *necessity* for man to love man' ([1957] 1974: 231; emphasis mine). One must distinguish between different levels in Ambedkar's argument—his view of the human condition, an individual ethics and a social code of conduct he advocates—and bring out some of the inherent difficulties and paradoxes, before one can deal with its 'canonized' social status.

The first difficulty concerns the relationship between society and the moral order, and the part of the individual within it. On the one hand, society is to be based on moral principles (an objective); on the other hand, the moral order for society is already, transcendentally, given. Buddha's 'discovery' of *dhamma* was the discovery of a pre-conceived principle of order *and* was the invention of a system of rules to be followed. Thus one can speak of 'Buddha's dhamma', or 'his dhamma' ([1957] 1974: 83, 227 etc.; see also the title of the book). At the same time, Ambedkar makes the objectivist claim that moral order is something determinable, something which can be 'proved' like the 'order in the physical world' ([1957] 1974: 170), and the opposite claim that it is something to be achieved constantly, that it 'rests on man and on nobody else' ([1957] 1974: 172). The moral order depends on 'men's' actions: 'The kingdom of righteousness lies on earth and is to be reached by man by righteous conduct.' ([1957] 1974: 201) Ambedkar here introduces the concept of *kamma*, for 'man's action', and *vipāka*, for its effect ([1957] 1974: 172).

'The law of *Kamma* has to do only with the question of general moral order. ... It is concerned with the maintenance of the moral order in the universe.' ([1957] 1974: 172, 173)

Ambedkar emphasizes the law-like functioning of *kamma*. At the same time, every person is ethically free to act. There is good (*kuśala*) as well as bad (*akuśala*) *kamma* ([1957] 1974: 172). Bad action, or *kamma*, leads to a 'bad' moral order—indeed, men may even decide to give up *dhamma* altogether: 'Society may choose not to have any Dhamma, as an instrument of Government.'[22] Thus, the moral order which was introduced as something given, and therefore universal, has developed into something which is constantly in danger, something one has to work for, something which needs regular reenactment. This repeats the issue of theodicy, well known to Ambedkar ([1957] 1974: 171), which denotes a confrontation of ontological and ethical propositions. Ambedkar uses 'moral order' in two different meanings: as a term for a cosmic mechanism, i.e. the mechanics of the working of *kamma*, which allots differential effects to action, and as idea of righteousness.

But in what sense is this moral order, the *dhamma*, religious? This question indicates a second difficulty which is implied in Ambedkar's argument. To be more specific: is Buddhism, *in principle*, interchangeable with other religions regarding the depiction of the moral order and the selection of moral principles? Or does the desired relationship delineated before, rational and secular, between moral order, society and individual, pertain only to Buddhism? As a matter of fact, Ambedkar uses 'religion' in two different ways, on the one hand as a generic term, as is usual in religious and social studies, on the other hand *in opposition* to *dhamma*. Ambedkar had started, as we have seen, from a comparison of religions. In his earlier article on 'Buddha and the future of His Religion' and also in several instances in his book on Buddha's teachings, he takes Buddhism as one religion amongst others ([1957] 1974: 83, 151, 173, etc.), which distinguishes itself 'only'—but fundamentally—by the fact that in Buddhism alone morality has attained a pivotal position, occupying a place which other religions reserve for God. 'Morality has been given the place of God', he states ([1957] 1974: 173). In the central part of *The Buddha and His Dhamma* on the other hand, he contrasts Buddhism with religion, presenting Buddhism thereby as non-religion. Religion is 'personal',[23] whereas *dhamma* is social. Religion 'is concerned with revealing the beginning of things', *dhamma* is not. 'The purpose of Religion is to explain the origin of the world. The purpose of Dhamma is to reconstruct the world.' ([1957] 1974: 226, 229, 231) Religion connotes 'belief in God, belief in soul, worship of God, curing of the erring soul, propitiating

God by prayers, ceremonies, sacrifices, etc.' ([1957] 1974: 226).[24] *Dhamma* does not. Morality 'is not the root of religion,'[25] while it is the 'essence of Dhamma' ([1957] 1974: 231). Hinduism especially is without a moral basis; it is a religion of ritual and observances ([1950] 1970: 5).

Depending on which formula we take, all religions, or all *other* religions besides Buddhism, are deficient. 'In other words Buddhism is the only religion which the world can have.' ([1950] 1970: 13). Only the Buddhist *dhamma*, as an ethics of social action, can, according to Ambedkar, bring morality back into society, thus bridging the gap between different, or opposite, spheres of life. Only Buddhism is able to remould society, to give society a new lease of life. Thus *dhamma* takes the place of religion, but at the same time surpasses, or undercuts, religion: it transposes the moral impetus—the one which is central for Ambedkar—onto another level. What Ambedkar looks for might be called 'elementary' or 'essential' religion: a rediscovery of the minimum prerequisites or basic requirements of any moral order, of human sociality; a humanistic, universalistic project.

Canonicity: *La religion civile*

Buddhism becomes the universal yardstick against which religions are measured. It is in this sense that Buddhism achieves a canonical status with Ambedkar, canonical in respect to all religions. This, however, implies a peculiar contradiction: Ambedkar looks for a universal religion or ethics in the name of Buddhism, i.e. in the name of a particular religion or morality.

In Ambedkar's conception of religion, which ultimately is geared to contemporary society, two perspectives are mixed: *religion as identity, as acceptance of a particular belief system* or distinctive construction of the world (which may give expression to universalist claims), and *religion as 'elementary' moral basis of all social life* (which voices universal principles like equality, liberty and solidarity that precede every particular expression). Ambedkar wants to create a religion for his particular community along with a religion for civil society at large.

What Ambedkar relates to in this second aspect is the idea of *religion civile* as it had first been broached by Jean Jacques Rousseau. But Ambedkar also carries with him all the equivocations this concept contains (above and beyond the combination with a particular religious tradition and community). 'Civil religion' as implicitly invoked in Ambedkar's exposition is meant in the sense of a fundamental, reasonable (*Vernunft-, vernunftmäßiges*) principle of 'sociality', which all men have to accept, and not in the narrow sense of collective ideas and sentiments ('national religion'), a 'religion' which integrates a particular social entity, as Durkheim had in mind in certain instances. That is, Ambedkar seems to be looking for a post-religious religion, a religion which transcends religious distinctions, that is: religious and social discrimination,[26] and also a religion which overcomes the cleft between religion and politics, between morality and society. Buddhism is to provide the grounds from which to draw out this general and foundational principle. Ultimately it is in this that we can grasp the meaning Ambedkar gives to the project of making a traditional faith viable for modern times.

This project of a new civil religion shows a distinctive resemblance to, but also a significant difference from, Dewey's ideas. Ambedkar shared impulses with Dewey, if he did not receive them from him, but Dewey took another route from the common proposition and drew a different conclusion. He was heading for a different and even greater impasse. It is worthwhile to briefly compare the two ventures, for this will shed new light on Ambedkar's vision and bring Ambedkar's endeavour into clearer profile.

Dewey pursues the idea of a 'secular religion' or 'sacralization of democracy' (Joas 1997).[27] Dewey considers modern secularization not as symptom of moral and cultural decay but as a change of the form of religion. Religion is being liberated from dogmatic doctrines and restrictive institutional patterns (as found in the established religions). Dewey wants to get to, and work out, the implicit rational core of all religious attitudes: to make explicit what he calls 'the common faith of mankind' (Dewey [1934] 1962: 87). He thus attempts to cling to the power of ideals and values, generated by the imagination, while speaking against belief in supernatural powers from which the pursuance of ideas and values is to be separated. Already in his earlier writings Dewey had pleaded for the sacralization of democracy, of everyday communication and of interaction with nature (i.e. of science), and thus for the surpassing of Christianity. The new, secular form of religion would no longer detach ideals and values from reality, thus impoverishing the everyday and distracting attention from intersubjective relationships, as had happened in the old religions. Instead it would acknowledge what might be termed immanent self-transcendence: the dimension of the imaginary, the human faculty of imagination (*Einbildungskraft*), as the site of the religious, and place it within social (and physical) experience. In the eyes of Dewey, religion, the definition of values and ideas and the striving for an integral existence, refers to an *ongoing creative process of idealization of contingent possibilities* (Joas 1997: 180). For Dewey it is decisive to see this common core of religion and this process as an intersubjective and interactive one and it is the experience of communication which becomes central, not only in an instrumental sense. Democracy as an institutionalized 'way of living together' signifies the highest ideal.[28]

For Dewey this reinterpretation of human experience and action marks the final release of the true religious impulses. But what is missing in Dewey is the interpretation of concrete religiosity. Dewey wants to be religious without following any particular religion. He heads for what Joas calls 'an empty universalism' (1997: 193). Thus, Dewey's sacralization of democracy ends in a paradox different from Ambedkar's. While Ambedkar attempted to reinstitute a specific, albeit universalist religion, or ethics, as foundation of society and social relationships in general, Dewey refrained from connecting his concept with any particular religion. He replaced the supernatural symbolism and language which had allowed believers to express themselves and their religious aspirations by an abstract ethics, de-culturalized and de-socialized, a dissociated religion. Against this, Ambedkar's endeavour, itself paradoxical, seems more considered, expressing a genuine (sociological) difficulty.

A general religion of or for society, a common social value base—a 'civil religion'—must be compelling for everyone, but it also has to first gain assent. The rationalist notion of establishing consent through submission to reason, free of constraints, is not able to cope with this dilemma. Besides, such an endeavour, which opts for a re-entwinement of religion and politics, is indissolubly caught in the dilemma that religion and politics constitute different spheres and follow different inner logics, above all in modern society.[29] Ambedkar himself did acknowledge that religion and politics operate on different lines and only partly intersect,[30] but he obviously did not apply this observation to *dhamma* or civil religion. He also acknowledged this differentiation in his practical and strategic actions. Luhmann sketches the double dilemma in which an attempt such as Ambedkar's gets embroiled, in a discussion of Rousseau's concept of *religion civile*.

> Now, is this *religion civile* only a useful, or is it a true religion, a religion of reason or a religion of the heart? Is this religion convincing, convenient and befitting, considering the historically given differentiation between religion and politics, or can it overcome this difference and capture that in which the human being realizes her/his humanity? (Luhmann [1981] 1991: 298; translation mine)[31]

Dewey's and Ambedkar's options taken together indicate the spectrum of alternatives, and of aporias, of public religion in a modern context, of a foundational ethics for a democratic, 'civil' society.

Possibilities and Pragmatics: Situational Creativity

It is not clear from the text of *The Buddha and His Dhamma* to what extent Ambedkar recognized the dilemma inherent in any attempt to create and institute a 'civil religion', inherent, for one, in the plea for re-entwinement of politics and religion, but as well in the merging of a particular religious tradition and the idea of a general civil religion. Perhaps it was just the simultaneous search for a community religion of self-respect which made it difficult to realize the dilemma. But it is important to stress that Ambedkar was not a mere utopian, drifting away from social reality and venturing a pre-fabricated model for society. He was well aware, or became aware in the battles he fought, of the contingency and limitations of institutions and the long way he and the Dalits had to go to overcome these difficulties.

Ambedkar operated on two levels. While bringing out his vision of what I called 'civil religion', wrapped into the terminology of a particular religious tradition, he sounds very rigorous and principled, but abstract. However, the way he operated in the public field appeared different. It seems that in his political action he took Buddhism, or Buddhist civil religion, as a kind of counter-factual foil which was to serve as a referential frame for himself and for his followers. This becomes understandable if, by way of trial, one links it with the pragmatist influences he had been exposed to. On closer inspection, this finds unexpected corroboration in his interpretation of Buddhism.

Ideals are conceded a particular social power by Ambedkar for the struggles he fought. Ideals reveal, if we read the remarks of John Dewey, his one-time teacher, cited at the beginning, the possibilities which show up in reality, 'the hard stuff of the world of physical and social experience', and they show the directions in which action was to be taken. They are thus related to the contingencies of a situation. This way of functioning builds on, and helps to develop and further, the faculty of distanciation and self-distanciation: A 'new vision emerges through seeing ... old things in new relations serving a new end which the new end aids in creating.'[32]

Ambedkar's distance towards social arrangements showed in his practical actions. He was always prepared, or had to inevitably learn, to modify modes of procedure and alter the institutions he had himself created. He tried out several ways of organizing social change, switching when he realized that a scheme did not suit his ends or that he did not get the expected response. Think only of his strategic shifts between class-oriented and caste- or *varṇa*-oriented political organizations (Independent Labour Party, Scheduled Castes Federation, Republican Party of India). He had always been aware of the overdetermined situation of those at the bottom of society which gave little space for manoeuvre but made it all the more necessary to broaden this space in every possible way. He always related to circumstances, to the conditions of a situation. Ambedkar developed and kept the ability to transcend institutions by moving to a deeper level of sociality. Following a broad (moral) idea, he acknowledged that he was implicated in interactive relations: It is thus a notion of *situational creativity* à la Dewey (cf. Joas 1992: 196f).

In Buddhism Ambedkar found this corroborated—or read it into Buddhism. I distinguish three steps in his argument in this respect. He starts with what he calls 'the doctrine of impermanence'. Society keeps changing just as the individual human being 'is always changing, always growing'. Ambedkar disputes any 'permanent and fixed system of classification of men', as written into the *varṇa* scheme. On the side of the individual, he sees the relative position of the *guṇas* in continuous need of rebalancing and tuning. A human being 'is not the same at two different moments of his life.' It is the composite character of beings and things which make them ever-changing ([1950] 1970: 10; [1957] 1974: 169).

'Being is becoming', Ambedkar depicts this Buddhist notion with a phrase in which the European dialectical tradition resounds ([1957] 1974: 169). Thus, questioning traditional concepts of identity opens up space for development. This is the second step I want to distinguish. Ambedkar refuses interpretations of the Buddhist notion of *śūnya* or *śūnyatā* (Pali: *sunnata*) as 'nihilism'. Instead, he emphasizes what we would today call the 'emergent side of things'. 'Very few realize that it is on account of *Sunnyata* that everything becomes possible; without it nothing in the world would be possible. It is on the impermanence of the nature of all things that the possibility of all other things depends.' ([1957] 1974: 170) A two-pronged moral frame, and this is the third step, can be drawn out from the theory of impermanence: on the one hand detachment from what is contingent, detachment from property, from friends, etc., on the other, if not hope, then at least non-pessimism, the possibility for improvement of worldly relationships, and thus a certain 'activist', or pragmatist tinge ([1950] 1970: 10; [1957] 1974: 170, cf. 78, 90).

Ambedkar gives Buddhism an anti-essentialist reading which parallels pragmatism. Ambedkar's thought and pragmatism share basic assumptions: the emphasis on potentiality, on non-manifest possibilities which inhere in things and social relations and which may come to constitute a social force. It is the power of distanciation, of the (social) imaginary, which allows to discern the possibilities open at a time.

Third Idiom: Translating and Transcending Particular Experiences

It is the admixture of identity religion to civil religion, and the principled dilemma of civil religion, as indicated above, which makes for the problematics of Ambedkar's endeavour in the last instance. But in addition to this, on a more pragmatic level, it is the difficulty in transcending the opposition between Hinduism, as a self-proclaimed entity, and Dalit(ness), between two ways of expression, two languages, which threatens to frustrate Ambedkar's cause.

Buddhism in India today has a limited range. Ambedkarite Buddhism particularly is treated as a sect, a young and deviant branch of 'real' Buddhism and the religion of mainly one *jāti*, the Mahars.[33] It has become a communalized affair, and, in the eyes of many, a replication of casteist thinking. We can now see more clearly the difficulties and aporias inherent in the project itself, besides the resistance of the larger society which was not able, or was unwilling, to distinguish between the idiosyncratic religious form (of Buddhism) and the general, 'civil' message and which also in large degree was, and is, not prepared to accept Ambedkar as a 'national' leader.

We find already in Ambedkar signs of wavering in the universalist drive. Not fully accepted or acceptable as moral authority, and fighting for the cause of those most oppressed socially, culturally and economically in Indian society, he could not but first of all address himself to what is taken as his 'natural constituency'. He himself largely refrained from and even opposed the prevalent racist ideas about the different origins of 'Untouchables' and 'Touchables', which declared the Untouchables or Dalits the original, non- and pre-Aryan, inhabitants of India. However, in an attempt to invent a past and a tradition for his people, he also played with an ethnic notion and fleetingly, in his last public speech on the day after the *dīkṣā* or 'conversion' ceremony in Nagpur, voiced the supposition that the Untouchables are the descendants of the ancient 'Nagas' of the Buddhist days who had been considered as enemies by the 'Aryans' and had been 'suppressed and oppressed' by them (Ambedkar [1956] 1993: 75). Even while rejecting the idea of an Aryan and a non-Aryan race, M.S. Gore argues, Ambedkar still accepted the idea of a distinct Aryan culture, 'dominated by the ritual of sacrifices, characterised by warfare, regional expansion and subjugation as well as the absorption of conquered peoples.' (Gore 1993: 240) This meant that he too pursued a divisive strategy in some of his statements and actions—difficult to avoid anyhow under the prevailing circumstances. In this he is part of, and has reinforced, a strong tendency of contemporary Indian socio-political reality. The developments in independent India have further deepened the chasm between the large, newly-defined social categories and imagined communities.

Still, Ambedkar's endeavour to break out of this vicious circle was the most forceful of all Dalit endeavours in his days in India. Other Dalit or 'Untouchable' groups too pursued the idea of a universal(ist) religion and an equitable social order. They founded new religious movements to cut themselves off from Hinduism in its hegemonic forms, while still building on Hinduistic, i.e. in many cases *bhakti*, traditions—the SNDP (Sri Narayana Dharma Pariplana) in Kerala or the Satnamipanth in Chattisgarh, or the Ad Dharm in Punjab—which built upon the veneration of *sant* Raidas. The aspect of group identity remained in the foreground in all these cases.[34] Or some others joined, or let themselves be brought into the fold of, alternative universal religions: Islam and Christianity were the foremost options. Ambedkar on the other hand, while clear about his anti-Hindu position, did not let any 'Hindu' notions creep into the articulation of a new vision. He chose, or rather revived, a universal religion which was not only 'of Indian origin', but, being defunct in the main part of India at that time, was also not controlled by an established body of religious experts and ritual functionaries. The choice of Buddhism, while being one of the universalist 'world religions', allowed Ambedkar and the Dalits to lead themselves, to go ahead without the consent or approval of others, the leaders of the more established religious communities, and to determine the outline of the moral order themselves.[35]

Ambedkar was not content with reconstructing a specific Dalit tradition or counter-tradition, a 'subaltern' tradition, standing out against the hegemonic mainstream. He rather tried to bridge this distance and transcend parochialism. Buddhism, in the guise of civil religion, for Ambedkar served as a 'third idiom' in the Dalit struggle for recognition, i.e. as a mode of translation that tries to introduce an idiom which transcends the limitations of two conflicting positions, discourses or frames of reference, in this case between a hierarchical idiom, which makes ontological distinctions between categories of people, and a counter-discourse, which rejects ontological discriminations. This can serve as a strategy to overcome a confrontational deadlock, or lack of understanding, by changing the level or idiom of communication. It means re-writing, re-casting, trans-scribing in the full sense of the term—not only one's ideas and one's language but *also the boundaries* which divide, or seem to divide, two opponents. The one who tries to translate his or her concerns and perspectives has to relativize and transcend his/her own traditions and language, his or her own frame of reference, as s/he has to relativize that of the opponent and transform it into the third idiom.

Ambedkar translated the specific experiences of oppression and marginalization, of disrespect and stigmatization the Untouchables have had to undergo, into a language and a social imaginary which others would, or should, comprehend: into a universalist ethics and a project of social reconstruction and self-organization, which it is not easy to dismiss on intellectual and moral grounds. Understood thus, it is not very meaningful to argue about the 'authenticity' of Ambedkar's interpretation of Buddhism and the sources of his construction, or whether he had engaged with 'Western' readings of the Buddhist message.

To transcend one's own traditions and mode of expression is difficult enough, but the whole endeavour requires something even more difficult at the other end. To be really successful the translation (into a third idiom) would have to happen on both sides. The position *against* which one is fighting tends to obstruct the endeavour to develop a reciprocal understanding. The problem is to establish a third idiom *as that* level of discourse to which both sides, and others as well, may link.

Besides, the danger in this switch to a third idiom (the level of civil religion) is, of course, that it gets disconnected from the everyday struggle for survival of the non-intellectual, non-middle class Dalits. Ambedkar's third idiom transcends the restrictions of instituted co-ordinates, opens up an imaginary space. But this kind of translation also serves to transpose the Dalit struggle. It lies in the nature of transposition that not only are issues phrased differently from how they are experienced in the original context, many experiential dimensions are also marked off and excluded by this kind of translation: they cannot be expressed in the detached language which Ambedkar's third, mediating idiom has to offer.

Does this mean that the switch to a religious discourse and the choice of Buddhism displaces the 'real' issues with which Dalits and Ex-Untouchables are faced today? Does the switch to general(ist) principles of civil religion overlook the specificity of the Dalit cause? And does the pragmatist approach, the idea of social possibilities and imaginations, still offer the hope of coming to grips with the situation of Dalits when Hindu nationalist forces seem to want Dalit integration into a reformulated, empowered Hinduism, whereby they may identify with their opponents?

On the pragmatic-political level as well as at the level of principle, Ambedkar's quest can be seen, and should be discussed much more thoroughly, as a paradigmatic attempt to make cultural traditions meaningful for the modern world and its central problems, through reappropriation and reinterpretation. His effort seems equally a paradigmatic example of the aporia this creates, of the dilemmas into which the attempt runs.

Notes

1. See esp. Zelliot (1986), Rodrigues (1993), Gore (1993), Narain & Ahir (1994), Baxi (1995), Herrenschmidt (1996).
2. If one includes the political level, things become even more complicated. The strong and meanwhile often purely ritualistic and opportunistic celebrations around and after the 100th anniversary of Ambedkar's birthday in 1991 met with renewed attacks on Ambedkar. He has been used, especially by Dalit politicians, to forward politics in the name of Dalitness (see especially the recent manoeuvres of the Bahujan Samaj Party, [BSP], in Uttar Pradesh). Other parties, and most significantly the Hindu nationalist ones, like the BJP (Bharatiya Janata Party) and Shiv Sena, long regarded as organisations of upper-caste and/or the regionally dominant middle-caste interests in Maharashtra and elsewhere, tried to incorporate Ambedkar. They use his sayings out of context in order to win the support of voters from amongst the 'Ex-Untouchables.' Against this, there are increasing attacks (not to mention the continuing atrocities on scheduled-caste members in rural areas) on the symbol Ambedkar has become, physically on his statues (e.g. in Bombay in July 1997. This led to riots in which the police killed ten people, most of them Dalit), ideologically to undermine his integrity and to demonstrate his anti-nationalist and pro-colonial, pro-British stance, as in a recent volume written by the leading Hindu nationalist journalist Arun Shourie (1997).
3. See for this: Dalit Sahitya (for English translations see e.g. Anand & Zelliot (1992); Dangle (1992), also Daya Pawar's *Balute* in several translations [orig. in Marathi in 1978]); for general evaluations Zelliot (1992), Gokhale (1990) and (1993), Nagaraj (1993), Omvedt (1994).
4. See Ambedkar's remarks on Dewey in his article 'Annihilation of Caste' (Ambedkar [1936] 1989: 79).
5. Dewey's thinking on democracy and education dates from an earlier period; similarly, his leanings towards a sacralization of the issue of democracy have earlier roots. The ideas of Dewey that Ambedkar was confronted with in his student days can be made out indirectly through his respective publications. It is striking that no one seems as yet to have taken up the task of comparing Dewey's and Ambedkar's propositions on democracy, or on education, besides their concepts of religion for contemporary society, which I will hint at here. The present contribution is only a first step.
6. For quotations from Ambedkar's publications I will omit his name hereafter and only indicate the year ([1950] 1970 and [1957] 1974 respectively).

7. Besides, Buddhism was easier to convey to others and to defend against his slanderers than, for example, Islam or Christianity, for it was a religion of Indian origin. Ambedkar had also considered Sikhism as a choice.
8. For 'spheres of value', or 'orders of life', their respective inner logic and their separation and tensions, as characteristic for the secular process of rationalization, see Weber (1972: 536–73).
9. C. Queen has pointed out that Ambedkar takes an argument and image of Dewey's to depict Buddha's teachings. In his 'Annihilation of Caste' Ambedkar quotes Dewey, without indicating the source, as pronouncing:

   > Every society gets encumbered with what is trivial, with dead wood from the past, and with what is positively perverse ... As a society becomes more enlightened, it realizes that it is responsible *not* to conserve and transmit the whole of its existing achievements, but only such as make for a better future society. ([1936] 1989: 79; emphasis Ambedkar's)

   In 'Buddha and the Future of His Religion' Ambedkar writes, continuing the sentence quoted above in the main text:

   > He (the Buddha, MF) wished, his religion not to be en(c)umbered with the dead wood of the past. He wanted that it should remain ever green and serviceable at all times. That is why he gave liberty to his followers to chip and chop as the necessities of the case required. No other religious teacher has shown such courage. ([1950] 1970: 4)

   Cf. Queen (1996: 64); not included in the 1994 version of Queen's article.
10. At this instance Ambedkar does accept the concept of the ten lives a Buddha has to go through to reach final enlightenment. The *bodhisattva* seems to develop some super-human qualities. In his seventh life he becomes 'one with Infinity', in his tenth and final stage, he 'attains the infinite divine eye of a Buddha' ([1957] 1974: 56–7). Ambedkar compares the 'theory of the Jatakas or the birth stages of a Bodhisatta' to the 'Brahmanic theory of Avataras'. While within the conception of *avatāra* God may be 'very impure and immoral in his conduct', the concept of Buddha is one of ever greater perfection of purity ([1957] 1974: 57).
11. The 'Path of Purity' or the Five Precepts are: not to kill, steal, speak untruth, drink and indulge in lust; the 'Path of Virtue', which contains ten articles, is drawn from the traditional *pāramitās*, or states of perfection, like *karuṇā*, loving kindness, *maitri*, extended fellow feelings, etc.
12. In the introduction to *Buddha and His Dhamma* Ambedkar even doubts that the 'Four Aryan Truths' (on the existence, origin and overcoming of suffering and the path to be followed) form part of the original teachings of the Buddha, because they would 'deny hope to man' and thus be 'a great stumbling block in the way of non-Buddhists accepting the gospel of Buddhism' ([1957] 1974: xli–xlii).

13. Ambedkar places less emphasize on those Truths, which 'in effect blame the victim for the cause of suffering' (Queen 1994: 113, 116).
14. As in the idea of exclusivist moralities ([1957] 1974: 233).
15. For the text of the vow, see Zelliot (1992: 215).
16. Main festival days celebrated amongst the Buddhist community are Ambedkar's birth and death (14 April and 6 December respectively), Buddha Jayanti and the Dhammacakra Pravartan Din, the anniversary of the initial conversion or *dīkṣā* ceremony (14 October).
17. The same may have been true of the Kabirpanthis, to which Ambedkar's father adhered.
18. The person who founded and inspired both organizations, Sangharakshita, alias Dennis Lingwood, had met Ambedkar three times between 1952 and 1956. Research on the Trailokya Bauddha Mahasangha has recently been conducted by Alan Sponberg (1996) and Johannes Beltz (for first results see Beltz 1997). I owe thanks to Johannes Beltz for discussions on Ambedkar and for his information on recent developments in Maharashtrian Buddhism. For controversies between a political and a 'soteriological' line amongst today's followers of Ambedkar, see the exchange between Gopal Guru, a political scientist, and Dhammacari Lokamitra (alias Jeremy Goody), who had been instrumental in instituting and building the TBMSG, in the pages of the *Economic and Political Weekly* in 1991 (also covered by Sponberg and Beltz).
19. The canonicity of these depictions is not at issue here.
20. *Saṃsāra* being disconnected from the concept of soul can here only refer to the 'rebirth' of matter (see above p. 254).
21. Taking the traditions of the 'sociology of religion' one can see in this also an opposition between a Weberian and a Durkheimian perspective on the relationship between religion and society.
22. 'Society has to choose one of the three alternatives. ... Society may choose not to have any Dhamma, as an instrument of Government. For Dhamma is nothing if it [is] not an instrument of Government. ... This means Society chooses the road to anarchy. ... Secondly, Society may choose the police, i.e. dictatorship as an instrument of Government. ... Thirdly, Society may choose Dhamma plus the Magistrate wherever people fail to observe Dhamma. ... In anarchy and dictatorship liberty is lost. ... Only in the third liberty survives.' ([1957] 1974: 226f)
23. 'Religion, it is said, is personal and one must keep it to oneself. One must not let it play its part in public life.' ([1957] 1974: 226)
24. This describes only the final state of religion which does not include Buddhism. Ambedkar, in line with religious studies of his time, assumes an evolution of the idea of (non-*dhammic*) religion through three stages ([1957] 1974: 225f). As is well known, Émile Durkheim, too, did struggle with the question whether Buddhism, or more precisely Theravada Buddhism, should be included in the generic term religion, because of the a-theism of its basic assumptions.
25. 'Every religion preaches morality but morality is not the root of religion. It

is a wagon attached to it. It is attached and detached as the occasion requires.' ([1957] 1974: 231)

26. 'Buddhism is the only real religion and those who do not accept this *must revise their definition of religion*.' ([1957]1974: 329; emphasis mine)
27. The following summary of Dewey's conception of ideals, values and religion profits from and follows in many respects Hans Joas' recent discussion of Dewey's ethical and religious thought (Joas 1997: 162–94). The central text of Dewey in this regard is his *A Common Faith* ([1934] 1962).
28. As I indicated before, it would be worthwhile to have a thorough look into the commonalities between Dewey's and Ambedkar's concepts of democracy.
29. But not merely in modern society—in India this differentiation dates to ancient times.
30. Cf. quotation in fn.22 above.
31. Gandhi's attempt could be discussed accordingly. Luhmann's statement allows only an approximate translation into English. The German original of the quotation above reads:

> Ist diese Religion nun eine nur nützliche oder eine wahre Religion, eine Religion der Vernunft oder Religion des Herzens? Überzeugt sie als Konvenienz angesichts der historisch gegebenen Differenzierung von Religion und Politik oder trifft sie in der Überwindung dieser Differenz das, was den Menschen als Menschen verwirklicht? (Luhmann 1991: 298)

32. See the opening quotation of the article. In the context of his recourse to Dewey cited above ('Annihilation of Caste', Ambedkar [1936] 1989: 79; c.f. fn 9, above), Ambedkar emphasizes life's orientation to the future, the emergent nature of the present.
33. D.C. Ahir, as reported in Kantowsky (1997), distinguishes five groups of Buddhists in contemporary India: 'survivals of the Buddhist period' (in Ladakh, Himachal Pradesh, the Northeast, plus the Baruas of Bengal); 'ethnic overlaps' from Nepal and Burma especially; those attracted to Buddhism as result of the missionary activities of the Mahabodhi Society; the followers of Ambedkar; and the Tibetan refugees of 1959 and after.
34. Even if the slogan was, as in the case of the SNDP, 'one God, one religion, one caste'.
35. Herein lies one reason for the current conflict between more 'political' and more 'religious' followers of Ambedkarite Buddhism in Maharashtra.

References

Ambedkar, Bhimrao Ramji. [1950] 1970. *Buddha and the Future of His Religion*. Jullundur (Punjab): Bheem Patrika Publications.

———. [1957] 1974. *The Buddha and His Dhamma*. Bombay: Siddharth Publication.

———. [1936] 1989. Annihilation of Caste with a Reply to Mahatma Gandhi. In *Dr. Babasaheb Ambedkar Writings and Speeches*, comp. Vasant Moon, 23–96. Bombay: Education Department, Government of Maharashtra.

———. [1956] 1993. The Great Conversion. In *B. R. Ambedkar*, ed. Verinder Grover, 74–91. New Delhi: Deep & Deep.

Anand, Mulk Raj and Eleanor Zelliot (eds.). 1992. *An Anthology of Dalit Literature: Poems*. New Delhi: Gyan Press.

Baxi, Upendra. 1995. Emancipation as justice: Babasaheb Ambedkar's Legacy and Vision. In *Crisis and Change in Contemporary India*, ed. Upendra Baxi and Bhikhu Parekh, 122–49. New Delhi: Sage.

Beltz, Johannes. 1997. Spiritualiser le dhamma? L'implantation contestée du Trailokya Bauddha Mahasangha en Inde. *Asiatische Studien / Études Asiatiques* 51.4: 1055–71.

Dangle, Arjun (ed.). 1992. *Poisoned Bread. Translations from Modern Marathi Dalit Literature*. Bombay: Orient Longman.

Dewey, John. [1934] 1962. *A Common Faith*. New Haven: Yale University Press.

Gokhale, Jayashree B. 1990. The Evolution of a Counter-ideology: Dalit Consciousness in Maharashtra. In *Dominance and State Power in Modern India. Decline of a Social Order*, ed. Francine R. Frankel and M. S. A. Rao, 212–77. Delhi: Oxford University Press.

———. 1993. *From Concessions to Confrontation. The Politics of an Indian Untouchable Community*. Bombay: Popular Prakashan.

Gore, M. S. 1993. *The Social Context of an Ideology. Ambedkar's Political and Social Thought*. New Delhi: Sage.

Herrenschmidt, Olivier. 1996. 'L'inégalité graduée' ou la pire des inégalités. L'analyse de la société hindoue par Ambedkar. *Archives européennes de sociologie* 37.1: 3–32.

Joas, Hans. 1992. *Die Kreativität des Handelns*. Frankfurt: Suhrkamp.

———. 1996. *The Creativity of Action*. Chicago: University of Chicago Press.

———. 1997. *Die Entstehung der Werte*. Frankfurt: Suhrkamp.

Kantowsky, Detlef. 1997. Buddhisten in Indien heute: Ein Literaturbericht insbesondere über die Neo-Buddhisten. In *Bauddha Vidyasudhakarah. Studies in Honour of Heinz Bechert on the Occasion of His 65th Birthday*, ed. Petra Kieffer-Pülz and Jens-Uwe Hartmann, 361–96. Swisttal-Odendorf: Indica et Tibetica Verlag.

Luhmann, Niklas. [1981] 1991. Grundwerte als Zivilreligion: Zur wissenschaftlichen Karriere eines Themas. *Soziologische Aufklärung 3. Soziales System, Gesellschaft, Organisation*, 293–308. Opladen: Westdeutscher Verlag.

Nagaraj, D. R. 1993. *The Flaming Feet. A Study of the Dalit Movement in India*. Bangalore: South Forum Press & Institute for Cultural Research and Action (ICRA).

Narain, A. K. and D. C. Ahir (eds.). 1994. *Dr. Ambedkar, Buddhism and Social Change*. Delhi: B.R. Publishing Corp.

Omvedt, Gail. 1994. *Dalits and the Democratic Revolution. Dr. Ambedkar and the Dalit Movement in Colonial India*. New Delhi: Sage.

Pawar, Daya. [1978] 1988. *Balute. Autobiographie eines Unberührbaren*. Frankfurt: Yvonne Landeck.

Queen, Christopher S. 1994. Ambedkar, Modernity and the Hermeneutics of Buddhist Liberation. In *Dr. Ambedkar, Buddhism and Social Change*, ed. A. K. Narain and D. C. Ahir, 99–122. Delhi: B.R. Publishing Corp.

———. 1996. Dr. Ambedkar and the Hermeneutics of Buddhist Liberation. In *Engaged Buddhism. Buddhist Liberation Movements in Asia*, ed. Christopher S. Queen and Sallie B. King, 45–71. Albany: State University of New York Press.

Rodrigues, Valerian. 1993. Making a Tradition Critical: Ambedkar's Reading of Buddhism. In *Dalit Movements and the Meanings of Labour in India*, ed. Peter Robb, 299–338. Delhi: Oxford University Press.

Shourie, Arun. 1997. *Worshipping False Gods. Ambedkar, and the Facts Which Have Been Erased*. New Delhi: ASA.

Sponberg, Alan. 1996. TBMSG: A Dhamma Revolution in Contemporary India. In *Engaged Buddhism. Buddhist Liberation Movements in Asia*, ed. Christopher S. Queen and Sallie B. King, 73–120. Albany: State University of New York Press.

Weber, Max. [1920] 1972. *Gesammelte Aufsätze zur Religionssoziologie*. Vol. 1. Tübingen: Mohr.

Zelliot, Eleanor. 1986. The Social and Political Thought of B. R. Ambedkar. In *Political Thought in Modern India*, ed. Thomas Pantham and Kenneth L. Deutsch, 161–75. New Delhi: Sage.

———. 1992. *From Untouchable to Dalit. Essays on the Ambedkar Movement*. New Delhi: Manohar.

Swadhyaya and the 'Stream' of Religious Revitalization

GITA DHARAMPAL-FRICK

I have nothing new to offer, I am only restating what has already been said.

Pandurang 'Shastri' Athavale

Remember it is God's grace that gives you success.

Bhagvad Gita 7, as paraphrased by Athavale

The Swadhyaya family works according to the divine teachings of the ancient sages.

Dada

One of the inherent characteristics of Indian traditions is that they are continually being reformulated, which means there is constant social and cultural regeneration. Swadhyaya, a phenomenon of the latter half of the twentieth-century, bears exemplary testimony to this heritage. Representing a movement of religious revitalization, it is preferentially referred to by its own adherents as a *pravah* (i.e. a stream), a term which appropriately underscores its dynamism and fluidity; and as such it could be characterized as a process or continuum, paradigmatically reflecting the similarly fluid status of religion in the Indian context.

In this short paper[1] I intend to trace the contours of this regenerative process, aptly called 'a silent but singing revolution',[2] which is gathering momentum, and yet which has remained relatively unknown in the Western academy. In consonance with the *leitmotif* of this volume, my specific aim here is to highlight how Swadhyaya exemplifies the symbiotic functioning of charisma and canon. At the outset, let me explain how I interpret these two terms. Succinctly defined, charisma represents the force of human agency in bringing about change in societies, transforming existing cultural relationships through the mediation of religion.[3] In addition to this standard definition, I understand it to represent above all, an inherent quality which is imputed to people presumed to be connected with some kind of 'divine' power, transcendent or immanent. Further, this charismatic quality can be perceived as existing both in a more intense form in particular individuals, as well as in a relatively attenuated or dispersed form[4]—a 'double feature' which is of crucial essence to an understanding of Swadhyaya's impact. As for canon, adapting its Western heritage to suit the South Asian 'climate', I interpret it as 'sacred tradition' (practised, spoken or written), constituting a criterion of legitimacy, and occupying a central position within Indian culture;[5] in conjunction with this rather sweeping functional definition, I wish to underscore the flexibility and inherent elasticity of Indian canonic ideals and traditions—hallmarks which account for their longevity, for traditions of mere eternal repetition cannot survive historical change.[6]

Of late too much attention has been drawn to religion as a source of division, but in the phenomenon I am dealing with it is the integrative role of religion, as a source of solidarity, that features predominantly. Indeed, it is the emphasis on the harmony between the 'self' and the 'other', representing the insignia of Swadhyaya, that sets it apart from other movements defining religious identity through rejection of the 'other' as alien or false.

II

The literal meaning of *swadhyaya* is the study, knowledge and discovery of the 'self'.[7] Explicitly in accordance with vedanta philosophy that holds *brahman* to be central to man's self-awareness (*aham brahmasmi*), it is maintained that, through the understanding of one's true or inner self, i.e. *atman* (as distinct from the individual ego), one attains, in the Swadhyaya idiom, a realization of the 'indwelling' God. The significance of this experiential (as opposed to theological) spirituality, and its capacity to meet contemporary needs was realized and propagated since the late 1950s by a Maharashtrian Brahmin scholar, Pandurang Vaijnath Athavale, endearingly known by millions as *Dada* (elder brother, in Gujarati and Marathi). Respected for his erudition (hence referred to by some as *Shastriji*), he is considered to be an exceptional communicator, presenting a very amenable philosophy and possessing extraordinarily persuasive powers as a teacher. Labelling him the *founder* of Swadhyaya is somewhat debatable, since he sees himself as merely revitalizing what he perceives to be already there; hence *initiator* may be the more appropriate term.

As indicated in biographical sketches,[8] about four decades ago Athavale realized he had a 'mission' in life. This was prompted by his attending the Second World Religious Congress in Japan in 1954, at which he stressed the salience of Vedic teachings and in particular the contemporary relevance of the philosophy of the *Bhagvad Gita*. However, when asked whether a single community in India lived by these ideals, he was greatly perturbed, being aware of the discrepancy between the existing reality and his vision of how Hinduism ought to be practised. Yet accepting this as a challenge, he decided on his return to work towards the restoration of these 'cultural ideals' in contemporary India.[9]

Athavale resumed his teaching at the Pathshala[10] in Bombay, set up by his father in the 1920s. He soon had a following of young urban professionals who were seeking spiritual edification and religious orientation to stem the tide of modern secularism. Under Athavale's guidance they became familiarized with the spirit of Swadhyaya, or self-knowledge which links the 'self' to divinity. He validated this link by citing canonical authority, namely the Upanishadic 'truth' *tattvamasi* (Thou art That, i.e. the identity of man and God) which, according to his exposition, represents the culmination of man's spiritual development. The two steps by which this ultimate truth is realized were elucidated by Athavale as follows: *tena tvam asi* (you exist because of him), which he interpreted as 'God's grace and presence is within you'; *tasya tvam asi* (you belong to him), i.e. 'in owing our life to God', he elaborates, 'we are all His children' (DD: 6).[11] By emphasizing the active presence of God in all humans, the existence of charisma in a dispersed form (as mentioned above) is implicitly underscored. To attain realization of this 'divine immanence', Athavale recommended the path of *bhakti*, or devotion, as propounded by Krishna to Arjun in the *Bhagvad Gita*,[12] which represents the canonical master text for Swadhyaya.

At this juncture, the question arises whether Athavale's thinking is governed by essentialist formulations of tradition and thereby ignores the existing plurality of religious beliefs and practices. Well aware of this implied criticism, Athavale himself validates his exegesis of what he terms India's 'philosophical heritage' by maintaining that it contains 'eternal truths' that he is rerouting from the past, using them, through inspired rationalization, as creative elements in the living present. (LL: 6; Srivastava 1997: 9). By thus revitalizing 'canonical' ideas, he views his endeavour as an attempt to rehabilitate their original meaning; adding nothing new of his own, he claims to remain true to the sources of inspiration. And as such he sees himself more as a 'renovator' than as an innovator. Strictly speaking, this 'renovating' trait is at variance with

Weber's definition of a charismatic figure being a 'great innovating personality' (Weber 1922, 2: 832–73). Yet, in the Indian context, it is the former (i.e. being true to tradition) that endows him with charisma in the eyes of his devotees.

This would also apply to Athavale's interpretation of *bhakti* which he views, in tune with the precepts of the *Gita*, not only as the activation of an individual's relationship with God ('Bhakti is our understanding of God's love for us and our response to that love.' HH: 32) but also as a socially regenerative force ('Intense love for God and His creation cannot make us passive spectators of social evils prevalent in the society.' HH: 32). Transposing the traditional threefold path leading to spiritual enlightenment (namely that of *bhakti*, *karma*, selfless action, and *jnana*, knowledge), he elucidates that the original purport of *bhakti* has two important aspects: the first is termed *bhav bhakti*, or 'mystic euphoria and contemplative surrender' which leads to individual transformation in thought and action by recognizing the 'inner essence' as the mirror of the divine, and thereby enhancing the individual's self-reverence (*asmita*),[13] as also perceiving others similarly in the image of divinity. Secondly *kriti bhakti*, or the 'creative principle of devotion to promote communal good' (Srivastava 1997: 15), leads to cultural regeneration, governed by a feeling of identity with the human and natural world for enriching collective existence. 'Bhakti must generate power and dynamism in a person. And this power and dynamism must be used for removing the disparities and social evils prevalent in a society. Bhakti-devotion is a social force.' (HH: 33) Using the idiom of *bhakti*, Athavale, like Gandhi (whom he, surprisingly, rarely refers to explicitly), strikes deep cultural chords, and thereby seeks to activate and render dynamic the 'divinity' (or attenuated charisma) latent in all members of society.[14] It is, however, the *religious* quality or impulse of *bhakti* that he emphasizes, categorically denying the equation with 'social service'—a significant distinguishing feature as against Gandhi's quasi-sanctification of *seva*. To quote 'Shastriji' verbatim: 'service to God is infinitely superior to the idea of service to man.' (DD: 18). Yet the ultimate goal of both Athavale and Gandhi is basically the same, namely 'to restore human dignity so that man may reconnect himself to God and to others',[15] to form a fellowship of mankind.

III

Concrete expression to transform *bhakti* into a socio-religiously relevant force was given in 1958 when Athavale urged his Bombay disciples to venture into rural and marginalized villages for the purpose of bringing to fruition the 'message' of Swadhyaya. Emphasizing the 'great moral responsibility' of his chosen adepts, he quoted from the *Gita*: 'action must be performed for the sake of *lokasangraha*', i.e. the welfare of the human race (EE: 22). This was to impress upon them their 'religious duty' to actively realize the principle of true *bhakti* among the rural populations. At the same time, to foreground the spiritual rather than social aspect of this 'outreach programme', Athavale stressed the following: 'but you will be going to the villages with no motive other than your own spiritual development.' (*The Systems*: 86), a development in self-knowledge that was to be attained, nonetheless, through the establishment of relationships with one's fellow-beings.

That these 'devotional visits' or *bhaktipheri* (as they were soon to be called) started from Saurashtra, 'the land where Krishna performed heroic deeds' (*The Systems*: 87), induces a disciple to make the following comment: 'It was as if Vedic culture was giving a clarion call through revered Dada.' (87) Thus, the 'canonic' connection is made to endow an innovatory practice with cultural legitimacy and a sense of revitalized continuity. Even at the outset, Athavale was intent on incorporating this activity within the sphere of recognized religious praxis, as is evident from the ingenious suggestion made to his spiritual recruits to 'treat this bhakti pheri as their mode of observing *ekadashi*' (*The Systems*: 86).[16]

In consonance with Swadhyaya's rationalized spirituality, the traditional *ekadashi* fasting days (i.e. two days a month) for the group of urban educated Swadhyayees were to be transformed into society-oriented spiritual acts by their using this occasion to go on regular visits to village communities. To lend cultural legitimacy to this unconventional expression of solidarity, a new Sanskrit term was coined, namely *atmiyata*, translated in a modern idiom as 'we-feeling'. Participation in *bhaktipheri* also exemplified for the well-to-do city dwellers the familiar adage *tan-man-dhan* (lit. body-mind-money), which meant, according to Athavale's exegesis, that a pious act consisted first in giving one's time and energy, then one's mind and devotion, and only then one's money.[17] In particular, emphasis was laid on *nishkama karma* (selfless action), a central tenet in Krishna's sermon to Arjun, which was likewise to guide the devotee's conduct: according to Athavale's 'briefing', a Swadhyayee was not to be motivated by the desire for proximate ends, neither by considerations of convenience, nor pecuniary advantage.[18] Thus, routine (ritualized) religiosity is replaced with religiously inspired actions, à la Weber, with their ideational mainsprings embedded in the foundational cultural ethos (à la Gita). Another interesting innovatory distinction to the practice of traditional religious itinerants is that a person on *bhaktipheri* is not supposed to accept any material hospitality from his rural hosts so as 'not to be a burden'—a feature that would seem to reflect 'modern' considerations. Indicative of Athavale's 'pragmatic' outlook, it also testifies to his desire to enable religious praxis (be it rooted in canonic tradition) to remain astride the times. Admittedly, it also represents an explicit attempt to instil the term *pheri* (etymologically this incorporates the seemingly pejorative connotations of a 'begging round') with new esteem.

The *bhaktipheri* is a key feature of the mobilizational activities of Swadhyaya, and has been crucial to integrating divergent communities into what is known as the *Swadhyaya parivar*. Indeed, the family metaphor (as distinguished from 'conventional' *sampraday* or sects) is integral to its non-institutionalized functioning, in which (as emphasized by 'liberal-minded' adherents) there is no membership, no oath-taking and no dress-code. It now reaches out to more than 100,000 villages, covering 14 Indian states with over 15 million people calling themselves Swadhyayees, from amongst whom 'dedicated activists', called *motabhais* (i.e. 'big brothers'), would number about 200,000.[19] In recent years, it also seems to be spreading among expatriate Indians in various parts of Asia, Africa, Europe and the Americas.

IV

In view of these expansivist tendencies, it would be pertinent to enquire into the contextual reasons for Swadhyaya's (and Athavale's) 'charismatic' attraction. Firstly, from a socio-political angle, in view of the decay or exhaustion of the Nehruvian political paradigm, the very notion of *Entzauberung* (i.e. the notion, according to Max Weber, of modernization, rationalization, secularization and so forth) has itself been *entzaubert*, that is, has lost a good deal of the fascination it may have held in the early days of Independence. In the situation of instability which became more pervasive from the mid 1970s, when formerly propagated slogans began to ring hollow and post-independence India seemed to be undergoing a crisis of identity, holistic visions, providing coherence and orientation in the present, must inevitably have exerted a forceful appeal. Set against the over-centralization and over-bureaucratization of the state, the family-like functioning of Swadhyaya—with its non-hierarchic and self-reliant localized networks stressing individual integrity, social altruism and spiritual mutuality—appeared for many to present a viable antidote to the seemingly indomitable 'evils' of corruption, casteism and communalism.

Secondly, from a more specifically religio-cultural perspective, a population disenchanted with the prevailing state of affairs and experiencing both a normative as well as a spiritual vacuum would necessarily be susceptible to the utopian promise of a new cultural order—avowedly inspired by fundamental principles of its religious heritage—rather than latching on to the superficial and tactical manoeuvring of party politics. Not only does Athavale (his charisma enhanced due to his high ritual standing as a brahmanical scholar) fill the gap brought about by the decline of traditional cultural mediators, but also the intensity with which his charisma is experienced (and the power of its motivation) is greatly influenced by the deep-rooted Indian cultural propensity for the sacred. Perhaps I could also venture to state that, though the village communities visited by urban Swadhyayees on *bhaktipheri* may be considered, in objective terms, as deprived and disadvantaged, their very marginalized status (and hence bypassed by modern secularism) may indeed have enabled them to preserve this inherent cultural sensitivity and responsiveness to the sacred and its embodied personification in charisma.

Another significant reason for the success of this grassroots 'awakening' is that the basic tenets of Swadhyaya (for instance the concept of the in-dwelling God) are not viewed as basically alien. Coupled with the familiarity of the message, its very simplicity underscores its fundamental appeal. At a theoretical level, this assertion implicitly questions the construction of a two-tier model of religion, namely that of the élite and the popular.[20] Indeed Swadhyaya, through the intermediary of a charismatic personality, and in emphasizing the all-pervasiveness of the dispersed charisma which it seeks to activate, foregrounds what it perceives as a common religious framework that 'glues together' the entire society.

This does not mean that the dissimilarities between the religious perceptions of the élite and those of the populace are totally disregarded. And some scepticism may be in order regarding the deprecation by certain activists of the 'degenerate' state of Hinduism in the villages, prior to contact with Swadhyaya.[21] Impelled by Athavale's zeal to restore the vitality of Hinduism, are the village communities being changed into a mirror image of *Sanatan* Hinduism? Or in streamlining 'rebellious' elements in the society, is one merely eliminating the 'otherness of the other'? These queries do raise a moot point, which perforce must remain 'hanging in the air' for the moment. Only as a partial reply could I advance that, through the onslaught of modernity, these local traditions would have been bulldozed in due course anyway. And partly in support of Athavale's reasoning, it seems more salutory to undergird the religio-cultural 'roots', even if, in the process, due to emulation, some elements of popular religious practice become discarded—but not exterminated. For indigenous cults, I would aver, have a tendency to reassert themselves once their practitioners have regained their sense of self-worth and dignity.

V

Indeed, Athavale's recognition of 'Indians' loss of self-respect'[22] was the prime instigation for him to embark on his mission of spiritual revitalization. Impelled by a firm belief that the 'disinherited' must be reinstated to achieve a just society, not only were they to be uplifted by *bhaktipheris*,[23] he also started coining a set of new nomenclatures of 'canonic ancestry' for social groups located on the periphery of the Hindu social order. Inspired by epithets from puranic literature, these were titles such as *bhumiputra* (son of the earth goddess and consort of Vishnu) for cultivators, *sagarputra* (son of the sea), emphasizing the descent of fishermen from *Matsyavatar* (the first of Vishnu's incarnations, who is said to have retrieved the Vedas from the depth of the ocean, cf. Frédéric 1987: 735); coolies received the illustrious title *Vasudev sena* (i.e. the army of Vasudev, father of Krishna who carried his son in a basket on his head across the flooded river Yamuna); *vaghris* were renamed *deviputri* (children of the mother goddess, their chief deity).[24] This constituted for Athavale not just a formal 'christening' ritual, but rather a meaningful exemplification of the shared heritage of these social groups. Enhanced with a charismatic aura befitting the 'progeny of the gods', and on a more prosaic level being boosted by the human interest and respect shown to them, these communities do appear to be gaining new self-confidence and a sense of pride in their respective occupations, becoming also empowered to 'remodel' their lives to a certain extent. I would also venture to state that these 'corrective mythologies' (Srivastava 1997: 53, n3) do not merely represent a 'rewriting' of the social grammar of Indian society, but rather are tantamount to a 'rediscovery' of it.[25] Also abiding, in principle, by the tenets of tradition, they are all the while sanctioned by dharma. Needless to say, though Athavale (as a *sanatani*) is a supporter of *varnavyavastha* (the four-fold division of ancient Indian social order), he finds it necessary to reinterpret canonic authority in the following manner: 'everyone who does God's work is a brahman, since God resides in him',[26] and quite logically, then, *asprashya* (untouchable), defined as 'one who has been deserted by God' (Srivastava 1997: 22) is non-existent in the Swadhyaya universe. In order to lend the force of reality to his reinterpretations, Athavale has bestowed the *yagnopaveet* (sacred brahmanical thread) upon fishermen and other low-caste Swadhyayees, a 'revolutionary' act befitting a charismatic personality, but considered blasphemous in the eyes of the orthodox.

Another crucial innovation is Swadhyaya's promotion of Sanskrit, making it accessible to hitherto marginalized sections of society, and thereby empowering them through a regenerated form of 'Sanskritization'. This forms part and parcel of Athavale's strategy to use canonic tradition as a source of cultural enrichment for the masses and by revitalizing it to turn it into, what he terms, 'a living faith' (LL: 51). A paradigmatic example is the introduction of the Sanskrit *trikal sandhaya* prayers into all Swadhyayee communities, whereby thanks are offered to God at morning, noon and night for waking, food and sleep—a Swadhyaya ritual serving as a constant reminder of the nearness of God, and with group prayers, sung in the well-known tradition of the *satsang*, instilling a new sense of community interconnectedness. As such, Swadhyaya could be interpreted to be functioning as a 'hinge' connecting popular religiosity to that of the scriptural traditions, not unlike many a religious reform movement of previous centuries.

VI

Despite Swadhyaya's emphasis on individual realization of the 'indwelling God', Athavale also stresses the need for temples, especially in rural areas, not only as places of worship but even more as centres of community life. Thereby his professed aim is to 'resurrect them to the status and glory they enjoyed in Vedic times' (*The Systems*: 125). Entitled *loknath amritalayam*, i.e. eternal abode (or literally, 'repository of divine nectar') of the lord of the people, these hut temples[27] are constructed in villages where at least 90 percent of the community are Swadhyayees, so that they may really serve as a socio-religious focus. As regards the central element of any temple, namely the deity, a few observations are called for: notwithstanding the belief in the spiritual *nirgun* form of divine immanence, Swadhyaya also insists on the *sagun upasana* (the worship of God with specific attributes),[28] and its chosen divinity is *Yogeshwar Krishna* (the lord of the yogins) of the *Bhagvad Gita*. For the purposes of religious ritual, a new set of images has been devised which consists of *Yogeshwar*, astride the globe with the *chakra* in his right hand and a conch in the left, accompanied by a novel adaptation depicting *Parvati* with baby *Ganesh* in her lap, along with *Shiva*, in a conventional meditative pose. *Parvati/Lakshmi* and *Ganesh*, harbingers of prosperity and good fortune in traditional Hinduism, have been enhanced here to symbolize the image of family love (a concept dear to Swadhyaya).[29] But even more intriguing is the unavoidable evocation (be it inadvertent) of a certainly more canonized trope of maternal love, namely that of the Virgin Mary with baby Jesus.[30] An element of innovatory revitalization is apparent, too, with regard to the temple priest: here, the role of *pujari* is performed *in turn* by each couple (i.e. husband

and wife) in the village for the duration of a week. This innovation is only partial for, as Athavale points out, marriage and the sacerdoce are not in contradiction according to canonic authority.[31] That the privileged sanctity of the sacerdotal office should be enjoyed actively by all conforms with the Swadhyaya belief in individual 'divineness', which, by this exercise in democratic religiosity, is to be rendered more explicit. At the same time, Swadhyaya's 'this-worldly' *grahastha* oriented philosophy (in line with the teachings of the *Gita*) is underscored (*The Systems*: 38).

To realize its function as a socio-religious centre,[32] the *amritalayam* serves as the location for morning and evening assemblies in which an hour of community prayers is followed by discussions about individual or community issues and problems. Voluntary collections[33] are made, the proceeds of which are distributed in part as *prasad* (and so free from the taste of 'charity' with its inferior-superior implications) to the needy of the village and the remainder is kept in a village fund to be used for community projects. All in all, these religio-cultural centres, initiated by Swadhyaya, aim to contribute to individual and community renewal, and thereby remain independent of state control.

VII

Apart from temple institutions, religious activities such as traditional regional festivals[34] and pilgrimages[35] have been similarly transformed with the goal of creating a spiritually and culturally revitalized 'brotherhood' (or *biradari*, to emphasize its indigenous embeddedness) where social and economic distinctions become superseded by religious aspirations. Above all, the ingenuity of Athavale's approach is exemplified in his keenness to experiment with new ideas, which he interprets as *participating* in God's divine and creative play (*lila*), thus dynamizing the conventionally passive relationship of man being considered a 'helpless puppet in the hands of the supernatural being' (LL: 10). Through Athavale's emphasis on this 'participatory' ludic force (intuitively grasping its appeal to the sensibilities of rural Indians), which is given free rein in numerous socio-religious experiments and innovations, Swadhyaya is seen as reinvigorating and rendering more meaningful religious tradition, thereby enriching not only it but also the lives of the participants.

In the following I shall describe in brief some of these *prayog* (experiments) among marginalized and peripheral groups in rural Gujarat[36] which, in the spirit of Swadhyaya, stress community participation as a revitalized form of *yajna*.[37] Here religiosity is expressed not through means of a vedic rite but through uniting to perform *shram-bhakti*—'the act of offering the best and the most useful in one for the welfare of others' (LL: 40)—in accordance with Krishna's rendering of *yajna* as 'self-dedication free from attachment' (*Bhagvad Gita, Karma Yoga* 9). Though the practical benefits are not a prominent concern in the 'theory' of Swadhyaya, they are no doubt a factor which enhances the attractiveness of these new ventures from the perspective of popular religiosity.

One of the most popular 'experiments' called *Yogeshwar krushi*, i.e. farming in the name of the Swadhyaya deity, is being practised, according to statistical data, in about four thousand villages (where 60 per cent of the population are Swadhyayees). To start with, a plot of three to five acres is rented or bought[38] by the village community and then cultivated by villagers taking turns in *shram bhakti* for a day or two about twice a year, and as God's labourers on the 'divine farm' they have the status of *pujaris*. The produce, naturally, belongs to God too, due to the devotional character of the labour. One-third of its income, termed *apaurusheya lakshmi* (i.e. impersonal wealth), is offered to indigent members of the community as *prasad* (as in the *amritalyam*), and the remaining two-thirds kept in a trust-fund called *madhavi raksha sankalp* (i.e. where the blessings or grace of *Lakshmi* are safeguarded), to be used for community needs.[39]

Apaurusheya lakshmi, one of the central concepts crucial to the functioning of these experiments, derives from Athavale's rendering of the *Isha Upanishad*'s initial query implying that all wealth belongs to God (Srivastava 1997: 41). Governed by the simple reasoning that if the production of wealth is divinely inspired, it follows (at least for charismatically endowed persons!) that its distribution and utilization should be equally determined by divine criteria. Another core element, i.e. *shram bhakti* (exemplifying the idiom 'work is worship') unites, according to Athavale's exegesis, two opposing human tendencies, namely *nivritti* (the renunciatory disposition) and *pravritti*, i.e. the desire to embrace the material world (42), to achieve both personal spiritual growth and community development, in the wider sense. The *leitmotif* of *kritibhakti* is further enhanced by lacing in another distinguished ideal, namely *nipunata* (i.e. excellence, expertise, efficiency), thereby exhorting the individual Swadhyayee in a revitalized manner to sustain 'divine' work by offering his 'skills' (interpreted as 'divine' gifts) for the welfare of the community (*The Systems*: 108).

In like manner, the lives of fishermen along the coast of Gujarat, Maharashtra and Goa have been affected. Previously impoverished and notorious for their alcoholism and smuggling activities, through contact with Swadhyaya these *sagarputra* have not only developed a new sense of pride in their inherited calling, but pooling together their earnings for one day in a fortnight (*ekadashi*) they were able to buy (or build) motorized boats which were named *Matsyagandha* (after the legendary fisherwoman, *Satyavati*, mother of *Vyas*). Treated as floating temples, these boats (now about sixty in number) are manned by a volunteer crew of six to ten from a pool of more than a million fishermen; this means that each individual fisherman (acting as a *pujari*) gets a chance to go on such a trip only once a year. The disbursement of the *apaureshya lakshmi* derived from the catch of the *Matsyagandha* follows the same scheme as with *Yogeshwar krushi*; just as an indication of the success, in mere monetary terms, of this Swadhyaya inspired venture, according to statistics over two million rupees are being distributed as *prasad* every year (Srivastava 1997: 32).

Yet another experiment called *vrikshamandir* (tree temples) testifies to Swadhyaya's reverence for the environment whereby canonic sayings[40] are shown to have contemporary ecological relevance. Starting with a tract of barren land, which is acquired by Swadhyayees from fifteen to twenty surrounding villages, rotating teams of 'pujaris' from these villages, by exercising *shrambhakti* a couple of times a year, transform this wasteland into 'divine orchards' or *upavan*, which are named after vedic sages. Creating an immense source of wealth (in accordance with the familiar scheme), the predominant aim of these *vrikshamandir* projects is to bring together economic and social unequals into the Swadhyaya *biradari* for their spiritual, cultural and socio-economic well being. Likewise with another experiment called *shreedarshanam* (i.e. a vision of prosperity); allegedly inspired by Lao Tse's concept of one 'completely self-sufficient village', Athavale's 'visionary' project 'aims at self-reliant villages which can have a relation of affinity with other villages'. (Srivastava 1997: 60). Representing an extended version of *Yogheshwar krushi*, it is a single large farm of about twenty acres or more on which Swadhyayees from about twenty villages come together to work. Fostering a feeling of inter-village community, this experiment inevitably recalls to mind Gandhi's seemingly utopian vision of 'oceanic circles of villages'.

These and numerous other Swadhyaya activities,[41] provide a new taxonomy of socio-cultural and economic living which aims to enhance not only community co-existence, but also the autonomy, initiative and enterprise of local groups. By reconstructing sacred space through reference to canonic authority, the strength of religious practice and belief is heightened. Yet these experiments do not only constitute 'corporate symbols of the workings of divinity' (according to the Swadhyaya idiom), but, more prosaically speaking, they link up with the socio-cultural equipment of rural India, i.e. that of control over land, labour and patronage, thereby bringing about a reordering of contemporary structures. Last but not least, despite the fact that Swadhyaya explicitly avoids any formal political involvement, its very influence does inevitably have a political dimension, in as far as it regenerates an alternative form of polity through 'spontaneous rooted-in-culture' and 'problem solving mechanisms' (Srivastava 1997: 15), totally independent of the established bureaucratic and administrative framework.[42]

VIII

Aspiring to larger transformations by reinstating religion in revitalized forms, and by replacing ritualized religious practice with 'inspired' actions, Athavale, through the medium of Swadhyaya, exemplifies not only the socio-cultural significance of charismatic authority but also discloses its revolutionary potential. His very reference to canonic tradition, I would proffer, serving both as a source of legitimation as well as of enrichment, diffuses the inherent disruptive tendencies and instead transforms charisma into a regenerative force.

Before concluding this overview, a few observations should be made regarding the mechanisms involved in institutionalizing Athavale's charismatic authority: firstly, in refusing to be called a guru, he appears to be playing down the traditional tendency to idolize, and prefers the less referential label *dada* (elder brother). So, in conformity with the Swadhyaya leitmotif that encourages individual efforts at realizing one's innate divinity, he would tend to see himself as *primus inter pares* in the extended family of devotees. Yet, over the years, though he would continue to see himself as a *bhakta*, his charismatic authority has been considerably 'elevated', no doubt also through the agency of his enthusiastic devotees. For instance, by naming the dais from which he delivers his *pravachans*[43] the *Vyaspith* (after Vyas, the vedic sage, par excellence), his imputed charisma is greatly enhanced by linking it with an established canon of interpretation. Further, his charismatic aura is considered intense enough for his own birthday to be celebrated on a grand scale as 'Human Dignity Day'—a celebration that connects Athavale's person to the *conditio humana*, thus underscoring the universalist dimension of charisma. This, again, has very recently been exemplified by Athavale's nomination for two prestigious distinctions, namely the Magyaysay (1996) and Templeton (1997) awards, lending him international recognition and 'institutionalizing' his charisma in the eyes of his followers. Albeit, to critical observers, his acceptance of such 'worldy honours' detracts from the quality of renunciatory holiness associated with a 'purist' interpretation of charisma.[44]

Needless to say, in the twentieth century, the power, reach and accessibility of charisma could be magnified by using modern media which, given the 'this-worldly' orientation of the movement, are by no means shunned by Swadhyayees, as is evident from the systematized use of video technology[45] to multiply Athavale's presence and message *ad infinitum*. Rather than condemn this celluloid projection as a 'desacralization' of religious experience, I would be inclined to acknowledge this innovatory device as testifying not only to the adaptability of so-called 'traditional' praxis and contexts, but also to the inherent malleability and transformative nature of religious phenomena (not only in the Indian sphere!). What's more, the videotaped transmission of charismatic *Dadaji* to Swadhyayee village communities (or as far afield as Chicago suburbs) is likened to the multiformity of *Krishna*'s divine apparition to the *gopis*[46]—a 'canonical' archetype for the *bhakta* of the media age! Tantamount to a reconstitution of the sacred, Athavale's charismatic authority is, in the process, almost inevitably being institutionalized.[47] Yet to employ the Weberian term 'bureaucratization' seems inappropriate, for *Dada*, the enraptured *bhakta* as a 'magician of orality'[48] (presiding *in persona* or projected on a screen) continues to charismatically enthral his audience, be it based in the East or the West.[49]

In summa: Acting as a catalyst, in initiating a process of religious regeneration under the auspices of the Swadhyaya *stream*, Athavale could be seen as revitalizing Weber's 'enchanted' universe,[50] endowing it with cultural meaning and the strength of human agency to enact transformations that could have far-reaching consequences.

Notes

1. Having very recently (in September 1997) had the opportunity to witness at first hand the impact of Swadhyaya in rural and urban Gujarat, this 'narrative' is based primarily on field notes, oral information, documentary and statistical material (supplied very generously by Shri Mahesh Shah, Shri Rajiv Vora, Shri Baldev Mehra and Dr. Raj Srivastava, research fellow at the Centre for the Study of Developing Societies, Delhi), published transcripts of speeches (see note 7), and on the proof-copy of a book on Swadhyaya, edited by R. K. Srivastava (1997).
2. Cf. Rahnema (1990: 19–27).
3. Cf. also the concise definition of 'charisma' in *The International Encyclopedia of Sociology* (1984: 38).
4. This is in line with the 'authorized' elucidation by Edward Shils (1968).
5. For an enlightening discussion regarding the use of 'canon' in comparative religion, see Sheppard (1987).
6. This is in partial juxtaposition to the thesis presented by Arjun Appadurai (1981: 201–19), who disputes that the past is an infinite and plastic symbolic

resource; instead it is argued that there exists a culturally variable set of norms whose function is to regulate the inherent *debatability* of the past.

7. Cf. Srivastava (1997: 11).
8. Gleaned from the documentation of the *Sat Vichar Darshan*, Swadhyaya's own publishing 'trust' in Bombay; the books and pamphlets quoted from (with the respective abbreviations employed) are as follows: *The Systems* (1996), *Hope of Humanity* (HH; 1997)—both anonymous publications on Swadhyaya, containing extended extracts from Athavale's speeches—*Light that Leads* (LL; 1991), *Eternal Ecstasy* (EE; 1996), *Dawn of Divinity* (DD; 1997) (published transcripts of Athavale's speeches, delivered on lecture tours to the United States).
9. Athavale's refusal of academic posts in America as well as of financial assistance from Radhakrishnan, then vice-president, is emphasized by his disciples as testifying to renunciation, moral integrity and singular dedication, defining traits which contribute towards the projection of an aura of purity and holiness and which are conducive to the concomitant building up of a charismatic personality.
10. Entitled the *Shrimad Bhagvad Gita Pathshala*, it is 'a seat of non-formal learning in vedic thought.' (Srivastava 1997: 18)
11. To a Westernized audience, Athavale preaches (not unlike fervent German pietists of the late seventeenth and early eighteenth centuries): 'Do not keep God in heaven. Do not keep God in temples and churches. Bring God with you.' (*The Systems*: 6).
12. In particular 'the chapters on Vibhutiyoga and Vishvarupdarshan make the Bhakta a really God-integrated personality' (EE: 21); Athavale is referring to the following verse: 'I am the Self, O Gudakesa, seated in the hearts of all beings. I am the beginning, the middle and also the end of all beings.' *Bhagvad Gita*, *Vibhuti Yoga*, 20.
13. '*Asmita* or ego-consciousness also means the awareness that "I am great, but the other person is not small or lowly".' (*The Systems*: 16).
14. 'When we look around, we find that a noble concept like bhakti is misinterpreted. (...) The devotees (...) have now become lethargic. (...) They forget that God does not work *for* them, He works *with* them. Bhakti (...) must instil in a person tremendous self-confidence and generate in him the confidence that he can do and achieve the seemingly impossible.' (HH: 33) Or more succinctly: 'The approach of devotion is the approach of love to a personal God. Its foundation is faith, and the response it gets is "grace".' (EE: 25).
15. Srivastava (1997: 9). Whereas this is said with specific reference to Swadhyaya, I would maintain that the commonality between Gandhi and Athavale, at least with regard to their goal (a fact that has been largely overlooked in Swadhyaya literature), is of the essence, and that, in this respect, Athavale is following in Gandhi's footsteps. A detailed study would be necessary to do justice to this topic.
16. Here, a few words of clarification will also highlight Athavale's revitalizing

and transformatory approach: according to his exposition the traditional Hindu practice of keeping a fast on the eleventh day of each lunar fortnight (*ekadashi*) derives from the fact that on this particular day the eleven elements (i.e. the sum of the five sense organs, five motor organs and the mind) of an individual's make-up are to be offered to God. But whereas fasting traditionally means withdrawing the senses from worldly objects (i.e. by non-feeding) and focusing them on God, Athavale, seeing 'no spiritual purpose in starving the body when the mind feasts on the pleasures of the world' (*The Systems*: 30), suggests an alternative reading: hereby he interprets *upvas* (fast), as 'time to sit near God' (from *up* near and *vas* sit or reside), and propounds that the best way to experience God and to be near him is through performing His work (Srivastava 1997: 54, n16).

17. I am indebted to Mahesh Shah for this explanation.
18. This corresponds very closely to the defining traits of a 'charismatic personality' as elaborated in Shils' article (1968: 387).
19. Figures supplied by Mahesh Shah and corroborated by Raj Srivastava (Srivastava 1997: 13). Other sources estimate the number of Swadhyayees to be more than 30 million. Needless to say, given the absence of formal criteria in Swadhyaya, numbers as such have only relative significance.
20. This corresponds to similar reflections made by Oberoi (1994: 22f.).
21. A full-scale investigation of the socio-cultural background of the 'regenerated' communities needs to be undertaken.
22. 'Self-respect is the spinal cord of human existence and we have lost it.' *Dada's Vision* in Srivastava (1997: 56).
23. Swadhyaya's activity includes developing intimate personal contact with the inhabitants of the *chawls* or poorest slum areas, and has so far brought about radical socio-cultural and economic changes in about one-fourth of all slums in Ahmedabad.
24. Srivastava (1997: 22, 39) where more examples are also cited.
25. Athavale could be seen as acting as a spokesman for these communities, in endeavouring to give voice to their own cherished myths, which itself would account for his effectivity. To investigate the validity of this supposition (i.e. regarding Athavale unlocking underlying knowledge) ethnological work needs to be undertaken on the micro-level cultural histories of these communities, for instance, taking into consideration their *jati puranas*.
26. For an elaboration on the regeneration of the 'true Brahmin' see *The Systems:* 34–6.
27. Built of rural materials such as bamboo, leaves and grass, this impermanent structure is purposefully chosen, since it requires constant care by the devotees and thus serves as a concrete object of *shram-bhakti* or devotional labour, an important ingredient of Swadhyaya activities.
28. Srivastava (1997: 26). On the 'rationale' behind *murtipuja* Athavale has elaborated at length, cf. LL: 18–24; *The Systems*: 26ff.
29. Cf. also the contribution by Daniel Gold (1997: 176–90, esp. 187).
30. This symbolic parallel needs to be investigated further. In another instance,

this kind of 'religious re-aggregation' could be taken to task as manipulation of the sacred: Athavale's including Mohammed and Christ as the eleventh and twelfth *avatars* of Vishnu, judged by some as being tantamount to 'scholastic trickery', has been criticized for 'outstretching' Swadhyaya's universalistic creed ('we're all children of one God') and thereby underestimating the cultural specificity of religious sensibilities not only of Christians and Muslims but also of Hindus.

31. 'A priest who worships God need not renounce his family, his work and his duties. The ancient sages were householders; and yet they could devote themselves wholeheartedly to the service of God and Vedic culture. Why not we—their descendants follow the same path?' (*The Systems*: 111). Further, it is interesting to note that this 'vedic' practice is still in vogue in the Chidambaram temple, it being believed that marriage sanctifies the priestly office. Could Athavale be restoring a practice that was more generally pervasive and more recently than in vedic times?
32. It was emphasized by the Swadhyayees I interviewed that Muslim and Christian rural inhabitants are welcomed in these centres, but that no explicit attempts are made to proselytize them. According to oral testimony, villages affected by Swadhyaya exhibit a high degree of communal harmony, even when riots erupt in surrounding areas.
33. These are legitimated by interpreting Krishna's injunction to Arjun in the *Sraddhatraya vibhaga yoga* vs. 20 and transposing it into the 'modernist' idiom of Swadhyaya as follows: since God is one's 'working partner', one owes a part of one's earnings 'as a sign of gratitude to God' (*The Systems*: 127).
34. For details, cf. *The Systems* (141ff).
35. In November 1979, 3000 Swadhyayees went on pilgrimage (visiting 1300 villages en route) to Kurukshetra (battlefield of the *Mahabharat* and location for the *Bhagvad Gita*)—a canonic spatial reference for Swadhyaya. (*The Systems*: 43).
36. Participating recently in a *prayog-darshan* (the Swadhyaya term for a 'guided tour' of the 'experiments') I was able to observe at first hand a number of these 'co-operative' community activities in the rural areas of Western Gujarat.
37. The following is Athavale's interpretation: 'The word *yajna* comes from the root verb *yaj* which means to worship, to unite. When people get together to perform a *yajna*, they reaffirm their faith in God and devotion to Him. Their coming together strengthens a feeling of unity and friendship.' (*The Systems*: 31).
38. Ideally this should be a joint venture to foster community self-reliance.
39. Srivastava (1997: 30). On the management of this 'divine' fund I have no concrete details, but it is supposed to be administered fairly in accordance with the Swadhyaya 'family ethos'.
40. Cf. Athavale's reference to the 'instructions of the ancient sages to see God in plants and trees.' (*The Systems*: 95f.).
41. Besides farming, fishery and forestry they also include irrigation projects

(innovating or rediscovering traditional techniques of water harvesting *nirmal neer* and conservation *bhugarbh jal sanchay*), co-operative *parivar* dairy farming, trading (*parivar* stores), rural medical clinics (*patanjali chikitsalaya*), educational and cultural centres for women and children (*mahila kendra*, *bal samskar kendra*) and an institute of Higher Learning in Philosophy and the Humanities (*Tattvajnana Vidyapith*) in Thane, near Bombay.

42. To what extent this regenerated polity derives inspiration from traditional (or regional) forms of political organization needs to be investigated.
43. These 'religious discourses', held for one hour every Sunday at the Bombay *Pathshala* to an audience numbering several thousands, represent 'dialogic narratives' (in the Bakhtinian sense): elucidating a couple of *shlokas* from a canonic text by means of cultural retellings, Athavale's indigenous exegesis is interspersed with references to Western 'authorities' (such as Marx, Freud, Russell etc.) to lend additional significance to the substance of his talks by endowing them with a measure of universalist contemporaneity. In line with canonic tradition which holds 'inspired orality' in high esteem, Athavale's expositions are contained exclusively in his *pravachans*, for, it is maintained, he does not use the written form. For more details, cf. Little (1997: 268ff.).
44. The discrepancy between these differing perspectives underlines the fact that the attribution of charisma is also a relational experience, depending on the responsiveness in the beholder to signs of 'greatness'.
45. Cf. Little (1997: 254–83) which obviates the need for me to discuss this innovation in detail.
46. An appealing comparison made by a Swadhyayee in Bombay, and also mentioned by Little (1997: 280).
47. Considerable attention has been paid of late to 'grooming' a suitable successor, namely *Didi*, Athavale's adopted daughter.
48. Rahnema's (1990: 25) poetic coinage.
49. To a gathering in America he concluded one of his lectures by exclaiming: 'I behold the Geeta as a love letter, and I lose myself in it.' (EE: 30).
50. Inspired by Oberoi's (1994: 139ff.) usage, this term is being employed metaphorically in connection with the notion of 'dispersed charisma'.

References

Appadurai, A. 1981. The Past as a Scarce Resource. *Man* 16 n.s.: 201–19.

Frédéric, Louis. 1987. *Dictionnaire de la civilisation indienne*. Paris: Robert Lafont.

Gold, D. 1997. Swadhyaya Parivar: Contemporary Religious Community in the Image of the Traditional Family. In *Vital Connections. Self, Society, God*, ed. R. K. Srivastava, 176–90. New York: Inside-Out Corporation.

Little, J. T. 1997. Video Vacana: Swadhyaya and Sacred Tapes. In *Media and the Transformation of Religion in South Asia*, ed. Lawrence A. Babb and Susan S. Wadley, 254–83. Philadelphia: University of Pennsylvania Press.

Oberoi, H. 1994. *The Construction of Religious Boundaries. Culture, Identity and Diversity in the Sikh Tradition*. Delhi: Oxford University Press.

Rahnema, M. 1990. Swadhyaya: The Unknown, the Peaceful, the Silent yet Singing Revolution of India. *IFDA Dossier* 75/76: 19–34.

Sheppard, G. T. 1987. Canon. In *The Encyclopedia of Religion*, ed. Mircea Eliade, vol. 3: 62–9. New York: Macmillan.

Shils, E. 1968. Charisma. In *The International Encyclopedia of the Social Sciences*, ed. David Sils, vol. 2: 386–90. New York: Macmillan.

Srivastava, R. K. (ed.). 1997. *Vital Connections. Self, Society, God*. New York: Inside-Out Corporation.

Weber, M. 1922/1956. *Wirtschaft und Gesellschaft: Grundriß der verstehenden Soziologie*. 4th ed. 2 vols. Tübingen: Mohr.

Swadhyaya literature

Anon. 1995. *Experiments Conducted Under the Aegis of Swadhyaya*. Statistical Information, Typescript Presentation at the Workshop on Hunger and Poverty, Brussels, 16–18 November.

Anon. 1996. *The Systems*. Bombay: Sat Vichar Darshan.

Anon. 1997. *Hope of Humanity*. Bombay: Sat Vichar Darshan.

Transcripts of lectures by Pandurang 'Shastri' Athavale

1991. *Light that Leads*. Bombay: Sat Vichar Darshan.

1996. *Eternal Ecstasy*. Bombay: Sat Vichar Darshan.

1997. *Dawn of Divinity*. Bombay: Sat Vichar Darshan.

The Advent of the Avatar: The Urban Following of Sathya Sai Baba and its Construction of Tradition*

SMRITI SRINIVAS

The cult of Sathya Sai Baba (b. 1926)is unrivalled among modern South Asian religious movements in terms of its spread across Asia, the sheer visibility and social prominence of many of the devotees, and the well-established nature of its cult organization. What is surprising, however, is the paucity of sociological literature on this cult. Most of the available writing consists of collections of speeches given by Sathya Sai Baba on various occasions and the official publications of the organization, or is hagiographical. One of the few ethnographic studies is the work of Lawrence Babb (1986); his thesis is that the cult has a largely urban or middle-class following which suffers from alienation, a certain biculturalism, and loss of meaning of traditional value systems, creating an investment in the charisma of Baba. He focuses on miracles as central to the cult which make the world of the devotee somewhat like 'an enchanted garden'. My article, instead, examines specific institutions and processes of the cult and its urban constituency as deploying a set of representations about tradition, modernity and charisma. It is part of work in progress on different aspects of the Sai Baba movement.[1]

I would like to preface this paper with certain theoretical observations: the distinction between the renouncer and such roles as the householder, the king, and the priest is familiar to most scholars of religion in India. This distinction is, in part, based on the relationship between the three 'worldly' ends of life (*dharma*, *artha*, and *kama*) and the fourth goal, liberation (*moksha*). For some, as Louis Dumont (1960 and 1962), the

* I am deeply indebted to V. Geetha, Meena Kaushik and Srilata Raman for their comments on this article.

elementary triad of religion in India is the brahmin, the king and the *sannyasi*, Hinduism being based both on the system of caste and its renunciation. It has also been suggested (Uberoi 1994) that the culture of medieval India displayed a parallelism between the structure of Hinduism (the priest/brahmin, the king and the renouncer) and that of Islam (the sufi, the sultan and the ulema). Sathya Sai Baba falls into the category of the renouncer—whether we derive this from the ancient or the medieval period. An understanding of his charisma *vis-à-vis* his following depends on how he has restructured the relations between other social roles. First, among his devotees Baba as renouncer is seen as the source of a new social order that is contrasted with the system of caste. The householder and the student—who completes his or her life-cycle by entering the institution of marriage within which the householder is implicated—are the focus of his charisma, but renunciation is largely abjured for them and is replaced with the activity of service. Second, the role of the priest or religious functionary, and the place of worship as a separate institutional-legal locus, are integrated into the householder's domain through the practices of neighbourhood devotion in which women too play a significant part.

The issue is also how these roles and categories are constrained and fashioned anew by the institutions of modern India, such as the state, which may be, in many ways, inadequate in dealing with charisma, or simply based on a different kind of rationality. Thus, the cult of Shirdi Sai Baba in nineteenth-century Maharashtra was very much part of the climate of the colonial transformation of India. Sathya Sai Baba poses before his constituency many of the same questions as the other Baba, but the cult derives its solutions differently. There is here not only the role of the renouncer *vis-à-vis* the canon, but also independent India's icons—sovereignity, science, democracy, and so on. In terms of historical time, a mere hundred years or so have passed between the two Babas, but in terms of symbolic time the architectonics of representation reveal that the passage from regional to national history has an insistent legitimacy of its own. What we are now witness to is the birth of a number of social classes associated with the new regime—scientists, lawyers, doctors, engineers, teachers, and so on, both in the field of civil society and the state—and their involvement in a range of new religious movements.

This article deals with these issues; it is divided into three sections. The first section deals with the different elements of the representation of Sathya Sai Baba's persona. The second outlines the structure of knowledge within which his charisma and his urban following are situated, and the millenarian vision of the latter. The third section contains concluding remarks.

The Representation of Sathya Sai Baba

Two groups form the most vocal and visible constituency of the cult: non-Indian devotees and Indians of the diaspora, and urban middle-class and upper-class Indian nationals. The latter group of Indian devotees, of which there is no possible numerical estimate, is the focus of this paper. It is estimated, however, that over 1,000,000 people gathered in his ashram for the celebration of Baba's seventeeth birthday alone.

Two recurring motifs appear in representations about him by urban devotees; here I use some of the literature on Baba produced by these devotees rather than, for the time being, his own works.[2] The first motif is that Sathya Sai Baba is the incarnation of Shirdi Sai Baba, a Maharashtrian saint (d. 1918) who was often compared to Kabir. Although I cannot discuss this in detail here, the relationship of Shirdi Sai Baba to certain Sufi orders in Maharashtra and Bijapur in Karnataka (especially the Chisti) has been speculated about (Rigopoulos 1993; Shepherd 1985). Many of his practices link him to the Nathpanthi order (White 1972). It is possible to show that the structure of worship at Shirdi is based on that of Pandharpur and has connections with the Maharashtrian Bhakti tradition that popularized this centre and Krishna worship in the region.[3]

The second motif is that Sathya Sai Baba is an avatar who has come to usher in the golden period of righteousness in this benighted dark age. Both motifs owe themselves to events and declarations in Baba's life.

Sathya Sai Baba was born on 23 November 1926, in Puttaparthi village (Anantapur district, Andhra Pradesh) as Sathya Narayana Raju to a landed family apparently known for their piety as well as for their musical and dramatic involvement in the village. At the turn of the century the village had about 200 houses and was situated near the Chitravati river, the region being a drought-prone, dry-land area. Sathya seems to have had a fairly ordinary childhood, although biographers and oral accounts claim a number of mysterious events at the time of his birth (such as musical instruments playing at night and the appearance of a cobra near his cradle) and during his school-years (such as his ability to materialize various objects). At the age of 14, on 23 May 1940, after a prolonged period of 'illness' (when he exhibited strange and erratic behaviour which the family thought was a sign of possession), Sathya declared: 'I belong to Apasthamba Suthra; I am of the Bharadwaja Gothra; I am Sai Baba.' (Kasturi 1968, 1: 43) A few months later, in October, he cast off his schoolbooks and said he was no longer the Sathya they knew, but Sai: 'I am going; I don't belong to you; Maya has gone; My Bhaktas are calling Me; I have My work; I can't stay any longer.' (47) He lived in the house of a Brahmin woman, Subbamma, till about 1950, when the construction of a separate ashram was completed. This house belonged to the 'Karanam', a liason officer between the government and a cluster of villages. In the interim, he continued to perform miracles, grant boons, give visions to various devotees who were beginning to pour in, and visit, occasionally, some towns and cities in south India. A second ashram came up subsequently in Whitefield near Bangalore called 'Brindavan', and a third summer ashram in the hill-station of Ootacamund. Baba also maintains residences at Hyderabad, Madras, and Bombay. Four festivals have been celebrated at the ashrams since the early years: Baba's birthday, Sivaratri, Guru Poornima and Dasara. Today, a whole host of others, such as his mother's birthday, Christmas, Onam, the Tamil and Kannada new-year festivals, Rama Navami, and so on have been added to the list and the form of many of the older festivals has also changed.

In 1957, Baba left on a north-Indian tour to visit temples and sites in Delhi, Rishikesh, Mathura, Srinagar, and other places. This marks a watershed in his career for after this year his public role came to be voiced more explicitly. In 1958, the *Sanathana Sarathi*, 'devoted to the moral and spiritual upliftment of humanity through Sathya, Dharma, Santhi and Prema', was inaugurated. This was brought out at first in Telugu and is now published in over eleven languages, including English. On the first day of the Dasara festival held in 1961, he declared: 'Rama was the embodiment of Sathya and Dharma; Krishna of Santhi and Prema. Now, when skill is outstripping self-control, when Science laughs at Sadhana, when hate and fear have darkened the heart of man, I have come to embody all the four – Sathya, Dharma, Santhi, and Prema.' (Gokak 1983: 304)

At his birthday celebrations the same year, his official biography written by N. Kasturi (*Sathyam, Sivam, Sundaram*) was inaugurated. On Guru Poornima day in 1963 he announced: 'I am Siva-Sakthi born in the Gothra of Bharadwaja according to a boon won by that Sage from Siva and Sakthi. Sakthi herself was born of the Gothra of that Sage as Sai Baba of Shirdi; Siva and Sakthi have incarnated as myself in his Gothra now; Siva alone will incarnate as the third Sai in the same Gothra in Mysore state.' (305) On Rama Navami day in 1964 he announced the establishment of an all-India academy of Vedic scholars. This was inaugurated the following year on his birthday as the 'Sathya Sai Veda-Sasthra Patasala', when he also declared that he had four missions: fostering the Vedas (*vedaposhana*), fostering of learning (*vidwatposhana*), protecting devotees (*bhaktarakshana*), and protecting dharma (*dharmarakshana*).

1967–8 signalled a movement to the pan-Indian and even international role of Baba and the beginnings of a cult organization. The First All-India Conference of Sai Seva Organizations was held in Madras in 1967. At the First World Conference of Sathya Sai Seva Organizations at Bombay in 1968, after inaugurating the centre of the World Council of Sai Organizations in Bombay called 'Dharmakshetra', Baba announced that he was the avatar of Sai and had come to establish dharma:[4]

At the present time, strife and discord have robbed peace and unity from the family, the school, the community, the society, villages, the cities and the State ... I have come to correct the 'Buddhi'—the intelligence—by various means. I have to counsel, help, command, condemn and stand by as a friend and well-wisher to all, so that they may give up their evil propensities and recognising the straight path, tread it and reach the goal. I have to reveal to the people, the worth of the Vedas, the Shastras and other spiritual texts, which lay down the norms ... Continue your worship of your chosen God along the lines already familiar to you. Then you will find that you are coming nearer and nearer to Me, for all names are Mine and all forms are Mine ... many hesitate to believe that things will improve, that life will be happy for all and full of joy and that the golden age will recur. Let Me assure you that this Dharmaswarupa—this Divine body—has not come in vain. It will succeed in warding off the crisis that has come upon humanity (Sathya Sai Baba 1976: 23–9).

In June the same year, he left for a tour of East Africa, his first and only foreign visit so far. 1968 was important in other ways too. He established the Sri Sathya Sai Arts and Science College for Women in Anantapur; a similar institution came up in 1969 for men in Brindavan near Bangalore. The 'Summer Courses in Indian Culture and Spirituality' for college students began in 1972. Baba's discourses during these courses are published in *Summer Showers in Brindavan*. In 1981, the 'Sri Sathya Sai Institute of Higher Learning', deemed a university, was set up. In recent years, two super-speciality hospitals have been established, one in Puttaparthi set up in 1990–1, called the 'Sri Sathya Sai Institute of Higher Medical Sciences' and another in Bangalore to be inaugurated in 2000. One of the most ambitious of Baba's new projects provides drinking water for the entire Anantapur district in Andhra Pradesh covering 751 villages and 11 towns completed after only a year's work in 1996.

In the fifty years since the declaration of his identity, the Puttaparthi area has changed radically. A small hamlet earlier, it was declared a taluk headquarters of the Sri Sathya Sai Taluk in 1991 carved out of Penukonda taluk in 1980. In 1981, the new taluk had a population of about 101,500. Since 1991 it has an airport as well. The Sri Sathya Sai Central Trust owns the entire area of the township-ashram of Prasanthi Nilayam at Puttaparthi.[5]

The growth of Puttaparthi into a miniature city with international links after the mid-1960s parallels three phases in the representation of Baba's persona. The first phase stretches from 1940 to 1960, when he declared on various occasions that he was Sai Baba of Shirdi reborn. Then there is an intermediate phase till 1968 when there is a suggestion of his avatar-hood but chiefly as an avatar of Siva and Sakhi. At the first world conference in 1968 came the explicit declaration that he was an avatar who had come to restore dharma for all humanity. The two giant architectural symbols of this latter period of avatar-hood are the arch at the entrance of the temple at Prasanthi Nilayam and the 'Sarva Mathaikya Stupa', also known as the 'Sarva Dharma Stupa'. The pillars of the arch have statuettes of the ten avatars of Vishnu, the tenth depicting the future Kalki avatar seated on a white horse. The second is an enormous pillar between the temple and an auditorium designed to hold a lotus on its peak; its base is made up of five sides with five symbols—the Om, the cross, the crescent, the wheel of dharma, and the sacred fire.

Both representations of Baba—as Shirdi Sai reborn and as avatar—have significant features. There are continuities: certain symbols within the cult of Shirdi Sai Baba, for instance the use of sacred ash, the festivals celebrated by him, his role as a healer, his attempt to mediate between two or more religions, are also features of the cult of Sathya Sai Baba. The paradigm of avatarhood presents some unique characteristics. Not only has Baba explicitly declared that he is an incarnation of Siva-Sakti but also, in the cult of Sathya Sai Baba, differentiation is made between previous avatars and the present incarnation in terms of the possession of certain attributes of divinity—of which there are sixteen. It is claimed that only Krishna was an integral avatar (*purnavatar*) like Baba (Gokak 1983: 15). It is precisely for this reason that it is difficult to unambiguously state that Baba's dominant identity is with Siva, as has been done by other scholars (Babb 1986; Swallow 1982). The symbolism of the cult spills over onto other images. It is as if a neo-epic is being written: the little village of Puttaparthi and the environs of Penukonda are a Brindavan of the new *purnavatar*. Brindavan is also the name of the ashram at Bangalore in which stands a giant statue of Venugopal, the youthful Krishna with the flute. With the Dharmakshetra declaration in Bombay that Sathya Sai Baba had come to establish 'Sanatana Dharma', Puttaparthi became the site of 'Prasanthi Nilayam', the 'Abode of Eternal Peace'. The Sarva Dharma Stupa effectively symbolizes the movement in the writing of this epic story from Shirdi and a regional tradition of devotion to an international ashram. This internationalism is not a medieval syncretism but a theosophical universalism. Baba himself has constructed his life in terms of three time periods: the first sixteen years of his life is a period of childhood miracles (*bala leelas*); the second period is one where divine miracles (*mahimas*) dominate; after his thirty-second year, Baba states that his task is preaching (*upadesa*) and guiding humanity back into Sanatana Dharma. It is as if the whole nation and even the globe are sites of this epic journey in time and space. During his birthday celebrations, for instance, Baba's chariot is drawn by one or more white horses and many devotees regard him as the Kalki-avatar of the new millennium.

The central issue is not so much what kind of tradition (Saivite, Vaishnavite or any other) he represents, but that the idea of Baba as avatar and the construction of Shirdi Baba posthumously as one as well signals a shift in the parameters of society after the passing away of Shirdi Baba. If the previous cult had largely participated in regional traditions of worship and depended on the presence and power of a living saint, after 1918 new figures were needed to represent the vast terrain created by print media, the railways, bureaucracy, and urban centres. The role of a local saint had to be replaced by that of a global avatar. This replacement occurred through a series of redefinitions of categories of place, time, knowledge and ritual processes. Thus, sacred spaces were created out of Puttaparthi, Bangalore and Ootacamund— a dry land agricultural area, a 'science city', and an ex-colonial hill-station. The ritual calendar of the cult was, in many ways, reminiscent of the avowedly 'secular' Indian state. Not only was the nature of piety and faith redefined (as, for instance, in the creation of *Sanathana Sarathi* and in the declarations between 1961–8), but so was the structure of knowledge through the establishment of many institutions of pedagogy and science. This charisma has, thus, what sometimes appear to be distinctly unlikely and novel co-ordinates.

The Transformation of Civil Society

The representation of Baba as an avatar and restorer of dharma in the age of Kali is linked to three sets of institutions and programmes. The first of such programmes and institutions are the Sathya Sai service organizations set up in various states and districts in India and other countries. The second set of programmes are pedagogic in nature, beginning with the first colleges set up in the 1960s, the Summer Course, and so on. Although a hospital was built by Baba at Puttaparthi in 1957, the Sri Sathya Sai Institute of Higher Medical Sciences set up in 1991 replaces the old centre. This is not to say that these are the only programmes at work, but each of these illustrates some special feature of the cult's world-view.

Although these institutions base their rationale on Baba's general philosophy and aims—the establishment of four goals, *sathya*, *dharma*, *shanti* and *prema*, (a different quartet of ends from *dharma*, *artha*, *kama* and *moksha*)—the workings of these programmes appear to be geared to a transformation of civil society, science, religion, and the nation, with the middle-class being largely the agent of transformation. I will examine, in the section below, how these transformations are mapped: first, between civil society and science through the medical institute; and second, between civil society and religion through the service organizations. The third, the mapping between civil society and the nation through pedagogy, I will deal with in the concluding section of this paper.

The Relation between Science and Society

Prasanthi Gram is a township developing around the nucleus of a hospital, the Sri Sathya Sai Institute of Higher Medical Sciences (SSSIHMS). The full significance of such an institution in medical super-specialities in India can be fully appreciated when we recognize that, in this country, only two other such institutions exist on the same scale. One is an outcome of Protestant piety started in Vellore in Tamil Nadu in the early years of this century by Ida Scudder, whose father was an American missionary. The other, planned half a century later, the All-India Institute of Medical Sciences at Delhi, is a symbol of national pride.

The SSSIHMS has the latest medical facilities. Doctors at the hospital have been trained all over the world and their services are voluntary, as is the service of the other staff. The hospital functions on a principle of service, is intended for the disempowered and economically backward, and all treatment, in-patient and out-patient, is free. Its philosophy is based on two premises—cure and care—and makes a distinction between art and science, the practice of modern medicine in treating the disease and the attitude of service towards the patient. This brings us, in a sense, to the structure of dualisms that the institutions of the movement and the world of the devotees are embedded in. A publication of a study group set up by the Sathya Sai Trust in Bombay in 1983 entitled *Spirituality and Science* (1985) examines both the accomplishments and failures of modern science and its compatibility with spirituality.[6] A major part of the analysis is based on a distinction between pure science and technology. It states that the responsibility for the ills of modern science is the use to which its products have been put at the hands of technologists. Further, modern science born in the West has upheld the material world as the ultimate reality and reason and sense perception as the only dependable faculties in man to seek truth. While this has resulted in a mechanistic universe, a similar philosophy of pragmatism in religion has had the beneficial effect of reform and resulted in a historical trend towards the rationalization of religion.

'This reform also stimulated a realistic study of scriptures and epics to find out the bearing of their symbolic and esoteric message, the ethical and cultural bases common to all world religions which reveal the unity of these faiths, and so on.' (Spirituality and Science 1985: 11) The report states that the birth of a cosmopolitan faith will bring to modern society the essential truths of all religions. However, what is necessary is that science, which has largely ignored Man's total being, finds a meeting point, a complementarity, and even an interpenetration with spiritual tenets. 'Spirituality, the central point on which all World Religions converge, is also the meeting point of Science, inasmuch as both have the common objective of search of Ultimate Reality.' (23)

It argues that whereas science approaches reality from an external point of view, spirituality approaches it from the point of Man's inner being. The report tries to show the correspondences between Vedic truths, yoga, non-mainstream philosophies of science, and modern scientific theories.

Despite the attempt to achieve some level of theoretical correspondence between modern science and spirituality, this analysis reproduces a structure of dualisms that, in fact, underlies the structure of modernity. First, it creates monolithic constructs of the domains of science and religion writing a linear history for both. Second, science is believed to be that which excludes magic and art or at least to have evolved from them to a higher level of understanding, while religion is believed to be the domain of mysticism and the symbolic. Third, not only does this view produce a separation of spheres, it also posits that for every pure discipline there is an applied technique. Fourth, exclusions of various kinds operate: the ills of one domain, superstition in religion or the use of science, become a result of something extraneous to that domain.

The issue is neither whether such a perspective is affirmed by historical record nor whether the study group does in fact accurately represent the Baba's views on science. It is rather that such a perspective has an elective affinity with the life-world of urban and middle-class devotees of the movement and is legitimated, curiously, by the terms of the scientific regime within which they are located. For many of these devotees, this structure of separations and distinctions between various spheres gives rise initially to a sense of disquiet with the modern world, the memory of worlds that are lost and past. This leads in time to the possibility of not just an accommodation between tradition and modernity but a magical transformation of modernity itself. This transformation is not merely in terms of 'miracles' that Baba works, but through a shift in the notion of time itself. The cult's most visible and vocal following is overwhelmingly urban—administrators, doctors, lawyers, scientists, businessmen, and teachers forming the bulk. Their world appears to be constructed in terms of certain oppositions—tradition and modernity, religion and science, the individual and the state, and so on. Further, Baba's own persona is represented and perceived in a dual fashion: as a global avatar and as the incarnation of a Maharashtrian saint. This set of correspondences or non-correspondences between different types of elements appears to give birth to a teleological vision of science and spirituality coming together in the future as man and society ascend to a higher level of evolution. This lies side by side with the belief in the cyclical notion of time and the possible dawn of a golden age. Indulal Shah, a long-time convenor of the Sathya Sai Seva Organizations and a member of the Sathya Sai Central Trust, states that there are four ages (*yugas*) that constitute a spiritual cycle which in turn influence human culture: 'The Satya yuga, "where eternal Truths are codified for humanity"; Treta yuga "where the Truths are put into practice"; the Dwapara yuga "where life is governed by laws of Truth which becomes convention"; and the Kali yuga, "the age of chaos, where these laws are mechanically followed without understanding the spirit of the codes defined in Satya yuga."' (Shah 1980: 81–2) He states further that the Kali age is coming to an end and the Satya age is dawning with the Sathya Sai era, a spiritual renaissance in which we have to play a role. Nowhere is this millenarian vision more apparent than in the *seva* organizations of the movement.

Religion and Society

In terms of chronology, the service (*seva*) organizations (sometimes just called *samiti*) are one of the oldest institutions and programmes initiated by Baba. The first Sai Seva Organization was registered in Bombay under the Societies Registration Act in 1965 and the growth of organizations was such that, in 1967, the first all India Sai Organizations conference was held in Madras. A 'Seva Dal' explicitly for service purposes was formed in 1967, and in 1968 a 'Mahila Vibhag' for women was added. The history of Sri Sathya Sai Organizations over the two decades was reviewed by the World Council of Sai Organizations on Baba's sixtieth birthday in 1985: By the year 1985 there were nearly 1200 centres and *samitis* operating in 19 states in India.[7] Their activities usually started with a nucleus of one of a few objectives—as a devotional centre, a study circle of literature, or service activities. They gradually developed to encompass official directives to result in three wings, a social-services wing, an educational wing for children (called at first the 'Bal Vikas' programme and then the 'Education in Human Values' programme), and a spiritual wing.

The path laid down by Baba for the *samiti* comprises the traditional exercises of devotional singing (*bhajan*), meditation and study that many organizations such as the Ramakrishna Math and the Aurobindo Ashram also follow. The *bhajan* sung at Sai centres are essentially utterances of the names of God. But there is a degree of codification at the centres that is perhaps not common to other non-monastic organizations. The code of conduct for members of the service organization involves individual spiritual exercise (*sadhana*), family *sadhana* or spiritual exercises at the family level, and community *sadhana* or service to society through the institutional framework of three wings.[8] This reflects the philosophy of Baba that, of the nine types of devotion, *seva* is the most important.

The Sai organizations at the local level appear to be the most successful in trying to bridge the separation between different spheres—the individual, family and the neighbourhood—through service work and spiritual exercises. Theirs is a liberal programme of social reconstruction; many of the organizations are city—and *mofussil*-based. While most of the leadership is male, the women also play roles as Bal Vikas teachers, as priestesses during the *bhajan* sessions, and in service work. Yet, the mediation between spheres occurs through a different kind of logic than simply the outward act of 'service' of inner spiritual labour: the daily life of the devotee is constructed in terms of miraculous events and synchronicities. The appearance of Baba in dreams for guidance, the outpouring of sacred ash and honey on photographs in homes, stories of healing and so on, form an ever-growing fund of folklore within the *samiti* related to the foregrounding of such events by Baba himself, who has referred to these as his 'calling cards'. The life of service and the inner life of devotion merge for most *samiti* members. Even the spheres of home and business, the professional/public and familial domains, achieve an abstract resolution through the construction of everyday life in magical terms. Baba's hidden figure and intention is perceived behind daily events for many devotees.

This 'enchantment of the world', however, is based on a very specific process: it has as much to do with the construction of Baba as a cosmic avatar with a world mission as with that of an accessible magus. The localization of his charisma is very much a function and feature of neighbourhood devotion and is, indeed, heightened through the structure of worship at the *samiti*. The aspect of Baba as magus is reminiscent of

Shirdi Baba who was petitioned for mediation in a variety of afflictions and whose power was conveyed through gesture, words, touch, and dreams. In this somewhat shamanistic and saint-like role, Sathya Sai Baba is a part of the devotee's everyday life and familial affairs. The return of the magical in these domains, however, is curiously balanced against the frame of modern urban existence that is premised on the negation of magic and synchronicity and is based instead on an ever-increasing rationalization of life. There is a process of accommodation by the devotee to modern life because, behind the vast spaces of the public, the professional and the national stands the figure of Baba who, in his other role as avatar, transcends time, space and context.

It is equally noteworthy that this Spiritual Revolution ushered in by Bhagavan Baba is taking place simultaneously on two planes viz., individual and global. Firstly, Bhagavan is revolutionising the individual's approach to spirituality by giving new dimensions to his sadhanas consistent with the demands of the present age. In this new approach, spirituality is synthesised with science, woven into our day-to-day living and the individual's sadhana is expanded into family and community sadhana; above all, it has transformed service to man into a spiritual sadhana to realise the Divinity in all. Secondly, on the global plane, Bhagavan is revolutionising the bond between man and man by upholding before all mankind One God (the truth of Divinity in Man), One Religion (selfless love), One Language (that of the heart) and One Caste (Humanity). (Shah 1980: 129)

Conclusion: The Nature of the 'Nation'

The normative vision of this cult and its construction of tradition lie at the point of intersection of the representation of Baba as magus-avatar and the social being of its constituency. One aspect of this construction is the casting of the relationship between ancient tradition and modern circumstance in terms of a cyclical movement from the Satya age to the Kali age and back to eternal truths with the inauguration of the Sai golden age, a millenarian process in which followers have a role to play. This aspect has been dealt with in previous sections of this paper. The other aspect is the definition of the 'nation' offered by Baba, which I will comment on briefly, and by way of conclusion, since many of its elements have been examined earlier in this article.

There are three features to this definition. First, a theosophical universalism that is central to the spread of the organization and the cult within and without India. Second, in spite of this universalism, the casting of Sanatana Dharma is not in terms of an international religious synthesis, but a 'Vedic' and 'national' one. Third, this rendering of Sanatana Dharma is constantly balanced by internalistic readings. The definition explicitly distances itself from inscribing political power within the definition of concepts and categories.[9] For instance, in a discourse titled 'What the Upanishads teach us', he states that we should forget that the battle of the Mahabharatha was fought in Hastinapura between two armies and instead remind ourselves that the battle occurs within our bodies and our hearts, between our good qualities and our bad qualities. Further that the citizens of 'Bharat' should not regard themselves as belonging to a country ruled by King Bharatha but Bharatha is one who takes pleasure in divinity (*Summer Showers* 1972: 46). Again, that the Vedas, which are the bases for Indian culture, have taught two main principles—to speak truth and to practice righteousness (*Summer Showers* 1990: 7).

The ability to move from a universalistic construction of Indian culture and nationhood to an inner and, sometimes, philological reading of scriptural traditions, from an emphasis on Vedic truths to pragmatic formulae, gives Baba's discourses a certain ambivalence. This is matched by the dualities that mark representations about his persona and the institutional mappings between civil society, religion, and science. For example, the somewhat paternalistic world of the organization and the magus-like presence of Baba behind it; the separation between cure and care; and the role of the devotee-citizen being at once based on the Brotherhood of Man as well as on the image of the dharmic warrior. The ambivalence of Baba's discourses may be necessary given the context of the reformulation of social roles within the new order that is held to be inaugurated by him. It appears that the householder now encodes into himself/herself the roles of the priest and the renouncer and a distance is created from political power as a defining social value, even though many devotees have access to that power. What it suggests, perhaps, is not just a symbolic and existential incongruity between elements, or alienated personal identities, but a double-voicedness within the urban middle-class and at the heart of national society itself.

Notes

1. See Srinivas (1999a) and Srinivas (1999b).
2. There is a vast literature by and on Baba which we can classify into six categories:
   (a) accounts of experiences of devotees;

(b) official publications of the Sathya Sai Central Trust which includes the *Sanathana Sarathi*, a monthly journal;
(c) accounts by devotees who have or had important roles to play in the organization;
(d) analyses of researchers (who are also devotees) of Baba and his philosophy;
(e) biographies; and
(f) Baba's own discourses and works, a vast list, which includes:
— volumes of discourses titled *Sathya Sai Speaks*
— *Summer Showers in Brindavan*, which are discourses given to college students;
— a set books called *Prema Vahini*, *Dharma Vahini*, *Sandeha Vahini*, and so on, which are discourses on specific themes; and
— works which are his exegeses of different scriptures—*Upanishad Vahini*, *Geetha Vahini*, *Bhagavata Vahini*, *Ramakatha Rasavahini*, and *Sutra Vahini*.

3. According to most accounts, Shirdi Sai Baba began his long period of residence at Shirdi (a small village in Ahmednagar district of Maharashtra) in 1858. He began to stay in a dilapidated mosque and acted in the manner of many Muslim saints. In the early period of his residence, village folk would come to him for medicines that he made and for his miracles. The majority of the populace at Shirdi, which contained about 200 households, were Hindu; the Muslims were a minority. Most of them were artisans or labourers and formed the main body of his clientele. In 1897, the practice of holding a festival in commemoration of the death of a Muslim saint (*urs*) was begun at Shirdi. In 1912, certain devotees decided to hold a Rama Navami festival to celebrate the birth of Rama along with the *urs* since the two coincided and this became an annual feature at Shirdi. The context of this shift deserves mention here: by the end of the first two decades of this century, the construction of the Godavari–Pravara canals transformed the famine-prone Ahmednagar district into the prosperous sugar belt. The devotees who began to gather at Shirdi in increasing numbers included a number of rich businessmen, administrators, and a growing middle-class. There was a gradual layering of Baba's largely Sufi practices with Hinduized forms that coincided with the creation of an incipient industrial-commercial economy. In 1918, Baba had an attack of fever and passed away on Vijayadashami day (the final day of the Navaratri festival, Dasara). A dispute followed about where he should be buried; the Muslim devotees wanted him to be interred in an open place and a tomb constructed over it. It was decided after a plebiscite to place him in a building where a Krishna idol was to have stood.
4. Shirdi Baba's assurances that even after his passing he would continue to help his devotees, and reports from certain devotees that he would find reincarnation as a boy of eight allowed the possibility among believers that his rebirth was imminent. The most important case of claim of

reincarnation is that of Sathya Sai Baba. On 28 September 1990 Sathya Sai Baba revealed certain details about Shirdi Baba during a discourse at Puttaparthi. He stated that towards the end of his life, Shirdi Baba told Abdul Baba, a close devotee, that he would appear again after eight years (*Sanathana Sarathi* 1990: 296–7). Shirdi Baba did not designate heirs nor give initiation. The idea of incarnation used by Sathya Sai Baba, therefore, solves the problem of the reproduction of his charisma because it needs no genealogical transmission of spiritual power.

5. In early 1994, there were 1200 family units and 40 community halls, the latter of which could each accommodate about 200 (Rao 1995: 146). The number of persons at various festivals celebrated at Prasanthi Nilayam is certainly larger than this number.
6. The study group was set up following a symposium held at Dharmakshethra. The study group had as its members, Dr A. K. Ganguly (Bhabha Atomic Research Centre), Dr V. S. Venkatawardhan (Director, Nehru Planetarium, Bombay), S. Ramakrishnan (Executive Director, Bharatiya Vidya Bhavan), Dr C. Ramaswamy (retired Director-General of Observatories, Govt. of India), Dr S. Mahapathra (Indian Institute of Technology, Bombay) and Dr Brahmanand S. Mavinkurve (retired Director of Economic Research, Reserve Bank of India).
7. The first Sai Baba centre outside India was opened in 1967 at Sri Lanka. In the USA, a centre in Hollywood and a book centre at Austin were opened in 1969, both in California. In the same year, the first centre started functioning in the UK. Centres then opened in South Africa (1973), Italy (1974), Mauritius and Australia (1978), and the West Indies (1983). By 1985, there were 421 Baba centres reported around the world, excluding India. Of these, 149 were situated in the western hemisphere, the USA leading with nearly 100 centres; 136 in South-East Asia, Malaysia leading with 78 centres; 72 in Europe, United Kingdom contributing 45; 25 centres in South Africa and 27 others in the African region with 15 centres in Madagascar alone. For co-ordination of such a world-wide programme, the reorganized World Council (1987–8) at the headquarters in Prasanthi Nilayam had the overall responsibility. The large number of centres in some regions, for instance, South-East Asia, is obviously due to the Indian diaspora there (See Rao 1995: 252–5).
8. The rules of this have been drafted: (1) every day meditation and chanting will be undertaken; (2) there will be *bhajan* with all members of the family once a week; (3) there will be participation in Bal Vikas programme by children of the family; (4) participation in community work and other programmes of the organization (these activities include programmes such as coaching classes for school and college students and adult education; health and hygiene activities such as medical camps, immunisation programmes; and rural service activities such as the improvement of sanitation, provision of drinking water and other facilities in the village); (5) attendance of *bhajan* or 'Nagara Sankeertan' (the singing of *bhajan* through the streets of the

neighbourhood) at least once a month; (6) regular study of Sai literature; (7) to speak softly with everyone; (8) not to indulge in talking ill of others; and (9) 'Narayana Seva' which involves some cereals to be kept aside separately everyday to feed the needy and to form the habit of not wasting food (*Manual* 1985).

9. Although it would take a separate article to deal with these issues, it must be mentioned that Baba has on various occasions spoken against the concept of Hindutva and the postures assumed by the Hindu Right.

References

Babb, Lawrence A. 1986. *Redemptive Encounters. Three Modern Styles in the Hindu Tradition*. Berkeley: University of California Press.

Dumont, Louis. 1960. World Renunciation in Indian Religions. *Contributions to Indian Sociology* 4 (o.s.): 33–62.

———. 1962. The Conception of Kingship in Ancient India. *Contributions to Indian Sociology* 6 (o.s.): 48–77.

Gokak, V. K. 1983. *Bhagwan Sri Sathya Sai Baba. An Interpretation*. New Delhi: Vikas.

Kasturi, N. 1968. *Sathyam Sivam Sundaram*. 3 vols. Prasanthi Nilayam: Sanathana Sarathi.

Manual of Sri Sathya Sai Seva Dal. 1985. Prasanthi Nilayam.

Rao, M. N. 1995. *God and his Gospel*. Prasanthi Nilayam: Sri Sathya Sai Towers Hotel Pvt. Ltd.

Rigopoulos, Antonio. 1993. *The Life and Teachings of Sai Baba of Shirdi*. Delhi: Sri Satguru Publications.

Sanathana Sarathi. 1990. vol. 33, no.11: 296–7.

Sathya Sai Baba. 1976. Why I Incarnate. In *Sai Baba and His Message*, ed. S. P. Ruhela and Duane Robinson, 23–9. New Delhi: Vikas.

Shah, Indulal H. 1980. *Sixteen Spiritual Summers*. Prasanthi Nilayam: Sri Sathya Sai Books and Publications.

Shepherd, Kevin. 1985. *Gurus Rediscovered: Biographies of Sai Baba of Shirdi and Upasni Maharaj of Sakori*. Cambridge: Anthropographia Publications.

Spirituality and Science. 1985. Dharmakshetra, Bombay: Sri Sathya Sai Trust.

Srinivas, Smriti. 1999a. The Brahmin and the Fakir: Suburban Religiosity in the Cult of Shirdi Sai Baba. *Journal of Contemporary Religion* 14,2, May: 245–61.

———. 1999b. Remembering Sai Baba: Sai Baba: la double utilization de l'ecriture et de l'oralité dans uns mouvement religieux moderne en Asie Sud, *Diogene* 187, Juillet-Septembre: 114–29.

Summer Showers in Brindavan. 1972. Dharmakshetra, Bombay: Sri Sathya Sai Education Foundation.

Summer Showers in Brindavan. 1990. Prasanthi Nilayam: Sri Sathya Sai Books and Publications Trust.

Swallow, D. A. 1982. Ashes and Powers: Myth, Rite and Miracle in an Indian God-man's Cult. *Modern Asian Studies* 16: 123–58.

Uberoi, J. P. S. 1994. The Elementary Structure of Medievalism: Religion, Civil Society and the State. *Contributions to Indian Sociology* (n.s.) 28.1: 1–34.

White, Charles, S. J. 1972. The Sai Baba Movement: Approaches to the Study of Indian Saints. *Journal of Asian Studies* 31: 863–78.

Convergences and Contestations: Contemporary Trends

Fluid Canons and Shared Charisma: On Success and Failure of a Ritual Performance in a South Indian Oral Tradition

HEIDRUN BRÜCKNER

The Tuḷu speaking population of the coastal South Kanara district of Karnataka still adhere to their oral religious tradition, which finds its most comprehensive expression in annual festival rituals held in honour of local deities. These deities can be lineage-, caste-, or village deities. Over the centuries, some of them have attained the status of 'princely' deities (*rājandaiva*) if they happened to be family deities of local rulers or owners of large estates. Such families generally belong to the dominant—matrilinear—caste of Baṇṭ agriculturalists, one of the highest of the local non-Brahman castes. The deities are closely associated with the lands of the estates which they protect. The annual festivals therefore have an element of thanksgiving and are intended to secure and renew the fertility of fields, cattle and people.

The success or efficiency of the festival rituals depends strongly on the proper functioning of three groups of people: the patrons, the possession priests or media, and the professional impersonators of the deities—whom I shall call god dancers in this paper.[1] Their acting in the rituals in their respective functions is legitimized by a formal authorization by the community based on eligibility as well as individual capacity and learning. The actual performance of those individuals, again, depends as much on transmitted knowledge as on personal ability. In this paper, I shall attempt to apply the notions of charisma and canon to these performance traditions.

In order to test the usefulness of the notion of 'charisma' in such a context I want to take the original meaning of the term as a starting point. According to the dictionary the ancient Greek word *charisma* means '(divine) gift of grace'. For this meaning the new testament of the Bible is given as reference. Cognates are the noun *charis* meaning 'comeliness, kindness, charm, grace, favour' and the verb *charein*, 'to be happy, rejoice, take pleasure in something'.[2] The use of the term *charisma*, often in the plural, *charismata*, is mainly attested for in the case of the apostle Paul. In his understanding, the *charismata* comprise divine gifts of grace such as prophetic speech, speaking in different tongues, and the capacity of healing. In contradistinction to such gifts, normally associated only with a chosen few, Paul also includes categories such as 'office' among the *charismata*. In late Christian theology, however, the charismatic person came to be viewed in opposition to the office-holder and office itself was considered as invested with charisma. Charisma thus became institutionalized and controlled by the church. Personal charisma received directly from God was no longer needed for the legitimization of institutionalized religion and lost theological significance. In modern religious studies, the notion of charisma is often applied in the context of the formation of religious sects (Kehrer 1990). In common parlance, charisma refers to the personal 'radiance' or aura of an individual.

In order to try and apply these notions developed in a European context to the religious tradition under consideration, especially to the roles of the patron, the possession priest and the god dancer, I take the original meaning of '(divine) gift of grace' to coin the term 'divine charisma' which manifests itself in ritual interaction. As the following discussion will show, it is a divine entity that favours a human being with its charisma. The association of the early use of the word charisma with prophetic and inspired speech as well as with healing fits well into the specific religious context examined here. The distinction between divine charisma in this sense and the institutionalized charisma of an 'office' available to its legitimate bearer has analytical significance since it points to the universal problem of religious legitimization. The same applies to Weber's assigning a legitimizing function to the belief or faith of followers in the charismatic person.

In a restricted sense the term 'canon', as I use the term here, will be taken to refer to the totality of orally transmitted texts recited, sung, and spoken during a given festival ritual. In an extended sense, it will be taken to refer to the 'performance text' (Schechner 1983: *passim*), i.e. the total presentation of a set choreography or 'staging' co-ordinating speech, movement, dance, etc. into a patterned behaviour. In contradistinction to the absolute fixity of an oral textual corpus such as the Veda, the oral texts under consideration partly allow variation and improvisation and thus provide space for individual creativity and personal style.

This situation raises a number of questions: does a fixed performance text (canon) put limits on variation and improvization, or, put more radically, what are the minimum requirements for a ritual performance to 'function' and when can it be considered to have 'failed'? To what extent do the limits of improvisation and variation depend on the 'charisma' of a performer and his acceptance by the participant audience? Is it possible or useful in this context to distinguish between divine and human agency, especially with respect to charisma?

In order to explore these questions, I shall briefly sketch the social position of priests and god dancers, take up the first aspect of charisma involved in the authorization of members of the three groups to act in festival rituals, and provide a general description of their roles in the festival rituals. This will be followed by an analysis in terms of 'charisma' and 'possession'.

II

In the social and ritual configuration considered here, possession priests are drawn from the Biruve caste of 'toddy tappers', ranging—in the local caste hierarchy—below the Baṇṭ patrons but clearly above the castes of god dancers. In the older social setup—still relevant in a ritual context—Biruve families were in charge of the palm trees of an estate besides being tenants of the estate owner. Members of one of the castes of god dancers, such as the Pambadas, lived on the borders of the cultivated area of an estate. They made their living by making mats and umbrellas from palm leaves, by collecting forest products, and by working as agricultural labourers during harvest time.[3] Patron family, tenants and various service castes such as oilpressers and washermen contributed to the annual festival of the patron family's deity, which, being in charge of the entire estate, was also worshipped by all the other groups living on 'its' lands.

The possession priest or medium of the deity came from among one of the Biruve families of the estate or small principality, thus restricting eligibility. At the same time, the deity had to make its own choice by possessing a particular person from among the eligible candidates during a special session. Conversely, an eligible person had to prove his qualification by making himself the vessel of the deity's presence. He could then be installed into the office of its priest (Pātri, lit. 'vessel'), if this was also approved by the patron and/or the community. During his first performance, he could be guided by the chief or managing priest who did not himself become possessed but supervised the entire ritual. In many cases, one of his older relatives may have held the office earlier. Controlling possession, too, is a matter of practice for which previously observed behaviour serves as a model.

In the case of god dancers, transmission of performance knowledge and choosing a new performer is slightly different, whereas eligibility is analogous to what has just been described for the priests. A performer is normally accompanied to a festival performance by relatives who help him with the preparation and donning of elaborate costumes and paraphernalia. A nephew or son who shows special interest and talent is gradually integrated into the performance: first, by acting as a small 'Bāvana' (apprentice) who may dance a little during a break in the major rituals, sometimes along with his performing father or uncle. In a second step, the boy may take over the part of an assistant deity, Baṇṭe, who does not speak. This step requires acceptance by the patron, since it involves his formally invoking Baṇṭe onto the impersonator. For some Baṇṭe performers, this is a transitory role which they use in order to improve their dancing and other set behaviour, and to pick up speeches from the senior impersonator. They then move into the senior role when required and accepted. In some cases, the Baṇṭe impersonator remains in this role for the rest of his career—because he may be lacking the power of speech or the intellectual capacity and maturity to act as an arbitrator in the court sessions.

Both possession priests and god dancers normally have a certain number of temples and estates where they are entitled and obliged to perform. This is termed their *ajalu*. Whereas the priests serve only one particular deity at a number of places, the Pambada god dancers may impersonate different deities of similar status, such as the five or six princely deities. As for the Baṇṭ patron of the festival rituals, he is normally a respected senior married man managing the family estate. In the matrilinear system, property is handed on in the female line, but public representation of the family and the management of estates are the tasks of males which they normally carry out for their sisters, not for their wives (Claus 1978). If the extended family and an eligible male agree, the latter undergoes the authorizing ceremony of 'taking *gaḍi*' (lit. incision, border). It is conveyed on him by the deity itself, as represented by its possession priest. Only a Gaḍipattunāru, a *gaḍi*-holder, is entitled to address the deity directly in the public rituals. The commitment of all three, the patron, the possession priest, and the god dancer is marked by a special golden bangle worn on the right wrist.

Focusing on the respective tasks of the patron, the priest, and the god dancer, the all-night festival rituals can be sketched as follows: all the people of an estate and guests from neighbouring estates or villages assemble at the small temple of the deity or a temporary open shed erected in the fields. The area has been cleared and decorated, the paraphernalia of the deity have been carried in procession to the shrine where they are displayed on large benches in front of the temple or in the shed or on a large swing in an open hall in the temple compound. Patron, priest and dancer have observed special rules of purity for the last few days. The dancer has confirmed his readiness and obligation to perform by accepting a token gift of paddy, betel nuts and betel leaves from the patron in front of the deity's shrine. Before starting his make-up, he stands in front of the shrine with his tembarè drum and recites the myth-legend (Bascom 1984) of the deity, called *pāḍdana*.[4] These texts frequently describe the origin and wanderings of the deity and the special circumstances that brought it to the present locality where it obtained a temple and a festival. The recitation functions as a first invocation to attract and invite the deity to the present festival. The singer then puts on facial make-up, costumes and ornaments, especially the sacred anklets (*gaggara*). When he is ready, the patron and other dignitaries assemble in front of the temple and the patron whispers an invocation requesting the deity to descend upon the body of the dancer. Kepula (*Ixora coccinea*) blossoms are thrown on him and the orchestra starts playing with full power. The dancer begins to tremble and shake, marking the onset of possession, and then performs a dance that includes features of pantomime.[5] He presents himself to the dignitaries and wider audience in the light of torches carried by two helpers and repeatedly exposes his body to the flames. Later, the possession priest appears before the dancer who takes hold of his right hand and causes him to tremble or shake, thus transmitting the divine presence or 'charisma' to him. After a short while, the priest comes back to his senses. This initial phase of the festival rituals, in which the deity is represented by the dancer, concludes with a procession around the temple.

In the second stage, the priest takes over. Wearing a red silk cloth, he stands in front of the patron and is given a silver belt and a silver sword as well as a yak-tail whisk and a bell from the paraphernalia of the deity by the patron who is assisted by the managing priest. After jointly circumambulating the sacred *homa*-fire, patron and possession priest move to the open space in front of the temple where the dignitaries are lined up and the audience holds its breath. The priest—in a stiff gait typical of the onset of priestly possession—lifts his sword up high, takes hold of a five-armed torch carried by one of the accompanying torchbearers, and walks up and down the row of dignitaries headed by the patron. He bends his bare chest deep into the flames in front of each man until the person addressed implores him by gestures to stop, since he is considered to have sufficiently displayed and, proved the presence and power of the deity. Then the orchestra stops suddenly and, in a moment of high dramatic tension, the priest presses the bell against his belly and starts speaking in the loud, coarse and frightening voice of the deity who inhabits him. He addresses the patron and eventually other *gaḍi*-holders among the dignitaries by their ceremonial names, other Baṇṭ family heads by their family names, as well as other castes and 'the people of the kingdom' in general. The deity speaks of itself, its origin and its coming to the present festival in self-glorifying ceremonial terms. It praises the ongoing event and the arrangements made by its human hosts and assures everybody of its continued protection. After a procession around the shrine, the deity holds court. It is at this point that family and village affairs may be discussed, and the deity brings up matters concerning the management of its temple, etc. For personal and medical problems remedies are recommended, sometimes involving applications of *prasāda* sandalpaste given by the deity.

This second stage of the festival rituals again concludes with a procession and the transmission of 'divine charisma' from the priest to the god dancer who will be in charge again for the third stage. The dancer now wears even more elaborate costumes, including a halo-like structure tied to his back. In a different tune, he again recites portions of the *pāḍdana* about the deity whose large facial mask of brass or silver is now fixed on top of his head and attached to the frame on his back. The dancer is handed the sword and bell so far held by the priest, who now throws flowers on him. At this moment, the priest emits a cry and.is left by the deity and carried away while the deity descends upon the dancer. The dancer starts trembling and the deity inhabiting his body begins to dance, showing itself in full attire and beauty like a living decorated idol. As via the medium of the body of the priest in the second stage, it now grasps the five-armed torch via the dancer and displays its power in front of the patron, dignitaries and audience. Then the dancer starts speaking in the voice of the deity, again formally addressing the people. The subsequent text is very close to the *pāḍdana* the dancer had sung earlier in third-person narrative. Now, the deity itself speaks through him quickly, in a loud voice, in the first person. The sequence follows the lines of the *pāḍdana*, shorn of all musical and metrical embellishment. The patron finally interrupts the delivery, addressing the deity directly by its name. He tells that—as everybody knows—its deeds are manifold and wonderful and cannot be measured—as little as the stars in the sky and the sand in the sea.

In the meantime, the priest has prepared a brass pot filled with *prasāda* (sandalpaste folded in leaves) and locked with a ripe coconut. He and the god dancer enact a graceful dance playing with the 'pot of plenty' by throwing it up into the air, catching it again, etc. until the deity finally catches hold of it after 'hunting' the priest. They open the pot and ceremoniously hand over the coconut to the patron as a special privilege and token of his office. They then distribute the content to the participants whom the deity also blesses with words and with its sword. Next, the deity and its followers move out of the compound to visit and inspect its fields. If it owns a wooden conveyance such as a tiger, horse or boar, it will use it now. Then, with reduced paraphernalia, it is offered food and drink in front of the shrine. After the meal, there may again be court sessions and consultations before the deity finally takes leave of its followers. In a final speech it expresses its satisfaction and pleasure and grants its blessings. The dancer returns the deity's sword, bell and yak-tail whisk, removes the head ornaments and falls down on the steps of the temple.

This is, in rough outline, the standard course of events of the annual festival rituals of a princely deity in the Banṭ-Biruve-Pambada configuration. Major ritual interaction takes place between the deity acting and speaking through its possession priest and dancer and the patron, who is entitled to carry on verbal exchanges with his god. The presence of these three people is thus indispensable and their roles are of central importance. In addition, the managing priest plays a major though unspectacular and therefore largely unnoticed role in directing ritual action. In terms of agency and power, it is ultimately only the deity and the patron, the divine and the human ruler of the realm, who annually confront each other in person in order to negotiate their affairs in public, reconfirm their status and identity and renew each other's power. Without the patron, the deity cannot become present or manifest; without the deity's annual public manifestation through members of other social groups, the power of the patron and his clan lacks legitimization.

III

Returning to the discussion of charisma and *charismata*, I should like to emphasize that in the South Indian religious tradition under study there is no founder figure, though there is a first divine self-manifestation reported in many of the myth-legends (*pāḍdana*) mentioned above. The deity shows its presence and power by possessing a person or an animal, mostly a Biruve 'toddy tapper' or a valuable water-buffalo.[6] Aided by a soothsayer, people find out the identity and wishes of the possessing entity which can harm as well as help them. A place of worship is set up and rituals are held regularly. The deity who first came on its own, causing affliction, is now invited and invoked in a fixed ritual setting. Its raw powers are channeled and made beneficial. Its rough first onslaught is transformed into a prolonged, artfully choreographed presence. Once established, it becomes a permanent source of 'divine charisma' which can be tapped and made to flow into human communities through specific channels in a particular setting such as the annual festival rituals.

In this context, the notion of 'divine charisma' may help to describe the phenomenon of 'possession'. We may say that the flow of divine charisma is brought about in a state often termed 'induced' or 'controlled' possession, as opposed to 'spontaneous' or 'uncontrolled' possession. This distinction, made by scholars for analytical purposes,[7] is to my knowledge not made in any of the Dravidian terminologies,[8] probably because the phenomenon itself is considered basically the same, the distinctions actually made refer to the identity of the possessing entity, to the way of handling it and to context.

Analytically, 'spontaneous' possession would normally occur to a passive human 'victim' incapable of handling it satisfactorily. The identity of the possessing entity would not be known, it could be a harmful and malevolent being. The 'victim', very often a woman, would be in a liminal, inauspicious or vulnerable condition. The space and time of the attack would not be predictable, they may also be inauspicious. Conversely, 'controlled' possession takes place at a fixed auspicious time and place by a known, predominantly benevolent divine being. It is actively induced by invocations and other means and handled skilfully by experienced specialists. In the material just described there is continuity between the two modes in two respects: Firstly, in the myth-legends, a deity initially makes itself known by means of 'spontaneous' possession before it receives regular worship, including its 'controlled' manifestation. Secondly, spontaneity comes into the picture in the context of identifying a new possession priest, who subsequently practices induced possession if chosen for the office. It should be noted that the first reported appearances of deities, again, are not unique unprecedented events, but follow set cultural patterns within a group of interrelated religious traditions.

In terms of religious legitimization in the context of an established cult, three conditions must be fulfilled: the first concerns the selection for an office. It involves inherited eligibility as well as personal receptivity for the divine charisma on the part of the candidate. The final choice is made by the deity inhabiting the body of the candidate and thereby marking him as its desired human vessel. Thus, spontaneous possession indicating charismatic contact is decisive for the conveyance of the office itself. Being a legitimate office-holder, i.e. a professional possession priest, in turn becomes a precondition for the functioning of induced possession in the setting of the annual festival rituals. The visible onset of possession in this public context proves that the chosen person is rightfully holding the office and that the way of performance of the rituals meets with the approval of the deity. The third condition is acceptance by the patron and audience, who believe that the deity is actually present within the body of the priest or the dancer. This belief is indispensable for meaningful ritual interaction.

IV

Against the background of these specifications, I want to return to my initial questions about the limits of variation in ritual performance and about the role of charisma. I shall base my discussion on the analysis of a set of incidents during festival rituals which departed from the 'normal' course of events. These departures as recorded in my fieldnotes between 1986 and 1992 refer respectively to problems involving the legitimation ('office-charisma') and/or performance of a patron, a priest or a dancer and which sometimes caused considerable changes in the total performance text (canon).

The first set of examples concerns the patrons. At several localities, I encountered the situation that an old patron holding *gaḍi* had died and a successor had either not yet been agreed upon or was hesitating to take the *gaḍi*. Still, the annual festival rituals were conducted successfully either by inviting a *gaḍi*-holding relative or even a Brahman priest as speaker to address the deity or—more often—by the proposed person taking charge provisionally. In the latter case, direct interaction between deity and patron was reduced to gestures on the part of the patron, who was not supposed to address the deity verbally. The deity did not touch the patron by taking his hand, which is otherwise a common gesture of confidence performed dramatically by the god dancer. In one case, the dancer integrated the patron's standard statements and questions rhetorically into his own speeches ('Isn't it that ...'). Invocations still worked without the patron addressing the deity verbally, since all the other required elements were in place. In another instance, a patron's distant relative had died very shortly before the beginning of the main festival night. Because of the consequent pollution, the patron was not allowed to enter the inner courtyard of the temple. He came and stood at the outer gate and performed his part from a distance.

In my last example, a very powerful and dominant old patron—possessing personal charisma in the everyday sense of the term—had been upset with the possession priest of his deity. He delivered a rather careless invocation, combining his address to the main and assistant deity. Only the second deity, Baṇṭe, manifested itself in its priestly medium.

Yet the old man started proceeding to the festival arena. After a few steps, Baṇṭe pulled him back, gesticulating and screaming inarticulately. The managing priest and some of the dignitaries also pointed out to him that the priest had not moved from the spot and the deity clearly had not yet inhabited his body. The patron had no choice but to return and perform the invocation properly. The deity came immediately and showed its dissatisfaction with the patron's behaviour. Only then were the rituals continued.

These examples make it evident that the main criterion for success, in spite of deviation, or failure, is the acceptability of the deviation by other performers and supposedly the deity, as also by the dignitaries and the larger audience. In the first instance, the dancer collaborated with the patron by taking over the speeches. The acceptance of this proceedure was probably facilitated by the fact that the deity—through the dancer—pressed the patron to take the *gaḍi* soon, and that this was promised. In the last example, the personal pride of the patron was not acceptable to the possession priest as well as the managing priest and the dignitaries. To avoid a complete failure of the rituals, which would have involved an expensive repetition, the patron had to give in.

Thus, deviations are acceptable if there is a consensus that they are due to temporarily unavoidable circumstances. They are then considered less dramatic than the offence of not conducting the annual rituals at the proper time or skipping them altogether. But deviation due to personal capriciousness is not tolerated and pressure is exercised to set it right.

Concerning the performance of possession priests, I recorded two examples of 'deficiencies'. In the first instance, the old local possession priest had died just before the annual festival. At very short notice, another priest of the same deity was invited from another village to perform that night. He was not familiar with the people and the affairs of the village. Since he arrived late, there was hardly any time for a briefing, and he had to be heavily prompted by the managing priest during the ritual performance. Thus, the names and titles of some of the dignitaries had to be whispered into his ear. He reduced his speeches to a minimum of conventional phrases, and consultations were largely skipped. Instead, the very experienced senior god dancer, in the third stage, took over most of the consultations and the court session. In the second instance, a newly appointed young possession priest appeared not fully capable of handling possession, of delivering speeches, and of swaying the deity's sword powerfully, etc. His deliveries were cut short, the managing priest guided his movements, and the more experienced dancer later performed the duties of the deity more comprehensively. Thus, in both cases, the deficiencies were in part compensated by the deity's dancer-medium and were tolerated by the participants and audience.

Concerning the god dancers, certain younger 'media' may perform beautiful and powerful dances, but they lack experience and inspiration in speeches and the proper handling of consultations and court cases. Such situations are normally resolved by the possession priest taking over more of these responsibilities. Shifts in both directions—from dancer to priest or priest to dancer—are not considered problematic, since the deity speaks equally through both types of media. In a more dramatic case, an elderly dancer impersonating the assistant deity Baṇṭe collapsed at the beginning of the third stage of the performance during the recitation of the *pāḍdana* while the patron and priests were approaching to conclude the second stage of rituals. The patron sprinkled holy water on the dancer. Then the main deity's dancer addressed him, then Baṇṭe's possession priest, and finally the main deity's priest. For a moment, Baṇṭe's priest also fell unconscious. When he came back to his senses, the second stage of the rituals was formally brought to an end. Next, an attempt was made to invite both deities on the bodies of their dancers. The invocation worked and the rituals were continued. While the main deity, Jumādi, delivered speeches, Baṇṭe's dancer was sitting on a stool supported by Baṇṭe's priest and a helper. Watching his condition, Jumādi's priest suggested that he be sent to the temple hall to rest. Jumādi's dancer took this up in his possession speech and gave an order to this effect. The dancer was led aside and some of the heavy costumes were removed. When it became clear that he could not perform any more, the rituals were continued with a single dancer. He declared that the assistant deity would take its ride into the fields seated on its vehicle 'in invisible form'—if a consensus about such a proceeding could be reached in the assembly ('the entire kingdom'). This was accepted by the patron, Jumādi's priest and the dignitaries. The ride and the final processions were performed in this manner and the rituals brought to a conclusion.

The old dancer was finally taken to hospital. It turned out that he had suffered a stroke. People said that he was punished for performing as a substitute for his cousin, although he was exclusively appointed at another locality for a different deity whose festival was to take place a few days later. The dancer was blamed, because he did not observe his obligation to the other deity not to perform at any other place for a certain period of time before the latter's festival, i.e. the problem was the personal lack of legitimacy of the dancer. This led to intervention by the deities. There were no further attempts to find out reasons for the accident from the deities themselves by questioning their priestly media.

A precisely similar procedure was resorted to in my last and most comprehensive example. In this case the ritual was actually disrupted and had to be repeated. It has to be noted here that the beginning and the end of the annual festival, rituals are marked by the ceremonial hoisting and lowering of the deity's flag in front of the temple in the presence of its possessed priests. The opening (1st day) and concluding (4th day) rituals take place in daytime; the central festival rituals described above are held on the second night. In March 1986, on the third night, i.e. before the final flag ceremony, at about 4 a.m., the flagpole broke and fell on the roof of the central shrine, partly destroying it. A watchman who had slept in a hall opposite the central shrine immediately reported the accident to the patron family.[9] They had the main deity's possession priest called, invoked the deity Jumādi into his body, and questioned it as to the reasons for the accident and the proper steps to be taken. Jumādi explained that his assistant, vigorous young Baṇṭe, had broken the flagpole because the patron had not kept his promise to renovate the shrine. Baṇṭe had only wanted to warn their devotees. Otherwise he would have destroyed the pole the night before and killed people. The deity assigned the main responsibility to the old patron who had kept postponing the renovation despite his public promises. He declared that the entire festival would have to be repeated. The old flag in human shape, which lay torn on the ground, would have to be buried far out in the Arabian Sea immediately. This was done the same night.

With a newly cut areca-palm tree as flagpole and a quickly stitched temporary flag, the festival rituals were repeated on the following night. Many people from the village had come; they had long wanted to join in the administration of the temple and the organization of the festival. They were willing to make substantial financial contributions. It turned out in the course of that night's discussions between deity and patron that the patron family alone would not be in a position to finance a new construction. With the consent of the deity a village committee was formed which collected nearly two lakhs of rupees in the following months. At the end of the same year, the temple roof was dismantled under the direction of the deities who possessed their priests. The new temple was inaugurated two months later and a special festival was held on the occasion. Representatives of the village committee occupied places of honour near the old patron with the approval of the deity. The incident initiated and sped up the last phase of a process by which social change finally came to be expressed and reflected in a 'traditional' ritual originally based on older social structures.[10]

V

To sum up the argument: the total performance text ('canon') is created through a balanced interaction among the major functionaries and between the functionaries and the larger participant audience. Elements of duplication, especially in the actions of the god dancer and possession priest, appear as wise provisions to allow shifts of certain performance slots from one performer to another. Both are equally entitled to carry out the ritual programme, first as 'office-holders' (cf. 'office-charisma') and second as 'vessels' into which divine charisma has been made to flow by means of invocations, etc. Normally, the person more experienced and more inspired to perform certain items within this programme will do so. This also facilitates interaction between the audience and the divine through the medium of the performer.[11]

Central events such as the onset of possession are not effected by a single cause such as an invocatory address by the patron, but by a whole set of conditions, including preliminary purificatory rites; personal preparation of the performer; recitation of a portion of the deity's myth-legend; the use of make-up; costumes and anklets in the case of the god dancer; a belt and divine weapon in the case of the priest; the throwing of flowers by dignitaries in which other audience members can join; and the sudden onset of powerful music played by an orchestra. There is thus a range of people, actions and objects that contribute to the coming of the deity, or of its charisma. As my examples have shown, the substitution of the patron's verbal address by mere gesture is a tolerable flaw in the total performance text, if all other conditions are fulfilled.

The 'success' of a performance manifests itself in the very process of being performed without major intervention or disruption; in the belief of the participants that the rituals are being carried out properly; and in the feeling of sharing in divine charisma. The personality of an individual performer may heighten the impact, but is not essential for the manifestation and efficiency of divine charisma. In terms of the indigenous, i.e. emic, perception of agency, it is the deity who speaks and acts through the performer.

Canon in the more restricted sense of a corpus of oral texts delivered during the rituals shows a high degree of flexibility—extension as well as reduction—and scope for improvisation. But again, certain items such as the recitation of parts of the myth-legends, the divine address to the patrons and dignitaries, the deity's account of his origins, and the formulaic expression of blessings, appear indispensable. Both canon as textual corpus and canon as 'performance text' cannot be separated from 'charisma' in the sense of divine presence in the human media, since in an oral tradition the text is manifested exclusively in its performance in the festival rituals. The divine speeches are never pronounced or 'rehearsed' in any other context. Their words would not make sense and would not be efficient if not uttered by the deity itself. The priests say they could not even remember and pronounce the words out of context, because it is not they who are the speakers. The ritual performance provides a setting for the self-manifestation of the divine that shapes and continuously reshapes its own 'canon' through its human media, and within a range acceptable to the participant community. Canon thus remains inseparably interlinked with and dependent on divine charisma.

Notes

1. See Diehl (1956: 221 and passim) for this expression which he uses for the Tamil terms *cāmiyāṭi* and *kōṭaṅki*.
2. See Gemoll (1979). *Charisma* (göttliche) Gnadengabe (NT) [(divine) gift of grace]. *Charis*, 1. Anmut, 2. Gefälligkeit, Gnade, Gnadengabe, etc. 3. Huld, Gunst, etc. 4. Erkenntlichkeit, Dank, etc. [comeliness, kindness, charm, grace, favour]. *Charein*, froh sein, sich freuen, Vergnügen an etwas haben [to be happy, rejoice, take pleasure in something].
3. Nowadays, the total number of performing families has decreased, leading to an increased demand for the remaining performers and to their near-exclusive specialization on god dancing. Thus, performers may impersonate a set of five or six different deities at fifty or sixty places during the season between December and May. Their women have often taken to bīḍi-making to secure a regular basic income for the rest of the year.
4. For a detailed terminological discussion see Brückner (1995: 18–9).
5. See Brückner (1995: chap. 3) for an elaborate description and analysis of the complete festival rituals.
6. Thus, in the former case, the manifestation takes place among people involved in handing down the oral myth-legends.
7. See Schömbucher (1993) for a discussion of recent scholarly approaches to possession.
8. See Freeman (1993) for the Malayāḷam terminology of the Teyyam tradition of Northern Kerala.
9. He later said a whirlwind had carried him to the side and saved him. There are, in fact, several instances in *pāḍdana* texts for the appearance of deities in whirlwinds. My own observation was that a heavy storm took place that night and woke me up. This factual aspect was of no interest whatsoever for the interpretation of the incident by local people. When I arrived at the patron's house the morning after the event, I found that a deep depression reigned there, as if a family member had died.

10. It was during the inauguration ceremony that the old patron's first attempt to invoke his deity failed—a case reported above; and it was during the extra-festival that Baṇṭe's god dancer collapsed (see above).
11. In one instance, even the necessity for the deity to be manifest in a human medium during the festival rituals was temporarily suspended by declaring that the deity would take a ride on its wooden horse in its 'invisible form'. This ingenious solution is also resorted to when, for technical reasons, a person cannot sit on a deity's vehicle. Often, there are permanent wooden representations of a deity seated on its vehicle and taking the ride during festival rituals.

References

Bascom, William. 1984. The Forms of Folklore: Prose Narrations *The Sacred Narrative. Reading in the Theory of Myth*, ed. Alan Dundes, 5–29. Berkley: University of California Press.

Brückner, Heidrun. 1993. The Place of a Tuḷu Pāḍdana among Interrelated Oral Traditions. In *Flags of Fame. Studies in South Asian Folk Culture*, ed. Brückner, H., Lutze, l. & Malik, A., 283–334. Delhi: Manohar.

———. 1995. *Fürstliche Feste. Texte und Rituale der Tuḷu-Volksreligion an der Westküste Südindiens*. Wiesbaden: Harrassowitz.

Brückner, H., Lutze, L. & Malik, A. (eds.). 1993. *Flags of Fame. Studies in South Asian Folk Culture*. Delhi: Manohar.

Claus, Peter J. 1978. Terminological Aspects of Tulu Kinship: Kin Terms, Kin Sets, and Kin Groups of the Matrilinear Castes. In *American Studies in the Anthropology of India*, ed. Sylvia Vatuk, 211–41. Delhi: Manohar.

Diehl, Carl Gustav. 1956. *Instrument and Purpose*. Lund: Gleerup.

Freeman, Richardson. 1993. Performing Possession: Ritual and Consciousness in the Teyyam Complex of Northern Kerala. In *Flags of Fame. Studies in South Asian Folk Culture*, ed. Brückner, H., Lutze, l. & Malik, A., 109–38. Delhi: Manohar.

Gemoll, Wilhelm. 1979. *Griechisch-Deutsches Schul- und Handwörterbuch*. München, Wien: Freytag.

Kehrer, Günter. 1990. Charisma. In *Handbuch Religionswissenschaftlicher Grundbegriffe*, ed. Hubert Cancik, Burkhard Gladigow and Matthias Laubscher. Vol. 2. Stuttgart: Kohlhammer.

Schechner, Richard. 1983. *Performative Circumstances from the Avantgarde to Ramlila*. Calcutta: Seagull.

Schömbucher, Elisabeth. 1993. Gods, Ghosts and Demons: Possession in South Asia. In *Flags of Fame. Studies in South Asian Folk Culture*, ed. Brückner, H., Lutze, l. & Malik, A., 239–67. Delhi: Manohar.

Canonicity and Divine Interference: The Tulkus and the Shugden-Controversy[1]

MICHAEL VON BRÜCK

Religions are systems of social communication which at the same time create images of reality which become normative structures of perception, and these in turn define what is considered 'real' in a given society. In this way the legitimacy of social structures as well as structures of perception and thinking are established. Religions develop different ways of creating these patterns and structures, or rather these different patterns and structures are called *religions*. In course of time, these patterns change. Therefore, 'orthodoxy' versus 'heterodoxy' or 'canonicity' versus 'changing interpretations' are only temporally established sets of communication which stabilize each other mutually. The 'canon' is more than just a set of scriptures and their generally accepted mode of interpretation: it is also a model of social relations and values. But religions also refer to what is not (yet), and thus negate what *is*. Their very structure includes an 'ought' which, in many cases, is imbued with a charismatic emphasis inasmuch as it is a potential or actual criticism of the status quo. Paradoxically, religious institutions are the subject and object of this critique at the same time. In this way, religion itself is the meta-critique of its own legitimation of reality. Therefore, canon and charisma or religious institutionalization and 'divine interference' are two aspects of the same subject matter. My paper demonstrates this interconnection by looking at the present Tibetan Shugden controversy.

As W.C. Smith has shown, we need to be aware that religions are cumulative traditions and, as such, are syncretic. Organized religion tries to channel syncretic processes in order to establish a longer lasting canonicity or stability, but this process itself bears syncretic traits. Identity, after all, is not an object but a process in which norms and patterns of argument are continuously being challenged by events. The result is a process of assimilation and dissimilation which follows pre-established criteria as long as a society can agree on the rules of the process. It seems that these criteria can be subsumed under two categories: (a) an *aesthetic logic* which determines the limits of that which can be integrated; (b) the *power structure* in a given community. Both give each other legitimacy.

The actual controversy on Shugden is an example of how canonicity is being defined and redefined in the ever-changing context of power structures. However, 'power' is not just political or economic; it is also that which is convincing and plausible, that which asserts itself successfully and becomes a pattern of interpretation for historical events. That is why celestial hierarchies not only reflect mundane hierarchies—the celestial aspect also informs and changes the mundane aspect. Both are in correspondence, or in a dialectical relationship.

Tibetan Buddhism is a highly syncretic and pluralistic form of Tantric Mahāyāna Buddhism which has integrated elements of Tibetan Bon, Shamanism, Manichaeic tradition and animistic beliefs. Though Tantric Buddhism was introduced into Tibet rather rapidly during the reigns of the kings Songtsen Gampo (AD 620–49) and Trisong Detsen (755–98), a variety of different forms can be observed from the very beginning: more scholastic systems (represented by Śāntirakṣita and Kamalaśīla) of a graded path to awakening rival the tantric form (represented by Padmasambhava) and the sudden experience of awakening as practised in Chinese Ch'an (represented by the monk Hoshang at the 'council' in the first Tibetan Buddhist monastery at Samye [792–4]). Later, different schools developed during the so-called second spread of Buddhism in Tibet after the tenth and eleventh centuries. From that time the Sakya school develops next to the Kadampa (later Gelugpa), the Kagyüpa and the old Nyingma school. The distinctive character of these schools is established not so much by differing philosophical views (though there are differences in interpreting the classical tradition), as by different chains or lineages of master-and-disciple relationships, because in Tibetan Buddhism the oral tradition and charismatic leadership of a master (skt. *guru*, tib. *lama*) plays a very important role. Even later, when one or the other school became dominant politically, there was never a dominant single religious lineage but rather a polycentric interaction of different traditions. Since the heads of different schools and/ or powerful monastic institutions were regarded as charismatic incarnations of their predecessors, each lineage could develop on the basis of its own authority and authenticity which, at times, could create tensions and conflicts with the religious and political desire to create a generally accepted canonicity in the tradition so as to form a consistent framework of a pan-Tibetan identity.

This paper is a case study of such a conflict between the plurality of charismatic interpretations and the claim of a unified canonicity within Tibetan Buddhism at the present time.

In Tibetan Buddhism religious authority rests mainly on two grounds:

1. The scriptural tradition, i.e. the canonical Vinaya, Sūtra and Tantra texts translated and collected over centuries and finally codified by Bu-ston (1290–1364) in the Kanjur (*bka' 'gyur*) and the commentaries of the Tanjur (*bstan 'gyur*).[2] However, Bu-ston's selection and arrangement shows a bias against the older Nyingma school (*rñiṇ ma pa*), which finally contributed to an antagonism of the new (reformed) schools and the old one.
2. The reincarnated Lama (Tulku, *sprul sku*), who embodies lineages of tradition that have shaped a specific monastic interpretation of Tibetan Buddhism and a social allegiance that has given Tibetan Buddhism its (regional) coherence. The concept of the Tulku has its roots in the Mahāyāna-*bodhisattva*, though its religious and political implications are unique to the Tibetan tradition. The Tulku represents spiritual authority due to his karmic *puṇya* acquired over countless lifetimes. He exercises authority for he embodies and combines both the charismatic presence of the spiritual force *and* ecclesiastical approval of the religious and political hierarchy. However, these different aspects can also lead to conflict as the recent controversy on the legitimacy of Shugden shows.

That Tibetan history was impregnated by those conflicts can be observed by referring to three areas of conflict:

- The tension between the authority of different Tulku lineages and the centralizing power of the more powerful lineages (such as the Sakyapas in the twelfth and thirteenth centuries and the Gelukpas after the sixteenth century).
- The tension between the canon of the *triratna*, i.e. Buddha, *dharma*, *saṃgha* as embodied in the Kangyur and the specific 'root-teacher' who is usually a reincarnated Lama responsible for the perpetuation of his specific lineage.
- The tension between the Buddhist canon and pre-Buddhist practices of the propitiation of deities which have been incorporated into the Buddhist universe but often are not accepted by all Tibetan Buddhists in the same way.

All three areas of conflict were closely tied to Tibetan geography and history—with the vast areas of sparsely populated land inhabited by nomadic, semi-nomadic and settled groups only loosely connected with each other. One reason for this is that cultivation of land was possible only in valleys which far from each other, were connected only by difficult paths over the mountains. This situation fostered independent social developments. Wider parts of Tibet were unified only after the eighth century, precisely the time when Buddhism was introduced into Tibet. In fact, the Buddhist establishment of administration, the introduction of a script, and a more general Buddhist creed contributed to the unification of Tibet. King Songtsen Gampo (620–49) probably used the structure of Buddhism to unify the country, even more than King Trisong Detsen (755–98). However, local forces and the old establishment of the Bon tradition (with its countless deities and localized cults) resisted both the unification and the canonization of religious beliefs and practices through Buddhism. This conflict shaped Tibetan history over centuries, and in some ways it is present even today, though in a different form. The conflict is both a religious problem of a generalized canonicity versus individual 'charismatic' claims and a struggle between centralized power and the plurality of local traditions.

The present controversy concerning the deity Dorje Shugden (*rdo rje shugs ldan*) known also as Dolgyal is a reflection of the problem of transmission and canonicity in Tibetan Buddhism. The issue is rooted in a controversy at the time of the 5th Dalai Lama (1617–82), was revived at the time of the 13th Dalai Lama (1876–1933) and gained momentum since the 1970s when Tenzin Gyatso, the 14th Dalai Lama, distanced himself from the worship of this deity, for he felt that Buddhist refuge is refuge in the *triratna* and not in minor deities. A controversial book by the late Zemed Rinpoche (Gaden monastery) in 1976 defending the Shugden worship and counter-arguments by Jadral Rinpoche (Nyingma) and others aggravated verbal hostilities. In July 1996 the controversy increased after the Dalai Lama took a stand[3] against the worship of Shugden in his personal surroundings and in institutions connected with the Tibetan Government in exile for basically two reasons:

- The cult of Shugden as the defender of the 'pure' Gelukpa doctrine as against other schools is divisive on sectarian lines.
- The sole authority and place of refuge for Buddhists should be the Buddha and his teaching alone, not minor deities.

A number of abbots and monks in Gelukpa monasteries resisted this order of the highest Tulku of the Tibetan tradition and formed a 'Dorje Shugden Devotees Religious and Charitable Society' in New Delhi in

July 1996. Besides, the Gelukpa Geshe Kelsang Gyatso in England formed a 'New Kadampa' order openly attacking the Dalai Lama on the Shugden issue and political issues as well. Fifteen abbots and Geshes of Kelsang's original monastery, the Sera Je Dratsang (now in Bylakuppe, Karnataka) issued an open letter against Kelsang[4] stripping him of his membership in the monastery, calling him an 'apostate'[5] and comparing him to Mohammed of Ghazni.[6] Samdhong Rinpoche, President of the Tibetan Parliament in Exile, visited the monasteries of Gaden and Drepung in July 1996 in order to explain the Dalai Lama's position on the issue. Monks at Sera and Gaden announced a demonstration against the presence of their own leader. The monastic authorities curbed any demonstration. However, some monks staged a silent demonstration and thus were charged to have broken their vow of obedience to the monastic authorities. The monks felt they were not guilty. But eleven monks were expelled from Gaden. The last tragic event was the murder of Abbot Geshe Losang Gyatso, Director of the Buddhist School of Dialectics, and two of his disciples in Dharamsala on 4 February 1997—the three Gelukpa monks had been known as outspoken critics of the Shugden worship.[7]

The dynamics of the controversy are not surprising: in Tibetan history, time and again, the differences between different schools of Tibetan Buddhism were reflected in antagonisms between different deities and/or *dharma-protectors* who were supposed to protect a specific monastery, tradition, lineage or school. However, the problem today is aggravated because of its political implications concerning the authority of the Dalai Lama and the endangered unity of the different Tibetan traditions (in exile).

Two Aspects of Transmission: Tulkus and Protector Deities

Formally, religious authority is derived from the transmission only of the dharma. But dharma is embodied in several ways, viz. the traditional Buddhist monastic transmission of the teaching, including the special reincarnated teachers (Tulku) and the spiritual powers which have been 'tamed' by Buddhism and were changed into Buddhist deities representing mental forces which may powerfully protect (or harm) the dharma. So far this is not a development in Tibet only, for in other Buddhist countries, such as Sri Lanka, Thailand, etc. actual religion in the villages (and often in the monasteries too) is shaped by a combination of the veneration of the *triratna* and worship of deities and local spirits. What is unique to Tibet is the fact that those deities may become associated with specific

Tulkus and/or lineages, so that these lineages are connected with the authority of transtemporal deities. That is to say the Tibetan issue of canonicity and 'charisma' is the fabric of a hierarchical universe where *temporal transmission* of the dharma and *transtemporal succession* of higher powers are interconnected.

The Tulku (sprul sku)

The Tulku is a physical manifestation of higher levels of consciousness, in the exceptional case of Buddha consciousness (*buddhatva*) itself. Tulkus are countless in number and different in the degree of their spiritual realization. The highest ones are considered 'beings' reborn not because of karmic necessity but due to their spiritual freedom to fulfil their *bodhisattva* vows. That is to say, Tulkus are embodied not to work out and counterbalance negative karmic imprints, but to help sentient beings in continuity with their *bodhiṣattvic* presence in former rebirths. There are many Tulkus, acclaimed and selected by their respective monastic institutions, but most Tulkus have no more than local appeal. Since the sixteenth century the most famous Tibetan Tulku is the Dalai Lama. He holds spiritual power as one of the main leaders of the Gelukpa sect,[8] and he represents political power in as much as the Gelukpas became the dominant group during the sixteenth century.

Generally speaking, the Tulku tradition in Tibet has two different roots: a spiritual-philosophical development in Indian Buddhism, i.e. the *bodhisattva* doctrine, and a political development in Tibet in relation to the Mongolian connection. It will be necessary to focus on the structural problem of spiritual-philosophical authority in order to clarify the canonical function of the Tulku in the Tibetan system.

The concept of Tulku is connected with the *trikāya* doctrine in Indian Buddhism, for *sprul sku* is the translation of the Sanskrit *nirmāṇakāya*. In Tibetan Buddhism, the Tulku represents the presence of the Buddha in his *rūpakāya* in the midst of the (monastic) society. Hence, the presence and authority of the Tulku represents the completion of *triratna*, complementing the dharma (which is the object of study and realization of the monks) and the monastic community (*saṃgha*).

The concept of Tulku reinterprets the former *bodhisattva* ideal in terms of the Tantric *siddha* tradition. The Tulku may have greater spiritual and magical powers, he may obtain different bodily forms etc. As this kind of incarnation happened deliberately, it needs to be distinguished from the general karmic chain of causation which makes ordinary beings reappear inevitably according to the karmic structure of consciousness. Though there are levels of higher Tulkus (such as the Karmapa, the Dalai

Lama, the Panchen Lama, etc.) who have the freedom to choose the circumstances of their reincarnation, and lower Tulkus who have fewer spiritual achievements and therefore less freedom from karmic bondage, Tulkus are classified according to the realization of the traditional *bodhisattva bhūmis* (Ray 1986: 41). In any case there is enough stability, so that Tulkus return into a predictable spatial and social situation such as a specific monastery, etc. Tulku lineages have a beginning, and once they have started they become a personalized expression of the cumulative tradition. Tulkus have a higher reputation than ordinary Lamas, but they have basically the same function, though, because of their reputation, they bring more material support and wealth from the laity to the monastery (Ekvall 1959: 216). Tulkus are bound to become high Lamas, for they have a better start than other beings due to their karmic imprint. This belief is demonstrated by the fact that Tulkus can jump classes in their monastic colleges. Tulkus, it is said, are manifest where they can enact most effectively their *bodhisattva* vows to liberate all sentient beings. Their manifestation is always *purposeful*. Therefore, the general quality of consciousness of enlightenment (*bodhicitta*), i.e. their *karuṇā*, is actualized and historically defined. This in itself is an interesting development in the Buddhist philosophy of history, but we have to limit our presentation to the Tulku issue in Tibet.

To sum up the argument so far, we can state that a Tulku is a *bodhisattva* who is reincarnated, discovered, and ritually 'canonized', viz. re-installed into the seat of religious-political power of his predecessor by becoming a Lama (Ray 1986: 44).

The Tulku may or may not be a charismatic figure, though any touch of charismatic character would certainly enhance his fame and importance in society. Politically speaking the Tulku system gave the monastic succession greater stability at a time when the Sakyapa—and later Karmapa and still later Gelukpa monasteries—gained considerable political power due to their changing alliances with the military power of the Mongols. Hence, from the very beginning the Tulku lineages not only represent spiritual authenticity but also political power and stability.[9] The decentralized system of monastic lineages and regional centres of spiritual and political power and centralizing forces which culminated in the takeover of power by the Gelukpas in the sixteenth century came into conflict. And this is precisely where the Shugden issue needs to be located politically, for Shugden arises at a period of conflict as regards the centralization of power by the 5th Dalai Lama. To delineate this conflict it is imperative to deal first with the hierarchy and function of different deities within Tibetan Buddhism, as Shugden is a deity whose status is debatable.

Deities (lha)

In Tibetan Buddhism there exist countless beings above the level of beings with a gross physical body. They are systematized in different classes depending on their spiritual quality. At the highest level, some of them are emanations (*sprul pa*) of the highest aspects of the Buddha: Mahākāla (*Nagpo chenpo*, in 75 forms), Yama (*gShin rje*), Śrī Devī (*dPaldan lhamo*), Vaiśravaṇa (*rNam thos sras*), etc. Some are deities (*lha*) which have a universal appearance and meaning (such as higher *dharmapālas*, Tib.: *chos skyong* or *srung ma*), some are only local ghosts. The highest beings are beyond any conceptualization and have the function of personal tutelary deities (*yidam*), they are nothing other than the radiation of universal Buddha consciousness or Buddha nature. Those lower beings that are ambiguous have been tamed and bound by oaths—they are the lower *dharmapālas*. Generally speaking, all *dharmapālas* are classified into two different groups: those beyond *saṃsāra* and those within *saṃsāra*. The last group again comprises beings in very different situations concerning their level of being. In order to make contact with the human plane, they use human media who fall into trances. However, there is no generally recognized classification and even within one school or tradition there are significant differences and contradictions of interpretation and classification.[10] This sometimes causes conflict because of the complexity of the subject, and regional as well as sectarian differences. A generally accepted canonization has never been possible.

In the context of this essay, it is most important to understand the difference between the tutelary deity (*yidam*) and dharma-protector (*dharmapāla*), for to confuse the two may have significant consequences. The present Shugden controversy might have to do with such a confusion of categories: *yidams* are *always* trans-mundane, for they are emanations of the Buddha. The meditational practice regarding these *yidams* is *identification* with the deity, which is possible through complete surrender or the 'life-entrustment' of body, speech and mind by special initiation. The practice is aimed at a complete union with the deity. Hayagrīva (*rta mgrin*), Yamāntaka (*gshin rje gshed*), Kālacakra etc. are considered to be *yidams* (*iṣṭadevatā*), though Hayagrīva is a rather rare case where *yidam* and *dharmapāla* converge. *Dharmapālas*, however, are usually not trans-mundane but *samsaric*, only some of them are trans-mundane.[11] *Dharmapālas* are only helpers to practice the *triratna* and remain external, the meditational practice relating to them is never unification for they cannot substitute the refuge in the *triratna*. Concerning all these deities, we have to add that some of these higher deities have Indian origins (such as Mahākāla, Śrī Devī, etc.), and they have acquired a number of different forms in Tibet. Others—mainly of the lower class whom Padmasambhava had bound by a specific oath—are of Tibetan background.

This vow or oath (Skt.: *samaya*, tib.: *dam tshig*) by which those spirit beings have been bound is of great importance. It is, however, different from the three types of vows human beings can take in order to foster their spiritual progess: *vinaya* vow, *bodhisattva* vow and Tantric vow. Out of these, the Tantric vow means that the disciple hands over his/her whole life (body, speech and mind) to the spiritual power visualized as that deity and represented by the Lama. The Tantric vow binds teacher and disciple together in an exclusive connection of total obedience on the side of the disciple. This is even more so in the relation to one's 'root Lama' (*rtsa ba'i bla ma*), who is the teacher who transmits all the three aspects of the tradition as a single person: (a) the oral transmission of the texts; (b) commentaries on the texts; (c) empowerment into the practice of a specific deity. Such a relationship to the root Lama creates a special karmic situation and is absolutely binding. To change or correct the transmission handed down by a root teacher is not possible unless the relationship has been dissolved and the vow has been returned formally. The one who breaks the vow (*dam nyams*) commits such a serious 'negative deed' that he/she will definitely be reborn many times in hell.

Taking these different levels and beings into account, conflicts concerning loyalty can often arise. Whereas some of the highest deities, such as Mahākāla, Tāra, Avalokiteśvara, Yamāntaka, Pehar, etc. are common to all schools of Tibetan Buddhism, certain schools have preferences even for different manifestations of the highest beings. Among the protectors, too, some are claimed to be protectors of special sects, groups, regions or individuals. The quality of these highest beings is undisputed in the tradition, they are 'canonical', but the authenticity of the specialized protectors can be disputed. The lower beings can become jealous and vindictive if a person looks for help to another protector. Next to faith in the highest beings, each lineage of Tulkus has special protectors as well. If Tulkus get into conflict with each other, so do protectors.

The Conflict of Authenticity—Aspects of the Shugden Controversy

At present a deep conflict has developed within Tibetan Buddhism, especially in the school of the Gelukpas around the Dalai Lama. This conflict reflects precisely the issue of different levels of canonicity earlier outlined: the universal *versus* the regional, the scriptural canon *versus* the charismatic interpretation as embodied in the Tulkus—whose lineages are authorized in addition by their special connections to deities. The problem is the classification or canonical status of a given deity, in our case the deity Shugden.

Shugden (*rdo rje shugs ldan*) should be considered a deity (*lha*) belonging to the lower realm, as can be seen by his historical origin. However, the issue is disputed. Obviously, Shugden has been linked to Gelukpa monasteries and became one of the main protectors of the Gelukpas, but there is also a relationship to the Sakyas. He comes from all directions (and monasteries!) in order to protect his worshippers, to fulfill wishes, to purify the dharma, etc. (Nebesky-Wojkowitz 1993: 141) His character is fierce and violent and he destroys all enemies. Animals are sacrificed to him symbolically. His abode is full of skeletons and human skulls, weapons surround him and the blood of men and horses form a lake. (Nebesky-Wojkowitz 1993: 136–7) His body has a dark-red colour and his facial expressions are similar to the well-known descriptions of *rākṣasas*. However, all these attributes are not unique, they are more or less stereotypes for dharma-protectors in general. Different traditions focus on different forms and colours, e.g. in the Gonkhang (*mgon khang*) of Geluk monasteries such as Gaden, the deity Shugden is propitiated in his red form, whereas as *dharmapāla* of the Sakya monastery he rides a black horse. How and when these different iconographic details developed cannot be established.

Shugden has obviously been quite popular in the Southern Himalayas. He is invoked to protect 'the prestige of the Buddha, dharma, and sangha' and to dissipate 'the obstructions that hinder attainment of the *bodhisattva* mind' (Mumford 1990: 262). So far this description testifies to the noble intentions of the deity and relates it to the refuge in the *triratna*. At the same time, Shugden is connected with 'human wealth, food, life, and good fortune' and asked to grant long life and the fulfilment of all desires, particularly in this life, and invoked against bodily and mental sickness (Mumford 1990: 262–3). This, too, is not at all a deviation from other incantations to protector deities. He is addressed as 'great king', 'religion-protector', 'wish-fulfilling gem' who 'protects the dharma and prevents its destruction' and is asked to 'repel external and internal enemies of the ten regions.'

Like Pehar, Nechung and other deities Shugden takes possession of mediums, or Kuten (*sku rten*), which are his physical supports. A famous Kuten of Shugden lives in the Gaden monastery of the Gelukpa sect, which has been approved by the monastic authorities and is tested regularly. I do not intend to elaborate on this aspect since I have dealt with the history and experience of this Kuten elsewhere.[12] It suffices to say that to my knowledge no sectarian tendencies have appeared—at least in connection with this Kuten.

History of Shugden

The 5th Dalai Lama: In order to determine the quality and nature of Shugden his history needs to be taken into account. However, there is little documented historical evidence before the beginning of this century, though many oral traditions—sometimes mutually contradictory—have to be taken into account.[13]

The story of Shugden[14] goes back to the 5th Dalai Lama (Ngawang Losang Gyatso, 1617–82). He lived at a time of struggle for power in Tibet. It was also the beginning of the Gelukpa dominance over Tibet, and the 5th Dalai Lama consolidated his power and centralized the state on the basis of Mongol military power. In order to unify the Tibetans he was interested in an 'ecumenical approach', i.e. he wanted to find a new approach to sectarian strife by recognizing their 'unity in difference'. Hence, he took instruction not only from Gelukpa teachers but also from Nyingma teachers. In the beginning he wielded a strong hand towards the Kagyüpas, but became more tolerant and accommodating in later years (Schulemann 1958: 235). This was certainly controversial among some Gelukpas, and the following story might well have a historical basis in those controversies.

At the Dalai Lama's upper residence (*bla brang*) in Drepung (*'bras-spungs*) monastery there was a Tulku Drakpa Gyaltsen (*sprul sku grags pa rgyel mtshan*) who was supposed to be a reincarnation of the Panchen Sonam Drakpa (1478–1554), the disciple of the 2nd Dalai Lama, whereas the first incarnation was Dulzin Drakpa Gyaltsen, a disciple of Tsongkhapa (1357–1410). It is hard to establish this reincarnation lineage historically, it is rather a matter of belief.[15] Tulku Drakpa Gyaltsen had probably been one of the contenders to be chosen as the 5th Dalai Lama (Yamaguchi 1995: 12), and this must have caused tensions, especially since the Dalai Lama intended to minimize the number and importance of other Tulku lineages at Drepung in order to centralize power. Due to his wisdom Tulku Drakpa Gyaltsen had an increasing number of followers which caused jealousy among the adherents and in the household of the Dalai Lama. Certain circles of government officials connected with the Dalai Lama (including the Regent) decided to kill Tulku Drakpa Gyaltsen. Different versions are handed down as to whether he was killed or killed himself. His main disciple asked him not to leave the world but to come back in proper form and take revenge on his enemies. All sorts of misfortunes happened to the Tibetan government, and even the Dalai Lama suffered. Nobody could stop this evil spirit or bind him. When the Tibetan government realized that the spirit could not be subdued, they requested him to co-operate and, instead of causing harm, to become a protector of the Gelukpa sect. The spirit of Tulku Drakpa Gyaltsen agreed and became Shugden, the protector deity.

Historical evidence is not clear and the details contradict each other. We cannot even be sure that the events relating to the death of Tulku Drakpa Gyaltsen and the worship of Shugden in the nineteenth and twentieth centuries concern the same deity or at least form a continuous tradition. The problem is that he seems to be an evil spirit causing harm to the monastic institutions and the Dalai Lamas, but at the same time he is regarded as dharma-protector of a higher rank.[16] One thing is quite clear: the story of the link between the death of Tulku Drakpa Gyaltsen and the worship of Shugden has its roots in the power struggles of the 5th Dalai Lama and the successful centralization of power in his hands after the death of the Mongol Gushri Khan.

Developments in the nineteenth and twenthieth centuries: The contemporary controversial Shugden worship starts probably with Tagphu Dorje Chang (*stag phu bstan p'ai dngos grubs*, 1876–1922), the teacher of Phabongkhapa (1878–1941), who handed down the practice to Trijang Rinpoche (1901–81), the junior tutor of the 14th Dalai Lama. It is here, at the turn of this century, that Shugden (Dolgyal) enters the Gelukpa tradition, whereas before many textual references hint at the Sakya school. And only at that time the deity seems to become a sectarian protector.

Phabongkhapa: This sectarian emphasis or exclusivity is evident in Phabongkhapa (1878–1941). Phabongkhapa (*pha bong kha pa byams pa bstan 'dzin phrin las rgya mtsho*) is a key figure in the history of the Shugden controversy. He was a charismatic teacher and member of the Sera Me monastery. Whether he received the Shugden tradition and the controversial Sogde (*srog gtad*, i.e. life-entrustment)[17] from his teacher Tagphu or not, he preached it forcefully, initiated many disciples into it, and made this practice popular among high Gelukpa Lamas. In his 'Initiation texts for the practice of the visionary teachings'[18] which he had received from Losang Choekyi Wangchuk (*blo bzang chos kyi dbang phyug*), there are teachings on Amitāyus, Avalokiteśvara, Vajrapāṇi, Tārā and the Guru Yoga, and there is no mention of Shugden because the text deals with high Tantric initiations. That Shugden is not mentioned in this context suggests that he considers the deity not among this high class of deities. However, in his text 'The profound blessing of life-initiation of Shugden, the most powerful *dharmapāla* of Jamgön (Tsongkhapa), the jewel chariot bringing forth a mass of blessings'[19] he gives a detailed account of the Shugden practice and remarks—

> I have written this at the request of Shugden, because in the past there was a tradition of Sogde (*srog gtad*) to Shugden[20] but later neither the tradition nor the text could be found—they have become like flowers in the sky—so Shugden has asked me two times to write a new initiation text. I have passed on the practice of initiation (*dbang*) to some disciples in accordance with my own experience, and (a text) has been written as a seed for (a detailed text). But only that would be not reliable and something like an illegitimate son. Therefore, I explained it in detail to my master Tagphu Dorje Chang and presented this draft to him. ... (501) He took that draft and wrote his text down, combining this seed text with his own vision. Tagphu commented about the five types of Shugden, the respective colors etc., the offerings to be arranged, thus at the time of initiation the large Lamrim text should be there on the altar, a cakra representing one's life, ḍamaru, dorje etc. The practitioner has to utter the life generating words of Vajrabhairava and to make torma[21] offerings. ... (502) The initiation can be given to somebody who has received initiation into Vajrabhairava and keeps the commitments connected with it. ... (502–503) Though there are so many different traditions and philosophies in Tibet, only this tradition of Tsongkhapa is the supreme, the top of the victory banner, the most complete, the essence of the teaching. ... (505) To bring Shugden into one's own service is a very powerful blessing. In order to receive this initiation the disciples visualize themselves as the *yidam* (Vajrabhairava) and as such invoke and control Shugden. The *dharmapāla* (Shugden) is presented to the disciples as the one who abides by their commands.

He goes on to explain how master and disciple visualize themselves as Vajrabhairava and Yamāntaka and then receive initiation into the five aspects of Shugden—including *mantras*, colours etc.—which emanate from the altar (505). The emanating energies are finally dissolved into the heart of the disciple, with full awareness that he controls the protector.

In order to interpret Phabongkhapa properly we have to distinguish several aspects of initiation in Tibetan Buddhism. There are two types of 'initiation', and the first comprises two aspects:

(1) (a) The initiation into the realm or presence of the positive emanation of a deity (*dbang*) which corresponds largely to the Indian rite of *abhiṣeka*;

(b) the permission to continue the practice of a deity (*rjes gnang*) after initiation (a) proper. This requires control of the deity, and high masters are supposed to be able to have the power to control the deity.

(2) Life-entrustment initiation (*srog gtad*) which is a complete surrender

of the person's whole life and unconditional refuge—this commitment can be made only to the Buddha or the *yidam* as his perfect emanation on the personal level.

On this basis Phabongkhapa's text has two characteristic marks:

— It does not say that only Gelukpa teaching leads to liberation, but calls Tsongkhapa's teaching the highest and the essence of all teachings. But this is traditional parlance and not an exaggerated exclusivity.

— The text quoted does not say that master and disciple actually take refuge in Shugden. The *yidam* and Shugden are kept apart, and the *dharmapāla* is to be controlled. The master transfers the power to control Shugden to the disciple, and this is common practice. However, in so far as the disciple merges with the Shugden energy an *identification with Shugden* takes place, and this is against the genuine Gelukpa tradition. There can be no life-entrustment initiation (*srog gtad*) concerning a *dharmapāla*, for the *dharmapāla* is a minor being and not a *yidam*.[22]

Thus, the whole controversy focuses on the interpretation of the status of Shugden. There is a contradiction concerning Shugden that cannot be resolved. On the one hand it is argued that Shugden is a wrathful, mundane protector deity with such and such an origin in history, and to deal with such a spirit one has to have control over him. On the other hand, those who propitiate Shugden maintain that Shugden is a high deity beyond the mundane level and therefore deserves life-entrustment (*srog gtad*), i.e. complete surrender, like emanations of the Buddha. Whether the sectarian issue (Gelukpa exclusivity) is connected with this problem is a different question. It depends on the interpretation of Shugden, and this varies, as has been demonstrated.

The issue was taken up by the 13th Dalai Lama and the Tibetan government, who managed to stop Phabongkhapa propitiating Shugden. The Tibetan government argued (1) that Shugden was in competition with Nechung who, being very close to the government and the Dalai Lama personally, was the protector of the Drepung monastery; and that taking refuge in Shugden was to belittle the refuge in the Buddha-Dharma-Saṃgha (*triratna*).

Whether Phabongkhapa's Shugden practice led to violent sectarian attacks particularly on Nyingma institutions, is not quite clear. Tsetan Zhabdrung, a famous scholar from Amdo, reports that followers of Phabongkhapa destroyed Padmasambhava's image and those of other peaceful and wrathful deities.

Trijang Rinpoche: Trijang Rinpoche (1901–81), the disciple of Phabongkhapa and junior tutor of the 14th Dalai Lama, had a tremendous influence on a whole generation of Tulkus and higher Lamas of the Gelukpa order. His residence at Gaden Shartse monastery (in exile near Mundgod, North Karnataka, India) ensured a close relation of this monastic establishment to his teachings. He also practised the Shugden tradition, and most of the present Gelukpa Lamas, who oppose the order of the 14th Dalai Lama to give up on Shugden, do so with reference to Trijang Rinpoche as their teacher. He mentions his stand on Shugden in his autobiography[23] and in a text called 'Commentary on Phabongkhapa's Praise to Shugden.'[24]

Trijang argues that the deity Shugden already has had a relation with Tsongkhapa, and that it arose as *dharmapāla* in accordance with the wishes of Nechung. He addresses Shugden—'Praise to you who had the courage to take up the wish of Nechung, the most powerful protector, who time and again asked you to arise as this *dharmapāla* specifically for the Gaden tradition.' (98) Thus, he implies that there is no contradiction between Nechung and Shugden. Trijang further maintains that the 5th Dalai Lama and Tulku Drakpa Gyaltsen *could* not have had this controversy, but that this misfortune was due to the followers of both Lamas—the seeming difference was an *upāya* (means for spiritual success) between the Dalai Lama and Tulku Drakpa Gyaltsen in order to manifest the power of Shugden (115). He quotes a hymn which the 5th Dalai Lama is said to have written in praise of Shugden (Tulku Drakpa Gyaltsen):

> ... your might and power is like lightning, you possess the courage and confidence to discriminate between right and wrong, I invite you faithfully, so come here to this place. ... You subdue various spirits of cremation grounds. I arrange varieties of outer, inner and secret offerings and tormas. I confess that previously due to my selfishness I could not leave this attitude of being so strict (against this spirit), but now I praise you humbly and respectfully with body, speech and mind ... may we always be protected by the *triratna*.

The problem is that this position has no historical evidence, neither in the biography of the 5th Dalai Lama or elsewhere. It could be assumed that had the Dalai Lama known about any connection between Tsongkhapa (Nechung) and Shugden (Tulku Drakpa Gyaltsen) he would have acted differently. Because of the very different position and rank of the two it is rather unlikely that the 5th Dalai Lama would have written such a hymn of self-correction.

We could go on quoting several oral traditions which are related by Trijang Rinpoche to establish and defend the Shugden tradition. Trijang wants to show that Nechung and Shugden do not clash or, in other terms, that there is no contradiction between the general protection of the whole of the Tibetan Buddhist tradition and the specific protection of the Gelukpa school only. Looking into the history of the struggle between different schools in Tibet and judging from the heat of the present controversy there is more to say. It is clear that by historical evidence the authenticity of that tradition on Shugden cannot be decided.

The Dalai Lama's Arguments against Shugden

When the Tibetans went into exile several Lamas, such as Trijang Rinpoche, Zong Rinpoche and others—many of them connected with Gaden Shartse monastery—brought the Shugden practice with them. Especially Zong Rinpoche, being a student of Trijang Rinpoche, was engaged in the practice and passed it on to many disciples, first in Buxa Duar (North India), later in South India. However, it needs to be mentioned that most of the Lamas who received this initiation had been devotees of Shugden long before, and it is obvious that this practice had been widespread for at least two or three generations. This was so not only in Nepal, as mentioned, but also in other areas of the Southern Himalayas such as Ladakh and Spiti. The 14th Dalai Lama himself had been initiated into this practice by his tutor Trijang Rinpoche. But the Dalai Lama publicly expressed doubts about Shugden and stopped this practice, first for himself in 1976, and since 1996 by asking all official institutions and disciples, who had received initiations from him, to give up Shugden. This is to be seen in connection with his interest in finding common ground in the main schools of Tibetan Buddhism (Dalai Lama 1984: 200–25) so as to overcome precisely those exclusivist tendencies that Shugden is said to protect.

The 14th Dalai Lama himself has taken up the issue several times. His statements on Shugden have been collected and published recently in Tibetan.[25] In order to investigate the canonical status of Shugden and his practice, he applies basically three methodological devices or arguments: (1) historical evidence, (2) political reason, (3) spiritual insight.

(1) *Historical evidence*: In order to examine the authenticity of the Shugden tradition the Dalai Lama refers back to the historical origin, implying that at the origin the purity of the tradition is still maintained and therefore the judgement on canonicity on this basis is valid. However, two 'origins' have to be distinguished: the general origin of the Buddhist tradition (the Buddha who has preached the dharma and thus established the *saṃgha*), and the particular origin of the Gelukpa tradition (Tsongkhapa and his teachings). The Dalai Lama defends his views in arguing that Buddhism is refuge in the *triratna*, and that this is the yardstick of

canonicity. Any additional practice may help in practising this refuge in the *triratna* but can never be a substitute. In fact, if such an additional practice leads to obscuring the *triratna*, it is to be given up. Therefore, he refutes the practice of life-entrustment (*srog gtad*) to Shugden. Otherwise Tibetan Buddhism would become a kind of Shamanism.[26] He also attacks the practice of Shugden as a corruption of the original *dharmapāla* practice for worldly gains.[27]

> Propitiating spirits is a practice originating in pre-Buddhist Tibet. However, when Guru Padmasambhava was helping to establish Buddhism in Tibet in the eighth century, He recruited some spirits such as Nechung, the State Oracle, to protect the Buddhist doctrine. Due to his high spiritual attainments, he was able to subdue such spirits and bind them by oath. Propitiating of spirits, therefore, is not a Buddhist practice itself, but a means to help sustain spiritual practice. Over the centuries the practice of propitiating spirits has instead become widespread as a means to achieve fame, fortune and the general well-being for this life, concerns that run counter to the general Buddhist outlook.

At the same time he needs to link his arguments to the *specific* origin of Gelukpa tradition, to Tsongkhapa. There cannot be a contradiction, for if Tsongkhapa interprets the Buddhadharma rightly, he himself refers back to the *triratna*. That is to say, that canonicity is to be founded in the *triratna* as interpreted by Tsongkhapa.

(2) *Political reason*: The Dalai Lama is part of the Gelukpa tradition but at the same time responsible for all of Tibetan Buddhism. This is a structural problem, for if the interests of the two conflict, the Dalai Lama is caught in between. His arguments here are based both on historical comparison and general reasoning. He refers to the life of the 5th Dalai Lama and the 13th Dalai Lama, takes these predecessors as examples of a pan-Buddhist spirit which has rejected the sectarian approach, and he himself follows the same line. In both cases the historical evidence has already been highlighted. The 5th Dalai Lama, for instance, established the political power of the Gelukpas, but in course of time he integrated Nyingma and Kagyüpa teachings and balanced the interest of these groups. He thus achieved political stability—unheard of before. Likewise in the present situation: he wants all Tibetans to be united in the refuge to the *triratna*, to respect the differences of the traditions by seeing them in relation to each other (Dalai Lama 1984: 200–25) so as to overcome all divisive forces. The 14th Dalai Lama goes on and argues: it is said by the Shugden propitiatiors that Nechung had asked Tulku Drakpa Gyaltsen several times to arise as this wrathful deity Shugden (77). Even if this were the case, it is Nechung who would be the subject and originator of the whole tradition. But because of the sectarian spirit, this cannot be.

(3) *Spiritual insight:* Since the argument is about deities in conflict (Nechung *versus* Shugden) a direct insight into the nature of these spiritual levels would be necessary to judge the authenticity. The Dalai Lama—as all the Dalai Lamas before him—relies on Nechung and repeatedly argues that he had approached Nechung (in a special spiritual communication which is not accessible to everybody) and Nechung had told him to bring up the issue (49–50). Accordingly, Nechung is in conflict with Shugden and therefore propitiating Shugden is to be given up. But even here the Dalai Lama judges the authenticity of Nechung by reason.

He states:

> Even if my master says something I compare it with what Je Tsongkhapa said and examine it on that basis. Likewise, I do not right away believe, even if it is said by a dharma protector. I think about it and do divination, I am very careful ... Some may think that I am easily believing everything that Nechung says ... but this is not so ... It is said that we Gelukpas appreciate the power of conventional reasoning. So we have to keep up with it. Hence it has to be questioned whether Shugden is the reincarnation of Tulku Drakpa Gyaltsen or not. Even if it were so, it would be on the basis of a conflict between Tulku Drakpa and the 5th Dalai Lama ... It is to be judged reasonably ... But to judge the exceptional (the deities) on the basis of the level of ordinary beings is impossible. (77)

However, in spite of these arguments, opposition against this interpretation of the Dalai Lama and the Exile government is still strong on two grounds:[28]

- the truthfulness and commitments to one's root teacher
- religious freedom

Many of the present Lamas of the Gelukpa tradition have received their teachings from Trijang Rinpoche or Zong Rinpoche. In those cases where he is the 'root Lama' (*rtsa ba'i bla ma*) who has handed down all three aspects of the tradition (oral transmission of texts, commentaries, the empowerments), the relationship to him is absolutely binding. This is an essential part of Vajrayāna practice. Otherwise, according to Tantric tradition he might be regarded as a person who has broken the Tantric vow (*dam-nyams*) and this would concern the Dalai Lama himself as having been initiated by Shugden practice.

Conclusion

The present Tibetan Shugden controversy can be interpreted as a problem of the general validity of arguments based on canonical judgements versus particular religious forces as embodied in special protector deities linked to specific sects and Tulku lineages. This issue is personalized in the institution of the Dalai Lamas. The Dalai Lamas are being interpreted as reincarnated Lamas of the highest spiritual power. They are incarnations of *Avalokiteśvara*, the *bodhisattva of compassion* for all sentient beings. As such their scope is universal or at least related to the whole of Tibet, both in religious and political terms. On the other hand, the Dalai Lamas belong to one sect of Tibetan Buddhism, the Gelukpas, who have been engaged in power struggles with other sects and groups. Since the identity of these groups is largely shaped by Tulku lineages, the lineage of the Dalai Lamas is in this respect one among many—a fact reflected in the different interpretations of protector deities, which are connected with those groups, sects and lineages.

These lineages are shaped not only by transmission of the canonical texts but also by Tantric *initiations*, which transfer spiritual power directly from teacher to disciple. However, the efficacy of Tantric initiation requires truthfulness and commitment to one's root teacher. Thus, if the root teacher has transmitted the Shugden practice to a disciple, he should not give it up, even if he wishes to. This is the tragic dilemma in the present controversy. That is to say, *the present controversy clearly reveals the clash between the need to critically establish canonicity and obedience to the Lama*. Therefore, the present controversy and the Dalai Lama's call to focus on the essentials of Buddhist practice are significant events in establishing canonicity within non-textual aspects of Tibetan Buddhism.

Notes

1. I wish to thank H. H. the Dalai Lama for his personal advice and help in getting access to the archives and informants at various offices in Dharamsala. I am also greatly indebted to Ven. Tenzin Tsepak, Dialectic School at Dharamsala, who helped me to locate and translate important texts in the archives and library at Dharamsala.
2. The 100 volumes of Kanjur (*bka' 'gyur*) contain 13 volumes of *Vinaya*, 21 volumes of *Prajñāparamitā–Sūtras*, 45 volumes of other *Sūtras*, and 21 volumes comprising various *Tantras*. Tanjur (*bstan 'gyur*) is divided into three parts: (1) 64 hymns in one volume; (2) 2664 commentaries on the *Tantras* in 86 volumes; (3) a collection of several texts that can be subdivided into 15 volumes of commentaries on the *Prajñāparamitā*-literature, 18 volumes of *Mādhyamika-Śāstras*, 10 volumes of further *Sūtra*-commentaries, 10 volumes of *Yogācāra-Śāstras*, 30 volumes of *Śāstras* on early Buddhist texts, 30 volumes on logic, medicine, crafts and trade (mostly translations from Sanskrit), and 13 volumes of Tibetan texts on various topics.
3. Statement of H.H. the Dalai Lama on the Shugden issue, 1 July 1996,

Archives Private Office of H.H. the Dalai Lama, Dharamsala 1996. Cf. Shobhan Saxena's interview with the Dalai Lama in *The Times of India*, 17 August 1996.

4. Open letter 'To the Tibetan Buddhists around the world and fellow Tibetan compatriots within and outside Tibet', no date (summer/autumn 1996), Archives of the Council of Religious and Cultural Affairs, Dharamsala.
5. 'To the Tibetan Buddhists' (5).
6. Ibid. (9).
7. *Tibet und Buddhismus* 11.41 (1997): 36–7.
8. The Dalai Lama (seat in Lhasa) is not the only and uncontested leading figure of the Gelukpas. The Panchen Rinpoche (seat in Shigatse) and the abbots of the three great monastic universities near Lhasa (Ganden, Drepung, Sera) are important too. In history we observe power struggles between the Panchen Rinpoche and the Dalai Lama which are linked with regional rivalries between the provinces of Ü (Lhasa) and Tsang (Shigatse).
9. Ray (1986: 42) suggests that from the beginning the concept of Tulku and divine kingship as understood in Tibet are connected.
10. Nebesky-Wojkowitz (1993: ix) states that even Lamas of the same sect 'very often disagree in their explanations of the more complicated religious theories or in the translation of obscure passages in Tibetan works.'
11. The cult of local protector deities had become very popular at the time of the *Mahāparinirvāṇa-Sūtra* for it is explicitly justified in that text. See Klimkeit (1990: 144).
12. See von Brück (1996).
13. Some material is collected in Kashag (ed.), *Dolgyal gyi jungrim* (Historical development of Dolgyal). Dharamsala, 1996 [manuscript].
14. Parts (or rather a few hints) of this can be found in the autobiography of the 5th Dalai Lama, but it is retold by Trijang Rinpoche and others, lately also by Nebesky-Wojkowitz (1993: 134–5).
15. See Losang Gyatso (1996: 2).
16. Losang Gyatso refers to the collected works of Phabongkhapa and criticizes him, for he regards him as a great deity and emanation of the Buddha but mentions at the same time that many regard him as a lower spirit which causes harm on account of his bad *karman* (Losang Gyatso 1996: 5).
17. *Srog gtad* is complete surrender of body, speech and mind to the deity. The disciple who entrusts his whole life to the Buddha or an emanation of the Buddha can do this only to the highest spiritual beings, not to lower ones.
18. The full title reads *Dpal stag phu'i gsaṇ chos rgya can bcu gsum gyi smin byed dbang chog chu 'babs su bkod pa don gñis 'bras bus brijd pa'i yoṇs 'du'i dbang po* and was printed from the block prints of 1935 from Lha klu House in Lhasa in 1979.
19. Phabongkhapa, *'Jam mgon bstan srung thu bo rdo rje shugs ldan gyi srog dbang dzab mo'i byin rlab rin chen dbang po 'dren p'ai yid ches nor bu'i shing rta*. In *Collected Works*. Vol. 7. 498ff. Delhi, n.d. (Library of Tibetan Works and Archives Acc. No. 457, Acc. 1622).

20. He refers to a lost text by Lama Rinchen Wangyal.
21. Tormas (*gtor ma*) are offering cakes used in rituals made of barley-flour (*tsam ba*) and butter.
22. However, there is evidence that *srog-gtad* or *rjes-gnang* is being practiced also with regard to other dharma-protectors. Hence, Shugden seems to be no complete exception.
23. Published in Tibetan in Delhi in 1978.
24. The full title reads *Dge ldan bstan pa bsrung b'ai lha mchog sprul p'ai chos rgyal chen po rdo rje shugs ldan rtsal gyi gsang gsum rmad du byung b'ai rtogs pa brtod p'ai gtam du bya ba dam can rgya mtsho dgyes p'ai rol mo*. (Dharma protector of Gaden, Supreme Deity, manifestation of the deity Dorje Shugden ...) in Trijang Rinpoche (1978: 98ff.).
25. See Dalai Lama (1996).
26. Statement in a personal talk with the author on 19 October 1996 at the Dalai Lama's residence in Dharamsala.
27. The Dalai Lama quoted in *Principal Points of the Kashag's Statement concerning Dolgyal*. Geneva: The Tibet Bureau, 1996.
28. Letter to all Tibet Support Groups by the Dorje Shugden Devotees Religious and Charitable Society, New Delhi, November 1996 (Archives of the Private Office of H.H. the Dalai Lama, Dharamsala). The letter expresses 'a great deal of anguish among a large number of Tibetans and the followers of several prominent Lamas who spread the Dharma to thousands of non-Tibetans around the world', for the prohibition of the Shugden practice 'is forcing almost all of the Gelugpa Lamas who have spread the Dharma to the West to break their vow and commitments to either His Holiness or to their root Guru, who is also the root Guru of His Holiness, Kyabje Trijang Rinpoche.'

References

Bleichsteiner, Robert. 1937. *Die Gelbe Kirche*. Wien: Josef Belf.

Dalai Lama. 1984. *Kindness, Clarity and Insight*. Ithaca: Snow Lion.

———. 1996. *Gong sa skyabs mgon chen po mchog nas chos skyong bstan phyogs skor bk'a slob snga rjes bstsal pa khag cha tshang phyogs bsdebs zhus pa* (Complete Collection of Statements of H.H. the Dalai Lama on the Reliance of Dharmapālas). Dharamsala: Sherig Parkhang Publications.

Dharma Losang Dorje. *Rigs dang dkyil 'khor rga mtsho'i khyab bdag heruka dpal ngur smrig gar rol skyabs gchig pha bong kha pa bde chen snying po dpal bzang po'i rnam thar pa don ldan tshangs p'ai dbyangs snyan* (Life Story of Phabongkhapa), *Phabongkhapa, Collected Works* Vol. 14, Lhasa Edition, Library of Tibetan Works and Archives, Dharamsala, Acc. No. 1622.

Ekvall, Robert B. 1959. Three Categories of Inmates within Tibetan Monasteries: Status and Function. *Central Asiatic Journal* 5.1: 206–220.

Klimkeit, Hans-Joachim. 1990. *Der Buddha. Leben und Lehre*. Stuttgart: Kohlhammer.

Ladrang Kalsang. 1996. *The Guardian Deities of Tibet*. Dharamsala: Little Lhasa Publications.

Losang Gyatso, Losang. 1996. *Shugs ldan gyi skor gsal bsha'i gsum pa* (Clarifications about Shugden). Dharamsala.

Losang Tayang. *'Jam mgon rgyal ba gnyis p'ai bstan bsrung thun mong ma yin pa rgyal chen rdo rje shugs ldan rtsal gyi chos skor be bum du bsgrigs p'ai dkar chags gnam lcags 'khor lo'i mu 'khyud phrin las 'od bar*. Dharamsala: Library of Tibetan Works and Archives Acc. No. 614.

Mumford, Stan. 1990. *Royal, Himalayan Dialogue. Tibetan Lamas and Gurung Shamans in Nepal*. Kathmandu: Tiwari.

Nebesky-Wojkowitz, R. de N. 1993. *Oracles and Demons of Tibet*. Kathmandu: Tiwari.

Phabongkhapa. n.d. *Collected Works* Vols. 7 and 14. Lhasa edition. Dharamsala: Library of Tibetan Works and Archives.

Ray, Reginald. 1986. Some Aspects of the Tulku Tradition in Tibet. *The Tibet Journal* 11.4: 35–69.

Richardson, H.E. 1958. The Karma-pa Sect. A Historical Note. *Journal of the Royal Asiatic Society of Great Britain and Ireland*, Pt. 1: 140–64.

Rock, Joseph F. 1935. Sungmas, the Living Oracles of the Tibetan Church. *The National Geographic Magazine* 68.4: 475–8.

Schopen, Gregory. 1985. Two Problems in the History of Indian Buddhism: The Layman/Monk Distinction and the Doctrines of the Transference of Merit. *Studien zur Indologie und Iranistik* 10: 9–47.

———. 1987. Burial 'ad sanctos' and the Physical Presence of the Buddha in Early Indian Buddhism. *Religion* 17: 193–225.

Schulemann, Günther. 1958. *Geschichte der Dalai Lamas*. Leipzig: Harrassowitz.

Stein, R.A. 1972. *Tibetan Civilization*. Stanford: Stanford University Press.

Tibet und Buddhismus 11.41 (1997): 36–7.

Trijang Rinpoche. 1978. *Dge lden bstan pa bsrung b'ai lha mchog sprul p'ai chos rgyal chen po rdo rje shugs ldan* (Commentary on Phabongkhapa's Praise to Shugden). *The Collected Works* Vol. 4. New Delhi.

von Brück, Michael. 1999. *Religion und Politik im Tibetischen Buddhismus*. München: Kösel.

von Brück, Michael and Regina. 1996. *Die Welt des Tibetischen Buddhismus*. München: Kösel.

Yamaguchi, Zuihō. 1995. The Sovereign Power of the Fifth Dalai Lama: sPrul sku gZims-khang-gong-ma and the Removal of Governor Nor-bu. *Memoirs of the Research Department of the Toyo Bunko* 53: 1–27.

Ānanda Yoga: A Contemporary Crossing between Ṣūfīsm and Hinduism[1]

GIAN GIUSEPPE FILIPPI AND THOMAS DÄHNHARDT

Rāmcāndr Caudharī was born at Fatehgarh, a small town in the United Provinces, present-day Uttar Pradesh, on 2 February 1873. He was the eldest son of Bhakṣ Rāy Caudharī, a small employee of the British administration, who belonged to the *kṣatriya* caste of the *kāyasthas*. Bhakṣ Rāy left his village of Bhugrama, in the Manipuri District (U.P.) for Fatehgarh after the tragedy of the Mutiny. The information collected on Bhakṣ Rāy discloses that he had also been the guru of a school of Ramaite Yoga which allowed its members to maintain the condition of married ascetics or *gṛhasthi yogīs*.[2] The legend adds that the wife of Bhakṣ Rāy Caudharī was sterile and middle-aged when she was blessed simultaneously by a *faqīr* and a *sant*. The double spiritual influence cancelled the infertility of the woman and after nine months she delivered Rāmcāndr, soon followed after twenty months by the second son, Raghubar Dayāl, who was born on 7 October 1874. Among the Ānanda yogīs the miracle of these two births is to the day considered as a sign of the spiritual revival of the Yogic path inherited by the children. It seems, in fact, that the internal situation of that Ramaite school was in disarray. The authority and personal charisma of the gurus reached its lowest point in the mid-nineteenth century. The sincere devotional attitude of its decreasing number of members was in no way supported by an efficient method or a clear doctrine. The exceptional piety, the intellectual capacity and the undeniable charm of Rāmcāndr and Raghubar Dayāl Caudharī seemed to promise a renewal.

In fact, nobody could have imagined the tortuous ways chosen by Providence in order to accomplish this task. In Aligarh, at that time, Ḥazrat Khvājā Maulvi Fazl Aḥmad Khān Rāypuri held the chair of *Pīr* of the *ṭarīqa naqšabandiyya—mazhariyya,*[3] fifth after the founder of this Ṣūfic branch, the great saint Ḥazrat Mīrzā Mazhar Jān-e-Jānān (1700–91). Starting from the time of Jān-e-Jānān, the outlook of the *ṭarīqa* had been intellectually open towards Hinduism. Jān-e-Jānān had himself, despite being undoubtedly an orthodox Muslim, studied the *Upaniṣads* and declared the Veda to be a book inspired by God, and Hinduism a revealed religion, equal to Judaism and Christianity (Murādābādī 1309 A. H.).

In a dream Ḥazrat Fazl Aḥmad Khān saw an angel who suggested to him that he give the Ṣūfic initiation, the *bai'at*, to the most gifted boy he would meet. Fate determined that Ḥazrat Fazl Aḥmad Khān recognized the young Hindu Rāmcāndr Caudharī as the most worthy person to receive his complete initiation. Rāmcāndr Caudharī received the *bai'at* from the hands of the Ṣūfī master on 23 January 1893. Ten months later on 11 October, Rāmcāndr obtained from the *Pīr* (he addressed him by the mixed title of *Huzūr Mahārāj*) the appointment to the role of Master and successor, *pūrṇa adhikāra aur guru padvī*. After a few days, the younger brother Raghubar Dayāl also became a disciple of the Muslim master. Right from the beginning, these occurrences display a very peculiar feature, namely that the disciples of the *Pīr* did not become Muslims, but remained *gṛhasthi yogīs*.

Thus the new guru Mahātmā Rāmcāndrjī Mahārāj continued with this kind of dual spiritual and social life. He was an employee of the Rāj just as his father and performed privately the function of master of yoga. His position compelled him to be transfered frequently and therefore the Ānanda Yoga became known throughout the United Provinces.

In 1907 Ḥazrat Khvājā Fazl Aḥmad Khān died and his brother Ḥazrat Maulvi Shāh 'Abdul Ghanī Khān succeeded in the regular Ṣūfic line *mazhariyya*. He recognized an appropriate spiritual co-operation with the Ānanda Yoga, and during the year 1913 he renewed the acknowledgement of the title of *pūrṇa adhikāra aur guru padvī* for his Hindu brother Rāmcāndr Caudharī. After this second Islamic recognition, the Hindu guru at times accepted Muslim disciples in his *sampradāya*.

Mahātmā Rāmcāndrjī did not recognize a worthy successor among his own sons and therefore turned his attention to the child of his brother Raghubar Dayāl. The birth of the Paramsant Mahātmā Brījmohanlāljī in April 1898 had also been propitiated by Fazl Aḥmad Khān with a peculiar blessing. Soon Brījmohanlāl displayed his exceptional intellectual capacities to such an extent that Ḥazrat Maulvi Fazl Aḥmad Khān appointed him as successor in the Hindu lineage. The boy was raised under the guidance of his uncle Rāmcāndrjī. Imitating the small boy's affectionate way of address, all the disciples began to call their guru uncle, *cācājī*, and the brother of the master *lālajī*, i.e. beloved father. After receiving the *dīkṣā* from uncle Rāmcāndrjī, Brījmohanlāl was initiated to the Ṣūfic *ṭarīqa naqšabandiyya* by Ḥazrat Maulvi 'Abdul Ghanī Khān, with the Islamic name of Muḥammad Sa'id. In 1928 the Islamic *Pīr* raised him to the honour of the supreme guru. Under his charismatic guidance the *sampradāya* reached several thousand disciples, gaining the respect of the Brahmans of the Ganges Valley.

Paramsant Mahātmā Rāmcāndrjī Fatehgarhi died in 1931. Brījmohanlāl Sāhab took over the guidance of the *sampradāya* and disseminated the Ānanda Yoga throughout North India due to the mobility required by his job. He was superintendent of the police and within a period of twenty years he was transferred from Kanpur, where his family had established residence in 1937, to Ujjain, Bombay and Lucknow. It was in Lucknow that he finally retired in 1951, dedicating the last years of his life to his family and his disciples. There are accounts of many miracles performed by Brījmohanlāl in these years. It also seems that, during the *satsang sabhā* with groups of *dīkṣitas* coming from the four quarters of the subcontinent, he often experienced *samādhi*. It was during a *samādhi* of three days that Brījmohanlāljī Mahārāj left the human world, on 17 January 1955. Subsequently, his body was conveyed to Lucknow and burnt in the cremation ground three days later. In the description of the funeral rites for Brījmohanlāljī the local newspaper compared him with Kabīr.[4] The article informs us that Svāmī Brījmohanlāljī, known in the Islamic milieu as Baba Shams ud-Din, had been a *gṛhasthi faqīr*, member and master of the Ānanda Yoga and of the *naqšabandiyyah ṭarīqa*. For this reason the mourning procession escorting his body was composed of Hindus and Muslims alike. On the crematory, *śmaśāna*, an *'ulamā* uttered for his intercession the *namaḥ-e-janaḥa*, before he was cremated. The ashes gathered after the *antyeṣṭi* were divided in two parts: the first part was thrown in the Gomati River, the second buried in the Islamic cemetery.

The designated successor was his son Dineś Kumār Omkārnāthjī, born in 1937. When his father died, he was not yet spiritually fit to rule the *āśrama*. For this reason the leadership of the mastery was maintained by his mother Śrīmatī Śakuntalā Devī upto the year 1974. The wife of Brījmohanlāljī Mahārāj had been a lady of delicate health, and her husband had retired before his time to take care of her. She outlived her husband by nineteen years, dying in Kanpur in 1974. She was cremated and her ashes were put in the *samādhi* of Brījmohanlāljī in Lucknow, where every Daśaharā festival is accompanied by an important pilgrimage, *yātrā*, in their honour. The period when the mastery was under the authority of Śakuntalā Devī marks the moment of release of the *sampradāya* from the

Ṣūfic ward. The pilgrimages of *yogīs* toward the sacred tombs of Delhi and Sirhind became less frequent, while the Islamic *Pīrs* stopped visiting the Ānanda Yoga centres. This independence has been attained without any conflict between the two schools. The *ṭarīqa* simply recognized the maturity of the *sampradāya*: on the other hand the Ānanda yogīs maintained an attitude of brotherhood towards the Ṣūfīs.

Mahātmā Omkārnāthjī is the present guru of the Ānanda Yoga in Kanpur, and the number of his disciples amounts to about 100,000.

The doctrine of the Ānanda Yoga is undoubtedly based on the *yogadarśana* of Patañjali, whose *Yogasūtras* are invoked as the scriptural canon with an absolute authority. The spiritual discipline is put into practice with the purpose of reaching the union with Īśvara through a process of successive *ekāgratās*. In the absence of written records, we had recourse to the oral tradition of the Ānanda yogīs maintaining that the yogic doctrine of the *sampradāya* comes from the very *nātha paramparā*, before the Ṣūfic influence had been exerted. This is confirmed by the observation that the *naqšabandiyya* Ṣūfīs follow the Islamic orthodox teachings of the founder of their Indian branch of the *ṭarīqa*. In fact Šaykh Imām Rabbānī Mujaddid fil Alfi Thānī Aḥmed Sirhindī (Hazrat Aḥmed Sirhindī s.d.) regarded the belief claiming the union between the creature and its Creator as *širk*, that is to say as the sin of association of some relative being with the absolute reality of God. From this point of view, the Ānanda Yoga and the *naqšabandiyya* doctrine seem to be incompatible. The Islamic doctrine identifies the supreme stage of the spiritual Ṣūfic path with the proximity or nearness to Allah. The initiated members of both the Islamic and Hindu ways mutually recognize the equality of the concepts of proximity and unity. This is further confirmed by the names designating the doctrine, which correspond to this spiritual experience: *brahmavidyā* and *'ilm-e-Ilahi*, which are basically synonymous terms.

In the Hindu terms of the Ānanda Yoga, the path leading to the goal starts from the heart, which is the eternal site of immortality, the *amṛta*. There, the empty space is permeated by the divine vibration. Through the *dīkṣā* the *yogī* is able to concentrate in this inner space and enjoy its bliss. Therefore the prescribed spiritual way is called Ānanda Yoga. In the opinion of Śrī Brījmohanlālji the path of Ānanda Yoga begins where Rāja Yoga comes to an end. A further element of Ānanda Yoga, which is absent in Rāja Yoga is grace, *kṛpā*, acting with the help of the guru.[5] The presence of the concept of grace points to the *bhakti* feature of the Ānanda Yoga, further emphasized by the devotion of the *sampradāya*'s members to Rāma, the seventh *avatāra* of Viṣṇu. The guru of this path must be able to offer the practice of the method, the pure doctrine and the means to obtain divine grace, that is to provide the synthesis of the three *mārgas* of the classical Yoga: *karman*, *jñāna* and *bhakti*. The tripartition is elaborated in this perspective, in order to correlate *karman* with the bodily level, *jñāna* with the mind and *bhakti* with the Spirit:

> Man is composed of the body, *śarīra* or *jism*, soul, *man* or *nafs*, and spirit, *ātmā* or *rūḥ*. The body holds the bodily elements, *śarīrātva*, and the organic consciousness, *śārīrik caitanyatā*; the soul along with the mind holds the mental elements, *mānātva*, and the spirit holds the spiritual consciousness, *ātmik caitanyatā*. These three components form our living individuality, *jīva*. The plane of the organic consciousness is called *karmakāṇḍa* or *šarī'a*, that of the psychic consciousness is called *upāsanākāṇḍa* or *ṭarīqa*, and the plane of the spiritual consciousness, *jñānakāṇḍa* or *ḥaqīqa*.[6]

The mentioned tripartition appears also in a dynamic perspective, as three steps in the *sādhanā*, the spiritual way of realization:

> You have to find a *guru* with a pure *antaḥkaraṇa*, who attained the realization of the *laya*, degrees in the *śarīrī*, *mānasī* and *ātmik* levels, during his way of attraction. His inside and outside life must be a mirror of pureness *pavitratā*, an example of an experienced spiritual realization, whose help will effect a true knowledge of the *karman* and of the *dharma*.[7]

The first spiritual influence of the guru on the disciples would be the infusion of his mental concentration through an effort performed during a meditation session. The disciple will feel a strong heat springing from the master, pervading his body. Simultaneously, the disciple will experience an inversion in the stream of his thoughts, *mānasī dhārā*, toward his own inner centre. The result of this mental retraction is the *mānasī śānti*, experience of the inner peace, from which the spiritual stream, *ātmik dhārā*, starts its vertical flux toward God: 'In this way the disciple, permeated by love, will be caught by a strong feeling of spiritual bliss, *rūhānī ānanda* in his state of mental peace.' (Brījmohanlāl 1958: 230–1)

The two different *dhārās* are consecutive and coincide with the two phases of the *Yoga*, the individual *ekāgratā* and the supreme *ekāgratā*, the union with God. But in the doctrine of the Ānanda Yoga the presence of grace seems to be necessary in the course of the second and higher route. We found a parallel concept in the doctrine of the *naqšabandiyya*, where there are two ways toward Allah. The first one is the *sulūk* (trail) way covered in laps by the Ṣūfis performing the methodical rituals prescribed by the *ṭarīqa*. The second is the *jazb*, the way without laps, that only exceptional Ṣūfis can enter with the grace of God. *Jazb* means attraction, and in fact only an individual chosen by God can obtain this way of realization. In our opinion, there is a difference in this regard between the Ānanda Yoga position and the Ṣūfic view. In the Islamic doctrine, the two ways lead to the same goal, but their existence is necessary for two different human types. In the Hindu doctrine, the two *dhārās* are two phases of the same spiritual way of realization. In the present case, obviously, the *mānasī dhārā* is the lower and the preparatory stage for the second conclusive phase of the spiritual development, the *ātmik dhārā*.

Till now we have examined the considerable and frequent points of contact between Ṣūfic and Yogic doctrines which fostered their reciprocal understanding. It is in the domain of the practice and method of initiation however, that the direct influence of the *naqšabandiyya* is particularly evident. First of all, the *mantram* used by the Ānanda yogīs is the *japa* Rām Rām or Om, silently uttered, with the technique called *surat śabda yoga*, beginning from the *ājñā cakra* in the forehead near to the bridge of the nose and addressed to the cavity of the heart.[8] The members of this yogic way do not disdain the use of the name of Allah as *mantram*. 'Regarding the utterance of the heart, one must focus and understand its subtle significance hidden in the inner recesses. One attains it through the invocation of one of the two names Om or Allah. They are the two *mahāmantrams* of our *sādhanā*.' (Śrī Mahārāja Rāmcandra 1971: 31)

The oral tradition of the *sampradāya* refers explicitly to the Upaniṣadic teachings[9] on the heart as uncreated centre of the creature. However, the other *cakras* do not correspond with any other Hindu conception of the subtle physiology of the human being. The *cakra* of the heart, *hṛdaya cakra*, is situated in the region of the ribs, approximately two inches under the left nipple: the following *cakra* is placed at the same position but on the right side of the chest. The third *cakra* is in the left breast, two inches above the nipple, but towards the centre of the chest. Analogically the fourth *cakra* is situated in the same position but on the right side. The fifth *cakra* is placed in the inner of the top of the sternum. The complex of these five principal *cakras* forms exactly an equilateral triangle. Therefore the subtle 'geography' of the human body for the Ānanda Yoga differs greatly from the vertical structure of the principal subtle centres of the classical Yoga, situated beside the backbone. The structure in the shape of equilateral triangle is an exact copy of the placement of the subtle centres, *laṭīfas*, in the *naqšabandiyya* method:

Then the *laṭīfa* of the heart, *qalb*, which is the source of the ether, is placed two fingers under the left nipple, toward the side ... The *laṭīfa* of the breath, *rūḥ*, origin of the element air, whose dignity in the domain of the order, *amr*, is higher than

> the *qalb*, ... is on the right side of the chest, two fingers under the nipple. The *laṭīfa* of the mystery, *sirr*, source of the element water, higher in dignity than the *rūḥ*, is situated between the nipple and the empty centre of the left breast. The *laṭīfa* of the secret, *khafi*, principle of the fire, whose dignity is higher than the *sirr*, ... is near the right nipple, between the *rūḥ* and the centre of the breast. Further up, in the centre between the nipples is placed the *laṭīfa* of the supreme mystery, *akhfā* whose rank is higher than the *khafi*, source of the earth, which is the most excellent and pure among the *laṭīfas*, and is the nearest to Allah the Highest ... [10]

The names of the *cakras* in the Ānanda Yoga method are also the exact translations of the Ṣūfic *laṭīfas*: these are in order *hṛdaya*, *prāṇa*, *rahasya*, *gupta*, *sugupta*.

Another important feature of the Ṣūfic method shifted to the Hindu *sampradāya* is represented by the inverted succession of the gross elements corresponding to the *cakras*. In fact, in the Yoga rooted in the classic tradition,[11] the interior path starts from below and moves upwards. In this way the lowest *cakra* corresponds to the element earth, and the higher *cakras* successively to the elements water, fire, air and ether (Filippi 1996). Proceeding in this ascent, the *yogin* should activate the *ājñā cakra*, and, overcoming the gross constituents of the body, move to the stage of control over the mind. Finally, the *sādhaka* can rise from this subtle frontal centre to the supreme lotus of thousand petals. As mentioned above, the Ānanda yogī begins his spiritual experience after the *dīkṣā* starting from the *ājñā cakra* which is rekindled by the guru by means of *upāsanā*. From that moment on, the awakened mental consciousness of the disciple is able to realize the potentiality of the *cakras*. The first centre, the *hṛdaya*, is the lowest, but it is the source of the ether, the purest among the elements. In this way the spiritual realization of the *yogin* ascends through the *cakras* of the breast with a zigzag movement, which is at the same time a descent in the hierarchy of the gross elements, from ether to earth. In the opinion of the disciples of Ānanda Yoga, it is as if the preliminary realization of the *ājñā cakra* implies the virtual realization of the lower *cakras*, which are realized *in extenso* proceeding from the upper centre, namely from the principle to the consequences.

After taking back the *cakras* and their elements into the mental centre, the *sādhaka* achieves the total realization of his individual possibilities, awakening the seventh *cakra*, the *rūpa*, which is spread over the whole surface of his body. This is the first phase of the spiritual path which allows him to overcome the domain of the body and the psyche through the destruction of the *saṃskāras* (Brījmohanlāl 1958: 137–8). This domain is the sublunary world, the *candra loka*, or the world marked by the two conditions of *nāma* and *rūpam* (200). 'The human being is composed of three parts: the gross body, *sthūla śarīra*, the subtle body, *sūkṣma śarīra*, and the causal body, *kāraṇa śarīra*.' (33) After the realization of the last *cakra* of the *rūpam* the *yogī* gets in contact with a person not human, *puruṣaḥ amānavaḥ*,[12] who then will be his interior spiritual instructor, the *sadguru*. Through the *tanmātras* and *guṇas* of God, the *sādhaka* completes the realization of the causal manifestation, and settles perpetually in the condition of *savikalpa samādhi* within the solar world, the *sūrya loka*, the highest step in the Universe. In this condition the *yogin* will wait for the *pralaya*, when his perfect *brahma vidyā* allows him finally to unite with Īśvara (Brījmohanlāla 1958: 33–4).

Concluding this brief presentation of the Ānanda Yoga, we would like to point out some peculiarities. First of all, the members of Ānanda Yoga are regular Hindus, who maintain the Hindu caste and *āśrama* prescriptions, usages and customs. Nobody adopts the obligatory rules of the Islamic Religion, the five *arkān*, of the *šari'a*. They only adopted the pilgrimage to the tombs of the Muslim saints from Islam, but this is just an optional article of faith, which is moreover much disliked by the modern rampant Islamic fundamentalism.[13]

The second point is that the doctrine of the *sampradāya* does not deviate from the yogic and Ramaite principle of origin. The only innovation deals with the recognition and the use of the semantic equivalence of some Ṣūfic terms. But the irreducible concepts and their Arabic, Persian or Urdu forms are not employed.

The third point is the total acceptance of the *naqšabandiyya* method of spiritual realization, along with all the complementary techniques. In this case the terminology utilized can be either yogic or Ṣūfic. In our opinion such a careful symbiosis cannot be considered a pure syncretism like, for instance, the weak attempts of Akbar and Dārā Sikūh. The accurate and protracted examination of this experience, and the success in the results, induce us to regard the present situation of the Ānanda Yoga as a good example of synthesis in the parallel history of Hinduism and Islam in India (Filippi 1993: 117–26).

Notes

1. This article is the result of research in progress. Being a new field of research, the information has proceeded from the direct oral tradition, taken in the milieu of the *sampradāya*, rather than from written records. I am also very grateful for the information Thomas Dähnhardt provided me with during the elaboration of his dissertation, the unpublished thesis Analisi comparativa della metodologia Mujaddidī e della sādhanā dell' "Ānanda

Yoga", discussed at the University 'Ca' Foscari' in Venice in February 1993. I owe further thanks to Shree Hazari Mull Banthia for his support of my research in Kanpur.

2. The internal tradition of the *sampradāya* traces the origin of this lineage to the person of the great *nirguṇa bhakta* Kabīrdās (1398–1518?). He combined two important spiritual heritages among others: the initiation link of the Rāmaite guru *paramparā* of his Master Rāmānanda (1390–1470?) inspired in him the devotion towards Rāma. The second initiation link has been with the *nātha yogīs*, who gave to the poet his peculiar monistic doctrine, very similar to the Islamic absolute monotheism. As the reader can infer, this feature of the *Kabīr Pantha*, transmitted through the centuries, facilitated the development of the crossway between the Hinduism and Ṣūfīsm analysed here.
3. The *ṭarīqa naqšabandiyya* was founded in Bukhārā by Khvāja Bāhā ud-Dīn Naqšband (1318–89), and was afterwards introduced into India. It became one of the four most eminent Indian Islamic orders, mostly under the authority of Aḥmed Farūqī Sirhindī (1563–1626), whose role has been considered to be of such importance for the Islamic religion that he is known as 'Renovator of the second millennium.' His sixth successor, Mazhar Jān-e-Jānān, was the first master of this *ṭarīqa* interested in Hindu spirituality with a mind free from any prejudice.
4. *Pioneer*, Lucknow, 21 January 1955. The comparison with Kabīr is a recurrent topic, not only among journalists, whenever somebody is related both to the Hindu and the Islamic spheres. In fact, in an earlier study we noted that Kabīr was indeed a Hindu *sant* with mixed notions of Islam (Filippi 1978: 137–41). The case of the Ānanda Yoga could be compared with that of Sai Baba of Shirdi. Cf. Rigopoulos (1993).
5. Brījmohanlāl (1958: 28–9). The *Tattva Prabodhanī* and the Ānanda Yoga are the only speculative texts of the *sampradāya*, but being written in Hindī and not in Sanskrit, these two books are not considered canonic.
6. Brījmohanlāl (1958: 242). We have already underlined the important correspondence between the terms *jīvān-ḥayā*, life, *śakti-qudra*, power and *jñāna-'ilm* in the common language of the *sants* of the *bhaktikāla* (Filippi 1974).
7. Brījmohanlāl (1958: 29). *Antaḥkaraṇa* in this context refers to the state of realization of the guru's soul, instead of indicating the inner cause, as in the technical language of the *Sāṃkhya darśana*.
8. It is interesting to highlight that the *nāstika* sect of *Rādhāsvamins* of Beas, in Panjab, also practice the utterance of a silent *mantram*, starting from the concentration on the *ājñā cakra*.
9. Chāndogya Upaniṣad, III. 14.3.
10. Abul Hassan Zaid Faruqi (1404 H [1983]: I. 3). About other Indian Ṣūfīc methods see Bausani (1960).
11. *Yogasūtra*, 3.29; *Haṭa Yoga Pradīpikā*, 3.107–8.
12. Exactly according to Ch.U., IV.15.5.
13. We have already mentioned the *yātrā* of Lucknow. Ever so often the Ānanda

yogīs perform also a *yātrā* to the Ḥazrat Mīrzā Mazhar Jān-e-Jānān tomb in Delhi. The Ṣūfic milieu in India is often troubled because of the cult of the tombs of saints is discouraged by the Islamic fundamentalists, especially by the members of the *Islāmī Jam'āt* and *Tablīghī Jam'āt*, very active in U.P. On the contrary, the cult of the *samādhi* of the saints is encouraged by the followers of Hindutva. Their hostility is focused on the political and šara'itic components of the Islamic community, keeping a singular detachment (sometimes respect) towards the Ṣūfīs. Therefore the Ānanda yogīs did not suffer any harassment, even during the events in Ayodhya in autumn 1992.

References

Abūl Ḥassan Zaid Fārūqī. 1404 H. [1983]. *Madarij ul-Khair va Manahij ul-Sair*. Delhi: Sāḥ Abūl Khair Academy.

Bausani, A. 1960. Note su Shah Waliullāh di Delhi. *Annali* 10.

Brījmohanlāl. 1958. *Ānanda Yoga*. Kanpur: Sant Prakāśan.

Filippi, Gian Giuseppe. 1974. Gli attributi divini secondo la Bhakti hindu e l'Islam. *Verifiche*, Trento 2.

———. 1978. Des composants culturels dans le Granthavali de Kabir. *Indologica Taurinensia* 6: 137–41.

———. 1993. The Polar Function of the Tasawwuf. In *Contemporary Relevance of Sufism*, ed. Syeda Saiyidain Hameed, 117–26. New Delhi: Indian Council for Cultural Relations.

———. 1996. *Mṛtyu: Concept of Death in Indian tradition*. New Delhi: D.K. Printworld.

Hazrat Aḥmed Sirhindī. s.d. *Maktūbāt*. Istambul, m. XXII.

Murādābādī. 1309 H. Makatuba. In *Kalimat-e Tabi'at*. 2nd ed. Dilli: Mujtaba'i.

Rigopoulos, A. 1993. *The Life and Teachings of Sai Baba of Shirdi*. Albany: State University of New York Press.

Śrī Mahārāja Rāmcandra. 1971. *Tattva Prabodhinī*. Fatehgarh: Śrī Rāmcandr Publications League.

Resistant Gināns and the Quest for an Ismaili and Islamic Identity among the Khojas

FRANÇOISE MALLISON

Although it might be correct to say that a religion in itself cannot provide sufficient cultural identity to an area or region, this is just what any fundamentalist ideology would deny. But, it may happen that the religious identity of a group relies to a large extent on a regional culture.

The cultural identity of Gujarat certainly results from the interaction of the multiplicity of religious currents that found shelter there. None were isolated from the other; instead, mutual influence and interpenetration tended to prevail.[1] A striking instance of this is provided by the Ismaili Nizārī Shiite Muslims, also called Khojas or Satpanthīs, who, in conformity with the definition of Ismailism as 'an esoteric Islam clad in a regional culture',[2] live their beliefs, celebrate their rites and holidays, and rule their daily lives according to customs which appear to be eminently Hindu. These customs are reminiscent of the bhakti of the Nirguṇī Sants of northern India or even the popular Tantrism of Saurashtra and Kutch. The Khojas revere a body of texts they consider sacred and to which they are fervently devoted: i.e. the Gināns, which occupy for them the place held by the Qur'ān in the rest of the Islamic world. Their peculiar adoption of Hindu customs and beliefs allowed the Khojas—when in danger, due to their extremist position with regard to Islamic orthodoxy—to hide themselves under the cloak (*taqiyyah*) of Hinduism—as their Iranian co-religionists did under the cloak of orthodox Sufism.

The Khojas

At present, the Khojas form a community which functions like a caste. Their well-to-do members, who range from small shopkeepers to businessmen, are educated above the average Muslim of the subcontinent. They do not form the only branch of Ismaili followers of the Aga Khan, who, in addition, heads communities in Iran, Syria, Afghanistan, Central Asia and even China, not to speak of communities living in the Hunza valleys (distinct from the Sindhi Khojas) in Pakistan. However, the Khoja community from Sind, Panjab, Mumbai and primarily Gujarat, but also those which emigrated from there to East Africa, Europe, North America and Australia, exceeds in number all the other traditional groups. Where did they originally come from?

The Khojas belong to the Nizārī branch of the Ismaili (or Sevener) Shiite Muslims. Ismailism branched off from Shiite Islam in AD 765 when there was disagreement concerning the authority of the successor of Ja'far al-Ṣādiq, because Ja'far's son and successor Ismā'īl had died before him. At that time Ismā'īl's followers acknowledged his son Muhammad as the seventh and last Imām, thus founding Ismailism, whereas the Shiite branch, which was to acknowledge twelve Imāms, chose as successor Ismā'īl's brother Mūsā' al-Kāzim. The Nizārī branch of Ismailis, whose followers are known as Khojas in the Indian subcontinent, was the outcome of a schism within Ismailism when in 1094, at the time of the decline of the Fatimids in Egypt, Nizār's followers fled to Persia, establishing themselves at Alamut from where they sent missionaries to India. They were neither the first nor the only Ismaili missionaries to India but they were present at the origin of the Khoja community and of their religious Ginān literature.

The story of the conversion of Hindu groups to the Ismaili faith brought about by the activities of the early missionaries or Pīrs hailing from Iran, and eventually from Egypt, may be reassessed only through legendary hagiographic tales.[3]

The first missionary Satgur Nur (*ca.* 10th/12th centuries), seventh of the Pīrs sent by the Imām, belongs to legend. His hagiography tells how, he converted the famous Hindu Solaṃkī king of Gujarat, Siddharājā Jayasiṃha (1093–1143). His mausoleum is located at Navasari in southern Gujarat. Among the later missionaries, three are traditionally associated with the composition of the Gināns: Pīr Shams, the 23rd Pīr (14th century) who was active in Kutch and Multan where his tomb may be seen; Pīr Sadruddīn, the 26th (*ca.*1400) who was at the origin of the *Jamā'atkhāna*, or private places of worship, and named *khwājā* (i.e. *Khoja*: Lord), his converts belonging to the Lohāṇā caste of Kutch; and finally Pīr Hasan Kabīruddīn, the first born in the subcontinent, son of Pīr Sadruddīn. Since Pīr Hasan Kabīruddīn had eighteen sons, his succession was difficult. His first successor was his brother, Pīr Tajuddīn, followed by the 29th Pīr, *Pīr*

Pandiyāt, who actually was not a person but a book of instructions written in Persian prose (*Pandiyāt-e javānmardī*). This was said to be the work of the Imām Mustansir Billah II (d. 1480), who may have been sent in order to solve the succession crisis. The replacement of the guide responsible for the community of the Indian faithful, to whom the Imām traditionally delegated his powers, by a book entitled *Pīr Pandiyāt*, is a remarkable fact, recalling the fate of the *Guru Granth* of the Sikhs. But here the similarity ends. Indeed the content of the *Pandiyāt*, being essentially didactic, is meant to reaffirm the exclusive authority of the Imām of the present time as the only gateway to salvation, the only possible support of allegiance—an authority which seems to have been questioned at the time.[4] This text, apparently of canonical status and meant to replace the charismatic person of the Pīr and function as his successor, was known and read in vernacular translations (Sindhi, Gujarati). It never reached the position held in the heart of the faithful by the Gināns, lyrical devotional compositions attributed precisely to the different Pīrs. Neither did the *Pīr Pandiyāt* succeed entirely in resolving the succession crisis. The son of Pīr Hasan Kabīruddīn, Imām Shāh, assumed, under the aegis of his son Nur Muhammad Shāh, the state of Imām, thus creating the dissident branch of the Imāmshāhīs at Pirāṇā near Ahmedabad.

The remaining sons and their descendants, called Sayyids, continued preaching the Nizārī faith not as Pīrs on a mission from the Imām, but as the successors of the early Pīrs. Actually, orthodox Khojas regard Imām Shāh and Nur Muhammad, who authored Gināns, as Sayyids. In the following centuries, Sayyid families were active in Kutch and Saurashtra, though the links with the Imāmate became very loose on account of new difficulties in Persia after the renaissance of Anjudan (15–16th century). This continued to be the case until the nineteenth century.

The preaching of the Pīrs aims at teaching the doctrine of the Imāmhood as defined by the successive Imāms from Alamūt in Persia and specially by Hasan 'ala dhikrihi al-Salām who, in 1164, proclaimed the *Qiyāma*, 'the great resurrection', i.e. the fulfilment of the time cycles, the end of the supremacy of the law (*sharī'a*) and the beginning of a new era during which only the spiritual life of the soul mattered. The Imām becomes the divine manifestation of the creative mind which the faithful must strive to come to know, to acquire its vision (*darśana* or *didāra*) either through pilgrimage to see the Imām, or just mentally, in order to achieve union in god. The Ismaili Nizārīs are the only Shiites to have a physically present Imām: the Aga Khan, who is considered to be the receptacle of the Divine Light, the perfect manifestation of god as the Imām of the present time. The faithful must undertake a spiritual quest leading them to mystic union, the hidden sense of which can only be revealed with the help of a guide, the Pīr, and a formula of meditation, the *dhikra* or *bola*, which corresponds to the mantra given by the Hindu guru to his disciple at the time of initiation. Indeed, the missionary practice of the Pīrs seems to have consisted of transmitting the Ismaili doctrine of Islam with the help of ideas, concepts, and a vocabulary borrowed from the Hindu world of their local congregation, of which they seem to know the language and the customs. They thus continue the Ismaili practice of isolating the Islam they teach from its Arabic cultural context, in order to make it universal. Ismailism thus appears as the last stage of a salvation process which had been prepared through the observation of Hindu beliefs and customs, but the true meaning of which is revealed by the Pīr to the neophytes who embrace a new religion without becoming acculturated. There are several borrowings from Hinduism, such as the belief in re-incarnation, or in certain cases the burning of the dead, the wearing of the Brahmanic thread, the observance of Hindu festivals, or even the adoption of the *mitākṣara* code. The tales of conversion as transmitted in the Gināns see the emergence of a certain type of personality playing an essential role in the process of inculturation of Hinduism. These are the local disciples, converted by the Pīrs, who, often in pairs, assist their spiritual leader although they may outwardly remain Hindus: Gaṅgā Bāī and Chāch or Matang, together with Satgur Nūr; Vimras and Sūrbhāṇ, with Pīr Shams. With Pīr Sadruddīn one finds associated Sahadev Joshi, alias Hariścandra, who, sometimes, is said to be the very Pīr Sadruddīn himself.[5] However, if these legendary figures may be met in other Hindu contexts in Saurashtra and Kutch, the present-day tradition of the community does not any longer recognize the authenticity of their Gināns; only Pīrs and the Sayyids descending from missionaries directly sent from Iran are included in the modern corpus.

The Gināns

The Gināns, lyrical compositions used as hymns, are sung during religious celebrations and regularly at the three daily prayer sessions by the faithful, collectively or individually. *Ginãna* derives from the Sanskrit *jñāna*, 'knowledge acquired through meditation'. These poems of varying length number about 700 to 800, depending on the collections and whether they include texts less well known and less sung. They were composed in different languages of northern India such as Sindhi, Kacchi, Punjabi, Multani, Hindi-Hindustani and Gujarati between the thirteenth and the end of the nineteenth or the beginning of the twentieth centuries, depending on the supposed date of death of the last of the authors, a woman, Bibi Imām Begam.

In several points, such as origin, form, transmission and utilization, the Gināns resemble the *pada* and *bhajana* of the Vaishnava *bhakti* of northern India. The oral transmission rendered them fragile and subject to change, and the composite language in which we know them now hardly contains any archaic features which would make them anterior to the eighteenth century or even to the period of the Pīrs. The first manuscripts date back to the eighteenth century (the first one to 1736) although the practice of writing Gināns might already have started in the sixteenth century (Shackle / Moir 1992: 15). According to tradition, Pīr Dādū (d.1593) was told by the Imām to collect in written form the teachings of the early Pīrs. A special alphabet called Khojkī, an adapted business script unique to the Khojas, was devised and put into use, exclusively for the transcription of the Gināns (34–54). With the progress of time it also acquired a sacred character. About 500 manuscripts are said to be extant. The habit of ritually destroying them after having been copied or printed explains the relative paucity of the manuscripts.

A majority of the Gināns uses the *chaupāī* and *doha* metres. The shorter ones have four to ten verses, the longer ones more than 500. In the latter case they are given a name indicating their theme and called *grantha* in order to distinguish them from the shorter ones. Each Ginān contains the oral signature, or *bhaṇitā*, of its actual or presumed author. It seems unlikely that the early Pīrs were the authors of the 600 to 640 Gināns with which they are credited, and many Gināns seem to bear the mark of the period of the Sayyids (i.e. 1600 to 1850) who, in their own name, are the authors of the remaining sixty Gināns, each being credited with one or two of them—with the exception of the ten last which belong to Imām Begam (17–9). It seems that the Sayyids drew on the teachings of the Gināns to maintain and foster the spiritual destiny of the community, and it has been suggested that the traditional oral signature at the end of a hymn meant 'for' and not 'by' in the case of the early Pīrs (Asani 1996: 268–74).

Each Ginān is sung according to an orally transmitted *rāga* and it happens that the same *rāga* is used for several texts, which might undergo metrical changes in consequence. As in the case of the poetry of Hindu devotion, the musical element is essential for the expression of the sacred message.

Ali Asani (1991) remarks that, in contrast with the Ismaili writings in Arabic or Persian, the Gināns do not speak of any theological or doctrinal problem, nor do they open any philosophical or intellectual debate. He distinguishes five groups of inspiration specific to the Gināns:

1. The theme of conversion: The Gināns show Ismailism as the completion of the Hindu tradition. Ali and his incarnation in the Imām of the present time are shown to be nothing but the tenth *avatāra* of Vishnu, Kalki or Naklanki (the 'Immaculate') who is expected to save the world by putting an end to Kaliyuga. This is the doctrine of the *Daśa avatāra*, the Gināns of which were quite frequently recited and favoured by the faithful until recent decades.[6] Belonging equally to this category are the Gināns putting forward traditional Hindu mythological figures such as Hariścandra, the Pāṇḍavas and Draupadī, Prahlād and Bali, as well as the hagiographic tales of early Pīrs.
2. The themes of cosmology and the end of time: The Gināns narrate the tales of the creation of the world reproduced from the Hindu context, or the stages of the soul having reached superior levels, or the prayer for the intercession of the Prophet Muhammad.
3. The didactic theme: The Gināns enumerate the rules of good conduct, reminders for the faithful, emanating from both religious traditions.
4. The ritualistic theme: The Gināns are used for the celebration of certain holidays or rites such as Navrūz, funerals, the birthday of the Imām.
5. The theme of the mystical experience: The category most important according to Asani, contains the mystical Gināns recounting the spiritual return of the soul to its origins 'in the transcendant and ineffable God', in an esoteric mode, the *bāṭin*. These Gināns, frequently describing a mystical experience with the help of the symbolism of the Nirguṇī Sants and of the Nāth-yogīs, are quite popular.

It has often been said that the Gināns had borrowed from the Vaishnava bhakti of the Sants of northern India, together with a shaktic or tantric element. According to G. Bowering, 'the devotional phase, from the fifteenth century onwards, developed Nizari Isma'ili instruction ... in India through the legendary *Jnans* of Hindu *pirs*, amalgamating popular tantric lore and the avatara doctrine with Islamic topics.' (1982: 130)

Indeed, for anyone familiar with the *Sant-vāṇī* tradition of Saurashtra, a strong resemblance of style, metaphors and teaching exists between the *bhajana* of the Mahāmārgī Sants (also called Mahāpanthīs, Bījapanthīs, etc.) of Saurashtra and Kutch and the Gināns attributed to the Khoja Pīrs and Sayyids. The Mahāmārgīs are a tantric sect with secret yogic rites sometimes involving sex. They mainly belong to the Untouchable caste of the Meghwals of Saurashtra. Their non-secret practice of the *bhajana* reveals texts and even authors they have in common with the Khojas, such as Sahadev Joṣī, Devāyat Paṇḍit, Ramdeo Pīr. They share for instance, the eschatological expectation of the saving *avatāra* Naklanki, who is to come from the country of Dailam and the city of Alamut, according to their own *Āgama-vāṇī*. They also share the same esoteric symbolism in the texts: *vayaka*, for instance, denotes the call of the Mahāmārgī guru to his disciple, as does *hukam* the call of the Pīr. The number of examples is unlimited. In spite of preliminary work[7] involved in trying to find an explanation for this connection, it remains impossible to come to a conclusion, especially as present-day Khojas ignore the Mahāmārgī tradition. While the Mahāmārgīs acknowledge their borrowings from what they correctly call the Satpanthīs,[8] they admit that they often do not understand the terms coming from the Islamic terminology in the texts they use.[9] The following explanation could be proposed: the Ismaili Pīrs might have converted a sizeable part of the Meghwals or other Untouchables while borrowing, according to their particular technique, from their Hindu culture. In time, these groups might have ceased to be a part of the Khoja community, when the latter structured itself in the middle layers of society. This happened possibly after a first wave of reforms which tended to diminish the Hindu influence that had taken place in the sixteenth century, precisely the time of the dispatch of the *Pīr Pandiyāt*. At that time, the need of consigning in writing the teaching of the Pīrs made itself felt and thus the Ginās were attributed to the missionaries who had come from Iran. It seems likely that those called the Hindu Pīrs, such as Rāmdeo Pīr, more or less disappeared from the authorized body of writings at that time (Ali 1995: 28–9). However this may be, the tradition of the Kathiawadi *Sant-vāṇī* is flourishing and well appreciated by all levels of Gujarati society, and the Mahāmārgī *bhajana* seem to generate the same emotion in their Hindu public as the Ginās do among the Khoja faithful. The Untouchable Sant-Kavi call their *Āgama-vāṇī* the 'Fifth Veda', exactly as the Ismaili Pīrs do the Ginās. And whatever the reason for this fact, it remains evident that a strong 'inculturation' of the Khoja persuasion was at work ever since the beginning of missionary work.

The tradition of the Ginās, sacred and revered as it is and recalling more appropriately the status of the *Guru Granth* among the Sikhs, has not received the same attention from contemporary historians and scholars of Ismailism as that given to the Perso-Arabic tradition and Fatimid history (Kassam 1995: 9-26). It is impossible to assert that this aspect is obfuscated on purpose, but it is definitely not the outcome of fortuitous negligence either. The events that upset the Khoja community during the latter half of the nineteenth century provide a sufficient explanation for this marginalization.

The Constitution of the Corpus of the Gināns During the Nineteenth and Twentieth Centuries

The Ginān manuscripts, most dating from the nineteenth century, show in the extant texts as found in the *pothi* (Moir 1997) a variety of items including the Hindu *bhajana* and even *ākhyāna*, that is, puranic tales in classical Gujarati, an inclusion that tends to prove the ease with which the Sayyids comprehended the ambient Hindu culture in their teaching. Some of them, like Imām Begam, gathered Hindu renouncers around themselves. It does not appear, however, that the community had to suffer any major persecution from the orthodox Muslim authorities. Whether Hindu or Islamic, the identity of the Khojas does not seem to have been a problem until the mid-nineteenth century, and the corpus of the Gināns, not yet closed, remained unquestioned.

In 1840, the Imām of the Nizārī Ismailis, Hasan Ali Shah (d.1881), the first Aga Khan, left Iran for political reasons and took refuge in Sind. From 1845 onwards he was at Bombay where he installed his headquarters among his Indian faithful, and among whom he tried to reaffirm his authority, which had grown weaker with time. The ensuing dissensions and internal struggles within the community were solved thanks to a judgment pronounced by the Bombay High Court presided by Justice Arnould in 1866. This was the famous *Aga Khan Case*, instrumental in corroborating the authority and status of the Aga Khan as the Imām of the Khojas, themselves defined as being 'a sect of people whose ancestors were Hindu in origin, which was converted to and has throughout abided in the faith of Shia Imāmi Ismailis, and which has always been and still is bound by ties of spiritual allegiance to the hereditary Imām of the Ismaili' (Asani 1987: 35). Curiously enough, the Gināns were included among the documents proving the claim and the Khoja faithful were then requested to produce and explain this sacred literature written in a secret alphabet. This resulted in a new scholarly appraisal of the texts by the members of the community and even outsiders.[10] In spite of the secession in favour of the Sunni current of some wealthy and influential families and in spite of additional secessions during the following years towards Shiism, notably in 1908 after the *Haji Bibi Case*, the Aga Khan recovered his authority to lead the spiritual destiny of his faithful and to receive the tithe directly without any further intervention by the Sayyids. The sermons of the Sayyids, based on and illuminated by the Gināns, were replaced by the Farmans issued directly by the Imām, henceforth the only legitimate commentator of the religion, and were published and translated into the different languages of the faithful. This explains why no new Gināns were composed. According to Zawahir Moir,

> though sincerely dedicated to the faraway Imāms and forever yearning for their presence, the Ginanic tradition was also in some sense socially and culturally predicated on their absence. Thus once the Imām crossed that wide divide to make direct contact with his followers, it was perhaps inevitable that much of the old Ismaili Khoja Dawa, including the Ginan tradition, would begin to crumble.

Concerning Imām Begam, the last composer of Gināns who left Bombay for Karachi between 1845 and 1860, she adds 'In this situation too, it is somehow fitting that the last composer of the Ginans, Imām Begam, should have felt moved to leave the Bombay of Hasan Ali Shah for Karachi, thus restoring a traditional measure of distance between herself and the Imām to whom she had pledged eternal fidelity.' (Moir forthcoming 1)

It shows that the extent of attachment to the charismatic person of the hereditary Imāms was transmitted by the Pīrs and Sayyids through the corpus of the Gināns during the estrangement of the devotees in India from the Persian Imāmate. What, then, happened to the Gināns?

Even though they ceased to be a living tradition, replaced as they were by the Farmans, the Gināns did not disappear. They had rather to suffer some transformations when they were cleared of their more evident Hindu elements, checked and somewhat re-interpreted. The Imām Aga Khan I, who was part of Persian culture, was a foreigner to India and did not speak the 'ginanic' languages. He had arrived in Bombay at a time when problems of religious identity were on the increase due to political and historical reasons. At the time, neo-orthodox groups, both Hindu and Muslim, decided not to tolerate mutual borrowings any longer and forced all those who found themselves to be half-way between the two religions to make a choice. After he was freed from his opponents (some of whom chose to be Sunnis or Shiites), all went in favour of the Aga Khan and his successors, who imposed on the Khoja community a stronger Perso-Arabic identity.[11] The Islamic re-orientation of the ginanic tradition was mainly the work of Aga Khan III, Sultan Muhammad Shah (1877–1957).[12] His work was continued by Prince Karim (b.1936), the present Aga Khan IV. Among the decisions taken was the replacement of the daily *Duā* prayer in Sindhi in 1952 which was attributed to Pīr Sadruddīn (but which may have been put into words by Pīr Dādū). It replaced the names of Imāms and Pīrs with a prayer in Arabic containing Koranic verses and a mere genealogy of the Imāms. As regards the Gināns, the recitation of those which appeared too directly under the influence of Hinduism was discontinued—for example the *Daśa avatāra*. Equally, the texts themselves were changed. Excessively Hindu-sounding terms were replaced by corresponding Islamic ones. Thus, *Hari* became *Alī*, *Sāmī* (*Svāmī*) became *Maula*.

But above all, an authorized canon was established, entailing the census of all existing texts from the different manuscripts which were dispersed among numerous local collections and which were until then beyond the centralized control of the Aga Khans. Begun under Aga Khan II, the recollection was continued under Aga Khan III, who conferred the task of receiving and evaluating manuscripts to Mukhī Lāljī Devrāj of Bombay in order to have them edited and published. The publications by Devrāj are not critical but rather unsystematic reproductions. His anthology of selected Gināns, *Elam sār: saṅgrah rāg mālā* (1905) became very popular. But as increasing numbers of manuscripts reached Bombay, the publication in five volumes of 100 Gināns each by the Khoja Sindhi Press from 1915 onwards, first in Khojkī characters and later re-edited in the Gujarati script, came to be considered the authorized version. Along with this, Devrāj published in 1915 the catalogue of the approved Gināns, entitled *Tapasil Buk*, for it was evident that he had to—and actually did—eliminate texts considered non-Ismaili from the manuscripts. Once published, the manuscripts were destroyed and 3500 of them were buried in Bombay. The editorial work accomplished by Devrāj remained the norm until the political changes brought about by the independence of India, when links with England were severed and new links with Pakistan established, thus pushing the 'Islamic purification' of the Khoja tradition even further. The first consequence was another revision of the authorized version and the publication of the *Ginān-e Śarīf* in two volumes at Karachi;[13] this time it was printed in the Gujarati script because acquaintance of the faithful with the Khojkī script has gone down considerably. The *Ginān-e Śarīf* is not an independent version but a selection from Devrāj, excluding the more compromising texts and replacing words and phrases considered inappropriate.

Thus, recent history has witnessed two stages in the establishment of an authorized version of the Ginanic tradition, but one may consider that the pre-modern period can be divided into two stages. The first consists of an exclusively oral tradition relying on the system of the *bhaṇitā*, aimed at establishing for the Gināns the legitimacy of the early missionary Pīrs. The second stage consists of the manuscript tradition, resulting from an expression of the spiritual authority of the Imām of the sixteenth century at a time of re-organization of the movement, when Pīrs were no longer sent but replaced by the *Pīr Pandiyāt*, and when, consequently, further efforts at conversion ceased. Perhaps the community started to consider itself as a well-defined social group and eventually dropped certain members of low castes who were considered to be already too Hinduized. We may catch a glimpse of these pre-modern traditions through non-canonic publications, the collection of oral traditions from Kutch, and from Saurashtra at the end of the last century—such as the *Khojā vrattant* by Nanjiani or the *Khojā Komanī Tavarīkh* by Edalji Dhanji Kabā.[14] This evolution of the tradition of the Ginān s into a canonical writing at the service of Islam could only give birth to a permanent and unresolved tension between its local Hindu character and its efforts towards acceptance by the Ismaili Shia community within the Islamic world at large.

The Ginān s Nowadays

Ali Asani, quoting Papanek (1962), concludes his article with the following words:

> Within the short period of fifty or sixty years, the Khoja sense of identification with the larger Islamic tradition has become so strong that many young members have come to regard their community's earlier beliefs as belonging to a phase in history when the early pirs (missionaries) had to make concessions to the Hindu milieu. At the present time, they affirm 'they are merely returning to their proper fold in Islam.' (Asani 1987: 38)

One might regard this as the radical position of an extreme fringe of the Khoja population considering that the Ginanic tradition has had to adapt itself to change and to evolve with the times. This happened precisely because, without the Ginanic tradition, the religious identity of the majority of the followers of the Aga Khan would have been lost.[15] The Aga Khans have understood this perfectly. Thus, Karim Aga Khan, while delivering a talk at Karachi in 1984, remarked, 'Many times I have recommended to my spiritual children that they should remember *ginān s*, that they should understand the meaning of these *ginān s* and that they should carry these meanings in their hearts. It is most important that my spiritual children ... hold to this tradition which is so special, so unique and so important ...' (Asani 1992: 101) Such quotations concerning what the Aga Khan calls 'the wonderful tradition' can easily be multiplied. Not only are the Ginān s inseparable from the religious life of the Khojas—certainly the Aga Khans have not forgotten them—but they were also instrumental in justifying the position of the Imām within the community when it was imperilled. It appears as if the Imāms themselves felt the challenging power of the Ginān s and fought for an Islamization of their content, but at the same time understood that the role assumed by the Gināns was supporting the attachment of the community to their person. The consequence was an ambivalent attitude of the Imāms, repressing the exuberant Hinduism of the texts, while consecrating them through granting them canonical status. After the epoch of the Sayyids, the Imāms, exclusively vested with the authority to comment on the sacred scriptures, were able to find a solution to the difficult problem of the status of the Qur'ān within the Ismaili Khoja community. Without recognizing the superiority of the Qur'ān as the Holy Book, it is difficult to preserve an Islamic identity. Indeed, the Gināns admit the importance of the Qur'ān, saying it is a *veda* or *purāṇa*, but their own function and importance for the religious life of the community exceed those of the Qur'ān. Aga Khan III chose to let the Ginanic literature appear as a sort of commentary on the Qur'ān in the vernacular languages for non-Arabic speaking populations. Since he added that their real aim was to initiate the audience into the hidden meaning (*batin*) of the Qur'ān and not into its external aspects (*zahir*), the Gināns continued to play their important role (Asani 1992: 108). One understands quite well the need for such an interpretation, and the texts of the Gināns, under pressure to render a meaning for which they were not composed, offer more or less resistance to the different solicitations they have to answer.

The overwhelming desire not to be put outside Islamic identity led the Khojas to employ other arguments or means than a mere reshaping of the Gināns. For example, to continue protecting the texts from any outside inquisitiveness is recommended. Only members of the community should have access to them. It is now also deemed useless to explain the institution of the Imām by means other than those of the religious history of Islam; no allusion to Hindu mythology is considered necessary. Finally, it was devotion to the pan-Islamic cause, social and educational work assisted by powerful financial means resulting from the institution of the tithe tax, and great tolerance and flexibility which enabled Nizārī Ismailism to win the esteem of the Muslim world, not the evolution of the corpus of the Gināns. For this purpose it has not been necessary 'to return to the proper fold of Islam'—at least not for all Khojas. The attachment to the Ginanic traditions may indeed vary with local communities. In 1984, in the preface to the English translation of a selection of Gināns, Allana recalls childhood memories at Karachi:

I see exactly at 3.45 a.m., my mother, Sharfibai, start singing a *ginan*. Her voice was unmatched. Everybody listened to her bewitching voice singing a *ginan*. No other person, as is normally customary, dare join his or her voice with her to sing in chorus, whether she sang a stanza or a *ginan* or the refrain of the *ginan*.

The fragrance of that spritual atmosphere still lingers in my mind. One seemed to live and be so near to the presence of the Omnipotent and Omniscient One. The weights of life's burden dissolve. (Allana 1984: 2)

Far from the Indian subcontinent, in Africa, North America or Europe, the Gināns continue to convey a sense of belonging and meaning to the community. Whatever the tribulations in the history of their transmission, the Gināns go on to incarnate the primacy of local Indianness above the universality of Islam in the heart of the Indian Ismaili Nizārīs, and, as Ali Asani states (1992: 109), they powerfully attest the contribution of Indian vernacular literature to the development of Indo-Muslim civilization.

Notes

1. See Mallison (1996).
2. According to Dr Rahmatoullah at an interview in Paris in May 1989.
3. On the difficulties encountered with this type of historic reconstruction see Nanji (1978) and Kassam (1995).
4. It also reminds its audience of the absolute duty to pay tithes. See Boivin (forthcoming).
5. Cf. Moir (forthcoming 2).
6. Cf. Khakee (1972).
7. On the common heritage of Satpanthīs and Mahāmārgīs, see Rajyaguru (1995. 72–81). Similar occurences were observed in the Rajasthani cult of Rāmdeo Pīr by Dominique-Sila Khan (1997).
8. One of the names given in Gujarat to the Khojas, but at present mainly denoting the dissident community of the Imāmshāhīs.
9. See the introduction to the *Āgama-vāṇī* of Devāyat Paṇḍit by N. Gohil, *Āgama-vāṇī*. Mumbai: Navabhārata Sāhitya Mandir, 1994: 52–5.
10. This was the case with W. Ivanow, who actually initiated scholarly studies on Ismaili Khoja literature; cf. Ivanow (1936) and (1948).
11. One of the decisions taken by Aga Khan III was to ask, in 1908, the so-called 'gupti' Khojas, i.e. those who had chosen to live their Nizārī faith secretly although outwardly appearing as Hindus, to come forward as Muslims and drop their Hindu names and customs. Though the majority of the Guptis (maybe half of them), mainly from Punjab and Gujarat, complied with this command, a few chose to return to Hinduism, where some adhered to the Arya Samaj (Moir forthcoming 3).
12. The reign of Aga Khan II lasted only for a few years, from 1881 until 1885.
13. The most recent edition was published in 1992 and the first one in 1978–9.
14. Both belong to the debate undertaken during the second half of the nineteenth century by Indian Ismaili writers and proposed to criticize Indian Khoja Ismailism. Sachedina Nanjiani in his *Khojā Vrattant* (Ahmedabad,

1892) remains sober and informative despite the fact that he himself had opted for the Ithna Asharis, unlike Edalji Dhanji Kabā, one generation later, who was quite polemical in his criticism of his erstwhile co-religionists in his *Khojā Komanī Tavarīkh* (Amreli, 1912). See Moir (forthcoming 3).

15. Religious identity was at the centre of the debate on the origin, nature and history of Indian Ismailism led by Indian Ismaili authors at the end of the nineteenth century and the beginning of the twentieth century. Among them, a group called by Zawahir Moir, the 'Revivalists', who were Aga Khani loyalists, defended successfully the Khoja religious identity through reaffirming a 'sense of Ismailism containing the essence of both Islam and Hinduism' (Moir forthcoming 3).

References

Allana, G. 1984. *Ginans of Ismaili Pirs*. Vol. 1. Karachi: His Highness Prince Aga Khan Shia Imami Ismailia Association for Pakistan.

Ali, M. A. T. S. 1995. Ramdeo Pir: A Forgotten Ismaili Saint. *Sind Review* 32: 24–9.

Asani, A. S. 1987. The Khojahs of Indo-Pakistan: The Quest for an Islamic Identity. *Journal Institute of Muslim Minority Affairs* 81: 31-41.

———. 1991. The Ginān Literature of the Ismailis of Indo-Pakistan: Its Origins, Characteristics and Themes. In *Devotion Divine: Bhakti Tradition from the Regions of India*, ed. D. L. Eck and F. Mallison, 1-18. Paris: École Française d'Extrême-Orient, and Groningen: Egbert Forsten.

———. 1992. The Ismaili Gināns as Devotional Literature. In *Devotional Literature in South Asia*, ed. R. S. McGregor, 101–12. Cambridge: Cambridge University Press.

———. 1996. The Isma'ili Gināns: Reflexion on Authority and Authorship. In *Medieval Isma'ili History and Thought*, ed. F. Daftary, 265–80. Cambridge: Cambridge University Press.

Boivin, M. 1994. The Reform of Islam in Ismaili Shi'ism from 1885 to 1957. In *Confluence of Cultures: French Contributions to Indo-Persian Studies*, ed. N. F. Delvoye, 197–216. New Delhi: Manohar.

———. forthcoming. A Persian Treatise for the Isma'ili Khojas of India: Presentation of the Pandiyat-i Jawanmardi (end of 9th/15th century). In *Confluence of Cultures: French Contributions to Indo-Persian Studies II*, ed. N. F. Delvoye. New Delhi: Manohar.

Bowering, G. 1982. Identity Problems of an Islamic Sect. In *Identity and Division in Cults and Sects in South Asia*, ed. P. Gaeffke and D. A. Utz, 128–34. Philadelphia: University of Pennsylvania.

Daftary, F. 1990. *The Ismā'īlīs: Their History and Doctrines*. Cambridge: Cambridge University Press, and New Delhi: Munshiram Manoharlal.

Engineer, A. A. 1989. *The Muslim Communities of Gujarat: An Exploratory Study of Bohras, Khojas and Memons*. Delhi: Ajanta Publications.

Gaborieau, M. 1997. Les débats sur l'acculturation chez les musulmans indiens au début du XIXe siècle. In *Altérité et identité: islam et christianisme en Inde*, ed. J. Assayag and G. Tarabout, 221–37. Paris: École des Hautes Études en Sciences Sociales.

Ginane Sharif. In 2 vols. Karachi: The Shī'ā Imāmī Ismā'īlī Tarīkā and Religious Education Board for Pakistan.

Ivanow, W. 1936. The Sect of Imam Shah in Gujarat. *Journal of the Bombay Branch of the Royal Asiatic Society* 12: 19–70.

———. 1948. Satpanth. In *Collectanea*, 1–54. Leiden: E. J. Brill.

Kassam, T. R. 1995. *Songs of Wisdom and Circles of Dance. Hymns of the Satpanth Ismā'ilī Muslim Saint, Pir Shams*. Albany: State University of New York Press.

Khakee. 1972. The Dasa Avatara of the Satpanthi Ismailis and Imam Shahis of Indo-Pakistan. Ph.D. diss., Harvard University.

Khan, Dominique-Sila. 1997. *Conversions and Shifting Identities – Rāmdev Pīr and the Isamailis in Rajasthan*. New Delhi: Manohar.

Mallison, F. 1989. Hinduism as Seen by the Nizārī Ismā'īlī Missionaries of Western India: The Evidence of the Ginān. In *Hinduism Reconsidered*, ed. G. D. Sontheimer and H. Kulke, 93-103. New Delhi: Manohar.

———. 1991. Les chants Garabī de Pīr Shams. In *Littératures médiévales de l'Inde du Nord*, ed. by F. Mallison, 115–38. Paris: École Française d'Extrême-Orient.

———. 1992. La secte ismaélienne des Nizārī ou Satpanthī en Inde: Hétérodoxie hindoue ou musulmane? In *Ascèse et Renoncement en Inde ou La Solitude bien ordonnée*, ed. S. Bouez, 105–13. Paris: L'Harmattan.

———. 1996. Hymnologies vishnuites, jaina, parsi, tantrique et islamique en gujarati: mode de transmission et thèmes convergents. In *Traditions orales dans le monde indien*, ed. by C. Champion, 273–87. Paris: École des Hautes Études en Science Sociales.

Mallison, F. and Z. Moir. 1997. 'Rencontrer l'Absolu, ô ami ...': Un hymne commun aux hindous tantriques et aux musulman ismaéliens du Saurashtra (Gujarat). In *Altérité et identité: islam et christianisme en Inde*, ed. J. Assayag and G. Tarabout, 265–76. Paris: École des Hautes Études en Sciences Sociales.

Moir, Z. 1997. Khojki Manuscripts. *South Asia Library Group Newsletter* 44: 18–22.

———. forthcoming 1. Bibi Imam Begam and the End of the Ismaili Ginanic Tradition. In *Proceedings of the VIth International Conference on Early Literature in New Indo-Aryan Languages, Seattle 1994*, ed. by H. Shapiro *et al*.

———. forthcoming 2. Hagiographical and Historical Elements in the Ginans of Sayyid Nur Muhammad Shah. *Journal of the Royal Asiatic Society*.

———. forthcoming 3. Historical and Religious Debates Amongst Indian Ismailis. 1840–1920. In *Proceedings of the VIIth International Conference on Early Literature in New Indo-Aryan Languages, Venice, August 1997*, ed. M. Offredi.

Nanji, A. 1978. *The Nizārī Ismā'īlī Tradition in the Indo-Pakistan Subcontinent*. Delmar, N.Y.: Caravan Books.

Papanek, Hannah. 1962. Leadership and Social Change in the Khoja Ismailia Community. Ph.D. Thesis, Radcliffe College.

Rajyaguru, N. 1995. *Bījamārgī gupta pāṭa upāsanā ane Mahāpanthī: Santanī bhajanavāṇī*. Gandhinagar: Gujarāt Sāhitya Akādamī.

Shackle, C. and Z. Moir. 1992. *Ismaili Hymns from South Asia: An Introduction to the Ginans*. London: School of Oriental and African Studies.

Canons, Charismas and Identities in Modern Islam

JAMAL MALIK

Islam is often politically projected as being homogeneous. Yet the question remains, how and by what means are Islamic social and cultural realities dealt with and negotiated, and what type of significance are they given by different social groups? It seems important to me to consider this question in the context of the making of canon, charisma, and identity.

A Complex and Heterogeneous Culture

Especially in ethnically, religiously and socially complex and heterogeneous societies such as those of Muslim South Asia, generalizing orientalist assignments of identity and Islamic canon do not hold. This can be elaborated with respect to folk religion and notions of mystical ideas and orders, where a variety of charismatics and canons can be observed.

Indeed, syncretist elements and accretion were preconditions of the creative interaction between local and foreign ideas and institutions in most of the regions inhabited by Muslims. For example, there is the translation of Islamic dogmas into Indian religious cosmology and vice versa (Eaton 1993). The prophet (*nabī*) becomes the incarnation of the divine (*avatār*). Ontological monism blurs the borders between religions—which is a precondition of the functioning of a Muslim minority—because if 'Everything is He' then even the non-Islamic must contain the sublime. A variety of religious and cultural hybridizations may be observed.

Holy sites which gradually developed around the graves and sarcophagi of mystics and holy men always served as centres of diffusion, providing different levels of identity and social interaction. They monumentalized and actualized the memory of particular groups. The centripetal and centrifugal functions of these places of social identification which are popular in agrarian and nomadic as well as, increasingly, in urban societies go back to the activities of those who maintain the tradition and heritage of these institutions: the charismatic *sajjādah nashīns*, *mutawallīs*, *mujāwirs*. They legitimize themselves through different genealogical, mythological and charismatic relations (*isnād*, *silsilah*) and miracles (*karāmāt*) (Gramlich 1986), on the basis of which they represent the moral authority for local people, thereby guaranteeing participation in blessing and grace (*barakah*). This blessing and grace is hereditary and at the same time lends status. The authority is renewed and secured through cyclically repeated rites at graveyards, especially during specified annual and monthly ritual periods when 'sacred time is dramatically separated from secular time' (Turner 1979: 97). This process can be observed in the cult around Sidi Ahmad al-Badawī in Tanta in Egypt, or the one around Salār Mas'ūd in North India (Mayeur-Jaouen 1994; Gaborieau 1975).

As important social events, ritualized collective visits to holy shrines promise emotional and psychological satisfaction; they also generate revenue. Connected with the physical movement to holy sites is a spiritual one, e.g. the elevation from a lower level of consciousness into a higher, or, more profanely, the elevation from one social group into another, or at least the overcoming of individual predicaments and social barriers (Gellner 1985; Geertz 1968). An egalitarian identity under one leader is created, the sufi songs (*qawwālī*) sing of the equality of all (Burckhardt-Qureshi 1986). These pilgrimages thus become the *hijra* into *dār al-islām*, i.e. the emigration into a pure, Muslim-dominated territory. Hence, they are often called small *hajj*. In this way the local small tradition supersedes or alternates with the all-embracing centre-oriented institution in Mecca. A complex sacred geography is created, the centre-periphery system is dissolved, periphery becomes centre, the main canon is replaced by alternative canons (Eickelman and Piscatori 1990; Bulliet 1994).

Indeed, because of social change especially in many cities, peasant migrants find an alternative source of satisfaction in an organized associational life of shrines and mystical orders. These identity-giving institutions and their cultures of pilgrimage therefore have therapeutic, social, economic and political significance; and in contrast to mosques, they provide an alternative source of communication and identity for women. Since a variety of activities takes place, these centres structure social reality and identity and therefore must be regarded as microcosms of local canonic and charismatic Islam. This facet of Islamic culture stands in contrast to the so-called scripturalist tradition (Geertz 1968).

Political Islam: One Among Many Facets

Religious fundamentalism or political Islam does not represent a monolithic block of cultural articulation. Rather, it is an outcome of colonial encroachment, as well as a demarcation against both folk-religious tradition and colonialism. From a socio-historical perspective the formulation of this religious identity can be analysed as follows.

The incremental social complexity is, among others, connected to the establishment of the colonial space that emerged parallel to the traditional sector in the nineteenth century. Colonial and traditional sectors are both—ideally speaking—socially coherent. However, amid these two extreme poles certain intermediary social groups have emerged, borderliners between the milieus, marginals or intersections (Schulze 1985; Riesebrodt 1990). It is important to note that these groups are not closed formations but, being segments of different formations which overlap, they oscillate between fixed positions and are ambivalent in their constitution—hybrids, so to speak. For analytical purposes we can say that their area of production (work and power) is mostly located in the colonial or postcolonial economy, and their area of reproduction (cultus, living) is to be found in the traditional realm. One may suppose that these intermediary sectors are not socially coherent but highly hybrid—because of structural differences which are manifest in traditional and modern economic and social formations—and thus offer totally different levels of identity. The swift social change, however, has called the matter in question, and the collective liability as well as the lack of an innate, inborn or traditional charisma results in the vulnerability of their own identity and authority. It results in identification problems and reorientation. In other words, identity does not correspond to former social standardizations, so that the frame of reference has to be enlarged and redesigned. This identity-critical situation or crisis of mind may confront a person with the question: Do I want to be as I am, or, am I a good Muslim?

This is particularly true in the era of post-colonialism and globalization; what we have are mixed sectors or hybrid cultures. Because of this cultural hybridization, and because of the detachment from canonized social ties, and due to the lack of an internal arrangement, one increasingly depends on networks of social relations, while network behaviour is seemingly less popular among citizens firmly embedded in institutions and among members of so-called primitive societies. The more detached from social relations (i.e. not coherent, e.g. border-liners in a liminal space), the greater the effort towards popularity and hence the establishment of social network relations (Streck 1985: 579).

If one follows post-colonial discourse, this hybrid perspective of the traveller between two worlds—between two border conditions—in principle enables one to elaborate upon the historical and present reality under totally new aspects—re-reading, re-writing, re-worlding: 'From the margin—the other—'all experience could be viewed as uncentred, pluralistic, and multifarious. Marginality thus became an unprecedented source of creative energy.' (Ashcroft *et al.* 1989: 12)

This means to initiate an inter-cultural hybrid dialogue in a steady oscillating process between different social poles, and thus to furnish a variety of new charismatic visions and canons. Certainly, this 'range of differential knowledges and positionalities' may estrange identity, but at the same time it produces 'new forms of knowledge, new modes of differentiation, new sites of power.' This double-vision (Bhabha 1994) would produce the presupposition for 'newness', for a creative discourse which would enable a reconstruction and revaluation of identity towards 'I want to be different,' a re-birth! This identity-critical conflict situation between a modern field of work, such as an assembly line, and a traditional life world, such as the *birādarī*-system—can be negotiated in at least three different ways (Schulze 1985; Malik 1996):

1. To adjust the 'own' tradition, which in the case of Muslim societies is articulated Islamically, to modern circumstances: thus integrationism.
2. To enrich or replace the modern field of production through tradition, or even isolate oneself from it: thus isolationism, or a most interesting field which, however, is difficult to qualify and quantify.
3. To create some kind of substitute culture which may have escapist features in order to provide a temporary refuge from the sharp contrast between modern and traditional, such as urban crime, the consumption of narcotics, or the world of cinema;[1] the veneration cult may also be considered here.

The choice in favour of one way as against the other depends on the type of work, the material conditions, the social position and social prestige. The degree of personal wealth seems to be decisive for the pattern of negotiating with the conflict: The higher in colonial or post-colonial hierarchy, the more inclined towards modernization of the area of reproduction or de-traditionalization—religion being the reservoir of the social and cultural experiences and the common frame of reference, e.g., integrationist political Islam. And the lower one is at the social ladder, the more the tendency towards a traditionalization of the area of production: here an isolationist political Islam can be observed—as in the case of most of the Taliban.

Indeed, leading Islamists hail from the field of tensions between traditional and modern sectors: border-liners, representatives of the middle ranks of administration, the military, lawyers, doctors and engineers, new professionals (Schulze 1985; Riesebrodt 1990; van Nieuwenhuijze 1995)—i.e. professional fields that are integrated into the post-colonial system. Thus, they represent rather high social formations. And due to their integration into the dominant post-colonial system they adopt and adapt its main terms and recognize them as part of their own biography, as can be seen in different neologisms. Islamic terms like *sunna*, *dastūr*, *shūrā'* etc. are extricated from their religious context and given new ideological order and value—such as parliament and constitution. They revalue such terms by giving them new meanings and develop them further, without, however, renouncing their Islamic identity—party system, nation state and constitution etc. are interpreted as having been Islamic from conception. With this normative replacement it is possible to transcend traditional boundaries. They also postulate appropriating God's message individually and independently through the revealed text (*ijtihād*), which stands in contrast to *taqlīd*. In doing so they 'more generally refer to the central tradition of Sunni Islam in its period of development' (Hourani 1962: 149)—the salafis, the best predecessors—*salaf sālih*. In this way these Islamicists can legitimize modern developments within Islamic semiotics, stabilize their own position and expand their area of action. In this process of the ideologization of Islam and the reinvention of tradition, *code-* or *identity-switching* is most important and can be applied according to different addressees. To the outsider, the colonial public, the Islamicist argues ideologically, limiting the use of Islamic symbols to the indispensable. To the insider, the traditional society, he/she pursues the theological argument. The Islamic cult is reinforced, the theological discussion is, however, of disputable theological value.

One of the first to have ideologized Islam was Abūl-A'lā Maudūdī (d. 1979) from Aurangabad, whose political ideas about an Islamic state became quite popular, even among Arab Islamicists, such as the Muslim Brotherhood in Egypt and Syria. Maudūdī, like many other contemporary Islamicists such as Hasan al-Banna (murdered 1949) and Sayyid Qutb (executed 1966), was not a religious scholar but an autodidact and journalist, a 'hybrid' so-to-speak among both colonized and colonial societies. As we will see, Maudūdī started to 'islamicize' the political discourse of the nationalists—Muslims did not constitute a nation but the party of God.

The new rising élites around Islamicists regarded themselves as being in opposition to the power assertions of the national élites which they considered to be westernized, corrupt and privileged state classes. With the help of a small religious élite that had mass appeal but little political power, the Islamicists articulated and generalized this common experience in a common language and symbolism. The aim was to establish one single canon for the whole Muslim community, to enhance their own cultural identity *vis-à-vis* the other, and to mobilize politically. Naturally, this self-conceptualization needed a common enemy, such as the followers of traditional Islam and folk piety, as well as Western society, and both were essentialized by Islamicists.

However, in contrast to politically and ethnically constructed identities, religious—and especially Islamicist—forms of solidarity can claim a special missionary conscience and zeal. They usually promise a righteous society here and now through catharsis, e.g. a transformation from corruption to purity, from disbelief to belief, from un-godliness to Islam. They call for the reconstruction of an idealized pure and pre-colonial cultural context—*imitatio muhammadi*, which would guarantee the iteration of the original mythical establishment. This re-birth (*ihyā'*) and moral renewal (*tajdīd*), the transnational notion of the Golden Age and the rejection of the original chain and inherited canon, all imply a breaking-off from tradition.

This breaking-off and radical revaluation of tradition seems to be grounded in a heritage under which the handed-down canon was blurred and lost due to the obliteration and appropriation processes of colonial power. Therefore, the only way to legitimate the necessary rebirth and revival was to go back behind this obliterated canon. Consequently, a new normative and formative past was created. And because of their untied historicity these Islamicists could regard themselves as exponents of the projected imagined Islamic society—they are the avant-gardes, or the hegemonical identity that considers itself to be authorized to create the new canon and re-establish the sharia which stands for *tajdīd* —renewal.

Thus, the concept of *tajdīd* presupposes a particular historical perspective; it is determined by the notion of decay:

> the whole past history of the *Ummat* presents a spectre of unchecked decline and continuous decadence and the history of the middle period appears to Maudūdī a barren desert and wilderness and in this immense darkness, there were only occasional flashes in some corners of the world of Islam of the lightning of religious endeavour and reform. (Maudūdī paraphrased in Nadwi 1982: 45)

> History reveals that the ideal *Mujaddid* (*mujaddid-e kāmil)* is yet to be born. Caliph 'Umar bin 'Abd al–'Azīz might have attained this position but he did not get a chance to achieve it. All the *Mujaddids* who appeared after him accomplished work in one or the other particular aspect only but none achieved the distinction of becoming the ideal *Mujaddid* (*mujaddid-e kāmil*). (Maududi 1963: 38)

Interestingly enough, Maudūdī, the charismatic leader of this movement, recurred to Islamic mystical tradition and symbolism—which he otherwise criticized—when he hybridized the sufic terms *insān kāmil* (perfect man) and *mujaddid* (renewer of century or saviour) into *mujaddid-e kāmil* (for the terminology see Chitticks 1989). He also linked his identity to *salafīs* by referring to the second Caliph.

However, it is important to note that Islamicists repeat the colonial version about the Orient: a classical or formative period, followed by decline, followed by renewal. Thereby they receive the colonial critique, adopt and adapt it. Either they tend towards self-exoticization when victimizing the Muslim world, or the West is pilloried as a collective other (Riesebrodt 1990: 155f; Maududi 1980: 37–40). Hence, they criticize moral decline, particularly the sexual moral code of the West. Promiscuity and agnosticism, unlawful renovations of modernity and the culture, civilization and society of the twentieth century are rejected and considered to be the modern version of the pre-Muhammadan times of ignorance: *jāhilīya* (Maududi 1976; 1963: 5–34).

This critique is brought together into a doctrine of salvation and developed into an *integriste* plan. This, however, has clear integrationist features, e.g. to modernize Islamic tradition. Ideally, a new Islamic society is to be built up, which would correspond to Western achievements—in the realm of technology as well as ideology. This in turn is only possible in a centralized Islamist state, which the Islamists as brokers of Allah's monarchy, as *Hizb Allāh* or *Jamā'at-e Islāmī*, want to control. Maudūdī calls for God's sovereignty (*hākimīyat-e illāhi*) on earth within an universal, ideological Islamic nation. 'The Qur'an not only lays down principles of morality and ethics, but also gives guidance in the political, social and economic fields. It prescribes punishments for certain crimes and enunciates principles of monetary and fiscal policy. These cannot be translated into practice unless there is a State to enforce them. And herein lies the necessity of an Islamic State.' (Maududi 1980: 158f)

In contrast to folk-religious rites that use the prophet-cult, the legend of a saviour, the reconstruction of the Golden Age and millennarian postulates and symbols, mediated through paralinguistic modes of communication like music and religious songs, colour symbolism, dreams and calligraphy (Malik 1997a), Islamicist messages are translated in a more sober way and without much ritual. Ritualization becomes relevant only as post-mortem. After Maudūdī passed away, he came to be charismatically styled *mujaddid* and *mujāhid* (*Zindagī* 1979; Nasr 1996).

At this stage of Islamicist discourse, ideas such as pluralism, democracy and human rights have little value in an imagined Islamic state, since the main concern is to establish a real Islamic identity. On the other hand, these kinds of pan-Islamic ideas are always postulated within the boundaries of a nation state; the nation remains untouched as the prime frame of reference. It is not only an important feature for cultural autonomy, but also offers space for an all-embracing cultural identity which can integrate particular and regional identities. Here are the limits of Muslim unity and Islamic identity.

Political Islam then provides the imagination of the realization and reconstruction of a society within a nation state. This is particularly true in post-modern times, when political Islam has failed, because Islamicist promises were not realized. Analogous to this failure, new alternative canons have emerged, reflecting the interaction of different social realities and cultural identities in a pluralizing society, in which also Islamicists have started increasingly to use ideas of mythical re-establishments to demarcate their social and spatial space, albeit within the existing nation state (Eickelman and Piscatori 1996). This phase of post-Islamicist discourse is characterized by pluralism (*al-ta'addudīya*), in which different positions are re-negotiated, especially since the 1980s (Haddad 1996; Kian 1997), though this has been the case in India since long. One may have the impression that different Islamicists have learnt from the Indian experience. Even groups like the *Islamic Society of India* (*Jamā'at-e Islāmī Hind*), a pendant to the Pakistani *Jamā'at-e Islāmī*, have opted for a quietist and pluralist approach in secular India. In this context the critique of Sayyid Abū'l Hasan 'Alī Nadwī (born 1913), head of the internationally reputed *Council of Islamic Scholars*, the *Nadwat al-'Ulamā'* in Lucknow (Malik 1997), is a case in point.

As a representative of traditional Islamic scholarship (*'ulamā'*) and leading member of many Muslim organizations, Nadwī represents the pluralist trend among Muslim thinkers. Due to his positive stand in relation to mysticism and his Indian experience, he is able to redefine the independent position of Islamic scholars and to negotiate new cultural demands in a most dynamic way: In his reply to Maudūdī's Islamicist conceptions, Nadwī in contrast considers, that:

> Life is a continuous movement and development and changes and alterations take place in it. This is not its defect but a quality, it is not a departure from nature but is natural. It goes on changing its outer garment, languages, ways of thinking, reasons, and causes inciting inner conflicts, the methods and means employed for their satisfaction, questions arising internally and their answers all go on changing. (Nadwī 1982: 15)

Hence—according to Nadwī—anti-colonial Islamic scholars were quite active in the nineteenth century while many Muslims in the twentieth century adopted Western ideas and, like Maudūdī, harmed Islam. His Islam had a political colouring and revolved around the concepts of 'Sovereignty of God' and 'Kingdom of God' (*sultānī-ye rabb*), thus reducing the purpose of the revelation of the Koran and Islamic preachings to the establishment of the Kingdom of God. Moreover, his negative approach was a misguided technique and strategy calculated to build up his 'own edifice on the ruins of Islamic history and Islamic thinking'—though he did not evolve such a technique in a planned manner, the consequence of this type of presentation was inevitable (Nadwī 1982: 53).

However,

it is true that belief in God and acceptance does entail belief in Lordship of God and servitude of man, but this is only a fraction and not the totality of the attributes and essence of God, and His relationship with His creatures and that of His creatures with Him. In reality the relationship between the Creator and the created, between the worshipped and the worshipper is far greater, wider, and deeper and far subtler and delicate than that of Lord and servant, a king and his subject, a commander and the commanded. (Nadwi 1982: 63)

Even Ibn Taymiya wrote that the relation between the worshipper and the worshipped is infinitely wider, deeper and comprehensive and in this association gnosis (*ma'rifat*), penitence (*inabat*), love (*muhabbat*), sincerity (*ikhlas*) and constant remembrance (*dhikr*) are all included. For a ruler humility (*khudu'*), meekness (*tadhallul*), obedience (*ita'at*) and subordination (*inqiyad*) alone are needed on the part of the subject. (Nadwi 1982: 65f)

While Maudūdī considered prayers (*'ibādāt*) to be the way to the reconstruction of theocracy, for Nadwī the struggle against the carnal soul or holy war (*jihād*) and the political system are merely means to establish prayers (*aqāmat-e salāt*). The reconstruction of a Kingdom of God and the development of human culture were only a means and of secondary value. Purification of the soul was the way to overcome predicaments. And this was only possible through mystical experience:

It is the profoundest experience of human life that mere knowledge, investigation and research, bare laws and regulations, order and system, are not sufficient for staking one's life or even for producing the spirit and willingness to sacrifice. It requires greater motivation, a stronger devotion, a spiritual ambition and certainty of nonmaterial gains in the face of which this life appears a cumbersome burden. (Nadwī 1982: 90)

Consequently, Nadwī does not speak of an Islamic Society, *Jamā'at-e Islāmī*, but of a Society of Muslims (*Jamā'at-e muslimīn*), which would accept the sovereignty of religion (*dīn-e haqq kā ghalbah*) and establish its pillars.

The way to establish Islam was, however, a highly flexible one: 'instead of presenting total opposition [it must be] (...) the course of counselling and rectification, reformation instead of elimination (*tafhīm o islāh awr mashwara o salāh*).' (Nadwī 1982: 102) According to Nadwī, social change can only come about if there is change at the individual level.

However, notwithstanding Nadwī's harmonizing postulates and his call for national integration in India, his ideas are determined by the perception of an Islamic cultural hegemony: 'The lands they [i.e. the Muslims] conquered were actually reborn, with a renewed zest and vigour, in a new and brighter world' (Nadwī in Hai 1977: 3), while the founder of the Mughal empire, Babur, plays a prominent identity-giving role. Moreover, Nadwī considered Zia ul-Haqq's Islamicization policy to be a promising Islamic revolution; he considered Zia's death as a martyrdom (*shahādat*) and a big setback for Muslim society (Nadwī 1980: 312).

It is these different, apparently contradicting opinions that reflect the competition of Islamicist discourses. This is especially true in the field of the supposed latent and open tensions between Muslim scholars, sufis and intellectuals. Do Islamicists and mystical orders really compete with each other or are social and economic overlappings and cross-connections or personal unions not powerful enough to deal with their social and cultural realities in similar ways? Do not many contemporary managers of holy sites replace the holy man and his miracles (*karāmāt*) on account of their cultural hybridization? Do they not link their double vision to a new, wider discourse, and with a multiplicity of canons and anti-canons, thereby enjoying multiple legitimacy?

These overlappings certainly lead to cultural multi-dimensionality: the given boundaries and standardizations are being shifted, displaced, and extended. Even Islamic women increasingly appear and act in public within Islamicist discourse and seem to find a new revalued identity (Göle 1995) in the course of re-canonization. According to the theory of cultural hybridization, the most creative forms of identity are realized precisely at these points of friction and at the margins of the life realities of collectives, thereby creating a variety of standardizations, as can be discovered in recent post-Islamicist discourses in Iran, Pakistan and India. This is especially true for the Islamic diaspora, where inter-cultural understanding is particularly difficult because the cement of a common language, history, standardization and organization is lacking. On the other hand, the European majority seems hardly to be prepared to comprehend Muslim concerns (Nielsen 1995: 152ff). Therefore the degree of sacralization and theologization of identity may increasingly lead to distinctively enhanced identities, as also to the development of anti-identities.

Thus, making sense of history, and of Muslim identities, canons and charismas can only be possible if these complex and dynamic perspectives are contextualized. Indeed, there is no monolithic political Islam. Instead, there are Islamicist canons and charismatic figures—likewise a variety of folk Islams—and they must be seen as articulations of particular social and cultural realities that are negotiating for their spaces.

Note

1. In South Asia cinema plays a fairly important socio-psychological role since for the majority it suggests a fantasy world away from the hardship of everyday life (Dickey 1993).

References

Ashcroft, B. *et al.* 1989. *The Empire Writes Back: Theory and Practice in Post-Colonial Literatures*. London: Routledge.

Bhabha, H. 1994. *The Location of Culture*. London: Routledge.

Bulliet, R. 1994. *Islam. The View from the Edge*. New York.

Burckhardt-Qureshi, R. 1986. *Sufi Music of India and Pakistan. Sound, Context and Meaning in Qawwali*. Cambridge: Cambridge University Press.

Chitticks, W. C. 1989. *Ibn al-'Arabi's Metaphysics of Imagination: The Sufi Path of Knowledge*. Albany: State University of New York Press.

Dickey, S. 1993. *Cinema and the Urban Poor in South Asia*. Cambridge: Cambridge University Press.

Eaton, R. M. 1993. *The Rise of Islam and the Bengal Frontier, 1204–1760*. Berkeley: University of California Press.

Eickelman, D. and J. Piscatori. (eds). 1990. *Muslim Travellers: Pilgrimage, Migration, and the Religious Imagination*. London: Routledge.

———. 1996. *Muslim Politics*. Princeton: Princeton University Press.

Gaborieau, M. 1975. Legende et cult du saint musulman Ghazi Miyan au Népal occidental et en Inde du Norde. *Objets et Mondes* 15.3: 289–310.

Geertz, C. 1968. *Islam Observed: Religious Development in Morocco and Indonesia*. New Haven and London: Yale University Press.

Gellner, E. 1985. *Leben im Islam. Religion als Gesellschaftsordnung*. Stuttgart: Klett-Cotta.

Göle, N. 1995. *Republik und Schleier: die muslimische Frau in der modernen Türkei*. Aus dem Türkischen von P. Lorenzi. Berlin: Babel Verlag Hund & van Uffelen.

Gramlich, R. 1986. *Die Wunder der Freunde Gottes: Theologien und Erscheinungsformen des islamischen Heiligenwunders*. Wiesbaden: Franz Steiner.

Haddad, Y. Y. 1996. Islamicist Depictions of Christianity in the Twentieth Century: The Pluralism Debate and the Depiction of the Other. *Islam and Christian-Muslim Relations* 7.1: 75–89.

Hai, H. S. A. 1977. *India During Muslim Rule*. Lucknow: Academy of Islamic Research and Publications.

Hourani, A. 1962. *Arabic Thought in the Liberal Age*. Oxford: Oxford University Press.

Kian, A. 1997. Women and Politics in Post-Islamist Iran: The Gender Conscious Drive to Change. *British Journal of Middle East Studies* 24.1: 75–96.

Malik, J. 1996. *Colonialization of Islam*. New Delhi: Manohar; Lahore: Vanguard.

———. 1997. *Islamische Gelehrtenkultur in Nordindien*. Leiden: Brill.

———. 1997a. Muslimische Identitäten, autochthone Institutionen und kulturelle Hybridität: Einige Forschungsperspektiven. *Mitteilungen der Anthropologischen Gesellschaft* 127: 67–78.

Maududi, A. A. 1963. *A Short History of the Revivalist Movement in Islam*. Lahore: Islamic Publications.

———. 1976. *Islam and Ignorance*. Lahore: Islamic Publications.

———. 1980. *Islamic Law and Constitution*. Lahore: Islamic Publications.

Mayeur-Jaouen, C. 1994. *Al-Sayyid al-Badawī: Un grand saint de l'Islam égyptien*. Le Caire: Institute Français d'Archéologie Orientale.

Nadwi, A. H. A. 1982. *Appreciation and Interpretation of Religion in the Modern Age*. Lucknow: Academy of Islamic Research & Publications.

Nadwī, Abūl-Hasan 'Alī. 1980. *'Asr-e hādir men dīn kī tafhīm o tashrīh*. Lakhna'ū: Dār-e 'Urfāt.

Nasr, S. V. R. 1996. *Mawdudi and the Making of Islamic Revivalism*. New York: Oxford University Press.

Nielsen, J. 1995. *Muslims in Western Europe*. Edinburgh: Edinburgh University Press.

Riesebrodt, M. 1990. *Fundamentalismus als patriarchalische Bewegung: Amerikanische Protestanten (1910–28) und iranische Schiiten (1961–79) im Vergleich*. Tübingen: J. C. B. Mohr.

Schulze, R. 1985. Islamische Kultur und soziale Bewegung. *Peripherie* 18/19: 60–84.

Streck, B. 1985. Netzwerk: Der transaktionale Einspruch gegen das Paradigma der struktural-funktionalen Ethnologie. *Anthropos* 80: 569–86.

Turner, V. 1979. *Process, Performance and Pilgrimage*. New Delhi: Concept Publishing House.

van Nieuwenhuijze, C. A. O. 1995. Islamism—A Defiant Utopianism. *Die Welt des Islams* 35.1: 1–36.

Zindagī (Lahore) 10/42 (1979).

The Vishva Hindu Parishad: A Nationalist but Mimetic Attempt at Federating the Hindu Sects

CHRISTOPHE JAFFRELOT

> Remember, it is the VHP that has given these sants legitimacy and exposure. Their only audience consisted of old men and women. Now they have a large audience.
>
> *A Vice-President of the BJP*[1]

> The leaders have let us down too many times. If the sants and sadhus had not called us, we would not have come this time.
>
> A *kar-sevak*[2]

The Vishva Hindu Parishad (VHP; World Hindu Council) can only be understood in relation to the Rashtriya Swayamsevak Sangh (RSS; National Volunteer Organisation), of which, in many respects, it constitutes an affiliate. Not only does the movement draw its ideology from the RSS, its structure is also derived from it. Indeed, the backbone of the VHP is embodied in the figure of the *pracharak*, a full-time 'preacher' and organizer of the RSS. These *pracharaks* are specially trained in Instructors' Training Camps and then at the Officers' Training Camps of the RSS. Though they are often well educated they have renounced career and family life to devote themselves more completely to the cause of Hindu nationalism. Besides, they are bound to an itinerant life because their mission is to pervade the network of RSS *shakhas* (branches).

Pracharaks conceive of their mission, their self-denial and austerity, in a manner similar to renouncers. They are perceived as such by several young *swayamsevaks* of the *shakhas*, who may even regard their *pracharak* as a guru. The RSS thus constitutes a kind of nationalist sect.[3] It presents itself both as a 'brotherhood in saffron'[4] inspired by the Hindu sect pattern, and in the words of its founder Hedgewar, in his last speech delivered in 1940, as the 'Hindu Rashtra [Hindu nation] in miniature'[5]

The affinities that the RSS *pracharaks* entertain with the Hindu sects are especially important for their activities in the VHP since this organization has been created to bring together the largest possible number of religious figures. However, the VHP does not draw its inspiration from the traditional Hindu sect, except for the self-professed asceticism of its *pracharaks*. Interestingly, it has undertaken its mission by imitating the ecclesiastical structure characteristic of 'Semitic religions', Christianity and Islam, so as to more effectively resist these very religions—which it perceives as posing a threat to Hinduism.

RSS *Pracharaks* and 'Modern Gurus'

The first project director of the VHP was Shiv Shankar Apte, a Maharashtrian Brahman born in Baroda. Apte studied law in Bombay before becoming an advocate in the sphere of influence of K. M. Munshi, a Congress leader known for his traditionalist Hindu positions.[6] Attracted by journalism, Apte collaborated for a time with the United Press of India, but his encounter with Golwalkar, head of the RSS from 1940 to 1973, led him to embrace the career of *pracharak* (*Shraddhanjali Smarika*: 28). In 1961, Apte published three articles in *Kesari* (a paper founded by B. G. Tilak) on the need to hold a meeting to bring together all the currents of Hinduism in order to create greater coherence.[7]

Soon after, an article by Swami Chinmayananda echoed his thoughts:

> It seemed to me, in a way that was still vague, that it was time to call for a *World Hindu Council* [the English name which the Vishva Hindu Parishad gave itself] by inviting to Delhi or Calcutta delegates from throughout the world to discuss the difficulties and needs concerning the survival and development of Hindu culture. In this Council, we would elaborate the plans and programmes making it possible to bring the family of Hindu dharma together. (*H.V.* 1980: 19)

Chinmayananda was a disciple of Swami Shivanand, founder of the Divine Life Society in Haridwar. Coming from a respected family in Kerala, he attempted to pursue his studies in Madras but, not able to enrol at the university, he left to study law in Lucknow in the early 1940s. He then became a journalist in Delhi. It was in this capacity that, in order to investigate sadhus whom he suspected of deception, he went to the Himalayas and eventually became a disciple of Swami Shivanand. After having been initiated into the Adi Shankaracharya order at the *math* in Sringeri by his guru, Swami Tapovanand, he gave lectures on *jnana yajna* (the sacrifice of knowledge) in the 1950s. He described these sermons as a metaphor for Vedic sacrifice. He assembled five pandits around the *kund*, where the fire is lit, who were responsible for making sacrificial offerings *(ahuti)*. Thereby, the human body is the *kund*, its five senses replace the priests, their perceptions are the offerings of the soul—the kindling of which is analogous to the flame.[8] The verve with which Chinmayananda described the 'sacrifice' bears testimony to his rhetorical ability. It was the latter to which he owed unforeseen popular success; his lectures attracted thousands of disciples and he began to make all-India tours in the 1950s. The social milieu which he wished to address most was the middle classes, whom he described as 'modern educated illiterates'. This was without doubt the reason why he established his ashram, the Sandypani Academy, in Bombay, the gateway to Westernized India. He soon awakened the hostility of the 'orthodox'—starting with his guru and the monastery with which he was affiliated, Sringeri—by promoting English as the medium of communication and acknowledging Hindus of all castes, irrespective of gender, and allowing them all access to spiritual knowledge. His sermons attracted, primarily, disciples from the middle class, not only in India but also in South-East Asia and the United States. Van der Veer thus sees him as a precursor of the 'modern guru'[9] a category which can be defined on the basis of a few of Chinmayananda's characteristics. His spiritual practice rested on a discourse which valorised individual development and a moral code as a factor in social success. To these themes the middle class in Western countries and in India were responsive.

Secondly, he did not fit into a precise sectarian tradition; the sectarian affiliation diminished in value relative to the 'Hindu' allegiance. He founded his own ashram. He began quite early to increase his lecturing throughout the world, and this was well in tune with the form he had chosen for his teaching, for in his arena the personal relation of master to disciple became less significant than public discourse. Swami Chinmayananda, moreover, did not initiate his *shishyas* (disciples) by whispering a mantra in their ears. He held such practice to be obsolete because elitist. He gave his mantra 'from the dais' to the entire audience. From this perspective, Chinmayananda was heir to neo-Hindu socio-religious reform movements. Ramakrishna too did not initiate disciples either, and they too were recruited precisely from the Westernized middle class (Sarkar 1992: 1543–66).

S. S. Apte was of course interested in the article written by Swami Chinmayananda in 1963. The encounter of these two men is significant because they are representative of the two categories which were to form the keystone of the Vishva Hindu Parishad: Hindu nationalists and the modern guru. Apte, in effect, undertook to contact the greatest possible number of sect leaders with a view to founding the VHP in 1964, but he primarily rallied modern gurus. He travelled for nine months through India to find people interested in his project. He was in communication with roughly 800 people, of whom 150 were guests at the inaugural conference of the VHP (*H.V.*, Sept.-Oct. 1980: 19).

The VHP: Council of 'Hinduism'?

Apte saw in the VHP an instrument of consolidation through the unification of Hinduism. Its foundation ensued mainly from the sentiment that Christian proselytism[10] constituted a threat to Hinduism, and that it was therefore necessary to emulate its techniques so as to offer more effective resistance. Indeed the VHP gives a good illustration of what I have called the Hindu nationalist strategy of the stigmatization and emulation of so-called threatening others. For the RSS leaders and their followers, Hindus are vulnerable to Muslims and Christians because these communities are supported from outside India and because they then expand (through conversions or high birth rates), but also because they believe Hindus are weak and divided into too many castes and sects. One of the remedies lies in imitating their 'threatening others', mainly Christians, in the view of the VHP.

Even though the project of such an organization developed over a long period, its formation was precipitated in 1964 because of the Pope's visit. The Pope announced, in August, that the International Eucharistic Conference was to be held in Bombay in November. The organ of the RSS, *Organiser* (*Org.*), spoke out against this 'invasion' after the announcement had been made, maintaining that 'Catholicism [was] not only a religion, but a formidable organisation allied with certain foreign powers .... The conversion of tribals on a large scale in the industrial heart of India [in Bihar] constitute[d] a threat for national security because, in the case of conflict between their country and the church, the allegiance of Catholics [would] always be foremostly to the Pope!'[11] This image of an enemy whose strength was derived from organizational rigour and its transnational dimension underlies the objective of Hindu nationalists to provide their religion with the ecclesiastical form of a church. This sheds light on the task assigned to the VHP, created on 29 August 1964, as well as on its structure.

S. S. Apte explained the foundation of the movement in the following terms:

The declared objective of Christianity is to transform the entire world into Christendom, just as it is that of Islam to make a Pak[istan]. Beside these two dogmatic and proselytising religions, a third has appeared, Communism [...] The world has been divided into Christian, Islamic and Communist [zones], and these three consider Hindu society to be a very good and very rich food upon which they feast and grow fat. It is therefore necessary, in this age of competition and conflict, to think of organising the Hindu world to save it from the evil eyes of these three. (*Org.*, *Divali Special* 1964: 15)

The main example offered by the author in support of his argument was the 'separatism' of the Naga tribes in the North-East which had just been granted Nagaland in 1963 . The RSS attributed this move to the 'denationalization' of the aborigines by the missions.[12] The RSS decided to react to this 'aggression' by using the weapons of the 'aggressors': the Hindus had to borrow Christians' techniques to resist them more efficiently. Hence the church-like structure of the VHP, for it is intended to be a centralized federation of the sects of Hinduism. S. S. Apte was explicit on this point in his opening speech at the founding conference of the VHP:

Vishnuites, Saivites, Lingayats, Advaits, Dalits, Vishnuite-Dvaits, Sikhs, Jains, Buddhists—in fact all the *panth* denominations of our very diverse society, as well as the people [Hindus] living in foreign countries, can make their difficulties disappear and come together to recognise the unity behind the diversity. Our effort is to promote a harmonious mutual understanding and a new order in accordance with the genius and spirit of our ancient noble heritage, while answering to the exigencies of the modern scientific age. (*H.V.* Sept.-Oct. 1980: 4)

The founding conference brought together representatives of different sects—for example Tara Singh and Gyani Bhupendra Singh, the president of the SGPC[13]—which constituted for the Hindu nationalists a current of Hinduism. In addition, the VHP provided itself with an 'advisory council grouping the *shankaracharyas*, the holy leaders and the gurus of all the Sampradayas and Panths' (*Org.*, *Divali Special* 1964: 15). It was also decided to organize a large international conference in Allahabad on the occasion of the Kumbh Mela in 1966, in which 'the learned of all sects' were to participate.[14]

To bring the different *shankaracharyas* together into the VHP was all the more difficult as they traditionally argued over pre-eminence. The first World Hindu Conference in Allahabad, which was given the old Sanskrit name Prayag, on 22–24 January 1966, suffered from the defection of *shankaracharyas* from Badrinath and Sringeri. Among 25,000 delegates, at least as many founders of ashrams or heads of modern associations were to be found as were spiritual masters initiated and invested, according to the rules of sects, with an ancient tradition. Among the former, the presence of two individuals in particular should be mentioned.

Prabha Dutt Brahmachari had participated in the independence movement, attracted by Gandhi and by Hindu traditionalists such as M. M. Malaviya, P. Tandon and Sampurnanand. In the 1920s, these traditionalists invited him to join the editorial staff of *Aj*, a Hindi paper in Banaras. Shortly thereafter, however, he became a renouncer and founded his ashram in Jhuri, near Allahabad, where he participated in the organization of the Kumbh Mela. In 1948, the head of the Allahabad RSS, Rajendra Singh, who became chief of the RSS almost fifty years later, made his acquaintance. M. S. Golwalkar also drew close to him. During the 1951–2 elections, he followed the suggestions of these men and stood against Nehru in the name of cow protection and in opposition to the Hindu Code Bill (*Org.*, 26 Oct. 1990: 9). Prabhu Dutt Brahmachari was the true exemplar of the category of 'modern guru'—*sadhus* who had founded their own ashrams and were active in politics.

Another important modern Hindu leader present at the first VHP conference was Sant Tukdoji. As president of the Bharat Sadhu Samaj (Society of Indian Sadhus), Sant Tukdoji was more representative of the 'Hindu traditionalist' current of the VHP.[15] He attributed his going over to the VHP to the need to protect Hinduism against Christianity and Islam, as well as against the anti-Hindu stance of the government (*Org.*, 26 Dec. 1965).

Among the representatives of historical religious currents, the most significant was Swami Vishvesh Tirth of Pejawar *math* (Udupi, Karnataka), the spiritual leader of the Vishnuite Madhva sect (*Org.*, 30 Jan. 1966: 1; 3 May 1981: 4). Born in 1931, he had been initiated to this order at the age of seven, and subsequent to apparently rigorous studies, notably of the Vedanta; he was named head of the Sri Krishna *math* in Udupi in 1951. He then established his reputation as a defender of Hindu culture through the Madhva Mahamandal, an institution principally active in the area of education (for the promotion of the learning of Sanskrit and the *shastras*) (*H.V.* May 1981: 39).

The under-representation of spiritual masters at the head of prestigious sects suggests that the VHP attracted, above all, swamis who sought additional legitimacy or a valorising platform. This was a question of weakness but not necessarily of an insurmountable handicap insofar as the authority of a Hindu spiritual master can be derived from a source other than official investiture at the head of a recognized sect. Knowledge of spiritual texts, an ascetic discipline, and rhetorical talent can compensate for these and help make it possible to proclaim oneself as a religious spokesman.

Despite its poor representativeness, the meeting in Allahabad was intended to be a kind of parliament[16] and repository of Hinduism. A sub-committee was designated to 'elaborate a code of conduct suitable to promote and strengthen the Hindu *samskars*' (*H.V.*, 30 Jan. 1966: 2). This Vidvat Parishad (Learned Assembly) then met to simplify the rites of purification, to give an official status to five principal festivals of the Hindu calendar, and above all to elaborate the much-vaunted code of conduct. Significantly, the process was accomplished in reference to Christianity and Islam:

> Christians and Muslims generally observe in a strict and scrupulous manner certain rules of religious conduct. Every Christian and Muslim, moreover, possesses outward symbols indicative of his religion. The Parishad has felicitously arrived at a 'code of conduct' which is suitable for all sects and beliefs. It has decided that the *pratashnan* (morning ablutions) and the *ishwarsmaran* (the reciting of the name of god) would constitute the minimal rules of conduct. (*H.V.*, 11 June 1967: 14)

Beyond these efforts to enact a code of conduct, the VHP also sought to establish its central authority over an entire religious network which was scattered through monasteries and temples. Priests were thus called upon at the Prayag assembly to make these latter places centres for the 'propagation of dharma and sanskriti' (*H.V.*, 30 Jan. 1966: 15).

At the end of January 1979, a second World Hindu Conference was held in Allahabad under the auspices of the VHP. As in 1966, this conference was intended to be a comprehensive gathering, but in a more credible manner, considering the number (estimated at 100,000) and representativeness of the delegates. The 'different currents' of the 'Hindu nation' were, in effect, represented: Buddhism by the Dalai Lama, who inaugurated the conference; the Namdhari Sikhs and the Jains by two dignitaries from those communities; the disciples of Shankara by the *shankaracharya* of Badrinath; the 'dualists' by two Jagadgurus from Udupi; and the Nimbarkis, the Vallabhis, the different schools and disciples of Ramanuja, the Ramanandis, the disciples of Chaitanya, those of Kabir, the Naths of Gorakhpur, the Arya Samajists, the Ramakrishna Mission and the Divine Life Society by various personalities.

The logic of these unitarian efforts remained that of a strategic mimetism: Hinduism was threatened by the proselytising religions which imperilled its majority status.[17] This implied the eradication of untouchability, which was a factor in conversions, and the unification of Hinduism via a coherent whole. These two remedies were once again proposed by reference to the cultural characteristics of Christian and Muslim 'aggressors'.

From this perspective the VHP again proposed a 'minimum code of conduct for the daily life of every Hindu', the objective of which was once again the unification of religious practices and references. Article 1 called for the veneration by all, morning and evening, of the sun; Article 2 for the systematization of the symbol 'om' (on lockets, visiting cards, etc.). Article 3 was yet more explicit: 'The Bhagavad Gita is the sacred book of Hindus, regardless of their sect. It contains the essence of Hindu philosophy. All Hindus should have a copy in their home.' (*H.V.*, Mar.-Apr. 1979: 89) Notwithstanding the number of delegates present in Prayag in 1979, those endowed with real authority were either absent (such as the more important *shankaracharyas*), or not very active in the VHP (such as the *shankaracharya* of Badrinath). The main religious figures significantly involved were not recognized as sect leaders, but as heads of their own ashrams, such as a newcomer who was to become a pillar of the VHP, namely Satyamitranand Giri.

Born in Agra in 1932 into a Brahman family, Satyamitranand Giri pursued his studies in the establishments of the Arya Samaj and the Hindi Sahitya Sammelan until receiving his M.A. in Hindi literature. He then embraced the calling of a renouncer and made his way to the Himalayas. Initiated in Rishikesh by the *shankaracharya* of Jyotirmath, he accepted, at the age of twenty-eight, the directorship of the Bhanpura *math* (Mandsaur district in Madhya Pradesh), the foundation of which is attributed to Shankara. He assumed this responsibility for three years as *shankaracharya*, then resigned so as to travel more freely. His journeys to southern Africa and the United States showed him that the spiritual addresses asked of him in these regions were more highly valued and lucrative than what he made by teaching his Indian disciples, despite their becoming increasingly numerous, particularly among the Patels of Gujarat.[18] One year, after having given up the office of *shankaracharya*, Satyamitranand Giri participated in the foundation of the VHP, which had offered him a prestigious platform.[19] However, he only joined the core influential people in the organization a few years later, after constructing a Bharat Mata Mandir with a pedagogic aim in Haridwar.[20]

Among the most active sect leaders in the VHP now figured the *mahant* Avaidyanath who, in the 1970s, had succeeded his guru Digvijay Nath as head of the sect of Naths in Gorakhpur. Like his father, he was invested with important responsibilities in the Hindu Mahasabha, a small Hindu nationalist party. He was elected MLA from the district of Gorakhpur in

1962, 1974 and 1977, then to the Lok Sabha in 1970, 1989 and 1991 (Parliament of India 1992: 43). At the same time, he occupied positions at the head of the Congress-backed Bharat Sadhu Samaj of the region in the 1960s.[21]

From its foundation in 1964 to the 1970s, the VHP thus endeavoured to group together the largest possible number of religious figures so as to provide Hinduism with an ecclesiastical structure. This undertaking attracted, above all, modern gurus who sought a valorizing platform, indeed legitimization, while the heads of 'historical sects', not having the same needs, showed more reserve—a few personalities excepted—in relation to the type of organization which was until then unknown to Hinduism, and which would undermine their independence.

When the VHP was founded, Apte was aware of the need to introduce new principles into Hinduism in order to defend the idea of a greater organization of sects: 'modernisation is a *sine qua non* for the continuity and eternal survival of a society.' [22] Swami Chinmayananda recognized that the very idea of the VHP was at odds with Hinduism:

> I know that religious organisation is contrary to the very principle of Hinduism, but we must evolve with our times [...] If one remains unorganised, one has neither strength nor vitality. Consequently, in the spiritual domain, even if progress and development are accomplished on the individual level, religion must also organise itself to serve society [...] If we do not organise ourselves, there will be no integration. And that is a matter of urgency. If we are not integrated despite the 82% of the population which we represent, our voices will never be heard. While the 18% [*sic*] Christians and Muslims are well organised. Their demands and their needs are well taken care of by the democratic government ... (*Shraddhanjali Smarika* n.d.: 69)

Chinmayananda thus justifies the organization of Hinduism by means of the VHP on the basis of the threat which the Muslim and Christian minorities represent.

This change was thus legitimized by the higher stakes involved, also by the so-called Hindu tradition. Apte declared during the founding conference of the VHP:

> It has been our tradition, since Vedic times, to come together in moments of crisis to reform society and cure its disorders. There were Jain assemblies, Buddhist councils and gatherings of the Sikh Panth, in which we sought solutions to the scourge which encroached more and more on society. If I had to, I would say that there has not been a united and representative gathering of all the *panths* and sects of our multi-petal society since the epoch of Harsha. We have today the possibility to create it. (*H.V.*, Sept.-Oct. 1980: 19)

The VHP also compared the conferences of 1966 and 1979 to that called by Emperor Harsha in the seventh century. At Prayag he had brought together representatives of different religious currents in India to induce them to live on good terms. This practice, however, reflected the Buddhist influences to which Harsha had been exposed (Devahuti 1970: 96, 157). But the relevance for Hindu nationalists lay in finding a 'national' reference suitable for legitimizing this type of gathering which was not really in character with Hinduism. A prestigious past was evoked so as to present a cultural import—the principle of an ecclesiastical structure. The mimetic aspect of the VHP's mindset had to be concealed somehow, even though it was more or less acknowledged by Apte himself.

Soon after its creation in 1964, the VHP succeeded in implanting its network throughout India, notably by employing on the one hand the ideological affinities which associate the *pracharaks* and the *sadhus* as variants of the figure of the renouncer and, on the other hand, the relationship between the notable-cum-patron (*rais*, *jajman*) and the religious figure (*brahman*, *sadhu*).

The Swayamsevak, the Notable and the Renouncer

The Vishva Hindu Parishad is not only inscribed in the Hindu nationalist project of the RSS, but is also part of the strategy of the movement. In addition to its purpose of becoming a council of Hinduism, the organization is intended to enable the structure of the Hindu nationalist movement to pervade national and local levels by bringing together notables and sadhus imbued with its ideology.

Succeeding each other as general secretaries of the organization were senior *pracharaks* who ensured a liaison with the leadership of the RSS, located in Nagpur. In 1982, the VHP was assigned a new general secretary, Har Mohan Lal, a diamond merchant from Agra and *swayamsevak* since 1947.[23] Most significantly, a secretary, Ashok Singhal, an Arya Samajist from Aligarh and former *pracharak* of the RSS for the Kanpur region, was appointed. Singhal became general secretary at the death of Har Mohan Lal in April 1986, and his office of deputy general secretary fell to Acharya Giriraj Kishore, *swayamsevak* since 1940 and then *pracharak*.[24] The preponderance of men from the RSS at the head of the VHP is confirmed and reinforced by the action of Moropant Pingle, a member of the general staff of the RSS who, as a 'trustee' of the VHP, exercised a strong influence on the conduct of the organization from the 1980s onwards.

These men benefited from the patronage of notables who often held positions as 'trustees', generous members who were benefactors. Eminent people linked with land or business affairs were attracted to this organization for the defence of Hinduism. These activities conform with their traditional function of providing patronage to Hindu institutions.[25] Thus, the Maharaja of Mysore presided over the VHP before being replaced by the Maharaja of Udaipur in 1968 (*Org.*, 12 Apr. 1968: 6). Another princely figure actively involved in the direction of the VHP, Vijaya Raje Scindia, never occupied an official position other than that of 'trustee', but as such she made numerous donations to the organization. Apart from princely families, notables patronizing the VHP were above all recruited from among Marwari industrialists : V. H. Dalmia—elder son of Jaidayal Dalmia (1904–93), founder of an industrial group who also patronized the VHP's cow-protection activities,[26] is president of the VHP; S. B. Somayya is one of the former vice-presidents, and G. H. Singhania is a 'trustee' of the organization. The presence of these eminent personalities serves to enhance the respectability of the VHP. The VHP also benefits from the patronage of retired Congress members,[27] or of former reputable advocates.[28] It has also attracted the patronage of retired policemen and army men: its former vice-president S. C. Dixit was director-general of police in Uttar Pradesh from 1980 to1984 and joined the movement subsequent to his retirement. He was also vice-president of the Lucknow branch of the Chinmaya Mission, the institution founded by Swami Chinmayananda (*Parliament of India* 1992: 198). Once again, patronage appears to be addressed to the VHP, as also to other institutions of which the purpose is more religious than ideological; however, it is precisely this distinction which becomes blurred.

While members of the RSS occupy governing positions in the VHP and notables occupy the more honorary posts, sadhus have places in the deliberative areas of the organization's structure. The organizers' endeavour is to woo them in order to institutionalize the collaboration of Hindu nationalist militants and religious leaders. In 1981 the VHP strengthened its Central Margdarshak Mandal (central circle of those 'who show the way'), the members of which were 'to conduct and guide religious ceremonies, morals and ethics of Hindu society'.[29] The members in question, numbering thirty-nine, represented quite comprehensively the sects of Hinduism: four *shankaracharyas* were at the head, then the Nimbarki, Ramanuji, Ramanandi and Goswami Jagadgurus, as well as other minor *acharyas*. Parallel to this instance, the VHP founded a Sadhu Sansad (Parliament of Sadhus), of which the seventeen sadhus were to enable the 'power (*shakti*) of the sadhus [to] play a greater role in the activities of national construction.' (*H.V.*, Sept.-Oct. 1980: 30–1).

These institutions evolved over the years; the Margdarshak Mandal, strengthened in its status as permanent organization, was raised to two hundred members who were called upon to meet twice yearly to the purpose of 'advising the VHP in socio-religious domains'.[30] The Sadhu Sansad became, in 1984, a Dharma Sansad comprising hundreds of participants and meeting to discuss 'vital problems' of the country at very irregular intervals. This informal character is found in the Sadhu Sammelans (assemblies) which are called at random.

Parallel to the effort of structuring the religious milieu connected with the VHP, the movement attempted to branch out to the local level. The basic unit of the movement, similar to that of the RSS and BJP, but called *upakhanda*, corresponds to a territory of 2000 inhabitants; then there are the *khanda* (20,000 inhabitants), the *prakhand* (100,000 inhabitants), the district, division, and finally the state. The *pracharaks* provided by the RSS numbered 150 in 1982, but the VHP also undertook to train its own *dharma pracharaks*; one hundred among them were 'initiated' by the heads of the seven *akharas* in Haridwar, in July 1982 (*Org.*, 28. 11. 1982: 11; 01. 08. 1982: 1). They were primarily active at the levels of district, division and state. The cadres of the VHP attempted to rally religious leaders at these different levels so as to form equivalent substitutes for the Margdarshak Mandal of the district, division and state.

The example of Ujjain in Madhya Pradesh suggests that the mainspring of this enterprise was also constituted at the local level by activists trained by the RSS and receiving the patronage of notables. In this town, the presidency of the local VHP was occupied until 1984 by a former town mayor and member of the Congress. In 1984, the post of president went to a Baniya from the Agarwal caste, Babulal Har Lavaka, who owned an electronic components shop in the town's centre. This man did not belong to a party but was known for his activity in a religious association with philanthropic connotations, the Gayatri Parivar.[31] It was by virtue of his status as a notable patronizing certain forms of social work with Hindu accents that the local RSS leaders asked him to preside over the Ujjain VHP.[32] He never belonged to the RSS and even disapproved of 'certain activities' of the movement.

Lavaka was assisted by a secretary from the *soni* (silversmith)caste, who came from the RSS. He was active for twenty years in the Jana Sangh and the BJP before becoming uninterested in political matters, preferring to work in the VHP.[33] His transfer to this organization corresponds to the desire of RSS leaders to appoint its cadres to offshoots of the movement with which they have the greatest affinities. In addition to the office of secretary in the local VHP, that of *sangathan mantri* is also occupied by a member of the RSS. The *sangathan mantri* supervises six districts around Ujjain. There is, however, no doubt that he represents the kingpin in the organisational structure of the local VHP insofar as he is the favoured correspondent in the hierarchy of the movement.

Compared to the poles constituted by notables and activists, the milieu of religious figures is by far the most interesting in the Ujjain VHP. Ujjain, no doubt by virtue of its status as a 'holy town' alongside a river which is much venerated by Hindus, shelters numerous monasteries. One of the main monasteries, the Sandipani Ashram, is considered by the Vallabhis to be the seventy-third seat of Vallabhacharya, who is said to have held a discourse and to have planted a pipal tree there in the sixteenth century. Ujjain also assumes a particular importance for the Naths. One finds on the periphery of the town the caves where Gorakhnath and Matsyendranath are said to have stayed, as well as the tomb of the latter (Rath n.d.). Despite the significance of the Vallabhi, Nath and Udaisin monasteries, no member of these *sampradayas* participated in the activities of the VHP at the time of our field-work in the early 1990s.

The sadhu representing the religious pole in the local VHP, Swami Shanti Swaroopanand, did not belong to a traditional order. In 1984 he took over the administration of the ashram which had been founded in the 1930s by Swami Akhandanand. Apparently he had been initiated, like Sadhvi Rithambara, by Swami Parmanand in Haridwar. He was thus trained in an activist practice of 'monkhood' centred on propaganda. It was during a tour—which he compared to those by Vivekananda—intended to 'awaken and organize' (*jagaran aur sangathan*)[34] Hindus that he discovered Ujjain and settled at the Akhand Ashram.

Shanti Swaroopanand no doubt represents a category of sadhus who have chosen the career of renouncer less because of the discipline and doctrine of a sect than for ideological reasons. Like the majority of these sadhus, he came from a well-off, educated milieu. The son of a Rajput family, he received his M. A. in philosophy. He initially became interested in 'monkhood' by listening to the sermons (*prachans*) of sadhus passing through his village. Shanti Swaroopanand was clearly attracted by the very ideological discourses held by Swami Parmanand and it is by way of his own rhetorical capacity (which is, in fact, remarkable and in a heavily Sanskritized Hindi) that he was solicited by leaders of the VHP.

The ideology which he propounds is in no way distinguishable from the Hindu nationalism of the RSS and its affiliates. Anti-Islamic xenophobia appeared at once as the central motif in his discourse. He invokes the desecrations and persecutions of the Mughal Empire, the separatism of Kashmiri Muslims, and generally those in India who support the Pakistani cricket team and give their allegiance to Arabian countries. The Muslim threat ensues not only from this transnational position but also from the demographic growth of this minority, the males of which, according to Swami Shanti Swaroopanand, marry four times and have on average twelve children. He demands the nationalisation of this community, which is to take place through the adoption of a uniform civil code and the recognition of an ancient Hindu culture as the national culture—which does not prohibit the practice of Islam in the private sphere.

Faced with what he considers the Muslim threat, he holds the entrance of sadhus into politics to be a matter of urgency for, on the one hand, awakening and organizing Hindus, and on the other to oblige politicians in New Delhi to desist from serving the minorities in exchange for their votes, but rather to recognize the preponderance of Hindus.

All these arguments have been codified by the RSS and adopted by the VHP decades ago, so that Swami Swaroopanand cuts a much better figure as '*swayamsevak* in saffron' than as renouncer. This is all the more so the case as he shows only scorn for sadhus who have withdrawn to the mountains or ashrams, while the real fight, in his eyes, is in the world. This inclination for a life in the world can be inferred from his publicity equipment. He travels in a Maruti van upon which is mounted a loud speaker. His interest in the West is another indication of this and one of his disciples in the ashram, an American, discussed it with him. He was concerned about the price of airline tickets to Europe, where he hoped to be able to hold a few paid lectures on yoga.

This type of sadhu is not only distinguished from renouncers of traditional *sampradayas* by worldly activities, but also through the devalorisation of sectarian adherence. He acknowledges being Sivaite in the Paramahans tradition (*parampara*), but wants above all to be 'Hindu'. In addition to his seat in the Margdarshak Mandal, Shanti Swaroopanand is the Pramukh Dharmachari of Madhya Bharat and the patron (*sanrakshak*) of the VHP in Ujjain.

On the whole, the VHP has branched out to the local level on the basis of a potentially influential sociological trilogy, the innovation residing above all in the rallying of religious figures who had previously been more on the margin of the RSS. The network thus formed made possible the meeting of the first Dharma Sansad on 7–8 April 1984 in Delhi, assembling 528 religious representatives of the different currents in Hinduism—in the wider sense as understood by the Hindu nationalists (*H.V.*, August 1990: 15).

The important fact to be emphasized regarding the last two or three decades is the increase in the number of 'modern' sadhus who do not all have the status of guru. Most of them have been trained by men of the generation of Swami Chinmayananda, Satyamitranand Giri, Brahma Dutt Brahmachari and Swami Parmanand. Shanti Swaroopanand was trained that way by the latter, like the famous Sadhvi Rithambara. This daughter of a Punjabi farmer belonging to the Kshatriya caste is reputed to have attained 'nirvana' at 16 years of age during a visit by Swami Parmanand to her village. Having followed the latter to his ashram in Haridwar, she was primarily instructed in oratory, like her co-disciple Shanti Swaroopanand. In 1986, at 23 years of age, she developed the art of the *dharmik pravachans* and was soon engaged in agitation for the VHP—with which her guru had links—and then for the BJP in 1989.[35] However, her discourses were apparently presented as being those of another *sadhvi*, Uma Bharti, whose career had been comparable.

Coming from a low-caste (*lodhi*) family, Bharti was noticed in her village in Madhya Pradesh for her oratory in matters of a religious nature when she was 6 years old. Rajmata Scindia, whose guru lived in a neighbouring district, having been impressed by her sermons, encouraged her to present herself for the 1984 elections as a candidate for the BJP (*Sunday*, 1. 9. 1991: 27). This attempt was, however, unsuccessful. Uma Bharti only began to show what she could achieve in 1989. During the electoral campaigns of 1989 and 1991 her speeches (apparently made by Sadhvi Rithambara when first recorded on cassettes) revealed a fervent capacity to manipulate religious symbols to political ends.[36] Elected as a member of parliament from Khajuraho, where she is sometimes venerated as a *devi*, at the age of 30 she declared herself a 'religious missionary' by profession in *Who's Who in the Lok Sabha* (*Parliament of India* 1992).

Significantly, this profession was claimed by three other sadhus elected on the BJP ticket in 1991, with sometimes the additional comment '*dharmacharya*' or 'social worker' (ibid.: 776–8). These indications confirm that the differences between this kind of religious figure and militant Hindu nationalists, who readily designate themselves in the same way, are very tenuous, all the more so as Uma Bharti and others like her were not initiated into any sect before their entry into the VHP.

The Infiltration of Religious Institutions

So far, the VHP has not been able to make exceptional inroads among the leadership of orthodox Hinduism; the Shankaracharyas, for instance, remain aloof from the organization, while it recruits its main supporters among 'modern gurus'. However, the movement is deploying a strategy of infiltration regarding temples as well as religious festivals.

One of the departments of the VHP is devoted to the training of *pujaris*, *purohits* and *pracharaks*. The people responsible for these activities in Madhya Pradesh justify them by alluding to the deterioration of services rendered by priests. Their practice being routinized, they no longer know the meaning of the formulas they recite and have lost all vocation as intermediaries between the devout and god. They are accused of being primarily concerned with earning the money necessary to support their families, and sometimes more.[37]

This diagnosis led the VHP towards involvement in the training of priests. To this end the organization has engaged the services of Sanskritists responsible for collecting knowledge from old *pujaris*, and to subsequently open *gurukuls* where children are taught. At the same time, sessions of 'professional training' are offered to priests who are already in service.

This plan of action enables the VHP to enter the temples. Its presence can be observed, apart from the ideology of the priests, in physical terms, as witnessed at the Mahakal temple in Ujjain.

This temple shelters one of the twelve *jyotirlingas* of Mahadev and constitutes as such a highly regarded place of pilgrimage. The procession of the deity Mahakal also attracts dense crowds every year. Vijaya Raje Scindia patronizes the procession from the top of the Gopal Mandir[38] which the Scindia family constructed in 1848–56. She is, in fact, heiress of the dynasty which patronized the religious events and institutions of Ujjain at a time when the town was part of Gwalior State. Daulat Rao Scindia, founder of the dynasty, had the authority to sanction the temples' management to a family of Tailanga Brahmans (Verma and Guru 1982: 373). One sees here the advantage which the VHP can derive from the presence in its ranks of princely notables such as Vijaya Raje Scindia.

Her influence, moreover, is not irrelevant to the presence of the VHP in the Mahakal temple itself. One of the buildings on the side of the tank of the temple was transformed into a *dharamsala*, the immense hall of which is used by the VHP for its meetings.[39] This infiltration into a sacred space by an ideological movement aroused no objection on the part of the roughly fifty *pandits* officiating at the temple. One of them, who underscores his adherence to the same *biradari* as M. M. Malaviya, considers the VHP to be the base of Hindustan. Hinduism constitutes the national culture of India and should be recognized as such.[40] Another, the descendant of a prestigious lineage of Vallabhi gurus,[41] himself came from the RSS and was elected as municipal councillor on the Jana Sangh ticket before occupying the presidency of the BJP in Ujjain.[42] He too emphazises the generosity of the Scindia family's official patronage of the temple, and this is a factor in his allegiance to the Rajmata. This individual, Vishwanath Vyas, is a member of a Brahman caste association, as well as president of a Panda Samiti which includes numerous *pujaris* and *purohits*, among whom he can expound the Hindu nationalist ideology.[43]

In addition to infiltrating temples, the VHP uses festivals. Hindu festivals constitute advantageous moments, from the point of view of the VHP, to spread its message as, in most cases, all sects are represented on these occasions. It is keen, then, to prevent the reassertion of differences and rivalries between *sampradayas*, and to promote the notion of Hindu festivals as crucibles of national unity.

To this end, the VHP, developed a department for the coordination of Hindu festivals (*hindu parva samanvaya*), to which was assigned the objective of 'awakening love of Hinduism'. Festivals, from this (ideological) point of view, should be vehicles of national fervour which alone will eliminate the weaknesses of Hindu societies which originated with its enslavement (*goulabi*) by the Muslim conquest, and later, colonisation.[44] Its priority is the standardization of festivals in such a way that they become national festivals (*rashtriya tyohar*). It is thus necessary to combat the diversity which the 'jatis, sampradayas, panths, mohalles, pradeshes' bring to each celebration, so that all celebrate these festivals in unison (*sammilit*). To do this, the VHP establishes societies for the co-ordination of festivals (*hindu samanvaya samiti*) in as many places as possible, and primarily in places of pilgrimage. Significantly, the model of national festivals spontaneously evoked by Santosh Tridevi, the man in charge of these questions in the VHP, is the Muslim prayer:

> The Muslims perform *namaz*, and one thus sees Islam, a thousand Muslims who bow down and rise up; it is the strength of Islam which one sees. In our festivals, one does not see the identity [in English in the original] of the Hindu, one does not see the strength of the Hindu. This is why the first thing to accomplish is a Hindu reawakening [*hindu jagaran*] during the festivals so as to bring about mobilisation [in English in the original].[45]

This type of discourse well illustrates the process of strategic mimetism involved in the emulation of cultural traits which are supposedly the source of the strength of the Other, the Muslim in this case, in order to more effectively combat it. In this practice the VHP attempted to exploit the calendar of festivals without really succeeding in playing the role of pan-Hindu co-ordination. The organization was founded on the date of Krishna's birth and, above all, it organized its first World Hindu Conference on the occasion of the Kumbh Mela in Allahabad. Afterwards, the sessions of the Dharma Sansad were held quite regularly during the Kumbh Melas in Haridwar and Allahabad, or during the Magh Mela organized every year in that town. During the Kumbh Mela in Allahabad in 1989, the VHP strove to exploit the presence of a very popular sadhu, Devraha Baba. This hermit from Vrindavan, who was quite readily ascribed an age of 300 years, was visited by such dignitaries as Indira Gandhi, who came to seek his blessings, bowing and touching her head to the feet of Baba, who used to be perched on a platform on the bank of the Yamuna. The VHP succeeded in having Devraha Baba on their tribune at the beginning of the Kumbh Mela, in front of a captivated audience (Tully 1992: 100).

The example of Ujjain—another large place of pilgrimage where the VHP attempted to exploit the festivals—illustrates the range, as well as the limitations, of this strategy.[46]

The participation of the VHP in the Mahakal procession would appear to be very revealing in this regard; concerned to affirm their presence, the cadres of the organization took part in the march, clad in their distinctive caps and ochre scarves. But in so doing they appeared to be one of the components in the Hindu mosaic, just like the other *akharas*, and not like an encompassing force. This contradiction emerges yet more clearly from the action of the Hindu nationalist camp during the Kumbh Mela at Ujjain in April 1992.

This festival, organized every twelve years and called *Simhastha* because it is celebrated when Jupiter enters the house of Lion (*Simha*), is the only Kumbh Mela to have been organized in a town that belonged to a princely state until 1947. And the Scindias, because they financed half the expenses incurred during this event, derived a prestige which continues today to be reflected on Vijaya Raje Scindia. The Simhastha attracts millions of devotees and thousands of sadhus each time it is held. In 1968, some one hundred *akharas* representing 30,000 *sadhus* are said to have participated (Verma and Guru 1982: 379). In 1992, approximately ten million pilgrims went to Ujjain, from 17 April to 16 May, for a simple bath on a particularly auspicious date, or for a longer stay (*National Mail* 15 and 17. 5. 1992). The gathering, of course, represents a prime target for the VHP, which participated there in several forms.

Vijaya Raje Scindia, who presided over the committee responsible for the organization of the Simhastha, supervised the preparation of the festival for several months (*National Mail* 12. 3. 1992). Hindu nationalists participated in a Sanskrit Sammelan, opportunely organized at the time of the Simhastha and presided over by Karan Singh.[47] The VHP also made use of this occasion to hold annual sessions of the Bajrang Dal and the Durga Vahini of the Madhya Bharat. The latter, located near the Mahakal temple, was inaugurated by Satyamitranand Giri, who took advantage of the situation to 'reconvert' some hundred tribals to Hinduism.[48] Above all, the VHP employed the framework of the Simhastha to convoke a Sant Sammelan presided over by Avaidhyanath. The latter reaffirmed the determination of his movement regarding the construction of the temple in Ayodhya where the Babri Masjid was to be destroyed nine months later. Ashok Singhal, who dominated the meeting, specified that the Ram temple would be completed in two years' time and he called upon all the sadhus present to spend the next '*chatur mas*' (four months around the monsoon season when sadhus are not supposed to travel) in Ayodhya to continue to exert pressure on the government.[49]

The reactions of some sadhus to the presence of Hindu nationalists at the Simhastha cast light on the limitations of the VHP strategy. Isolated individuals, such as Swami Yogeshwar Videhi Hariji, denounced the political dimension of the movement in favour of the Ram temple (*National Mail* 10. 5. 1992). Above all, sadhus took umbrage at the collusion of certain religious leaders with the BJP government of Madhya Pradesh, a collusion in which the VHP was instrumental.

The organization of the Simhastha had been entrusted to a minister in the BJP government in Bhopal, Babulal Jain, a member of the state assembly from Ujjain district and member of the RSS since childhood. This man also had a seat in the committee over which Vijaya Raje Scindia presided. It appears that they together managed the few hundred million rupees which the state government allotted to the Simhastha from 1990 to 1992. The VHP made use of this formidable ally to further 'its' sadhus, a majority of whom were Saivaites. But the Saivaites were in a minority compared to the total number of sadhus present. When they asked that there be only one '*shahi snan*', to which the authorities agreed, the Vishnuites protested, saying that their traditions prescribed the organization of three baths; Babulal Jain had to find a compromise (*National Mail* 19. 4. 1992). The simple fact that this kind of conflict can still arise is an indication of the weakness of the VHP in representing all sadhus and, above all, is a sign of its inability to neutralize ancestral rivalries. It would once again appear as one group among various others, and that is why the organization needed the support of the government.

This process was again to be observed at the concluding ceremony of the Simhastha. The responsible officials, Babulal Jain and Vijaya Raje Scindia, invited different sect leaders to the Grand Hotel. However, they did not respect the order of precedence. Sadhus close to the VHP were given place in the first rows, while prestigious *mahants* were not even offered a seat. The latter protested and left the hall, taking their *mandaleshwars* with them. Babulal Jain and Vijaya Raje Scindia were obliged to extend their apologies to these outraged *mahants*.[50]

Conclusion

In this study of the Vishva Hindu Parishad, I have tried to show that this organization applies a form of strategic mimetism through its efforts to erect an ecclesiastical structure and to hold pan-Hindu festivals on the model of Christian and Muslim 'aggressors' in order to unify Hinduism and thereby offer greater resistance to rival religions. The VHP is, in this respect, only to a certain extent Hindu, even if it seeks to legitimize its innovations by claiming to replicate the assemblies of the time of Harsha. Its organization has, all the same, reproduced a traditional sociological articulation between the notable-cum-patron and the sadhu which is to be found at local and national levels. This configuration has been converted to strategic ends to make the establishment of the movement easier at the local level. However, the VHP has been more successful in recruiting 'modern gurus' than important sect leaders. It is trying hard to rally more orthodox and prestigious leaders around its cause but the strategy of infiltration, which consists of the VHP penetrating temples and festivals, shows its limitations, as many religious figures disapprove of the methods of the movement and fear for their own independence.

Notes

1. Quoted in *India Today*, 30 April 1995: 35.
2. One of those who went to Ayodhya to prepare for the construction of the Ram temple prior to the demolition of the Babri Masjid. *Times of India*, 5 December 1992.
3. For more details on this interpretation, see Jaffrelot (1996).
4. To employ the title of the book by Andersen and Damle (1987).
5. Quoted in Deshpande and Ramaswamy (1981: 185–6).
6. After independence, he became one of the proponents of the reconstruction of the Somnath temple—destroyed by Mahmud of Ghazni (Van der Veer 1992: 89-93).
7. See *Hindu Vishva* (*H.V.*) (Sept. – Oct. 1980): 18.
8. Interview with Swami Chinmayananda in Puteaux, 10 June 1993.
9. See van der Veer in Marty and Appleby (1994).
10. Andersen and Damle (1987: 133–4). One of the VHP's objectives, assuming a prominent place in its statutes, concerned the establishment 'of an order of missionaries, both laymen and initiates', as well as the opening and

management of 'seminaries or training centres for these missionaries' (H. V. Sept.–Oct. 1980: 27).

11. The obsessive fear of Christian 'separatism' continued until the 1980s, to which this excerpt from the 'opinion column' in the *Hindu Vishva*, organ of the VHP, bears witness: 'The Christian rebels, after having formed a separate state named Mizoram with a special status, are now preparing to extend their terrorist activities to Orissa, Bihar and Madhya Pradesh so as to form new theocratic states named Kolham and Jharkhand.' (*H.V.*, June 1987: 21).
12. Four-fifths of the people included in the census declared themselves Christians, which is an indication of the extent of conversions.
13. Shiromani Gurudwara Prabhandak Committee, the committee for the management of Sikh temples.
14. *Organiser* (21 June 1969). S. S. Apte repeated in 1969 his will to promote 'the integration and unification without rift of all strata, castes, communities and sects, in such way as to make of this multi-petal [*sic*] society a great living organism.'
15. This institution, in Nehru's mind (he presided over it in the year of its foundation: *Statesman*, 27 March 1957: 4) was intended to lead the *sadhus* to participate in economic development through *shramdan* (voluntary work) (*Hitavada*, 15 April 1956: 4). This project revealed above all the mark of Gandhian values, as shown by the themes of *bhoodan*, of the prohibition of alcohol and cow protection (*Hitavada*, 2 March 1956; 1 May 1956: 5; 24 September 1956: 7 and 25 September 1956: 6).
16. *H.V.* (*Republic Day Special Number* 1966: 9). S. S. Apte considered his members to be 'representatives' of Hindus dispersed throughout the world and of different persuasions.
17. According to an old neurosis which the 1971 census had already 'revived'. See for example Misra (1973). The census of 1971 showed a diminution in the proportion of Hindus from 83.4 per cent in 1961 to 82.7 per cent, while the Muslims went up from 10.7 per cent to 11.2 per cent.
18. This biography is derived from chapter 5 of the thesis by McKean (1992).
19. Satyamitranand Giri contributed to the introduction of the VHP in Anglo-Saxon countries, beginning in the 1970s (*H.V.*, March 1978: 55).
20. Each of its seven storeys contains figures symbolizing one aspect of the Hindu nation. (Jaydee 1984: 39–41). This 'temple' was inaugurated in the presence of Indira Gandhi in 1983.
21. *Who's Who in the UP Legislative Assembly 1962–1967* (1993: 10).
22. World Hindu Conference (n.d.: 95).
23. *Shraddhanjali Smarika* (13 April 1986: 2).
24. Interview with Acharya Giriraj Kishore, 18 November 1989 in New Delhi and *H.V.* (July 1982: 34).
25. Regarding patronage of the Puri temples by the rajas, see Kulke (1978: 133).
26. *Times of India* (10 March 1993).

27. Such as K. M. Munshi and Shivnath Katju, son of a minister of Nehru and president of the VHP prior to Dalmia.
28. Such as the former Chief Justice of the Calcutta High Court, who became working president of the VHP in 1966, older brother of Shyama Prasad Mookerjee and son of Ashutosh Mookerjee, vice-chancellor of the University of Calcutta from 1906 to 1914 and 1921 to 1923, and illustrative representative of the bhadralok élite (*Shraddhanjali Smarika* 13 April 1986: 56).
29. Vishva Hindu Parishad (n.d.: 28). 'First the Margdarshak Mandal was defined in the constitution of the VHP as a simple "advisory council" comprising *dharmgurus*, saints, scholars and philosophers of different sects of Hinduism to advice the Board of Trustees every now and then on points of philosophy and the code of conduct when their opinion was sought.' (*H.V.*, Sept.-Oct. 1980: 30). Its role would at present appear to be much more active.
30. Interview with Acharya Giriraj Kishore in New Delhi, 10. 10. 1991.
31. Founded in Haridwar by Acharya Shri Ram Sharma and his wife, the Gayatri Parivar combined an enthusiasm for ancient India and an admiration for science, which is described as deriving from spirituality and Brahmanic ritualism. His ascetic ethics were deliberately orientated towards the world, as this organisation maintained it provided through its discipline spiritual realisation and material success. See McKean (1992).
32. Interview with Babulal Har Lavaka in Ujjain, 25. 8. 1992.
33. Interview with Hari Narayan Soni in Ujjain, 25. 8. 1992.
34. Interview with Shanti Swaroopanand in Ujjain, 24. 8. 1992.
35. *Times of India* (19.7.1992: 13). Sadhvi Rithambara attempted to found her own ashram, between Vrindavan and Mathura, on land which the BJP government had ceded at a throw away price, notwithstanding prevailing laws (*Frontline*, 12. 3. 1998: 100).
36. Regarding the special effects which lend these cassettes an almost superhuman intensity, see Sarkar (1992), as also the essay in this volume by Tanika Sarkar.
37. Interview with Dinesh Vaidya in Ujjain, 25. 8. 1992.
38. She only comes down for the *puja* to the deity Mahakal, who arrives at the end of the procession. Formerly, she saluted and threw *malas* to various *akharas* who marched past her for several hours (observations made on 26. 8. 1992).
39. I attended the celebration of the anniversary of the local VHP on 23 August 1992. All the speeches and pamphlets distributed at the entrance focused on Hindu nationalist themes.
40. Interview with Jai Shankar Sawalji in Ujjain, 23. 8. 1992.
41. His grandfather was the Raj Guru of the Maharajah of Dewas, and his father a *purohit* of repute, to whom the Birlas, as *jajman*, gave the building bordering another side of the temple tank.
42. Interview with Vishwanath Vyas, 26. 8. 1992.
43. As regards the opinion of a few priests chosen at random, the majority of whom favour the construction of a temple in Ayodhya. See *Sunday* (8. 2. 1993: 32-3).
44. Interview with Santosh Trivedi in Indore, 28. 8. 1992.

45. Ibid.
46. The same phenomenon could be illustrated by the participation of the VHP at the Mahamaham festival in Tamil Nadu. In 1992, the VHP seems to have wanted to install its tribune at the centre of this festival, which is organized every twelve years, notwithstanding police opposition (*Sunday* 8. 3. 1992: 72).
47. *National Mail* (5. 5. 1992). Karan Singh, former maharajah of Kashmir and minister under Indira Gandhi, had been close to the VHP since the 1980s. For more details on this point, see Jaffrelot (1996: Chap. 10).
48. *National Mail* (12. 4. and 9. 5. 1992). The Shiv Sena also gave an exhibition, near the Datta Akhara, in which the corruption involved in the organization of the Simhastha was denounced in images (*National Mail* 21. 3. 1992).
49. *National Mail* (14. 5. 1992). Singhal also announced on this occasion that the VHP availed of eighty million rupees in the bank for the construction of the temple.
50. Interview with Shanti Swaroopanand, 25. 8. 1992.

References

Andersen, W. and Damle, S. 1987. *Brotherhood in Saffron—The Rashtriya Swayamsevak Sangh and Hindu Revivalism*. New Delhi: Vistaar Publication.

Deshpande, B. V. and Ramaswamy, S. R. 1981. *Dr Hedgewar, the Epoch-Maker*. Bangalore: Sahitya Sindhu.

Devahuti, D. 1970. *Harsha: A Political Study*. Oxford: Clarendon Press.

Dharma Marg. January 1984.

Dumont, L. 1966. *Homo Hierarchicus*. Paris: Gallimard.

Frontline. 12. 3. 1993.

Gross, R. L. 1979. Hindu Asceticism: A Study of the Sadhus of North India. PhD diss. in Anthropology. Vol. 2. Berkeley, University of California.

Hayat, S. 1984. Hindu Revivalism: Genesis and Implications. *Regional Studies* 2.4.

Hindu Vishva. [H.V.] 30. 1. 1966; Republic Day Special Number 1966; 11. 6. 1967; March 1978; March-April 1979; September-October 1980; May 1981; July 1982; June 1987; August 1990.

Hitavada. 2. 3. 1956; 15. 4. 1956; 1. 5. 1956; 7. 9. 1956; 24. 9. 1956; 25. 9. 1956.

Jaffrelot, C. 1993. *Les nationalistes hindous—Idéologie, implantation et mobilisation des années 1920 aux années 1990*. Paris: Presses de la FNSP.

———. 1996. *The Hindu Nationalist Movement and Indian Politics*. Delhi: Viking.

Jaydee. 1984. Bharat Mata Mandir. *Dharma Marg* 1.4: 39–41.

Kulke, Hermann. 1978. Royal Temple Policy and the Structure of Medieval Hindu Kingdoms. In *The Cult of Jagannath and the Regional Tradition in Orissa*, ed. A. Eschmann, H. Kulke and G. C. Tripathi, 125–37. New Delhi: Manohar.

Mauss, M. 1953–54. La nation. *L'année sociologique* 3me série: 5–68.

McKean, M. 1992. Towards a Politics of Spirituality: Hindu Religious Organizations and Indian Nationalism. PhD diss. in Anthropology. Sydney, University of Sydney.

Misra, S. K. 1973. Will Muslims Outnumber Hindus? *Motherland*, 26 August.
National Mail. 21. 3. 1992; 12. 4. 1992; 19. 4. 1992; 5. 5. 1992; 9. 5. 1992; 10. 5. 1992; 14. 5. 1992; 15. 5. 1992; 17. 5. 1992.
Parliament of India. 1992. *Tenth Lok Sabha Who's who*. New Delhi: Lok Sabha Secretariat.
Rath, S. [n.d.]. *Temples of Ujjain*. Ujjain: Devasthan Administration.
Organiser. *Divali Special* 1964; 26. 12. 1965; 30. 1. 1966; 12. 4. 1968; 3. 5. 1981; 1. 8. 1982; 28. 11. 1982; 26. 10. 1990.
Sarkar, S. 1992. 'Kaliyuga', 'Chakri' and 'Bhakti': Ramakrishna and his Times. *Economic and Political Weekly*, 18 July: 1543–66.
Seshadari, H. V. 1981. *Warning of Meenakshipuram*. Bangalore: Jagarana Prakashan.
———. (ed.). 1988. *RSS: A Vision in Action*. Bangalore: Jagarana Prakashan.
Shraddhanjali Smarika. [n.d.]. New Delhi: Vishva Hindu Parishad.
Statesman. 27. 3. 1957.
Sunday. 1. 9. 1991; 8. 3. 1992; 8. 2. 1993.
Times of India. 19. 7. 1992.
Tully, M. 1992. *No Full Stops in India*. New Delhi: Penguin.
Turner, V. 1969. *The Ritual Process, Structure and Anti-Structure*. Chicago: Aldine Publishing House.
Van der Veer, P. 1992. Ayodhya and Somnath: Eternal Shrines, Contested Histories. *Social Research* 59.1.
———. 1994. Hindu Nationalism and the Discourse of Modernity: The Vishva Hindu Parishad. In *Accounting for Fundamentalisms*, ed. M. Marty and S. Appleby, 653–68. Chicago: University of Chicago Press.
Verma, R. and Guru, S. D. 1982. *Madhya Pradesh District Gazetteers—Ujjain*. Bhopal: District Gazetteers Department.
Vishva Hindu Parishad. [n.d.]. *The Hindu Awakening – Retrospect and Promise*. New Delhi: Vishva Hindu Parishad.
Who's who in UP Legislative Assembly 1962–1967. Lucknow: UP Legislative Assembly Secretariat.
World Hindu Conference n.d.

Aspects of Contemporary Hindutva Theology: The Voice of Sadhvi Rithambhara

TANIKA SARKAR

'*Khūn kharābā hotā hai to ekbār ho jāne do*' (If there has to be bloodshed, let it happen once and for all). Sadhvi Rithambhara, a young *sannyasin* (female ascetic) spoke these words at a crucial moment during the Ramjanmabhumi campaigns organized by Hindutva forces between 1986 and 1992. A recording of her speech was made and released shortly before 30 October 1990, when the Vishwa Hindu Parishad (VHP), the religious façade of the Sangh combine, was about to lead its first attack on the historic Babri mosque at Ayodhya. The speech was repeatedly broadcast from temples across the Hindi belt and recited at several *sadhu sammelans* (assemblies of ascetics) organized by the VHP.[1] I shall attempt to lay out a conceptual grid with which to better understand the context in which Sadhvi Rithambhara's words were spoken.

Rithambhara has delivered a large number of speeches in different parts of the country. She was, for instance, chief speaker at the historic VHP rally at the India Gate in Delhi on 4 April 1991, when the VHP announced its decision to support the Bharatiya Janata Party (BJP: the electoral wing of the Sangh combine), in the coming elections. Slightly earlier, she was a leading speaker at the Dharam Sansad, the apex body of sadhus affiliated to the VHP. Some of her speeches were filmed on VHP video-cassettes, titled *Bhaye prakaṭ kṛpāla* and *Prāṇ jāye par vacan na jāye*.[2] These speeches, originally delivered 'live', constitute only minor variations on her more famous audio-cassette. I will separate out these speech-acts from her career, her personality and her life-story, because her live appearances have been overshadowed by her recorded speeches. The details known of her life are few; at public appearances her physical gestures are minimal. Unlike Uma Bharati, another sannyasin active in the VHP cause, Rithambhara is no parliamentarian capable of suiting words to contexts. There is an immense austerity in Rithambhara's, deployment of her figure: she is pure voice, bare words.

The importance accorded to this young female ascetic by Hindu religious institutions is unusual. Moreover, it is an honour exceptional inasmuch as it is vested in a sannyasin who ran only a minor ashram at Rishikesh and who, unlike Uma Bharati, had no reputation of great religious learning behind her. Even the precise sect that her ashram is part of seems largely unknown. The lack of information about her doctrinal affiliation is important: by such erasures the VHP attempts to obscure the considerable and significant sectarian differences among Hindus.

Rithambhara has amply justified the importance vested in her. Her ringing exhortations to Hindus to arise and kill Muslims have paid rich dividends in the form of anti-Muslim pogroms even in places earlier free of communal conflict. At the small western UP town of Khurja, for instance, the old lanes were strewn with nearly 200 Muslim corpses after two bouts of violence in December and January 1990–1. Interviewing some of the inhabitants we were told that though old habits die hard, and though peaceful coexistence had been one such old habit, repeated broadcasts of Rithambhara's cassette over successive days at local temples had finally done the trick.[3] Priests from Basti in UP informed us that they had suspended their normal programmes of recitation from sacred texts at temples in order to continuously play the cassette.[4] The Pesh Imam of the Babri mosque at Ayodhya pleaded with P. K. Datta, a member of our investigating team, help ban the cassettee via an agitation. He said that this cassette had by itself 'erected a wall of hatred between hearts'. So widespread was the cassette's public use, he had no idea that a ban was already formally in place (Datta 1993: 66).

In the voice of Rithambhara I hear a communal ideology that draws its force primarily, or at least considerably, from a religious vision. This vision depends on novel forms of support. Although it emerges as the utterance of a young ascetic—a conventional enough vehicle—the figure relaying the message is intentionally charismatic and forceful. Behind the voice lies a movement organized by an elaborate institutional complex for several years, successfully disguising the fact that the message derives its charge from something quite other than instant revelation. This is both an affirmation and a fundamental revision of the idea of the charismatic moment. The words of seeming revelation are, at one level, detached from the living presence of the charismatic person and, being endlessly and mechanically projected to listeners, seek to make them respond as to a direct and immediate command. The medium, instead of distancing the author and the message, merges with them. These are some of the new co-ordinates of contemporary bhakti, and they require serious analysis.

II

Communalism is shrugged off far too easily as plain politics masquerading as religion. This ignores much of the specific resonance that communalism has acquired among its votaries, and leaves unexplored some of its real sources of power. While communalism is certainly part of a political agenda, religion, however instrumentally used by certain politicians, possesses several separate cognitive categories and practices. I would therefore argue for re-examining the religious elements that go into the making of a communal movement.

The Ram-centred, RSS-led Hindutva movement is far too unproblematically held up as a telling example of something that effectively addresses godless, 'secular' modernity which shows up the secularized, disenchanted, and deracinated middle classes who have lost their former anchor in real, living faith. Faith supposedly lives on among the common people, and can only return to higher levels in a distorted and repressed form. I would partially reverse this argument and suggest that modern Hinduism, over 200 colonial and post-colonial years, has systematically tried to absorb the public and political spheres within its fold; and that in fact this only continues its age-old practice of being closely connected with political processes in pre-colonial times. Moreover, it has been precisely the modern middle classes that have from the start been most preoccupied with questions of faith; many have even derived their primary identity via such religious preoccupation. They have experienced and articulated their sense of changing times as a crisis of faith, and they have come to terms with the cognitive disorders spawned by modernity through new religious resolutions. The nineteenth century yielded a large number of cults, sects and orders whose understanding or uses of religion, or whose relationship with the sacred, were transformed away from traditional understandings in fundamental ways. Religious beliefs and practices have, similarly, gone through profound breaks and transformations in many previous historical periods as well and what we have witnessed recently via the Ram movement is not therefore radically new.

One aspect of change in this sphere within the nineteenth-century, was an enlargement of the discursive domain connected to matters of faith, and an expansion of the scope of debates over its basic terms. Another change was manifest in the proliferation of social groups that participated in these debates, thanks to the growth of print and vernacular prose; the latter led to translations and popularizations of a far larger range of texts than ever before. Vernacular journalism began its career in Bengal with religious newspapers. Till the end of the nineteenth century, about three-fifths of all Bengali publications included in the National Library's holdings in Calcutta were on religious matters (Sarkar 1992). Fatwas issued by Deoband maulvis were printed and widely disseminated, generating a second level of commentaries; and these, in their turn produced yet another round of public speeches and debates or *bahas* (Metcalf 1982). Orality and print became thus interconnected and available as regularly handed down theological issues to large, popular audiences and readers. Lutgendorf (1990) has pointed out that sacred texts like the *Ramcharitmanas* now entered individual homes through print. This created a deeper, more continuous and intimate relationship between text and devotee, a relationship that went beyond the occasional collective listening to recitations and expoundings of texts. In a sense, therefore, Rithambhara's cassette reflects yet another moment in this process process and promulgates a new dependence on the spoken word. We need to locate the Ramjanmabhumi movement within these long-term institutional and communicational media changes within modern Hinduism.

Communalism is part of a process in which modern political concepts draw many of their valences from the realm of sacred meanings. We also need to remember a fact about communalism which is constitutionally embedded within it. This is the fact that communalism cannot ever name itself, it cannot articulate its authentic and specific agenda. Its agenda is to redraw the boundaries of religious identity and community in exclusively antagonistic and vindictive terms.[5] Deprived of the exact words for its own enterprise, it can only live as a parasite. I suggest that communalism inserted itself into and drew its life from two modern forms of bhakti: *deshbhakti* and Rambhakti. Of these two due, deshbhakti is a relatively new form of devotion, while Rambhakti, an older tradition, was refigured through new usages during the anti-colonial movements.

III

In colonial times, both society and country were thought out and thought about very largely within the realm of the sacred. I use the word 'country' deliberately because the ubiquitous words 'nation' and 'nation-state', which have emerged these days as the nearly exclusive terms with which to read nationalist or anti-colonial discourses, seem unsatisfactory in the context of my analysis. The *country* as birthplace, as homeland, as ancestral property, had meanings that are not collapsible within, nor historically or conceptually coterminous with, the vision of the modern nation-state. The latter has had a far more restricted, discontinuous and specific orbit of influence. It is important to recover the word *desh*, for *desh* was a visualization of the country as divine mother goddess, or as a deified Motherland, and this was the term that created the first major form of modern bhakti—*deshbhakti*. The new deity rested on a synechdochal understanding—where the whole is greater than the sum of its parts or as in this case, where the deified Motherland is detached from and valorized over the land and its people. From the late nineteenth century, *deshbhakti* began to acquire the character of a vivid icon which became an object of worship; a demonology; the distinctions between believers and unbelievers; a holy chant; a mode of worship; and a concept which could demand acts of sacrifice.

More than anyone else, it was the late-nineteenth-century Bengali novelist-satirist-polemicist Bankimchandra Chattopadhyaya who, in his widely celebrated nationalist novel *Anandamath*, created the icon, elaborated the new bhakti, established its proper act of worship, and composed a sacred chant or mantra for this new deity—the chant of *Vande Mataram*. Bankimchandra, and especially his patriotic novel *Anandamath*, have been very significant resources for the Sangh combine. In the Sangh complex at Jhandelwalan in Delhi, the VHP leader-cum-erstwhile BJP MP, B. L. Sharma 'Prem', talked about Bankim's inspirational writing. So did Asha Sharma, leader of the combine's womens' front, the Rashtrasevika Samiti. The Suruchi Prakashan Bhandar, an RSS bookstall at Jhandelwalan, sells cheap posters that depict the core song, *Vande Mataram*, taken from Bankim's novel. The song is chanted in full, at prescribed times, at all daily *shakhas* or training sessions of the RSS. To the combine, this remains the real national anthem. Rabindranath's song, *Jana Gana Mana* —the official anthem of the Indian state—is widely condemned as a paltry substitute. Rithambhara's speech pours anger and scorn over the substitution; changing one for the other was the ultimate betrayal of Hindu interest, she declares. It was forced on us by Muslim and pseudo-secularist pressure. As soon as the BJP government came to power in Delhi, it made *Vande Mataram* the compulsory anthem at all government-run schools.

The song begins in Sanskrit, then turns into Bengali, and ends with Sanskrit passages. It evokes the country in the form of the goddess of the Motherland, but it breaks up the new goddess into three distinct and older divine forms. Each of these older forms is made to correspond to a different state of the land and its history— the bounteous land of the past, corresponding to Annapurna, the giver of food; the starving, ravaged land of the colonized present, evoking the naked and angry Kali; and the triumphant yet gracious land of the glorious future, the state of Durga, the demon slayer. The future will belong to the Mother and her children only if the demon is slain.

Appropriately, the song first appears in the novel at the moment when a battle is about to commence. The novel itself is ambiguous about who the Mother is fighting against. It is set at a transitional moment in the eighteenth century, when the British ruled through a puppet Muslim sovereign whose misrule had led to a devastating famine. A band of ascetic warriors helped by starving bands of villagers has taken up arms against the political order. The rebellion ends the puppet Muslim dynasty, but instead of this being followed by the restoration of Hindu power the British now assume direct government. The leader of the ascetics is heartbroken but a divine prophecy assures him that the transfer of power to the English is providentially designed. Later nationalists interpreted this conclusion as a reminder that the war was unfinished, and the leader still awaits the expulsion of the British. The RSS, which never participated in an anti-colonial struggle of any sort, reads this conclusion and the song as an exhortation to war against Muslims. Significantly, the song was later detached from the novel. It achieved a life of its own as a slogan in mass nationalist rallies. Ironically, it was also a slogan used invariably in times of communal violence (Chattopadhyaya 1969: 726; Sarkar 1996).

The song initially enters the novel as a sacred chant in Sanskrit which is meant to be recited within a prescribed ritual sequence. However, a new mode of worship is soon composed around the song which introduces important shifts and breaks: in the first place, a few Bengali stanzas break through the Sanskrit. Second, it is actually first heard on the eve of battle, and not within the prescribed ritual sequence. War thus takes the place of a ritual act of worship. The song is chanted not by a brahman priest but by a mixed crowd of ascetics and villagers and here resembles the congregational devotional music accessible to all in public sessions among Vaishnavas. Yet, instead of being sung as part of a peaceful contemplation of Krishna's *leela*—which is the normal purpose of Vaishnavite congregations—it is here sung to mobilize the spirit of war and violence which are simultaneously introduced as aspects of ritual sacrifice, compulsory in the worship of goddesses. In spirit therefore the song is closer to the *Bhagavad Gita*, where Krishna is an inspiration for holy war, rather than to the erotically playful Krishna of Bengali Vaishnavism. Rithambhara's inaugural words in the cassette too invoke the spirit of the battleground as a new mode of worship, requiring a new order of sacrifice. She too encapsulates the mood of both *Gita* and *Anandamath*. In the song devotional music is loosened from its original form as a chant and made to sacralize war through a politic displacement or transference of its context. At the same time, this hymn/song becomes the battle-cry that transforms a congregation of devotees into the single body of a disciplined army. If a Hindu community is here being imagined, then from the very start it is conceived as a community of people at war.

These imaginative resources towards a violent agenda are immensely enriched and extended, paradoxically, by the simultaneous evocation of gentle and peaceful images as aspects of the very same deity. Bankim introduces dramatic juxtapositions of lush, flowing sounds as well as harsh and jagged ones; images of bounty and nurturing alternate with those of fierce violence; deep piety is placed beside naked aggression. These rather shocking and astonishing transitions are held in place within the brief and continuous duration of a single song.

The rhetorical charge and power of the Hindutva project are often trivialized by assuming that this project has made a simple transition from the gentle quietism of past religion to the violence of the present. But *Vande Mataram* widens and complicates that notion and suggests, rather, a binary movement between tolerant Hinduism and violent Hindutva. And in this binary force the song is not alone. Violence is related, even by Hindutva spokespersons, to quietism and gentle religious beliefs in multiple and complex ways. Rithambhara's speech, perhaps the purest condensation of the violent impulse, still retains the supple movement between the two domains of peace and aggression: Ram is intrinsically *udar* (tolerant), and so are Hindus. Yet, the actions of demonic Muslims necessitate a violence which requires the transformation of Ram's fundamentally tranquil character. Several priests at Ayodhya told Datta that the ordinary *sevak* is mistakenly enthusiastic about the destructive dimensions of the movement. Rithambhara asks insistently for unadulterated violence, yet like the priests she too needs to frame this demand within an overarching principle of benevolence. The weaving together of the *madhur* (sweet) and the *krodhit mudras* (angry gestures) of Ram, are thus enabled by the organizing principles of the song. And so it transpires that it is the Muslims—a factor extrinsic to Hindus and their peaceable worldview—who call forth violence in a fundamentally peaceful Ram and his Hindu community (Datta 1993).

Bankim gives *deshbhakti* its entire imaginary as well as its devotional and rhetorical repertoire. Bhakti is now directed towards a feminized figure who contains the tripartite aspects of *shakti* (divine life-force or energy), namely nurturing, violence and power. These aspects are embodied in the three different manifestations of the Goddess—Annapurna, Kali and Durga. The three aspects are pulled together to compose a 'historical' narrative of India—her glory, her decline, and her future triumph. Bankim describes this bhakti as a fusion of the three forms of *yoga* or religious practice—*jñānayoga*, *karmayoga* and *bhaktiyoga*—the paths of knowledge, action and devotion. By this he lays claim to the entire resources of self-discipline and self-cultivation within all yogic forms.

Bankim also introduces two crucial departures in older forms of bhakti, both of which were destined to influence Hindutva theology. The devotee now expresses his bhakti ideally and with optimum effectiveness through a war against the Muslim. The devotee becomes the demon-slayer himself, performing an act that the theory of divine incarnation or *avatarvad* had reserved for the *avatar* alone. At the same time, by so acting the devotee participates actively in the life of the divinity. In Vaishnava theories of *leela* or divine sport, the *bhakta* can do this in two ways. He can identify with a companion or associate of the deity and participate in the *leela* through an assumed persona. Or alternatively, as in *tathastha bhakti* enjoined upon Bengali Vaishnavas, he can stand transfixed at the shore of the *leela* and watch it as a spectator in rapt contemplation. In the new bhakti of Hindutva, however, he is given access to divinity via an immensely more activist and intrusive mode. He can enter the divine life in his own earthly being and, indeed, intervene in the life of the deity and even transform it through an act of war. He can become the saviour hero.

It is an immensely empowering mode. I was privileged to read out a paper on the RSS at a session organized by a Delhi womens' organization for their area activists, who came from slums dominated by the RSS/VHP. I asked them why the Ramjanmabhumi message was so powerful, even though this theme is absent from all major textual traditions. They replied, 'We are always asking God for so many things. When he comes to us and asks for his home, who can resist?'

The appeal is heightened by some of the visual images used in the VHP media. Their videocassette *Bhaye prakaṭ kṛpāla* deploys a lovely, dark child in the sequence when the deity is miraculously supposed to have manifested itself in the Babri mosque in order to reclaim it. Instead of the more widely-used visuals of the warrior Ram, this sequence shows a child playing hide-and-seek in his old home, in the birthplace he has lost. It is a long sequence. It builds itself on the beauty and pathos of an irresistible appeal—the appeal of a homeless male child.

IV

The RSS makes other, more extended uses of *Vande Mataram*. In its *shakhas* the hymn is always chanted *in toto* and in the original language. The RSS thus restores the song to its old status as a sacred chant, not a word of which can be altered. Neither the Bengali nor the Sanskrit passages may be translated, since the original words are supposed to contain sacred energy. When I asked why the song is never abbreviated, members of the organization told me that it is symbolic of the integrity of the Motherland. It is always displayed against a map of undivided India, expressing the organization's refusal to accept the partition of the subcontinent.[6]

Partition—always described by them as the result of Muslim culpability—comes to acquire new and more terrible meanings when it is filtered through the grid of this theological understanding. It is no longer a human disaster or a territorial division: it is the mutilation of a sacred body, an act of desecration committed by Muslims. The mutilation can be symbolically healed by chanting the hymn—the image of the undamaged body—in its entirety. In this way the chant sanctifies the divinity of the land and embodies its essential integrity. Simultaneously, it underscores the gross violation of its integrity.

Integrity emerges here as a condition of the sacred. Integrity and sacrality are conjoint in the single body of the Motherland, and by this semantic leap the political is absorbed into the religious, and political acts become imbued with religious significance. This sacred frame then goes on to refigure other political acts as desecratory. Rithambhara's speech abounds with figures of fissiparous, centrifugal politics, she evokes the horror of disintegration. Central to this horror is disinterring the wholeness of divinity. The images deployed to this end include reactions of the majoritarian Hindi/Hindu heartland to the separatist movements in Kashmir, Punjab and the North East, as well as to the dismantling of the highly centralized national polity now increasingly influenced by regional parties.

The map of India becomes the divine idol—at once sacred and vulnerable, and this explains the anger against Rabindranath's anthem *Jana Gana Mana*.[7] The latter detaches divinity from the body of the land and transfers it to the heavenly father. The country, now demystified, reverts back to the land and its people. More immediately, the synechdochal operation is undone and Tagore's India is invoked through a recitation of its many parts—the different and separate regions, the many peoples, the diverse geographical features. Rabindranath's map of the country, once again, represents a territorial region which can go through many histories and be redrawn in different ways. But in his vision the magical wholeness which, since Bankim's hymn, had reduced the diversity of the parts to insignificance, is unpacked. In that very literal sense, the Indian national anthem is in fact an indeed, an act of 'disenchantment'.

Reification and mystification of the country have been fundamentally necessary for the political project of Hindutva nationalism. The premise of this project is an authoritarian, militaristic and overcentralized polity. The image of threatening neighbours outside and of treacherous Muslims within—both of whom are united by a common Muslim identity—is intended to keep the nation to an aggressive and unstratified whole.

There is also a necessary spillover of meaning from the territorial to the social. Internal divisions of class and caste are seen as forms of divisiveness that desecrate the wholeness of the *desh*. These divisions, therefore, are not to be interrogated but submerged under a political piety that suspends all manner of criticism which might expose social hierarchies. Such criticisms, whenever encountered, are elided into the metaphor of a divided and mutilated, yet sacred body which has to be reconstructed as non-stratified so that it can continue singular and integrated. The sacrality of an integrated and, aggressive yet perpetually threatened female body is the organising principle that holds the edifice together. The argument loses its power, its charge, if the country is allowed to be seen as a piece of land with flesh and blood people living within it. The power of this vision is further undone if the mystical description of people as soldiers in a holy war lapses into one in which they are social beings with very real social problems. Rithambhara warns untouchable dalits against violating the sacred unity of Hindus by the lure ('candy') of the Mandal issue. The problems of territorial diversity and social division require endless transcendence; a replay on many registers of the long history past mutilations desecrations of an inviolable, sacred body. The loss of the Ramjanmabhumi, Partition, Hindu disunity, lower-caste protest—all these are ranged together as enactments of the same terrible sin.

V

This new mode of bhakti through which the devotee actively participates in the life of a deity makes it necessary to fuse the mythological and the historical, the time of Muslim invasions and the time of the epics, *voila*! and—the devotee restores the birthplace to the deity and Babur becomes the real adversary of Ram. There is indeed a semantic conjuration at work in all this. Rithambhara is the magus who blurs boundaries between communally-constructed history, epic and present-day politics so completely and with such perfect ease that, today, Ram's children can be beheld as locked in combat with Babur's sons.

Before Gandhi, the icon of the sacred Motherland had long sunk deep into the nationalist imaginary through successive phases of the anti-colonial struggle. It had left a deposit of images, symbols, rhetoric and belief. With the advent of Gandhian mass movements, the attention shifted away a little from *desh* as a feminine icon to the formulation of the same concept as a sacred and ideal post-colonial political order. Ram and his realm, the most popular objects of worship in India's north, emerged as the dominant inspirational resources, dimming the lustre of the Mother Goddess a little. Ram was invoked as the rebel who fought against royal power with an army of monkeys and squirrels. He was also king himself, the great lawgiver. As Gandhi chanted the name of Ram as monarch, peasant leaders such as Baba Ramchandra, struggling in autonomous ground-level movements, simultaneously had more in mind had the rebel figure of Ram. Anti-colonial and popular movements thus stretched out the boundaries of Rambhakti, grounding it in popular political action and, in turn, reinscribing political action as acts of worship and sacrifice.

The RSS used the aura of Ram as well as the aura of the Goddess by founding its first *shakha* on the day of Vijaya Dashami, when Ram is supposed to have received the blessings of the Mother Goddess in his war against the demon (Basu *et al.* 1993: 5). Nationalism had already fused these two forms of bhakti. With Hindutva the inspiration was initially male-centred: the RSS is an exclusively male organization and until the 1990s women were not allowed into its political movements. In fact, a womens' wing was only founded in the RSS eleven years after the organization's own foundation. And as for the VHP, its present and future movements are oriented by three male deities—Ram, Krishna and Shiva. Savarkar had defined Bharat as the *pitribhumi* (Fatherland) of all Hindus, departing significantly from the *matribhumi* (Motherland) ideal (see Basu *et al.* 1993: 12–55).

VI

In post-independence India, however, there were important currents of change in devotional patterns, particularly in the north. Most significant among these changes was a proliferation of female cults in a region that had been markedly bare of them. The Vaishno Devi temple at Jammu, dedicated to a goddess, emerged as the most popular pilgrimage for affluent devotees. Religious sessions dedicated to Bhagavati became standard, and a part of regular neighbourhood activities. A film expounded the cult and ritual for an instantly-invented goddess—Santoshi Ma—and immediately her worship became routinized among various middle-class and lower-middle-class households. A new penchant for devotional music is now abundantly fed with cassettes dedicated to Jai Mata Di, Bhawani Ma, Mamta Ma, and Shakti Ma. The icons of these various goddesses have generated an abundance of calendar art, small images and posters. Everyday audio-visual spaces have been saturated with celebrations of goddesses. New, film-created goddess-centred mythologies and miracle-lore have filled up the devotional imagination. At a VHP satyagraha at Ayodhya in January, 1991, women *sevikas* spun out their own theories about the superior significance of Sita within the Ramayana (Datta 1993).

The Sangh combine needed to absorb all these reorientations in order to keep up with the times and appeal to a changing Hindu audience. Shakti has special connotations for women in electoral constituencies as well as in violent campaigns against Muslims, where women have been very active in recent years. It also has rich inspirational meanings for men who are about to initiate violence. So far, the only female icon to have reigned with her glory undiminished has been the Motherland. The Rashtrasevikas, however, have their own icon of an eight-armed Ashtabhuja Durga, whose weapons are objects of devout contemplation (Sarkar 1993): she presides over womens' *shakhas* alone. From the nineteen-eighties, the VHP deftly set about appropriating these new icons. The Ramrath—re-created by a DCM Toyota touring India with L. K. Advani as chief charioteer—was preceded by *rathyatras* to honour Bharatmata and Ganga. The huge Ekatmata Yajna rallies used the icon of Jai Mata Di, worshipped at the Vaishno Devi temple. The VHP also constructed the towering Bharatmata temple at Hardwar (McKean 1996: ch. 5). Gradually therefore the goddess has worked her way up and percolated: she features in recent RSS *Vande Mataram* posters as well. These are topped by an identical two-armed, lion-riding goddess in a pink and gold sari, holding aloft a saffron flag. Sangh hymn books are replete these days with songs dedicated to various goddesses, and Savarkar's term *pitribhumi* is now abandoned for a revitalized *matribhumi*.[8]

Rithambhara's centrality is partly responsible for restoring the female inspiration within a movement, led by the Dharm Sansad and the RSS, which otherwise remains scrupulously male. Yet she is delineating not simply the significance of the sacred as female, she is relocating it within a particular order. Ram has definitively emerged, as a result of VHP campaigns, as an all-encompassing icon who dwarfs the emergent goddess cults and annexes them as auxiliaries within a movement strongly centred around him. VHP priests explain that Ram's aspects sum up all possible diversity in religious texts, beliefs and practices. Recent pilgrimage manuals at Ayodhya make the Ram temple coextensive with every significant moment in the entire history of India (Datta 1993). Ram encompasses in this view the entirety of both religion and country.

This movement has managed to stitch up the two forms of bhakti, for Ram and for *desh*, in a terribly potent brew. With an admirable husbanding of existing resources, it has combined the various energies associated with Ram and the Motherland into a singular and composite noun—Ramjanmabhumi. In fact, the insistent projection of Ayodhya as Ram's birthplace is intended to appropriate the emotional-devotional weight associated with the term '*janmabhumi*' (birthplace) as a synonym for *desh.* According to a pilgrimage guide of 1893, written for Bengali pilgrims, Ayodhya's sanctity derived from the fact that it was the place where Ram *died.* It was also referred to as Ramgaya, since the association with his death and funeral meant that pilgrims were required to perform their ancestral rites here, as in Gaya (*Tirthamukur* 1893). It is in order to link up with the older *deshbhakti* and its reliance on the Motherland being the *birthplace* of us all, that Ayodhya now, in contrast, needs to be beheld primarily as a birthplace.

This 'spatialization' of the object of devotion, i.e. the sacred as a specific place or space which needs to be recovered through a struggle, moves the struggle for sacred country into the more bounded notion of struggle for a sacred birthplace—not of the people, but of Ram. In the videocassette *Bhaye prakaṭ kṛpāla*, the map of India has a green blinking light to indicate the birthplace of Ayodhya. If Christianity has its Bethlehem and Islam its Mecca, the green light of Hindutva shines with Saffron favour upon Ayodhya. As Jaffrelot points out in his essay within this volume, the techniques of propagating Hindutva are frequently borrowed paradoxically from the very religions that are being opposed. The map of India is still sacred, but now it is made more a protective larger covering which guards the sacred heart that is the birthplace. *Ram's* birthplace now sheds its sanctity upon India. Through this process of reworking old material, and through a series of transferences and displacements, India's sacredness is simultaneously emphasized and yet made derivative of Ram's birth in the country. The struggle for the country is replayed within a narrower territorial confine as the struggle for Ram's birthplace. Rithambhara's voice brings back the call for *desh*, the feminized sacred force. Yet she dedicates the country itself to Ram—'*yah deś Rām kā hai, yah pariveś Rām kā hai.*' This country belongs to Ram, this environment belongs to Ram.

VII

Rithambhara gives this divine hierarchy an earthly counterpart. As a *sannyasin* she embodies *shakti* (divine energy) within her self. But she also calls Hindu men to action, to vengeance—'*vīr bhāiyo jāgo!*' (Brave brothers, awaken!) She uses emasculation and eunuchs frequently as tropes while relying on images of combative masculinity. Women are also invoked, and there are things for them in her speech: anecdotes about other brave women; images drawn from food and cooking; homely and humorous tales referring to domestic concerns; the domestic politics played out among daughter, mother and sister-in-law. There are heroic images too with which women can identify, and Rithambhara reverently refers to *matrishakti*—the shakti that specifically resides in the mother goddess and, by extension, in mothers. Women must internalize the Ramjanmabhumi agenda, they must fill their hearts with anger and take their place in the struggle. She leaves them in no doubt about what role they should play. Their hearts angry, their bodies hard with the desire to avenge, they must produce sons who will kill Muslims. She begins by calling them mothers, she ends up addressing them as wombs (*kokhs*). This is a form of motherhood that almost brutally transgresses the known forms of emotion and gesture associated with motherhood. In her story, Bhagat Singh's mother weeps after her son's execution not because her only child is dead, but because she has no other son who can die in the holy war. She hungers to re-experience her loss. Reproduction and mothering are viewed primarily as acts of anger, and this represents a crucial departure from the known emotional universe. The woman in this vision of Hindutva conceives and nurtures her sons as instruments of revenge; she gives birth to violence; the space for this violence is reserved for men: 'Make yourselves into a clenched fist, my brothers!'

VIII

Rithambhara's voice is distanced from the combatants, yet her words, when it is time for action, will speak through the bodies of these combatants. The rhetorical use of repetition is therefore necessary, for the call to violence has to be embedded within the body via exhortation. Violence is transgressive, and therefore its necessity can be most powerfully communicated when the demand for it emanates from an agent who is seemingly and conventionally distanced from it—an ascetic and a woman. Her appeal seems all the more cogent because she seems to stand to gain nothing from it: in fact, her hortatory voice seems to transgress her calling, to make a sacrifice of her own need for ascetic peaceableness, and thereby gains all the more in credibility. The VHP claims that *sadhushakti*—the sacred energy of ascetics—leads the movement, but it deploys every communicative technique to ensure that the urge seems both holy and universal. The presence of the *sadhvi*, the female ascetic, is both an example to men and an indication that no-one is immune from the desire for violence. To make it a pure desire, *sadhushakti* is made to appear detached from all aspirations that sadhus might have for themselves: it conceals material incentives, which are considerable. The Ramjanmabhumi made ashrams, *akharas* and temples, run by *mahants*, sadhus and priests, a most lucrative real-estate investment at Ayodhya, and thus added vast financial power to the resources of organized religion. Shortly after Independence, the state had imposed various forms of financial control on religious establishments that were irksome to *mahants* and priests. The 1957 electoral manifesto of the Jan Sangh (predecessor of the BJP) had promised such people protection (McKean 1996: 100). As a matter of fact, the *maths*, the *mahants*, the older pilgrimages—the older religious leadership, in short—had somewhat lost their importance with the proliferation of new temple networks, media-produced cults and godmen. The VHP has forefronted this old guard and vested them with renewed claims to supremacy, power and resources.

This link-up is part of an old agenda based on mutual benefit. But in the present movement no mention is heard of such mundane calculations—in contrast with what had been candidly expressed in the 1957 manifesto. *Sadhushakti* now came out to demand the birthplace for the sake of Ram: other motives were piously discounted or absent. This time the sadhus were held up seemingly with less spuriousness as an alternative to the corrupt political order that Rithambhara denounced with revulsion. The image of the sadhu as a form of pure disinterestedness and complete innocence of worldly gains was recovered in order to oppose it with dirty trade-offs in the political world. Rithambhara reclaims sadhus as the guardians of pure religious passion: images of greed and corruption, in her speech, encompass merely the entire world of electoral politics. Sadhus, guided by Ram, are held up as leaders of the good society. The cassette was produced before the VHP decided to publicly support the BJP in the elections, and before the BJP depoliticized as well as sacralized its electoral slogan: '*Rāmrājya kī or caleṃ, BJP ke sāth caleṃ*.' (Move towards Ramrajya: Move with the BJP). This seems to introduce the concept of rule by sadhus, and sure enough the sadhus did soon publicly nominate the BJP as their agent. By October 1990 everyone knew that this was going to happen. Rithambhara, however, made no mention of this possibility in her cassette, thereby positing *sadhushakti* as a disinterested alternative to the corruption of the electoral system. The nomination of the BJP by this disinterested *sadhushakti* seeks, then, to divest the BJP of the taint of politics.

Rithambhara's speech carefully distances itself from a political address. Rather, it uses some of the conventions of the *katha* mode, or the public recitations and explanations of sacred texts. These techniques include what in music would be called a *rondo* movement, i.e. repeatedly coming back to the same point from a variety of discursive paths. In Rithambhara's case these discursive routes take the form of exhortations, homilies, anecdotes and stories, and couplets that embed the moral ineffably in the memory.

The linguistic range behind the speech is remarkable—chaste, Sanskritized Hindi is used when reciting names of holy places and people, Urdu-dominated Hindustani for the couplets, a domestic and homely Hindi for the stories. The tone moves quickly from tremendous passion to humour to nearly-obscene and earthy parables. The overriding impression is that of sustained anger, passion, continuous urgency, but it is deftly broken up by this wonderfully clever variety of narrative modes.

Sacred myths alternate with communalized histories, folk-tales and proverbs to reiterate the same points. However, there is not even one full citation from any of the sacred texts, not one complete recall of any mythological event. This is not simply the deliberate evacuation of real religious content; it is also the making of a new religious mode. Ram is entirely detached from the epic frame and a novel and original VHP theology is crafted with ingredients drawn largely from the new form of *deshbhakti*. There is a surprising omission of sacred texts in RSS books, printed discourses, and in the VHP's religious material. Though the VHP does recognize the Bhagavad Gita as the canonical text of Hindus, they make little use of it. What we really see is a return to sacred orality, the eviction of older canonical traditions to clear the space for a new mythology and canon of bhakti. This is not a canon that would bear scrutiny if examined in the light of the established religious texts. This is the theology of instant bricolage, an arsenal of on-the-spot fragments. Any coherent totality of texts and myths is conspicuous by its absence here.

Rithambhara's speech sums up the entire wisdom of the new theological discourse and renders it accessible and memorable. The great utility of the cassette is its effacement of all trace of technological manipulation, its metronomic cadences of complete spontaneity. Freshly recaptured each time before new audiences who hear the cassettes under very different circumstances, and who bring their very different experiences and understandings, the cassette infinitely stretches out the meanings of the original words to spur listeners to action and enlist allegiance to the new Hindutva.

If, as I suggested at the start of this essay, communalism is structured by the unsayable, if it has to seek homes in the discourses of others—*deshbhakti* and Rambhakti—then there is the real risk that it may not be able to adequately preserve its own distinct identity, thereby losing its purpose in a different discursive world. Rithambhara's function is to enunciate and preserve what is normally, or most often, unsayable—to spell out the agenda of violent aggression that distinguishes communalism from its two foster homes. A VHP *sannyasin* can best give homespun credence to communal violence via representing the private face, the intimate domain of the Sangh combine. Her excessive speech, her 'feminine unaccountability', her hysterical emotiveness—all suggesting the inner domain where religious life is conventionally assigned—are thus most effectively and powerfully deployed to mobilize the world that lies outside, namely the masculine world of political, communal action. The disguise, the masquerade of a supposedly peace-loving renunciant who has been awoken from godly slumber into divine fury—these are accomplished theatre, even as they make no secret of their aims and purposes. The words of self-revelation, of self-description cannot be spoken by all; they can be uttered only at very special circumstances of sustained violence. For that very reason, even as they are *enacted*, they need to be *enunciated* with absolute clarity, with unambiguous stridency, with an undisguised declaration of intent. That is why the charismatic utterance seems so single mindedly, *purely* and *divinely* violent—'*khūn kharābā hotā hai to ekbār ho jāne do*.'

Appendix
Vandemataram: Text and Translation[9]

Text

vandemātaram
sujalām suphalām
malayajaśītalām
śasyaśyāmalām
mātaram

subhrajyotsnāpulakitayāminīm
phullakusumitadrumadalaśobhinīm
suhāsinīm sumadhurabhāṣiṇīm
sukhadām varadām mātaram

saptakoṭikaṇṭhakalakalaninādа karāle
dvisaptakoṭibhujairdhṛtakharakaravāle
avalā kena mā eta bale
bahubaladhāriṇīm namāmitāriṇīm
ripudalavāriṇīm mātaram

tumi vidyā tumi dharma
tumi hṛdi tumi marma
tvam hi prāṇā śarīre
bāhute tumi mā śakti
hṛdaye tumi mā bhakti
tomāri pratimā gaḍi mandire mandire

tvam hi durgā daśapraharaṇadhāriṇī
kamalā kamaladalavihāriṇī
vāṇī vidyādāyinī
namāmi tvam

namāmi kamalām
amalām atulām
sujalām suphalām
mātaram

vandemātaram
śyāmā saralām
susmitām bhūṣitām
dharaṇīm bharaṇīm
mātaram

Translation

I bow to thee, Mother
richly-watered, richly-fruited
cool with the winds of the south
dark with the crops of the harvests
the Mother.

Her nights rejoicing in the glory of the moonlight
her lands clothed beautifully with her trees in flowering bloom
sweet of laughter, sweet of speech
the Mother, giver of boons, giver of bliss.

Terrible with the clamorous shout of seventy-million throats
and the sharpness of swords raised in twice seventy-million hands
who sayeth to thee, Mother, that thou art weak?
Holder of multitudinous strength,
I bow to her who saves
to her who drives from her the armies of her foemen
the Mother.

Thou art knowledge, thou art conduct,
thou art heart, thou art soul,
for thou art the life in our body.
In the arm thou art might, O Mother,
in the heart, O Mother, thou art love and faith,
it is thy image we raise in every temple;

For thou art Durga holding her ten weapons of war
Kamala at play in the lotuses
and speech, the goddess, giver of all lore,
to thee I bow.

I bow to thee, goddess of wealth
pure and peerless

richly-watered, richly-fruited
the Mother.

I bow to thee Mother,
dark-hued candid
sweetly smiling, jewelled and adorned,
the holder of wealth, the lady of plenty,
the Mother.

Notes

1. On the movement and its organizers see Gopal (1991) and Basu (1993).
2. Both were filmed at the J. K. Jain Studios, Delhi, in 1990.
3. Interviews at Khurja, December 1990 and January 1991, conducted by Uma Chakravarti, Prem Chaudhuri, Pradip Datta, Zoya Hasan, Kumkum Sangari and Tanika Sarkar.
4. Interviews in Basti, 1991, conducted by Sambuddha Sen and Pradip Datta.
5. I owe this observation to Pradip Datta, introduction, *Carving Blocs* (Delhi: Oxford University Press (1999).
6. Interview with Asha Sharma, Rashtrasevika Samiti, Delhi, 1990.
7. For the full text of the song, which is the official national anthem of the Indian state, see Tagore (1931: 697).
8. See recent RSS texts like Krishna Behari's *Pranamya matri devata*. Lucknow: Lokhit Prakashan, 1994; *Sangh Geet*. Jaipur: Gyan Ganga Prakashan, 1997; Vande Mataram poster, published by Suruchi Kala Niket in Delhi, 1997.
9. Translated by Sri Aurobindo and published with kind permission of the Sri Aurobindo Ashram Trust, Pondicherry.

References

Basu, Tapan *et al*. 1993. *Khaki Shorts and Saffron Flags: A Critique of the Hindu Right*. New Delhi: Orient Longman.

Behari, Krishna. 1994. *Pranamya Matri Devata*. Lucknow: Lokhit Prakashan.

Chattopadhyaya, Bankimchandra. 1969. *Anandamath*. In *Bankim Rachanabali* ed. J. C. Bagal. vol. 2. Calcutta: Sahitya Parishad.

Datta, Pradip Kumar. 1993. VHP's Ram: The Hindutva Movement in Ayodhya. In *Hindus and Others: The Question of Identity in India Today*, ed. Gyanendra Pandey, 46–73. Delhi: Viking.

———. 1999. *Carving Blocs*. Delhi: Oxford University Press.

Gopal, S. (ed.). 1991. *Anatomy of a Confrontation: The Babri Masjid–Ramjanmabhoomi Issue*. New Delhi: Penguin.

Lutgendorf, Philip. 1990. Ram's Story in Shiva's City: Public Arenas and Private Patronage. In *Culture and Power in Benaras: Community, Performance and*

Environment, 1800–1980, ed. Sandria Freitag, 34–61. Delhi: Oxford University Press.

McKean, Lise. 1996. *Divine Enterprise: Gurus and the Hindu Nationalist Movement*. Chicago: University of Chicago Press.

Metcalf, Barbara Daly. 1982. *Islamic Revival in British India: Deoband 1860–1900*. Princeton: Princeton University Press.

Sangh Geet. 1997. Jaipur: Gyan Ganga Prakashan.

Sarkar, Tanika. 1992. The Hindu Wife and the Hindu Nation: Domesticity and Nationalism in nineteenth century Bengal. *Studies in History* 8.2 n.s.: 213–35.

———. 1993. Women's Agency Within Authoritarian Communalism: The Rashtrasevika Samiti and Ramjanmabhoomi. In *Hindus and Others: The Question of Identity in India Today*, ed. by Gyanendra Pandey, 24–45. Delhi: Viking.

———. 1996. Imagining Hindurashtra: The Hindu and the Muslim in Bankimchandra's Writings. In *Making India Hindu: Religion, Community and the Politics of Democracy in India*, ed. David Ludden, 162–84. Delhi: Oxford University Press.

Tagore, Rabindranath. 1931. *Sanchaita*. Calcutta: Vishwabharati Publications.

Tirthamukur. 1893. Calcutta.

Oppositional Tellings in the Ramayana Tradition

PAULA RICHMAN

The core concept of 'canon' suggests explicit agreement upon a set of authoritative texts within a religious community. The Ramayana tradition, in contrast, encompasses a wide range of tellings of Rama's story.[1] Given that situation, whether Rama's story can function as a canon within the Hindu tradition proves a contentious issue. In order to explore it, I examine the following questions:

1. To what extent does the story of Rama consolidate the distinctiveness of a community?
2. To what extent do leaders of religious communities see it as authoritative?
3. And to what extent does it function to exclude certain groups of people from representation in the literary canon?

In order to answer these questions I first evaluate various meanings of the term 'canon'. Next, I assess various ways of conceptualizing the diversity of the Ramayana tradition. Finally, I analyse three case studies of communities that have generated 'oppositional' tellings of Rama's story. In each case study, I consider whether the use of the story of Rama should be termed 'canonical'.

Defining Terms

Although scholars use the words 'the Ramayana' quite loosely, because of the complexity of the issues explored in this paper such a phrase can lead to confusion. Instead, I use the terms 'story of Rama' or 'Rama's story' (a translation of *Rām-kathā*) to refer in general to a narrative that—as a minimal requirement—recounts or takes for granted Rama's birth and youth in Ayodhya, his marriage to Sita and subsequent exile to the forest, the abduction of his wife by the demon Ravana, Rama's search for her with the aid of his army of monkeys, and Rama's defeat of Ravana and his army.

When I discuss a particular telling of this story, such as the *Rāmāyaṇa* attributed to Valmiki,[2] *Rāmcaritmānas* by Tulsidas, or the Rāmlīlā of Ramnagar in Benaras, I refer to the specific name of the text, author, or performance. If I refer, as a collective, to the diverse set of tellings that relate the story of Rama in different ways, languages, and media, I use the term 'the Ramayana tradition'. This phrase indicates a set of tellings, rather than some single telling or some synthesis of the many tellings.

The use of the term 'canon', as well, needs some clarification at the outset. As noted in the introductory essay, the influence of Max Weber has shaped the sociology of religion in myriad ways, most notably for the discussion at hand in terms of his theories about the role of canon. To a prophet Weber attributes the ability to articulate 'a unified view of the world', presented as an 'ordered totality' (Weber 1964: 59). Weber claims that after a prophet's death, religious specialists routinize his charisma by closing the scriptural canon, thereby maintaining doctrinal orthodoxy. As he puts it, 'Priests systematized the content of prophecy or of the sacred traditions by supplying them with a casuistical, rationalistic framework of analysis, and by adapting them to the customs of life and thought of their own class and of the laity whom they controlled.' (69) A canon, thus, takes the particular form that it does because religious authorities at the time shape the canon in ways that consolidate the distinctiveness of their community.

Weber's formulation of canon does not apply as well to Hinduism as it might to a religious tradition with a single founder. Since the Hindu tradition possesses no single 'prophet' whose teachings become the basis of an entire religion, Rama's story may function in canonical ways only for certain groups, rather than as the basis of the entire religious tradition. Lord Rama does serve as an exemplar of dharma, but the stories of his trials and victories have not become the single canonical text of Hindu tradition. Furthermore, the sheer diversity of tellings of Rama's story suggest that no single 'ordered totality' exists that would function as the kind of unified worldview Weber has described (Richman 1991). Instead, Rama's story has played a unifying role only for certain communities of devotees.

Etymological understandings of 'canon' illuminate another way in which the term can function. 'Canon' derives from the ancient Greek word, *kanon*, denoting a 'rod' or 'reed' used as an instrument of measurement. This primary meaning led to the development of a secondary usage, 'rule' or 'law'. *The Oxford English Dictionary* provides a range of definitions for the term, the most germane of which include 'a standard of judgement or authority; a test, criteria, or means of discrimination' (s.v. 'canon'). The canon of a particular community enables those within it to articulate standards for discerning whether a certain entity may be judged good or authoritative.

Many scholars have implicitly or explicitly used this notion of canon as standard of judgment in their assessments of the earliest *Rāmāyaṇa*, attributed to Valmiki. In fact, many secondary sources on the Ramayana tradition assume that if one compares a particular telling of Rama's story with Valmiki's telling, one can determine to what extent the former can be judged correct or authentic. It would not, however, be accurate to say that Valmiki's telling of Rama's story has functioned in an authoritative manner for all communities within the Hindu tradition, let alone all the communities for whom devotion to Lord Rama plays a large role, as the rest of this essay will illustrate.

Yet a third deployment of 'canon' occurs among literary critics debating the processes by which certain works of literature have obtained places within the English literary canon. John Guillory, a scholar examining the debate, shows how all three meanings of the term canon have overlapped in recent debates. He begins with the canonizers of early Christianity, who 'acted with a very clear concept of how texts would "measure up" to the standards of their religious community, or conform to their "rule". They were concerned above all else with distinguishing the orthodox from the heretical.' Guillory then summarizes how critics have seen a similar process at work in English literature: 'In recent years many literary critics have become convinced that the selection of literary texts for "canonization" (the selection of what are conventionally called the "classics") operates in a way very like the formation of the biblical canon. These critics detect beneath the supposed objectivity of value judgments a political agenda: the exclusion of many groups of people from representation in the literary canon.' (Guillory 1990: 233)

Some scholars of English literary curricula argue the canon has silenced or marginalized non-élite voices and promoted certain 'correct' ways of viewing texts. In a similar vein, some critical studies of research on the Ramayana tradition have argued that Western scholarship has treated Valmiki's telling as the canonical telling of Rama's story, thereby excluding or marginalizing other tellings of the story (Richman 1991).

In order to adjudicate claims about whether Rama's story functions as a canon and, if so, whether it facilitates certain kinds of exclusion, we must examine the fundamental nature of diversity within the Ramayana tradition.

Conceptualizing the Ramayana Tradition

Throughout the centuries, many authors and performers in India have produced—and many patrons have supported—diverse tellings of the story of Rama in numerous media. In addition to the widely-known *Rāmāyaṇa* by Valmiki, hundreds of other tellings of the story of Rama in India exist, not only in written form but in visual media and varied performance traditions. In confronting the diversity of the tradition, how can one best articulate the relationships among these tellings?

Many Indologists trained in philology and specializing in Sanskrit literature view the *Rāmāyaṇa* attributed to Valmiki according to a perspective that emerged from scholarly studies of manuscript transmission. They tend to take Valmiki's work as the '*Ur*-' or 'original' text, and, by extension, as the authoritative telling of Rama's story. Such scholars view all other tellings of the story as derivative in relation to Valmiki's *Rāmāyaṇa*.

This assessment of Rama's story possesses several notable advantages. It rightly recognizes the status of Valmiki's poem as the first full literary telling of the story of Rama. It also takes into account the text's long history of transmission by brahmanical *literati*. Furthermore, this model reflects the aesthetic renown that won Valmiki the title of *Ādi-kavi* (First Poet) so celebrated in Sanskrit lore (Raghavan 1980: 1–2). Most significant, this view also accurately reflects the extent to which Valmiki's *Rāmāyaṇa* has influenced many of the tellings that followed his text.

Figure 1 illustrates this first way of understanding the relationships between Valmiki and other tellings. For example, this figure clarifies the extent to which the anonymous author of the *Adhyātma Rāmāyaṇa* drew upon Valmiki, as well as the ways in which Tulsidas built upon the work of Valmiki and the author of the *Adhyātma Rāmāyaṇa* in composing his *Rāmcaritmānas* (Whaling 1980). The figure also illustrates the relationship between selected performance traditions and the texts upon which they have been built. Figure 1, for instance, indicates how the performers of leather puppet plays in the Palghat region of South India incorporate verses from Kamban's Tamil *Irāmāvatāram* into drama with improvised commentary (Blackburn 1996: 27).

Figure 1.

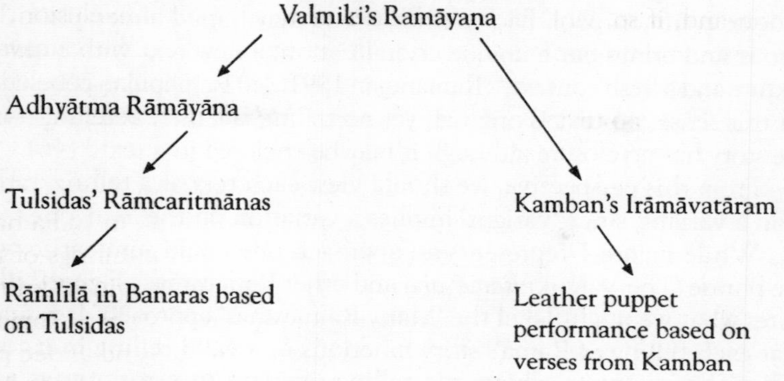

No doubt exists that Valmiki has produced one of the earliest poetically sophisticated tellings of the story extant. Nonetheless, one cannot rule out the possibility that *Dasaratha Jātaka* appeared earlier (Cowell 1956: 78–82; Gombrich 1985). And some scholars have wondered whether the kernel-like telling of the story of Rama that appears in the *Mahābhārata* might have preceded Valmiki's telling (Weber 1870; van Buitenen 1975: 207–14).

Chronological controversies aside, however, this model still contains some implicit judgments that oversimplify the complexity of the Ramayana tradition. The model represented by Figure 1 implies that one must view all subsequent tellings of the story of Rama as derivative, suggesting that they possess lesser authority and primacy. Such a view of the Ramayana tradition, consequently, creates a hierarchy of tellings that tend to induce comparison of all other tellings to Valmiki's text. Thus, it locates the best and most 'authentic' telling in the Sanskrit élite telling of Rama's story.

The vast majority of Hindus today cannot read Sanskrit, nor could they in the past; knowledge of Sanskrit remained primarily the intellectual property of the upper three varnas in society, and of brahmin males in particular. In contrast, most Hindus have learned the story of Rama by hearing it in their local or regional language. The model represented in Figure 1, thus, privileges a telling that excludes the vast majority of Hindus.

A. K. Ramanujan developed an alternative model of the Ramayana tradition that deserves our attention. As a specialist in the field of folklore, he knew about the creativity, scope, and diversity of oral tellings in India. He argued that we should abandon the notion of 'The Rāmāyaṇa' and 'its variants'. Instead, Ramanujan suggested that the story of Rama takes multiple forms in a series of tellings. Likening the Ramayana tradition to a pool of signifiers he said, 'These texts not only relate to prior texts directly, to borrow or refute, but they relate to each other through this common code or common pool. Each author, if one may hazard a metaphor, dips into it and brings out a unique crystallization, a new text with a unique texture and a fresh context.' (Ramanujan 1991: 46) Ramanujan concluded: 'In this sense, no text is original, yet no telling is a mere retelling—and the story has no closure although it may be enclosed in a text.' (46)

From this perspective, we should view each text as a telling, rather than a variant, since 'variant' implies a variation on the 'real' one.

While Figure 1 represents an approach one could summarize with the phrase 'The Valmiki *Rāmāyaṇa* and other Ramayanas', Figure 2 illustrates what we might label the 'Many Ramayanas' approach. It assumes that each telling of Rama's story functions as a valid telling in its own right. The extent to which one telling overlaps in certain ways with another telling is informative, but does not provide the basis for judgment as to whether it is more or less pure. Figure 2 enables us to attend to how certain tellings are in consonance with religious affiliation, region, language, historical period, literary conventions and teller's social location and experiences. In such a model, Tulsidas, Kamban, the participants in a Rāmlīlā performance, the author of the *Dasaratha Jātaka*, and Valmiki tell the story in their own ways. Valmiki's work is rooted in a particular social and ideological context, just as the other tellings are. This model suggests a less hierarchical set of relationships between various tellings within the Ramayana tradition.

Figure 2

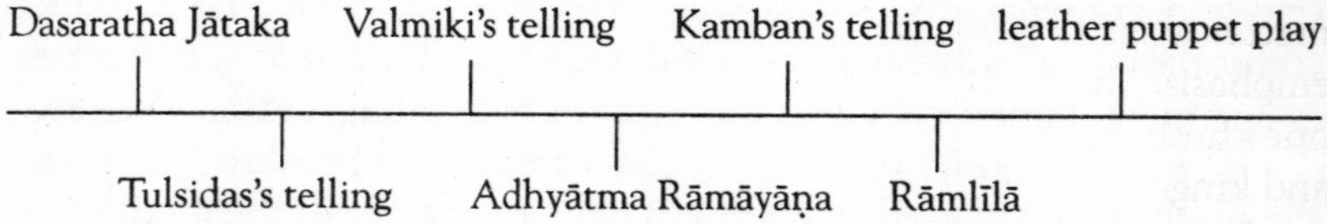

Figure 2 eschews a Valmiki-centred understanding of the story of Rama, emphasizing instead the multiplicity that constitutes the Ramayana tradition. Its strength is that it makes room for the many different tellings of the story—oral and written, read and performed, recited and depicted in visual forms—without representing each one primarily in terms of its relationship to Valmiki's telling. Although this model has the disadvantage of flattening out chronology, it does represent more accurately than Figure 1 the impact of many different tellings across India, including places where people have never heard a word of Valmiki's Sanskrit text.

Yet, Figure 2 does not acknowledge differences in status and political significance among tellings of Rama's story. It would be naive to ignore the issues of power that govern reception among different tellings of Rama's story. For example, millions of people know sections of the *Rāmcaritmānas* of Tulsidas by heart, particularly since Hindi speakers dominate much of North India. Far fewer people have heard or read Nagachandra's Jain telling, *Rāmacandracaritapurāṇa*, composed in Kannada (Aithal 1987: 4–6). Differences in size of audience, prestige of the patron(s), and extent of access to media attention shape the reception of tellings of Rama's story. For example, the televised (Doordarshan) Ramayana reached a far larger audience, found a far more influential patron (the Indian government), and won far more publicity than, say, a single performance by a shadow puppet troupe in Palghat region would.

Tellings with wide audiences and pan-Indian status can be called 'dominant tellings'. Valmiki earns the title of a 'dominant telling' due to the pre-eminent status of Sanskrit, the pan-regional dissemination of the text, the attention paid to it historically by both brahmin élites and recent Indian and Western academics. The *Rāmcaritmānas* functions as a 'dominant telling' because of its centrality in North Indian bhakti, its use as the basis for many performance traditions, its influence among several significant groups of overseas Indians, and its recent appropriation by the BJP/VHP in Indian electoral politics.

In general, those with extensive power and status in society often praise these dominant tellings as providing models for dharmic action or exemplars of true devotion. Dominant tellings tend to affirm the values of social order. More specifically, dominant tellings of Rama's story advocate the need to perform one's brahmanically-defined dharma—no matter what the cost of doing so. Exegesis of these texts also tends to emphasize that one must carry out one's prescribed duties in relation to one's husband, wife, parents, elder brother, family, master, lineage (*kula*), and kingdom.

In contrast, 'oppositional tellings' supplement, revise, question and sometimes subvert dominant tellings. These oppositional tellings provide multiple perspectives on the characters, thereby enriching the diversity of the Ramayana tradition. At the same time, their effect usually remains fairly limited, especially when these tellings are confined to a particular sex, jati, religious community, or region. Certain women's oral tellings question or supplement male tellings. Some low-caste tellings subvert texts that affirm brahmanically-based hierarchy. Regional tellings often localize characters by identifying local sites with particular Ramayana incidents.

To avoid oversimplification, one must also assure that 'oppositional' and 'dominant' are understood as relative and partial descriptions. A particular telling may support or oppose dominant tellings to a lesser or greater extent. Furthermore, a text may have specific oppositional tendencies around certain issues, but reaffirm dominant norms in other areas. For example, a Jain Ramayana may be oppositional in relationship to Valmiki's brahmanical status, but dominant in contrast to tellings that question the patriarchal aspects of both Valmiki's and Nagachandra's telling. Furthermore, one particular group that develops an oppositional telling may view their own telling as the only real and authoritative telling, thereby claiming dominant status for their telling. In contrast, another oppositional telling may claim that what others view as the dominant telling has no authority, nor should any telling of Rama's story be seen as authoritative.

In order to take into account multiple factors that shape the power and influence possessed by different tellings of Rama's story, Figure 3 provides for multiple dynamics, often ones that take place simultaneously. This figure has four levels of interactions, but more could be added to take into account other factors that shape the status and power of any given telling of Rama's story.

Figure 3.

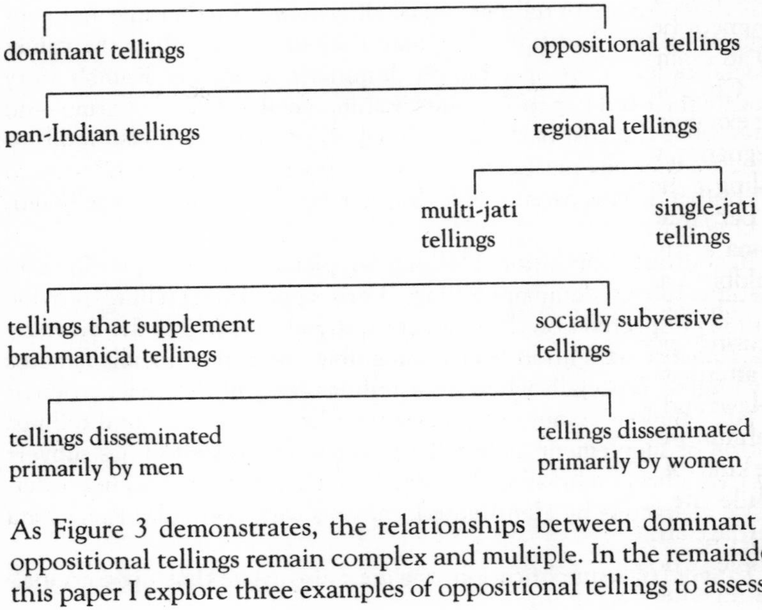

As Figure 3 demonstrates, the relationships between dominant and oppositional tellings remain complex and multiple. In the remainder of this paper I explore three examples of oppositional tellings to assess the extent to which such tellings can be conceived in relation to the notion of canon. I have chosen my three case studies to explore how issues of gender, caste, and region shape attitudes towards canonicity within the Ramayana tradition.

Gentle Supplements: A Set of Women's Songs

As a child when he sat with his mother and aunts in his brahmin joint-family in northeastern Andhra Pradesh, Velcheru Narayana Rao heard a set of Telugu songs based on characters in the Ramayana that focused almost entirely on the experiences of women. Both the men and the women in his family recognized the authority of Valmiki's Sanskrit telling of Rama's story and attended public recitations based on it. Nonetheless, although the men in his family associated Valmiki primarily with his Sanskrit *Rāmāyaṇa*, the women viewed Valmiki primarily as the character in the story who recorded events and took Sita to his ashram after she gave birth to her twin sons in the forest.

Although the women respected Valmiki's text, it did not speak directly to many aspects of their ordinary lives. In their free moments, they quietly supplemented Valmiki's telling with songs that related to the activities that filled their days. Since Narayana Rao has analysed this song cycle at great length (Narayana Rao 1991: 114), for the purposes of my argument here I focus only on (1) the topics addressed in the songs and (2) an example of the kinds of ideal relationships presented in them.

Childbirth and childcare provide the main subject of several songs. For example, one recounts details of Kaushalya's morning sickness during pregnancy, while another depicts how she clung to ropes hung from the ceiling as she pushed her baby into the world. One piece presents a lullaby to Baby Rama, while yet another narrates how Kaushalya gives Baby Rama a bath. These songs pass on information about the process of childbirth as well as affirm the significance of children to these women.

The marriage process figures prominently in another set of songs focusing upon specific experiences of women during the ceremony and its aftermath, such as when Sita's parents entrust their daughter to her in-laws and when Sita begins the journey to her new home. The Telugu brahmin women also sing about the contents of Sita's dowry, and even the kinds of games that Sita and Rama play during the wedding ceremony. While the subject of dowry signals the economic aspects that shape marriage arrangements, the songs about wedding games depict how two people (who may not know each other) begin the process of creating a life together in the midst of a community. The singers deal with the negotiations of living in a joint family on an everyday basis, a process that each of them had to experience when marrying into a joint family.

Songs about Sita's trials in Lanka, during the fire ordeal, and in the forest at Valmiki's hermitage emphasize the suffering that Sita experiences and how her sons defend her name. For example, in one song Lava and Kusha force Rama to acknowledge some of his past misdeeds in relation to Sita, thereby ending a long period when Sita's goodness has been insufficiently honoured. This set of songs presents situations from Sita's perspective, particularly with regard to the children whom she has borne and raised at the cost of great personal sacrifice.

As does Valmiki's telling, the song cycle of the Telugu brahmin women also depicts ideal relationships between members of a family. As does Valmiki as well, these songs celebrate a commitment to behaviour that may often seem beyond the ability of ordinary humans to perform. In Valmiki's *Rāmāyaṇa*, Rama nobly upholds his father's honour by setting out for the forest, even though he was just about to be crowned king. One of the Telugu songs, 'Sita Locked Out', portrays an equally extraordinary example of unselfishness within the family.

In this story, conscientious Sita has been working to complete her household chores until long after her husband has retired for the night. After waiting impatiently for Sita to come to bed, Rama angrily locks her out of their room. When weary Sita finally completes her work, she finds the door bolted, and pleads with Rama to let her in. He refuses, so she turns in despair to her mother-in-law, who takes her side and commands her son to let his wife in. As Narayana Rao notes, 'Kausalya is represented here as the ideal mother-in-law every daughter-in-law dreams of in a joint family, a mother-in-law who shows warmth and support for her daughter-in-law and who helps to bring her closer to her husband.' (1991: 121) Although many mothers-in-law would take the son's side against a wife who was seen as wanting her own way, this fairminded mother-in-law recognizes the new bride's virtue and stands by her. These ideals, which do not receive emphasis in Valmiki's telling, matter to singers of Sita's story.

The women in this orthodox Telugu-speaking brahmin community do not seek to undermine Valmiki's text or its veneration by their husbands. Although the songs in no way question Valmiki's status, the range and content of the songs do suggest certain gaps in Valmiki's text, even though Valmiki's telling supposedly provides all kinds of models for ideal behaviour to guide one through life. To fill such gaps, the women supplement Valmiki with a vocal tradition of Ramayana narratives that encompasses the experiences of wife and mother featured in the lives of the singers. Their oppositional telling of Rama's story can be seen as taking Valmiki's telling for granted but then adding to it, in an unassuming and non-confrontational manner, to make it suited to their own experiences as women.

Abridging Tulsidas: Caste Distinctions Rejected

A community of people living in the Chattisgarh region of Madhya Pradesh have refashioned the *Rāmcaritmānas* (henceforth abbreviated as *Mānas*) by Tulsidas in a way that they consider authoritative. Calling themselves the 'Ramnamis' because of their emphasis on the power of Ram's name, they have rejected certain passages from the *Mānas*, and their rejection of those passages is closely linked with their social identity. High-caste people in the area consider them Harijans, due to their hereditary occupation as leather-working Chamars. The ethnographic account of this group by Ramdas Lamb relates how they have abridged Tulsi's *Mānas* into a text of radical egalitarianism (Lamb 1991: 235–55), and used it as the basis of a performance tradition centred upon chanting Ram's name and appropriate verses from their revised version of Tulsidas. The Ramnamis would not probably conceive of themselves as telling Rama's story in opposition to Tulsi's text; instead, they *know* that their telling provides the only correct understanding of the story.

The origins of the Ramnamis lie in a miraculous event. When a man in their community with leprosy became well, he credited his dramatic cure to chanting verses about the compassion of Ram from the *Mānas* of Tulsidas. In gratitude he became even more devoted to the *Mānas*, many verses of which he had memorized. Though illiterate, he and his followers memorized and recited additional verses from it and participated in bhajans in which, gathered in a circle around the book, they performed puja to the *Mānas* and chanted verses together.

The situation changed, however, when several younger Ramnamis had educational opportunities denied to their elders. Attending local government schools and motivated by a love of Tulsi's text, they learned to read not only colloquial Hindi but the older Hindi of the sixteenth-century *Mānas*. When they became familiar with the entire telling, they encountered many verses that portrayed Rama as affirming caste hierarchy, praising the purity of brahmins, and denigrating Untouchables as polluted. Yet the Ramnamis believed in the radical equality of all people. Furthermore, the Ramnamis identified Ram's most salient characteristic as compassion, praising him for giving his love to all devotees without consideration of caste status. How were they to reconcile their view of the *Mānas* with the written text they now faced?

Ramnamis cite a famous legend about the *Mānas* as corroboration for their subsequent refashioning of the text. According to that story, at the time that Tulsidas composed his telling of Rama's story, brahmins in Varanasi denigrated it because Tulsidas composed it in Hindi. Only Sanskrit, the perfected language, was good enough for Lord Ram, they said; a Ramayana in Hindi would be unworthy. God apparently disagreed with this view, as the denouement of the legend shows. To settle the question once and for all, the brahmins took the *Mānas*, put it at the bottom of a stack of Sanskrit books, on the top of which was Valmiki's Sanskrit *Rāmāyaṇa*. They set this pile down before the image of the deity in the inner shrine of the temple and bolted the door. Imagine their surprise the following morning, when they unlocked the door: the *Mānas* sat on the top of the stack. Lord Ram had indicated that he wanted his story to be disseminated in a vernacular text. That way everyone, not just brahmins, could read it (Lamb 1991: 237).

That being so, reasoned the Ramnamis, the verses supporting the caste system could not have originally appeared in Tulsi's telling of Rama's story. These problematic passages must have been later interpolations, added by brahmins. Ram displayed his divine greatness through his love and compassion for all creatures, so he *could not* have legitimized caste prejudice, they felt. The Ramnamis, therefore, proceeded through Tulsi's telling verse by verse, excising from their chanting repertoire verses that portrayed Rama as confirming caste hierarchy, praising the superior status of brahmins, or denigrating lowcaste people. When they finished their labours, they identified the remaining 400–500 verses (out of a much larger text) as the *real Mānas*, the one at the centre of Ramnami study and practice. When asked what gave them the authority to discard large portions of the text, the Ramnamis cited the power of the text itself, saying, 'This *Rāmāyaṇ* is so great we cannot possible damage it; we can only make it better!' (Lamb 1991: 251). The Ramnamis believe that they improved the previous version of the text by taking out the later additions that obscured the central message of the text, Ram's love for all living creatures.

This use of the story of Rama possesses a number of elements that one associates with canon. First, the Ramnamis see Tulsi's telling as the repository of their worldview, encompassing the totality of their wisdom and ideals. Although they also chant verses from other texts that conform to their beliefs about the *Mānas*, it remains the text around which they orient their lives. Lamb discusses the kinds of recitation styles, debates, and conversations that all build upon specific verses from the *Mānas* and shows how they form the centre of community life (Lamb 1991: 240–2). He also notes how the Ramnamis foreground Rama's loving relationships with tribal chieftains, Shabari, monkeys, and ferrymen, using them as prooftexts for the divine sanction of radical equality (Lamb 1991: 242).

Second, the Ramnamis have created a text that they conceive of as the *real Mānas*. By removing the spurious verses, they claim to have returned to the text that portrays the true, fundamental, and unarguably compassionate nature of Ram. Thus, they possess some standard of judgment, some measuring rod that enables them to distinguish between what they see as authentic verses and later interpolations. Using the notion that the heart of the *Mānas* lies in Ram's compassion, they can evaluate precisely what does and does not belong in the text.

Third, the text does function as a means to distinguish members of the Ramnami community from other devotees of Ram. Since only Ramnamis have embraced this particular version of the *Mānas*, it both bestows upon them a unique interpretation of the text and distinguishes them from other groups who venerate the text. In fact, one could argue that the Ramnamis use the *Mānas* in a manner exactly opposite to the manner in which canons are said to function, according to some who participate in the 'canon wars' in literary circles. Rather than a dominant group closing a canon in a way that marginalizes oppressed groups, in this case an oppressed group uses the notion of a canonical text to redefine what is canonical and create a distinctive view of Ram that fits their philosophy of radical egalitarianism.

Full-scale Attack: A Regional Telling

One of the most oppositional tellings of Rama's story gained prominence beginning in the late 1920s in and around Madras in South India. There a set of social critics promulgated an interpretation of Rama's story which viewed it not as a mythical account of Lord Rama's conquest of the demon kingdom of Lanka, but as a thinly veiled history of a brahmin-supported subjugation by Aryan warriors of the Dravidian land to the south. This interpretation of Rama's story rests on an Aryan/Dravidian dichotomy, first proposed as a linguistic category to classify different families of Indian languages. Later, social thinkers appropriated these linguistic terms as a way to classify Indian cultures, with Dravidian culture seen as equivalent to a pre-brahmanical culture that flourished in ancient South India. The dominant regional element of this story—identification of Rama and his army with Aryan power and the identification of the demons and the monkeys with peaceful and honourable Dravidians—seemed to explain why brahmins possessed such high status in the southern region and why so-called shudras, the majority of South Indians, had such low ritual status. This oppositional telling of Rama's story neither supplements nor rewrites a dominant telling. Instead, it attacks any telling of the story that takes Rama as divine and brahmins as worthy of respect.

E.V. Ramasami (1878–1973), avowed atheist and social revolutionary, did more to publicize this reading of Rama's story than any other figure of the time, so my analysis focuses upon him. Ramasami assembled an attack-cum-telling of Rama's story to function as a component of his assault on brahmanical beliefs, Hindu ritual, and caste hierarchy. Ramasami, a militant non-brahmin who advocated 'Rationalism' instead of religion, led and spoke for the Dravida Kazhagam (Dravidian Federation), propagating the belief that Dravidians should throw off rule by brahmanically-legitimized invaders. Ramasami argued that Hindu myth, ritual, and caste rankings functioned as the means for Aryan warriors and brahmins to subjugate Dravidians; these Hindu institutions brainwashed Dravidians into accepting their subordinate position in society.

The Ramayana, according to Ramasami, presented evidence of the Aryan conquest and subsequent oppression of Dravidians. He saw Rama and his brahmin advisors as devious and power-hungry marauders from the North who adhered to barbaric practices, such as cutting off the nose and breasts of Dravidian women. His interpretation argued that the so-called demons, Ravana and the citizens of his realm, were actually the indigenous inhabitants of South India, whom Rama and his armies slaughtered, enslaved, and reduced to self-hatred by instilling in them the idea that they were shudras. Because Ramasami took Rama's story as prime evidence recounting the source of Dravidian oppression, the text played a major role in his public speeches.

In the pamphlets that Ramasami wrote and reprinted over a period of more than thirty years, he moved through the Rama story systematically, character by character, identifying what he saw as the moral failings of Rama and his brahmanical advisors and the virtuous nature of Lanka's monarch and citizens. In the process of assembling and communicating his interpretation of Rama's story, he put forward certain ideals for behaviour; Rama provided negative examples, while Ravana provided positive examples (Richman 1995: 636–8).

Ramasami reproached Rama for upholding the caste system, and singled out for extensive comment a relatively short incident in Valmiki's telling: the story of Shambuka, a shudra who performed harsh ascetic practices to gain religious salvation. Orthodox texts prohibit such penances because asceticism can only be practised by members of the upper three varnas. In contrast shudras must perform their duties as servants well in order to win rebirth in a higher varna in the next life. Since Shambuka broke this rule, his ascetic practices upset the order of dharma in Rama's kingdom and, as a result, a young brahmin boy died. The brahmins of the kingdom insisted that Rama take action in order to restore proper dharma in his land. In response, Rama went into the forest, located the errant Shambuka, and killed him. At the story's culmination, flowers rained from heaven and the brahmin boy returned to life, celestial signs that dharma had been restored. Ramasami saw this incident as a clear example of Rama's collusion in the subjugation of shudras, as well as his recourse to violence in order to maintain a repressive social order. Rama, thus, provided a negative example of proper behaviour: a righteous king would never have performed such a deed.

Conversely, Ramasami interprets King Ravana's deeds as righteous and honourable. For example, Ramasami contrasts Rama's treatment of Surpanakha with Ravana's treatment of Sita. Rama first humiliated Ravana's sister, Surpanakha, with insults, jokes, and expressions of contempt, and then directed his brother Lakshmana to cut off her nose and ears. In contrast, Ravana kept Sita in a lovely pleasure garden and politely asked her to marry him. He never hurt her or even attempted to force her to accept his attentions. To Ramasami, Rama's behaviour seems barbaric, while Ravana's behaviour honourable. In fact, one of the front-page cartoons for the newspaper Ramasami edited depicts Lakshmana cutting off the breasts of Surpanakha, at the instruction of Rama. The caption asks bluntly, 'Is this man a God?' to imply that no righteous figure would stoop to such a degraded act of mutilation (Richman 1995: 642).

Research reveals that Ramasami's knowledge of the story of Rama came primarily from translations of Valmiki's *Rāmāyaṇa* into Tamil (Richman 1991: 187), but he also studied and responded to Kamban's Tamil telling of Rama's story as well. Notwithstanding, Ramasami drew his evidence from any source that helped his case. If he wanted to lambast Rama, he cited Valmiki's presentation of the killing of Vali, in which Vali reproaches Rama for his action. Yet, if he wanted to prove the nobility of King Ravana, he cited Jain *Rāmāyaṇas* that portray Ravana as a tragic and learned fellow. If he sought to show that his quasi-historical interpretation of the text was correct, he cited as his authority Jawaharlal Nehru. In each case, one thread runs through Ramasami's attack on Rama's story: Rama's story functions as a central text of Hinduism. Since he seeks the heart of brahmanical Hindu belief in order to rip it out, he focuses on Rama's story with an intensity greater than any of his simultaneous critiques of incidents from other religious texts.

Ramasami's relentless attacks on Rama's story demonstrate his recognition of its authoritative power. Precisely because Hindus have given dominant tellings of Rama's story so much veneration, Ramasami used it to win people's attention, whether the attention he won proved admiring or shocked attention. In other words, E. V. Ramasami assumed canonical status for Rama's story in order to attack it with the most dramatic effects possible. He was drawn to the tale because Hindus considered it so sacred. One could, therefore, argue that because Ramasami assumed that Hindus viewed Rama's story as canonical, he attacked it. So, in a sense, Ramasami confirms its canonical status, adding even more status to it.

Some would argue that this final example of an oppositional telling, a most extreme one, does not even belong within the boundaries of the Ramayana tradition. Yet even Ramasami used the story of Rama as a source of exemplary behaviour. Ramasami's moral evaluation of the deeds of particular characters differs from that of the dominant tellings; the exemplary characters stand on the opposite side of the conflict, Ravana's side. Rama's story remains one that contains a set of ideals but what is done in the *Rāmāyaṇa* by the 'heroic' characters is exactly what Dravidians should not do.

Conclusions

From the discussion of meanings of 'canon', with which this paper began, three issues seem salient: (1) whether Rama's story consolidates a group's distinctiveness; (2) whether it functions as a standard of judgment by which people can declare certain beliefs canonical; and (3) whether it excludes certain groups. Unlike the Christian canon, upon which much of the theoretical discussion of canons has focussed, the story of Rama takes many different forms rather than a single unchanging form. The diverse tellings of incidents from Rama's story reflect the sex, social location, and regional identity of teller and intended audience. Thus, one could argue that because the Ramayana tradition encompasses such a diverse set of tellings, one cannot call it a canon.

One could, however, consider whether the Ramayana tradition possesses *certain* characteristics of a canon for particular groups. For example, do stories within the Ramayana tradition consolidate distinctiveness? In each of the three case studies, the answer proves to be 'yes'. The Telugu women's song-cycle consolidates the women's distinctiveness from their husbands. They sing their songs in their own part of the house when their wifely duties have been completed. Their tellings depict certain kinds of behavioural ideals that they can strive to achieve in their own lives and pass on to the next generation of women with pride. Similarly, the Ramnamis deliberately edited the Tulsidas *Rāmcaritmānas* so that it reflected their own distinctive worldview. In it, Rama acts according to their ideals of compassion and egalitarianism. Since they remain the only group that has adopted this particular abridged version of Tulsidas as its sacred text, it certainly consolidates their distinctiveness. Finally, E. V. Ramasami's telling makes his interpretation of Rama's story an argument about the differences between Aryans and Dravidians. He uses Rama's story as a proof-text to illustrate how the history, power, and distinctiveness of the pre-conquest Dravidians has been suppressed, thereby emphasizing their distinctiveness in relation to the Aryan conquerors who later subjugated them.

Do discriminating people declare Rama's story to be authoritative and use it as a standard of judgment? The Telugu brahmin women venerate Valmiki; the Ramnamis venerate the *Rāmcaritmānas*; and E. V. Ramasami attributes authoritative status to Valmiki's telling within Hinduism. Yet the Telugu brahmin women see nothing wrong with supplementing Valmiki's telling, just as the Ramnamis have few qualms about abridging Tulsi's telling. E. V. Ramasami uses Valmiki's telling (as translated into Tamil) as a standard of judgment, but he uses the text in a way that shocks and insults those who consider it a sacred text. If the text were not considered authoritative, his critique would not be so threatening.

Does the Rāmāyaṇa prevent certain groups from having access to the canon? No doubt exists that certain tellings of the story, particularly the brahminical Valmiki version and certain sections of Tulsidas, have been used by those who seek to keep certain groups at a lower status than their own in the gender and caste hierarchy of Hindu tradition. Yet these lower-status groups have created alternative tellings of the story. Although we cannot know precisely under what circumstances the song cycle of the Telugu brahmin women came into being, we know exactly how the Ramnamis came to create their own edition of the *Rāmcaritmānas*. The sacred status of the text seems not to have excluded them, but instead encouraged them to abridge it. Although E. V. Ramasami sees dominant tellings of Rama's story as oppressive, in his pamphlets he takes control over the telling and creates a counter-*Rāmāyaṇa* in which King Ravana becomes the hero of the tale and Rama the scoundrel. Thus, the Ramayana tradition seems elastic enough to encompass *both* tellings that exclude certain groups from a particular community and tellings that oppose dominant groups and values.

Finally, how do these three groups relate to Rama's story according to different models of the diversity of the Ramayana tradition explored in the second part of this paper? The Telugu women venerate Valmiki but whether they view his telling as an *Ur*-text seems relatively unimportant to them: they respect Valmiki's story of Rama, but they lavish their devotional attention on their songs that relate to their everyday experiences. We might place them in the model proposed in Figure 2. They see both Valmiki's telling and their song-cycle as tellings of the story and do not seem particularly concerned with the exact source of their telling. The Ramnamis, in contrast see Tulsi's telling as the authoritative text, but they want to 'return' to the pure version that Tulsi truly wrote. That is, like modern Indologists who seek to separate out the layers of the text to isolate the earliest ones, they use their view of Rama to liberate the 'original' Tulsidas. This notion seems much like the view of an *Ur*-text illustrated in Figure 1, except that it assumes the *Rāmcaritmānas*, rather than Valmiki's *Rāmāyaṇa* as the fundamental standard. E. V. Ramasami's text might be seen in light of Figure 3, because he tells the story in a way that combines a regional perspective with an oppositional thrust that openly subverts the values of a dominant telling.

One could say that the notion of canon helps us to see certain aspects of the Ramayana tradition in new ways. Although 'canon' is helpful, it is not sufficiently capacious to provide an explanation for the complexity and diversity of the Ramayana tradition in India. The notion of canon assumes a single unchangeable telling that remains at the core of a religious tradition, but in Indian textual tradition, many tellings of the Rama story appear, circulate, and continue to be transformed.

Notes

1. In order to keep diacritical marks to the minimum, I have used them only for the names of individual texts and for words in Indian languages that are in italics.
2. Henceforth for simplicity's sake, I will simply refer to Valmiki as the author of this telling of Rama's story, although much controversy surrounds the issue of his supposed authorship, at least partially because he appears as a character within his own text.

References

Aithal, Parameswara. 1987. The Ramayana in Kannada Literature. In *South Asian Digest of Regional Writing*, ed. Hermann Berger, Vol. 12: 1–12. Heidelberg: South Asia Institute, University of Heidelberg.

Blackburn, Stuart. 1996. *Inside the Drama-House: Rama Stories and Shadow Puppets in South India*. Berkeley: University of California Press.

Cowell, E. B. (ed.). [1913] 1956. *The Jātaka: or, Stories of the Buddha's Former Births*. 7 Vols. London: Luzac and Co. for the Pali Text Society.

Gombrich, Richard. 1985. The Vessantara Jātaka, the Rāmāyaṇa and the Dasaratha Jātaka. *Journal of the American Oriental Society* 105.3: 427–37.

Guillory, John. 1990. Canon. In *Critical Terms for Literary Study*, ed. Frank Lentricchia and Thomas McLaughlin, 233–49. Chicago: University of Chicago Press.

Lamb, Ramdas. 1991. Personalizing the *Rāmāyaṇ*: Rāmnāmis and their Use of the *Rāmcaritmānas*. In *Many Rāmāyaṇas: The Diversity of a Narrative Tradition in South Asia*, ed. Paula Richman, 235–55. Berkeley: University of California Press.

Lutgendorf, Philip. 1991. *The Life of A Text: Performing the* Rāmcaritmānas *of Tulsidās*. Berkeley: University of California Press.

Narayana Rao, Velcheru. 1991. A *Rāmāyaṇa* of Their Own: Women's Oral Tradition in Telugu. In *Many Rāmāyaṇas: The Diversity of a Narrative Tradition in South Asia*, ed. Paula Richman, 114–36. Berkeley: University of California Press.

Oxford Etymological Dictionary. 1974. 2 vols. Oxford: Oxford University Press.

Raghavan, V. 1980. The Ramayana in Sanskrit Literature. In *The Ramayana Tradition in Asia*, ed. V. Raghavan, 1–19. Delhi: Sahitya Akademi.

Ramanujan, A. K. 1991. Three Hundred *Rāmāyaṇas*: Five Examples and Three Thoughts on Translation. In *Many Rāmāyaṇas: The Diversity of a Narrative Tradition in South Asia*, ed. Paula Richman, 22–49. Berkeley: University of California Press.

Richman, Paula. 1991. The Diversity of the *Rāmāyaṇa* Tradition. In *Many Rāmāyaṇas: The Diversity of a Narrative Tradition in South Asia*, ed. Paula Richman, 3–21. Berkeley: University of California Press.

———. 1995. Epic and State: Contesting Interpretations of the Ramayana. *Public Culture* 7.3: 631–54.

Van Buitenen, J. A. B. 1975. *The Mahābhārata*. Vol. 2. Chicago: University of Chicago Press.

Weber, Albrecht. 1870. Ueber das Ramayana. *Abhandlungen der Königlichen Akademie der Wissenschaften zu Berlin*, 1–118.

Weber, Max. 1964. *Sociology of Religion*. Boston: Beacon Press.

Whaling, Frank. 1980. *The Rise of the Religious Significance of Rama*. Delhi: Motilal Banarsidass.

Select Bibliography of the Writings of Heinrich von Stietencron

A. Books

Indische Sonnenpriester: Sāmba und die Śākadvīpīya Brāhmaṇa. Wiesbaden: Harrassowitz, 1966. (Indian Sun Priests.)

Gaṅgā und Yamunā: Zur symbolischen Bedeutung der Flußgöttinnen an indischen Tempeln. Wiesbaden: Harrassowitz, 1972. (Gaṅgā and Yamunā: The Symbolic Meaning of the River-goddesses on Indian Temples.)

Der Mensch und sein Tod (co-author). Ed. J. Schwartlaender. Goettingen: Vandenhoeck und Ruprecht 1976. (Kleine Vandenhoeck-Reihe 1426). (Man and his Death.)

Christianity and World Religions: Paths to Dialogue (co-author, with Hans Kueng, Josef van Ess and Heinz Bechert). Bantam Doubleday Dell Publishing Group 1986. Reprint Maryknoll, New York: Orbis Books, Fourth printing 1999. Original German edition Muenchen: Piper Verlag, 1985.

Das alte Indien. (co-author). Ed. H.G. Franz . München: Bertelsmann Verlag, 1990. (Ancient India.)

Hahnenkampf. Gedichte von Sitakant Mahapatra, ausgewählt und aus dem Oriya übertragen. Frauenfeld: Waldgut, 1991. (Cock-fight.)

Der Begriff der Religion (co-author). Ed. Walter Kerber, (Fragen einer neuen Weltkultur Bd. 9). Muenchen: Kindt Verlag, 1993. (The concept of Religion.)

B. Books edited

Der Name Gottes. (Ed.) Düsseldorf: Patmos Verlag, 1975. (The Name of God.)

Dämonen und Gegengötter. Antagonistische und antinomische Strukturen in der Götterwelt. (Ed.) Saeculum 34,3–4, 1983. (Demons and Anti-gods. Antagonistic and Antinomic Structures in the Realm of Gods.)

Theologen und Theologien in verschiedenen Kulturkreisen (Ed.) Düsseldorf 1986. (Theologians and Theologies in Different Cultures.)

Krieg und Kultur (Ed.), Seaculum 37.2, Freiburg 1986. (War and Culture.)

Angst und Religion (Ed.), Düsseldorf 1991. (Schriften der Katholischen Akademie in Bayern Band 139). (Fear and Religion.)

Epic and Purāṇic Bibliography (up to 1985), annotated and with indexes. (joint ed., co-author) (Purāṇa Research Publications, Tübingen 3), two parts. Wiesbaden: Harrassowitz, 1992.

Töten im Krieg. (Ed., with J. Rüpke) Veröffentlichungen des Instituts für Historische Anthropologie 6. Freiburg: Karl Alber, 1995. (Killing in war.)

Representing Hinduism. Constructions of Religious Tradition and National Identity. (Ed., with V. Dalmia.) New Delhi: Sage Publications, 1995.

C. Papers

Suicide as a Religious Institution. *Bharatiya Vidya* 27 (1967 [1969]): 7–24.

Bhairava. *Zeitschrift der Deutschen Morgenländischen Gesellschaft*, Supplementa I, Teil 3, 1969: 863–71. (XVII Deutscher Orientalistentag, in Würzburg 1968, Vorträge).

Yašt X, 126 an Incomplete Stanza? *Zeitschrift der Deutschen Morgenländischen Gesellschaft* 119.1 (1969): 93–7.

Daṇḍanāyaka und Piṅgala. *Indo-Iranian Journal* 13.1 (1971): 1–19.

Zur Rolle der Religion in der pakistanischen Staatskrise 1970/71. *Internationales Asienforum* 4 (1972): 332–41. (The Role of Religion in the State Crisis of Pakistan in 1970/1.)

Bemerkungen zur Gaṅgādhara-Mūrti des Śiva. *In Indologen Tagung, 1971. Verhandlungen der Indologischen Arbeitstagung im Museum für Indische Kunst Berlin, 7.–9. Okt. 1971*, 273–82. Wiesbaden: Steiner, 1973. (Remarks on the Gaṅgādhara-mūrti of Śiva.)

Name und Manifestation Gottes in Indien. In *Der Name Gottes*, ed. H.V. Stietencron, 50–65. Düsseldorf: Patmos, 1975. (Name and Manifestation of God in India.)

Traditional Patterns of Social Security in Hinduism. In *German Scholars on India, Contributions to Indian Studies, vol. II, 286–95*. Bombay: Nachiketa Publications, 1976.

Moral im zyklischen Denken: Die Auswirkung der Wiedergeburtslehre auf soziale Werte und Normen. In *Religion und Moral*, ed. by B. Gladigow, 118–35. Düsseldorf: Patmos, 1976. (Morals in a Cyclical World Concept.)

Das Kunstwerk als politisches Manifest. *Saeculum* 28.4 (1977): 366–383. (The Work of Art as a Political Manifesto.)

Vom Tod im Leben und vom Leben im Tode: Bemerkungen zur hinduistischen Auffassung von Tod. In *Der Mensch und sein Tod*. ed. J. Schwartländer, 146–61. Göttingen: Vandenhoek und Ruprecht, 1977. (Of Death in Life and Life in Death: Remarks on the Hindu Concept of Death.)

The Date of the Jagannātha Temple: Literary Sources Reconsidered. In *Sidelights on History and Culture of Orissa*, ed. M. N. Das, 516–32. Cuttack: Vidyapuri, 1977.

Orthodox Attitudes Towards Temple Service and Image Worship in Ancient India. *Central Asiatic Journal* 21.2 (1977): 126–37.

The Advent of Viṣṇuism in Orissa: An Outline of its History According to Archaeological and Epigraphical Sources from the Gupta period up to 1135 AD. In *The Cult of Jagannath and the Regional Tradition of Orissa*, ed. A. Eschmann *et al.*, 1–30. Delhi: Manohar, 1978.

Early Temples of Jagannātha in Orissa: The Formative Phase. In *The Cult of Jagannath and the Regional tradition of Orissa*, ed. A. Eschmann et al., 60–78. Delhi: Manohar, 1978.

The Śaiva Component in the Early Evolution of Jagannātha. In *The Cult of Jagannath and the Regional Tradition of Orissa*, ed. A. Eschmann *et al.*, 119–24. Delhi: Manohar, 1978.

The Jagannātha Temples in Contemporary Orissa. In *The Cult of Jagannath and the Regional Tradition of Orissa*, ed. A. Eschmann *et al.*, 469–75, maps. Delhi: Manohar, 1978.

Die Rolle des Vaters im Hinduismus. In *Vaterbilder in Kulturen Asiens, Afrikas und Ozeaniens*, ed. Hubertus Tellenbach, 51-72 and 169–72. Stuttgart 1979. (The Role of the Father in Hinduism.)

Vedische Religion und Hinduismus. In *60. Schopenhauer-Jahrbuch für das Jahr 1979*: 17–30. (Vedic Religion and Hinduism.)

Angst und Gewalt: Ihre Funktionen und ihre Bewältigung in den Religionen. In *Angst und Gewalt: Ihre Präsenz und ihre Bewältigung in den Religonen*, ed. H. v. Stietencron, 311–37. Düsseldorf: Patmos, 1979. (Fear and Violence: Their Function and their Sublimation in Religions.)

Zur Theorie von Ordnung und Strafe im alten Indien. In *Entstehung und Wandel rechtlicher Traditionen*, ed. W. Fickentscher *et al.*, 537–55. Freiburg: Karl Alber, 1980. (On the Theory of Order and Punishment in Ancient India.)

Die Stellvertreterrolle des Narasiṃha im Kult des Jagannātha. *Studien zur Indologie und Iranistik* 5/6 (1980): 245–78. (Narasiṃha's Role as a Deputy in the Cult of Jagannātha.)

Weltherrschaft oder Selbstbefreiung. Ein südasiatisches Modell Gesellschaftlicher Toleranz für alternative Lebensziele. In *Staat und Religion*, ed. B. Gladigow, 205–24. Düsseldorf: Patmos, 1981. (World Dominion or Self-liberation. A South Asian Model of Social Tolerance Towards Alternative Goals of Life.)

Jagannātha-Narasiṃha : A Unique Syncretistic Stone Image Based on an Episode from the Skanda Purana. *Journal of the Orissa Research Society* 1 (October 1981): 3–7.

The Liṅgarāja Temple at Bāliā – An Unknown Temple of the Bhauma Period. In *Aspects of Indian Art and Culture (S. K. Saraswati Commemoration Volume)*, ed. J. Chakrabarty and D. C. Bhattacharyya, 68–80. Calcutta 1983.

Die Göttin Durgā Mahiṣāsuramardinī. Mythos, Darstellung und geschichtliche Rolle bei der Hinduisierung Indiens. In *Visible Religion vol.II: Representations of Gods*: 118–66. Leiden: Brill, 1983. (The Goddess Durgā Mahiṣamardinī in Myth and Art and her Historic Role in the Hinduization Process in India.)

Dämonen und Gegengötter: Überlegungen zur Typologie von Antagonismen. In *Saeculum* 34.3–4 (1983): 372–83. (Demons and Anti-gods. Reflections on the Typology of Antagonisms.)

Die Rolle der Religion in Modernisierungsprozessen. In *Indien-Probleme eines Schwellenlandes. Vorträge gehalten in der Reihe 'Länderseminare' des Instituts für wissenschaftliche Zusammenarbeit mit Entwicklungsländern*, 28–43. Tübingen 1984. (The Role of Religion in the Process of Modernization.)

Gedanken zur Theologie. In *Theologen und Theologien in verschiedenen Kulturkreisen*, ed. H.v. Stietencron, 9–24. Düsseldorf: Patmos, 1986. (Reflections on Theology).

Kalkulierter Religionsverfall: Das Kaliyuga in Indien. In *Der Untergang von Religionen*, ed. H. Zinser, 135–150. Berlin: Reimer, 1986. (Calculated Decline of Religion: The Kaliyuga in India.)

Political Aspects of Indian Religious Art. In *Visible Religion vol. IV-V: Approaches to Iconology*: 16–36. Leiden: Brill, 1985/1986.

Hinduismus. In *Theologische Realenzyklopädie* Bd. XV, Lieferung 3/4, 346–55. Berlin/New York 1986.

Hinduismus/Hindu-Religionen In *Lexikon der Religionen*, ed. H. Waldenfels, 288–96. Freiburg: Herder, 1987.

Heilige Schriften III: Hinduismus/Hindu-Religionen. In *Lexikon der Religionen*, ed. H. Waldenfels, 258–63. Freiburg: Herder, 1987. (Holy scriptures III: Hindu Religions.)

Gott VII: in Hindu-Religionen. In *Lexikon der Religionen*, ed. H. Waldenfels , 226–30. Freiburg: Herder, 1987. (God VII: in Hindu Religions).

Heil/Heilsweg II: Hinduismus/Hindu-Religionen. In *Lexikon der Religionen*, ed. H. Waldenfels, 245–8. Freiburg: Herder, 1987. (Liberation II: Hinduism/ Hindu Religions.)

Tod und Wiedergeburt im Hinduismus. In *Ein Leben nach dem Leben?*, ed. H. Waldenfels, 7–29. Düsseldorf: Patmos, 1988. (Death and Rebirth in Hinduism.)

Voraussetzungen westlicher Hinduismusforschung und ihre Folgen. In '... *aus der anmuthigen Gelehrsamkeit.' Tübinger Studien zum 18. Jahrhundert. Festschrift Dietrich Geyer*, ed. E. Müller, 123–53. Tübingen: Attempto, 1988. (Preconditions of Western Research in Hinduism and its Consequences.)

Hinduism: On the Proper Use of a Deceptive Term. In *Hinduism Reconsidered*, ed. G. D. Sontheimer and H. Kulke, 11–27. Delhi: Manohar, 1989. (Proceedings of a panel in the Ninth European Conference of Modern South Asian Studies, Heidelberg 1986).

Yoghinī, streghe dell' India medievale? *Abstracta* 41 (Oct. 1989): 32–41. (The Yoginīs: Witches of Medieval India?)

Geplanter Synkretismus: Kaiser Akbars Religionspolitik. In *Die Religion von Oberschichten*, ed. P. Antes and D. Pahnke, 53–72. Marburg: Diagonal Verlag, 1989. (Planned Syncretism: The Religious Policy of Emperor Akbar.)

Perspektiven des Faches Indologie. In *Die sogenannten Geisteswissenschaften. Innenansichten*, ed. Prinz and Weingart, 388–99. Frankfurt: Suhrkam, 1990. (Perspectives of Indology as an Academic Subject.)

Der Weise in Indien: Entsprechungen zur Weisheit in der indischen Tradition. In *Weisheit. Archäologie der literarischen Kommunikation III*, ed. Aleida Assmann, 271–88. München: Wilhelm Fink, 1991. (The Wise Man in India: Correspondences to 'Wisdom' in Indian Tradition.)

Von der Heilsträchtigkeit der Angst: Religionswissenschaftliche Perspektiven. In *Angst und Religion*, ed. H. v. Stietencron, 13–36. Düsseldorf: Patmos, 1991. (Salvific Aspects of Fear: The Perspective of the Science of Religions.)

Die purāṇischen Genealogien und das Datum Buddhas. In *The Dating of the Historical Buddha, part 2 (Symposien zur Buddhismusforschung IV,2)*, ed. H. Bechert, 148–81. Göttingen 1992. (The Purāṇic Genealogies and the Date of the Buddha).

Der Begriff der Religion in der Religionswissenschaft. In *Der Begriff der Religion. Ein Symposion*, ed. W. Kerber, 111–58. München: 1993. (The term 'religion' in the science of religions.)

Der Beitrag der indischen Religionen zu einem Weltethos. In *Weltethos. Kultur und Entwicklung. Zeitschrift für Kulturaustausch* 1993.1: 107–15. (The Contribution of Indian Religions to a World Ethos.)

Toleranz gegenüber der Natur?–Ein Blick auf die Sichtweisen der Hindus. *Dialog der Religionen* 3.2 (1993): 114–28. (Tolerance Towards nature?—The Hindu views.)

Languages, Nations and Peoples: Hermann Gundert and the trends of his time. In *Tellicherry Records* vol. 4 & 12, (Tuebingen University Library Malayalam Manuscript Series vol. II), ed. Scaria Zacharia and Pazhassi Rekhakal. Kottayam: D.C. Books, 1994.

Menschenrechte? Sichtweisen südasiatischer Religionen. In *Die Menschenrechte. Herkunft - Geltung - Gefährdung*, ed. W. Odersky, 65–89. Düsseldorf: Patmos, 1994. (Human Rights? The Position of South Asian Religions.)

Das Glück und die Schatten der Vergänglichkeit. In *Vom guten Leben. Glücksvorstellungen in Hochkulturen*, ed. A. Bellebaum, 153–78. Berlin: Akademie Verlag, 1994. (Happiness and the Shadows of Impermanence.)

Die Suche nach nationaler Identität im Indien des 19. und 20. Jahrhunderts. In *Die fundamentalistische Revolution. Partikularistische Bewegungen der Gegenwart und ihr Umgang mit der Geschichte*. (Historiae Band 7), ed. W. Reinhard, 111–32. Freiburg: Bombach Verlag, 1995. (The Search for National Identity in nineteenth and twentieth century India.)

The Purāṇic Genealogies and the Date of the Buddha. In *When did the Buddha Live? The Controversy on the Dating of the Historical Buddha*, ed. H. Bechert, 221–49. Delhi: Sri Satguru Publications, 1995.

Religious Configurations in pre-Muslim India and the Modern Concept of Hinduism. In *Representing Hinduism: The Construction of Religious Traditions and National Identity*, ed. V. Dalmia and H. v. Stietencron, 51–81. New Delhi: Sage Publications, 1995.

Die Erscheinungsformen des Hinduismus. In *Indien: Kultur, Geschichte, Politik, Wirtschaft, Umwelt. Ein Handbuch*, ed. D. Rothermund, 143–66. München: C. H. Beck'sche Verlagsbuchhandlung, 1995. (Manifestations of Hinduism.)

Religion: Vom Begriff zum Phänomen oder vom Phänomen zum Begriff? *Ethik und Sozialwissenschaften. Streitforum für Erwägungskultur* 6.4 (1995): 492–5 (Kritik zu Ernst Feil: Zur Bestimungs- und Abgrenzungsproblematik von 'Religion'). ('Religion': To Proceed from the Term to the Phenomena or From the Phenomena to the Term?)

Töten im Krieg: Grundlagen und Entwicklungen. In *Töten im Krieg*, ed. H. v. Stietencron and J. Rüpke. (Historische Anthropologie 6), 17–56. Freiburg: Karl Alber, 1995. (Killing in War: Basic Structures and Developments.)

Die mythische Dimension von Kampf und Krieg. In *Töten im Krieg*, ed. H. v. Stietencron and J. Rüpke. (Historische Anthropologie 6), 17–56. Freiburg: Karl Alber, 1995. (The Mythic Dimension of Conflict and War.)

Macht und Markt im Wettbewerb der Religionen und der Ruf nach Toleranz. In *Markt und Macht in der Geschichte*, ed. H. Breuninger and R. P. Sieferle, 297–321. Stuttgart: Deutsche Verlags-Anstalt, 1995. (Power and Market in Religious Competition and the Call for Tolerance.)

Hindu Religious Traditions and the Concept of 'Religion'. Fourth Gonda lecture held on 1 November 1996. Royal Netherlands Academy of Arts and Sciences, Amsterdam 1997, 30 pp.

Die Zusammenkunft der Götter.—Ein Bericht über das Doḷasammeḷaṇa-Fest in Orissa. In *Nānāvidhaikatā. Festschrift für Hermann Berger*, ed. Dieter B. Kapp, 214–47. Wiesbaden: Harrassowitz, 1996. (The Meeting of the Gods—A Report on the Doḷasammeḷaṇa Festival in Orissa.)

Ethik in der Wirtschaft: Welche Werte gelten noch? In *Ethik, Moral, Wirtschaft* (Vortragsreihe der Industrie- und Handelskammer Nordschwarzwald 1), 26–56. Pforzheim: 1997. (Ethics in Business: Which Values Continue to be Valid?)

The Non-existence of Impurity and the Legitimation of Kings. In *Lex et Litterae. Studies in Honour of Oscar Botto*, ed. Siegfried Lienhard and Irma Piovano, 487–508. Torino: Edizioni dell'Orso, 1998.

La pluralità del divino: costellazioni politeistiche. In *Studi e materiali di storia delle religioni (anno 1996).(Festschrift Dario Sabbatucci)*, 667–75. Rom: 1998. (The Plurality of the Divine: Polytheistic Constellations.)

Note on Contributors

- Michael von Brück, Professor of Religious Studies at the University of Munich, studied Theology, Sanskrit and Indian Philosophy, and is a teacher of Yoga and Zen. He has been a dialogue partner of the Dalai Lama for many years. His publications concerning Hinduism, Buddhism and interreligious dialogue include inter alia *Die Welt des tibetischen Buddhismus* (1996), *Buddhismus und Christentum* (with Whalen Lai, 1997) and *Buddhismus. Grundlagen, Geschichte, Praxis* (1998).

- Heidrun Brückner is Professor of Indology at the Department of Indology and Comparative Religion at the University of Tuebingen (Germany). Besides Advaita Vedanta and classical Sanskrit drama her research focusses on Dravidian oral literature and folk Hinduism. Her major publications include *Fuerstliche Feste. Texte und Rituale der Tulu-Volksreligion an der Westkueste Suedindiens* (1995) and *Flags of Fame. Studies in South Asian Folk Culture* (co-edited 1993).

- Martin Christof (Christof-Füchsle) is Research Fellow at the Department of Indology and Comparative Religion at the University of Tuebingen (Germany). His main areas of interest are Epic and Purāṇic studies as well as Hindi language and literature. Published *Rājputentum und Purāṇische Geschichtsschreibung* (1997).

- Catherine Clementin-Ojha, at École Française d'Extrême Orient (Paris), has written on the history and organization of modern Vaishnava sects and on the process of indigenization of Christianity in India. Her recent publications include *Le trident sur le palais: une cabale anti-vishnouite dans un royaume hindou de l'époque coloniale* (1999).

- Dieter Conrad, Senior Research Fellow at South Asia Institute, University of Heidelberg, was in charge of Department of Law till his retirement in

1998. He specializes in the legal and constitutional systems of South Asian countries and has published widely on constitutional developments in these countries. A collection of major articles is forthcoming: *Zwischen den Traditionen. Probleme des Verfassungsrechts und der Rechtskultur in Indien und Pakistan* (ed. by J. Lütt and M. P. Singh, 1999).

- Thomas Dähnhardt holds a Ph.D. from SOAS in London. He is Researcher in the Centre of Islamic Studies, University of Oxford, and Professor of Urdu Language and Literature, University 'Ca'Foscari' of Venice.

- Vasudha Dalmia is Professor of Hindi and Modern South Asian Studies at the University of California, Berkeley. Her research focuses on modern Hinduism and colonial and post-colonial Hindi literature. She has published *The Nationalization of Hindu Tradition: Bhāratendu Hariśchandra and Nineteenth-century Banaras* (1997) and co-edited *Representing Hinduism: The Construction of Religious Traditions and National Identity* (1995) with Heinrich von Stietencron.

- Gita Dharampal-Frick teaches at the History Department of the Augsburg University. She has published 'La religion des Malabars. La contribution des missionaires à la naissance de l'indianisme' (1982) and *Indien im Spiegel deutscher Quellen der Frühen Neuzeit* (1994). Presently she is researching the contemporary socio-religious movements in India.

- Gian-Giuseppe Filippi is Professor of Indology at the Department of Studies on Oriental Asia, University of Venice. His publications include *Mṛtyu: the concept of Death in Indian Traditions* (1996), *India: miniature e dipinti dal XVI al XIX secolo* (1997) and *Kāmpilya: Quest for a Mahābhārata City* (1999).

- Martin Fuchs, anthropologist and sociologist, teaches at Free University Berlin and at the South Asia Institute, University of Heidelberg. His main areas of interest are social and cultural theory, critique of representation, social movements and Dalits. He has published inter alia *Theorie und Verfremdung. Max Weber, Louis Dumont und die Analyse der indischen Gesellschaft* (1988) and *Kampf um Differenz. Repräsentation, Subjektivität und soziale Bewegungen—das Beispiel Indien* (1999). Currently he is involved in research on interculturality and on Dalit problems.

- Jörg Gengnagel is Assistant Professor at the Department of Classical Indology, South Asia Institute at the University of Heidelberg. His research interests include Shaivism and ritual literature of Shaiva Siddhanta. He has published *Māyā, Puruṣa und Śiva: Die dualistische Tradition des Śivaismus nach Aghoraśivācāryas Tattvaprakāśavṛtti* (1996) and 'Visualisierung religiöser Räume—Zur Kartographie von Benares' (1999).

- Friedhelm Hardy is Reader in Indian Religions, King's College, University of London. His main areas of interest are the religions and cultures of India, especially South India. Among his major publications are *Viraha-bhakti: The Early History of Kṛṣṇa Devotion in South India* (1983), *The Religions of Asia* (ed. 1990) and *The Religious Culture of India: Power, Love and Wisdom* (1994).

- Monika Horstmann (Boehm-Tettelbach) is Professor of Modern South Asian Studies at the South Asia Institute, University of Heidelberg. Her special research interests are in the field of North Indian Bhakti and the history of Bhakti groups. She has published *Dadu: Lieder* (1991) and *In Favour of Govinddevji: Historical Documents Relating to a Deity of Vrindaban and Jaipur* (1999).

- Christophe Jaffrelot is a research fellow at the CNRS-CERI, Paris and teaches at the Institut d'Etudes Politiques de Paris. He is editor in chief of *Critique* and author of *The Hindu Nationalist Movement* (1996). He has recently co-edited *The BJP and the Compulsion of Politics in India* (1998).

- Jamal Malik studied South Asian History and Islamic Studies and has worked on South Asian Islam and Islam in Europe. He published *The Colonialization of Islam* (1996, 1998) and *Islamische Gelehrtenkultur in Nordindien* (1997). He currently holds the chair for Muslim Religious & Cultural History, University of Erfurt.

- Angelika Malinar is research fellow and teaches at the Department of Indology and Comparative Religion, University of Tuebingen (Germany). Her main areas of research are Epic and Purāṇic literature, Sāṃkhya and Yoga philosophies and history of Vaiṣṇava traditions (presently in the context of a research project on sacred centres in Orissa). Publications include *Rājavidyā: Das königliche Wissen um Herrschaft und Verzicht. Studien zur Bhagavadgītā* (1996).

- Françoise Mallison is Directeur d'Etudes at the Ecole pratique des Hautes Etudes, Section des Sciences historiques et philologiques, Paris, where she holds the chair of Histoire et Philologie de l'Inde occidentale. Her main interests are in the field of religious culture of medieval India and Gujarat. She has published widely on hagiographical narratives and devotional lyrics of the Bhakti current as well as the acculturation of Islam in India.

- Denis Matringe is Director of Research at the CNRS, Paris. His publications include *Hir Varis Shah* (1988) and *Masnavis: Poèmes d'Amour de l'Inde moghole* (1993), as well as articles on Urdu and Panjabi literatures and on Sufism and Sikhism. He is currently engaged in a project on the urban morphology in Madhya Pradesh (Chanderi).

- Paula Richman, Irvin E. Houck Professor in the Humanities at Oberlin College, Ohio, USA, has published in the field of South Indian religious texts. Her most recent publication *Extraordinary Child: Poems from a South*

Indian Devotional Genre came out in 1997. She edited and contributed to *Many Rāmāyaṇas: The Diversity of a Narrative Tradition in South Asia* (1991) and *Questioning Rāmāyaṇas: A South Asian Tradition* (2000).

- Tanika Sarkar is a historian who teaches at Jawaharlal Nehru University, New Delhi. She is author of *Bengal 1928-1934: The Politics of Protest* (1987) and of several books and articles on issues relating to gender and history. She co-edited *Women and the Hindu Right* (1995). Her book *Hindu Nation, Hindu Wife* will appear soon.

- Peter Schreiner is Professor of Indology at the University of Zürich and does most of his research on the Sanskrit Epics and Purāṇas. His publications include *Sanskrit indices and text of the Brahmapurāṇa* (1987), *Brahmapurāṇa: Summary of Contents, with index of Names and Motifs* (1989), and *Nārāyaṇīya-Studien* (1997).

- Smriti Srinivas is Assistant Professor of Comparative/Cultural Studies of Religion at Ohio State University. She is the author of *The Mouths of People, the Voice of God: Buddhists and Muslims in a Frontier Community of Ladakh* (1998). Her research interests are in the study of the city, the frontier and contemporary religious forms and practices.

- Heinrich von Stietencron was Professor and Head of the Department of Indology and Comparative Religion till his retirement in 1998. His main areas of interest are Indian religions, Indian art and the comparative study of religions. Having done extensive work on the Jagannath cult of Puri as well as other religious traditions of Orissa, currently he is again engaged in a research project on the religious history of Orissa. He is the author of *Gaṅgā und Yamunā. Zur symbolischen Bedeutung der Flußgöttinnen an indischen Tempeln* (1972), co-author of *Christianity and the World Religions* (ed. Hans Küng, 1999), and editor of *An Epic and Purāṇic Bibliography* (1992).

- Robert Zydenbos holds a Ph.D. in Indian philosophy and religions from the University of Utrecht, the Netherlands. His special areas of interest are Kannada literature, Jainism, Virasaivism and Dvaitavedanta. Among his publications are *The Calf Became an Orphan: A Study of Contemporary Kannada Fiction* (1996) and *The Concept of Divinity in Jainism* (1993).